# THE REBIRTH
## — OF —
# FEDERALISM

# The Rebirth
# — of —
# Federalism

*Slouching toward Washington*

Second Edition

DAVID B. WALKER

**CHATHAM HOUSE PUBLISHERS**
SEVEN BRIDGES PRESS, LLC
NEW YORK • LONDON

THE REBIRTH OF FEDERALISM
Slouching toward Washington
Second Edition
Seven Bridges Press, LLC
135 Fifth Avenue, 9th Floor, New York, NY 10010
Copyright © 2000 by Chatham House Publishers of Seven Bridges Press, LLC

**Library of Congress Cataloging-in-Publication Data**

Walker, David Bradstreet, 1927-
    The rebirth of Federalism : slouching toward Washington / David
B. Walker. – 2nd ed.
        p.   cm.
    Includes bibliographical references (p.  ) and index.
    ISBN 1-56643-074-7
    1. Federal government – United States.   I. Title.
JK311.W16   1995
320.473 – dc21                                               99-6051

Manufactured in the United States of America
10   9   8   7   6   5   4   3   2   1

*To my mentors:*
*Guy Howard Dodge*
*William G. Colman*
*The late Edmund S. Muskie*

# Contents

Preface     xiii

Acknowledgments     xvii

Acronyms     xix

Introduction: A New System     1
*A Dozen Dimensions of Recent Change, 1961–98, 2*
*Conclusion, 15*

## Part 1
## FEDERALISM TODAY

1. Federalism and Its Many Faces: What Is Federalism?     19
   What Are Intergovernmental Relations?
   *Models, Metaphors, and Interpretations, 21*
   *Summary, 34*

## Part 2
## NEARLY FOUR CENTURIES
## OF AMERICAN FEDERALISM, 1607–1998

2. American Federalism and Its Intergovernmental Relations,     39
   1607–1789
   *How It Began, 39*
   *The Constitutional Convention: Creativity under*
   *   Difficult Circumstances, 45*
   *What Manner of System? 54*

3. Variations on Dual Federalism, 1789–1930     65
   *The Dual Federalism of the Rural Republic, 1789–1860, 65*
   *The Second Seven Decades: Dual Federalism*
   *   with a Few Dents, 1861–1930, 73*
   *Conclusion, 87*

4. The Rise and Maturation of Cooperative Federalism, 1930–60     89
   *The Court Crushes Old Dual Federalism, 90*
   *Operations of Functional Federalism, 94*
   *The Third Phase of the Third Party System, 111*

5. Cooperative Federalism's Conceptual Offspring, 1960–80          121
   *Creative Federalism, 123*
   *The New Federalism, 126*
   *Congressional Federalism: Creative Federalism Resurgent, 128*
   *The New Partnership, 133*
   *From "Picket-Fence Federalism" to "Bamboo-Fence Federalism," 136*
   *Conclusion, 140*

6. The Reactions to Cooperative (and Co-Optive) Federalism, 1981–   141
   *Campaign Themes and Reagan Goals, 142*
   *The Reagan Record, 142*
   *The Bush Aftermath, 151*
   *Clinton, Congress, and the Current IGR Condition, 156*
   *Our Federalism's Current Condition, 168*

## Part 3
## SOME DYNAMICS OF TODAY'S SYSTEM

7. The Federal Judiciary: Centralizer or Umpire?                   175
   *The Warren Court in the Sixties, 176*
   *The Burger Court, 179*
   *The Rehnquist (or Post-Powell) Court, 190*
   *The Supreme Court in Retrospect, 206*

8. Fiscal Federalism: The Fateful Dynamic                          212
   *Galloping Public Sector Growth, 212*
   *Intergovernmental Fiscal Transfers: Dramatic Expansions,*
        *Then Some Constraints, 226*
   *The Deficit That Disappeared, 255*

9. A Resurgent Role for the States?                                260
   *The Leading Intergovernmental Linkage, 260*
   *The Silent Revolution, 264*
   *The Fifty State-Local Fiscal and Servicing Systems, 269*
   *The States as Implementers of New Intergovernmental Programs, 277*
   *The States as Shapers of Local and Substate Regional Institutions*
        *and Processes, 281*
   *Eighteen Approaches to Regionalism, 286*
   *Afterthoughts, 298*

10. A New Political System?                                        300
    *The Devilish Dynamics, 300*
    *State and Local Parties Adapting, 311*
    *What Kind of Party System? 313*

## Part 4
### TOWARD A REBIRTH OF FEDERALISM

11. What of the Future?                                            321
    *General Findings and Observations, 322*
    *Five Paradoxes, 328*
    *Why These Conflicting Views? 336*
    *An Agenda for Reform, 342*
    *A Last Word, 354*

Notes                                                              355

Index                                                              385

# Tables and Figures

Table Int-1. Federal Grants-in-Aid Relative to State and Local        4
　　　　　　　Outlays, Total Federal Outlays, and Gross Domestic
　　　　　　　Product, 1960–2000

Table Int-2. Intergovernmental Relations (IGR) Trends, Fiscal Years    6
　　　　　　　1960–98

Table Int-3. Outlays for General-Purpose, Broad-Based, and Other      10
　　　　　　　Grants, Selected Fiscal Years, 1975–97

Table Int-4. State Finances and Manpower, Selected Years, 1967–94     13

Table 3-1. Federal Tax Collections, by Type of Tax, 1902 and 1927    77

Table 3-2. State and Local Tax Collections, by Type of Tax, 1902     77
　　　　　　and 1927

Table 3-3. State Intergovernmental Expenditures, by Function, 1902    78
　　　　　　and 1927

Table 3-4. Federal Intergovernmental Transfers, by Broad Functional  80
　　　　　　Category, Selected Years, 1902–27

Table 4-1. Share of Total Domestic Governmental Expenditures from     95
　　　　　　Own Funds, by Level, 1929, 1939, 1959

Table 4-2. State and Local Tax Collections, by Type of Tax, Selected  96
　　　　　　Years, 1927–58

Table 4-3. State Aid to Localities, by Function, Selected Years,      97
　　　　　　1932–58

Table 4-4. Federal Intergovernmental Expenditures, by Function,     100
　　　　　　Selected Years, 1933–59

Table 8-1. Federal, State, and Local Shares from Own Funds of Total  213
　　　　　　and Domestic Governmental Expenditures, Selected
　　　　　　Years, 1962–94

Table 8-2. Selected Federal Revenue Sources as a Proportion of Total 214
　　　　　　General Revenue, Selected Years, 1960–95

Table 8-3. Distribution of State and Local Revenue Sources,          217
　　　　　　Selected Years, 1957–94

Table 8-4. Changes in Effective Federal Taxes, 1977–96              221

Table 8-5. Federal versus State and Local Tax Revenue as a          223
　　　　　　Percentage of Gross Domestic Product, Selected Years,
　　　　　　1959–94

Table 8-6.   Tax and Nontax Revenues as a Percentage of Gross                223
               National Product, Selected Years, 1959–94

Table 8-7.   Pass-Through Federal Aid as Proportion of Federal to           227
               State Aid and State to Local Aid, Selected Years,
               1957–90

Table 8-8.   State Aid to Local Governments, Selected Years, 1964–96        228

Table 8-9.   State Aid to Local Governments, by Jurisdictional              229
               Category, Selected Years, 1960–96

Table 8-10.  State Aid as Proportion of Local Own-Source General            229
               Revenue, Selected Fiscal Years, 1960–91

Table 8-11.  Growth Rate of Federal Grants and State-Local                  233
               Own-Source Revenue, 1960–94

Table 8-12.  Federal Grants as Proportion of Total Aid, by Function,        235
               Selected Fiscal Years, 1960–95

Table 8-13.  Categorical Grant Programs by Eligible Recipients,             238
               Selected Fiscal Years, 1975–93

Figure 8-1.  Basic Forms of Intergovernmental Transfers                     242

Table 8-14.  Grant Design Features in Combination                           243

Table 8-15.  New Social Regulatory Enactments by Type and Over              247
               Time, 1930–90

Table 8-16.  Federal Grant Matching Ratios by Number of Programs,           249
               1960, 1976, 1991

Table 8-17.  Federal Per Capita Grant Allocations by States (FY 1994)       252
               Ranked by Per Capita Income

Table 8-18.  Average Fiscal Disparities for Common Sample of                254
               Metropolitan Statistical Areas (MSAs)

Table 9-1.   Centralized, Balanced, and Decentralized States, Selected      272
               Years, 1902–92

Table 9-2.   Composite Ranking of the Fifty States in Terms of State        273
               Centralization, 1957 and 1992

Table 9-3.   Comparison of Individual States with National Trends,          274
               1957–92

Table 9-4.   Local-Level Jurisdictions, Selected Years, 1962–97             285

Table 10-1.  Index of State Regulation of Political Parties                 302

Figure 10-1. Political Action Committee (PAC) Count, 1977 to 1995           306

Table 10-2.  Summary Financial Activity, All Congressional                  307
               Campaigns, 1996

Figure 10-2. Soft-Money Contributions                                       308

# Preface

This book is both a history of American federalism and an analysis of its current somewhat conflicted condition. It is not accidental that our entire system of domestic governance also is now encountering severe challenges. Federalism, after all, historically has been a facilitator far more often than it has been an obstacle. But this fact has been forgotten in recent years, in large part because people of vastly different political persuasions need the national government to achieve at least some of their programmatic goals. Federalism then has become the least constant, hence the weakest, of our constitutional principles. Were James Madison to magically reappear in Washington, D.C., he would find nearly all of his paramount precepts for the national Constitution in remarkably robust health. The partial separation of powers, checks and balances, judicial review (though more of a Hamiltonian principle than his), republicanism, respect for the document as basic law, and the concomitant respect for liberty and the protection of individual rights are in good to extremely good condition. With federalism or the geographic division of governmental powers and authority, his judgment would have to be "fair" in practice, though were his assessment to have been made a generation ago, it inevitably would have been worse. The operational role of the states after all became indispensable since the sixties. Without them most national programs would not be implemented; without their enhanced fiscal power and administrative capacity, national resources would be revealed as inadequate; without these reformed states, the center would be rendered catatonic. Moreover, the Supreme Court beginning in the early nineties began to hand down a cluster of cases that began to curb certain congressional powers and place the states in a stronger constitutional position than they had been in since the thirties.

So why the middling but still negative judgment regarding the health of American federalism today? It is because in the judicial, constitutional, political, and representational spheres, the states and their localities by implication occupy a secondary position when compared to the counterpart stance of the national government. The Court, as we shall see, has favored the states in an increasing number of instances in recent years. But the supremacy of the Federal government in the commerce power, the conditional spending sphere, which is the single most potent source of national constitutional power, the supremacy clause, and some recent cases in the taxing area only underscore the systemic and constitutional hurdles a conservative Supreme Court encounters when it seeks to protect "our Federalism," as Justice Hugo Black once described it.

When the centripetal tendencies of our recently acquired new political (not

xiii

party) system and its many actors and processes are probed, the cruel condition of the formerly all-powerful state and local politics, politicians, and organizations is revealed and with it the decline of their ascendancy for roughly 140 years in American national politics and policymaking. The strengthened national parties; the expansive growth of interest groups in number, types, influence, and systemic significance; the allied role of campaign financing political action committees (PACs); the variety of "hired guns" for individual candidacies; and above all the meddling, molding, and mostly mean-spirited role of most of the media combined to perpetuate a centralized governmental and political system, advocates of reassigning power and functions to subnational governments (devolutionists), states' righters, futurists, and dreamers notwithstanding.

But as noted at the outset, the states, localities, and other subnational instrumentalities occupy high ground in the realm of governmental operations, and this position along with an emerging sympathetic Court and public opinion help provide some substance for the claim (perhaps with a question mark) that a rebirth of federalism is at hand. Perhaps the most fundamental reason that the outcome is in some doubt is that mass public opinion and most of us as individuals adhere to totally ambivalent views regarding various facets of the bigger federalism issue. We love big Federal programs but hate big government; we bash bureaucrats but demand good services from them; we rank the Federal government last in terms of trust, reliability, and honesty, but we always turn first to that government when dire domestic or threatening foreign crises arise.

These ambivalent attitudes, centralizing political and judicial developments, and noncentralizing state and Federal developments — along with other lesser trends — combined to shape a system that is overloaded, seriously confused, and distrusted. The overload is not the overall systemic phenomenon many of us wrote of in the late seventies and early eighties. Instead, it is the current condition wherein the public still expects far too much of government — all governments — and where the national government still plays a major, if not the major, policy role in the domestic arena, even when its fiscal contributions to this sector have shrunk. The overload is reflected in the continuing centripetalism of key Court decisions, of the media, and of some pressure groups, and in the continuing rush, though slower in the nineties, to regulate and to preempt. It also manifests itself at the subnational level, where the states have taken on or have been assigned the heaviest ever administrative and implementing roles, especially since the enactment of the Personal Responsibility and Work Opportunity Reconciliation Act (PRWORA) of 1996 by the 104th Congress with the president's approval and most particularly its first title, the Temporary Assistance for Needy Families (TANF), the new block grant substitute, with fewer strings, for the sixty-one-year-old Aid to Families with Dependent Children (AFDC).

The system is conflicted insofar as it reflects tendencies that are simultaneously centralizing and decentralizing, cooperative and competitive, co-optive and more discretionary, symbolic and substantive, and activist as well as retrenching. Reconciling opposite values and propensities is a hallmark of the American political tradition, but some of the ambivalence reflected in these contrasting pairs is not healthy, and in some cases, notably the co-optive, it is destructive. This raises the topic of *distrust*. Among the intergovernmental partners of the federal system, distrust now is rampant. The "deficit-driven," "fend-for-yourself," and "pass-the-buck" fiscal trends that have dominated so much of Federal-state-local relations in recent years have wreaked havoc with the mutual confidence and shared sense of interlevel comity that formerly existed among the governments. Moreover, the perennial congressional habit of enacting symbolic acts and regulations and gutting regulatory and other agencies at both the Federal and state levels by budget cuts and executive branch political operatives have damaged intergovernmental relations and equally important the public's confidence in these relations.

An authentic federalism needs to be reformulated — one that remembers that the concept of federalism above all else signifies a geographical division of governmental labors. It also must assign a jurisdictional status to the constituent governments that gives them a very special status in the courts of the land, a status that their operational role today should have earned for them long since. It should include a strong territorial and subnational governmental representation in the nation's capital and a preeminent place for state and local elected officeholders in the deliberations of their respective national parties. It requires a restoration of a healthy spirit of interlevel comity among elected and appointed officials at all levels. And it must end "hollow government," bring life to unimplemented legislation and regulations, and revive anorexic agencies that are supposed to be carrying out the people's business. All this is needed to help solve the all too many top-priority policy challenges.

While the hurdles that are to be surmounted if a more balanced and a more functional federalism is to be had seem impossibly high to some, the recent record is far from totally negative as the subsequent chapter (and later ones) will indicate. Some of the emerging trends of the nineties suggest that intergovernmental reform is not outside the realm of possibility. A more state-sensitive Supreme Court, the modest decline in regulatory enactments, the presidential trust in the states as reflected in Clinton's permissive granting of waivers, the aggressive stance of state representational bodies, and the success that a united phalanx of all seven of the state and local generalist organizations that represent their discrete interests in Washington, D.C., can achieve are but a few of the more salutary developments that the 1990s have witnessed.

This brings us to the subtitle of this work, "Slouching toward Washington," an adaptation of a phrase in the last line of William Butler Yeats's poem "The Second Coming." In this work, remarkably contemporary though penned in 1920, the poet cautions:

> Things fall apart; the centre cannot hold;
> Mere anarchy is loosed upon the world, ...
> And what rough beast, its hour come round at last,
> Slouches towards Bethlehem to be born?

Metaphorically, the beast already has arrived, for it slouched into Washington, D.C., unannounced and not clearly noticed sometime during the seventies in the form of the "new political system." Its mating with the governmental system created yet a new beast, an even uglier animal, the Federal deficit, which was pure beast, but now subdued — at least for the moment. Yet the pressure group, PAC, and media components of this "new political system" are as voracious as ever, and there are few signs that we understand the corrosive effects of their combined actions on our federal polity. The United States has need of a "Second Coming," one that recaptures the functionality, constitutional viability, and common sense not of the old traditional federalism that defended racism as well as rationality but of an authentic rebirth of federalism that comes from a reformulation of traditional political, governmental, and administrative precepts for a twenty-first-century setting.

# Acknowledgments

It is not possible to thank everyone who has assisted in the writing of a book. However, I would like to express my gratitude to Darlene P. Williams for her invaluable logistical support and superb word processing skills, to G. Ross Stephens for sharing his wealth of current data on intergovernmental issues, and to Anthony Illionardo for his consistent capacity to locate hard-to-find data. I also want to recognize a number of people who provided technical data, support, and encouragement, including Patricia Atkins, William Barnes, David Beam, Jonathan D. Bruel, Carmen Cirincione, Timothy J. Conlan, Cynthia L. Cates, Brewster C. Denny, Kathryn A. Foster, Mathew W. Hart, Maureen Haynes, Lawrence Hush, Cindy Jasper, Laura S. Jensen, Annette Liseno, James Martin, Bruce D. McDowell, Paul L. Posner, Howard L. Reiter, David Russell, Scott Simoneau, Elizabeth T. Smith, Leigh Anne Tracey, Bruce A. Wallin, Larry Singer, and Justin D. Walker.

# Acronyms

| | |
|---|---|
| ACIR | Advisory Commission on Intergovernmental Relations (1959– ) |
| ACIR | American Council on Intergovernmental Relations (1996– ) |
| ADEA | Age Discrimination in Employment Act |
| AFDC | Aid to Families with Dependent Children |
| CBO | Congressional Budget Office |
| CDBG | Community Development Block Grant |
| CETA | Comprehensive Employment and Training Act (1973) |
| COG | Council of Government |
| DEFRA | Deficit Reduction Act (1984) |
| DOD | Department of Defense |
| EEOC | Equal Employment Opportunity Commission |
| EPA | Environmental Protection Agency |
| ERISA | Employee Retirement Income Security Act (1974) |
| ERTA | Economic Recovery Tax Act (1981) |
| FAP | Family Assistance Program |
| FDA | Food and Drug Administration |
| GAO | General Accounting Office |
| GDP | gross domestic product |
| GRS | General Revenue Sharing |
| IGR | intergovernmental relations |
| ISTEA | Intermodal Surface Transportation Efficiency Act (1991) |
| MPO | Metropolitan Planning Organization |
| MSA | Metropolitan Statistical Area |
| NAFTA | North American Free Trade Agreement |
| NPR | National Performance Review |

| | |
|---|---|
| OBRA | Omnibus Budget Reconciliation Act (1981, 1993) |
| OIRA | Office of Information and Regulatory Affairs |
| OMB | Office of Management and Budget |
| PAC | political action committee |
| PIG | public interest group |
| PRWORA | Personal Responsibility and Work Opportunity Reconciliation Act (1996) |
| RFRA | Religious Freedom Restoration Act (1993) |
| SPDD | State Planning and Development Districts |
| SSI | Supplemental Security Income |
| TANF | Temporary Assistance for Needy Families |
| TEA-21 | Transportation Efficiency Act–21st (Century) |
| TEFRA | Tax Equity and Fiscal Responsibility Act (1982) |
| TRA | Tax Reform Act (1986) |
| UMRA | Unfunded Mandates Reform Act |
| USDA | U.S. Department of Agriculture |
| ZBB | zero-based budgeting |

# Introduction

# A New System

A new system of domestic government evolved, unplanned, in the United States over the past four decades. Its level of policy centralization but continued reliance on subnational governmental implementation, its degree of complexity and interdependency, and its vastly expanded and then somewhat reduced scope of intergovernmental financing and servicing arrangements have been in marked contrast to the simpler, more separated, more predictable, and more intergovernmentally balanced features of the predecessor pattern of the New Deal and post–New Deal years.

The present system was shaped initially by a welter of dynamic forces — social, political, judicial, and fiscal; attitudinal, programmatic, and servicing — that were unleashed in the midsixties. These largely centralizing dynamics were actually strengthened in the seventies, despite the economic and public finance difficulties of that comparatively conservative decade. With the Reagan reaction, there was some reining in of the Federal fiscal role and some of the servicing roles in the federal system but also a continued expansion of the centralizing Federal regulatory, retrenchment, political, and judicial thrusts. There also was a marked increase in the states' responsibilities — a trend that had begun in the seventies. The Bush and early Clinton years, while very different in many respects, represent an eclectic merger of some of the domestic activism of the sixties and seventies along with some of the Reaganite conservative reaction to the earlier national policy activism and with increasingly more serious efforts to retrench in light of the deficit fallout from Reaganomics. The result is a special form of ambivalence because both centralizing and decentralizing, co-optive and collaborative, and activist and constraining tendencies can be found in nearly all of the many arenas in which intergovernmental relations occur. Moreover, and to a greater extent than in any other time of peace, the Damocles sword of soaring Federal deficits, an anemic economy (1978–83 and 1989–92), and continuing structural unemployment in certain regions combined to constitute a dominant conditioner of intergovernmental developments of the late eighties and early nineties, although the 1993 Clinton budget victory constituted a major response to the deficit challenge. But by the late nineties, the economy had enjoyed eight years of uninterrupted growth, inflation was practically nonexistent, and unemployment was hovering around 4 percent. In addition, the 1997 budget agreement committed the president and Congress to a balanced budget by 2002,

1

and for fiscal year (FY) 1999 the annual Federal budget deficit was eliminated, for the first time in thirty years.

Each of the three phases was different from the others. Operational and political overload summed up the Johnson-to-Carter years; immense Federal fiscal overload and continued political and judicial centripetalism with some modest devolutions characterized the Reagan years; and fiscal expenditure-revenue gaps impacted all levels, with enlargement of the orbit of systemic ambivalence and continued judicial and political centralism occurring during Bush's incumbency. Overload and imbalance, then, were prime features of each phase, though the specific type of each dysfunctionality differed. Throughout, the states assumed a greater role. Yet the preeminent Federal position was never really rolled back during the Reagan-Bush years in the regulatory enactments, preemptions, and categorical grants either in the judicial or political areas, despite the relative reduction in the Federal government's fiscal and, to a much lesser extent, programmatic and regulatory implementation roles. The first year and a half of the Clinton administration reflected a general trend toward a somewhat less conflicted system. But, during all of the Clinton years, including those wherein he was jousting with the conservative Republican 104th and 105th Congresses, there was and is conflict, some confusion, and even a dose of collaboration between the two national political branches and between them and the state and local governments.

Today, intergovernmental relations do not tend to any one direction, as many have contended, but are of an ambiguous nature, given the many conflicting trends within the various arenas of intergovernmental action. In the regulatory, judicial, program, and fiscal areas, no one tendency is consistently dominant. Whether this is transitional or more long lasting depends on later developments in the Clinton years and probably beyond.

To grasp fully the striking synthesis that produced simultaneously devolving and continuing centralizing tendencies along with resulting ambiguity, the dynamics of the centralizing years (1964–78) and then those of the mixed centralizing-decentralizing Reagan-Bush-Clinton years must be probed. This is done in chapters 5–10. Meanwhile the broad contours of overall change during this current period need chronicling.

## A Dozen Dimensions of Recent Change, 1961–98

What are some of the distinctive developments during this current period that set it apart from its immediate predecessor and that make it one period with three phases, not three periods? And what are the bases for assigning the labels *overloaded*, *unbalanced*, and *ambiguous* to it? The following points merit close attention.

1. *The initial deluge, then the brief decline during the early Reagan years, and the resumed rise of Federal aid dollars* involved nearly a tripling in current dollars between FY 1960 and 1969; a more than four-and-a-half-times hike from FY

1969 to FY 1981; an overall 38 percent increase during the Reagan years despite an absolute reduction in FY 1982 and later merely incremental increases; and a somewhat faster growth rate under Bush and Clinton. In constant dollars there was a doubling of aid during the Kennedy-Johnson years, nearly a doubling from 1969 to 1980, near-static growth from 1981 to 1992, but a 51.4 percent rise from 1989 to 1998 (see table Int-1, pp. 4–5). This suggests some reduction in the Federal domestic fiscal role.

2. *The number of grant programs steadily proliferated for twenty years, then a one-time Reagan contraction followed by a steady rise* during the second Reagan administration occurred. That ultimately produced the highest figure ever, over 660 grants by FY 1998 (see table Int-2, pp. 6–7). Most of the 125 grants that disappeared in 1981 and most of the 660 plus awarded in 1998, however, were pygmy project grants.

3. *A near-perfecting of the Johnsonian theory of panoramic partnership was followed by its nearly complete collapse,* for during the seventies all the jurisdictions eligible for LBJ's Creative Federalism grants (the states, some special districts, some cities and fewer counties, most school districts, and some nonprofit units) were still direct recipients, as were all other local units of general government, practically all school districts, and more than 1,800 substate regional bodies, for a grand total by 1980 of approximately 60,000 recipient subnational governments — compared with about 50 in 1960. This extraordinary expansion of Federal grant recipients was caused by the enactment of General Revenue Sharing (1972, which reached 38,000 localities); the Comprehensive Employment and Training Act (1973) and the Community Development Block Grant program (1974), two Federal-local block grants; and three countercyclical programs enacted to end the severe recession of 1975–77 whose eligibility and entitlement provisions converted a host of local governments into new direct recipients of Federal assistance. In the eighties, however, nearly all significant Federal-local grants were eliminated by consolidation or outright repeal, save for the entitlement Community Development Block Grant, Mass Transit monies, some drug funds, and later some policing funds. Direct Federal aid bypassing the states to localities went from 12 percent of the total aid (1968) to 24 percent (1974) to 29 percent (1978), then down to 24 percent at the end of the Carter administration, to 11.4 percent in 1994, and it is still dropping (see table Int-2, pp. 6–7). The decline was a major and largely unheralded result of the Reagan revolution.

4. *The shifting positions of the partners evolved,* with the states in the earlier phase occupying a lesser yet still powerful recipient position, receiving about 75 percent of all Federal aid to states and localities during the seventies. Cities, counties, and school districts, however, were assuming a more significant role, as the bypassing figures cited above suggest. Impressions in the seventies were that the shift was partly influenced by the various public interest groups representing the states, and especially counties, cities, and school districts, in Washington. Meanwhile the Federal government still played a senior-partner role fiscally, but its administrative capacity, collaborative intentions, and some program purposes were being questioned by the states and localities with considerable vigor. During

## Table Int-1
## Federal Grants-in-Aid Relative to State and Local Outlays, Total Federal Outlays, and Gross Domestic Product, 1960–2000

| Fiscal Year[a] | Federal Grants-in-Aid (Current Dollars) | | As a Percentage of | | | Federal Grants (Constant 1992 Dollars) | | Grants for Payments to Individuals | |
| | Amount[b] | Percentage Increase or Decrease (–) | Total State-Local Outlays[c] | Total Federal Outlays | Gross Domestic Product | Amount | Percentage Real Increase or Decrease (–) | Amount[d] | Percentage of Total Grants[d] |
|---|---|---|---|---|---|---|---|---|---|
| 1960 | 7.0 | 7.7 | 23.4 | 7.6 | 1.4 | 33.4 | 7.4 | 2.5 | 35.7 |
| 1961 | 7.1 | 1.4 | 21.2 | 7.3 | 1.3 | 33.8 | 1.0 | 2.6 | 36.7 |
| 1962 | 7.9 | 11.3 | 22.0 | 7.4 | 1.4 | 37.1 | 9.8 | 3.0 | 37.2 |
| 1963 | 8.6 | 8.9 | 22.7 | 7.7 | 1.4 | 39.3 | 5.9 | 3.3 | 38.0 |
| 1964 | 10.2 | 18.6 | 25.2 | 8.6 | 1.6 | 45.8 | 16.5 | 3.6 | 35.0 |
| 1965 | 10.9 | 6.9 | 24.9 | 9.2 | 1.6 | 48.7 | 6.3 | 3.7 | 33.9 |
| 1966 | 12.9 | 18.3 | 27.0 | 9.6 | 1.7 | 56.5 | 16.0 | 4.3 | 33.2 |
| 1967 | 15.2 | 17.8 | 28.5 | 9.7 | 1.9 | 64.8 | 14.7 | 4.8 | 31.3 |
| 1968 | 18.6 | 23.4 | 31.2 | 10.4 | 2.1 | 75.7 | 16.8 | 6.1 | 32.7 |
| 1969 | 20.2 | 8.6 | 29.4 | 11.0 | 2.1 | 77.7 | 2.6 | 7.2 | 35.9 |
| 1970 | 24.1 | 19.3 | 30.9 | 12.3 | 2.4 | 86.9 | 11.8 | 8.7 | 36.3 |
| 1971 | 28.1 | 16.6 | 31.4 | 13.4 | 2.6 | 94.9 | 9.2 | 10.5 | 37.5 |
| 1972 | 34.4 | 22.4 | 35.1 | 14.9 | 2.9 | 110.5 | 16.4 | 13.9 | 40.6 |
| 1973 | 41.8 | 21.5 | 40.2 | 17.0 | 3.2 | 128.8 | 16.6 | 13.9 | 33.2 |
| 1974 | 43.4 | 3.8 | 36.7 | 16.1 | 3.0 | 122.6 | –4.8 | 14.8 | 34.1 |
| 1975 | 49.8 | 14.8 | 36.7 | 15.0 | 3.2 | 126.6 | 3.3 | 16.8 | 33.7 |
| 1976 | 59.1 | 18.7 | 39.1 | 15.9 | 3.4 | 139.4 | 10.1 | 20.1 | 33.9 |
| 1977 | 68.4 | 15.7 | 41.2 | 16.7 | 3.5 | 149.7 | 7.4 | 22.7 | 33.2 |
| 1978 | 77.9 | 13.9 | 47.0 | 17.0 | 3.5 | 159.5 | 6.5 | 24.7 | 31.7 |
| 1979 | 83.4 | 7.1 | 43.2 | 16.5 | 3.3 | 157.4 | 1.3 | 27.5 | 33.0 |
| 1980 | 91.4 | 9.6 | 43.0 | 15.5 | 3.4 | 155.7 | –0.1 | 32.6 | 35.7 |

| Year | | | | | | | | | |
|---|---|---|---|---|---|---|---|---|---|
| 1981 | 94.8 | 3.7 | 39.6 | 14.0 | 3.1 | 146.4 | −6.4 | 37.8 | 39.9 |
| 1982 | 88.1 | 6.7 | 32.8 | 11.8 | 2.7 | 127.4 | −14.9 | 38.8 | 44.0 |
| 1983 | 92.5 | 5.0 | 34.0 | 11.4 | 2.7 | 127.7 | .3 | 42.5 | 45.9 |
| 1984 | 97.6 | 5.5 | 31.9 | 11.5 | 2.6 | 129.5 | 1.4 | 45.3 | 46.4 |
| 1985 | 105.9 | 8.5 | 32.0 | 11.2 | 2.6 | 135.6 | 4.7 | 49.3 | 46.6 |
| 1986 | 112.3 | 6.0 | 31.5 | 11.3 | 2.6 | 139.7 | 3.0 | 54.2 | 48.3 |
| 1987 | 108.4 | −3.7 | 27.1 | 10.8 | 2.4 | 131.4 | −7.1 | 57.7 | 53.2 |
| 1988 | 115.3 | 6.4 | 26.9 | 10.8 | 2.3 | 133.9 | 2.7 | 62.1 | 53.9 |
| 1989 | 122.0 | 5.8 | 26.6 | 10.7 | 2.3 | 136.2 | 1.7 | 66.5 | 54.5 |
| 1990 | 135.4 | 11.0 | 26.9 | 10.8 | 2.4 | 144.7 | 6.2 | 75.7 | 55.9 |
| 1991 | 154.5 | 14.1 | 28.3 | 11.5 | 2.6 | 158.6 | 9.6 | 90.7 | 58.7 |
| 1992 | 178.1 | 15.3 | 30.7 | 12.9 | 2.9 | 178.1 | 12.8 | 110.0 | 61.8 |
| 1993 | 193.6 | 8.7 | 31.5 | 13.7 | 3.0 | 188.6 | 5.9 | 121.5 | 62.8 |
| 1994 | 210.6 | 8.8 | 32.7 | 14.4 | 3.1 | 200.5 | 6.3 | 131.1 | 62.3 |
| 1995 | 225.0 | 6.7 | 33.2 | 14.8 | 3.1 | 208.2 | 3.8 | 141.2 | 62.8 |
| 1996 | 227.8 | 1.2 | 31.7 | 14.6 | 3.0 | 205.5 | −2.0 | 142.8 | 62.9 |
| 1997 | 234.2 | 3.1 | 31.2 | 14.6 | 2.9 | 205.8 | 1.5 | 144.2 | 61.6 |
| 1998e | 250.9 | 7.1 | N/A | 15.0 | 3.0 | 215.9 | 4.9 | 156.8 | 62.5 |
| 1999e | 271.3 | 8.1 | N/A | 15.7 | 3.1 | 228.3 | 5.7 | 166.0 | 61.2 |
| 2000e | 284.3 | 4.8 | N/A | 15.9 | 3.1 | 233.8 | 2.4 | 176.1 | 61.9 |

Sources: ACIR computations based on Office of Management and Budget, Historical Tables, Budget of the United States Government, FY 1992; Department of Commerce, Bureau of Economic Analysis, Survey of Current Business (monthly); ACIR, Characteristics of Federal Grants-in-Aid Programs to State and Local Governments: Grants Funded FY 1991, M-182 (Washington, D.C., March 1992); Significant Features of Fiscal Federalism, vol. 2, Revenues and Expenditures, M-185-11 (Washington, D.C., September 1993), 13; Historical Tables, Budget of the United States Government, FY 1999, on-line via GPO Access.

Note: Number of Federal grant programs funded: 1960, 132; 1967, 379; 1984, 404; 1985, 426; 1991, 543.

a. For 1955–76, fiscal years ended 30 June; subsequent years, 30 September.

b. See Special Analysis H of the 1990 Budget of the United States for explanation of differences between grant-in-aid figures published by the National Income and Product Accounts, Bureau of the Census, and OMB.

c. As defined in the National Income and Product Accounts.

d. Revised from previous editions of Significant Features of Fiscal Federalism.

e. Estimated.

## Table Int-2
## Intergovernmental Relations (IGR) Trends, Fiscal Years 1960–98

| | 1960 Total | Great Society | | New Federalism | | New Partnership Federalism | | 1980 Total | Reagan Federalism | | Bush Years | | Clinton Era | |
|---|---|---|---|---|---|---|---|---|---|---|---|---|---|---|
| | | 1964 | 1969 | 1970 | 1977 | 1978 | 1981 | | 1982 | 1989 | 1990 | 1993 | 1994 | 1998 |
| Number of grant programs | 132 | 397 ('67) | | 442 ('75) | | 492 ('78) | | 539 | 404 | 492 | 492 | 593 | 633 ('95) | 660+ ('97) |
| Grant outlays in current dollars (billions) | $7.0 | $10.2 | $20.2 | $24.1 | $68.4 | $77.9 | $94.8 | $91.4 | $88.1 | $122.0 | $135.4 | $193.6 | $210.6 | $250.9 |
| Grant outlays in constant 1992 dollars (billions) | $33.4 | $45.8 | $65.8 | $77.7 | $149.7 | $159.5 | $146.4 | $155.7 | $127.4 | $136.2 | $144.7 | $188.6 | $200.5 | $215.9 |
| Federal aid as a percentage of state and local outlays (own source) | 23.4% | 25.2% | 29.4% | 30.9% | 41.2% | 47.0% | 39.6% | 43.0% | 37.8% | 26.6% | 26.0% | 31.5% | 31.7% | 31.2% ('97) |
| Federal aid (current dollars) as a percentage of total Federal outlays | 7.6% | 8.6% | 11.0% | 12.3% | 16.7% | 17.0% | 14.0% | 15.5% | 11.8% | 10.7% | 10.8% | 13.7% | 14.4% | 14.6% |
| Grants for payments to individuals as a percentage of total Federal aid | 35.7% | 35.0% | 35.9% | 36.3% | 33.2% | 31.7% | 39.9% | 35.7% | 44.0% | 54.3% | 55.9% | | 62.3% | 62.5% |

| | | | | | | | | | | |
|---|---|---|---|---|---|---|---|---|---|---|
| Forms of grants[a] | 133C | 2B, 3T rest C | 5B, G, 2T 426C ('75) | 5B, G 492C | 4B, G, 534C | 12B, G, 396C | 14B, 478C | 15B ('93) 578C | 15B, 633C ('95) | 24B, 640C[e] ('98) |
| Percentage of aid bypassing the states | 8% | 12% | 24% ('74) | 29% ('78) | 23.6% | 24.2% | 14.5% ('88) | 11.2% ('92) | 11.4% ('94) | 11.56% ('97)[e] |
| Major IGR regulations | 2 | 7 ('61-'68) | 23 ('69-'76) | 5 ('76-'80) | 37 ('80) | 21 ('81-'88) | | 6 ('89-'92) | 11 ('94-95) | 6 ('96-'97)[e] |
| Federal preemptions | 89 ('59) | 47 ('60-'69) | 108 ('70-'79) | | 344 ('80) | 100 ('80-'89) | | 25 ('90-'91) | 7 ('93-'96) | |

Sources: Adapted from Advisory Commission on Intergovernmental Relations, *Significant Features of Fiscal Federalism*, 1985–86 edition, M-146, p. 19; 1989 M-163-II, pp. 18–24; David B. Walker, *Towards a Functioning Federalism* (1961), 100–131; U.S. Bureau of the Census, *Government Finances*, 1988–90 editions; ACIR, *Characteristics of Federal Grants-in-Aid Programs to State and Local Government*, M-188 (January 1994), p. 1; ACIR, *Federal Statutory Preemption of State and Local Authority*, A 121 (Washington, D.C., Government Printing Office, September 1992): 7, 9; 1992 data from OMB, *Budget Baselines Historical Data and Alternatives for the Future*, January 1993. ACIR, *Characteristics of Federal Grants-in-Aid Programs to State and Local Governments: Grants Funded in FY 1995*, M-195 (June 1995), 3; G. Ross Stephens, University of Missouri–Kansas City, private communication, 8 July 1998; *Historical Tables, Budget of the U.S. Government, FY 1999*, on-line via GPO Access; General Accounting Office, *Grant Programs, Design Features – Shape, Flexibility, Accountability, and Performance Information* (GAO/GGD-98-137) (Washington, D.C., June 1998), 7ff.

a. Forms of grant codes: B=block; C=categorical; G=general revenue sharing; T=target.

e. estimated

the Reagan-Bush years, the questioning of Federal intentions (especially those relating to devolution, retrenchment, and regulations) and state-local willingness to resort to litigation increased. But the premier position among the subnational governments was clearly held by the states; witness the preeminent place given the governors in the deliberations over the 1982 Reagan "Big Swap" proposal, which would have sorted out separate Federal and state responsibilities for a range of health and social welfare programs, the exclusive state recipient role conferred by the thirteen new block grants enacted in the eighties, and the major reductions in direct Federal-local links in these years. This resurrection of the traditional and paramount Federal-state connection was another largely unnoticed by-product of Reagan federalism and has not been reversed thus far. More recently, a local economic development package failed in 1993, and despite passage of empowerment zone legislation (which eliminated certain rules and regulations therein and provided for tax incentives) in the same year and the later policing and housing grants, Clinton did little to modify this downward slide, to the consternation of Democratic mayors and others.

5. *Expanding, then contracting, and finally some renewed Federal new-program thrusts* characterized the roller-coaster ride of national activism during the four decades. Exuberant expansionism in broad as well as increasingly more narrow functional areas occurred from 1964 to 1978, if not 1980. All of the major areas of intergovernmental and national significance (such as welfare, health, hospitals, transportation, and education) were assisted by Federal grants, and people-related programs experienced the greatest dollar and proportionate gain. Moreover, this was accompanied by the enactment of an array of grants for activities that in the fifties would have been considered state or local responsibilities (such as rural fire protection, car-pool demonstration projects, jellyfish control, estuarine sanctuaries, juvenile justice, libraries, and solid waste disposal). In some cases, Federal grants stimulated wholly new servicing roles among some recipient governments, as with community development and manpower training for certain cities and urban counties. The only opposite trend to the growing mingling of servicing responsibilities was the 1972 Federal takeover of the adult welfare categories in the Supplemental Security Income (SSI) program, but even this move was not total because state add-ons were permitted.

During the early Reagan years, especially the first, existing grants were slashed: 77 were merged into 10 new block grants, another 60 or so were scrapped, and outlays were cut for a range of programs, mostly social welfare programs. The reduction in grants from 539 to 404 did not last long: by 1988 the total had reached 492; by 1992, 593; and by 1998, an estimated 660 plus. Some of the growth since 1989 is explained by the presence of a revitalized Congress and a president more sympathetic to certain domestic programs. The results during the Bush years were major renewals involving expansion (for example, the Medicaid amendments, the 1990 Clean Air Act Amendments, and the landmark Intermodal Surface Transportation Efficiency Act [ISTEA]), a revamping of older, smaller programs (for example, Head Start, the Women, Infants and Children nutritional program [WIC], compensatory education), and the enactment of several small new grants. Clinton chalked up an 88 percent enactment record in 1993, but program cuts in the budget battle were part of this. Clinton and the Republican 104th Congress, because of a very different set of highly confrontational circumstances, enacted eight devolving measures, with welfare being the most significant, rejected at least eight other devolving bills, passed a dozen centralizing conservative acts chiefly in the criminal justice field, and enacted three liberal centripetal proposals — the minimum wage hike and two health insurance coverage enactments. Clearly the activism of the slovenly seventies and that of the conservative nineties along with the perennial use of both pigmy project grants and regulations for symbolic and policy purposes had not disappeared in the nineties.

6. Beginning in 1966, *diversification in the forms of Federal aid* (that is, the manner in which the funds are distributed and administered) was under way; the traditional types of categorical grants (see table Int-2, pp. 6–7) were still in heavy use, along with the new "no-strings" programs like General Revenue Sharing (GRS) and five block grants. Strict categoricals still accounted for 73 percent of the FY 1978 Federal aid package; block and other broad-based grants, 14.7 percent; and GRS, with other general-purpose aid, 12.3 percent. In dollar terms, local governments, especially cities and counties, benefited more from the emergence of GRS, two of the block grants, and the countercyclical programs, only one of which was really categorical in character. The states, on the other hand, were involved more with the categoricals, though they also shared in some of the newer forms of aid during the seventies. The paradox of the Reagan years was that the number of block grants reached a high at that time of fourteen, but their dollar outlays accounted for a mere 10.4 percent of the FY 1989 aid total (see table Int-3, p. 10). Moreover, GRS lost the states as recipients in 1980, survived renewal in 1983 only with presidential support, and was scrapped in 1986 as a part of an economy drive and with presidential blessing. The lesson here is that categoricals with all their constraints are the most popular form of U.S. intergovernmental fiscal transfer (82.5 percent of the FY 1997 total grant outlays) because of their complete compatibility with our pulverized political system.

7. *Creeping conditionalism and galloping social regulation* were among the most novel features of intergovernmental relations (IGR) developments during these three decades. Conditions came with nearly all forms of Federal aid, despite the earlier assertions that GRS and block grants were essentially "no-strings" and "few-strings" assistance programs. The procedural strings (civil rights, citizen participation, and auditing requirements) that were added to GRS in 1976 and the tendency of most of the then five block grants to pick up program and other constraints over time brought this about. Moreover, more than sixty national-purpose, across-the-board requirements in the equal rights, equal access, environmental, handicapped, historical preservation, and personnel areas (to mention only the more obvious) were attached to practically all Federal assistance. These and other new forms of Federal regulation of states and localities gave rise to a new and controversial phase of intergovernmental relations. During the Reagan years, hardly any of the crosscutting requirements (that is,

## Table Int-3

### Outlays for General-Purpose, Broad-Based, and Other Grants, Selected Fiscal Years, 1975–97 (Dollar Amounts in Billions)

| | 1975 | 1978 | 1981 | 1984 | 1987 | 1989 | 1991 | 1993 | 1997 |
|---|---|---|---|---|---|---|---|---|---|
| **Current Dollars** | | | | | | | | | |
| General-purpose | 7.0 | 9.6 | 6.8 | 6.8 | 2.1 | 2.3 | 2.2 | 2.4 | 2.3 |
| Broad-based (mostly block) | 4.6 | 11.5 | 10.0 | 13.0 | 13.1 | 12.7 | 16.4 | 21.8 | 41.04[a] |
| Other (categoricals) | 38.2 | 56.8 | 77.9 | 77.8 | 93.2 | 106.9 | 133.4 | 182.2 | 190.86 |
| *Total* | 49.8 | 77.9 | 94.7 | 97.6 | 108.4 | 121.9 | 152.0 | 206.4 | 234.2 |
| **Percentage of Total** | | | | | | | | | |
| General-purpose | 14.1 | 12.3 | 7.2 | 7.0 | 1.9 | 1.9 | 1.4 | 1.1 | .1 |
| Broad-based (mostly block) | 9.2 | 14.7 | 10.6 | 13.3 | 12.1 | 10.4 | 10.8 | 10.6 | 17.5[a] |
| Other (categoricals) | 76.7 | 73.0 | 82.2 | 79.7 | 86.0 | 87.6 | 87.8 | 88.3 | 82.4 |
| *Total* | 100.0 | 100.0 | 100.0 | 100.0 | 100.0 | 100.0 | 100.0 | 100.0 | 100.0 |

*Sources:* Outlay data from Office of Management and Budget Analysis, unpublished data, 1991. Constant dollar computation based on GNP Implicit Price Deflator, "Economic Report of the President, 1992." Advisory Commission on Intergovernmental Relations, *Characteristics of Federal Grants-in-Aid Programs to State and Local Governments: Grants Funded FY 1993*, M-188 (Washington, D.C., January 1994), 7. Catalog of Federal Domestic Assistance (Washington, D.C., August 1997).

a. Includes ISTEA and TANF.

conditions that apply to all relevant grants) were done away with because they were based on law, but others relating to retrenchment, regulatory issuances, and other topics were added. The new block grants of the eighties were handled initially in a most permissive fashion, but over time most, like their predecessors, acquired more conditions, thanks largely to congressional actions, though state representatives succeeded in warding off some agency-proposed new directives.[1]

By all odds, however, the most dramatic programmatic dimension of the entire era was the emergence of the "new social regulation" as a major centralizing dynamic in the system. Nine major intergovernmental regulations, including major civil rights ones, were enacted during the Kennedy-Johnson administrations, and twenty-seven in such areas as health and safety, the environment, and equal access were legislated between 1969 and 1980. Remarkably, the eighties and early nineties witnessed the enactment of twenty-six additional major regulatory statutes and amendments with significant intergovernmental effects along with 125 new preemptions (see table Int-2, pp. 6–7). All this, despite what was supposed to have been an age of Reagan-Bush deregulation. Enactment of the Unfunded Mandates legislation in 1995, which allows a "point of order" if a measure comes up for full consideration that mandates state and local outlays above a certain dollar figure, tended to curb some of the earlier congressional regulatory recklessness. But it did not deter passage of the minimum wage increase which had a pronounced fiscal impact on some subnational governments.

8. *Using and then scrapping most conditions that helped create new regional institutions* were largely unnoticed dimensions of the Federal role during the Johnson-through-Reagan years. Between 1965 and 1980 there were enacted nearly forty Federal aid programs that encouraged the establishment of more than 1,800 single-purpose, multicounty planning bodies. Though the 660 multi-purpose, generalist-dominated regional units (usually councils of governments) benefited from the A-95 grant-application review-and-comment process, the units were not designated, at least half the time, to carry out the functions of the other Federally encouraged regional programs. The substate regional scene of the seventies, then, was primarily a product of procedural and institutional strings attached to Federal aid programs enacted over the previous fifteen years. In addition, at the multistate regional level, two enactments in 1965 gave rise to Federal-multistate economic development (Title V) and river basin (Title II) commissions. By the 1980s there were eight of the former and five of the latter.

By late 1981 Federal support for and membership in these bodies ended because they were eliminated by the Omnibus Budget Reconciliation Act (OBRA-1981). Drastic changes also were instituted by OBRA among the various substate regional undertakings: twelve of the thirty-nine such programs were terminated, eleven experienced major budget cuts, nine lost their regional features, six were revised, and one was left intact.[2] At present, what Federal support there is can be found primarily in the economic development, areawide Agency for the Aged, manpower training, and especially the Department of Transportation's Metropolitan Planning Organization (MPO) programs. The last was given major new authority in ISTEA (1991) and its successor TEA-21 (1997). But clearly, the Federal role of the late sixties and the seventies as the prime architect of new multi- and substate regional bodies experienced a severe slashing under Reagan. This was another largely unnoticed success for his disengaging approach to federalism, and it left the states in a position of having to confront the regional issue largely alone. There has been some interest in asserting a revamped Federal role in substate regionalism that has been shown by a few Clinton administration officials, but thus far no concrete proposals have been forthcoming.

9. *The erosion of Federal-state tax comity* was one of the most distinctive public finance developments. Outside the realm of Federal aid, its conditions, and intergovernmental regulation based chiefly on the conditional spending and supremacy clause powers, states and localities beginning in the seventies had to focus closely on various Federal efforts to reduce the scope of reciprocal tax immunity, especially actions directly affecting municipal bonds.[3] As long as the bonds were used for traditional governmental purposes, the Federal tax exemption accorded to them retained strong congressional support. In 1968 the Revenue and Expenditure Control Act stipulated the first tests to differentiate between tax-exempt and taxable bonds. Subsequently and in wake of the growth of private-activity bonds, Congress and the Treasury escalated their responses; state and local outcries regarding the erosion of their sovereign taxing powers mounted.

Meanwhile, in light of the explosion in private-activity bond issuances and the soaring Federal budget deficit, congressional laissez-faire attitudes began to crumble. The Mortgage Subsidy Bond Tax Act (1980), the Tax Equity and Fiscal Responsibility Act (TEFRA-1982), and the Deficit Reduction Act (DEFRA-1984) in part reflected the new viewpoint by removing the tax exemption from some kinds of industrial development bonds, by marking others for greater targeting or extinction, and by excluding some types of public transportation from the exempt-bond category. In the Tax Reform Act (TRA) of 1986, Congress placed most private-activity bonds under a state volume cap, put maximum limits on independent higher education bonds, and eliminated certain purposes for tax-exempt bonding.[4] On the revenue front, state and local sales taxes under TRA were no longer deductible from the Federal personal income tax. Finally, in *South Carolina v. Baker* (1988), the Supreme Court held that the Federal income tax exemption for interest on bonds issued by state and local governments was not constitutionally protected.[5] All these developments presented a new and highly controversial arena for continuous intergovernmental conflict, an arena within which interlevel comity previously had prevailed.

10. *The states were revitalized but still reined in.* During the thirty-six years at issue, the states were "reformed, reinvigorated, resourceful," in the words of Mavis Mann Reeves.[6] In terms of reform, forty or so modernized their constitutions

- to expand citizens' rights, notably "freedom of information," public hearings, and open meeting guarantees;

- to give all but three governors four-year terms;

- to strengthen gubernatorial budgetary, appointive, and staff powers;

- to streamline legislatures and make them more responsive and professional;

- to integrate the judicial system (well over two-thirds of all states now have moderate to strong unification of state and local components); and

- to overhaul the state bureaucracy (at least three-fifths of all states made significant consolidations, and over three-quarters of all state permanent civil servants are now under some form of merit system).

Thanks to these undertakings as well as external pressures (from the Supreme Court in the form of reapportionment decisions and from Congress with the Voting Rights Act of 1966), state political systems became more open, responsive, and representative than they had ever been.

State policy processes also generally exhibited a level of initiative, innovation, and industry never really equaled in the past. This was reflected in revived or newly assumed systemic roles: (1) as "laboratories of democracy," comparable to their record from 1870 to 1932; (2) as the major implementers of most Federal domestic aid programs, which involved a beefing up of their much lesser responsibilities in this area than had obtained from 1933 to 1960; and (3) as more caring "legal parents" of their local governments than formerly had been the case.

## Table Int-4
### State Finances and Manpower, Selected Years, 1967–94

|  | 1967 | 1977 | 1990 | 1994 |
|---|---|---|---|---|
| State share of total state-local own-source general revenue | 51.10% | 56.80% | 56.70% | 55.10% |
| Specific state taxes as percentage of total revenues |  |  |  |  |
|     Sales, gross receipts | 58.80% | 51.80% | 48.94% | 49.79% |
|     Individual Income | 15.30% | 25.20% | 31.97% | 31.37% |
|     Corporate Income | 6.98% | 9.08% | 7.24% | 6.88% |
|     Other | 19.47% | 13.91% | 11.85% | 11.95% |
| Total state aid (millions of dollars) | $18,434 | $60,277 | $175,274 | $221,160 |
| State aid as percentage of local own-source revenue | 41.50% | 50.38% | 44.23% | 55.70% |
| State employment | 1,873[a] | 3,343 | 4,503 | 4,693 |
| State employment as percentage of total public sector employment | 18.60% | 22.60% | 24.50% | 24.23% |

Sources: Advisory Commission on Intergovernmental Relations, *Significant Features of Fiscal Federalism*, vol. 2, *Revenues and Expenditures*, M-180-II (Washington, D.C., February 1992), 70, 90, 116–19; Advisory Council on Intergovernmental Relations, *Significant Features of Fiscal Federalism — 1995*, vol. 2, *Revenues and Expenditures* (Washington, D.C., October 1997), 44–45, 74, 76–77, 159.

a. In 1964.

In terms of fiscal resources, the states' situation during these three decades constitutes the main reason for their enhanced role in the system. The diversification of revenue sources tended generally to increase the personal income tax proportion of overall state revenues (see table Int-4) and permitted a significant hike in state aid, especially to education. It also provided the fiscal basis for the states' assuming a major or dominant role in funding Medicaid, corrections, environmental protection, highways, welfare, and health care/hospitals.

It was providential that most of these reforms, revitalizations, and new resource acquisitions occurred before the Reagan years because, absent states with these strengths, intergovernmental relations in the eighties would have been much more negative in systemic terms than they actually were and citizens would have fared much worse. Yet politically and judicially, the states fared much less favorably.

11. *The Supreme Court served basically as a centralizing force.* In addition to the above ten developments in the realm of operational federalism, the extraordinary role of the Supreme Court during the thirty plus years must also be noted. The Court, after all, exerted a generally centralizing influence throughout most of the period. In federalism cases involving commerce, conditional spending, and generally the taxing powers of Congress along with the supremacy clause — in short

the key constitutional provisions, other than the Fourteenth Amendment, affecting the jurisdictional status of states and their localities — the Federal courts in all but a few of the key cases upheld the national position. This was clearly the trend with the Warren Court, but there was no major retreat by the Burger Court. No constraints were placed on the power of Congress to spend for the general welfare (which is the basis of Federal grants and the conditions attached to them) despite Congress's growing habit of appending highly restrictive regulations to grants during the seventies. In *National League of Cities* v. *Usery* (1976) an attempt was made to curb Congress's power to regulate interstate commerce and to give substance to the Tenth Amendment as a curb on the exercise of this power.[7] And this proved to be short-lived; the decision was specifically overruled nine years later. The Burger Court did exhibit some sensitivity to state autonomy and police powers in certain areas but, in most civil rights and civil liberties cases, proved to be almost as sensitive to racial justice and libertarian values as its predecessor.[8]

Even with the elevation of Justice William H. Rehnquist to the chief justiceship in 1986 and the appointment of three new justices by Reagan and three by Bush, creating an overwhelmingly conservative Court, there have been few signs of major retreats from earlier centralizing positions on Congress's commerce, conditional spending, and taxing powers and on the supremacy clause; the appointment of two Clinton justices only served to strengthen this tendency. Greater concern for state and local authority was expressed in various areas. On balance, however, the Court's recent actions in certain of its cases dealing with federalism issues have preserved national power, especially in the conditional spending, explicit preemption, and to a lesser degree the commerce powers fields, while accenting states' rights in procedural and lesser jurisdictional disputes as well as in some crucial Tenth Amendment and commerce power cases. This suggests a new role for the court — Solomonic arbiter of the system.

12. *The full emergence of a new political system was perhaps the most significant phenomenon prompting major IGR changes.* Historically, the decentralized structure of the major U.S. political parties served to keep the system noncentralized and to provide important vertical channels of influence and power in the nation's capital. For much of our history, this system to constrain national domestic policy initiatives and, if such undertakings occurred, enactment usually recognized or was protective of state and local interests. This was because in most instances state and local party organizations were able to influence, sometimes decisively, the nomination and renomination of national policymakers. Where individual members were powers in their own right, and there were many such senators (even before the Seventeenth Amendment) and representatives, their basic and sole constituency was the electorate of their states or local districts.

During the past quarter century, all this changed. Even before 1960, state and local party organizations had gone into something of an eclipse because of the decline of bossism, the loss of party control over primaries, and the judicial attacks on the white primary in the South. Yet in 1960 and even in 1964, ours was still deemed a decentralized party system. National committees and conventions

possessed few significant powers, nationally based interest groups were comparatively few (though not feeble), and the media were still in their political infancy.
After 1968 far more authoritative national party organs emerged.[9] At the same
time, the parties as a whole are "indisputably weaker today" than heretofore,
especially in terms of influence on Federal officials.[10] The rapid rise in the number of pressure groups, PACs, pollsters, consultants, think tanks, and above all
the escalation of the media's influence and cost of access produced other complexes of nationalizing political forces. And these became primary actors in most
political areas.

One result has been that state and local officials generally were not and are
not accorded the deference — before congressional committees and national
administrative bodies or in their respective national conventions — that was
automatically theirs, at least through the midsixties. Yet the Supreme Court
in *Garcia v. San Antonio Metropolitan Transit Authority* (1985) held that "state
sovereign interests are more properly protected by procedural safeguards in the
structure of the federal system than by judicially created limitations on federal
power."[11] In short, the use of state and local political clout within the national
political and policy processes is the proper way to protect states' Tenth Amendment rights. But it was, and is, precisely in these processes that their influences
now are so weak.

At the beginning of the Republican 104th Congress, leaders of the thirty-one
Republican governors took advantage of the new congressional leadership's offer
of easy access to national policymaking, and some actually set up shop next to
the House office buildings and helped formulate some of the planks in the Gingrich Contract with America. A candid interview with any of the governors at
the end of the second session of the 104th would reveal that while the states got
some items they wanted, they lost more than they won, and intrusive conditions
attached to grant programs experienced no real declines. State spokespersons
largely encountered closed doors with the 105th Congress. So much for state
clout in Washington, D.C., in an era of alleged devolution.

## Conclusion

The above twelve distinctive developments since 1961 — some nationally in-
spired, some state or locally initiated, some a direct product of changes in public
opinion — constitute fundamental changes in our system of governance. The
developments are not merely logical extensions of the intergovernmental legacy
of the New Deal or of the Eisenhower years. Transforming attitudinal, political,
representational, programmatic, and institutional shifts have occurred since the
early 1960s, and there is no way that a return to the simple "cooperative federalism" of yesteryear will ever occur, not to mention a drive back to traditional
dual (or compartmentalized) federalism as some pundits would have it.

Ours, then, is a system that currently seems to contain a remarkable cluster
of contrasting characteristics. For example, it is

- overloaded and undernourished — overloaded programmatically and undernourished fiscally;

- top heavy and bottom heavy — top heavy still in most policy areas and bottom heavy in its continuing dependence on the states and, to a lesser degree, on the localities and nonprofits to implement most Federal domestic programs;

- overregulated and underregulated — in the sense that statutorily Federal and state intergovernmental regulation remains excessive, and Federal executive-branch administration of key regulations and its supervision of the mushrooming contracting loan, loan-guarantee, and related government-sponsored enterprises (whose funds have soared while grant authorizations have risen incrementally) have been lax to criminally negligent in some cases;

- activist and passive — activist in reenacting most old and all popular programs and in pursuing and passing new policy proposals, some of which are simply symbolic, others of which have no proper place on the national agenda since they are of state, local, or private concern, and still others that are worthy and in the national interest; and passive in the sense that deficit worries until 1998, related and continuing retrenchment concerns, and populist conservative personnel and budget policies have combined to produce "hollow government," "shadow bureaucracies," and "dead law" at all levels, but especially at the national level, which combine to reflect agencies starved for personnel and laws that are not being implemented;

- co-optive and cooperative — in that arbitrary Federal (and state) regulations and grant conditions along with certain judicial dictates continued during the last third of the twentieth century even during the two Republican Congresses of the nineties; yet certain older grant programs, presidential waivers for welfare and Medicaid reforms, and more block grant enactments indicate that the earlier collaborative ethic is by no means dead; and

- competitive as well as collaborative — witness the state-local confrontations with the national government over mandates, regulations, and Federal threats to their revenue resources, but also the increasingly shared goals of all levels in confronting such challenges as educational reform, health care cost controls, crime, and transportation.

Today's federalism has been abused, in the sense of being callously ignored at times and severely overused at others. It also is an ambiguous and overloaded system or, in the parlance of the day, a "conflicted federalism," though it is less conflicted now than it was in 1992, 1988, or certainly 1980. Hence the first half of the title of this study: *The Rebirth of Federalism*. The next chapter deals in depth with how the multiplying interpretations of the system in the past and in recent years have helped generate this contemporary description.

*Part 1*

# Federalism Today

## Chapter 1

# Federalism and Its Many Faces:
# What Is Federalism?
# What Are Intergovernmental Relations?

As the history of federal systems lengthens, so do the variety and number of definitions. A simple one is suggested by the American record, as well as that of the other, older sister systems (for example, Switzerland, Canada, Australia, and Germany). It holds that federalism is a governmental system that includes a central government and at least one major subnational tier of governments; that assigns significant substantive powers to both levels initially by the provisions of a written constitution; and that succeeds over time in sustaining a territorial division of powers by judicial, operational, representational, and political means. This balancing arrangement avoids the hypercentralism of unitary systems, wherein sovereign power is located at the center, as well as the centrifugal chaos of confederations, wherein the constituent units are basically sovereign, thereby achieving the "middle ground" Madison sought well before the convening of the Constitutional Convention.[1]

The territorial principle of divided powers was and is the prime gift of the United States to the art and science of government. It is the formula to which emerging nations turn when confronting the ultimate systemic dilemma of how to achieve national unity for certain overarching purposes while preserving constituent governmental autonomy for reasons of area, regional, ethnoreligious, and/or socioeconomic diversity.[2] Currently, the federal format is experiencing a new popularity, given the challenges of a post–Cold War and increasingly democratizing world as well as of the resurgence of ancient, even tribalistic nationalisms. Federalism, then, is a constitutional principle involving a distinctive territorial division of powers, usually a special approach to representation within the national government, and mechanisms — both legal and political — to settle interlevel disputes. Its embodiment as a system is not easily established and usually is even more difficult to maintain. A balancing act, after all, is never easy to sustain. In most federations, the dynamics of modernization have tended to generate a heavy tilt toward the center, while the dynamics of revived old ethnocentrisms have tended toward a devolutionary result, if not disunion. Moreover, excessive nationalizing of policymaking, the persistent propensity to regulate, dissatisfaction with the performance of certain national and grant-in-aid programs, along with the decentralizing potential of the technological revolution in communications recently have nurtured drives to devolve functions, powers, and responsibilities to lower tier subnational governments in both unitary systems (as with the recent moves to enhance Scottish and Welsh autonomy in the United Kingdom) and federal systems; note the effort of the three new federalisms — Nixon's, Reagan's and Gingrich's.

In a constitutional democracy, *intergovernmental relations* (IGR) may involve a web, simple or complex (depending on the level of modernization in the system), of constitutional, electoral, representational, programmatic, fiscal, administrative, and judicial relationships — some formal, some informal — between and among the officials at all levels of government. Such relationships are found in all systems larger than a city-state and in authoritarian systems as well as constitutional democracies of the unitary type. In a federative system, however, the relationships generally have less of a central-command character and are more reciprocal and mutually interactional. Federations, to be sure, have special need for arrangements of this type because the extent of interdependence among levels is usually greater than in other systems, given the central government's modern tendency to rely on subnational governments to carry out many domestic national policies and programs.

In the history of American IGR, as will be demonstrated later, the earlier patterns were relatively simple; there was minimal interpenetration of each level's programmatic, personnel, functional, and fiscal spheres. Twentieth-century developments — Progressivism, the New Deal, and especially the Great Society and its aftermath, along with the emergence of an industrial and then a postindustrial socioeconomic system — produced an extraordinary labyrinthian maze of intergovernmental linkages. The present complex, however, is a little less complicated than its predecessor of 1980, but more on that later.

*What is the relationship between federalism and intergovernmental relations?* It is not a case, as one authority has described it, of where "federalism–old style is dead. Yet federalism–new style — is alive and well and living in the United States. Its name is intergovernmental relations."[3] Old-style federalism — the constitutional dual federalism of the Founders and of the Supreme Court until 1937 — is nearly dead, though the Court has not removed all the barriers to full national control of state and local governmental activities and has resurrected some during the past few years. Moreover, the operational roles of the state and local governments in the system have never been stronger. Federalism as a legal and operational precept, then, is still alive and acquiring some new strength. IGR have never been wholly separated from this constitutional doctrine but have been and are inextricably linked to it and its interpretation by the Court and by politicians. Federalism has been a constant concern since 1789, though more so before 1937 than after; IGR have emerged as a problem only since the thirties, when they began to expand and became essential to furthering national and subnational governmental goals. In quantitative and qualitative terms, the recent pattern of IGR has gone far beyond the political, electoral, legal, judicial, and especially the few programmatic linkages between the Federal and state governments that prevailed in the nineteenth century and in modified form during the first third of the twentieth century.

The complicated hallmarks of late-twentieth-century intergovernmental relations, as Deil Wright has summarized them, are "(1) the number and variety of governmental units; (2) the number and variety of the public officials involved; (3) the intensity and regularity of contacts among the officials; (4) the importance of the officials' actions and attitudes; and (5) the preoccupation with financial policy issues."[4] All of these traits are by-products of an expanding national government since Roosevelt and more recently of state governments as well. What is more, the traits resulted from political and judicial actions encouraging, or at least sanctioning (in the case of the courts), the expansion at both levels. Federalism and intergovernmental relations, then, are separate but interdependent. To understand the latter, one must probe the former, and the reverse is also true to some extent.

Unfortunately, *federalism* and *intergovernmental relations* are terms that today are frequently used almost interchangeably. But there is a difference. Federalism is chiefly a constitutional, legal, jurisdictional, power-political, and two-tier formal systemic concept. Intergovernmental relations are more encompassing; multitiered; more functional, fiscal, administrative in foci; and more flexible and informal, though not lacking formal features. They, like federalism, changed significantly over the past four decades.

## Models, Metaphors, and Interpretations

What federalism means specifically in terms of the territorial division of powers and of the appropriate mode of relationships between the two constitutionally recognized levels of government (national and state) has been the subject of contention, even violent conflict, during the past two hundred years. In part, this is because the Framers for good and practical reasons left many questions relating to federalism unanswered or unclear (for example, the locus of sovereignty, the nature of the Union, the scope of its powers), and in part the contention stems from their overriding desire to create a "flexible instrument concerned with functions and the practice of government."[5]

Politics and common sense encouraged later theorists, political leaders, and plain citizens to enunciate their own conceptions of federalism. These have been diverse, discordant, and numerous. They tell us much about federalism's evolution, enduring importance, and changing meanings, though the proliferation of models, metaphors, and glib single-factor-dominated labels in recent years has caused some to question their usefulness.[6] Those used here are helpful in that each touches on a significant feature or features of the system — past or present.

## Power-Centered Conceptions

A key factor conditioning the development of one group of contrasting theories is power and where most of it should reside. In the debates between the Federalists and the anti-Federalists, and later between the Federalists and Jeffersonian Republicans down to the present, there have been *nation-centered* and *state-centered* interpretations.[7] In the nineteenth century, the debate centered on whether the U.S. Constitution was a compact entered into by the states or a higher law emanating from its ratification by the people in the only arena then known to indicate popular acceptance: specially elected state conventions. Interpretation of the implied powers clause of Article I, Section 8, which stipulates that Congress may enact such laws as are "necessary and proper for carrying into Execution" the powers expressly stated in the same section, has been a perennial legal point of disputation between the two schools of thought. In the current era the Supreme Court's nationalistic interpretations of the Tenth Amendment and the conditional spending power, not to mention Congress's right to regulate commerce, have been bitter points of constitutional contention between the two camps.

In assessing IGR developments from 1937 to 1980, Michael D. Reagan and John G. Sanzone came up with the centripetal *permissive federalism* label to describe the evolving condition wherein "there is a sharing of power and authority between the national and state governments, but the state's share rests upon the permission and permissiveness of the national government."[8] These scholars have no doubt that the national government possesses the legal authority and the political clout to impose "whatever degree of restrictiveness it wishes." Many authorities today agree with Reagan and Sanzone and consider ours still to be a nation-centered system, despite some diminishment of the Federal role and a strengthening of that of the states since 1981. Others see the reemerging of a more balanced, if not a state-centered, system. A basic purpose of this book is to probe these interpretations and determine which is correct.

The earliest clearly articulated theory of *dual federalism* came from John Taylor of Caroline County, Virginia, in his *Constitutions Construed and Constitutions Vindicated* (1820), wherein the proposition was enunciated that an equal distribution of power between the two levels is the essential federalist feature of the Constitution. For Taylor, it was the clear duty of the branches of the national government and the states to maintain a parity of power. Under Chief Justice Roger B. Taney, the Supreme Court developed its own dual federalism concept, which was resurrected after the Civil War and served as a basis of negating both state and Federal actions deemed contrary to the Constitution.

Dual federalism, in this context, with its separate, equal spheres of power serves as the mean between the nation- and state-centered approaches. This version has survived to the present in the arguments of the many scholars, political pundits, and citizens who urge a righting of the centralizing imbalances in the federal system. It should be noted that the nation- and state-centered approaches were prevalent in the earlier eras when there was minimal national involvement with and assistance to state and local governments, and in the twentieth century when such entanglements became endless. Dual federalism as a balanced power precept has enjoyed considerable durability, but as an operational theory it enjoyed a different fate, as the following analysis indicates.

## Independent Competitive versus Independent Collaborative Concepts

A second cluster of theories is based on differing views of the proper functional and concomitant behavioral relations between the levels. On one hand, the compartmentalized concept posits that with the exception of the few concurrent powers cited in or inferred from the Constitution (for example, commerce, taxation, police) the functions, administrative personnel, and revenues of the national government are and should be essentially separate from those of state and local governments. This is the *operational version of dual federalism* and is partly derived from the equal-power version cited above. It was the implicit theory of most of the Framers, the explicit theory of some, and certainly the clear approach of the members of the Second Constitutional Convention (that is, the First Congress), which among many "fleshing-out" actions made it clear that there would be no reliance on state and local officials to implement national functions (notably, customs collections). As will be demonstrated later, dual federalism, or the "layer cake," or compartmentalized, theory, was almost exclusively the operational theory from 1789 to 1860; the dominant form from 1861 to 1932, given the meager Federal regulatory and grant-in-aid activities that emerged in this period; and a much reduced but not dead precept operationally from the inauguration of Franklin D. Roosevelt through to 1963, despite the emergence of cooperative federalism.

In the current era, the *New Federalism* of Ronald Reagan, in theory at least, constituted an effort to return functionally to a form of dual federalism. Reagan federalism emphasized a major reduction of the Federal role in the federal system by means of domestic program eliminations, devolutions, and cutbacks, along with a parallel drive to reduce Federal regulation of business and of subnational governments. The Reagan strategy did not succeed, but the level of intergovernmental entanglements is lower now than in 1980. But this, of course, did not constitute a return to dual federalism.

Collaborative or interdependent functional theories of federalism began with *cooperative federalism*, as was suggested earlier, yet isolated examples of interlevel cooperation can be found in the pre-1933 period.[9] In essence, the term was not coined until the fifties, though extensive intergovernmental collaboration in the form of Federal grants, services-in-aid, and other forms of interlevel assistance were prime features of the New Deal. The growth of Federal grants and the salutary character of most of their conditions have been used as basic indices of the evolution of cooperative or, to use its culinary metaphor, of "marble cake" federalism. *Creative Federalism* was a basic component of Johnson's Great Society. It was rooted in its simpler cooperative predecessor but was also markedly different from the intergovernmental system of 1960 or even of 1963. Its greater program scope, its dollar size, its inclusive-partnership theory (involving the range of sub-state governments and nonprofits, not just the states, as was predominant in 1960), its innovative plunges into new program areas, its use of new grant forms, and its urban focus combined to transform the earlier, largely two-tier, inexpensive, rurally oriented, and incrementally conditioned intergovernmental complex into something quite complicated, quite complex, and quite controversial. After all it added a second story to the modest Rooseveltian welfare state and converted the Lincolnian legacy of the Fourteenth and Fifteenth Amendments into live law.

Nixon's *New Federalism* was also a by-product of cooperative federalism because it focused heavily on ways to enhance a more genuine partnership among the Federal, state, and local governments through efforts to develop a more streamlined grant system, improved Federal field-office operations and expanded recipient discretion through block grants, as well as General Revenue Sharing and a strengthening of the intergovernmental communication and information systems. Success marked some of these efforts, and defeat or deadlock with Congress was the fate of others. Unlike Reagan's New Federalism, Nixon's assigned the Federal government clear and continuing fiscal and programmatic intergovernmental roles in a range of program areas.

Although each form of federalism reflects an increasing level of intergovernmental relations and hence of interdependence, *cooperative* is not a descriptor of all the varieties of intergovernmental behavior in the scores of program areas that were involved with Federal grants during the late sixties and especially the seventies. *Controversial, confrontational, conflicting,* even *litigious* would be just as appropriate in instances where program goals were new and untested at the state or local level, were redistributive in terms of their fiscal effects, or were geared to achieving individual or group behavior modification. Many of the Federal programs enacted in the Johnson and Nixon years incorporated one or more of these three objectives, and that meant problems, not partnerships.

Conflict did not produce disengagement or attempts to return to a dual federalism model. Reality and the resources required to achieve various policy goals indicated the continuing, even intensifying need to harness all levels to pull together, albeit reluctantly in many cases. By 1980 this phenomenon had produced an extraordinary degree of interlevel linkages, and by 1989 at the end of Reagan's second term, or even now after two Republican Congresses, only somewhat fewer IGR entanglements. These continuing linkages suggest the reality of significant interdependence, if not a large measure of reluctant, though necessary, collaboration. Such is the nature of much of today's cooperative federalism.

### Dominant Players and Policy Arenas

The modifier of *federalism* in recent years usually has signified the crucial or controlling role of a particular institutional player in an intergovernmental area. *Executive federalism* is not an American term but is frequently found in analyses of Canadian, Australian, and German federalism,[10] given the strength of executive leadership at the national and constituent levels in these three parliamentary federal systems. It depicts the corresponding capacity of the premiers at both levels in each system to meet regularly and to arrive at binding agreements. Three of the intergovernmental interpretations described above were products of presidential initiatives and pronouncements (Johnson, Nixon, and Reagan). Only in Johnson's case, however, can it be said that the president's intergovernmental initiatives were largely accepted by Congress. In terms of intergovernmental reforms generally, and especially grant reforms, it should be remembered that such undertakings from Eisenhower to Carter more times than not emanated from the White House. It is difficult to label all the Reagan and Bush or even Clinton IGR proposals as grant reformist in the conventional sense, but they certainly would have changed the system had all of them been enacted.

The term *bureaucratic or administrative federalism* is not commonly employed to depict the pivotal role of civil servants at all levels in the implementation, sometimes in the formulation, and certainly in the reformulation of assistance programs, but other terms and metaphors have been used. *Vertical functional autocracies* was a term first used by Meyer Kestnbaum, chair of President Eisenhower's temporary Commission on Intergovernmental Relations (1954–55), to describe dramatically the emerging programmatic power of professional grant administrators at the disbursing and receiving ends of the connecting IGR ladder. It was sometimes used to describe the emergence of "iron triangles," that is, the legislative, administrative, and interest group angles of tightly knit functional triangles, with a territorial basis to their strength, wherein the tightly knit administrative–legislative–interest group triad that each grant tended to generate at the national level was replicated at the state tier and sometimes at the local. With Terry Sanford's *picket-fence federalism* metaphor of 1967, the importance of the interlevel bonds between and among grant program specialists, such as educators and highway engineers, gained greater academic, political, and public recognition.[11] The corresponding weakness of generalists, whether in the executive or legislative branches at all levels, in facing down these particularistic phalanxes of program specialists and their allies led to efforts, especially under Nixon in Washington and by governors in the states during the early seventies, to counteract this threatening situation.

When Federal grant administrators were surveyed in 1975, a majority of the respondents revealed far fewer programmatic and professional rigidities than their predecessors of the midsixties.[12] Their greater flexibility in coping with the system's managerial, subnational personnel and with related concerns led this author to come up with the label *bamboo-fence federalism* to capture the Federal grant administrators' newfound capacity to bend with but not succumb to prevailing political winds. No new bureaucratic designations have been given to characterize the administrators' generally subdued, if not supine, IGR role in the eighties. All power to the professionals, after all, has not been a timely theme since the late sixties, and it is clout that generally prompts the coining of clever metaphors.

Turning to the courts, *judicial federalism* as a designational term is fairly recent,[13] despite the Federal judiciary's significant influence on the evolution of American federalism since the beginning. The judiciary's emergence as a "new" factor influencing federalism over the past three decades is due to the fact that the Supreme Court since the sixties has served as the initiator of certain fundamental changes in the federal system. Most of its key decisions relating to federalist issues have tended to uphold national authority,[14] but some also have strengthened subnational governments — as with the reapportionment and civil rights cases. In the seventies and even the eighties, with the continued expansion of national authority in the programmatic and regulatory areas by the political branches of the Federal government, the Court almost always upheld these actions when they were legally challenged. A whole new body of case law dealing with grants-in-aid is also illustrative of the Federal judiciary's new role in IGR developments.[15]

The Court has served generally as a major force for centripetalism from 1962 (some would say 1937) to roughly 1990. The Burger years produced as many reiterations and expansions of Warren Court precedents as modifications or overrulings. No special sensitivity to the inferior jurisdictional position into which the states (and their localities) were placed in the earlier era was reflected in the bulk of the Burger Court decisions relating to federalism questions. The chief exception to this broad generalization was *National League of Cities* v. *Usery*,[16] which proved to be aberrational. The same trend can be found in the record of the early years of Chief Justice Rehnquist's tenure. In more recent years, the Court has reflected more sensitivity to state prerogatives, while not touching in any substantive way the conditional spending power (the power of Congress to "spend for the General Welfare" and to append any conditions it wants to the grants that result from the exercise of this power) nor the supremacy clause (the Constitution, laws made pursuant to it, and treaties are the "Supreme Law of the Land"). The commerce power, however, has not been seriously circumscribed, but certain Tenth Amendment protections have been recognized in this decade. The Court clearly is a player in current intergovernmental relations — a major and sometimes the ultimate player — hence the frequent use of the term *judicial federalism* to capture the Court's expanding influence on the future of federalism.

Another major institutional actor is Congress. Yet the term *congressional federalism*, like its judicial counterpart, is of comparatively recent vintage, dating from the seventies.[17] Congressional conditioning of how American federalism evolved manifested itself as early as the First Congress, which really clarified the Founders' intent in several crucial areas — all to the advantage of the new national government. From Madison to McKinley (with the obvious major exceptions of Jackson and Lincoln, and the lesser ones of Polk and Cleveland), Congress was the prime arena within which national policies were developed or failed to develop. In terms of the fate of federal union, the great compromises of 1820, 1833, and 1850 were indispensable to preserving it during those forty fateful years prior to the Civil War. These were largely congressionally crafted, basically engineered by that master of interregional conflict resolution, Senator Henry Clay (Whig-Ky.).

Congress has almost always been a force to contend with in the twentieth century, and presidential leadership has been much more a factor to consider than previously. Yet in the seventies Congress emerged as the paramount player in formulation and enactment of expansionist national policies. This was a first. When Congress was strong in earlier years it usually had been a constraining, not an initiating, force in national policy development. Congress thus became the chief architect of the overloaded, if not dysfunctional, intergovernmental system in place by 1980, and it was the chief cause of the failure of many of the Reagan federalism proposals. To overlook Congress is to ignore one of the key forces for the recent centralization in the entire system.

The states are also major actors in the contemporary system, though the designation *state-centered federalism* is rarely used. Yet terms like "resurgent states" and "the maligned states" along with recent summary generalizations — for example, "State power needn't be resurrected because it never died"; "As federal policymaking ebbs, states are assuming new powers"; and "Although often overruled by the federal government, states are the primary domestic governors" — combine to suggest that a new, very special state role in contemporary intergovernmental relations has come into being.[18] The states currently perform all of their historical functions: as instruments (but not *the* instrument, as was the case before 1860) of social choice and of politics for their respective electorates; as "laboratories of experimentation," as they were in the 1860–1932 era and especially during its Progressive period (1900–1920); and as assistants in implementing Federal grant-in-aid programs, as they were from 1933 to 1963. In addition, as Samuel H. Beer has pointed out, the states today also plan and control big and frequently expensive intergovernmental programs and use their position as the major intermediate level of government and of politics to mobilize political support for these programs and for other modernizing undertakings.[19]

The states' blending of traditional and new intergovernmental functions has occurred against a backdrop of wide-ranging efforts — mostly indigenous but some externally prompted — to modernize the structures, finances, decision-making processes, administration, and politics of their governments. In operational terms, the states have become the paramount implementers of domestic governmental programs, given the Federal government's heavy reliance on them to carry out almost all of its domestic programs. States also implement their own policy initiatives in such areas as public education, the environment, consumer affairs, transportation, and welfare reform, and increasingly have assumed special and expanding parenting roles regarding their localities. In light of all these developments, perhaps the designation *state-dominated functional federalism* is appropriate, though awkward, to depict the newly acquired operational significance of the states for American federalism. The label, of course, stresses the operational facets of the current system but leaves out the judicial, regulatory, and political dimensions, where the states have fared poorly. Most recently in his *Disunited States*, John D. Donahue develops the theme that "by the measures that best gauge governmental power — authority, resources, and legitimacy — the tide is flowing away from Washington."[20] And he views what he takes to be a broad devolutionary development with no small amount of alarm, since it among other things menaces America's capacity to "engage a maturing global market system" and threatens a "balkanization" of the country. Later analysis will probe the accuracy of these various interpretations of the states' roles at present in our federal system.

## Processes That Impact

Along with the familiar power-oriented and interactional behavioral theories of federalism, as well as the more recent prime-actor approach, certain interlevel processes or functions — the regulatory, fiscal, and political — have experienced dramatic transformations in recent years with concomitant crucial impacts on Federal-state-local relations. Judicial federalism was analyzed under the institutional actor heading and appropriately so, given the pivotal position of the Supreme Court. Yet it could have been dealt with here because it also involves an interlevel process with various actors and certain results that resemble the other IGR processes described below.

Perhaps the most extraordinary new IGR activity affecting contemporary federalism's functioning is the rise of an unusual type of regulation at both the Federal and state levels beginning in the sixties and extending to the present — deregulatory drives notwithstanding. The activity has come to be known as *regulatory federalism.*

The perennially heavy use of narrow categorical grants from 1964 onward is one part of this story, despite the advent of the more flexible block grants. The latter, however, usually acquire more conditions and constraints over time. Of more significance were "the new social regulations," starting in 1964 and rapidly growing during the next decade. In the nondiscrimination, consumer protection, health and safety, environmental, and minority-participation areas, to cite the more significant, various types of IGR regulations were enacted by Congress.[21] Between 1960 and 1995, major such actions totaled 108, with hardly any letup during the Reagan-Bush years.

Fundamental differences between the new social regulation and the earlier type are the contrasting subject matter and the fact that the new regulations were and are directed as much against state and local governments as against the private sector. In the case of the states, they frequently have had to serve simultaneously as the objects and implementers of the same regulations. Not to be overlooked here are a series of Federal court decisions requiring state and local governments to reapportion their legislatures; eliminate prayers in public schools; notify defendants in criminal proceedings of their rights prior to questioning and detention; end legal restrictions on abortions; provide legal counsel to indigent defendants facing criminal charges; and do away with racial segregation in their public schools.[22] Yet another facet of this new and intrusive form of Federal regulation is "arbitrary" executive orders (such as the surgeon general's initial "Baby Doe" regulation issued in the early 1980s, which barred dissemination of any information on family planning in clinics funded by Federal grants) and the more than 280 Federal preemptions of state authorities that occurred from 1960 to 1991 with scarcely a ripple of reaction.[23] Clearly, the latter do not directly regulate state and local governments, but they do reduce the scope of the states' police power, which is the legal basis for most state regulatory actions. The many facets of this nationalizing brand of regulation are to add to the imbalances and ambivalences in the overall system, to undercut the collaborative underpinnings of IGR, and to strengthen Federal co-optive tendencies in current intergovernmental relations.

Finally, the states also regulate both the private sector and their own localities, and the incidence of the latter regulatory activity has picked up appreciably during the past three decades. From a local governmental perspective, state regulation frequently appears far more onerous than does the Federal. Of course, some state proscriptions were prompted by congressional enactments, but regardless of the proscriptions' origin, local governments for more than two decades have felt a kind of "double jeopardy" menacing them and their "home-rule" prerogatives, given the dual-pronged Federal and state campaigns in this social regulatory area.

Closely related to these recent developments in the IGR regulatory realm are those in the *fiscal federalism* sphere. Some explain the steady march of Federal mandates in terms of the continuing shortfall in Federal revenues in light of mounting expenditure demands and the corresponding ability of Washington to link regulations to grant funds, as has frequently been the case since the seventies.

The 1960s witnessed the longest broad economic expansion in the twentieth century, which helped sustain widespread optimism about the nation's economic future[24] and underpin the expansionist fiscal policies of the Johnson and early Nixon administrations. Despite (and partly because of) the emergence of various destabilizing factors — OPEC and soaring oil prices, a general rise in inflation, a major recession (1975–77), greater foreign competition, and "stagflation" — fiscal expansionism dominated the response of the national political branches. This pushed Federal aid numbers, grant outlays, and recipients far beyond the high-water marks of the sixties. Local government outlays from own-source revenues stabilized by 1974, and the same occurred with the states two years later. The continued growth in their respective expenditures occurred because of the continued flow of Federal aid funds.

During the eighties, fiscal federalism acquired a pair of subspecies. Domestic retrenchment, not rapid domestic fiscal expansionism, was the hallmark of the decade. Following up on his campaign promises, Reagan sought to cut taxes and domestic expenditures in 1981. He succeeded handsomely in both areas, though more in the former than the latter. Meanwhile, the worst recession (1981–83) since 1939 had set in and caused further reductions in Federal (and state and local) revenues. Despite tax hikes in 1982 and 1984 and the mandated rise in Social Security revenues in 1983, the reductionist goals of the 1981 Economic Recovery Tax Act (ERTA) were not really affected, but the radical reductionist domestic spending goals of the Omnibus Budget Reconciliation Act (1981) did not materialize. In addition, the comprehensive tax reform package of 1986 shifted $120 billion from individuals to corporations.[25] The impact of these various fiscal actions was to assault "the revenue base of the modern welfare state," as one authority phrased it.[26]

When the impacts of the recession, the revenue cuts, the outsize hikes in defense outlays (especially from FY 1982 to FY 1985), and the failure of Congress to adhere to the administration's calls for further drastic cuts in domestic expenditures are combined, the largest deficits in peacetime history resulted. Reagan's campaign promise of a balanced budget by 1984 had long since evaporated. The IGR fallout was a *deficit-driven federalism*, wherein national outlays in grant-in-aid assistance were held to a modest rate of growth, expenditures in the area of nontransfer payments were rolled back, and major new IGR ventures were barred.

The effects of this reining in of the Federal role in intergovernmental fiscal relations generated what John Shannon has termed *fend-for-yourself federalism*, a situation wherein the Federal budget deficits, the concomitant cut in real terms of Federal aid, and the near-elimination of direct Federal-local grant programs created an environment requiring state and local officials to become more self-reliant.[27] And this was not difficult from 1984 to about 1988, during which time state revenues and state aid increased, thanks to the return of prosperity.[28] With the onset in 1989 of a recession with minor rallies and three declines, state and local revenues were as adversely affected as those of the Federal government. It signaled the arrival of an *all-level deficit-driven federalism*, an even more potentially fratricidal version of the fend-for-yourself type. With the national government, this led to more deficit spending and greater efforts to curb it. For states and localities facing a prospective deficit during the rough 1989 to 1993 years, the only options were to raise taxes, reduce services, or both because they had to balance their budgets. The need to make these unpopular choices evaporated as the states began to accumulate surpluses in the middle and late nineties, though many localities did not enjoy the pleasure of acquiring fiscal cushions as a result of the continuing extraordinary expansion of the national economy.

To sum up, fiscal federalism in all its manifestations has probably been the most fundamental determinant of current IGR. Some argue that it is the controlling determinant and a centrifugal one at that. But this notion is rejected by others, who note the contrasting centripetal influences of the judicial, regulatory, and political processes. No one, however, can disagree with the generalization that fiscal federalism has been a powerful force contributing first to the activist and then to the reductionist transformations of IGR from 1964 to 1998.

A third process that has been influential in a power-political sense involves the countless interlevel activities that fall under the general heading of political. As with the judicial, regulatory, and fiscal forms of federalism, *political federalism* is a very recent designation, despite the fact that parties, pressure groups, and politics have long conditioned the development of both federalism and IGR.[29] Parties, especially the major parties, have — since Jefferson's departure from Washington's cabinet in 1793 — played the most salutary role of the three. Over their nearly two hundred years the parties have usually adhered to electoral, organizational, program, governing, and integrative practices that have supported the federal principle and interlevel comity, not centralization, separation, or intergovernmental confrontation. This has not been the same with pressure groups generally. Though not envisioned by Madison when writing *Federalist* No. 10, major parties have served more times than not as another means — within and partly outside the orbit of his governmental system of horizontal and vertical partial separations of powers — to help control "the effects" of "factions" (that is, interest groups).

For most of their history, the major parties have exhibited noncentralized organizational, heterogenous compositional, weak ideological, and poor disciplinary traits.[30] In the main, they served as a decentralizing force in the system. Moreover, until the 1960s they tried and sometimes succeeded in keeping controversial issues that divided their national ranks largely at the state and local levels.[31] What real political power and influence that existed were at the state and especially the local levels during the pre-1968 period.[32]

Use of the term *political federalism* stems directly from the decline of the parties and the arrival of a "new political system" in which the parties are only one player and not always the major one. The deterioration and demise of the "old party system" began at different times. A basic early causal development was the erosion of state and local party control over their own and national nominating processes, thanks to the increase of primaries, state regulations, and, in the case of the Democrats, constraining action by national party instrumentalities.

The rise of a new generation of more independent, issue-oriented voters free of the dependencies on state and local political organizations that many of their parents possessed is a generational political development that should be remembered. The rise of stronger national parties was a result of some of the centralizing actions cited above. In addition, Federal judicial intervention, Federal election reform, and national parties' renewal undertakings have contributed to this historic development.[33] National party organizations — the Republicans' more than the Democrats' — are stronger than they have ever been.[34]

Equally important is the fact that the parties at all levels have had to compete and sometimes collaborate with several new, tough competitors. In the process, they usually have come out the losers, with the state and local organizations suffering more than the national because they already were undermined by state regulatory and national party actions. Voter contact now is largely achieved through the mass media rather than by party stalwarts, leaders, and publications. The media have become the prime influence on how most voters form their views on issues and candidates. It is impossible to discount the evolving, ever more powerful role generally of television and of some of the press.[35] Closely linked to this development are soaring campaign costs, mainly due to the candidate's need to rely on the media to make a case before the electorate. Individual contributions still are the prime source of most campaign dollars for both state and congressional elections, but political action committees (PACs) are the second. Out of all this has come the "independent politician" with his or her own organization, fund-raising activities, campaign consultants, and, in big contests, pollster. It is a circumstance that has done little to aid state and local organizations' revival.[36]

In an overall systemic sense, the three-decade proliferation in the number, variety, and influence of pressure groups in Washington, D.C., constitutes the most significant threat to the major parties and to American federalism as we have known it. The number whose headquarters are in the national capital increased by 40 percent between 1960 and 1981.[37] The types of pressure groups operating in Washington mushroomed with the big increases in the number of citizens' groups for civil rights/minorities, social welfare, women, the elderly, and the handicapped, along with lesser but important growth in the trade and professional associational sectors.[38] The weakening of internal formal and informal congressional procedures and institutions by the democratic reforms of the early seventies also strengthened pressure groups' impacts on national policy developments, especially in the seventies. Congress was less porous during the eighties and nineties, thanks to the rigors of retrenchment and the paramount positions of the finance committees in both chambers.

All of this brings us back to Madison and his treatise on "factions." This most important Framer was primarily concerned with control by a majority faction. Today's dilemma is the impact of multiple minority factions who through modern communications and transportation have been able to pierce the geographic barrier and pursue their narrow goals nationally in a way that Madison could not have contemplated. "Federalism as safeguard against special interests became federalism as opportunity," as one authority summed it up.[39] Political federalism, as it operates today, undeniably is a prime factor and frequently a nationalizing one, though a few observers see some recent revival of state and local political party strength.

## Developmental Theories

A final group of introductory issues that merits attention is the differing interpretations relating to the development of American federalism. One approach focuses not so much on the direction of change as on a basic cultural value and a general attitudinal approach that combine to produce a "constantly evolving, problem-solving attempt to work out solutions to major problems on an issue-by-issue basis, resulting in modifications of the federal and intergovernmental systems."[40] For Parris N. Glendening and Mavis Mann Reeves, this *Pragmatic Federalism* generates an "elasticity of arrangements" that helps to maintain the "viability of the American System."[41]

Others focus on direction when probing the developmental question, and a preponderance of expert opinion tends to the view that the evolution of American federalism has been essentially toward greater accumulation of power in Washington, D.C. The modernization theories developed by sociologists and economists provide rationales for this development because they focus on economic, social, cultural, and the resulting political changes that mark the transition from a traditional, decentralized preindustrial society to a central-ized modern one. As Samuel H. Beer has explained it, this particular economic/technological interpretation holds that in any society, ever growing functional differentiation and the concomitant widening scale of economic activity cre-ate increasing dependencies, and the latter can be facilitated and regulated only by a centralized authority.[42] Political and policy centralization along with growing subnational governmental dependence on and subordination to the center thus become functional necessities for coping with a more integrated society.

In the U.S. case, Beer points to the dominance of differing types of coali-tions characteristic of each of the major phases of the economy's and federalism's development: "pork barrel" for the regional economy–dominated system of the Jacksonian, states'-rights era; "spillover" for the expanding industrializing, grad-ually centralizing, early regulatory Republican period of 1861–1932; "class" (coalitions) for the more centralizing, cooperative federal, New Deal years; and "professional/technocratic" for the postindustrial, even more centripetal, postwar period.[43] In terms of broad economic policy goals, each coalition type generates its distinctive thrust: distributive, regulatory, redistributive, and instrumental, respectively. And each type sets the stage for the next stage, with increasing centralization characterizing the overall developmental process. None of the types really disappears but is merely superseded by a more "advanced" coalition. Questions can be raised about certain aspects of this economic/technological developmental scenario, especially regarding the power of the professional/technological elites, the appropriateness of *technocratic federalism* as a relevant current label, the linear centralization progression, and the ignoring of distinctly American social, moralistic, and populist factors that also have conditioned our system's evolution. Yet the Beer interpretation merits close attention.

In contrast, other authorities have advanced cyclical theories interpreting American federalism's history. Richard P. Nathan and Fred C. Doolittle in their detailed probe of the impact of Reagan's New Federalism on the states concluded that its initiatives "activated state governments and enforced their role in the na-tion's governmental system."[44] Expanding on this finding and having examined past experience, they concluded that "the states tend to be more prominent in domestic policy in conservative periods"; in liberal or progressive periods, "the assertion of the role of the central government" occurs.[45] Political liberals and conservatives, then, should let their federalist theories be conditioned by the kind of ideological era in which they find themselves.

James E. Kee and John Shannon also reject the "straight-line projection" of an ever more centralized governmental system. In their 1992 study, cited earlier regarding its competitive thesis, they contend that the past decade "opened our eyes to a revolutionary development for our federal system — the great transfor-mation from a fiscal system that favored the national government to an open and competitive system in which the national government appears peculiarly unable to function without massive reliance on deficit financing."[46] Their analysis of fed-eralism's history shows that shifts in political ideology do exert marginal changes in the national government's domestic role but that a "great national consensus has governed this diverse and incredibly complicated American federal system."[47]

For the nation's first 143 years, write Kee and Shannon, a "constitutionally framed consensus" supported a largely limited Federal government domestic role. A "Washington-centered consensus" lasted from 1933 to 1980. It initially was sustained by the Great Depression, then by three wars — World War II, the Cold War, and the Korean War — and later by affluence and the resourceful national revenue system. The present era they describe as an emerging "dual-centered federalism," one that is "more open and competitive" then either of its predecessors.[48] In effect, there is no tilt here either toward Washington or toward the states because of the former's loss of its fiscal advantage. Now, so their argument runs, both levels must compete for voter approval when added tax revenues are required. The authors conclude that this neo-Hegelian synthesis of elements from both of the earlier eras amounts to "an uneasy compromise" and "the evolving dual-centered federal system will likely be viewed by some as the most uneasy compromise since 1787."[49]

## Summary

Federalism and its related networks of intergovernmental relations are fundamental features of the American system of governance, though many seem unaware of this basic fact. Both our history and our current condition indicate that power and influence in our system manifest themselves in many spheres, are subject to frequent shifts, and always have some sort of territorial dimension. Similarly, the functional relationships between and among the various governmental levels are ever changing and dynamic, with a strong tendency toward centralization of policymaking and devolution of policy implementation occurring through 1980, but a more mixed pattern seems to have emerged since then. In terms of behavioral IGR patterns, the present pattern appears to include the full range of possible attitudes that the history and practice of Federal-state-local relations has generated — from independent, competitive, and confrontational over to interdependent, collaborative, and collegial.

The shifting and continuing IGR roles of key institutional actors in our system highlight yet another dimension of the continuing dynamism and not-always-predictable direction of American federalism. And the pivotal position of federalism and IGR in such policy processes as the judicial, regulatory, fiscal, and political is one more reminder that these territorially based phenomena, while never static, remain a foundational feature of today's system, just as much as they were for earlier ones.

The conflicting interpretations of the history of our federalism should surprise no one. Different modes of analysis produce different developmental theories. In the chapters that follow, the evolution of federalism is traced from its beginning, which clarifies the developmental theory issue. The dynamics and legacies of that history are probed, and the questions raised above regarding current IGR power, operational, institutional, and policy process relationships are addressed. Out of all this should come a better understanding of the continuities and extraordinary changes in our federal system, especially since 1964, as well as a deeper appreciation of federalism's worth and of the complex challenges now confronting it. Finally, the many reasons for assigning the labels *overloaded, unbalanced, ambivalent,* and especially *conflicted* to the federalism of the nineties will complete this analysis, along with recommendations for making federalism a stronger foundation for a new American agenda.

*Part 2*

# Nearly Four Centuries of American Federalism, 1607–1998

*Chapter 2*

# American Federalism and Its Intergovernmental Relations, 1607–1789

Most thinking observers on both sides of the Atlantic believed before the Revolution that differences among the colonies in governance, denominational religion, and economic pursuits, as well as the rivalries, were so great that union was impossible. Hence, effective resistance against Britain was impossible.[1]

Such opinions were not uncommon among the members of the First Continental Congress. Fear of central governmental power, the absence of historical examples of successful free continental unions, the preference of the admired Montesquieu for small republics linked in a large, loose confederation, the continued and profound identification with things British, and the lack of any real American sentiment until 1776, as well as the powerful sense in each of the thirteen colonies of an identity as a distinct corporate entity, were controlling factors suggesting the unlikelihood of union.[2] If a union were to be effectuated, some agreed, it would be a heavily shackled one. The disparateness of the colonies was deemed by some British leaders to be their trump card in maintaining control.

## How It Began

The First American Republic (the Articles of Confederation) represented an institutional victory for the forces of nascent American nationalism that rapidly arose with independence, the hard-fought war, the behavior of the British army, and the widespread popular participation in the struggle.[3] The Second Republic, established by the Constitution of 1787, was, on the other hand, a less probable development. Human ingenuity, as much as the legacy of the past and the impact of recent events, was crucial in shaping a new federative regime in little more than a decade after the signing of the Declaration. Why the modest national victory in establishing the First Republic in contrast to the creative and successful statecraft that established the more nationalist Second?

The Articles of Confederation were drafted in 1776–77 and adopted in 1781. They formalized the institutional arrangements that had come about during the First and Second Continental Congresses. These, of course, involved a unicameral deliberative body at the national level based on equal representation of the states, with basic powers to act in regard to defense and foreign relations but not taxation, the regulation of commerce, and other crucial areas, where the states were authoritative. A confederal formula — a strong one compared to other such arrangements — evolved during the Revolution and was formally adopted in 1781, the year of Yorktown. That was all that was possible at the time.

## The Colonial Conditioning

The more than a century and a half of British rule had produced a strong pattern of local self-government (colonial towns and the colonies were "virtually synonymous" at the outset, as Leach notes[4]) and a high degree of partial autonomy and authentic assertiveness on the part of the colonial assemblies. These developments were due to the sustained strength of transplanted English local governmental customs; the distance from the mother country; and the long period of "salutary neglect," as historians have described it, by Great Britain. Moreover, signs of colonial assertiveness emerged despite the powerful formal role of the royal governors in eleven of the thirteen colonies during the greater part of the colonial era.

Reinforcing the separateness of the thirteen colonies' evolution was the fact that formal contacts (intergovernmental relations[5]) with London were bilateral and irregular relationships between a single colony and the pertinent imperial agency or official. In short, there was a distance between and among the colonies, as well as between each of them and London.

## The Pre-Revolutionary Debate

Colony separateness was further reflected in the arguments developed by the colonial spokesmen in their off-again, on-again debate with London over the various imperial policies enacted by Parliament during the period 1764–75. In the first phase of the controversy, certain powers of Parliament were questioned. Whether it was a matter of taxing internally (the Sugar and Stamp Acts) or of taxing externally for revenue purposes (the Townsend Acts), the contending colonial leaders relied heavily on the rights of Englishmen, especially the right to direct representation (clearly feasible in their separate colonial assemblies but rejected by most as impossible in Parliament), and the compact as well as the rights-guaranteeing character of their charters from the crown as major argumentative weapons. Some of the colonial leaders, like Governor Stephen Hopkins of Rhode Island and John Dickinson of Pennsylvania, developed a clear functional federative theory of the British empire based on a division of legislative powers, with the power to tax in any form rejected, Parliament's power to regulate trade acknowledged, and colonial assemblies having sole revenue-raising authority.

Following a four-year calm triggered by Parliament's repeal in 1769 of all duties on colonial imports (except tea), a measure to shore up the sagging fortunes of the East India Company was enacted. This produced a major crisis in 1774, including the Tea Party in Boston Harbor. The subsequent passage of four punitive parliamentary acts at the behest of the ministry of Lord North brought the

colonists to the point of forming for the first time instruments of extralegal government: the committees of correspondence, provincial congresses, and the First
Continental Congress. The so-called Intolerable Acts also prompted an outburst
of renewed colonial pamphleteering, with Sam Adams, the youthful Alexander
Hamilton, James Wilson, and John Adams rejecting the power of Parliament to
enact any laws (including those regulating commerce) that were binding on the
American colonies. The last three developed a definite dominion theory of empire wherein the level of the colonial assemblies' authority was raised to that of
Parliament and the crown served as the imperial link. John Adams explained the
new theory this way:

> I contend that our provincial legislatures are the only supreme authori-
> ties in our colonies. Parliament, notwithstanding this, may be allowed an
> authority supreme and sovereign over the ocean...; our charters give us
> no authority over the high seas. Parliament has our consent to assume
> a jurisdiction over them.... Our allegiance to his majesty is not due by
> virtue of any act of a British parliament, but by our own charter and prov-
> ince laws.... It follows from thence, that he appears king of Massachusetts,
> king of Rhode Island, king of Connecticut, etc.[6]

By the spring of 1775, the insurgent colonial leaders had developed the idea
of dominion status for each of the thirteen provinces, with an imperial tie that
had little practical significance because the king would have only nominal authority.[7] The idea forecast the confederation of sovereign states that is now the
(British) Commonwealth of Nations. The earlier idea of a functional federative
system based on a division of legislative powers had been scrapped for a futur-
istic concept that was totally rejected by the loyalists on this side of the water
and by the dominant body of leadership on the other. After all, it conflicted
head-on with the "King-in-Parliament-is-supreme" doctrine that had emerged as
the dominant British constitutional principle from the "Glorious Revolution of
1689." Yet like the British constitutional precept, it too did not recognize the
actual territorial division of functions that had existed in the empire.

### Rising Nationalism as a Conditioner

These pre-Declaration developments cannot be fully understood without considering the slow rise of elements of an emerging American nationalism. The
colonies, despite their pronounced socioeconomic differences, actually were
gradually becoming more alike after the 1680s, thanks to the looseness of
mother-country control until 1763, the vast supply of land and other exploitable
resources, and entry of the colonies into an intercoastal and then a "broad Atlantic" trading system.[8] These conditions combined to bolster prosperity and to
foster "more developed, complex, differentiated, and pluralistic societies" as well
as "more autonomous personality types" in all of the colonies.[9] The looser the
ties with Britain, the greater was the colonies' emphasis on their common historical experience, their shared social and political ideology, and their similar

institutions. This "growing convergence" among the colonies was, as one expert expressed it, "the most important pre-condition for either the American Revolution or the emergence of an American national government and an American nationality."[10]

Collective loyalties, then, were rooted in a common culture but also reinforced by common interests. The growing awareness of Britain's effort after 1763 to subvert to subordinate status what in practice had been equal was one major issue here. Another was the great fear after 1774 of division and disunion; hence the growing sentiment among members of the First Continental Congress that a national union was vital, not only to combat Great Britain but to prevent internal chaos.[11] These were some of the general concerns that gave the rising sense of Americanism a basis in self-interest and in shared cultural values. They also served to undercut the still powerful pull of intercolonial separatism.

### The Impact of Independence

Against the background of the constitutional contentions of the colonials, of special socioeconomic and psychological developments, and of the series of punitive acts taken in London to crush the rebellion, Tom Paine's *Common Sense* can be better understood. Published in January 1776, it became an instant success. Two themes dominated the American tract: a scathing attack on the institution of the British monarchy, and a dramatic call for immediate severance of all political, governmental, and emotional ties with the mother country. Parliament was ignored for the most part. These ties, after all, already had been cut in the dominion theory of John Adams, James Wilson, and Alexander Hamilton.

The political mind and national spirit of America were being prepared for the high drama of June and July of 1776 and the introduction by Robert Henry Lee of Virginia on 7 June of a resolution in the Second Continental Congress declaring that "these United Colonies are, and of a right ought to be, free and independent States." From the committee of five to which the resolution was referred came the Declaration (largely from the pen of Thomas Jefferson, with the minor modifications made by Benjamin Franklin and John Adams). Following the eloquent appeal to world opinion and the statement of the fundamental American political principles of natural law and natural rights, the compact basis of the state, the doctrine of popular sovereignty, and the right under certain circumstances to revolution, there appears a lengthy indictment of George III largely unfamiliar to contemporary readers.

Though most of the "long train of abuses" listed flowed from acts of Parliament, the monarch was singled out as a source of despotic government, reflecting Jefferson's and the Congress's acceptance of the recently developed dominion theory of colonial status within the empire. Because the crown was the only imperial link under this theory, the crown itself became the focal point of the grievances cited in the Declaration. It was the authoritative institution from which "the political bands" were severed. The Declaration, then, ended the transatlantic debate over theories of empire, theories that constituted varying approaches to organizing the intergovernmental relations between Great Britain and its thirteen American colonies, and theories of divided and of undivided powers on a territorial basis. With the cutting of political ties, the Continental Congress and later the states assumed the authority of the crown (and Parliament), and, in effect, a new debate began. This time it was a wholly intra-American affair.

### The First Republic: A Confederacy

Once independence had been decided on, there was nearly general agreement that the confederative formula was the proper one for structuring the relations between the states and the new national government. It underscored not only the continuing strength of their sense of separateness and the continuing appeal of the dominion theory of empire, but also the growing crisis-based awareness of the need for a union government. Now it was an American empire and an American pattern of intergovernmental relations that were being constructed.

The drafting of the Articles, it should be remembered, was done by a Continental Congress "harried by the rush of daily business — most of it, at any given point, more urgent than the task of confederating."[12] Throughout the disjointed deliberations, confederation was viewed not as an end in itself but as a mechanism for advancing the battle against Britain. In the protracted drafting process, strangely little attention was paid to the key confederal question of the division of powers between the constituent and central governments. Other issues seemed more significant: the voting in Congress, which generated heated clashes between large and small states; the appropriate formula for apportioning the expenses of the Union among the states, which produced interregional clashes; and the future of the unsettled western lands, which divided "landed States" from the "landless."[13] On the powers of the Union, drafts by Benjamin Franklin (1775) and John Dickinson (early 1776) foresaw a confederation that would exercise a wide range of powers in domestic and foreign affairs. Once independence was declared, however, the debates produced a much more constrained definition of powers.

The final document allotted to Congress powers that it already had been utilizing (to wage war and make peace, to enter into treaties and alliances, to dispatch and receive ambassadors, to regulate Indian affairs, and to establish a postal system) and that had been exercised by the crown and Parliament in the old days of "benign neglect" prior to 1763.[14] The key powers denied to Congress (regulation of trade and taxation) were those that the colonials had denied to Parliament and that had triggered the dispute with and ultimate departure from the British system. It was around the two powers, of course, that the earlier federative and dominion theories of empire were fashioned. In denying both, the Framers adhered primarily, but not wholly, to the dominion theory.

A "confederacy," then, was established and was so designated in Article 1: "each State . . . retains every power, jurisdiction and right not expressly granted to the United States, in Congress assembled." Recent scholarship has raised several arguments that tend to modify this stark and simple confederative characterization of the Articles:

- First, it was the First Continental Congress that issued the call for the former colonies to establish state governments, and this provided the basis for a nationalist interpretation of the origins of the new system.

- Second, the Framers in effect adhered to a dual federal approach to dividing the governmental powers on a territorial basis, albeit unbalanced: those relating to war and peace were assigned to Congress; those relating to taxation, to legislation affecting "the fabric of daily life," and to the dispensation of justice were left to the states.[15]

- Third, the "so fatal an omission," as Madison phrased it a decade later, of Congress's not having the power to force the states to obey its decisions arose largely because the Framers did not perceive it to be a problem, given the supportive stance of most states in the mid-1770s and their general confidence that "the justice, the good faith, the honor, the sound policy of the several legislatures would render superfluous any appeal to the ordinary motives by which the laws secure the obedience of individuals."[16]

- Finally, there is the matter of the limits on, and interstate responsibilities assigned to, the states that obviously restricted their authority.[17]

What has emerged from this mode of analysis is that the "process by which the American union was formed is too...complicated to support either a national or a compact [by the states]-theory of its origin," and that from the First Continental Congress on through to the Articles, the Union involved a division of powers in which Congress and the states in their separate spheres exercised certain functions of sovereign government.[18]

After the war, the errors made in this division became manifest both at home and abroad. The difficulties in collecting state revenue allotments, in paying war veterans, in meeting loan payments, in properly garrisoning the western territories, and in having to depend on the states for its revenues were but some of the more obvious signs of the fiscal disability of the Congress under the First Republic, thanks largely to the lack of a direct taxing power. The inability to enter effectively into commercial treaties (because Congress could not guarantee state compliance), to retaliate against discriminatory foreign trade policies, to curb "trade wars" between and among the states, and to enforce provisions of existing treaties revealed the new regime's frailties abroad. This, of course, stemmed from the lack of effective national authority in regulating interstate and foreign commerce and from Congress's inability to gain acceptance even in those areas where it was supposedly authoritative. All of this suggests a state-centered variety of intergovernmental relations arising from the need of the central government (1) to rely on the states as its primary implementing agents and (2) to achieve state cooperation if almost any of its functions were to be discharged successfully. It also underscores the full import of the unanimous-approval requirement for amendments: a 1783 proposed amendment to firm up Congress's finances failed because of only a few negative votes.

Nonetheless, not all of the postwar difficulties can be attributed to the deficiencies in the confederal formula and the state-centered intergovernmental relations that flowed from it. The economic dislocations caused by the war and by being outside the British imperial system and the resulting postwar depression would have occurred regardless of the nature of the new regime.

What is more, there is a legacy from the Articles that is salutary and lasting, not negative and "imbecilic," the favored adjective used in its condemnation. For some, the Articles have constituted a "democratic" alternative to the conservatism of the Constitution. For others, the positive achievements of Congress under the Articles are stressed, such as the improvement in the management of the executive departments, whose importance increased as Congress's declined, and the settlement of the conflicting territorial claims of the states. The many linkages between provisions of the Articles and those of the Constitution also should be noted. Many of the Articles' prohibitions on the states, their comity clause, their assignment of foreign policy and war-making roles to Congress, and the power of Congress (because of an amendment to the Articles) to regulate territorial development all found a place in the Constitution of 1787.[19]

Despite these positive features, the drive for constitutional change derived impetus from Congress's weaknesses in the foreign, fiscal, and economic areas, as well as from Congress's inability to prevent states from issuing their own paper money. Conflicts between hard- and paper-currency factions sprang up in several states and led to Shay's Rebellion in Massachusetts. By 1787 nearly all of the new nation's leading statesmen had come to recognize the defects in the design of the first constitution, and the drive for reform became irresistible. At the same time, as noted, not all of the provisions of the old charter were scrapped, and the experience under it was a critical factor in formulating a more balanced federative principle. Confederalism, after all, is a variant of federalism; it simply incorporates a different division of powers between the center and the periphery.[20]

## The Constitutional Convention: Creativity under Difficult Circumstances

Shortly before the fifty-five delegates to the Constitutional Convention gathered in Philadelphia, Madison laid out their essential task: to construct a polity that was neither a wholly centralized regime nor merely a confederation or league.[21] This was the issue that Parliament under the pre-1763 empire had settled by allowing a significant gap to arise between the theory of the indivisibility of parliamentary sovereignty and the practice of significant colonial autonomy. It had been the prime assignment (as Edmund Burke so eloquently framed it) that Parliament had been unable to discharge during the dozen years prior to independence. It was the basic issue that prompted the development of the federative, then dominion theories of empire by colonial spokesmen during the same period. And it formed the polar points of tension in this required geographical division of governmental powers that the Articles of Confederation had failed to reconcile in their version of a division.

The Framers, then, came to their task with the old imperial practices, their own experiences during the antecedent and actual Revolutionary periods, and the record of the Articles clearly in mind. They had witnessed and written about a range of patterns of intergovernmental relations: superior-subordinate, independent versus interdependent, conflicting versus heavily commingled, center-oriented versus constituent unit–based. Allocating powers was not as difficult as how to formulate, establish, and maintain the principle of union. The former, after all, had a fairly lengthy historical record to fall back on; the latter was still a matter of theories and interpretations at odds with one another. It would require superlative statecraft to solve the question of imperial order, but the nation had sent its best to Philadelphia (save for John Adams in London and Jefferson in Paris), and they proved fit for the transcendent task.

### Would It Be a Government?

The Randolph (or Virginia) plan was largely the work of Madison, was introduced first, and soon was used as the basis of the convention's work. It turned out to be the main nationalist option and called for a bicameral Congress, both chambers to be based on population; direct election of the lower house and selection of the upper by the lower; the assigning to Congress of all powers of the Continental Congress, as well as the power to "legislate in all cases in which the separate States are incompetent, or in which the harmony of the United States may be interrupted by the exercise of individual legislation"; and the power to disallow state enactments that constrained "the Articles of Union." The plan clearly involved no merely minor changes in the Articles. Moreover, the proposed authority of Congress "to call the force of the Union" against recalcitrant states suggests a compliance device that would have been unimaginable in the old confederacy, though the plan's overall prolegislative features were less exceptional.

Subsequently, the convention went into a committee of the whole, wherein Edmund Randolph of Virginia immediately moved — at the urging of Gouverneur Morris of Pennsylvania — the temporary setting aside of the first item in his plan in order to present a new resolution. Its purpose was to establish the basic intention of the convention and to do so in strongly nationalist terms. It declared that no "Union of the States merely federal" or any "treaty or treaties among the whole or part of the States would be adequate," and concluded "that a national government ought to be established consisting of a supreme Legislature, Executive, and Judiciary." The first two principles were accepted with practically no discussion. The third generated debate over the meaning of a "federal" (confederal) as against a "national, supreme Government." Yet it was adopted only six days after the convention was organized, with Connecticut alone dissenting. It was an early and remarkable victory for the nationalist viewpoint and, in some respects, the first and most significant convention decision relating to the nature of the system to be devised. Despite a subsequent resurgence of small-state and anticentralist strength, the question of whether it was a government or a strengthened league being formulated was answered by this vote. It was to be a government that would interact directly with the citizenry.

But how was such a government to be composed? With what powers and what kind of separation of powers? With what relationship to the states and to the citizenry? With what representational devices? With what form of mediation, if any, between the levels? All these and other issues were yet to be settled, and the drama of the convention from then on turned on the delegates' proposals, reactions, and compromises on the vital questions that flowed from the pivotal decision of 30 May.

One way of classifying the decisions that shaped the Constitution's bases for federalism is to separate the major ones that occasioned much debate from those that occasioned little. In addition, less significant actions — some contested, some consensual — merit mention here.

## Major Contested Decisions

*"The Great (or Connecticut) Compromise."* Following the 30 May vote, attention shifted back to the Randolph plan, and Congress's composition immediately dominated the discussion. Both the method of election and the mode of apportioning representatives were disputed. The bicameral principle itself was not an issue, reflecting the defensiveness of the small-state confederationist members. They advanced no real opposition to the Randolph proposal that the lower house be popularly elected, and that resolution was approved. But some nationalists and the antinationalists rejected the plan's call for election of the upper chamber by the lower chamber.

A week later John Dickinson moved that the Senate be elected by the state legislatures. Nationalists like Madison and Wilson urged popular election, and small-state leaders like Roger Sherman argued for representation of the states as such. The Dickinson resolution finally was adopted unanimously.

The even greater difficulty of apportionment remained. Should representation in the two houses be based on population or on state parity? The nationalists defended the proportionate principle largely in terms of popular representation and contended that citizens of small states would thereby have a voice equal to that of the larger states. The opposition countered with heated arguments against proportionate representation and its undercutting of state sovereignty.

Sherman offered a compromise that called for such representation in the lower house and state equality in the upper, which the nationalists successfully vetoed. Rufus King then moved that the lower house be based on "some equitable ratio of representation." The motion carried, whereupon Sherman moved that each state should have one vote in the Senate, but that was rejected. A bare majority then sanctioned a resolution stipulating that the upper house adhere to the same rule of representation as the lower. The nationalists had carried the day, but the drama was far from over.

With the arrival of additional delegates from small states and a growing awareness of their embattled position, the antinationalists launched a skillful and partially effective counterattack with the so-called Patterson (or New Jersey) plan, which was "purely federal" (confederal, in today's terms). It called for a revamped Continental Congress with added powers (taxation and commerce regulation), an executive selected by it, the authority to coerce recalcitrant states, and legal supremacy accorded to all treaties and congressional acts. However, it provided no change in the equality-of-the-states precept in its basis of representation.

A near-nasty debate on the defects of the Articles ensued, and the nationalists defeated the proposal. The amended Virginia plan was subsequently reported from the Committee of the Whole, but the state parity principle was by no means dead. For two days Luther Martin of Maryland argued the inseparability of state equality and the "federal idea." Madison observed that the small states had nothing to fear from the larger because the individual interests of the latter differed greatly. Franklin urged the institution of daily prayer to help avoid the impending impasse.

After nearly a week and a half of diligent and disputatious debate, the convention again sanctioned proportionate representation for the lower house. Three days of protracted argumentation followed in which moderates urged the need for a compromise and for recognition that "we are partly federal, partly national," as Connecticut's Oliver Ellsworth put it. When it ended, the antinationalists succeeded in achieving a tie vote on a resolve placing the upper house on a proportionate representational basis. At this point, the moderate nationalists, at the urging of C.C. Pinckney of South Carolina, suggested establishment of a committee to devise a compromise.

The resulting recommendations called for a lower house based on population, with one member for every forty thousand inhabitants; the origin of all revenue-raising measures in this chamber; and equal state representation in the upper house. With the later amendment that members of the Senate vote as individuals rather than as state delegations, the convention accepted the committee's report with no other major changes. The "Great Compromise" was achieved.

Though later events proved the accuracy of Madison's forecast of no real large state–small state controversies in the real political world, the composition question was more than just a minor difficulty for the convention. Without the representational compromise, the dead end would probably have resulted in the breakup of the assemblage. The direct recognition of state interests within the very structure of the central government inflamed the more ardent nationalists, but it served until very recent times as a sustaining force for federalism. Moreover, without it, no plan for a "more perfect Union" or any national, albeit limited, government would have been possible.

**Coercion: by Force or Law?** Another controversial decision of critical import for the future of the new system dealt with a question that all federal polities must confront: Who is to judge in cases of disputes between the central and constituent governments, and by what means? Both the Randolph and Patterson plans answered it by empowering Congress to coerce states that violated the treaties or duly enacted laws of the United States. The former plan also included the prior right of Congress to disallow contravening state enactments.

As the convention progressed, it became increasingly apparent to the nationalists, if not their opponents, that coercion was more in harmony with the idea of a league, not a government — hence the provision for it in the New Jersey plan. Many delegates also began to recognize that a national government in many of its most essential actions would be operating directly with individual states. But who was to define and maintain the respective spheres of national and state powers? Both camps had great fears on this score: the nationalists were troubled by the prospect of state erosion of national authority; the antinationalists by the potential reduction of the states to the status of "mere corporations."

The scope of the national and state areas of authority also entered into the debate. The enumeration of Congress's powers, as we shall see, meant a rejection of the broad empowering approach, and the proposed disallowance authority was subject to increasing criticism from a few nationalists and many moderate and state-oriented spokesmen. Sherman, speaking for the latter, argued that the device of the congressional negative was the wrong approach because state laws not negated would remain in effect even though some might be contrary to the fundamentals of the Constitution. Hence, Congress would have to assess every state law to determine compatibility with Federal acts and the Constitution — a practical impossibility.

Gouverneur Morris, a nationalist, also condemned the approach as "terrible to the States" and as essentially unnecessary because a law that contravened the Constitution would not be upheld by the courts, thus raising for the first time the possibility of a judicial alternative.[22] Despite Madison's strong defense of disallowance, the convention scrapped the proposal. At that point, Martin resurrected the largely overlooked supremacy provision of the New Jersey plan. After minor changes, it was adopted. By making the treaties enacted under the "Authority of the United States" (so phrased to cover those concluded under the Articles), the Constitution, and laws "made in pursuance thereof" the "supreme law of the Land," and by stipulating that "the judges in every State shall be bound thereby" notwithstanding any contrary provisions in state constitutions or statutes, the delegates set the Federal judiciary as the arbiter of interlevel conflict. The courts — all courts — now had to consider the Constitution to be law enforceable in their respective halls of justice.

Leading nationalists fought the idea, and James Wilson of Pennsylvania led a last-ditch defense of congressional disallowance. Yet the Martin resolution was approved. But why would small-state defenders advance this resolution and regard its adoption as a kind of victory? The answer is that it eliminated the powers of congressional disallowance and coercion, which though part of the New Jersey plan, were now seen as dangerous, and state courts — it was assumed — would have the lion's share of the adjudicative burden. What is more, the required establishment of inferior Federal courts already had been rejected by the convention, 5–3, apparently because of moderately sized states' and small states' fears that a lower Federal judiciary would assume direct jurisdiction in certain classes of cases, thereby causing a further loss in state court status.

Subsequently, Madison and Wilson managed adoption of a resolution permitting the national Congress, at its discretion, to establish such tribunals. The right of appeals from state tribunals to a national supreme court already had been accepted by some delegates, though some authorities believe that the convention "did not regard the right of appeals as establishing a general power in the federal judiciary to interpret the extent of state authority under the Constitution."[23] Other authorities maintain that the "existence of this judicial power [that is, to pronounce state and congressional acts void] was by most delegates taken for granted."[24] In any case, the supremacy of the Constitution and laws, when linked with the establishment of a supreme court and the right of appeal from state courts (whose bases were clearly detailed in the Judiciary Act of 1789, as was the establishment of lesser Federal courts), laid the foundation of the Supreme Court's ultimate right to define the nature and extent of state and national authority. Ironically, the adoption of the New Jersey plan's "supreme Law of the Land" provision achieved the goal that Madison and Wilson sought, but by means that not all in the convention clearly understood. It was a crucial and contested decision that most of the nationalists opposed, one that ultimately helped assure the legal supremacy of the national government and that heavily affected the future course of American federalism.

**Choosing the Chief Magistrate.** A third issue critical to the future of American federalism was endlessly debated: the method of electing the president. The overwhelming majority of the convention delegates — nationalists and state sovereignty men alike — were prolegislative in their institutional bias, reflecting their revolutionary and Whig heritage. Even so, confidence in legislative bodies was beginning to erode and all delegates advocated separation of powers, though like their state counterparts earlier, they were not sure how to incorporate the principle institutionally.

At first glance, the matter appears to be a horizontal one — assuring the independence of the executive, especially vis-à-vis Congress — but it had vertical aspects as well. The evolution of a separate presidency armed with adequate executive powers was "tortuous" indeed.[25] Both the Virginia and New Jersey plans, after all, called for congressional election, and the convention sanctioned this method on five occasions.[26] Yet a tiny minority led by Wilson, Morris, and Madison persisted in a push for a strong, separate chief magistracy with a silent assist from Washington, the convention's presiding officer and the inevitable first magistrate.

Both Wilson and Morris argued initially for popular election, only to be countered successfully by the legislative defenders. The Committee on Detail, as it turned out, dealt with this most important unresolved "detail" in a lengthy paragraph that set forth a compromise version of the electoral college concept. Each state was accorded the same number of electors as its total of congressional members and was to choose them "in such manner as its legislature may direct," thus recognizing the states, the possibility of popular election at the discretion of the states, and the partly "federal," partly "national" basis of congressional representation. The electors were to ballot for two persons; the man having the greatest number of votes would gain the presidency, provided the vote constituted an absolute majority of all electors. This feature of the Constitution, most authorities on political parties agree, was and is critical in explaining the coalition-building efforts of the major parties prior to the actual balloting for the office. Finally, the committee stipulated that if no candidate gained the required majority, the Senate would choose a president from the five men receiving the most votes, in this way recognizing the legislature and the state parity principle.

When the plan was placed before the convention, many delegates expressed the view that cases where a candidate gained the necessary majority would be rare, hence legislative selection would be a common occurrence. Strong-executive proponents agreed and fought the proposal, but it was sufficiently attractive to win over legislative-selection adherents to the electoral college concept.

The only basic change in the committee's proposal was adoption of a Sherman resolution calling for the House, not the Senate, to elect in instances of a no-absolute-majority winner. To assure that no combination of two or three states would dominate the process, the resolution also stipulated that each state delegation would vote as a unit and that a majority of state votes would be required to elect. Here, an effort to favor the more "democratic" of the two chambers was made, but the bias in favor of legislative selection remained along with the state parity principle. That feature of the electoral college remains unchanged to this day and is one of the key features of the formal presidential election process that has been singled out for criticism and reform, especially during the 1992 Perot candidacy for the presidency.

The complicated compromise appears on quick examination to be no compromise at all but rather a surrender to the legislative-ascendancy advocates and to the state sovereignty proponents. In truth, and with the benefit of over two hundred years of hindsight, it was a victory for the separation-of-powers principle, for a separately constituted and independent chief magistrate, and for nationalism and democracy, as well as for the states. Within a generation, presidential electors were popularly elected, and even earlier (thanks to the emergence of parties) they had been reduced to the status of party rubber stamps, thus rendering the electoral college a triumph for those who argued for a separate, popular, and national constituency for the office. At the same time, the need to run in each of the states, not the nation as a whole, and to acquire an adequate territorial spread of one's electoral votes — along with the later state-imposed winner-take-all requirement — has been believed by many to have exerted a moderating influence on presidential politics, to have strengthened the state basis of the two-party system, and to have buttressed the federal system. Contemporary proponents of direct election of the presidency, of course, would and do reject all such contentions.

## Major Uncontested Decisions

In retrospect, it seems extraordinary that so many issues that might have generated fiery convention debate did not. One reason for this was that only one Hamilton was in attendance and no Tom Paines or Patrick Henrys. Another was the amazing degree of agreement among most of the delegates on several fundamental precepts of representative government. That there should be a written constitution with a special amendatory process, a new government based on a separation of powers and its correlative checks and balances, a Congress with the power to legislate for and tax individual persons, and a lower house whose representation was to be based on population and whose members were to be popularly elected were issues of statecraft that required no compromises.[27] A deep sense of urgency, even of crisis, was a contextual factor that tended to facilitate agreement. In terms of the constitutional foundation, of the federal principle, three key issues were dealt with on a basis of near or complete unanimity.

**The Territorial Division of Powers.** Fundamental action involving the federal principle related to the powers of the proposed new government. Though it was settled largely in committee and with only minor debate, it was nonetheless a major decision. The Virginia plan, after all, left to the Congress a vague, almost plenary authority to "legislate in all cases in which the separate States are incompetent," and only a handful of delegates questioned the scope of this authority.

Yet the Committee on Detail, when it produced a constitutional draft in early August, set forth eighteen specific delegated powers, including, of course, those of taxation and of regulating commerce, which even the New Jersey plan had sanctioned, as well as a final nineteenth paragraph that set forth the doctrine of implied powers. This "necessary and proper" clause empowerment, of course, was the chief basis for later expansions of national authority, yet it was not singled out for critical debate. Some of the other individual powers proposed earlier by the committee or by individual delegates were rejected, however, including the power to emit bills of credit and the power to issue charters of incorporation.

Some authorities have conjectured that the moderate cast of the committee's membership may explain its action here. The supremacy of national acts would have been more difficult to sustain in state courts if Congress's powers were only broadly bounded, and enumeration of its powers could be used in arguments favoring the Constitution's ratification. Memories of having to contend with a deliberative body that claimed the whole orbit of legislative authority also must have played a role. In any event, the final listing was quickly accepted.

Though this decision was relatively easy and clearly rooted in tradition, it had immense implications for the future.[28] The later lengthy political and judicial debates over the nature of the expressed and especially the implied powers assigned to the national government would have assumed a very different character had the Randolph plan been adopted. Moreover, the evolution of intergovernmental relations doubtlessly would have been quite different, more direct perhaps, and less devious at times had the national government's power been as broadly encompassing as the Virginia plan contemplated.

**State Constraints.** Another federalist feature of the new Constitution that remarkably generated no really serious opposition was the series of sixteen prohibitions placed on state power that the convention adopted.[29] Even a cursory examination of this listing in Article I, Section 10 produces the inevitable conclusion that sovereignty formally conferred on the states by the Articles of Confederation was restricted in various operational ways by this approving action of the convention. The prohibitions along with the expressed and implied powers delegated to the national government began to provide the constitutional basis for the dual federalism formula for Federal-state functional relations that emerged with the adoption of the new charter.

## Lesser Contested Decisions

As a clear forecast of future political and economic disputes, regional jealousies and conflicting interests gave rise to the need for a cluster of compromises bearing on the future of federalism. Yet these were not on a par with the major decisions discussed above.

**Entry of New States.** East-West differences emerged in considering whether new states admitted into the Union would be allowed representation and other rights on the same basis as those accorded to the original states. In federalist terms, was the Union to be one of equal states or not?[30] Gouverneur Morris of Pennsylvania was the most vocal disparager of western frontiersmen and their future rights; Madison and George Mason argued eloquently for the principle of democratic equality. The convention refused to adopt limited and inferior representation for the future western states. Morris, however, did succeed in having the phrase "on the same terms with the original States" struck from the provision, thus effectuating a compromise whereby Congress was given the power to determine whether terms of admission would place new states on an equal or inferior footing with the old. History shows special terms have been congressionally stipulated to achieve entry, but once in the Union the new member enjoyed equal rank.

**Slavery and Representation.** A North-South division arose over whether slaves should be counted in determining the basis of representation. Initially, the proposal to enumerate three-fifths of the slaves appeared to be acceptable, but opposition arose later. Some deep South spokesmen argued for counting all slaves; some northerners contended none should be enumerated. James Wilson questioned: "Are they not admitted as Citizens? Why are they not admitted on an equality with White Citizens? Are they admitted as property? Then why not other property be admitted into the computation?" Without counting at least three-fifths of the blacks, North Carolina's Davie insisted his state would never "confederate." Morris's response was that the basis for representation *and* taxation should be the same, and this provided the basis for the compromise that then ensued: three-fifths of the slaves were to be counted for both purposes.

**A Tax on Exports.** Sectional differences arose over the desire on the part of most southern members to prohibit Congress from levying duties on exports. Some northerners perceived this as a halving of Congress's power to regulate commerce. But sectional lines were not so rigidly drawn on the issue as with some others, and the members from the then major exporting states had their way.

**The Slave Trade.** More serious sectional controversy arose over whether to give Congress the power to regulate the slave trade. Slavery, it is to be remembered, was found then in all states but New Hampshire, even though it was concentrated in the South. Spokesmen from Georgia and South Carolina argued in the negative, citing their states' need for more labor to till their fields; some middle-state members condemned the trade; and some New Englanders maintained it was better to allow continued importation than to deny any chance for a new constitution, arguing that slavery was on the wane and could not last. The Committee on Detail's draft of the Constitution denied Congress the power to levy a tax on importation of slaves and also the right to prohibit their migration or importation. The chance for compromise then was presented. The final deal called for no ban on the slave trade until 1 January 1808, and the right of Congress to impose a tax not exceeding ten dollars per imported person. This and other debates refute the contention that the Constitution was a compact between free and slave states. Opposition to slavery was almost as prominent in some southern delegations, especially Virginia's, as among some of the northern delegations. Only Charles Pinckney of South Carolina presented a full defense of it. The invention of the cotton gin only a few years later demolished the forecasts of slavery's early demise.[31]

# What Manner of System?

The Constitution was the crowning achievement in statecraft of that extraordinary first generation of Americans. In contrast to the document's predecessor, many of its basic features were not predictable or inevitable but, instead, products of inventiveness. It also represented a clean break with the past, in that it established a system unknown to political theorists and unlike any other in recorded history. Its distinctive blend of certain familiar principles drawn from "the science of politics," as Hamilton phrased it, and from American experience with wholly novel concepts and procedures engendered by the delegates' own creativity, and compromises in effect established a "unified, internally coherent and highly original model of a new kind of government."[32]

The one overarching goal of the convention that all the delegates shared and that was the ultimate conditioner of most of the compromises was "to form a more perfect Union." The imperfections of the old Union, both in its external (foreign policy, trade, and defense) affairs and in its internal operations, were acknowledged by nearly every delegate. The antinationalists, after all, were as bent on reform as the nationalists; their New Jersey plan by no stretch of the imagination can be described as a simple continuation of the old regime.

The confederation's frailties in foreign relations were the easiest to document, the easiest to resolve, and the easiest to dramatize in the later struggle for ratification. One authority has gone so far as to contend that foreign policy and military, not domestic, concerns were primary in the convening of the convention as well as the drafting and ratification of the Constitution.[33] But this goes too far.

The domestic disabilities of the old Union, especially those of the previous two years, obviously were deeply worrying to the delegates, and this concern extended to the states as well as to the Continental Congress. Their common objective here was the preservation of "republican liberty," that is, certain personal rights like freedom of conscience, protection of one's property, and political liberty, as well as the right to government "by consent of the governed."[34] Their fundamental differences were over the proper implementing principles and procedures. In essence, the nationalist-antinationalist divisions were rooted in wholly opposite views on the appropriate governmental arrangements for preserving this legacy of the Revolution. The differences, then, were primarily political and, as we have seen, at times sectional. Economic divisions based on class differences were practically nonexistent.

Roger Sherman and other like-minded antinationalist delegates as well as various later antifederalists opposed what they believed were the predominantly, if not wholly, nationalist features of the proposed Constitution because they viewed them as a basic menace to "republican liberty." This interpretation, as Martin Diamond explained it, "rested on two considerations. First, it argued that only small countries can possess republican governments. Second, it argued that, when such small republics seek the advantages of greater size, they can preserve their republicanism by uniting only in a federal [confederal] way."[35] Both at the convention and in *The Federalist,* Madison turned the "small-republic argument" on its head. Republicanism and the liberty it protects are menaced in small jurisdictions, he contended. Only a large country could counteract the destabilizing, antilibertarian tendencies of factions in small republics and secure "private rights and the steady dispensation of Justice."[36] More pointedly, he warned his fellow delegates, "Was it to be supposed that Republican liberty could long exist under abuses of it practised in some of the states?"[37]

In *Federalist* No. 10, he went into a deeper analysis of how factional (interest group) dangers to republican liberty would be checked in a vast "compound republic." The great diversity of interests in such a system would preclude the emergence of an arbitrary majority at the national level, and the existence of a stable, balanced government of the Union would serve as a positive force in respecting "the rights of every class of citizens" and in protecting the rights of local minorities against local majorities.[38] Hence, "In the extent and proper structure of the Union we behold a republican remedy for the disease incident to republican government."[39]

For the nationalists, then, a full-fledged national government was needed to correct the defects of the old confederacy in both foreign policy and do-mestic matters. Madison's skillful undermining of the basic premises supporting the small-republic thesis of Sherman and other antinationalists (not to men-tion Montesquieu) and his powerful libertarian argument for a great republic combined to place a heavy burden of proof on the state sovereignty men. His analysis also served as the major intellectual rationale for the 30 May decision to establish a central government, not a reconstituted league.

If a government was to be constructed to preserve "republican liberty," what should be its design? Here the Framers had little difficulty in agreeing on several essential features because political theory and the long course of American gov-ernmental experience, as was suggested earlier, joined in suggesting certain basic principles that ought to be institutionalized. The concepts of a written constitu-tion, separation of powers, checks and balances (or as one authority phrased it, a "balance of checks"), bicameralism, representation, and the ultimate sovereignty of the people were viewed as fundamental features of any genuinely republican frame of government.

These precepts of the "new science of politics" were dominated by the over-riding concern of many eighteenth-century political thinkers: how to achieve and preserve a free government. Based on a measured degree of distrust in human nature, a design was advanced that sought to protect liberty by divid-ing and balancing power and authority within the polity.[40] In this way, man's love for power and the tendency to abuse it would be restrained by barring "any monopoly of the instruments of power."[41] Hence the need for the devices cited above, so that these instruments would be appropriately divided and balanced.

Yet these principles had been "tested" only in the relatively small (and uni-tary) governmental context of the states, and the heavy weight of Montesquieu's counsel was that they could be applied directly only in a small country where the commonwealth is "more obvious, better understood, and more within the reach of every citizen."[42] Although the French theorist had developed the con-cept of a "confederate republic," it far more resembled the outline of the Articles of Confederation than the design of the Constitution of 1787.

Two major theorists, both of whom were known to the Framers, took a dif-ferent position on the virtues of smallness.[43] James Harrington in *Oceana* (1656) found in republican bigness a source of strength both abroad and at home. He rejected the dichotomy that a stable and large republic was an impossibility. Instead, he contended that with a proper constitution Oceana would endure. Why? Because with a constitution that set forth its precepts as "unalterably law," that was ratified and implemented by the whole people, that established a dif-ferently constituted two-chamber national legislature, that generated consensus as a result of a pluralistically rooted and rational system of debate, and that provided for a territorial division of powers, the necessary counterweights to arbi-trary power would be created.[44] David Hume, in effect, transmitted Harrington's great commonwealth ideas in modified form to the Framers. In his *Idea of the Perfect Commonwealth*, which first appeared in his *Political Discourses* (1754) four years after Montesquieu's *The Spirit of Laws*, Hume took issue with the small-republic theory, arguing that "a republican government" could be more easily sustained, "steady and uniform, without tumult or faction" in "a more extensive country than a city."[45]

On the other hand, the teachings of most of the other influential "republican" theorists led to the small-polity model. Colonial experience and the revolutionary debate were less clear on this point, as we have seen. A de facto division of powers within a large system had been achieved under the old, pre–Stamp Act empire, and John Dickinson and Stephen Hopkins sought to formalize this in their later federative theories. Yet in neither case were all the features of a free system dealt with satisfactorily (that is, popular consent, representation, a neutral arbiter, and so on). Moreover, Adams's dominion theory, the imperial organizational premise of the Declaration — not to mention the Articles — led to the small-republic governmental model and only a confederative arrangement at the national level.

Against this background, the dramatically different design of the Constitution can be more clearly understood. What the Framers did, of course, was to substitute a large-scale unitary model (the Virginia plan) for the confederative one (the Articles), and that in a formal sense at least incorporated most of the techniques for dividing and balancing the instruments of power that were found in or thought to be necessary for the small republic. But, thanks to the "small-republic" men (led principally by Sherman of Connecticut) and certain individual nationalists (Morris, Wilson, and sometimes Madison) who disliked some of the specifics in the Randolph outline, a series of modifications was made in the unitary draft. The cumulative effect of the changes was to establish neither a national nor confederal system but a federal one, in the modern sense of that term.[46]

What is more, the new federal formula gave Madison, not to mention Hamilton, a far better basis for arguing persuasively for ratification of the Constitution than would have been the case had the Randolph draft or especially some of Madison and Hamilton's own nationalist positions prevailed on the convention floor. The amendments to the Virginia plan, after all, could be and were described as additional, if not new, means of balancing power — not only at the center but between the center and the periphery. Madison's great-republic cure for the ills of factionalism was strengthened considerably by the "federalist" engravings on the unitary body of the nationalists' initial plan. Remember Madison's able exposition of the virtues of a "compound republic": "In the compound republic of America, the power surrendered by the people is first divided between two distinct governments, and then the portion allotted to each sub-divided among distinct and separate departments. Hence, a double security arises to the rights of the people."[47] How effective, how convincing, how "republican" would that have been had the national Congress of the new regime been assigned the broad, ill-defined powers, the authority to coerce states and select presidents, and the solely numerical representational base that the Randolph draft would have accorded it?

Madison's skillful detailing of the "national" and "federal" (confederal) features of the new basic frame in *Federalist* No. 39 would have been far less balanced and far more removed from the equilibrium ideal that late-eighteenth-century sophisticates so strongly favored had the dual representational formula for Congress (by territorial units and by the number of people), the fairly clear division of powers by governmental level, and the extraordinary high-wire performance of the electoral college been missing. The Virginian also was able to argue that the functional division and dual-level representational features of the "compound republic" provided a greater protection of "republican liberty" while also affording the people an unusual opportunity to play the role of ultimate balancer in the system.[48]

All this does not mean that the Framers were wholly clear about all of their actions or necessarily thought in terms of abstract political models. Still, the two opposing groups at the convention had contrasting views of the best means of preserving republican liberty, and both adhered to quasi-unitary formulas: one operating at the center and the other at the periphery. Thanks to the "compromises" a halfway house was found, and the modern concept of federalism involving "the division of powers between distinct and coordinate governments" was born.[49]

No great debate, however, occurred in the convention on the nature of this new form of federalism or even on its proper name. How could it? The bundle of critical decisions that established it were made in an ad hoc fashion, and their overall significance was not appreciated until later, though Madison and Hamilton's expositions in *The Federalist* reveal considerable awareness of what had been wrought in Philadelphia.

Understandably, then, certain crucial questions relating to the essential nature of the Union, nation-state relationships, and above all sovereignty were not clearly answered because of the manner in which the unique federative, compound republican formula evolved. Even in *The Federalist* different answers to some of them emerged. Hamilton viewed the new system as a "consolidated" one but only insofar as national concerns were involved; Madison, as we have seen, found it partly federal and partly national. On the question of the scope and significance of the powers assigned to the national Congress, the New Yorker wrote of "an entire change in the first principles of the system," but the Virginian soothingly asserted that they were less a matter of an "addition of New Powers, than the invigoration of its Original Powers."[50] Hamilton saw the delegated powers in the aggregate along with the "elastic clause" as adequate to meet the greatest and widest "variety of national exigencies"; Madison found the powers "few and defined" and chiefly important in times of "war and danger."[51] The seeds of future political antagonisms were already planted!

Another dilemma arises when it is remembered that both Madison and Hamilton at the convention opposed practically all of the compromises and decisions that established federalism, on grounds that they undercut the national features that the two believed were so necessary for the new system. The chief authors of *The Federalist*, who wrote under the pseudonym Publius, then were placed in the position of defending a regime that had many features they previously had considered dangerous. Does this mean that the eighty-five papers are all merely devious debating arguments and useless as a basis for understanding the new system? The answer is that *The Federalist* is both a campaign document and a work of political theory,[52] and care must be taken to try to understand where the two overlap and where they are separate. Care also must be used when encountering the term *federal* in the *The Federalist*. The term is frequently and confusingly used in its eighteenth-century, hence confederate, sense and some-times is used in its "new-system" sense of a balanced division of governmental powers between a national and a constituent government, with both exercising concurrent jurisdiction regarding the people in their separate spheres of author-ity. In light of these and other interpretative issues, much has been made in recent years of what *The Federalist's* true interpretation of federalism is, but a consensus has yet to emerge.

Martin Diamond, for example, held that *The Federalist* does "not regard the Constitution as establishing a typically federal, perhaps not even a primarily fed-eral system of government," and "as compared with its use of other important terms and concepts," it is fairly "inexplicit and ambiguous in its treatment of federalism."[53] This interpretation was based largely on Diamond's exclusive re-liance on the eighteenth-century definition of *federalism* as a means of divining Publius's intent; this, of course, led to the conclusion that the Framers created "a political order that, from the standpoint of 1787, was decisively national."[54] The new regime, he conceded, did have some federal features, and because the authors of *The Federalist* had to convince antifederalists that the system was suf-ficiently federal (confederal, in the eighteenth-century sense), they tended to overemphasize these features.

Many opponents of the new Constitution were not taken in by Publius's re-sounding rhetoric or its clever manipulation of the federal label. As one critic put it, "This abuse of language does not help the cause."[55] At the same time, from their severe strictures against the Articles, it is patently clear that both Madison and Hamilton totally rejected the prevailing eighteenth-century concept of fed-eralism and its resultant union government, which lacked a direct basis in and access to the people and which was inadequate for achieving a "more perfect Union."

Jean Yarborough has contended that Madison and Hamilton did not "al-ways explicate the principle of federalism in the Constitution" because "in some places, where one might expect to find a sympathetic discussion of federalism, there is silence."[56] This, her argument runs, gives *The Federalist's* treatment of federalism "a peculiar tilt," one that is "less a description of federalism as the framers invented it" than of a "far more consolidated national government than most of the Philadelphia framers intended."[57] In essence, this contention leads to her conclusion that Publius believed that the national government, not the states, would be the better preserver of individual rights. Her interpretation also prompted a heavy emphasis on Madison's forecast that "the people would over-come their natural tendency to love best what is near" and think of themselves as "citizens of the United States" and on her finding that for Publius "the proper

relationship between the states and the federal government should be administrative rather than political" because the states were seen as the basic threat
to liberty.[58] In this interpretation of *The Federalist*, federalism becomes merely
the first phase of an ongoing systemic development that ultimately leads to a
nationally dominated system.

Vincent Ostrom, on the other hand, contends that both Madison and
Hamilton recognized that the new system — sometimes designated "federal,"
sometimes "compound republic," sometimes "partly federal and partly national" — was new and involved "concurrent jurisdiction on the part of a limited
national government and state governments that independently exercised a limited jurisdiction with reference to individuals."[59] The limits, he stresses, are set
forth in relevant provisions of the U.S. Constitution and the various state charters. Those "residual powers are reserved to the states," and the overall format
of these governmental relationships corresponds closely to the modern definition
of *federalism*, in Ostrom's opinion. What is more, he argues that *The Federalist*'s defense of federalism was a "defensible" one,[60] even though the imprecise
use of certain terms clouded the meaning of some of Publius's arguments. The
term *federal* is interpreted by Ostrom as coming from the Latin *foedus*, which
he translates as "covenant," not "treaty," as Diamond and others did. This produces the definition that "a federal system depends upon the maintenance of
limits on the prerogatives of power," and this is the basic thesis of *The Federalist*
for him.

How does one react to these widely varying assessments of *The Federalist*'s interpretation of federalism? In the first place, the system that emerged from the
Constitutional Convention no doubt was viewed as second-best by both Madison and Hamilton. But in the real political world, and these two Founders were
preeminently in and of this world, the only options were the new Constitution or
the discredited Articles. Given their vehement disapproval of the latter, they had
no choice but to support the new charter with "rhetorical brilliance," generally
convincing arguments, and vigor.

To say that *The Federalist* is basically a nationalist document is a provocative interpretation that ignores certain obvious points. First, the number of times
where its authors' earlier nationalist passion reveals itself are not all that numerous, nor particularly prominent, save perhaps for a remarkable slip on the
part of Hamilton in *Federalist* No. 17.[61] Second, the contention that *The Federalist* implies that administrative decentralization is preferable to a federalist
constitutional division of powers misinterprets the primary paper dealing with
the subject. In *Federalist* No. 32, Hamilton expresses "a conviction of the utility and necessity of local administrations for local purposes,"[62] and this has been
viewed as a subtle argument for administrative decentralization but not for federalism. In the full context of this and the previous paper, the meaning is simple:
states and their localities should be left with the responsibility for implementing the vast range of domestic functions left to them by the provisions of the
U.S. Constitution and their own charters. In more specific terms, Hamilton was
arguing here in favor of the concurrent right of these subnational governments

to levy taxes to sustain this traditional pattern of state and local policymaking and administration.

A third topic that must be dealt with is the Diamond argument that *federalism* in eighteenth-century usage had to mean a confederative arrangement with a union government that represented the constituent units and especially one that possessed only the power to interrelate with these units. It is the full acceptance of this interpretation that generates most of the argumentation relating to the new Constitution's being nationalist. But this view ignores the writings of Harrington and Hume, the linkages between the mother country's central governmental instrumentalities and the colonial governments as well as the colonists, not to mention the federative theories of Hopkins and Dickinson. One could argue that a new federative theory was evolving throughout the eighteenth century and that it overtook and superseded the older confederative version with the creation of the Constitution.

A final factor to reckon with in this assessment of the nationalist character of the new Constitution is the question "If *The Federalist,* in fact, advocates a largely nationalist-oriented new form of government, how were the authors supposed to persuade the skeptical voters and delegates of the pivotal state of New York to ratify the new Constitution?"

Yet another contention is that *The Federalist* is neither sufficiently explicit nor explanatory regarding the various provisions establishing the new federative system. Another argument is that *The Federalist* overemphasizes the federal dimensions of what basically was a nationalist regime. The two need not be in total contradiction, but they do reveal the wide differences in this latter-day debate on a two-hundred-year-old topic. Nevertheless, in balancing the two arguments, one might conclude that Publius made a decent, if not good, defense of federalism as it emerged from the convention.

Regarding the forecast of a future weakening of the states, Madison and Hamilton made it clear that this would depend on changes in popular attitudes regarding the performance of the two basic levels of government. In *Federalist* No. 46, Madison phrases it this way: "If . . . the people should in future become more partial to the federal than to the State governments, the change can only result from such manifest and irresistible proofs of a better administration, as will overcome their antecedent propensities."[63] Clearly, there is nothing inevitable about this development. Hamilton is more certain but just as conditional about his forecast.

So what does *The Federalist* tell us about federalism? It tells us that the federalism of the Articles provided an inadequate basis for preserving the legacy of the Revolution, and it implies that despite a heavy slant toward the states, even the Articles undermined the general eighteenth-century meaning of *confederacy* because they assigned the union government domestic as well as foreign policy and defense functions. It sets forth a new modern definition of *federalism,* a definition that had been germinating since the early eighteenth century, if not the midseventeenth. It tells us that such a regime must be established by a written constitution (though it could have stressed this fact more); that a division of

substantive governmental powers between levels is of the essence in such a system; that constitutional limits on each level and each branch of government are
necessary; that representation of state and local interests within the policy processes of the national government is a vital protector of those interests (though
their emphasis on this could have been stronger);[64] and that there must be an arbiter of interjurisdictional conflicts — in some places the people are called upon
to play this role, and elsewhere the courts.[65]

When combined, these points add up to a fair, if not full, defense of the
federalism of the Constitution as it emerged from the convention. Moreover, it
also constitutes an eloquent exposition and application of republican principles.
The Framers after all were more republicans (Hamilton perhaps excepted) than
they were federalists, and the application of the republican principles was what
produced the limited national government that the modern critics contend with.
There was then not only a compounding of national and federal principles in the
new frame as Madison described it. But in *Federalist* No. 10, he also stressed that
in the extended orbit and the proper institutions of the Union "the republican
remedy for the diseases most incident to republican government can be found."
Therefore, "according to the degree of pleasure and pride we feel in being republicans, ought to be our zeal in cherishing the spirit and supporting the character
of Federalists." In short, the republican precepts of representative government
and of popular sovereignty along with all the other attendant checks were as
much required at the center as at the periphery, where the stability of the small
republics had been threatened by the absence of the former. To focus exclusively
on federalism and to ignore the republicanism of all the Framers is to overlook
the basic reason for which the new national government was sought. Federalism
was thus one more means of achieving republican liberty.

Turning to intergovernmental relations as such, little overt attention was
given to the subject either in the convention debates or in *The Federalist*. Yet
modern-day authorities find entirely different meanings in their readings of both.
Grodzins and Elazar contend that "the Constitution did not set up rigidly independent administrative establishments in both national and state governments.
On the contrary, cooperation between the national government and the states
was assured from the very first."[66] At the opposite end of the interpretative spectrum stands Harry N. Scheiber, who concludes that "the Framers conceived of
the central government and the states operating in different spheres."[67] Neither
the Grodzins-Elazar nor the Scheiber view would appear to be wholly correct.
On the one hand, the convention delegates, or at least the majority of them,
sought to extricate the new national government from having to rely on the
states for administering its basic functions. The Continental Congress's disastrous
dependence on the states in so many areas was a vivid reminder of a pattern of
intergovernmental relations that they abhorred; hence their focus on a national
government that had different powers and purposes from those of the states.[68]
Moreover, the scope of national authority assured that "jurisdiction is limited to
certain enumerated objects, which concern all the members of the republic, but
which are not to be attained by the separate provisions of any."[69] The assigning

of "clearly stated and clearly recognizable powers," as an authority of an earlier generation phrased it, was necessary to the viable, separate existence of the national government, and also to avoid "friction between governments."[70] These ideas of the Framers, then, support the later functional theory of dual federalism, a concept of separate state and federal governments that operate in distinct areas with little major overlap in the sharing of authority and functions.

Despite the foregoing, the Grodzins-Elazar assessment is not totally inaccurate. Several interlevel relationships and interdependencies were debated, recognized, or simply assumed by the Framers. The senatorial, judicial, and presidential selection connections with the states already have been noted, and all three arose from "compromises" engendered by small states. Yet there were others; suffrage requirements, the elections process and machinery, and the amending process were all constitutionally stipulated functions requiring state collaboration. In addition, the concurrent authority of both levels in the taxing area at least hinted at a future field of both intergovernmental conflict and "mutual forbearance," as Madison phrased it, and the militia was to be jointly administered.

In essence, some of the cooperative but far more of the dual federalism theory can find support in the convention debates and in the Constitution. The Framers, then, crafted an entirely new governmental model, known to later generations as a federal system. Its evolution during the course of the convention began with the introduction of a basically national, quasi-unitary draft for fundamental constitutional reform that then was subjected to a series of modifications chiefly led by small states. The result was neither a unitary regime nor a confederation but a federal system. A wholly novel governmental arrangement thus was launched, and America's greatest contribution to "the science of politics" was rendered.

The fundamental purposes of this new order were to gain respect and authority in foreign relations, and at home to promote social and governmental stability, protect "republican liberty," and defend the people's ultimate authority as master of all governments. Certain key questions regarding the operations of this great republic were not addressed or answered clearly during the convention's fashioning of the federal formula. The resolution of these questions and the new regime's record in achieving its great goals over the next two centuries will be dealt with in the four following chapters.

Other key questions were clearly addressed by the Framers, especially by Madison. From a contemporary perspective, however, it appears that some of the questions and the formulated answers to them have been ignored. The recent record, as noted later, suggests that contemporary Americans find Madison's warnings regarding the dangers of factions (interest groups) to individual liberty to be merely the alarmist admonitions of a late-eighteenth-century conservative. Moreover, the behavior of today's national policymakers indicates a widespread forgetfulness regarding the fundamental domestic role the Framers assigned to the national government: the regulation of factions. The failure on the part of the citizenry and the system to honor these early and elemental themes of our political tradition in no small measure explains why contemporary American federalism is not only untraditional but unbalanced and ambivalent.

Finally, from the vantage point of comparative federal systems and of more than two hundred years under the U.S. Constitution, the most critical decisions made by the Framers in terms of their impact on the future of federalism were (1) "The Great Compromise," with its incorporation of direct state representation within the national decision-making process, (2) the less controversial listing of Congress's delegated powers along with the implied powers proviso at the end, and (3) the beginning of establishing the Supreme Court as the ultimate institutional umpire of jurisdictional disputes within the system. The first gave rise to representational and ultimately political federalism. The second generated the long and still controversial history of functional or operational federalism, with all that involves in terms of confrontation and independence or cooperation and interdependence of the governmental levels in the programmatic, personnel, public finance, and regulatory areas. The last decision produced an authoritative judicial federalism, which has molded the system to varying degrees throughout its history. Subsequent chapters will demonstrate the critical conditioning role of these three fundamental federalist decisions of the Founding Fathers.

# Chapter 3

# Variations on Dual Federalism, 1789–1930

The evolution of American federalism, and the resulting intergovernmental relations, fall into four periods: pre–Civil War (1789–1860); from the firing on Fort Sumter to the advent of the Great Depression (1861–1930); the age of Roosevelt and the consolidation of federalism under Eisenhower (1930–60); and the current period, which began with the election of John F. Kennedy in 1960. The first two will be treated briefly in this chapter; the last two in the next three chapters.

Other historians have blocked out different periods. Yet there is a cohesion to the dominant themes of each of these periods, even though each exhibited its own share of conflicting, cooperative, centralizing, and decentralizing tendencies, as well as strong links to the past.

To fathom the character of each period, its constitutional, judicial, operational (for example, fiscal, servicing, and administrative traits), and political features must be probed. These, after all, are the chief conditioners of the evolving course of American federalism. When combined, they provide the basis of determining the general intergovernmental character of each period.

## The Dual Federalism of the Rural Republic, 1789–1860

The concepts of functional and power-based dual federalism, as developed by Edwin S. Corwin, included four postulates: "(1) The national government is one of enumerated powers only; (2) Also, the purposes which it may constitutionally promote are few; (3) Within their respective spheres the two centers of government are 'sovereign' and hence 'equal'; (4) The relation of the two centers with each other is one of tension rather than collaboration."[1] The period from 1789 to 1860, for the most part, reflected an adherence to most of these dual federalism themes — judicially, politically, and operationally. Madison's compartmentalized "compound republic," in short, was largely realized in the first seventy years under the Constitution. Only in the sphere of actual power relationships between the levels were dual federalism's equal centers of government not always realized.

## Judicial Dual Federalism

Notwithstanding the political conflicts between the national and state-centered schools of thought, most of the judicial developments of this period reveal much more of an adherence to the dual federalism doctrine. At the constitutional and judicial levels, and despite some conflicting crosscurrents, this certainly was the case. On the one hand, the Bill of Rights (1791) and the Eleventh Amendment (1798) (which barred access to Federal courts in cases where a citizen of one state sues another state, thus overturning the 1793 Supreme Court decision in *Chisholm v. Georgia*)[2] could be viewed as restricting national authority because both placed curbs on it. On the other hand, Madison piloted the Judiciary Act of 1789 through the House, a Federal circuit court first declared a state law unconstitutional in 1791, and twelve years later in *Marbury v. Madison* (1803) John Marshall successfully asserted the power of the Supreme Court to negate an act of Congress. All of these combined to establish the Federal judiciary as the ultimate interpreter of the Constitution and the arbiter of conflicts between the states and the nation.

The decisions of the Marshall Court clearly were crucial in determining the controlling significance of the supremacy, commerce, and contract clauses of the Constitution in cases where national and state powers came into conflict. (The "contract clause," in Article I, Section 10, prohibits states from "impairing the Obligation of Contracts.") These decisions, along with *McCulloch v. Maryland* (1819),[3] which sanctioned a broad Hamiltonian view of implied powers, laid the bases for applying the "nationalist" label to this Court.

At the same time, the Court recognized an array of legitimate commerce-related actions under the states' police power that were beyond national authority. It also developed the doctrine that a state could regulate commerce and navigation in the absence of congressional legislation; ruled that the Bill of Rights did not apply to state actions; upheld state bankruptcy laws; and denied that a state's tax power could be presumed to have been surrendered by the granting of a corporate charter.[4]

Clearly, the Marshall Court was protective of its own institutional independence, assertive of its authority to render ultimate judgment regarding unconstitutional actions of the nation's political branches and of the states, and selectively protective of Congress's powers under the Constitution. But just as clearly, it also was mindful that the national government's powers were by no means plenary; that the states were "for some purposes sovereign, and for some purposes subordinate," as Marshall phrased it in one of his most nationalist decisions;[5] and that the relationship between the two levels was essentially one of tension. This last proposition was rooted in the fact that during Marshall's tenure, the Court had declared unconstitutional some acts of half the states. State resentment of these individual decisions and of the Court's general arbitrating role was strong and fairly sustained.[6]

With the successor Taney Court (1835–63), adherence to the postulates of dual federalism was even more pronounced. In a string of commerce clause cases, it developed a rounded concept of "concurrent powers" only hinted at in the Marshall decisions. In *Briscoe* v. *Bank of the Commonwealth of Kentucky* (1837), it sanctioned establishment of a state-owned and state-controlled bank that was authorized to issue notes for public circulation.[7] Moreover, a broad interpretation of the states' police power emerged from a cluster of other cases. The famous *Charles River Bridge* case (1837) provided Taney with the opportunity to define it as "the powers necessary to accomplish the ends of its [the state's] creation."[8] In other decisions, Taney described it as the power of the states to "provide for the public health, safety, and good order," which was reserved to them by the Tenth Amendment as one of their "sovereign powers...complete, unqualified, and exclusive."[9] The combined result of these cases, of course, was to modify considerably the sanctity of contracts, to foster economic competition by ending monopolies, and to stimulate a rash of state banking enterprises.

Corwin believed that the Taney Court's decisions in the areas of commerce and state police powers were a basic threat to the supremacy clause.[10] Others have contended that the Taney Court was no radical champion of state sovereignty but, rather, the developer of the "doctrine of selective exclusiveness" — of a limited concurrent states' power over commerce that was both popular and realistic because most aspects of commerce then still were more within the powers of state than national regulation.[11] The broad dictum laid down by Marshall in *Gibbons* v. *Ogden* (1824) was never overthrown or even challenged, and the Court's right to control state judiciaries in matters of constitutional interpretation was vigorously upheld.[12]

The Taney Court, then, gave the principles of dual federalism a more powerful enunciation than did its predecessor. Without denying Federal supremacy in its proper sphere of operations, the Court viewed the existence of the states with their reserved powers as a limitation on Federal authority. The state police power, or state sovereignty as Taney phrased it, staked out "certain subjects as exclusively within the jurisdiction of the states and beyond the reach of the national government."[13] This aspect of dual federalism later permitted it to be used by the South to protect slavery against Federal encroachment. Despite this tilt toward the states, neither national supremacy in its very limited area of authority nor the Court's own role as ultimate judge of what is constitutionally permissible within the states' proper sphere of action was undermined by this reading of judicial dual federalism.

## Operational Dual Federalism

How did the constitutional and judicial doctrines of dual federalism correspond with operating practice? For the most part, closely. Administratively, a small but separate Federal bureaucracy came into being with the establishment of the national government, and so it remained throughout these early dual federal years. The fact that a separate national administration was established was a foregone conclusion, given the heavily nationalist tenor of the First Congress. Any lingering thoughts (and a few delegates had expressed them in Congress) that the new government would utilize only state agencies to discharge some of its basic functions (tax collection and the Post Office were cited) were put to rest by the establishment of the Departments of State, Treasury, and War in 1789 and Navy in 1798. The post of attorney general was created by the Judiciary Act of 1789, but it did not assume cabinet rank until 1870. The Post Office was given permanent standing in 1794, but again cabinet rank was not accorded until later (1829). The only other department to be formed in this antebellum period was Interior (1849).

Departmental functions for the most part clearly related to expressly delegated national powers and, in all but two instances (the attorney general and Interior), continued departments that had emerged under the Articles. Their administrative size was small, starting at approximately 1,000 civilian employees (1,300 military) in the Washington administration, going to 7,000 under Monroe, to more than 11,000 in the middle of the Jackson administration, to a little over three times that figure during Buchanan's last year in office. Accurate counterpart figures for the states and their localities are unavailable, but undoubtedly the bulk of public administrators — to the extent that there were public functions to be administered — was at these levels, especially the local.

In terms of finances, a clear division also emerged: the national government relied heavily on customs and receipts from the sale of western lands; the states, on excise taxes.[14] The national government assisted some or all the states by four largely ad hoc actions during this period:

- the cession of portions of the Federal land in western public-land states for the support of common schools as each such state was admitted into the Union (first enacted by the Continental Congress);[15]

- Federal assumption of state Revolutionary War debts (1790);

- congressional enactment in 1818 of a measure stipulating that 5 percent of the proceeds from the sale of remaining national lands within a state should go to that state's treasury; and

- the no-strings distribution of the Treasury surplus in 1837 (before the financial panic of that year wiped out the surplus), the only case of general revenue sharing until the 1972 enactment.

Efforts to allocate Federal funds to states for internal improvements or for other specific purposes were consistently rejected throughout this largely laissez-faire era. In the few instances where Congress was able to put together the necessary coalition, a presidential veto was inevitably forthcoming. In 1854, for example, an act sponsored by Dorothea Dix was passed to provide Federal aid to the states for the indigent insane. President Franklin Pierce vetoed it, contending that if

> Congress is to make provision for [paupers], the fountains of charity will be dried up at home, and the several States, instead of bestowing their own means on the social wants of their people, may themselves, through the

strong temptations, which appears to States as individuals, become humble suppliants for the bounty of the Federal Government, reversing their true relation to this Union.[16]

In terms of governmental functions and services, the states exercised an almost exclusive role (sometimes shared with their localities) in the areas of elections and apportionment, civil and property rights, education, family and criminal law, business organization, roads and bridges, local governmental organization and powers, and labor and race relations (including slavery).[17] During the three decades preceding the Civil War, the states also dominated banking and, as noted earlier, shared in making national monetary and commercial regulatory policies.

National functions, on the other hand, were still relatively few, and they became fewer after 1830. Witness the undermining of the second Bank of the United States by Jackson (1832) and the unsuccessful Whig efforts to resurrect it later (1842); the strict constructionist (and vetoing) approach toward "internal improvements" and toward aid for specific program areas on the part of nearly all of the presidents after 1800 (save notably for John Quincy Adams); and the growing disinclination of Congress to use the powers it possessed, especially under the commerce clause. Some have claimed that by 1850, the overall system resembled more the Confederation in the 1780s than it did the federal system under Monroe.

Not to be overlooked in this assessment of state and national functions is the emergence in this era, and even before, of a national role in the enactment and expansion of Federal entitlements. The Continental Congress passed exclusionary legislation that awarded pensions only to Revolutionary War officers. This was followed by congressional enactment of follow-up legislation awarding pensions for all Revolution veterans. An 1828 act granted full pay for life to various categories of surviving Revolutionary War veterans without reference to meeting any means test. These early and hotly debated national efforts to hammer out the nation's first entitlement policies set a precedent that would be repeated after later wars.[18] Ultimately with massive expansions into other recipient categories, the largest portion of today's Federal domestic outlays emerged.

## How Much Cooperative Federalism?

Where were the germinating seeds of cooperative federalism from 1789 to 1860? In very barren soil, with only isolated cases of collaboration springing up — more at the beginning than at the end. How could it have been otherwise? Domestic Federal program activities, after all, were few (in personnel terms, chiefly involving the postal service, customs collections, and Corps of Engineers, as well as organizing and providing for territorial governments). And although there obviously was a necessary interaction between the levels, especially in the areas of judiciary, militia, elections-machinery, commerce regulations, and Indian affairs, conflict was as much a part of these intergovernmental relationships as cooperation.

## The Political Backdrop

In political terms, these seven decades witnessed the rise and fairly rapid demise of the first party system and the emergence and collapse of the second. The Constitution and the national government came first, then the parties — first one, then its competitor. They were created at the center because the Constitution established a "new focus of power which promoted greater integration by requiring the articulation of a national will to decide these policy questions," which now had become the responsibility of a national electorate.[19] This led to efforts to bring together diverse interests under each party's umbrella; the chief element of persuasion was the contrasting policy positions the Federalists and the Jeffersonian Republicans assumed on foreign and domestic questions.[20] These were patently issue-oriented parties, and issues along with a modest dosage of patronage were the chief factors of party coherence. Corresponding state and local efforts arose in part at the behest of national leaders and in part on the parties' own initiative.

In integrationist terms, the parties divided even as they reunited, and this helped stabilize the new regime. Regarding the electorate, they activated theretofore passive voters rather than engineer any great extension of the franchise. In regional terms, they struggled to include members from all sectors, though the Federalists had more difficulty doing this than the Republicans because they basically were a northern party. The fact that it was a two-party system, not a four-party one, was due to the skillful proselytizing by the Federalists of former Tories and by the Jeffersonians of former antifederalists. The caucus, that is, all legislative members of a party, reigned supreme nationally and among some states and local units as the means of making party nominations, but other more informal techniques (for example, announcement of one's candidacy in a newspaper) also were used locally.

Another customary party function was the filling of appointive administrative positions as well as elective ones. Given the relatively limited political participation (compared to a generation later, but not to other countries), the gentry or equivalents tended to fill the posts by means of a system that combined merit and patronage.[21] Both parties utilized this patronage-of-the-elite system. With the Federalists, the principle of extended tenure, assuming good performance, as enunciated by Hamilton, was also a factor; Jeffersonians when out of power endorsed the republican rotation-in-office precept. As the first "out party" to confront the administrative consequences of an electoral triumph, the Jeffersonians used their leader's principle to remove several Federalists.[22] Yet the replacements were just as "gentlemanly" as their predecessors, and their tenure was sometimes longer. The first chapter in the history of public personnel administration left a legacy of government by competent, dedicated, honest, and generally politically loyal public servants. It was truly a "Government by Gentlemen," as Frederick C. Mosher described it, not ever to be repeated.[23] The first party system established a dualistic, nationally integrative, policy-generating, electorate-energizing, and government-running tradition — some of whose parts became permanent features of political federalism's record. Its collapse had many causes, chief of which were the Federalists' fairly outspoken elitism, their dwindling support in the South and lack of it in the new western states, and the Republicans' growing pragmatism once in power and their consequent support for various earlier Federalist programs.

In political and constitutional terms, the Federal and state-local governments were roughly on a par with one another during the first forty years of the Republic. In its own way, the first party system with its initial national political focus, integrative and contesting functions, leadership and other personnel roles, and spawning of state and local counterpart organizations did much to help produce this balanced result.

The second party system emerged more than a dozen years after the disappearance nationally of the Federalist party, and immediately after the only U.S. experiment with a one-party, though multifactional, system (1817–24). In its first phase, the Jeffersonian Republicans split into the National Republican (Clay-Adams) and the Democratic (Jackson) wings; the latter captured the White House for its hero in 1828. The second phase was marked by the coalescence of a variety of anti-Jacksonians into the new Whig party and the sustained ascendancy of the Democrats, save for two Whig presidential interludes (with four presidents). It ended with the collapse of the Whigs amid the turmoil over the admission of Kansas and Nebraska in 1854.

The second party system continued some of the trends of the first, but to a far greater extent it provided a foundation for the third. Regarding the federal system itself, the parties served as significant supporters. In constitutional terms, the parties like their predecessors were as much influenced by the basic frame as they were an influence on it. The representational facets of the Great Compromise (that is, the equal representation of the states in the Senate but of population — and growing northern numbers — in the House) proved to be of major import, especially with the surging of sectional rivalries after 1830. The office of the president assumed the same sort of central political focus as it had had from 1796 to 1816. It helped sustain a preelection coalition-building process by nurturing opposing mass parties that supported the perennial dualism in American politics. What is more, the selection of presidential electors became a wildly popular affair in this period, with state legislatures being shunted aside.

In its many integrative functions, this two-party system surpassed the Federalist–Jeffersonian Republican duo in several ways. First, it was both affected by and an energizer of the democratization of the electorate and of politics. The vote was expanded to the point where by 1850 practically all adult white males were enfranchised and voter turnouts had soared.[24] Popular participation and emotional involvement in party politics were widespread and deep. As in no other era, politicians were the folk heroes of the day. Of prime integrative importance was the effort of both the Democrats and the Whigs to run successfully in all the regions of the country, whether in the northern, middle, or southern states or in the new states across the Appalachians, whose number grew in the three pre–Civil War decades.

Alongside the theretofore unparalleled integrative functions were others that both complemented and supplemented them. Organizationally, an extraordinarily intricate interlevel system of conventions, interim committees, and professional politicians replaced the earlier less structured, caucus-oriented system.[25] The convention was viewed as a democratizing nominating device, despite its later oligarchical features; it was used in practically all jurisdictions; and it was geared not only to selecting winning candidates but to unifying the parties at the national and state levels by selecting factional representatives to balance party tickets and by adopting platforms that pacified divergent party interests. In the Democratic case, the two-thirds rule was adopted nationally in 1836 (not to be scrapped until 1936), and that assured the ultimate selection of a near-consensus presidential candidate. In 1848 the first Democratic National Committee was selected. Overall and to a far greater degree than the first party system, the second was decentralized in organization, authority, and ability to deliver the vote. In all these respects, "this stage of American political party development" established an "enduring significant form in party structure and action."[26]

In selecting leaders and filling administrative posts, new, more egalitarian approaches were taken by the parties, and this was in keeping with the times. Both parties had notably distinguished members in Congress, especially in the Senate, and although the Democrats focused on civilian candidates after Jackson, the Whigs nominated military heros in 1840 and 1848; Clay's three tries for the highest office were failures. At the appointive level and in nearly all jurisdictions, a new form of patronage arose that favored the "common man."[27]

Straightforward and blunt party patronage was first practiced openly in the new and egalitarian western states. With the first popular election of the first western president, it was sanctioned at the national level. Jackson insisted on competence as well as political reliability in government employees; some later presidents did not. The arrangement lasted well into the next political era, but in the second party period, it proved important in sustaining party loyalty because the diverse composition of both major parties, especially the Whigs, made principles and programs feeble foundations for party cohesion.

The breakup of this system in the 1850s, basically over the issue of slavery in the western territories, led first to a three-party experiment in 1856 and a four-party canvass in 1860, followed by a bloody war. The decentralized organizational, diverse compositional, loose programmatic, and weak national instrumental features of the second party system proved to be persistent, however. With but a few adaptations they reemerged as the dominant features of most of the long third era in U.S. political party history. Most authorities consider this confederative form of party system as a basic supporter of governmental federalism. And in the three decades prior to the Civil War, the growing difficulties in reconciling rising regional rigidities nearly converted the system itself into a confederative replica of its party component.

To conclude, the party system performed admirably in the integrative, organizational, and conflict-resolution areas until the issues of slavery and sectional differences overtook it. As long as these issues were suppressed, it continued, but by the mid-1850s they were irrepressible. Here the formal federal conditioning of the parties asserted itself, and when sectional interests linked with assertions of state sovereignty "took precedence over other cleavages," the parties — first the Whigs and then the Democrats in their 1860 Charleston convention — were unable to meet their greatest integrative and conflict-resolution challenge.[28]

### The Seven Decades in Perspective

A range of legal, economic, social, and political developments during the first seventy years — all heavily conditioned by the dominant egalitarian and localistic cultural norms — combined to sustain an operational adherence to Madison's "compound republic" and its implied functional dual federalism features. The national role was minimal (still restricted largely to "war and danger" and some very limited pork barreling); its few policies fell under various "distributional" headings; and its expenditures and personnel were consistently meager. The states, on the other hand, were the prime focal points of economic development, political and governmental reform, and after 1830, party organization. Their economic and social activism was in marked contrast to the laissez-faire policy generally adhered to by the national government.

Clearly, there were in this era two separate spheres of power, each roughly supreme in its own area of authority, with minimal overlap and with conflict — far more than collaboration — characterizing the interrelationships where overlaps existed. It was, then, a predominantly dual federal system but with questions arising in the later years as to whether the balance of power between the two levels contemplated by the Framers was being sustained, given the growing strength of the states (and of sectionalism). The growing doubts set the stage for a bloody fratricidal contest over whether a nation-centered or states-centered theory of federalism would prevail. Yet as we shall see, dual federalism was not obliterated by the outcome.

## The Second Seven Decades: Dual Federalism with a Few Dents, 1861–1930

The second major evolutionary period in the history of U.S. federalism and its intergovernmental relations also lasted for approximately seventy years, 1861 to 1930. It, too, had a dominant political and economic theme: "to perfect the free economy."[29] Moreover, and despite dramatic social, economic, and governmental changes over the period, the dominant theory and practice of federalism throughout still warrant the dual federalism designation. The second period, however, produced some very different interpretations and applications of the doctrine, as well as some departures from it. These set the period apart from both its predecessor and successor.

## Constitutional and Judicial Shifts

The Civil War settled several of the questions left unanswered by the Framers and *The Federalist*. It destroyed the doctrine that the Constitution was a compact among sovereign states, each with the right to interpose or nullify an act of Congress, and each with the ultimate right to secede legally from the Union.[30] The Supreme Court scuttled this state-centered concept in *Texas v. White* (1869), with a dual federal theory of perpetual Union articulated by Chief Justice Salmon P. Chase:

> The perpetuity and indissolvability of the Union, by no means implies the loss of distinct and individual existence, or of the right of self-government by the States. Under the Articles of Confederation, each State retained its sovereignty, freedom, and independence, and each power, jurisdiction, and right not expressly delegated to the United States. Under the Constitution, though the powers of the States were much restricted, still all the powers not delegated to United States, nor prohibited to the States, are reserved to the States, respectively, or to the people.... Not only ... can there be no loss of separate and independent autonomy to the States, through their union under the Constitution, but it may be not unreasonably said that the preservation of the States, and the maintenance of their governments, are as much within the design and care of the Constitution as the preservation of the Union and the maintenance of the National Government. The Constitution, in all its provisions, looks to an indestructible Union, composed of indestructible States.[31]

A partly national, partly federal decision, this one. The nationalist view of the Constitution as supreme law and as emanating from the people and of the Union as being perpetual clearly are accepted. Yet so were the earlier dual federal concepts of divided powers, of two separate spheres of governmental authority and autonomous activity, and of the constitutional guarantee of state autonomy.

Implicitly, Chase here accepts the Marshall-Taney view that the Supreme Court ultimately would serve as the valid interpreter of what were constitutionally permissible actions either by the political branches of the national government or by the states. And in the long period of judicial activism that extended throughout the rest of this span of time, the view had major implications for both the theory and practice of federalism. Between 1789 and 1860, only 2 acts of Congress and some 60 state enactments had been declared void by the Court; from 1874 to 1898, 12 congressional and 125 state acts were invalidated; and from 1898 to 1937, 50 Federal and 400 state laws were found unconstitutional.

The Civil War and its aftermath also produced three constitutional amendments (the Thirteenth, Fourteenth, and Fifteenth), a cluster of civil rights acts, and a highly intrusive, congressionally dictated approach to reconstruction in the southern states — all signs of an extraordinary assertion of national legal authority. Yet the Supreme Court itself ultimately put the brakes on drastic constitutional change in the civil rights area,[32] the net effect of which was to leave civil and voting rights matters pretty much to the states until the 1950s and 1960s.[33]

The main arena in which judicial conflict arose in this period was the scope of the states' police power as it affected commerce, manufacturing, labor relations, and social welfare — all areas that came to the forefront as ever advancing urbanization and industrialization transformed the landscape and political agenda.

By 1930 (and it did not really end for the Federal judiciary until 1937), the Supreme Court had built a half-century record of aggressively acting as the ultimate interpreter of the constitutionality of state laws enacted pursuant to their police power, as well as Federal statutes passed in furtherance of the national government's commerce or taxing powers. From the late 1880s on, the doctrine of substantive due process and a constrained concept of "commerce in commerce" were applied to a range of cases involving state and Federal statutes — admittedly with a somewhat moderating test of reasonableness emerging in both by the second decade of the twentieth century.

The general effect was to enhance the Federal judiciary and to sanction state actions in some areas but not others, as well as to sanction Federal laws in some areas but again not others. Over time Congress's regulatory authority (relying primarily on the commerce but occasionally the tax power) came out somewhat ahead of the states' police power. Earlier analysis led to the conclusion that the Supreme Court was supreme in this period. Yet even in the halcyon conservative interventionist years of 1887 to 1910, of the 558 cases involving due process challenges to the states' use of their police power, the Court in 83 percent upheld the state position.[34] Even so, the states continued to exercise a near-exclusive authority, with little to no Federal judicial or other intervention, in the areas of family and criminal law, elections, control over local government, and commercial law.[35] In addition, civil rights, following the 1896 *Plessy* "separate but equal" doctrine,[36] pretty much fell wholly under state jurisdiction, for better or worse, while criminal justice and civil liberties, and state enactments relating thereto, did not begin to become a due process concern of the Court until the 1920s. A major extension of Federal judicial power, especially in the Court's insistence on the right to review the reasonableness of legislation, and some expansion of congressional authority but not always at the expense of the states[37] — these were the main constitutional developments of the second period of American federalism.

What do these developments mean? In terms of power, especially constitutional power, the pitiful position in 1860 of the national government was ended, thanks to the Civil War–related amendments and to Court decisions. Whether one could accurately describe the state and Federal spheres as equal is debatable. But it is certain that the Federal portion of the dual federalism layer cake in 1930 was much greater than its 1860 counterpart. Moreover, although there appeared to be conflict between the two levels as to regulatory authority, in practical and political, if not legal, terms the states could not take on giant corporations operating on a national economic basis. These were matters for national attention. This produced a rough division of functional labor and partially preserved dual federalism in this operational area. But the Court, while sanctioning some of the state actions and other Federal actions, sometimes interpreted the due process clauses of the Fifth and Fourteenth Amendments to preclude any government from acting in a way that "seemed to alter market and property relationships too drastically."[38] The power vacuum enhanced the position and power of corporate America. The regulatory movement nevertheless was active at both levels throughout nearly all of the first two decades of the twentieth century and into the 1920s. Sometimes it scored legislatively and less frequently judicially, although the Supreme Court in a cluster of cases "confirmed the existence of a Federal police power under the commerce and taxing powers of Congress."[39] The general ascendancy of what has been described as "decentralized laissez-faire constitutionalism"[40] during most of this period and seven years into the next underscores the essential and enduring strength of judicial dual federalism.

## Finances and Functions: Still Divided, but a Few Signs of Sharing

As Riker points out, sole reliance on formal constitutional analyses of federalism can provide a highly distorted picture of the real relationship between the nation and the states.[41] An examination of the funding and servicing patterns of this period will help serve as a corrective to any of the minor distortions that the foregoing judicial analysis may have produced.

Basic changes occurred in the realm of public finance but not to the point of overturning the older stratified approach to revenue raising nor of generating any major fiscal imbalances between and among the governmental levels. Nationally, the prime shift was away from the tariff and sales receipts from western land to the income tax — a shift that took two Supreme Court decisions, a constitutional amendment, and several years' political pressuring to bring about in 1913. During the Civil War, a national income tax of sorts had been levied to help finance the Union effort, and it was not challenged in the courts. After more than a decade of agitation by agrarian radicals and eastern liberals, Congress in considering the Wilson-Gorman tariff (1894) accepted over considerable opposition an income-tax provision sponsored by William Jennings Bryan. It was immediately challenged in Federal courts, with some of the ablest legal talent of the day serving as the plaintiffs' lawyers.[42]

By some artful reasoning and ignoring of several Federal taxing precedents, the Court's majority concluded in the second *Pollack* case (the first had produced a 4–4 tie) that the tax in essence was direct, hence unconstitutional.[43] Apportionment in accordance with state population would, of course, violate the entire thrust of an income tax and the amendment approach ultimately

### Table 3-1
### Federal Tax Collections, by Type of Tax,
### 1902 and 1927 (in Millions of Dollars)

| Year | Income | Consumption | Other | Total |
|------|--------|-------------|-------|-------|
| 1902 | — | 487 | 26 | 513 |
| 1927 | 2,138 | 1,088 | 138 | 3,364 |

*Source:* Bureau of the Census, *Historical Statistics of the United States, Colonial Times to 1957* (Washington, D.C.: Government Printing Office, 1960), 724.

was used, though it took another fourteen years and a progressive congressional coalition to force it.

Some have explained the entire later course of American federalism in terms of the Sixteenth Amendment, which authorized a Federal income tax, and its assignment to the Federal government of the most lucrative of all public revenue sources. Yet in terms of the period under analysis here, the rates were quite moderate and the receipts relatively modest. Nonetheless, the income tax heralded a new era in Federal finance. It became the most important single source of Federal revenue (from nothing in 1902 to more than three-fifths of the 1927 total; see table 3-1), and shifted the bulk of Federal financing more onto the shoulders of the wealthier, a goal of the Populists and later of the Progressives, who advanced it as a means of redistributing the wealth. At the state and local levels, less drastic shifts occurred. The key shifts were a growing overall role of the states, the beginning of their own reliance on the income tax, and a slight hike in local governments' dependence on the property tax (see table 3-2).

Overall, state revenues rose from roughly 18 percent of the 1902 combined total to over one-quarter of the 1927 figure. A modest hike, perhaps, but still a contrast with the earlier period. The growing state role is explained by fifteen states (and one territory, Hawaii) enacting personal income taxes between 1901 and 1930; by sixteen (and again, Hawaii) adopting corporate income taxes during the same period; by forty-eight levying gasoline taxes; by twenty-seven

### Table 3-2
### State and Local Tax Collections, by Type of Tax,
### 1902 and 1927 (in Millions of Dollars)

| | Year | Income | Consumption | Property | Other | Total |
|-------|------|--------|-------------|----------|-------|-------|
| State | 1902 | — | 28 | 82 | 46 | 156 |
| | 1927 | 162 | 445 | 370 | 631 | 1,608 |
| Local | 1902 | — | — | 624 | 80 | 704 |
| | 1927 | — | 25 | 4,360 | 94 | 4,479 |

*Source:* Bureau of the Census, *Historical Statistics of the United States, Colonial Times to 1957* (Washington, D.C.: Government Printing Office, 1960), 722–24.

## Table 3-3
### State Intergovernmental Expenditures, by Function,
### 1902 and 1927 (in Millions of Dollars)

| Function | 1902 | | 1927 | |
|---|---|---|---|---|
| | *Dollars* | *Percentage* | *Dollars* | *Percentage* |
| Education | 45 | 86 | 292 | 49 |
| Highways | 2 | 4 | 197 | 33 |
| Public welfare | — | — | 6 | 1 |
| Other | 5 | 10 | 101 | 17 |
| Total | 52 | 100 | 596 | 100 |

*Source:* Bureau of the Census, *Census of Governments, 1957,* vol. 4, no. 2, *State Payments to Local Governments* (Washington, D.C.: Government Printing Office, 1959), 100.

moving on the cigarette excise front; by all but one charging for automobile reg-istration; and by twenty-two joining the twenty-three that had enacted death duties in the nineteenth century.[44] The mix of taxes varied considerably from state to state, reflecting a continuance of at least one facet of the previous era's competitive mercantilist practices. General sales, gift, and distilled liquor taxes, it should be noted, were part of none of the states' tax packages prior to 1930. The overall trend, then, was of gradual diversification, with a major reliance on individual excise levies, both new and old. Then, as now, the prop-erty tax was the chief local source of revenue (from own sources), accounting for 92 percent of the total in 1890 and 97 percent in 1927. Despite the emer-gence of some modest tax overlaps among the levels (personal and corporate income and a few excise taxes between some states and the Federal govern-ment, and between some states and their localities with the property tax), clearly the broad picture still was one of a basic separation of revenue sources by governmental level.

## Growth of Grants

By way of contrast, intergovernmental fiscal transfers on a continuing basis emerged as a significantly new development chiefly during the last three of the seven decades. Grants-in-aid represented a different kind of revenue source for recipient governments, and their emergence suggests the real beginnings of a cooperative Federal theme slightly denting the dominant dual federal principle. State aid to localities rose from a mere $52 million in 1902 to $596 million by 1927, accounting for a little over 6 percent of local general revenue in the earlier year and 10 percent in the latter.[45] The functional areas aided are highlighted in table 3-3. Four generalizations emerge regarding this first meaningful phase in the history of state aid:

- The amounts in absolute and relative terms were small, and not all states were involved.

- The areas aided were the same ones that dominated state efforts in the modern period.

- School districts and counties inferentially, except in New England, were the prime local governmental recipients.

- Above all, the paramount responsibility for funding the aided activities and all other local governmental functions rested with the localities themselves and their property taxes.

The emergence of Federal cash aid to the states, of course, constituted an equally dramatic break with the previous period, though again, the scale of Federal assistance was quite modest. A kind of prelude to this, of course, was the signing by President Lincoln in 1862 of the Morrill Act, opening the public lands to all the states for support of such agricultural and mechanical colleges as they wished to establish.[46] The Hatch Act of 1887 supplemented this earlier program by providing for the establishment of experimental stations at the agricultural colleges, but this time the funding was in the form of a cash grant. The first such program was the textbooks-for-the blind enactment (1879), but this involved a grant to a nonprofit body (American Printing House for the Blind). By 1900 five cash grant programs were in operation (textbooks for the blind, 1879; agricultural experiment stations, 1887; state soldiers' homes, 1888; resident instruction in land grant colleges, 1890; and irrigation, 1894). During the second decade of the twentieth century, six more were enacted:

- assistance to state marine schools (1911), which was the first open-ended matching grant (Federal matching of whatever states spent for the schools);

- state and private forestry cooperation (Weeks Act of 1911), which required the formal submission of a state plan and established minimum performance standards;

- agricultural extension service (Smith-Lever Act of 1914), which stipulated a dollar-for-dollar match;

- highway construction (1916), which also stipulated a fifty-fifty match as well as planning and state administrative requirements and contained a complicated three-factor allocational formula;

- vocational education (Smith-Hughes Act of 1917), which permitted the funding of teachers' salaries; and

- vocational rehabilitation (the Fess-Kenyon Act of 1920), a fifty-fifty matching program for disabled veterans.[47]

This legislation, save for the 1920 act with its ostensible intrusion into a purely state program area, enjoyed strong state support, additional revenues

### Table 3-4
### Federal Intergovernmental Transfers, by Broad Functional Category, Selected Years, 1902–27 (in Millions of Dollars)

| Year | Total | Education | Highways | Welfare | Other |
|------|-------|-----------|----------|---------|-------|
| 1902 | 7 | 1 | – | 1 | 5 |
| 1913 | 12 | 3 | – | 2 | 7 |
| 1922 | 118 | 7 | 92 | 1 | 18 |
| 1927 | 123 | 10 | 83 | 1 | 29 |

*Source*: Bureau of the Census, *Statistical History of the United States* (Stamford, Conn.: Fairfield Publications, 1965), 484–516.

being states' prime concern. Conditions, as has been noted, began to become more detailed. Each act, save the last, used the grant device as a means of supplementing national efforts and of avoiding the constitutionally doubtful direct-expenditure route.[48] And three of the six (not to mention three of the earlier five) had a clear rural bias.

In the early twenties, two new enactments generated considerable state opposition. The 1921 amendments to the Federal Road Aid Act of 1916 called for a periodic national evaluation of state highway departments to determine if they were able and empowered to coordinate and administer the grant to the satisfaction of the Federal administrator.[49] This was deemed a national intrusion by the states, though they wanted the added funding. With the maternity and infancy health program (the Sheppard-Tanner Act of 1921), a range of state and professional groups rose in opposition, questioning the need for the program, the degree of national intervention, and the extent to which it reflected national goals and priorities, not those of the states. Soon it was before the Federal courts, and in two cases, one initiated by the Commonwealth of Massachusetts and the other by a private taxpayer, the Supreme Court decided on its constitutionality. In *Massachusetts v. Mellon* (1923), the Court held that no violation or attack on state sovereignty was involved in the enactment, in that the grant-in-aid was merely an inducement and a state could (as some did) refuse to participate.[50] In *Frothingham v. Mellon* (1923), the Court decided that an individual had no standing in court in such a case because "after funds have been brought into the Treasury and mingled with other funds there placed, Congress has sweeping power to dispose of these funds."[51] These decisions were crucial in the later evolution of Federal grants, though the Sheppard-Tanner Act itself expired by 1929, under opposition from President Coolidge.

By 1930 fifteen grant programs were operating, with highway aid predominant (see table 3-4). With rising state tax receipts in the 1920s, the 1927 Federal aid total represented only about 2 percent of all state revenues for the year, hardly a significant sign of major efforts in cooperative federalism. Moreover, the aggregate of state aid to localities for the same year was nearly five times the Federal.

## Functional Assignments

As much in the foregoing fiscal and judicial analyses has suggested, fairly significant shifts in servicing responsibilities occurred during the seventy-year second
period. The national government, over time and not easily, acquired a functional
role that was in marked contrast to the one it held in 1860 or would hold in
1960. The most obvious functional development, of course, was the significant
growth in national authority, activities, policies, and programs. The dominance
of the national government in the military, foreign policy, monetary, and banking areas was established. Moreover, a new role was gradually carved out: the
national government was serving as a positive (not passive, as had been the case
formerly) regulator (and even reformer) of certain parts of the economic system,
subject of course to the curbs provided by the Supreme Court. The antitrust,
fair-trade practices, various interstate commerce prohibitions, and direct regulation of railroads and radio communications efforts combine to suggest a major
departure from the predominantly negative or neutral role the national government had assumed in such matters during most of the pre–Civil War era. And
the new promotional efforts in economic development, natural resources conservation, social welfare, and education — generally by direct action but sometimes
by grant-in-aid — suggest other contrasts with the past and movement toward
somewhat greater centralization.

Yet were the states and localities eclipsed or enervated by these developments? The answer, basically, is no. What the national government was doing
was responding gradually and with considerable uncertainty and conflict "to the
new national dimensions of business enterprises and labor organizations, and
to the consumer problems of an increasingly urbanized society."[52] Most of the
newly assumed functions were part of the response and most of them, by their
genuinely interstate and national scope, were beyond the effective control of
the states' police power. At the same time, this left a wide range of functions
primarily, if not exclusively, in state or local hands: primary and secondary education, public higher education, public welfare, public hospitals, police, fire
protection, and local sanitation, to mention only the more obvious of state-
and local-provided and wholly or almost wholly financed services. In all the
Federal-grant-aided areas, including the two largest — highways and vocational
education — the states were still the senior partners fiscally and administratively.

Toward the end of the era, the number of state and local personnel had grown
to more than four times the Federal figure.[53] In a similar vein, while Federal per
capita direct expenditures were increasing steadily over this period (beginning at
$2 per capita in 1860 and rising to $7.23 in 1902, thence to $35.84 in 1927),
overall state-local per capita expenditures were soaring from $13.83 in 1902 to
$65.61 by 1927. In short, although the states' regulatory power, intrastate com-
merce power, and in a few instances taxing authority were constrained by some
of the Federal regulatory efforts, these powers were not in any sense negated or
undermined. In some cases, expansion of the state police power was sanctioned.
Above all, perhaps, practically all of the growing number of public services pro-

vided directly to the public were decided upon, performed, and financed by state and chiefly local governments. In overall functional terms, the increase in national regulatory efforts vis-à-vis the private corporate sector was balanced by an increasing state and local direct servicing role (and without Federal incentives or controls).

## The Political Conditioner

The third party system was ushered in with the election of Abraham Lincoln and has lasted to the present. Scholars have described this more than 130 years of Republican-Democratic contesting as a "derivative stage," in that "the survival of early basic forms" during this broad sweep of political history makes this era "one of adjustment, rather than creativity."[54] Its first two major phases, probed here, were basically Republican ones and lasted from 1860 to 1932. Changes, however, occurred during all of the era's four phases — 1860–95; 1896–1932; 1933–68; 1968 to present — but for the first three the shifts were more incremental rather than basically creative. The current political phase presents special analytical problems, to be discussed later, but in various respects it is drastically different from the previous three and may merit the label *Fourth Political System.*

Regarding the two phases under analysis here, 1860–95 and 1896–1932, the first "saw the rise of the classical, corrupt, but assimilative boss and machine," and it brought "party loyalties to a pitch of almost military fervor" and voter turnout to all-time highs.[55] The next phase (1896–1932) witnessed various efforts to curb and cleanse politics, politicians, and parties. There was a rise in direct primaries and a decline in voter turnout, party loyalty, and the strength of the major parties generally. These and other developments during the two halves of this Republican period affected the integrative, public policy, leadership and personnel recruitment, socialization, and conflict resolution roles of the parties. They also influenced the management, public administrators, and finance and policy functions of the various levels of government, especially the local. Turning first to the derivative dimensions of the first phase, the egalitarian political style, the essential dominance of party dualism, the highly decentralized party organizations and interlevel power relationships, their heterogeneous makeup, and their efforts to integrate different regions, classes, and ethnoreligious groups into the political system were just as much hallmarks of this early phase of this third political system as they were of the second.

The party traits sometimes involved confronting new challenges and generating different outcomes. Put differently, some of these characteristics did not continuously characterize this phase. The decentralized designation, for example, was not applicable to the initial solidly Republican years that extended from the Civil War through much of the Age of Reconstruction because they exhibited strong centralizing tendencies.[56] The two-party ascendancy label is only roughly accurate because there were several third (and even fourth) parties during these years. With increasing industrialization, urbanization, and economic functional differentiation, as well as the emergence of a national economy to replace the separate regional ones of the prewar years, both of the major parties focused on the dynamics of the new developments, especially from 1876 to 1896. Against a seeming eastern ascendancy in both the major parties, agrarians rallied around the Grangers in the seventies, the Greenbackers in the eighties, and with southern support the Populists in the early nineties. The last was the most successful third party ever; in 1894 it captured the largest number of congressional seats of any third party and went on in 1896 to be the majority faction within the Democratic party under William Jennings Bryan. The Progressives began as a movement within both major parties, became a secessionist party under Theodore Roosevelt in 1912, and then a third party in 1924. There were third parties (chiefly antislavery or nativist in their thrust) during the second party system, but they lacked the scope and strength of these later protest parties.

To label the 1866–1930 years as a solidly Republican era also is not wholly valid. During the most hotly contested two decades (1876–96) in U.S. political history, one party dominated both political branches of the national government for only four of these years. Cleveland was in the White House for two separated terms and was the popular (but not electoral) vote winner in the 1888 contest for the intervening four-year term. The vote of the third parties was a factor in these and other races, but even more was the return of southern Democratic congressional delegations after the 1876 election. The Republicans, then, were regnant during the Civil War and Reconstruction years and became the clear majority party with the pivotal realigning victory of William McKinley over Bryan in 1896. The Wilson win in 1912 was the by-product of a severe Republican split, and his reelection was not settled until the California vote came in — a tribute more to him than to his party. Republican control in the twenties was unquestioned. So this seventy-year era was a Republican one but not steadily so.

The major parties were heterogeneous in their composition, but not as much as their Democratic and Whig predecessors. These post–Civil War parties were far more regionally rooted, with solid one-party domination in whole sections of the country, largely as a political result of this war. The geographic distribution made the intraparty integrative job easier, but it also made the task of sustaining the system more difficult. The dominant party, after all, had no southern support despite three attempts to acquire one, and this was the prime cause of the overall systemic dilemma. Others were the emergence of a white supremacist Democratic South after Reconstruction and the advent of the direct primary.

The emergence of split-level politics and political issues was another distinguishing new feature of the 1866–1930 years. Although railroads, the tariff, and trusts tended to dominate national-level policy and interparty debate, ethnoreligious, cultural, and community questions frequently were the dominant issues in state and local politics and in determining party affiliation.[57] This differentiation of policy issues by governmental level created yet another basis for dual federalism.

Another new, and in this case centralizing, political development was the arrival in Washington of clearly identifiable interest groups, chiefly economic.[58] It began with business groups that wanted to escape state regulation and to achieve "friendly" Federal enactments and with efforts by some farmers to lobby their cause. Labor followed, though weakly, and most of agriculture by the twenties had discovered that a strategy that involved interest groups outside Congress and bipartisan factional groups inside Congress was superior to its previous third-party approach.

With the arrival of organized unifunctional groupings, a new form of policy-making arose: one wherein "the private interplay among functional groups was basic to and more fundamental than their public interplay."[59] The failure of such groups to reach mutually satisfactory deals, according to Samuel Hays, led to the interjection of public agencies into the process. In this way, antitrust, railroad, banking, and agricultural enactments from the 1880s on to 1929 were more frequently the by-product of the efforts "of some segments of private business" to "restrict other segments when their objectives could not be reached through public accommodation."[60]

From Samuel Beer has come a somewhat different but not contradictory interpretation. Relying on the classical economists' concept of externalities, Beer finds there are political fallouts from the external consequences of economic activities that though incidental to an entrepreneur's main activity are also inseparable from it.[61] Such external effects may exert a favorable (a benefit) or an unfavorable (a cost) impact on other firms or individuals. A "spillover" political coalition then arises to achieve governmental intervention in order to curb the negative effects of specific economic activities (for example, the farmers' efforts to curb adverse railroad actions). In terms of governmental levels, early stages of economic modernization witnessed intervention by local governments, but the "increasing flow of interlocal and interstate costs (or benefits)" later tended to produce centralization of such efforts at higher jurisdictional levels.[62]

For this seventy-year political era, the initial sources of regulatory reform were the localities and then the states because they were the first to encounter the emerging problems of a "modernizing society," and they were the first to establish independent regulatory commissions. Though the central government gathered more responsibility and power as the interstate costs increased, it tended to model its policies "on precedents already provided by states and cities." Spillover coalitions, then, could and did operate at both the state and national levels.[63] When the Federal government expanded its regulatory role, the many remaining responsibilities were left to the states, and their response won for them the accolade of "laboratories of experimentation." In this fashion, Beer developed the spillover-coalition model as the interest group political basis for both state and national policy activism during this Republican era. He also found in it the basis of the new modified form of dual federalism.

Still another new political development, at least in its extent, was the rise of urban and sometimes state machines. The emergence of cities, the increase in the industrial working class, and the soaring numbers of foreign population groups were the main materials out of which they were fashioned, especially in the Northeast and Midwest.[64] Their leaders' prime concerns were with local social and ethnoreligious issues, patronage, and other rewards that the capacity to deliver a vote can bring.

During the first two party systems, national and state patronage generally was held by state legislatures, thanks to their own institutional powers and their influence over the selection of U.S. senators. In the first phase of the third party system (1861 to 1895), changes relating to the selection of senators that began in the last decade of the previous system shifted this control. Prior to 1850, senatorial candidates usually campaigned after the election of the state legislatures, and this placed the winners in a dependent relationship, even to the point of receiving state instructions. But during the 1850s some candidates began the contest before the legislative canvass and urged voters to elect representatives who favored their candidacies.[65] Such was the case in the historic Lincoln-Douglas debates in 1858.

By the 1870s, most Senate contests were waged in such fashion, with the outcome frequently deciding which party controlled the legislature. With this development, most U.S. senators acquired the previously unheard of opportunity to affect the distribution of both national (given the role of "senatorial courtesy") and state patronage. Local machines and other leaders consequently began in earnest to interest themselves in senatorial contests. By the 1880s, most northeastern and midwestern senators were either state bosses who sought the post to attain a pivotal position in their parties' state organizations or were the "handpicked representative of state or local bosses."[66]

Patronage also constituted the chief motive for local machine involvement in presidential elections. In return for their support in the nominating and electoral campaigns, presidential candidates adhered to the informal but usually binding rule relating to "senatorial courtesy": senators of the president's party acquired the right to control patronage within their respective states. Some of the most important political battles of the day involved presidents from Rutherford B. Hayes to Grover Cleveland who refused to acquiesce in turning over control of the New York Customs House to the senators from that state, Roscoe Conkling being the most notable and formidable. State and local organizations also exercised significant influence over the behavior of their House members in Washington, which led to brief tenures, high turnover, and a lack of seasoned political professionals in that chamber.

The overall political effects of the machine-motivated developments were to enhance state and local party organization, to sustain the split-level approach to the treatment of policy issues, in that the bosses were not interested in national policies but only in national patronage and in curbing national-policy activism.[67] The results plus the corruption, constrained national policy process, close ties with corporate America, and their combined impact on the conscience of middle-class America generated a sizable reaction to the more egregious features of this "Gilded Age."

The reaction constituted yet another unique phenomenon in this political period. The Progressive movement grew out of the merger of the Populist-Democratic agrarian revolt of the 1890s and the urban, largely middle-class, northeastern-midwestern, bipartisan reform drive of the early 1900s, though their respective motives were quite different. They agreed on one basic proposition, however: the "alliance between big business and party officials" was "the antithesis of good government."[68]

Both had a national reform agenda but an even greater state and local one. Among the most important items on the latter was the drive to transfer power over policymaking from corrupt legislatures to the people. Hence, they advocated the need for a secret ballot; the initiative, referendum, and recall; reliance on direct primaries for nominations; and direct election of U.S. senators. To advance clean and competent government, they also endorsed city-commission and city-manager forms of local government, the merger of nonviable local units, regional planning, and unified executive budgets.[69] The last was sanctioned for the national level as well, along with antitrust and other regulatory legislation in the economic sphere and the income tax amendment in the fiscal. The merit system was advanced as a means of paralyzing the old patronage system for staffing the national, state, and local bureaucracies.[70]

It took the assassination of a president by a disappointed office-seeker to trigger the transformation. But the Pendleton Act (1883) initially exempted over 80 percent of the Federal administrators from its coverage, thanks to the heavy lobbying of state and local bosses.[71] By 1901, 45 percent were covered, and thirty years later the figure reached 77 percent. Endorsement of public scientific managerial reforms came in the first decade of the twentieth century as a logical concomitant of good government. Progress in this area at the state and local levels came at a much slower pace, extending into the current era.

In reviewing the array of electoral, economic, and good government reforms, more emphasis was given by the populist Democrats and their allies to the electoral and economic reforms. The midwestern-northeastern bipartisan Progressives focused more on governmental effectiveness and accountability, along with the economic changes. What impact did their reform drives have? The number of presidential primaries rose from none to twelve to seventeen for the Democrats and from none to thirteen to sixteen for the Republicans from 1890 to 1912 to 1928. At best, the whole array of electoral improvements achieved only a marginal weakening of the urban machines. The latter's resilience and adaptability along with the continued strength of the groups that were aided by the machines guaranteed no quick retreat in the face of middle-class reformers. Machines, it is to be remembered, performed many significant integrative and assimilative functions by assuming social welfare, "fix-it," and Americanization responsibilities. Where machines were absent, populist and other interested groups were able to access the political arena more easily. In the South, however, the primary merely sent the last nail into the coffin of civil and political rights for blacks because it enthroned a one-party Democratic, white supremacist system. With the U.S. senatorial elections, no really drastic changes occurred, except in states where parties already were weak.

The merit and scientific management movements did affect personnel systems, but their impact at the state and local levels was nearly glacial. Other good government proposals that achieved great successes, again over time, were the city-manager and unified-executive-budget reforms. Finally, the Progressives did have a lasting effect with their successful sponsorship of the Sixteenth Amendment, which sanctioned a personal income tax, and with their lead role in enacting ten new grants-in-aid between 1901 and 1921 and in carving out a national police power that the Court ultimately upheld. All of these served as significant precedents for later New Deal and postwar actions.[72]

To sum up, various political developments from 1860 to 1932 challenged the derivation traits inherited from the second party system. But decentralizing forces, whether bosses in the Northeast and Midwest, racism in the South, or even populist electoral reforms in the West, combined to make sustained national programmatic activism very difficult. Spillover coalitions did arise and did succeed at times in increasing national power and responsibilities. In politics, parties, interest groups, and the system, these divergent trends combined in various ways to perpetuate dual federalism though with a few new centralizing and collaborative features.

## Conclusion

The dynamics of this period, 1789–1930, as reflected in the judicial, public finance, servicing, developmental, and political areas, all lead to the generalization that Madison's compound republic with its basically compartmentalized theory of functional assignment was still pretty much intact 140 years after it was established. It operated differently under the emerging industrial republic than it had under the old rural regime, but it definitely was a dual federal system. The national government clearly was in a stronger position — constitutionally, judicially, and fiscally, as well as in regulatory matters — than it had been in 1860. The states and localities also had grown in power and authority during the period. The emergence of servicing government, after all and quite naturally, began with these jurisdictions. Whether comparative revenue, expenditure, or personnel figures are used, the states and their localities were the senior operational partners under the federal system throughout the period.

What is more, hardly any of these expanding state and local undertakings involved any regular interaction with the national government, though they did accelerate the interaction between them. Fifteen Federal categorical grants amounting to a total of $100 million in 1930 did not add up to any major piercing of the traditional Federal-state separation-of-services barrier. Moreover, the informal, ad hoc, and largely sporadic contacts between parallel regulatory and administrative agencies at the Federal and state levels, while suggesting cooperation, were neither required (save in one instance) nor indispensable to the performance of either level's implementing and regulatory responsibilities. Local governments, of course, had implementing and regulatory roles, but most such units had no regular formal or significant informal contacts with the Federal government. To be noted here is the fact that it was during this period that the American regime's "statelessness" ended and evolved into a new "tempo-rary American state," as Richard J. Stillman II phrased it.[73] A series of secular challenges — the end of the frontier, urbanization, industrialization, foreign for-ays, and domestic crises — combined to force ad hoc and incomplete reforms in public personnel, national regulation of the economy, budget processes, execu-tive management, and administrative law. While rough and partial, this fleshing out of America's previously skeletonized governmental structure and functions helped thicken the Federal layer of the "layer cake" federal system of this period.

  Dual federalism dominance — such was the operational theory of federalism that characterized most of the intergovernmental relations of this second period of the emergence of the United States as a nation. The dents in this model, however, were a forecast of the future.

*Chapter 4*

# The Rise and Maturation of Cooperative Federalism, 1930–60

The third period of our evolving federal system encompassed the rise and maturation of cooperative federalism. Traditional dual federalism, for all intents and purposes, began its decline during the Great Depression. Cooperative federalism, the seeds of which were sown in the previous period, evolved fairly rapidly and reached a high point of maturation and acceptance in the fifties. Yet with the launching of the contemporary period in the sixties, a series of developments emerged that combined to undermine conventional cooperative federalism.

The concept of cooperative federalism appeared only a little later (that is, in the forties and fifties) than the idea of intergovernmental relations. And with good reason. Both primarily represented attempts to describe what had come about with the New Deal, though diligent efforts were made to trace the roots of the concept to the Articles of Confederation.[1] As the two previous sections demonstrate, sustained interlevel interaction in administration, servicing, or finances — whether cooperative or conflicting — ranged from nil to minimal throughout the 140 years following adoption of the Constitution, just as Madison intended.

What, then, are the postulates of cooperative federalism? In essence, as it emerges from the writings of its prime expositors, Grodzins and Elazar, it encompasses seven premises. These were meant to be descriptive but ultimately became prescriptive:

- "The American federal system is principally characterized by a Federal-state-local sharing of responsibilities for virtually all functions."

- "Our history and politics in large part account for this sharing."

- "Dividing functions between the federal government, on the one hand, and the states and localities, on the other," is not really possible "without drastically reducing the importance of the latter."

- "No 'strengthening' of state governments will materially reduce the present functions of the federal government, nor will it have any marked effect on the rate of acquisition of new federal functions."

- Real and reliable decentralization is that which exists "as the result of independent centers of power and . . . operates through the chaos of American political process and political institutions."

- "Federal, state and local officials are not adversaries. They are colleagues. The sharing of functions and powers is impossible without a whole."

- "The American system is best conceived as one government serving one people."[2]

In an analysis of this theory, certain of its more distinctive features need to be emphasized. Primarily, it is a functional interpretation, focusing heavily on the funding, administration, and rendering of public services. The dominant pattern of service provision, so the theory holds, is a shared one including practically all governmental functions. The uncentralized basis of our political parties and processes and the good representation and protection of state and local interests at the national level combined to sustain "noncentralization," to use Elazar's apt term, within the peripheral governments. In terms of structure and power, the institutionalized pattern of collaboration had come into being within a "dualistic structural pattern" and "the relative balance between the federal government and the states [had] not significantly shifted" since the Constitution was adopted.[3]

Attitudinally, officials at all levels behave as allies, not as enemies, in that they need and rely on one another, as well as operate under one system and serve one people. The melding of the powers and functions of the governments thus resembles the characteristics of a "marble cake," as Joseph McLean called it, rather than the "layer cake" of dual federalism.[4] So much for the theory, but what of its practice?

The real rise of cooperative federalism occurred during the Great Depression and the decade and a half following World War II. In terms of public finance, public programs, public administration, regulation, and politics, a broadly collaborative pattern, or at least a pattern of sharing — whether done in a really cooperative fashion or not — was the dynamic new feature of the intergovernmental relations of that period. The dollars, programs, and personnel involved, as well as the sheer scope of expanded and regularized intergovernmental contacts, were so much greater than the limited counterpart efforts of the earlier era that the cooperative federal label was wholly appropriate. At the same time, as this chapter shows, not all of the theory's premises were reflected in practice. Moreover, this basic shift in the development of American federalism would not have persisted for three decades (nor would the more recent pattern of intense intergovernmental relations have arisen as it has) without judicial sanction.

## The Court Crushes Old Dual Federalism

Intergovernmental relations, as the analyses of the predecessor periods indicated, were and are conditioned by judicial decisions as much as by any other single factor. This is not to say that justices are necessarily the paramount actors in the unfolding of the federal drama, but they were (and are) actors. Through most of 1937, the Supreme Court pursued a course that generally was the opposite of the course of political branches of the national government, resisting the New Deal's rapidly emerging cooperative federal shift in direct regulation and intergovernmental relationships and enunciating variations on the older judicial dual federal principles.

Unlike President Hoover, who rejected a broad construction of the Federal commerce power even as he urged certain relief measures (hence the 1930 dating of the beginning of this period), Franklin Roosevelt quickly scrapped his earlier states'-rights views and adopted a flexible approach to the constitutionality of the sweeping economic recovery and reform proposals he advanced in the wake of his first inauguration. In their entirety, the emergency programs enacted during 1933 added up to an extraordinary assumption of Federal authority over the nation's economy and a major expansion of the national government's commerce and taxing powers, in part as a result of broad delegations of congressional authority in both areas to executive branch agencies and officials.[5] Two lines of precedents, in effect, were before the justices when dealing with cases this legislation generated. The more limited one stretched back through the child-labor cases to *E.C. Knight* (156 U.S. 1, 1895), while the more latitudinarian followed a different course, leading to decisions that combined to create a broad Federal regulatory power.

It was not until 1935 that a New Deal statute came before the Court. Beginning in January of that year and continuing for sixteen months, ten major cases or groups of cases were decided. In eight, the majority voted against the New Deal. Only the emergency monetary measures and the Tennessee Valley Authority Act survived, largely on conditional terms.[6]

In the eight, the majority of the justices rejected the New Deal's great expansion of Federal authority, some of it at the expense of the states. More specifically, they rejected

- any delegation of broad rule-making or regulatory authority to executive or especially to quasi-private agencies in the absence of clear congressional guidelines;

- any real Federal control over production whether by means of the commerce, taxing, or general welfare clauses, thus harking back to the dual federalism approach to the Federal policy power; and

- any viable concept of constitutional growth in light of economic growth or emergency.[7]

The Court with its "anti-delegation" doctrine was not alone in its assault on the Roosevelt program. Political conservatives in both parties, business groups, and financiers, as well as former president Hoover, joined in a defense of limited constitutional government, the sovereignty of the states, and the free-market economy. With Roosevelt's campaign against the "economic royalists" and his tremendous electoral triumph in 1936, overtones — but only overtones — of class politics began to emerge and the stage was set for a confrontation with the Court.

Various proposals to curb the Court were advanced in Congress. In early 1937 the president presented Congress with a bill that would authorize him to appoint another judge for each one who had served ten years or more and had not retired within six months after his seventieth birthday. A maximum of fifty such appointments were to be permitted and the Supreme Court's size was to be raised to fifteen.[8]

The plan was clearly constitutional, but it split his own party, especially in the Senate. Yet the likelihood of its ultimate passage prompted some dramatically different decisions from the Court itself. In rapid succession, the Farm Mortgage Act of 1935, the amended Railway Labor Act of 1934, and the National Labor Relations Act and the Social Security Act of 1935 were upheld between March and June. The Court reorganization fight continued for a while before its demise, but its essential purpose already had been realized.

A new era of judicial construction had been launched. The commerce power was given broad interpretation in the cases upholding the Labor Relations Act. The older distinction between direct and indirect effects of commercial activity was abandoned and the more realistic "stream-of-commerce" concept adopted.[9] The scope of the Federal taxing power also was broadened expansively. In sanctioning the Social Security Act, the unemployment excise tax on employers was upheld as a legitimate use of the tax power, and the grants to the states were viewed as examples of Federal-state collaboration, not of Federal coercion.[10] The act's old-age and benefit provisions were deemed to be proper because "Congress may spend money in aid of the general welfare."[11] When combined, these decisions obviously amounted to last rites for judicial dual federalism.

In overall judicial and constitutional terms, the post-1937 Court sanctioned a permanent enlargement in the scope of Federal power.[12] Areas of authoritative action that previously had been left to the states' sphere of sovereignty or to the private sector now fell within the powers of Congress. The sale of securities, public utility operations, agricultural production and marketing, labor-management relations (including wages and hours), flood control, and regional development were only some of the more obvious new Federal policy areas that the New Deal carved out and that the Court ultimately found constitutional.[13]

The economy in all of its key phases had become a national responsibility, and no later Court or set of new political leaders ever seriously questioned this. State authority in many of these areas was not nullified, but the regulatory activities of the national government generally far outweighed those of the states, singly or collectively. Dual federalism as it had been applied judicially was a dead doctrine throughout the rest of the period. No longer could the justices fall back on the two lines of precedents when dealing with commerce or taxing-power cases because only the broad, liberal national tradition was deemed authoritative.[14] At the same time, the states' police power actually expanded during these thirty years, and well into the contemporary period. Moreover, as later analysis will show, the states became major implementers of several nationally initiated grant programs.

Judicial passivity in the economic and regulatory areas did not lead to passivity in all. Fears in the late thirties that the Court's role in the system would decline and that its traditional policy-making assignment would wither proved groundless. Before, but especially following, World War II the Court dealt with segregation, church and state issues, and subversive activities. As early as 1937, it began to enunciate a "preferred-freedoms" principle involving Federal constitutional protection of the rights "implicit in the concept of ordered liberty" and the principles "so rooted in the traditions and conscience of our people as to be ranked as fundamental."[15] This libertarian doctrine provided the basis for a new judicial activism.[16]

In application, the doctrine led to a case-by-case gradual incorporation of various First Amendment guarantees within the due process and equal protection clauses of the Fourteenth Amendment, thereby generating a new body of substantive due process in the civil liberties areas directed mainly against the states.[17] A few justices, notably Hugo Black, contended that the entire Bill of Rights should be covered by the amendment, and that this was the intent of its framers.[18] The full Court, however, was not persuaded.

Reflective of the postwar period was the regularity with which civil rights cases began to come before the Court. State-required segregation in interstate transportation was found unconstitutional in 1946, and state judicially enforced restrictive covenants were invalidated two years later.[19] Though earlier higher education cases had begun to chip away at the "separate but equal" doctrine as it applied to education,[20] it took the landmark *Brown* v. *Board of Education* (1954) to relate the principle to primary and secondary schools and in the context of midtwentieth-century conditions, not those of the late nineteenth. The doctrine was found to be in violation of the equal protection clause of the Fourteenth Amendment, less on legal and historical grounds and more on the basis of the impact of segregation on black children.[21] The famous phrase "with all deliberate speed" was an attempt to recognize that implementation of the decision would not be instantaneous, but that flexibility and inevitable delays would be part of the effort to achieve what amounted to a social revolution in the South.[22] "Interposition" and "massive resistance" were but two aspects of a broad pattern of southern formal and informal resistance to the decision. By the end of this period, school desegregation was still moving at a glacial pace.

In broad outline, what does this period's Court history suggest? It clearly indicates that Federal-state questions arising in diverse areas were the dominant concerns of the Court. It demonstrates that judicial activism in one area may be accompanied by passivity in others, with a majority of the pre-1937 justices generally exhibiting a strong predilection to assert their narrow view of the Federal commerce, taxation, and police powers, while rarely asserting themselves on civil rights or civil liberties issues. The New Deal Court, on the other hand, assumed a generally deferential posture vis-à-vis Congress's interpretation of its powers (thus leaving the question of constraint almost wholly to the political process), while civil liberties and a new version of substantive due process provided the basis for renewed judicial assertiveness.

In terms of the states, these various shifts in judicial outlook were not always threatening. The old Court's dual federalism doctrine obviously was beneficial to them (at least in a judicial sense) and the new Court's abandonment of economic substantive due process expanded the scope of their police power. Moreover, the conservatism of the postwar years helped produce a series of decisions that were more protective of states' police power than was the case during the years 1937–41.

Yet national authority in the economic arena was expanded tremendously during this period, and the Court ultimately found the crucial change to be within the framework of the Constitution. The desegregation cases in the fifties marked a renewal of this national assertiveness, though from the Court itself rather than from the president or Congress. Equally clear was the fact that some of this judicial enlargement of the Federal "sphere" was at the expense of the states and the private sector. In short, despite relative state gains during the period, the national government, in both absolute and constitutional terms, came out as the more authoritative partner in the system. Moreover, the Court remained something of an umpire of the federal system, even though it abdicated its role in the economic regulatory and conditional spending power areas, leaving both to the determination of the political branches of the national government. Yet it also espoused — sometimes vigorously, sometimes softly — a new type of activism, if not interventionism, in the areas of civil liberties and civil rights.

## Operations of Functional Federalism

### Governmental Finances: Great Growth and Some Diversification

Major public finance shifts occurred during this third period in the history of U.S. federalism — shifts that paralleled developments in the other areas of intergovernmental activity. One authority put it in these dramatic terms: "The decade of the 1930s brought more drastic change to the intergovernmental financial structure in the United States than did the preceding 140 years."[23]

The prime fiscal fact of this period, perhaps, was the extraordinary growth of governmental outlays, especially during the thirties. In GNP terms, the 1959 percentage for such outlays was 2.7 times greater than the 1929 percentage. In constant dollars the 1959 figure was more than four times the earlier one. The growth rates on a per capita and dollar basis for the period exceeded their counterparts for the earlier period, but the latter's figure in relation to the GNP remains unsurpassed.

The expenditure patterns by level of government also highlight equally dramatic developments. The Federal government for the first time assumed the dominant role; its outlays rose from 2.5 percent of GNP in 1929 to 18.7 percent in 1959. At the same time, the state and local share of GNP still surpassed

Table 4-1
### Share of Total Domestic Governmental Expenditures from Own Funds, by Level, 1929, 1939, 1959 (in Percentages)

| Calendar Year | Federal | | State | | Local | |
|---|---|---|---|---|---|---|
| | Total | Domestic | Total | Domestic | Total | Domestic |
| 1929 | 25 | 17 | 21 | 23 | 54 | 60 |
| 1939 | 51 | 47 | 21 | 23 | 28 | 30 |
| 1959 | 70 | 48 | 14 | 24 | 16 | 28 |

Source: Adapted from Advisory Commission on Intergovernmental Relations, Significant Features of Fiscal Federalism, 1978–79, M-115 (Washington, D.C., May 1979), 7.

the Federal domestic proportion (8.2 percent versus 7.7 percent) at the end of the period, as it had by narrowing margins throughout.

The steady growth in state expenditures was especially noteworthy: a nearly threefold hike in per capita terms and almost a doubling of its proportion of GNP. Local expenditures, on the other hand, declined as a proportion of GNP (from 5.3 percent in 1929 to 4.4 percent in 1959) and slightly in per capita terms between 1929 and 1949. The small rise (to 4.4 percent of GNP) in the fifties still left local governments with a per capita 1959 figure that was only 29 percent higher than its 1929 counterpart. Yet when state and local outlays are combined, their 1959 share of GNP was 8.2 percent compared to 6.9 percent in 1949.

The shift in the Federal, state, and local shares of total and domestic expenditures during this period provides another means of dramatizing the significantly changed character of public finances. The jump in the Federal share of domestic outlays from 17 percent in 1929 to 47 percent in 1939 to only a percentage point higher in 1959 really tells the story (see table 4-1). The relatively minor shifts in the state and local proportions in 1939 and 1959 also should be noted, suggesting rather stable trends during the period's last two decades and the continuing, though reduced, greater local expenditure role relative to the states'.

In terms of specific revenue sources, the Federal government relied somewhat less on income taxes during the thirties (because of the depressed economy) than it did in the previous decade. Yet the income-tax share soared steadily during the forties and fifties, to assume an ever greater proportionate dominance than it had in the twenties (1927, 64 percent; 1948, 77 percent; 1958, 79 percent).

State and local taxes also experienced major shifts. Overall, the state share of total state-local tax collections rose from 26 percent in 1927 to 41 percent in 1938, and then to a near-parity status of 49 percent in 1958 (see table 4-2, p. 96). This marked upturn in one sense represents a continuation of a trend that began in the latter part of the previous period. Yet the magnitude of the changed collections picture suggests a real departure from the earlier incremental growth pattern.

The adoption of new state taxes helps to explain this. Between 1939 and

### Table 4-2
### State and Local Tax Collections, by Type of Tax,
### Selected Years, 1927–58 (in Millions of Dollars)

|       | Calendar Year | Income | Consumption | Property | Other | Total |
|-------|------|--------|-------------|----------|-------|-------|
| State | 1927 | 162    | 445         | 370      | 631   | 1,608 |
|       | 1938 | 383    | 1,675       | 244      | 831   | 3,132 |
|       | 1948 | 1,084  | 4,042       | 276      | 1,340 | 6,743 |
|       | 1958 | 2,562  | 8,750       | 533      | 3,074 | 14,919 |
| Local | 1927 | 0      | 25          | 4,360    | 94    | 4,479 |
|       | 1938 | 0      | 120         | 4,196    | 157   | 4,473 |
|       | 1948 | 51     | 400         | 5,850    | 298   | 6,589 |
|       | 1958 | 215    | 1,079       | 13,514   | 653   | 15,461 |

*Source:* Bureau of the Census, *Historical Statistics of the United States, Colonial Times to 1957* (Washington, D.C.: Government Printing Office, 1960), 722–24, 727–29.

1960, seventeen states enacted a personal income tax (sixteen states in the thirties), and a like number adopted a corporate income levy (fifteen during the depression years).[24] Moreover, and in complete contrast to earlier behavior, thirty-five passed general sales tax measures (twenty in the thirties). In two specialized tax areas, thirty-nine instituted distilled liquor excises (thanks to the repeal of Prohibition) and fifteen enacted gift taxes.

In all, 114 enactments of eight types of taxes took place in the thirties; 29 additional enactments, in the forties; and 11, in the fifties. The total of 154 tax actions for the three decades stands in contrast to 183 for the entire pre-1930 period, of which 48 were death taxes and 49 were automobile registration fees. The mix and rate of taxes in any one revenue package varied considerably from one state to another, but unlike the earlier pattern, greater commonalities were emerging because more states were making use of the same diverse sources of revenue.

At the local level, the property tax continued to be the chief revenue raiser, even as it experienced some gradual slippage (from 97 percent in 1927 to 95 percent in 1938, 89 percent in 1948, and 87 percent in 1958). The modest erosion was the result of the piecemeal and highly selective adoption (mostly by cities) of sales, earning, and/or income taxes. Sometimes specific state authorization was needed for these actions and sometimes not, depending on whether home rule statutes conferred any real fiscal powers.[25] In absolute dollar terms, the property tax had regained all the ground by the fifties that it had lost in the thirties, demonstrating a strength that surprised some.

Despite all of these changes, the overall tax system at the end of the period was only slightly more "intergovernmentalized" than at the beginning. Ninety-six percent of the income taxes went to the Federal treasury in 1959, and 94 percent

## Table 4-3
### State Aid to Localities, by Function, Selected Years, 1932–58 (in Millions of Dollars)

| Function | 1932 Amt. | 1932 % | 1940 Amt. | 1940 % | 1948 Amt. | 1948 % | 1958 Amt. | 1958 % |
|---|---|---|---|---|---|---|---|---|
| Education | $398 | 49.7 | $700 | 42.3 | $1,554 | 47.3 | $4,598 | 55.8 |
| Highways | 229 | 28.6 | 332 | 20.1 | 507 | 15.4 | 1,167 | 14.2 |
| Public welfare | 28 | 3.5 | 420 | 25.4 | 648 | 19.8 | 1,247 | 15.2 |
| Health & hospitals | — | — | — | — | — | — | 150 | 1.8 |
| General support | 140 | 17.5 | 181 | 10.9 | 428 | 13.0 | 687 | 8.3 |
| All other | 6 | .7 | 21 | 1.3 | 146 | 4.5 | 390 | 4.7 |
| Total | 801 | 100.0 | 1,654 | 100.0 | 3,283 | 100.0 | 8,239 | 100.0 |

Source: Bureau of the Census, *1972 Census of Governments, Topical Studies*, vol. 6, no. 3, *State Payments to Local Governments* (Washington, D.C.: Government Printing Office, June 1974), 9.

of the property taxes were collected by local governments (a slight increase over 92 percent in 1927); although consumption taxes were levied by all levels, the general sales tax was almost exclusively in state hands, and the selected excises oftener than not were different for the different levels. Still, there clearly was some increase in tax overlaps because of the mounting diversification of state tax systems and, to a much lesser degree, those of localities.

### Intergovernmental Fiscal Transfers: Major Increases with Some Systemic Impacts

Far more significant than the changes in tax systems was the great growth in grants-in-aid during these three decades. More than any other single factor — save for the Court's shift — this development with all its administrative, servicing, and fiscal implications was the one that gave the phase its dominant intergovernmental character. Cooperative federalism, after all, depends heavily on grants as its chief means of reflecting functional collaboration in practice. This reliance on grants was a pragmatic national response to the perennial opposition to big government and to the powerful role of state and local organizations in politics of all levels.

State aid to local governments witnessed a remarkable rise. During the thirties, of course, its growth was modest, but its major postwar expansion made it the principal intergovernmental method of fiscal transfers ($8.2 billion versus $4.7 billion for Federal aid in 1958) by the end of the phase (see table 4-3).

Explicit and implicit in table 4-3's figures are certain significant trends. First, the amounts in both absolute and relative terms were impressive. Even in constant dollar terms, state aid registered a nearly fourfold increase,[26] a marked contrast to the slowly evolving pattern of the previous period.

Second, although the functional areas aided were pretty much the same as before, significant proportionate shifts occurred among them over time.[27] Welfare and general support payments fluctuated irregularly; highways declined steadily in proportionate terms; and education began high and after some decline during the depression had ascended to an even more predominant position by 1958.

Third, school districts and counties continued to be the chief local governmental recipients of the aid programs, though cities that administered a school system — like New York City, Philadelphia, Baltimore, St. Louis, Denver, and San Francisco — also benefited significantly.[28]

Fourth, the overwhelming bulk of state aid throughout the period was of the conditional variety, ranging from more than 83 percent of the 1932 total to more than 96 percent of the 1958 total. The funds had to be spent for a specific purpose; certain conditions had to be met (though these were far less intrusive than today's); most of the grant dollars were allocated pursuant to a legislatively determined formula; and the cost-sharing approach was frequently used for determining how much a recipient jurisdiction received.

Finally, local governmental finances were helped, and indirectly the pressures on the property tax were somewhat lightened by the rising tide of state aid. As a percentage of total local general revenue, it amounted to 14.1 percent in 1932; 23.8 percent in 1940; 28.9 percent in 1948; and 29.2 percent in 1958. Moreover, as a percentage of the states' own direct general expenditures, the figures for this period reveal another steadily upward trend.[29]

All of these developments are based on aggregate data, and they conceal varying state aid efforts in light of varying resources, varying preferences regarding program areas to be aided, varying degrees to which Federal aid was incorporated in the state aid figures,[30] and the varying state reliance on the direct servicing approach (as in Hawaii) rather than on intergovernmental fiscal transfers (as in New York and California) as a means of responding to the growing servicing demands of citizens. The three decades, in essence, were the formative years in the evolution of these systems because the states' intergovernmental transfer role had ranged from minuscule to meager in the earlier period.

Overall, then, state revenue raising and aid expanded extraordinarily during the latter part of this period. Although these developments varied considerably among the states, each state far more resembled a single fiscal and functional system at the end of the period than at the beginning; all had become more intergovernmentalized to a greater or lesser degree. Despite mostly malapportioned legislatures, real and widespread state-local fiscal and functional cooperation, then, was a distinctive and dynamic feature of the thirty-year period.

The Federal aid story for these years is almost as exciting as the state saga. For the thirties alone, it was the main attraction. Whether gauged in dollar amounts, kinds of services aided, or perfecting of the mechanism, the growth in Federal grants marked a major turning point in the history of U.S. intergovernmental relations. This growth and that of state aid were major factors accelerating the operational decline of traditional dual federalism. The conditional grant-in-aid, after all, became a major weapon in the arsenal of a national government initially bent on relief, reform, and economic recovery and then on defense and postwar rehabilitation and on development. During what some have called the

"First New Deal" (1933–mid-1935), new grant programs were enacted for distribution of surplus farm products to the needy, free school lunches, emergency highway expenditures, emergency relief work, general relief, administration of employment security, and support of general local governmental costs.[31]

From mid-1935 to 1939, during the "Second New Deal," additional aid programs were passed.[32] In dollar amounts, these depression-born programs generated outlays in 1939 that were more than fifteen times the 1933 total, a figure not reached again until the early fifties. With the advent of World War II and the economic recovery it stimulated, six emergency relief programs were terminated, and immediately following the war, five war-related aid programs were discontinued[33] — this partially explains the aid figure of less than $900 million for 1946.

During the Truman years (1946–52), grant programs were adopted for agricultural marketing services (1946), airport construction (1946), scientific agricultural research (1946), hospital construction (1946), mental health (1946), disaster relief (1947), cancer control (1947), heart disease (1948), urban renewal and slum clearance (1949), civil defense (1950), aid to the permanently and totally disabled (1950), fish restoration (1950), and school construction in Federally impacted areas (1950).[34] Aid outlays rose gradually to more than $2.2 billion in 1950, then to $2.4 billion in 1952 for seventy-one separately authorized grant programs.

Despite the ostensibly conservative Eisenhower years (1953–60), more grants-in-aid were enacted, including the interstate highway system (1956) and defense educational programs (1958).[35] The new grants and changes in ongoing ones produced 61 new authorizations for a total of 132 grants as of 1960, accounting for $6.8 billion in aid outlays, or two and a half times the figure obtaining when Eisenhower was inaugurated.

In terms of program emphasis, health and welfare programs dominated the New Deal grants — a marked contrast to the highway and specialized education predominance in the pre-1933 package (see table 4-4, p. 100). Agriculture, agricultural research, and other natural resource programs experienced a slow but steady incremental growth over the entire period, and education and general research grants and, especially, transportation and housing made significant gains during its final years. What really stands out is that as of 1960 four programs accounted for nearly three-quarters of the aid disbursements: highways (43.7 percent), old-age assistance (16.5 percent), aid to dependent children (9.1 percent), and employment security (4.7 percent). And in geographic terms, only a little over half of the 1960 total went directly or indirectly to urban areas.

The "numbers game" in Federal grants-in-aid is a perennial one, thanks to the problem of differentiating clearly between technical assistance and aid to individuals, private organizations, and business, on the one hand, and cash grants to state and local governments, on the other. Moreover, there is the quandary of whether to count separate authorizations, appropriations, and/or substantial amendments to existing grants. In terms of permanent aid programs, 15

## Table 4-4
### Federal Intergovernmental Expenditures, by Function, Selected Years, 1933–59 (in Thousands of Dollars)

| Major Functional Area | 1933 | 1936 | 1939 | 1946 | 1950 | 1956 | 1959 |
|---|---|---|---|---|---|---|---|
| Veterans' services and benefits | 758 | 568 | 720 | 20,238 | 15,277 | 8,091 | 8,316 |
| Health, welfare, and labor | 63,133 | 2,248,197 | 2,622,480 | 567,873 | 1,562,252 | 2,109,270 | 2,777,160 |
| Education and general research | 10,349 | 13,055 | 24,678 | 25,308 | 38,614 | 208,672 | 296,747 |
| Agriculture and agricultural research | 12,966 | 21,656 | 92,370 | 92,427 | 106,276 | 389,277 | 322,470 |
| Other natural resources | 1,523 | 1,473 | 2,474 | 8,274 | 16,957 | 26,606 | 34,481 |
| Commerce, transportation, housing, communication | 104,237 | 27,565 | 161,277 | 180,505 | 475,006 | 873,715 | 2,877,781 |
| Total | 192,966 | 2,312,514 | 2,903,999 | 894,625 | 2,214,382 | 3,615,631 | 6,316,955 |

Source: Advisory Commission on Intergovernmental Relations, Periodic Congressional Review of Federal Grants-in-Aid to State and Local Governments, A-8 (Washington, D.C., June 1861), 12–13, table 2.

were separately authorized by 1930; 15 were added between 1933 and 1940; 41 between 1941 and 1952; and 61 during the period's last eight years. As of 1960, 132 separate grant authorizations were subsumed under 58 basic program headings.[36]

Despite the absolute growth in grant dollars and number of programs, annual outlays from 1942 to 1958 hovered around 1 percent of GNP, and then reached 1.4 percent in 1959 and 1960. In addition, as a percentage of state and local revenues, they remained steady at 10 percent between 1952 and 1957, rising to 14 percent by 1959. As a proportion of all nondefense Federal expenditures, they went from 11.2 percent in 1952 to 14.1 percent in 1956, and to 17.1 percent in 1959.[37]

Regarding the recipients of Federal aid, the states were the prime partners in all but a handful of the ongoing regular grant programs. Put differently, the by-passing of the states was unusual and modest during most of the period, though it did occur frequently in the thirties because of the public works and local relief efforts. But these did not last, and the housing acts of 1937 and 1949, the 1946 airport legislation, and the urban planning and renewal program of 1954 were the pivotal local programs of the postwar period. All told, some fifteen programs of local aid that involved no state role whatsoever had been enacted prior to 1960. Yet the dollar amounts of all of these efforts were minuscule: $298 million in 1950 (10 percent of Federal aid) and $473 million nine years later (7 percent of Federal aid).

In design, all but one of the programs were categorical or conditional grants. The exception was shared revenue from western lands distributed to the states involved on a "no-strings" basis; this never accounted for more than 1 or 2 percent of total aid outlays in any one year. Within the categorical designation, however, four separate grant types emerged. All of the 132 programs enacted fell under one of these headings.

There were (and are) three types of formula-based grants, wherein funds were made available automatically to eligible recipients who met the requirements and conditions established by statute or regulation:

- *open-ended disbursements,* under which the Federal government matched approved expenditures without limit to the absolute amount (for example, the 1911 assistance to state marine schools and the aid-to-dependent-children program started by the Social Security Act of 1935);

- *formula grants,* whose dollar disbursements were dictated wholly by a congressionally specified or required allocation formula (for example, the highway programs of 1916 and 1956); and

- *formula-project grants,* under which a state's area funds were determined by an allocation formula, but the specific recipients and their precise disbursements were left to the process of state or Federal administrators deciding among numerous individual competing applications (for example, the 1946 airport legislation).

Pure project grants, the fourth type, had no allocation formula and no state area distribution constraints. For such grants, potential eligible recipients had to submit specific individual applications in the form and at the time indicated by the Federal grantor agency (for example, the 1937 public housing and the 1946 scientific agricultural research programs). Although formula grants always dominated the aid package in dollar terms, the number of project grants grew during the postwar period to where they exceeded the formula type by about two to one at the end of the Eisenhower years.[38]

The conditions attached to Federal grants reached a high level of maturation during this period. As one authority put it regarding the New Deal programs:

> Many were additions to the already established programs of the 1910's and 1920's. Since many of the services were new, and since the funding was generous, there were additional incentives for the attachment of greater conditions. Plans were required by almost every act and permanent programs had detailed administrative regulations.[39]

Of the fifty-eight basic programs in 1960, twenty-one required a state or other broad-gauged plan. Near the end of this period, the authors of the report of the Commission on Intergovernmental Relations (Kestnbaum Commission) to President Eisenhower wrote:

> The maturing of the grant as a means of stimulating and shaping particular programs, as distinct from a subsidy device, is reflected not only in increasing legislative attention to conditions, standards, sanctions, and methods of supervision, but also in the evolution of National administration machinery and procedures. The conditions attached to grants have not remained mere verbal expressions of National intent; National agencies have generally had funds and staff to make them effective.[40]

Closely linked to this maturing of the grant device was the attachment to certain programs of protective conditions aimed at enhancing the professionalism and political neutrality of recipient agencies and personnel. Thus, merit-system coverage was required in 1939 for state (and county) employees administering the Social Security Act programs, and under the 1940 amendments to the Hatch Act political activities of recipient employees paid wholly or in part with Federal grant funds were restricted. In an organizational sense, the "single state agency" requirement was used ostensibly to establish an administrative focus for implementing grant programs, but it was also used to isolate and insulate grant administrators and their personnel from the pressures — political and otherwise — from the rest of the state systems. Merit-system requirements (which by 1960 covered practically all of the health, welfare, and employment security programs), the political-activity prohibitions, and "single state agency" provisions combined to fashion a nonarticulated theory of grants administration that stressed the vertical, functional, bureaucratic linkages and the protective strengthening of administrative counterparts at the recipient level. Under it, the administrative role of elected chief executives and the administrative shaping powers of legislative bodies were deemphasized, if not ignored, in part because several states had no merit system for the portions of their bureaucracies that were covered by these Federal requirements.

To sum up, the growth in conditional grants, both state and Federal, was a major feature setting this period apart from its predecessor and serving as a prelude for its successor. It was this development that helped launch the study and definition of intergovernmental relations, even to the point of a temporary presidential commission on the subject being set up and a statute creating the permanent Advisory Commission on Intergovernmental Relations (ACIR) being enacted in 1959. It was grants-in-aid, more than any other form of interlevel collaboration, that generated the cooperative federal theory, and their operation prompted the "marble cake" metaphor.

That a "marble cake" had been baked during the three-decades-long period there can be little doubt. Whether it was done in a collaborative spirit by all the parties involved is another matter. And whether the cake was as "marbleized" as many writers have contended it was is still another. The following analysis of the functional assignment issue will shed more light on the character of the cake.

## Functional Assignments in a Time of Growing Collaboration

That the orbit of national authority formally expanded considerably over three decades cannot be doubted. The foregoing judicial, fiscal, and grant analyses provide ample bases for this assertion. The Great Depression, the most devastating war the United States has ever fought, and the aftermath of the two were sufficient — along with an ultimately supportive Supreme Court — to expand greatly the established though skeletal roles of the national government as regulator, reformer, and promoter of the economy.

Legally, as we have seen, no real barriers were placed in the path of the roles after 1937, to the extent that the political processes supported policies that furthered them. The power to spend for the general welfare and to regulate commerce produced a new concept of the national government's responsibilities in the entire economy. It covered practically all of the economy's most important phases: production, labor, unemployment, money and banking, social security, housing, public works, flood control, and conservation of natural resources.[41]

A national police power of far greater scope than its Progressive era predecessor thus emerged, and, as Theodore Lowi has emphasized, the regulatory role that the national government assumed in the New Deal far outweighed the significance of the ballooning Federal budgets.[42] The adoption of a range of new regulatory policies and the establishment over the entire period of fourteen new regulatory agencies (in addition to the fourteen established before 1930) were indicative of this new Federal interventionist thrust.

Federal domination of banking, monetary, and fiscal policies was stretched to points unimaginable in the earlier period, thanks to the depression, the establishment of the Board of Governors for the Federal Reserve system, and the gradual acceptance of Keynesian countercyclical concepts. Agriculture became a largely Federally "managed" sector of the economy, and a Federal presence was established in private labor-management relations with the Wagner Act (1935) as well as its Republican-sponsored major modifier, the Taft-Hartley Act of 1947. Regulation of communications (telegraph, telephone, and radio) was lodged with the newly established Federal Communications Commission in 1934, and a little later regulation of the operation of nonmilitary aircraft was assigned to the Civil Aeronautics Authority. The U.S. Maritime Commission was created to supersede the Shipping Board, and the powers of the Federal Trade Commission were expanded to curb false or misleading advertising. The Securities and Exchange Commission (1934) was given regulatory authority over stock exchanges and public utility holding companies. The Federal Power Commission (1930) was assigned oversight of large electric-power companies in 1935 and supervision of the construction of interstate natural-gas pipelines and the rates charged to big-city utilities' customers. The Tennessee Valley Authority (1933) constituted a rare venture into government ownership of the means of energy production, and in 1946 both the operating and regulatory facets of nuclear energy were lodged with the Atomic Energy Commission.

Despite this seemingly inexorable trend toward national regulation and centralization, certain caveats need to be cited:

- First, most of these undertakings were of such a clear interstate nature that the states separately could not have assumed them.

- Second, the vigor with which the national regulatory policies were pursued varied considerably from agency to agency, from time to time, and from administration to administration.[43]

- Third, although the net effect of these legislative (and supporting judicial) actions was largely to keep the states out of interstate commerce, admiralty, bankruptcy, and currency matters and to prevent them from imposing burdens on Federal instrumentalities, this did not mean, as noted earlier, that the states' police power in intrastate commerce or even some aspects of interstate commerce was fatally weakened.[44] The power to incorporate businesses, to tax and legislate in a way that established in very real terms the image of a "favorable" or "unfavorable" climate for expanding or relocating firms, to regulate insurance companies, to audit state-chartered banks, and to regulate the wide range of intrastate transportation activities (bus, rail, trucks, and ports) and such utilities as gas, light, telephone, and water were all left to the states.

- Fourth, no "constitutional no-man's-land" existed after 1937 wherein neither the national government nor the states could act in economic matters; either one or the other was, in effect, given the authority to legislate because of the New Deal Supreme Court's interpretations of the Federal commerce and taxing powers and of a state's police powers.[45]

- Fifth, the earlier practice of joint boards, representing regulatory agencies at both levels, was greatly expanded by law to cover such areas as motor carriers, communications, electricity, and natural gas.

Above all, perhaps, the scope and degree of separation of the direct-servicing responsibilities of the various levels must be weighed when considering the degree of centralization that emerged from 1930 to 1960. Here, the perspective of 1930 as well as that of the present are needed to arrive at a balanced assessment. On the one hand, the state and local services that received Federal aid and were subject to its accompanying conditions clearly were more numerous and more caught up with shared decision making and shared implementation than ever had been the case prior to the New Deal. On the other hand, major state and local servicing responsibilities were minimally affected or wholly untouched by the expansion of Federal grants during this period.

The range of new social welfare, public health, natural resource and conservation, airport and highway construction, public housing and urban renewal, and selective, specialized educational programs of aid to the states and, in a few cases, to their localities did give rise, however, to the cooperative federal concept of a collaborative commingling of funds, personnel, and program purposes to promote common goals. State highway, health and welfare, and natural resource and conservation agencies were most affected by this expansion of Federal grants-in-aid. Yet even these units were by no means wholly dominated by the Federal programs and their regulations.

- With highways, maintenance and rural roads were wholly under state purview and subject to heavy state direct and grant expenditures.

- In welfare, general assistance programs geared to filling the gaps left by the Federal programs were under state control and funding, and they were frequently administered by local units. Moreover, state and local welfare outlays constituted 60 percent of the 1958 total (chiefly for matching and general assistance), and even within the aided programs, payment levels and certain aspects of eligibility were left to the states to determine.

- Among state health programs, only one-fifth of the funds came from Federal grants by the late fifties, and state expenditures dominated the outlays for mental hospitals.

- With natural resource conservation, only about 2 percent of all state expenditures were earmarked for these programs (excluding those for agriculture), and Federal grants constituted only 7 percent of these funds.

All this suggests that some, not all, of the activities of these state agencies were conditioned by their heavy participation in Federal grant programs. This was even more true of state agricultural and educational agencies.[46] Many of the U.S. Department of Agriculture programs, after all, were carried out directly with state and county committees of farmers and farm experts with no formal linkages to state or county agricultural agencies, though informal ties were not uncommon. Thus, although Federal grants varied from 10 to 50 percent of the cost of running agricultural experiment stations and extension work, they averaged only about one-fifth of the states' own outlays for agricultural activities in 1958, aside from soil and conservation undertakings.[47]

In the case of education — the largest state and local revenue consumer — comparatively modest amounts of Federal aid were the prevailing pattern. For state universities, aside from the original land grants, there was assistance for agricultural college programs, experiment stations, and contract research; special grants under the National Defense Education Act (1957); and indirect aid by means of tuition funds for veterans. With public primary and secondary education, there was the U.S. Office of Education's program of collecting statistics, specialized research and demonstration grants, vocational educational assistance, support for teaching agriculture and home economics in high schools; and there was the U.S. Department of Agriculture's (USDA) school lunch program and aid to school districts affected by the presence of a Federal military or other installation within them. In short, state and local education efforts were only minimally affected by Federal aid programs, which amounted to only about 4 percent of state and local educational outlays in 1958.

Beyond these significantly and minimally aided state programs and agencies stood those that secured no Federal grant funds: the attorney general's office, the state police, corrections departments, court systems, economic development units, licensing boards, and regulatory commissions, not to mention the offices of treasurer and secretary of state.

At the local level, informal contacts with Federal officials increased, but ongoing intergovernmental administrative relationships grew only modestly. The pre-1930 pattern of receiving technical assistance from the Corps of Engineers, Public Health Service, Census Bureau, and the Department of Agriculture continued and expanded. Moreover, the emergency relief programs of the thirties (the Civil Works Administration, 1933; the Public Works Administration, 1933; and the Works Progress Administration, 1935) did pump sizable amounts of public works funds to cities and counties in an effort to provide jobs for the unemployed.[48] These programs as well as the direct financial assistance for local relief expenditures, however, disappeared with the end of the depression.

During the second half of this period, local contacts on an ongoing basis with Federal officials and agencies were relatively limited. The number of assistance programs for which local governments were directly eligible, after all, was small, twenty-five; only fifteen were wholly of the direct type, with no state role of any kind, and only five had local governments as the sole recipients (low-rent public housing, urban renewal, the two impacted-area education grants, and community renewal).[49] The bulk of the $347 million, then, that was distributed directly to localities in 1957 was accounted for by five programs, along with some airport, water-resources, and civil-defense aid funds. They represented 8 percent of 1957 Federal grant funds and 1 percent of overall local revenues.

In operational terms, of course, all of these Federal-local programs (save the impacted-area grants) were project grants, which, in light of the limited amounts of money, meant that comparatively few localities were continuing participants. Put differently, few local governments were continuing direct partners with the Federal government in shared program undertakings, and none of the major traditional functions of cities (servicing the physical environment and providing police and fire protection) were much affected by any of these aid programs. The same generalization, of course, could be applied to school districts because even those benefiting from impacted-area aid received it in "no-strings" disbursements.

In the case of counties, direct grant relationships were restricted to a few of their urban units, and hardly any of their customary functions (in criminal justice, roads, elections, and natural resources) were affected by these Federal-local grants. On the other hand, counties were significantly affected by certain Federal-state programs wherein the states mandated a county role, as in welfare and public health. Moreover, the USDA's extension system with its county organizational basis indirectly affected these local jurisdictions.

Regarding special districts and authorities, four of their categories (water and sewer, housing, renewal, and soil conservancy) expanded in number during this period, partially as a result of Federal aid in these program areas. These, of course, provide some early examples of bypassing local general governments, albeit at their own instigation in many instances.

The cooperative federal interpretation that emerged in the late forties and fifties, then, reflected the growth in Federal-state as well as state-local sharing of functional responsibilities that had occurred since the early thirties. Although its enunciators traced the roots of this development back to the Articles of Confederation, it seems clear that it was the 117 new Federal aid programs enacted during the three decades, not the 15 from the previous period, that provided the dynamic environment in which the concept crystallized. The ever greater state-local interdependence provided yet another backdrop to this development, though the Federal role initially was the chief focus of the cooperative federalism analysts. It was no accident that the interpretation emerged when it did. If there is any doubt, ponder the prospect of advancing it in the twenties. Impossible, given the dominant dual federalist pattern of the intergovernmental relations of that decade.

Yet it did capture the relatively structured, simple, and stabilized — though obviously somewhat complex — pattern of the final decade of the 1930–60 period. And the "marble cake" metaphor was apt. The "ingredients," after all, were almost wholly the Federal government and states: the chocolate and vanilla. The frequency of the major interweavings were few (four, in fact) — the cake of the fifties resembled the one that had been baked in the late thirties. None of these attributes characterize the contemporary cake, of course, for simplicity, relative stability, and structure are not among its ingredients. Unending complexity, some continuity but constant shifts, and a seemingly unstructured nonsystem are its main attributes, and no clever culinary metaphor really expresses it, except perhaps "fruit cake" federalism.

Transcending and sometimes subsuming major aspects of the new Federal regulatory and intergovernmental fiscal transfer efforts was the vast expansion during the postwar years of the national government's role as promoter of the economy and broker-subsidizer of major interest groups. In some respects, this was merely an extension of its 140-year record of subsidization, chiefly through tariffs, land grants, maritime support, and even some regulations. But in this period, the forms of subsidy multiplied, the cost in real dollar terms clearly escalated (though the real amounts were, and are, impossible to estimate), the number of benefiting groups skyrocketed, and a very old political strategy was given a very new application. The result was a drastic reformulation of the promotional role of the Federal government — not merely in its intergovernmental relations but in its private-sector relations as well.

The New Deal has been interpreted in terms of class coalitions and of redistributive politics and programs.[50] It also may be viewed as an effort, however, to satisfy the aspirations and needs of weaker socioeconomic groups (labor, agriculture, the poor, the unemployed, and even the middle classes) by a range of responses, all the while not threatening the fundamental role of, nor the system that conferred that role on, the older ascendant groups (business, finance, the well-to-do). This concert-of-interests approach dominated the "First New Deal" with its something-for-everyone strategy. As Richard Hofstadter described it: "Farmers got the Agricultural Adjustment Act (AAA) of 1933. Business got the National Recovery Administration (NRA) codes. Labor got wage and hour provisions and the collective bargaining promise of Section 7(a). The unemployed got a variety of Federal relief measures. The middle classes got the Home Owners' Loan Corporation, securities regulations, and other reforms."[51]

The "Second New Deal" reflected more of a redistributive and less of a pork-barrel thrust. The Wagner Act and fair labor standards legislation were a boon to labor and led to thoroughgoing and successful union efforts to organize (10 million members by 1939). The Agricultural Adjustment Act of 1938 carried forward the promise to agriculture of the 1933 legislation struck down by the Court. Trust busting was launched to appeal to the middle classes, and an inheritance tax, an estate levy, gift taxes to prevent evasion of the inheritance tax, and more steeply graduated taxes on large incomes were enacted as redistributive measures. The Social Security Act aided the elderly and a range of other beneficiaries. All reflected the more social democratic tendencies of the second phase of the New Deal.[52]

World War II put an end to much of this and the concert-of-interests approach again became fashionable, thanks to crisis conditions, near-full employment, boundless government procurement and defense contracts, and rising corporate profits. In the fifteen years following VJ Day, it was that approach far more than class politics that, in practical terms, conditioned the interventionist national role and especially its expanding subsidization activities.

Political rhetoric and political attitudes regarding the newly acquired class bias of the majority party notwithstanding, the statutory and institutional legacy of the New Deal and its extensions under Harry S. Truman's Fair Deal and during

Dwight Eisenhower's conserving years — not to mention the Cold War defense budgets — stressed distribution and pork-barrel politics far more than redistribution and class politics. The Full Employment Act of 1946, the Housing Act of 1949, its amendments of 1954, a cluster of other small categorical grants, some modifications in Social Security and its grant programs, and the desegregation decisions of the Court all nodded in the direction of redistribution. Yet the dominant practice was distributive. One basic reason was the ascendancy of the so-called Conservative Coalition in Congress from 1939 onward, which is discussed later.

The other basic reason, of course, was that the liberal nationalist ethic of the dominant political coalition throughout most of these years was pragmatic. With FDR, this meant, as he put it: "It is common sense to take a method and try it: If it fails, admit it frankly and try another. But above all, try something."[53] With the next generation of national politicians, it became the pragmatism of the political process. In effect, whatever agreement came out of the byplay among the basic socioeconomic interests was legitimate and in the national interest.

This 1950s version of "interest group liberalism" occurred because (1) no concept of a really authoritative national government emerged during the Roosevelt years; (2) the expansion of national government powers during this period was accompanied by attempts to deny it; and (3) the "concert-of-interests" strategy was more in harmony with the traditional pork-barrel political ethic than variations on a redistributive theme and more in accord with the heterogeneous composition of the major parties than with any presumed clear-cut class differences. And so it was that the agencies intended to regulate frequently collaborated with the regulated. At the same time, direct assumption of a responsibility usually was rejected in favor of relying on subnational governments by means of the grant device or on quasi-private or wholly private organizations by means of contracts and subsidies.[54]

Reflective of the Federal assumption and then abdication of authority was the relatively slow growth in its own bureaucracy during these years. Despite the ostensible accumulation of vast new Federal "managing" authority and responsibilities, employee count rose from 600,000 in 1929 to only 1,100,000 a decade later, then to 2,399,000 by 1959 (including postal, Social Security, and Internal Revenue Service workers). As a proportion of the nation's labor force, Federal employment peaked in World War II and declined ever after.

Another prime result of the "concert-of-interests" strategy was the swiftly multiplying number of subsidy programs. On a formal level, these may be described as promotional efforts by the national government to encourage various sectors of the economy in order to further development and to assist national defense.[55] At a more mundane and practical level, they reflected the interaction between more numerous interest groups, chiefly of the economic and professional variety, and the national government, as well as the brokerage response of a political process that was primarily conditioned by pork-barrel and spillover coalition politics.

In 1960 the Joint Economic Committee of Congress compiled a listing of "subsidy and subsidy-like programs of the U.S. Government."[56] It included programs, past and then current, that "by one criterion or another, might be considered to partake of or involve an element of subsidy regardless of original intent of any particular programs."[57] Ten types of subsidies were identified:

1. grants (five) to business firms and corporations to carry out specific objectives;

2. farm subsidy programs (eight);

3. tax benefits to specific economic groups;

4. various forms of indirect assistance to specific economic groups;

5. economic programs having incidental effects similar to those of subsidies;

6. free or below-cost national services (other than loans or insurance programs);

7. nineteen lending and at least thirteen loan-guarantee programs;

8. direct insurance programs undertaken by eleven national agencies in eleven different areas;

9. fifty-one grant programs to states and local governments; and

10. seventeen payment arrangements to individual programs.

About 140 of the "subsidy and subsidy-like" programs were operational in 1960; more than nine-tenths had been enacted between 1930 and 1960. Not covered were Federal regulatory efforts — some of which also had a subsidy-like effect[58] — which constituted an eleventh type. Thus, to a far greater degree than merely regulation or grant efforts as such, the expansion of the Federal government's subsidizing promotional role in this period stands out as the dominant form of national interventionism. Regulation itself was in part caught up with it, especially in the post–World War II years, and major Federal aid programs were merely one of its many (eleven) basic manifestations. Of greater significance, of course, were the grants to firms, farm subsidy programs, specialized tax breaks for and indirect aids to specific economic groups, preferential lending and loan-guarantee programs, and insurance programs.

The functional assignment picture changed greatly during the three decades. The national regulatory role expanded, though not to the extent of really undercutting the states' police powers in a range of critical social and economic areas. Federal reliance on grants-in-aid as a means of achieving a range of specific programmatic (as well as fiscally supportive and especially stimulative) purposes became much heavier during these years, and the cooperative federalism metaphor served as a roughly accurate description of this novel development. Yet it did not reach the point of affecting even a majority of most state functions or even any of most cities', counties', or school districts' basic service responsibilities.

In the Federal government's promotional efforts, however, a much more complicated, largely private-sector-oriented version of cooperative federalism emerged, which involved practically all of the basic organized sectors of the economy plus some of the not-so-well-organized sectors of society. Diverse direct and indirect subsidy programs were developed, including certain regulatory and grant-in-aid undertakings. When viewed in their totality, those supportive programs reflected an adaptation of the older, more narrow promotionalism in light of the interest group politics and policymaking of the fifties. It was this expansive adaptation that constituted the most significant shift in the functional responsibilities of the national government between 1930 and 1960.

## The Third Phase of the Third Party System

The largely Democratic third phase (1932–60) of the third party (Democratic versus Republican) system incorporated continuities with the past as well as novel developments suggesting the political future. It was in retrospect a transitional time politically, just as it was intergovernmentally. And this was not accidental or coincidental.

Like its Republican predecessor, this Democratic political phase had two parts: one solidly Democratic (1933–46) yet still characterized by many of the two-party, integrative, compositional, distributive, noncentralizing party traits of the past; the other (1947–60) was much less Democratic, given the election of two Republican Congresses (the 80th and 83d) and a two-term Republican president, and the pivotal power position in Congress of a bipartisan conservative coalition. Different economic, social, and foreign policy factors explain the contrasts between the subphases, and the parties were far more affected by these secular factors than they were conditioners of them. Moreover, despite the significant strengthening of national governmental regulatory, financial, assisting, and subsidizing roles, as well as the nationalizing of many policy issues during the New Deal, the political system still was decentralized at the end of the Roosevelt years. William N. Chambers has pointed out:

> In the era of the Great Depression . . . , parties did revamp their outlooks and to some extent their activities to cope with demands for welfare, the need to meet the effect of massive economic collapse, and problems of economic management in a mixed economy. Once again, however, the effect of a federally structured party system was often to fragment or federalize national policies or programs.[59]

Moreover, even with the addition of Cold War, new regulatory, and a few new domestic program responsibilities to the national agenda, the political system in 1960 was still largely noncentralized, as Morton Grodzins emphasized then.

Centralizing political tendencies manifested themselves in several ways during the Roosevelt years, however. In the first place, it was one of the few times prior to 1964 in which there was a sustained centralization of activist policymaking under the guidance of a new majority party and its leadership. The Republican party from 1861 to 1868 provided the last example of this kind of concentrated centripetal party policymaking.

The politics permitting this political centralization, of course, was the gradual emergence of a New Deal coalition in the 1932, 1934, and 1936 elections. It was an incredibly heterogeneous alliance made up of the Democrats' traditional regional preserve of the South; urban northern working-class whites; Catholics, Jews, and nearly all of the more recently arrived ethnic groups; and many intellectuals.[60] It was a membership that required extraordinary integrative party efforts to keep together. It was a coalition produced partly by conversions (for example, some progressive Republicans and native-born American workers), by the continued electoral activation of urban groups that first voted Democratic in the 1928 Hoover-Smith contest (for example, first- and second-generation women of the "new immigration"), and by the coming of age of their first- and sometimes second-generation children.[61] It was a remarkable mix of socioeconomic groups, along with some midwestern farmers, that prompted the shift from a vertical "concert of interests" to a more horizontal class basis for FDR's more redistributive policies of the "Second New Deal," noted earlier. It was generally the have-nots of the coalition that sustained this short rendezvous with redistributive politics. What is more, it was its polyglot composition that also sustained for a longer period both pork-barrel and spillover coalitions as well as the brief class-based ones in the midthirties.

Another centralizing phenomenon was the way the New Deal conferred direct programmatic as well as patronage and electoral benefits on northern and midwestern state and urban machines; the widespread impact was unique. The first New Deal program to confer such benefits was the emergency relief program administered by the Federal Emergency Relief Administration (FERA) headed by Harry Hopkins. Over more than three years FERA distributed more than $3 billion for relief purposes under an arrangement that left public welfare administration at the state level while operating under flexible nationally imposed guidelines.[62] Where state and local program management proved unsatisfactory, Federal takeover or the total cutoff of funds was permitted, and each occurred in a few instances. In 1935 another relief effort was mounted: the Works Progress Administration (WPA). This public works program was really run by national officials and required no state matching funds. Governors, southerners, and Republicans all complained about various aspects of this rare nationalized domestic undertaking — chiefly and with cause — on grounds that it was used to strengthen big-city Democratic machines; merit requirements did not enter into the picture until late in the decade.[63] Direct program benefits, not just patronage, thus became a basic conditioner of Federal-state and Federal-local political relations — a new phenomenon in U.S. party history.

National antimachine strategies, both intentional and unintentional, were reflected in other Federal actions. The Social Security Act with its national program of old-age assistance and its four Federal-state grant programs marked the beginning of the Federal government's gradually assuming some of the welfare functions that urban machines formerly performed. Paralleling this was the emergence, again for the first time, of a deep personal identification by many with a party and its leader on the basis of relating their specific economic coalition to the programs and electoral success of that party. This theretofore unknown politico-psychological phenomenon in its own way also began to undercut the need for local machines. Yet other antimachine moves were the application in 1939 of merit-based personnel standards to state and local employees administering Social Security Act grant programs and the extension in 1940 of the Hatch Act's political-activity restrictions to such workers in agencies receiving Federal aid funds.[64]

Roosevelt's intervention in the Democratic senatorial primaries of 1938 constituted a rare open attempt to discipline members of his own party. Congressional battles over his Court-packing proposal, the administration's reorganization bill, and wages-and-hours legislation produced cleavages within Democratic ranks. Incumbent Senator Claude Pepper of Florida, an administration supporter, and insurgent pro-FDR candidate Lister Hill of Alabama won their respective primary races with visible presidential blessing. In five other U.S. senatorial primaries, the candidate having the support of the state organization won, and the president, despite his immense popularity, was unsuccessful.[65] This unique presidential endeavor to "discipline" recalcitrant (in his eyes) congressional members of his own party and the election outcome underscore the continuing noncentralized character of the overall party system, even at the near-height of the New Deal. Despite this result, longitudinal studies of the extent of constituency influence on congressional election turnout indicate a continuation of its decline during the New Deal.[66] Put differently, national issues assumed a much greater role than they had during the Progressive era when this trend began.

One of the most remarkable both centralizing and decentralizing political developments of the late New Deal years was the Conservative Coalition in Congress, a development with both centralizing and decentralizing effects. Growing out of the Court-packing battle, the president's drive to discipline, and the GOP gain in seats in the 1938 election, a new breed of alliance emerged the next year in Congress — an alliance composed of conservative southern Democrats and conservative-to-moderate Republicans. The bipartisan block dominated national domestic policy for the remainder of this period and well into the next. This was true regardless of which party controlled Congress or the presidency. It was not true in the few instances where the two factions could not find common ground, as with Lyndon B. Johnson's Civil Rights Acts of 1957 and 1960 and the Housing Act of 1949.

Congressional rules, procedures, and leadership had not previously been a key factor in protecting decentralized government within the very core of the national policy-making process. The Court, the parties generally, public opinion, and the power of state and local organizations were adequate to the task. By the late thirties and subsequently, however, the Court, the parties, public opinion, and frequently a majority of the members of both chambers favored national action(s). What barred many such initiatives and what made for a highly incremental hike in domestic national governmental activism and in aid programs was the authoritative role of the Conservative Coalition. Its extended domination by means of the seniority system (and its assignment of power to members from one-party areas) and until 1961 conservative control of the House Rules Committee ensured its role at the "traffic cop" (as friends dubbed it) or "the guillotine" (as liberals described it) of the House.

The years from 1946 to 1960 also produced a different style of policymaking, different factional challenges to the parties, and a different pattern of Federal program benefits and beneficiaries. Some of the earlier approaches to providing party leadership and filling appointive posts continued, but innovations in party primaries occurred that amounted to a forecast of the future. The sustained centralized party control of the national policymaking of the New Deal collapsed, but there was no return to the twenties. Presidents were expected to propose, but Congress frequently rejected, redesigned, or recast wholly their legislative initiatives. Eight of the fourteen years, after all, were divided-governmental ones, though Truman fared nearly as well with the (in)famous Republican 80th Congress, as he did with the Democratic 81st and 82d. Moreover, Eisenhower had better relations with the Democratic Rayburn-Johnson led 84th, 85th, and 86th Congresses than he did with the Republican 83d — again, highlighting the workings of factional infighting within both parties.

Major "conservative measures" (for example, Taft-Hartley and the two McCarran acts), some "liberal legislation" (for example, the Full Employment Act of 1946, the Housing Act of 1949, its 1954 amendments, and two civil rights acts), and major foreign policy and defense measures were enacted. The Interstate Highway and National Defense Education legislation — the two major grant enactments of the Eisenhower years — were defended as much on defense as domestic-needs grounds, highlighting the generally incrementally based though occasionally crisis-conditioned national policy process of this era. Presidents were important, especially in foreign affairs, but Congress was prominent in domestic affairs and a necessary partner in ongoing Cold War policies requiring large appropriations. Party per se was less a conditioner of the politics of these years than external conditions and the pork-barrel coalition, spillover coalition, and the Conservative Coalition.

Much of the incrementalism related to the changed character of both the parties in the postwar years and the special integrative effort required to maintain even a semblance — in the case of the Democrats — of any cohesion nationally. The New Deal coalition no longer was made up of have-nots; it had acquired a "new-middle-class" component made up of the sons and daughters of FDR's immigrant supporters. It also had a strong "Big-Labor" component, so strong that the GOP 80th Congress felt the need to clip its wings a bit with Taft-Hartley. There was a new, large, and basically central-city cohort made up of northern blacks, resulting from their wartime exodus from Dixie. Race finally had become a national issue and a source of deep division among the Democrats. Truman, his Civil Rights Commission (1946), its recommendations, and the Dixiecrat walkout from the 1968 Democratic Convention over the civil rights platform plank brought some in the South to raise again the flag of rebellion — this time against the national party, which was favoring social policies that the same party in the South opposed locally.

The national Democratic party had become one of the most heterogeneous political entities ever. Truman's upset win over Governor Thomas E. Dewey of New York prompted some analysts to conclude that the party was the majority party and would be so permanently.[67] Truman's nomination had been opposed by the far left, the moderate left (for example, Americans for Democratic Action), the moderate right (for example, some old-time bosses), and the southern right. The left bolted first and nominated Henry Wallace; the right walked out of the convention to form the Dixiecrat party and to nominate Governor Strom Thurmond of South Carolina. Yet Truman won because he appeared, in contrast to each of his opponents, to be both conservative and liberal, and the protector of the New Deal legacy. He campaigned as a furiously maneuvering centrist who "systematically took advantage of each defection and brought its opposite group back into the fold."[68] Once elected, he pressed for several liberal measures: civil rights, aid to education, repeal of Taft-Hartley, health care for the aged, and a housing bill. In a few instances, he knew that the Conservative Coalition or others would scuttle them. And such was the case. Save for housing, compromise was the "unswerving objective of his Presidency" because it alone was the traditional Democratic approach to accommodating its internal divisions. But the cleavages among the component groups were so deep, thanks largely to race and, to a lesser degree, religion, that "the only form of compromise possible in Truman's administration was stalemate."[69]

General Eisenhower also confronted integrative challenges in carving out a winning Republican coalition in 1952 and in dealing with the GOP 83d Congress, the first to deal with a Republican president since 1930. He expanded greatly the northern suburban gains as well as the southern inroads made in 1948. He attracted the German-, Irish-, and Italian-American voters who had been leaning Republican since 1940 but voted for Truman in 1948. He won the farm, white-collar, and women's vote, all without irrevocably antagonizing traditional Taft Republicans. Once in power, however, the ideological cleavages between the conservative GOP congressional wing of the party and the moderate pragmatic presidential one prevented major policy gains. The fragility of the party bases and the forcefulness-of-personality foundation of the 1952 win were revealed more clearly with the Democratic congressional triumphs in 1954, 1956, and 1958.

Each party then had special problems in performing its historic integrative and stabilizing role. In a systemic sense, Eisenhower's ability to bring most Republicans around to accepting most of the New Deal was a constructive achievement, even as the Democrats' effort to deal openly and nationally with the oldest source of national division — race — marked the beginning of a destabilizing endeavor that was and is necessary ultimately for the long-term stability of the system. In terms of inter- and intraparty relations, there was a "strong tendency toward bimodality within each party," more so in the Republican than the Democratic case, yet still discernible in the latter, as Theodore Lowi has noted for this period.[70]

Turning to the issue of the political implications of Federal grant programs, contracts, loans and loan guarantees, and other forms of subsidies, more confusion and conflict seem to emerge. In addition to the beneficiaries of the early redistributive programs, veterans were aided greatly by the GI bill, farmers by crop and other subsidies, a range of industries by defense contracts, construction firms and Detroit by the highway program, and so on and on. Unlike the situation in the thirties, the numbers of the voters feeling a direct psychological connection between their immediate economic condition and the success or failure of a political party nationally had dwindled. But unlike the twenties, the number of citizens, economic entities, and social groupings that depended on various of the Federal government's diverse mix of redistributive, especially distributive, and regulatory programs soared during the fifties. All the groups then within the New Deal coalition or leaving it as well as groups tending Republican wanted something from the Federal government. This generated other kinds of collusion or dependency, noted by Eisenhower with his reference to the "military-industrial complex" in his farewell address. Hence, the expansion in the number of "iron triangles," the amount of interest group–conditioned decision making, the role of pork-barrel and spillover coalitions, and the clout of major pressure groups — business, labor, farm, and medical. To a far greater degree than the parties, these political actors played a dominant role during the bipartisan years of the fifties.

Leadership recruitment for elective and appointive positions experienced changes and some continuations of early trends during these years. In general, what party organizational control there had been at the state and local levels during the New Deal was significantly curbed or had disappeared by the fifties. In the Northeast and Midwest, some urban machines were still in existence by 1960, notably in Chicago, Albany, Buffalo, and Providence, among others. But these proved later to be relics of an earlier age. The spread of the merit system among municipal governments and in some states, the decline in the number of dependent populations (blacks and Hispanics excepted), the failure in most cases of urban machines to capture the new public welfare agencies, and the advent of a new communications medium and its use by rising politicians in primaries all combine to explain the accelerated decline of machines in this decade.

In the machines' place in some cities were municipal party organizations based on reform and recovery issues, as with David Lawrence in Pittsburgh, Joe Clark and Richardson Dilworth in Philadelphia, and Raymond Tucker in St. Louis. At the state level, major issue-related party changes sustained by the Stevenson image nationally and by socioeconomic developments geared to nurturing two-partyism occurred in various theretofore one-party or modified one-party Republican states. The direct primary itself had been weakening the minority Democrats in these states from 1940 to the mid-1950s. V.O. Key's classic study of state politics found that in one-party northern states "popular interest tended to concentrate in the primary of the stronger party."[71] This suggests that ambitious and talented young politicians (if not barred by background) were likely to gravitate toward and into that party, assuming they were not already within it. Under the convention system of the last half of the nineteenth century, second-party strength was generally greater in many of these states, despite the greater hostility then toward Democrats because of the legacy of the Civil War. In any event, the increase in two partyism helped curb this magnetic effect.

In at least twelve northern and western states, a competitive threat to theretofore fairly solid Republican ascendancy emerged in the fifties. In two cases it resulted from the merger of a secessionist (from the GOP) progressive state party with its generally weaker rival, the state Democratic organization. Elsewhere, a major revitalization of what had been a moribund state Democratic party was launched by what James Sundquist has described as "programmatic liberal Democrats."[72] Why this shift a generation after the New Deal? The emergence in some of these states of a larger urban population, more industry, and cleavages within farmer ranks are factors to be reckoned with here. In addition, the new Democratic insurgents did not reflect the conservatism, patronage concerns, and ethnoreligious minority status of the New Deal Democratic state and local leaders.[73] In these states, the revamped issue-oriented state and, in some cases, local organizations were able to master the primary process in ways that adaptable bosses formerly had done. Control here is too strong a descriptor, but strong influence is appropriate.

Despite southern resistance to *Brown* v. *Board of Education* and other national signs of civil rights concerns, moderate senators continued to be selected in Alabama, Louisiana, Arkansas, and Tennessee. At the same time, the "white primary" was having to confront change. In "rim" southern states and in some urban areas, the franchise was extended to blacks. This was even before certain Supreme Court cases that stripped this form of primary of the legitimacy accorded it in a 1935 decision that declared a party was a "voluntary association" and could constitutionally exclude blacks.[74] Six years later, the Court found that where a state had made a primary "an integral part of the procedure of choice," the right of an elector to have his or her vote counted in such a process is constitutionally protected.[75] In the landmark *Smith* v. *Allwright* case, the Court overruled its earlier upholding of the white primary, contending that it was an "integral part" of the state-established machinery for choosing officials and the procedure by which party-certified names were included on the general election ballot was stipulated by state law. Hence, discrimination by the party had to be considered discrimination by the state, and such action was prohibited by the Fifteenth Amendment.[76] Various attempts to circumvent this decision were made in the late 1940s and early 1950s, but none was upheld. After *Smith* v. *Allwright*, a real pickup in black voting occurred again in "rim" states and in cities, but not in jurisdictions with high black populations.[77] All this was a prelude to the Civil Rights Acts of 1957 and of 1960, which were geared to protecting voting rights, and to the historic enactments of the midsixties.

Clearly, the earlier party-leadership selection process experienced both transformation in some areas and reaffirmation in others between 1946 and 1960. Change was least apparent at the national level, where both candidates in 1952 were selected by power brokers of their respective parties with neither having to experience the trials of presidential primaries. Less than a third of the states held such primaries then and frequently they were nonbinding. At the state and local levels, transformation was greatest in theretofore one-party states, in most earlier boss-run urban areas, in the dramatic revitalization both organizationally and ideologically of grass-roots Democratic parties from Maine to Oregon, and in the beginning of growth in southern Republicanism. All this suggests organizational and candidate-selection differences among regions and among state parties, though not as great as was the case previously. Despite the contrasts, loosening of party organizational discipline could be detected in a majority of the state and local areas. Accompanying this trend was a parallel one wherein the political organizations of individual incumbents assumed greater significance, especially with members having greater tenure and greater congressional influence. James MacGregor Burns, reflecting on the politics of the fifties and early sixties, concluded, alternatively, that the many local and state party organizations had begun to serve basically as "holding companies" for individual candidates.[78]

The record of party involvement in filling administrative positions in the Truman-Eisenhower years was mixed, some gains and some losses. First, the merit system at the national level was pushed to its highest mark under Roosevelt and Truman, surpassing 85 percent by 1952. This was consistent with one of the recommendations of FDR's Committee on Administrative Management (more familiarly known as the Brownlow committee, after its chairman). The committee's prime concerns were with concentrating executive branch power and responsibility in the president and ensuring that executive power included administrative. To achieve these goals, classical organizational principles were applied to the untidy New Deal executive branch. Clear and uninterrupted lines of direction downward and of accountability upward, a reduction in the number of agencies by mergers and thus reporting to the chief executive, assignment of the nonjudicial functions of independent regulatory commissions to regular line departments, and the strengthening of the president's administrative capacity by creating a small White House Office and a presidential role in the Federal budgeting, personnel, and planning areas were called for.[79] The perennial policy-politics and administration dichotomy was given short shrift. The merit system was to be expanded to cover "all permanent positions in the Government service except a very small number of a high executive and policy-forming character."[80] In essence, the committee implicitly recognized that a properly functioning executive branch with an authoritative president at its head was as important politically as it was administratively. Poor administration, after all, hurts a chief executive politically, and political accountability is meaningless if the president lacks adequate administrative authority. FDR understood this and Truman came around to it after some patronage scandals hurt him.

In the postwar period, public administration itself was caught up with claims that administration was essentially a political process (Paul H. Appleby), and that given our undisciplined political system, a successful program manager had to assume a strong program support role (Norton E. Long).[81] Yet another intellectual leader contended that the dichotomy, properly understood, was still valid, and that true social scientists must develop a "true science" of administrative decision making founded on objective facts and rational analysis; value judgments would come from the electorate and its representatives (Herbert A. Simon).[82]

In practical terms, the newly elected Eisenhower administration was worried in 1953 about rendering a protected civil service responsible to new political leadership. This led to tension and suspicion between new political executives and their senior civil servants — a forecast here of later such episodes in 1961, 1969, 1977, 1981, and 1993. That certain protected civil servants were exercising policy-influencing roles was undeniable, and the conclusion was reached by the administration that merit had gone too far. Hence, Eisenhower established a new category (Schedule C) of persons involved in policy determination or in "confidential" matters at a high level that would be unprotected by Civil Service.[83] The second Hoover Commission (1955), on the other hand, reaffirmed the need for "numerous trained, skilled, and nonpartisan employees in the Federal service" and even called for a reduction in the number of political appointees at the top. The contrasting need for able noncareer executives to be selected by a successful political party was also underscored in the commission's effort to reconcile the claims of the contesting values in the dichotomy. In retrospect, the Eisenhower administration ultimately chalked up a good record in maintaining this balance, despite Schedule C and in light of later less successful endeavors.

The personnel and political battles were replayed at a much less furious pace at the state and local levels. Less furious because only about half of all full-time state employees were covered by a merit system by 1960, and in some instances only those affected by Federal merit requirements were involved. Thanks to the interstate highway legislation, the largest state agency in the late fifties was the department of roads, and it was rarely covered by state merit requirements and ostentatiously not covered by Federal requirements. In this case, state patronage was expanded by the largest Federal grant of the times. Counties, with the exception of welfare workers, were in most states also heavily patronage-oriented, but more cities were adopting the manager form of municipal government and merit systems along with it.

What conclusions can be drawn from this brief assessment of the politics of the New Deal and the Truman-Eisenhower postwar years?

- The centralized program-formulation role played by the Democratic party and its leadership from 1933 to 1938 had no permanent effect on the party system.

- National government policies were promulgated, but the confederate character of the national party system tended to "federalize" many of them, notably in the case of grant programs and especially in the postwar period.

- Most authorities at the time, including David B. Truman, E.E. Schatt-schneider, and Morton Grodzins, considered the party system to be decentralized or noncentralized, which made sense for the thirties and perhaps the forties, when state and local political organizations were potent. Yet it seemed to make less sense for the fifties, when these organizations began to lose their clout — unless one remembers that national party instrumentalities gained no significant powers during this time, except for (1) the 1952 Democratic Convention requirement that delegates use all "honorable means" to place the party's nominees on their respective state ballots and (2) the 1955 replacement, which held that state Democratic parties in selecting and certifying delegates "would place on their election ballots" under the Democratic party label "candidates for elector pledged to support the Convention nominees."

- Not to be overlooked is the crucial controlling national domestic policy role of the Conservative Coalition from 1939 through 1960. This amazing alliance was the key conditioner of the glacial growth of domestic programs, it explained why the new constitutionally sanctioned powers conferred on the Congress by the New Deal Court were not fully utilized until the 1960s, and it made sure that grant conditions and regulations were not intrusive and that grant administrators would refrain from interpreting statutory provisions in a similar way. In fact, it was the basic factor underpinning the Grodzins-Elazar thesis regarding the sensitivity of Federal decision makers to state jurisdictional prerogatives, not the potent position of state and local parties. It was conservative power at the center, then, as much as power at the periphery that helped sustain a decentralized political system.

- Despite the decline of most machines and the slow erosion of the white primary, state party organizational strength was aided by the increase in two-party competition, the programmatic liberal Democratic movement that helped engender it, and the continuing strong party-identification propensities of at least two-thirds of the electorate in the states experiencing this mix of political developments.

- Finally, it is clear that the multiple facets of political and representational federalism during this period had as great a role shaping the intergovernmental system as did any other force.

# Chapter 5

# Cooperative Federalism's Conceptual Offspring, 1960–80

The fourth, contemporary period (1960–) in the more than two-hundred-year evolution of American federalism has witnessed the ultimate realization of many of the tenets of cooperative federalism — tenets that previously had never been put fully into practice. This in turn produced the collapse of the concept as an accurate descriptive theory of intergovernmental relations, but not as an ideal prescription of what their relations should be. In effect, the demise in the sixties of the residual and delimiting constraints imposed by dual federalism provided the basis for a near-complete triumph of cooperative federalism, both at the national and state levels. The forces that were unleashed by this sweeping victory produced the "overloaded" federalism of the seventies, described at the outset, and the concomitant collapse of cooperative federalism.

Reagan federalism constituted a conservative reaction against most of the dynamics and manifestations of the operationally overloaded system. Though a major reduction of the Federal government's domestic role was a pivotal part of the Reagan strategy, the continuing strength of national activist groups frustrated the goals of a Reagan revolution in this area. The Bush period was basically characterized by a near-deadlock between the forces of activism and of restraint, with the latter being aided primarily by the imperatives of the mounting budget deficits, not the dictates of a conservative ideology. With Clinton, there initially was less deadlock and more cooperation, but the ambivalences continue. During Clinton's first two years, there was fairly significant collaboration with the major exception of his massive health care reform package in 1994 and in his relations with the Republican 104th and 105th Congresses. Confrontation, some collaboration, and stalemate were the key characteristics of the 1995–98 period with contrasting versions of federalism emerging from the two branches. Centralizing and devolutionary thrusts were part of the president's and Congress's intergovernmental strategies, but in each case the approaches differed, with the major exception ultimately of welfare reform.

## Pragmatic Thinkers, Not Theoreticians

All of the dominant theories of federalism of these years were enunciated by or derived from the actions of leaders in the government's political branches (chiefly at the national level). All, save for the Reagan version, constitute a variation, but only a variation, on the cooperative federal theme. Despite their many differences in emphasis, methods, and goals, the Creative Federalism of Lyndon B. Johnson, the New Federalism of Richard M. Nixon, the congressional federalism of the nation's legislature in the seventies, and the New Partnership of Jimmy Carter must be considered as subspecies of the generic cooperative federal concept.[1] All of them until 1981 were functional theories that stressed governmental activism as well as intergovernmental collaboration, sharing, and intricate interlevel linkages. Even the "picket-fence" concept and related operational concepts of the system that emerged from surveys of Federal administrators indicate no real departure from these norms but only other perspectives and approaches to achieving the collaborative concepts.

This is not to say that the advocates of the various "theories" were political theorists or even aware of all the principles implicit in their concepts. Creative Federalism, after all, never received a full presidential exposition. One of its best interpreters was not even a member of the Johnson administration but a journalist, and another was an independent-minded senator who was as much a critic as an ally of the administration.[2] One of the best analyses of Johnsonian federalism still lies buried in an unpublished doctoral dissertation at the American University.[3]

With the first New Federalists (Nixonites), there were far more presidential explanations, beginning with a largely unheard Nixon radio address from Williamsburg, Virginia, during the 1968 campaign, thence to presidential messages, and even to a televised presentation. There also were far more interpretative analyses from administration spokespersons[4] and from the media — both friendly and unfriendly. With Carter, dramatic labels were avoided for the most part, though the long-awaited and long-in-preparation "National Urban Policy," unveiled in March 1978, did produce the *New Partnership* label.[5]

Most of the exponents of Creative, New, and New Partnership Federalism, then, were people of practical, not theoretic, bent — concerned with political, programmatic, and/or administrative matters. Most did not attempt to formulate a comprehensive view of the system, and none sought to use the interpretations as full explanations of how it "works" or how it used to "work." In the case of Congress, its principles had to be inferred from its actions. With the Federal administrators, it was a cluster of concepts that emerged from opinion surveys that combined to suggest a certain view of the system.

All of them were operational theories, and all of them must be classed as variations of cooperative federalism. Their chief differences arise primarily from contrasting methods and values, differing views of the Federal role, and varying views of the partnership ideal.

The exceptionalism of Reagan's federalism was reflected in his reductionist goals for all governments, not merely the Federal; in his implicit acceptance of the "competitive-federalism" precepts of the "public choice" economists; and in his bias in favor of private communal action over any governmental involvement, except in instances of last resort.[6] To a greater degree than his recent predecessors, Reagan's intergovernmental imperatives were very much part of an overall philosophic, if not ideological, view of our governance system. Bush did not adhere to this philosophy, and neither does Clinton. But Gingrich and the 104th Congress did adhere to an even more ideological approach to government, the free market, certain moral principles, and federalism, but more on that later.

## Creative Federalism

The first major variation to emerge was, of course, Johnson's Creative Federalism. Governor Nelson Rockefeller coined the phrase for the Godkin Lectures at Harvard in 1962, but it was Johnson's use and practical application of the phrase that made it a major molder of this era's intergovernmental relations.

With Johnson's *expansive redefinition* of the partnership principle to include cities, counties, school districts, and nonprofit organizations, as well as the states, the older, primarily Federal-state focus of the cooperative federal concept as it had been applied in the late forties and fifties was scrapped. Moreover, it conditioned both politically and programmatically the successor versions: Nixon's New Federalism, congressional federalism, Carter's New Partnership federalism, and Reagan's New Federalism.

Philosophically, Johnson's Creative Federalism represented a *combination of four political traditions:* two were liberal (and in partial conflict with each other) and two were conservative. The first tradition draws on the thinking of Franklin D. Roosevelt, Theodore Roosevelt, and Herbert Croly (the "New Nationalist" philosopher of the Progressive era), and it incorporates the liberal nationalist reformist belief in the national government's capacity to solve basic economic and societal problems. Explicit in this, for Johnson, was the overriding national purpose of promoting the integrative, educational, economic, and redistributive goals of one vast commonwealth, of one Great Society. Johnson also shared a liberal federalist ideal that harked back to Franklin Roosevelt but thence to Woodrow Wilson and Louis D. Brandeis. From this perspective, the states and localities take on greater significance — as partners in the system, as implementers of national and subnational programs, as indispensable components, albeit politically independent, of our federal system. Hence, grants-in-aid became a prime mechanism for promoting partnerships to achieve national as well as state and local goals.

Despite his predominantly liberal outlook, Johnson's *pragmatism and fiscal and administrative conservatism* should not be ignored. In his "concert-of-interests" approach to legislative enactments, in his distributional approach to parceling out benefits, and especially in his dealings with individuals and groups, the pragmatist in Johnson was rarely missing. With his efforts to keep the budget under $100 billion in the midsixties; with his worry about deficits (small ones by recent standards) and about the conservative criticisms they would generate; with his hostility to welfare reform; and even with his antipoverty efforts, which after all were geared to producing "tax payers, not tax eaters," a strong streak of fiscal conservatism was clearly manifested. His heavy reliance on grants to achieve most of his program goals and his concomitant hostility to a heavily expanded Federal bureaucracy reflected his administrative conservatism. These traits in part suggest again the influence of Franklin Roosevelt, but Johnson's heritage as a Texan also cannot be overlooked as a conditioning factor.

Turning from the more philosophic *to the systemic,* the cumulative efforts of Creative Federalism on the overall system were profound. Intergovernmental relations between 1964 and 1968 became bigger (in dollars, programs, and jurisdictions involved), broader (in the range of governmental functions affected), deeper (in terms of intrusive grant conditions and of the expanding number of recipient local governments and nonprofit organizations), and certainly more complicated when compared to the relatively neat, narrowly focused, inexpensive, basically two-tier intergovernmental pattern of 1960.

Federal-state-local intergovernmental relations after Johnson would never return to the simpler days of Eisenhower and Kennedy. The marble cake metaphor that was used to describe what was presumably a complicated and convoluted network of Federal-state-local relations was a good one to use for the earlier era, but Creative Federalism dramatically modified its cooperative federalism predecessor, and the marble cake metaphor was no longer apt.

Seven basic shifts brought about this transformation. First, grant-in-aid outlays nearly doubled between 1964 and 1968, and given the relatively low level of inflation, this meant a 68 percent hike in terms of constant dollars (see table Int-2, pp. 6–7).

Second, a pronounced shift in favor of urban and metropolitan areas occurred in Federal aid allocations. Compared to the 50–50 rural-urban division in 1960, the split eight years later was 30–70, reflecting roughly the actual geographic distribution of the population. Part of this change was caused by the bypassing of the states and the increase in direct Federal grants to local, generally urban, governments. By 1968, 12 percent of all Federal aid was channeled to local governments, compared with 8 percent in 1960.

Third, more grant programs (210) were enacted during Johnson's five years than in all of the previous years dating back to the first categorical grant enactment (1879). Practically all were categorical, but two were block grants.[7]

Fourth, the range of purposes encompassed by the 210 new enactments greatly expanded the definition of what is in the national interest. From a historical perspective, nearly all of the leftover domestic items from Truman's Fair Deal, the congressional Democrats' legislative agenda of the fifties, and the Democratic platform of 1960 were enacted. Put differently, the national liberal programmatic pipeline was wholly decongested under Johnson. But Johnson (and in part Kennedy) pushed beyond the past and initiated programs that were not part of the liberal legacy. From antipoverty programs and Model Cities to Medicaid and numerous smaller grants, many Johnson proposals were newly conceived, thus adding fresh, frequently controversial, and vastly expanded programmatic dimensions to the national liberal implementation agenda.

Fifth, and as an outgrowth of much of the above, the partnership principle under Johnson's design took on a more panoramic character. With the increasing tendency to allocate Federal aid directly to substate jurisdictions, a growing number of cities, school districts, special districts, and some counties, as well as a range of nonprofit organizations, joined the states as recipients of grant funds. The president couched these efforts in terms of Federal actions needing "the cooperation of the State and the city, and of business and of labor, and of private institutions and of private individuals."[8] In most of his messages, he indicated that this intergovernmental cooperation had its roots in nineteenth-century as well as in New Deal practice. In some, however, he sensed the jurisdictional novelty of many of his proposals and talked of "new federal partnerships."[9]

Sixth, with Creative Federalism the beginning of a new regulatory era was launched — an era wherein states and localities became the objects of and/or implementers of Federal regulations. Relying on the Fourteenth Amendment, the commerce power, or the conditional spending power (and increasingly on the last), legislation was enacted that established new approaches to achieving national regulatory goals. With the Civil Rights Acts of 1964 and 1968 (Titles VI and VII, respectively), the Architectural Barriers Act of 1968, and the National Historic Preservation Act of 1966, four major crosscutting conditions were established (that is, requirements that apply to all or all relevant grant programs). The Highway Beautification Act of 1965 was one of the first examples of a crossover sanction, under which aid provided through one or more specified programs would be terminated or reduced if the requirements of another program were not satisfied. Finally, with the Water Quality Act (1965), the Wholesome Meat Act (1967), and the Wholesome Poultry Act (1968), three early case studies of partial preemption emerge (that is, the Federal government establishes the standards but their administration is delegated to the states, provided they adopt standards equivalent to those of the national government). These approaches represent a major departure — admittedly in areas of crucial national concern, for the most part — from the carrot of grant funds to the stick of coercive grant conditions.

Seventh, a largely unrecognized but significant managerial thrust was also part of Creative Federalism. In response for the most part to criticisms following the 1966 midterm elections from leading Democratic governors, a cluster of efforts were launched to improve grants management, to establish clearer lines of communication with the states and localities, to rationalize headquarters relations with field offices, and to reorganize the Federal bureaucracy. Not all of these undertakings occurred during Johnson's last two years, but it was during that time that the overall drive to apply systematically a group of fairly conventional public administration principles did occur.[10]

In more specific terms, the following points should be noted (for in many instances they set the scene for follow-up efforts lasting to 1980):

1. To provide better information and achieve better communication with states (especially) and localities, intergovernmental liaison officers were established in all the domestic departments; Circular A-85 was promulgated

to facilitate public interest groups' participation in the development of grant conditions; and trips were made by the "Flying Feds" to every state.

2. To help standardize and simplify certain phases of grants management, executive-branch attention focused on the "letter-of-credit" technique of disbursing grant funds in a timely fashion, the problem of separately required grant accounts, overhead costs (which resulted in Circular A-87), and audits (Circular A-74).

3. Efforts to improve headquarters–field office relationships were reflected in the experimental establishment of Federal Regional Councils and the development of plans for full-scale regional reform that came to fruition in June 1969 under Nixon.

4. Major drives to rationalize the Federal bureaucracy were marked by the reorganizations that produced the Department of Housing and Urban Development and the Department of Transportation.

Although most of these undertakings in better management and better communication proved by the late seventies to have their shortcomings, they conformed largely to the administrative reform principles of the day and were expanded and embellished by Johnson's three successors during the next decade. Yet even in the Johnson years a note of caution was voiced by Budget Director Charles Schultz when in 1967 he commented on the irrelevance of the hierarchic concept of management in intergovernmental relations and called for the development of techniques that would permit many government units, all of equal status, to work together voluntarily.

## The New Federalism

With Nixon's New Federalism, a reaction set in to many of the thrusts of Creative Federalism. It was ostensibly *anticentralization, anti–Federal bureaucracy, anticategorical, and antiadministrative confusion.* In positive terms, it supported greater decentralization within the Federal departments to their field units; a devolution of more power and greater discretion to recipient units; a streamlining of the service-delivery system generally; definite preferring of general governments and their elected officials; and some sorting out of some servicing responsibilities by governmental levels. As we will discover later, some of these Nixonian precepts were not part of the New Federalism II or New Federalism III's agenda. Moreover, there was some relationship between the theory and practice of the New Federalism, though less than was the case with Creative Federalism.

With *decentralization,* the field structure was reorganized in 1969, with ten standardized regions and common headquarters cities established. By the end of Nixon's administration, nine domestic departments or agencies were covered by this structure. In addition, their key field representatives served as members of the Federal Regional Councils (FRCs), which were assigned both an inter-departmental coordinative and an intergovernmental liaison role. Attempts to delegate "sign-off" discretion in managing grants from Washington to the field produced the assertion in 1972 that at least 190 grant programs had been decentralized administratively.[11] *Devolution* took the form of General Revenue Sharing (GRS) and six special-revenue-sharing proposals. The former became law in 1972, New Federalism's greatest legislative victory. With it, the discretion of states and general units of local government was strengthened because it could be, and was, used for a range of purposes: tax reduction, supplementing existing services, and/or launching new projects. Although none of the special-revenue-sharing proposals were enacted in their original form, these Nixon initiatives did lay the groundwork for block grant compromises, which contained more conditions (the essential difference between a block grant and special revenue sharing) than the administration sought. Yet the Comprehensive Employment and Training Act of 1973 (CETA) and the Community Development Block Grant Act of 1974 (CDBG) provided recipients with far more programmatic discretion than did their categorical predecessors. *Streamlining of the grant-delivery system* was largely subsumed by the interagency Federal Assistance Review (FAR) effort, which explored various ways to standardize and simplify administrative procedures and requirements. Its chief accomplishment was Office of Management and Budget Circular A-102, which sought to establish uniform phases of the grant application and management process. In addition, FAR launched the Integrated Grant Administration project, and twenty-seven pilot undertakings resulted from this experiment in jointly funding state, areawide, and local grant application projects. This in turn helped provide some of the momentum required to achieve enactment of the Joint Funding Act of 1974, a measure that had been proposed initially in 1967.

New Federalism's *preference for generalists* and general governments was reflected in the eligibility provisions of General Revenue Sharing and the new block grants (which flowed from the special-revenue-sharing proposals). In all of these new programs, special districts were excluded and elected officials of general governments favored.

The attempt to *sort out the system* somewhat was reflected in three endeavors. First, the special-revenue-sharing proposals, although continuing Federal funding, gave recipient state and local governments the bulk of the real decision making in the six functional areas covered: law enforcement, rural development, urban development, primary and secondary education, job training, and transportation. None of these was enacted as introduced by the president. Second, the unsuccessful but innovative Family Assistance Program (FAP) would have replaced a range of older welfare categoricals with a national system covering all low-income families with children. Third, the actual Federal takeover of the financing of the adult public assistance categories (old-age assistance, aid to the blind, and aid to the permanently and totally disabled, authorized by the 1972 Social Security Amendments) marked the first real sorting out of functions that occurred during this entire period.

In these diverse ways, the Nixon administration's New Federalism sought to reverse some of the trends in Creative Federalism, while not returning to the laissez-faire and narrow dual federalism of Hoover or to the mere conservative acceptance, with a few adaptations and a few new departures, of the inherited intergovernmental system, as had been the case with Eisenhower. The legacy, after all, was that left by the Johnsonians, and much of it was deemed unwise, unmanageable, or undermining of state and local governments by the Nixonians. Hence, their reform proposals: some fairly drastic (the special-revenue-sharing proposals and FAP) and others milder (unemployment insurance and job training). This assertive, revisionist stance on the part of the Nixon administration generated a range of initiatives for congressional consideration. Only a few survived, but they managed to dominate much of Congress's attention, to raise the suspicion of Creative Federalists among the congressional Democrats, and to generate a climate wherein halfway objective assessments of the Johnson programs proved nearly impossible.

Still, there were several continuities between Creative and New Federalism. The former, after all, was not all programmatic wind; it did have a managerial rudder, and this was shaped during LBJ's last two years in office, as noted earlier. During that biennium the "managing" problem was given major emphasis, with the launching of the A-85 and A-80 processes, with staff work on Federal regional boundaries, and with support for the Intergovernmental Cooperation Act of 1968.

In these and other ways, the Johnsonians began trends that the Nixonians continued, suggesting that Creative and New Federalism had some things in common. Yet the real story of the Nixon effort must be placed alongside that of the Democratic Congress, with which his New Federalism had to contend.

## Congressional Federalism: Creative Federalism Resurgent

As cited in chapter 1, the primary architect of the seventies' pattern of intergovernmental relations was Congress. Congress's operational concept of federalism had to be inferred from its actions, but these reveal a theory that more than any other dominated the workings of that system. What were the hallmarks of the theory? Its essential features may be described as incremental, confrontational, strongly categorical (as well as anti–block grant and anti–General Revenue Sharing), heavily conditional, and politically co-optive.

The *incrementalism* inherent in the concept merely reflected the perennial congressional tendency to cope with problems, programs, and pressures in an ad hoc, largely piecemeal fashion. The tendency was heavily reflected in dozens of discrete grant enactments and reenactments in the seventies, with little attention paid to the side effects of the programs or to the interrelationships among them. It also helped to conceal the drastically altered thrust of Congress's approach to intergovernmental relations, even though the many separate actions when combined clearly indicated the remarkable degree to which Congress played the role of state legislature, city council, and school board. Much of this stemmed from the high level porosity of the Congresses of this decade.

The *confrontational character* of Congress's concept of federalism suggests something fairly novel, however, because it underscores the newfound assertiveness in the seventies of Congress vis-à-vis presidents, department secretaries, Federal administrators, and interest groups — both private and public. The trait was distinctly a phenomenon of the decade, of dramatically different political conditions, and of weakened presidents.

The *antipresidential* overtones of many congressional actions were probably the most familiar. The Nixon initiatives, especially the special-revenue-sharing proposals and their seeming threat to the legacy of Creative Federalism, were the first conditioner of the congressional attitude, which was sustained by later presidential vetoes and impoundments of appropriated grant funds that triggered court cases. The latter produced the Budget and Impoundment Act of 1974 as an authoritative congressional response. President Gerald Ford's failing effort to achieve enactment of three "block grants" reinforced the attitude with the proposed merger of fifty-seven categoricals in the areas of health care, elementary and secondary education, and child nutrition.[12]

Nothing, perhaps, illustrates congressional assertiveness as well as the countercyclical programs. The chief Federal response to the severe recession of the midseventies, after all, was largely a congressional one, and it took the form of three enactments: the Local Public Works program (authorized by Title I of the Public Works Employment Act of 1976 and expanded by the Intergovernmental Anti-Recession Act of 1977); the Anti-Recession Fiscal Assistance Program (established as an add-on to GRS by Title II of the 1976 omnibus legislation and extended as part of the 1977 measure); and a major extension of the public service programs (Titles II and VI) of CETA in June 1977. The first two programs were almost wholly a product of congressional initiatives; the last was a joint effort between President Carter and Congress. Like many of the Creative Federalism programs, these heavily favored local governments. Finally, although Carter did not confront Congress with any really revisionist programs in the intergovernmental area, the earlier distrust of the White House remained, for reasons that will be discussed later.

The *antibureaucratic thrust* of many of Congress's intergovernmental actions was reflected in the rapid erosion in the seventies of the trust that formerly characterized Federal middle management–congressional committee (and subcommittee) relationships. With Nixon, and to a much lesser degree Ford, it was partly a matter of the congressional Democrats' belief that these posts had become politicized (that is, held by Republicans). With all three presidents, there was the congressional feeling that in all too many instances competent professionals did not occupy key administration posts. This feeling, along with the heavy turnover among the political executives in the departments, generated a sentiment among many congressional committees and their expanded staffs that their own expertise was at least equal to, if not superior to, that of the executive branch. A tendency to treat the administrators as mere functionaries, if not administrative agents of the Congress, emerged. Witness the tendency to include detailed regulations in the authorizing legislation (as with the Elementary and Secondary Education Amendments of 1978) and to spell out in specific terms the organizational relationship between the Federal agency and the recipient government (as with the Vocational Rehabilitation Amendments of 1973). In these and other ways, Congress confronted what it took to be hostile forces and developed its own oppositional approach to intergovernmental relations.

At the heart of the congressional approach was an expanded and *eager reliance on the categorical device.* Although attention in the seventies tended to focus on General Revenue Sharing and the enactment of three new block grants and a few categorical consolidations (chiefly in the educational area), an equally significant development was the passage of more than sixty new public health categoricals during Nixon's years in office and approximately thirty more under Ford.[13] Some of these reflected major new Federal initiatives (as in the case of the protection of the environment beginning in 1969), but most were by-products of the process by which the Great Society programs were reauthorized (as the dozens of programs that were part of Federal aid to primary and secondary education in 1980 demonstrated).

Part of this intensified preference for categoricals was mirrored in Congress's hostility to the two newer forms of intergovernmental fiscal transfer: General Revenue Sharing and the block grant. Enactment of the former, of course, was the result of the coming together of an unusual cluster of political pressures and an unusual political year, 1972.[14] Its renewal in 1976, although not thwarted, was marked by the addition of several new strings, including auditing, citizen participation, and tough civil rights requirements.

In the case of the block grants, the first — the Partnership for Health program — degenerated during the seventies into a minor part of the Federal government's overall efforts in public health. Beginning in 1970 and despite the protests of then HEW secretary Elliot Richardson, new categoricals began to be enacted, to the point where by 1980 a score of such grant programs surrounded what in 1966 had been trumpeted as the Federal government's prime aid program in this functional area. The Safe Streets program acquired new conditions and earmarks within and functionally related new grants outside it during the seventies. In Title XX, CETA, and CDBG, the familiar tension between achieving national purposes (that is, "strings") and maximizing recipient discretion (that is, cutting "strings") emerged in all three, with the resulting tilt favoring more conditions, especially during the Carter years. In all but a handful of instances, either administrative fear of congressional reaction or direct congressional action produced this binding of the block grants.

Closely linked with the concentration on categoricals was Congress's increasing *proclivity to enact "new social regulations."*[15] As noted above, the movement began in the sixties with the 1964 civil rights legislation, but only seven major regulations were enacted then. The seventies became the decade of dramatic national regulatory initiatives, reflected in twenty-seven major enactments (see table Int-2, pp. 6–7). In several of the areas covered, the new regulatory enactments directly impacted state and local governments more than they did the private sector — a novel departure from earlier Federal regulation. In legal terms, there was a reliance on the conditional spending and commerce powers and the supremacy clause. The first, it should be noted, tended to permit actions that might be voided under the commerce power and to hide a bit of the regulatory thrust of the enactment. These new regulatory approaches included (1) *direct orders,* which do rely on the commerce power and must be obeyed to avoid the threat of civil or criminal penalties (for example, the Equal Opportunity Employment Act of 1972, the Fair Labor Standards Act as amended in 1974, and the Occupational Safety and Health Act of 1970); (2) *partial preemptions,* which rely on the commerce power and the supremacy clause (for example, the Clean Air Act of 1970, Surface Mining Control and Reclamation Act of 1977, and the National Gas Policy Act of 1978); (3) *"crosscutting" requirements* that are based on the conditional spending power (for example, those prohibiting discrimination based on race, sex, or handicap, and others, which together numbered more than seventy by 1980); and (4) *"crossover sanctions,"* which also are conditional-spending-power based (for example, the Highway Beautification Act of 1965, the Emergency Highway Energy Conservation Act of 1976, and the Education for All Handicapped Children Act of 1975).[16] These regulations were much more intricate, more intrusive, and more pervasive than the programmatic strings that were attached to the grant programs of the fifties and sixties. In many instances, the direct impact of the requirements was not gauged; in practically all of them, the secondary and tertiary effects were not explored; and at no point was the cumulative impact of these intergovernmental regulations on individual recipient jurisdictions fully evaluated by Congress.

The *political process* from which all of the substantive intergovernmental traits of the congressional theory emanate was, of course, that of the seventies. The further decentralization of congressional power with the empowering of the more than three hundred subcommittees resulting from the liberal reforms of 1972–74, the quadrupling — at least — of the interest groups located in Washington, the initial breakthrough into several new program areas during the sixties, and the decline in Congress's traditional techniques for coping with outside pressures combined to help produce a new method — a co-optive political one — wherein during the reauthorization process all groups that were directly or even indirectly affected by the initial program were "pacified" one way or another. The typical vehicle was an omnibus bill that reflected the concerns of a wide range of interests — primarily functional subcomponents of a broad function, and even subcomponents of the subcomponents but also generalist public interest, sociomoralistic, and demographic. Categoricals, especially project grants, were the perfect device for satisfying the divergent claims of such diverse interests. And a regulation or special grant condition frequently was a valuable stratagem to employ when confronting interests that were more concerned with discrimination, safety, health, or the environment than money, program mechanics, or meaningful implementation. Here again the high porosity levels of the Congresses of the seventies are revealed.

Reflective of the vigorous representational efforts of all local governments was the congressional tendency to place all governments on a par and to channel funds directly to substate units as frequently as to channel them through the states. This greatly expanded concept of partnership produced a "pinwheel pattern" of grant administration, with each of the governmental and quasi-governmental recipient groups constituting a separate spoke in the wheel and with Washington (and by implication, Congress) serving as its hub.

This special brand of co-optive politics was, in a sense, only an extension of traditional logrolling but in a vastly expanded area and with infinitely more players. That it was congressional in character and in focus was undeniable. That it changed, if not clogged, the legislative process was also undeniable. That it shaped heavily the overloaded intergovernmental network of the seventies was again undeniable. And that it marked the complete collapse of the old decentralized party system is irrefutable.

Incrementalism, confrontation, more and more categoricals, and new conditions and new regulations, as well as a new variant of interest group–co-optive politics — these were the substantive and procedural hallmarks of the congressional approach to and theory of federalism in the seventies. In combination, they tended to place Congress at the center of the system and to make it the major molder of the pre-1981 pattern of intergovernmental relations.

The failure on the part of many to recognize the differences between Nixon's New Federalism and Congress's expansion of Creative Federalism explains many of the confused interpretations of the 1969–76 phase of this period. When the two are joined, certain very understandable paradoxes emerge:

- A conscious presidential effort to curb categorical grants was mounted, yet their number only multiplied.

- A serious presidential drive was launched to "devolve" greater decision-making authority to subnational governments, yet intrusive conditions and new regulations of various types increased.

- New forms of Federal aid emerged, but in time most of them came to resemble the older, categorical form.

- An effort was made to streamline the grant delivery system, but greater managerial confusion resulted — thanks to more programs, more recipients, and more conditions (both programmatic and regulatory, as well as procedural and institutional).

- Generalists and general governments were favored by presidential efforts, yet these, along with efforts of Congress, made no attempt to distinguish among subnational governments that were genuinely general, as in the case of General Revenue Sharing, and both branches failed to confront the array of special-program people and districting units at the substate regional level, which Federal grant programs with a regional component had encouraged.

- Finally, some sorting out of governmental functions was contemplated, with the special revenue sharing and the Federal takeover of the "adult categories," but the overall tendency was a tremendously expanded commingling of governmental functions.

## The New Partnership

To chronicle the components of Jimmy Carter's approach to intergovernmental relations is hazardous at best, given the eclectic character of his initiatives, the secondary emphasis given to Federal-state-local relations by his administration, and his need to shift gears halfway through his administration.

An enlarged Federal-state-local–private-sector partnership, a heavily urban/city focus, a wide range of expanded and new intergovernmental programs, the bypassing of state governments, greater targeting, and a leadership role for the national government in the system — such were the Johnsonian tenets that were reiterated initially by Carter.[17] Fiscal caution, greater devolution, curbing categorical growth by grant consolidations, overhauling the Federal executive branch, and injecting some rationality into the organization and behavior of its bureaucracy — these were the Nixon New Federalism themes that crept into his federalism. His early views, then, like most of the follow-up, reflected an artful effort to synthesize key concepts from both of the predecessor presidents' approaches to federalism, as well as from his own arsenal of technocratic and populist beliefs.

In his earliest phase, Carter focused his goals for improving intergovernmental relations and stressed (1) the need for a more precise targeting of Federal aid to the most hard-pressed communities and to the poorest in such communities as well as elsewhere, (2) greater use of public funds as levers in stimulating private investment, and (3) his intent to mount a full-fledged attack on red tape and the paperwork morass hindering efficient government at all levels.[18] He promised the governors not to "preside over an administration which ignores the lessons of my own personal experience," but the pressures on the new president were such that some of these lessons had to be ignored.[19] Not to be ignored were the problems of stagflation, a ragged economy, rising deficits, and serious foreign policy challenges, especially during his last two years.

Four basic Carter themes emerged: managerialism, greater access and improved intergovernmental procedures, fiscal prudence, and better-targeted existing programs and some new program initiatives. These four themes, in fact, dominated the Carter approach to intergovernmental relations during his first two years, but some of the managerialism and most of the new program thrusts were largely forgotten by 1979 and 1980.

Extraordinary efforts were mounted *on the organizational and reorganizational fronts.* In a strict sense, however, these improved managerial drives had little to do with Federal-state-local relations as such because they were largely based on the old public administration notions of executive leadership and of the president's obligation to structure the Federal bureaucracy "into a manageable hierarchy, establish firm control over expenditures, and render the civil service accountable to him."[20] As applied by Carter, this traditional philosophy produced five reorganizational undertakings.[21]

Carter's managerialism also led to a revamping of the executive budget process with the introduction of zero-based budgeting (ZBB) for FY 1979. Touted as a technique for prioritizing all expenditures for existing programs and activities, as well as for new proposals, ZBB was geared to providing each successive level of administrative authority (starting at the lowest) with the information needed to make more astute judgments about future spending plans.[22]

The third angle of Carter's managerial triangle was formed by his Federal Personnel Management Project, which ultimately came up with his civil service reform proposals. The "reforms" were largely accepted by Congress, and in the process the old public administration concept of personnel as a vital tool of executive management was given something of a boost. A key argument in gaining congressional enactment was the assertion that the old civil service system had erected "a pretty firm wall against effective management."[23]

A second basic theme of the Carter administration was its *stress on accessibility and on improved intergovernmental procedures.* Here, there was a clearer Federal-state-local focus and set of assumptions. One of the president's first acts was the appointment of Jack Watson, a long-time Carter associate, to the dual role of secretary of the cabinet and assistant to the president for intergovernmental relations. A directive to the departments shortly thereafter sought to assure that similar points of contact would be available to state and local officials throughout the executive branch and that such posts would be staffed with "high-ranking" officials. Accompanying this action was a presidential memorandum that specified that state and local inputs should be sought on any major policy, budgetary, or reorganization proposal.[24]

Carter administration efforts to simplify and enhance the coordination of the many procedural and some substantive requirements attached to Federal assistance programs were varied but persistent. The first step was taken on 9 September 1977, with a presidential memorandum geared to launching "a concentrated attack on red tape and confusion in the Federal grant-in-aid system."[25] A June presidential directive had called for a "zero-based" revision of all Federal planning requirements (more than 3,500 in some 160 aid programs), and a March 1979 executive order called upon existing agencies to adopt procedures that would produce regulations that were simple and clear, would achieve legislative goals efficiently and effectively, and would not impose unnecessary burdens on the economy, individuals, public or private organizations, or state and local governments.[26]

*Fiscal constraint and control* constituted another basic, albeit sometimes wavering, theme of the Carter approach to intergovernmental relations. Perhaps its firmest features were the budgeting procedures: ZBB, multiyear budgeting, and better use of existing programs. After ZBB's first year in operation, an OMB assessment declared that it had facilitated explicit identification of agency priorities, had helped curb the size of agency budget requests, and had increased management participation throughout the process. Shortcomings were conceded, however.

The more substantive but less consistent feature of Carter's fiscal constraint theme was his campaign pledge of a balanced budget by FY 1981, which he reiterated after his inauguration. Yet austerity was not part of his revisions of the Ford budget. This had to change.

With his proposals for FY 1980, a more concerted effort was made to reduce spending. Inflation now was recognized as a far more pressing problem than unemployment. At the heart of the proposals was the pledge to hold the Federal deficit to $29 billion, down from $33.2 billion in FY 1979 and $48.8 in FY 1978. Inflation was to be brought under control, and governmental restraint was needed. In political terms, this Carter thrust was intended to immunize Washington from Proposition 13 fever (Proposition 13 was a state-imposed restriction on increases in local property taxes in California) and to slow the mounting momentum behind a drive for a constitutional amendment requiring balanced Federal budgets. This shift from moderate expansion to fiscal contraction was one of the key shifts made during the Carter years that made his a difficult administration to assess.

The final theme that conditioned the Carter New Partnership was a concern with *improving and sometimes expanding the operations of old programs and with launching some new ones,* but all in a highly flexible fashion. In a real sense, the three other themes all reflected Carter's technocratic bent, but this one reflected his party affiliation. In his first year, a range of program and policy initiatives were launched (too many, some said). In the aggregate, they highlighted the diversity of initial program concerns and the traditional tendencies of a Democratic president to curb unemployment, to aid in one fashion or another divergent interests that helped elect him, and to rely heavily on conditional grants as the basic means of doing this.

Other than energy, probably the most prominent of Carter's new program undertakings during his first two years, and certainly the most significant from an intergovernmental perspective, was his promised national urban policy. Responsibility for its devising was lodged in the Urban and Regional Policy Group (URPG), but the group soon encountered major obstacles — political, programmatic, and procedural.[27]

The final report, *New Partnership to Conserve America's Communities,* made frequently inconsistent recommendations. Missing in these proposals and in the background report was any real recognition that Federal urban aid already was at an all-time high (thanks to the three countercyclical programs) and was moderately well targeted.[28] There was no real assessment of the vast array of existing urban programs, nor any proposed consolidation or elimination of any older programs. Moreover, no proposal relating to the Federal government's multiple and conflicting substate regional programs was advanced. Instead, certain of the existing grant programs were expanded; several new programs were proposed, chiefly of a conditional character; and a new cluster of members (the neighborhoods) was added to the already expansive membership of the old partnership.

The policy's defenders emphasized that its roots were quite different from those of early urban assistance efforts.[29] They stressed its pro-city emphasis, its new state role, and its striving to shift certain older Federal programs out of their former anti-city role (transportation, infrastructure subsidies, and so on). They contended that a new urban-conserving ethic was a basic conditioner of the policy and that more of a targeting and less of a formula-allocation strategy was reflected in it.

By the end of 1978, some thirteen urban-related measures had become law (five of which had not been part of the original urban policy package).[30] In the arena of administrative actions, four executive orders were issued as a follow-up to the urban policy. It would be going too far to compare this interest-group-conditioned product to FDR's "concert-of-interests" strategy, but this prime example of Carter's New Partnership certainly resembled it.

### An Inconclusive Conclusion

The confused and conflicting effects of Carter's managerialism, proceduralism, fiscal conservatism, and program flexibility underscore the absence of any consistent theory of federalism or approach to intergovernmental relations in his administration. The ambiguities arose partly because within the president the technocrat was in steady conflict with the need to be a Democrat. The technocrat had not moved much beyond the traditional public management precepts and had not confronted the intergovernmental administrative realities that previous Democrats, both presidential and congressional, largely had shaped. His fiscal conservatism also was at war with his Democratic self, though really only late in his administration and with little recognition of its possible use as an alternative means of achieving greater manageability in the system.

Despite these conflicting personal pressures, as well as the equally conflicting external pressures (in the form of the largest and most aggressive aggregation of interest groups ever to assemble in Washington up to that point and stark foreign policy challenges), what ultimately emerged from his principles and practices was not wholly unclear in intergovernmental terms.

# From "Picket-Fence" Federalism
# to "Bamboo-Fence" Federalism

Federal aid administrators, as noted in chapter 1, were primary participants in the intergovernmental relations (IGR) of the 1960s, thanks to the accelerating significance of Federal assistance programs. How influential a role these administrators played and how significant their views of the system were depended not only on how their power, influence, and position within the system were assessed but on the formal and informal constraints placed upon them by other key IGR actors — the Executive Office of the President, Congress and its oversight and appropriations committees, departmental political executives, nationally based public and functional interest groups, and state and local political and program leaders.

## Attacks on Theories of Administrators

During the Johnson years, professional civil servants played a major role in the formulation and obviously the implementation of various Creative Federalism programs. Moreover, from the fifties onward (as was also pointed out in the introduction), Federal aid officials formed an angle in a series of "functional iron triangles" that also included affected interest groups and relevant congressional committees and subcommittees.[31] Sometimes, but not always, this horizontal "iron-triangle" view was given a downward "vertical functional autocracies" dimension.[32] The linkage between the two is not wholly consistent because the latter was chiefly a bureaucratic interpretation involving "clear and unbroken lines of communication between and among functional specialists and their counterparts in the field."[33] Hence, some treat this view as a wholly separate explanation of Federal aid officials' influence and behavior.

In the seventies, and partly stemming from these two earlier views, *a pair of "whipping-boy" interpretations emerged.* Both embodied the belief that aid administrators were the paramount actors in the current intergovernmental drama. From the executive branch came the view that severe measures had to be taken — in terms of personnel actions, administrative reorganizations, budgetary and other fiscal actions, and program reformulation — if these officials were to be rendered accountable. From Congress came a range of antibureaucratic opinions that tended to lead to common conclusions: the Federal bureaucracy was out of control and beyond the will of Congress, as reflected in grant statute provisions that were was not being honored. Detailed statutory prescriptions of proper administrative behavior, better congressional budget procedures, "sunset" legislation (statutory provisions that require programs to be terminated if they are not renewed after being reviewed), and/or legislative review (or veto) of administrative regulations were utilized or proposed as means of establishing a pattern of proper accountability.

In one sense, both of these interpretations stemmed from the constitutionally based dual theory of administrative accountability, wherein the president and Congress share responsibility for organizing, directing, and controlling the civil administration. In another, they reflected the institutional and partisan conflicts of 1969–76 and the institutional divisions of 1977–80 despite one-party control of both the presidency and Congress. But from a systemic vantage point, they tended to reflect presidential and congressional frustrations, if not bewilderment, throughout 1969–80, with the immense change in Federal assistance efforts.

But what of *the views of the bureaucrats themselves?* In 1975 the Advisory Commission on Intergovernmental Relations conducted a survey of Federal grant administrators as part of its multivolume probe of the intergovernmental grant system. The poll and the pioneering 1964 effort of the Senate Subcommittee on Intergovernmental Relations were the only two of their kind and provide the basis for the following attitudinal analysis.[34]

*Respondents to the subcommittee's midsixties survey tended to reflect four behavioral themes in their replies.*[35]

- Functionalism, or the administrator's preoccupation with protecting and promoting the purposes of individual grant programs, was the most important single conditioner of comments.

- Professionalism, or a deep faith in the merit system principle and in the ethical and technical standards of the specialized group to which the grant administrators belonged, conditioned answers to numerous questions relating to intergovernmental personnel and state organization.

- Standpattism, or the vigorous defense of traditional practices and program principles, dominated many of the replies to items covering Federal aid, financial management, and metropolitan area problems.

- Indifference, or the seemingly cavalier dismissal of serious questions of broader intergovernmental, managerial, and fiscal import, was another theme embodied in the administrators' survey replies. This attitude was viewed as partly an extension of the other three but was singled out for special treatment in the subcommittee report because of its special significance for those seeking to reform the grant system.

In most respects the Federal aid administrators of the midsixties matched the assertive and basically antipolitical behavior assigned to them in Terry Sanford's "picket-fence" federalism metaphor,[36] described briefly in chapter 1. But *how did the general attitudes of Federal aid administrators in the seventies compare to those of their counterparts in the sixties?* Although the areas of inquiry in the later survey differed in many respects from some covered by its 1964 predecessor, certain identical questions appeared in both, and broad attitudinal themes can be gleaned from both.

The four earlier behavioral norms were present in the pattern of responses to the 1975 poll, but they were much less striking and strident, as chapter 1 noted. Certain new themes could be detected in their collective responses to several survey items.[37] Of the earlier four, functionalism, or program protectionism, emerged most fully intact. The moderate to strongly negative responses on consolidating programs, standard application and preapplication forms, the staffing size and organization of counterpart recipient units, congressional cuts in authorizations and appropriations, and departmental reorganizations highlight the continuing and not surprising strength of this collective attitude. Not to be overlooked here was each respondent's overwhelming satisfaction with most of the features of his or her grant program's design and fairly strong tendency to rate highly the performance of special-purpose, public, and quasi-public recipients over and above that of general-purpose governments. Yet this functional theme emerged less strongly from the 1975 survey than from the 1964 poll. Some of this can be explained in terms of the chastening effect of various efforts to curb narrow program commitments during the previous ten years. Equally significant was the emergence of other themes in the later survey — themes that do not necessarily reinforce the functionalist tendency.

Standpattism figured predominantly as a major bureaucratic norm conditioning a heavily status-quo orientation on a range of items in the earlier poll, but it was more than matched by a countervailing tendency toward greater flexibility in the later one. The moderate to favorable views on the management circulars, the A-95 process, and others clearly suggest adaptability and, in some cases, a shift of attitude from that of their predecessors.

Professionalism, or strong attachments to vocational and program standards or goals, was very much present in the 1975 attitudinal probe, but it presented a far less paternalistic image vis-à-vis state and local program personnel than it did in 1964. This was due primarily to the many positive changes that the later generation of Federal aid administrators found in recipient governments' personnel practices. Salaries, training, personnel turnover, and merit systems were all given much more favorable ratings than they had received earlier and deservedly so, given the real improvements in these areas in the seventies. More negative judgments about the "overall capacity" of recipient units suggested some continuing concerns, chiefly of a professional nature. But even here, the dominant views were not caustically critical.

Finally, the earlier collective sentiment of indifference toward serious questions of broad intergovernmental concern can hardly be discerned in the responses to the 1975 poll. Instead, it was replaced almost wholly by a spirit of skepticism, if not a sense of hard-headed realism. The strong "no appreciable effect" response to the management circulars, to incentives for improved recipient program administration or servicing, and to many of the regionalization and decentralization efforts underscores this, and the self-criticism reflected in the response pattern on agency monitoring of recipient performance and on the issuance of regulations suggests a realistic awareness of internal management difficulties rarely found in the previous attitudinal probe.

Overall, then, the 1975 aid administrators adhered to some of the behavioral norms of their predecessors. But their lesser commitment to standpat positions, their greater flexibility in confronting broad managerial and interlocal issues, their much more moderate professional concerns regarding state and local counterpart personnel, their rejection of their predecessors' cavalier indifference toward certain basic intergovernmental management challenges, and a certain skepticism regarding some efforts to reform grants management clearly indicate changed attitudes.[38]

*What kind of an operational theory of federalism emerges from all this?* Only a minority of the 1975 respondents implicitly favored the old "picket-fence" theory with all of its rigid, vertical functionalism that was endorsed by three-quarters of the respondents to the 1964 survey. But what of the majority? A fence still would appear to be the proper metaphor, but not the sturdy, solid-wood variety.

One of bamboo would be more apt — given its somewhat softer materials, its elaborate horizontal wiring system, and its greater capacity to bend to prevailing winds. Whether "bamboo-fence" federalism accurately captures the vertical functionalism, continuing professionalism, greater flexibility, and realism of the administrators of the midseventies depends in part on one's taste in metaphors. Yet it clearly suggests a marked contrast with the more rigid "picket-fence" variety, and a similar contrast was reflected in the general attitudes embodied in the two surveys of Federal aid administrators.

## Conclusion

Creative Federalism, New Federalism, congressional federalism, New Partnership, "picket-fence," and "bamboo-fence" federalism — such was the range of intergovernmental interpretations and ideas that helped shape the first two decades of the 1960–98 period. All were derivatives of cooperative federalism. None paid any homage to dual federalism. All were more than theories because each had an impact on the system. Some scholars said that the confusing and conflicting character of intergovernmental relations by 1980 in large measure was a direct by-product of the intellectual confusion that these diverse though ostensibly collaborative concepts reflect. Others believed their impact overall was for the good of the nation — assisting the elderly, the sick, the discriminated against, the ill-educated, central cities, and rural areas, to cite only a few of the beneficiaries of Federal grant programs in the seventies.[39] Still others found that the absence of any meaningful concept of the national interest, of any awareness of the finite nature of the nation's fiscal and administrative resources, and of any real resistance to the heavy interest group conditioning of the entire national domestic policy process produced a system whose policy agenda was much too broad, whose fiscal costs were too great, and whose interlevel jurisdictional entanglements were far too deep. Hence, the late seventies saw much criticism of an overloaded system.

*Chapter 6*

# The Reactions to Cooperative (and Co-Optive) Federalism, 1981–

A minor reaction to some of the excesses of the seventies set in during the last two years of the Carter administration, and a major rejection of nearly everything the inherited intergovernmental system stood for was the interpretation most observers placed on the election of Ronald Reagan in 1980, whether deserved or not. Johnson's Creative Federalism and its outsized programmatic legacy were major targets of Reagan campaign criticisms. Yet the trends of the seventies were a major conditioner of Reagan's campaign strategy, and these, as has been noted, cannot be wholly or even reasonably attributed to Johnson. Although it was never conceded, the Reagan domestic speeches in 1980 were addressed as much against his two Republican predecessors as against Johnson, the Democratic Congresses, and Carter. It was during their tenure, after all, that the entitlements were indexed, social welfare spending really soared, Federal regulation of subnational governments got seriously under way, large deficits became the norm, and defense outlays were significantly reduced. But Carter and the Democrats were the main objects of his strictures, even though the Georgian had hiked defense expenditures, curbed grant outlays, initiated an effort with Executive Order 12174 (1979) and the Paperwork Reduction Act (1980) to curb regulations, and even sponsored four block grants (though late and unsuccessfully).

Reagan then continued the trends begun under Carter, but with more flair, more force, and greater success at least initially. In its approach to federalism, the Reagan administration should be judged in terms of individual years because somewhat different intergovernmental strategies characterized each. Yet throughout these years, the themes of devolution and reducing the flow of Federal aid dominated, while deregulation and deinstitutionalization of Federal multistate and substate regional efforts were major subthemes. The one clear call for greater centralization occurred in the 1982 State of the Union address with the president's proposed "Big Swap."

During the campaign Reagan ignored, as did many politicians of both parties, the positive results of certain of the earlier enacted programs.[1] Between 1960 and 1980, the poverty percentage was cut in half and the gap between the economically stronger and weaker did not widen (as it might well have, given the great influx of new baby-boom-generation job applicants). Thirty million members were added to the national work force, in part because of certain Federal actions. Longer life expectancy and lower child mortality rates were achieved, and a fundamental revolution occurred in civil rights and civil liberties. These salutary aspects of the Johnson-Nixon-Ford-Carter years were overlooked, and the actual and alleged negative aspects were highlighted by Reagan and his associates.

## Campaign Themes and Reagan Goals

Most of the national expansionist developments of the previous sixteen years and their fostering dynamics were subjected to severe indictments. The Reagan campaign's economic goals were framed in terms of bitter criticisms of high Federal taxes, soaring domestic expenditures, rising levels of governmental borrowing, and increasing regulation. These, Reagan argued, hindered business initiative, productivity, competitiveness, private investment, and, as a result, national economic growth.

The Reagan administration's approach to public management basically paralleled its supply-side economic strategy. The approach, as James D. Carroll, A. Lee Fritschler, and Bruce L.R. Smith have pointed out, involved both program and top-personnel reductions, and it dominated most of the administration's basic decisions on financial and budgetary management, information policy, regulation, procurement, personnel, program, and grant administration.[2]

Reagan's New Federalism was as critical of the national government's past intergovernmental policies as his economic and management strategies were of past policies in their respective areas. Hence, he urged a surgical reduction in the Federal government's intergovernmental role, a devolution of various program responsibilities to the states (sometimes with the needed funding resources), a strong effort to deregulate, a return to the traditional Federal-state partnership principle, and a diminution in activism at the state and local levels, as well as at the national.

Although all this suggests a high degree of conceptual consistency among the components of the Reagan conservative antidomestic government, pro-big-defense, free-market radical creed, there were other conflicting values: "big business," Moral Majority, retrenchment, defense buildup, and political pragmatic concerns were also a major part of the Reagan arsenal of ideas.[3] Most of these could and did conflict with his devolutionary, decentralizing, degovernmentalizing, and deregulatory goals — in short, with the New Federalism II. What, then, were the achievements of the Reagan crusade? Was it merely a reaction? A mild rollback? Or was there a real "Reagan revolution"?

## The Reagan Record

The mix of wins and losses in *achieving Reagan's secular economic-growth goals* in effect left the country and its governments with greater destabilizing difficulties in fiscal policy than had been confronted in the seventies.[4] Initially the president succeeded handsomely in getting domestic expenditure and tax cuts with the Omnibus Budget Reconciliation Act (OBRA) and Economic Recovery Tax Act (ERTA) in 1981. Later tax hikes in 1982 and 1984, along with a gas tax increase (1982) and a mandated rise in Social Security revenues (1983), in no way seriously undercut the revenue-reduction significance of ERTA. With it, a 25 percent reduction in individual income tax rates and numerous corporate tax breaks produced more than $280 billion in forgone Treasury revenues. Presumably, the Tax Reform Act of 1986 was basically revenue neutral.

On the expenditure side, however, the OBRA scenario of steady and deeper domestic spending cuts in later years did not play out. In fact, domestic outlays increased by $212 billion between 1982 and 1988, most of it due to continuing heavy outlays for entitlement programs like Medicare, Medicaid, and food stamps. Moreover, Reagan's drive to accelerate greatly Carter's last-two-years' effort to build up defense pushed Department of Defense (DOD) annual outlays from $168 billion in 1981 to $306.5 billion by 1988. These expenditure and revenue trends combined to produce the largest budgets and the largest deficits in peacetime history. They also scuttled the Reagan campaign promise of a balanced budget by 1984.

Meanwhile, inflation was lowered significantly, thanks to the monetary policies of the Federal Reserve skillfully crafted earlier and to the worst recession (1982–83) since the Great Depression. The subsequent economic recovery, exuberant in certain regions and certain areas of economic activity, left some areas and activities (notably those dependent on international trade) in bad shape. A 6 percent, not 3 percent, unemployment level was now an acceptable target goal. Much of the expansion had been financed by heavy foreign investment, which dampened the worst effects of large deficits on capital formation. The trade deficit began to mushroom, but the decline of the dollar, triggered by the gargantuan domestic deficits, did not bring about any early turnaround. Serious efforts were made to reduce the deficit, ultimately including Gramm-Rudman-Hollings, which overhauled the congressional budget process by including new deadlines for budget decisions, specific targets for deficit reductions, and an automatic series of cuts if deficit reductions were not met. These efforts fell prey to a series of congressional-presidential standoffs, each side having very different budget priorities, especially after the return to full Democratic control of the Congress, though the 1987 budget summit did lessen interbranch friction in 1988 while making modest contributions to deficit reduction. Over the eight years, annual deficits ranged from $128 billion to $200 billion.

The cumulative impact of the economic, fiscal, and monetary developments was to dampen the ardor of policy activists in Washington, to curb domestic program growth, and to shackle the professional top managers.[5] The jump in the national deficit from $914.3 billion in FY 1980 to $2.9 trillion in FY 1989, not to mention the corresponding hike in interest payments on it, conditioned U.S. governance and the economy more heavily in the eighties and later than any fallouts from Reagan federalism.

The *supply-side approach to public management* at the national level rested in theory on two basic interrelated goals: slash the number of Federal governmental managers (and personnel generally) and cut back on the number and funding levels of Federally run or assisted domestic programs.[6] A reduction in the managerial cadre's size would discourage detailed Federal involvement in program operations, and with program eliminations and devolutions, the pressure to appoint more administrators would dwindle. Achieving both these goals, moreover, would tap into the managerial talent of state and local governments as well as the nonprofit and for-profit sectors. In behavioral terms, supply-side managers were more interested in operational efforts than in staff activities, more concerned with ultimate program results than with system or agency preservation, more presidentially oriented than congressionally or clientele centered, and more believing in management by objectives and performance ratings than in improved administrative procedures, reorganizations, and program analyses.[7]

Grants management and reform, as they had evolved since the midsixties, won little to no attention from the president and the Executive Office of the President. Reagan federalism, after all, viewed negatively practically all but the block grant aspects of the inherited grant system and sought to eliminate the dynamics that sustained it. Most of the components of "middle-range" reform (for example, measures of an organizational or procedural nature, which although intended to remedy some defects in the operation of the categorical grant system, still seek to preserve it) were rejected because they were geared to retaining the categorical system by reforming it. Hence the basic differences between Nixon's New Federalism and Reagan's New Federalism. Block grants for Nixon were a way of improving the administration of and recipient government discretion in these more flexible intergovernmental transfers without eliminating all categoricals or the Federal role in the block grant program areas. With Reagan, block grants — at least in theory — were a prelude to full devolution of their program responsibilities. Reagan federalism's goals were to devolve, deregulate, and decongest the overloaded intergovernmental system, all with a view to reducing dramatically the Federal role in the federal system, especially in its multiple categorical manifestations. Presidential appointive, budgetary, strategic-planning, and legislative powers were the weapons used to implement various phases of this New Federalism agenda. Executive Orders (E.O.'s) and administrative orders (for example, A-122) were issued to

- curb public interest groups (A-122);

- centralize review (and control) over regulatory issuances (E.O. 12291 and E.O. 12498);

- devolve communicational and coordinative grant processes to the states (A-95 thus became E.O. 12372); and

- achieve retrenchment objectives (A-129 and so on).

Grants management of a constraining, confrontational, controlling, even fancifully constitutional federalist variety (that is, E.O. 12612), in effect, did exist.[8]

Yet it reflected none of the collaborative, constructive, reformist goals of the earlier efforts.

As an administrative approach, the supply-side strategy was not so very novel or consistent. After all, use of a range of indirect techniques of program execution, many with weak Federal control features, had been a paramount aspect of the system since the thirties. A reliance on other than Federal managers and personnel to implement national program objectives had also been a prime trait of Federal domestic program implementation for more than fifty years. A concern with keeping the Federal bureaucracy comparatively small had been an important implicit goal for even longer. Detailed Federal managerial interventions in the operational undertakings of aided subnational governments and others were attempted primarily with the advent of the new "social regulation," but these congressionally mandated actions in reality were undercut by inadequate or hostile staff, or both; by the number of public, quasi-public, and private bodies covered; and by the large number of these new regulations and conditions (see table Int-2, pp. 6–7).

In terms of complementary concepts, this apparently simple administrative approach was riddled with conflict and confusion. Program and administrative curbs or devolutions were the primary means of carrying out this supply-side managerial strategy, yet extraordinary centralizations of policy formulation and administrative power were required to achieve these goals. Moreover, the reduction in the number and influence of professional Federal managers, in both theory and fact, involved an expansion of the size and roles of the political sector at the top.

In practice, these inconsistencies, along with the inherent conflict between this managerial approach and other key planks in the Reagan platform (notably a beefed-up Defense Department, nationally oriented business and Moral Majority concerns, and retrenchment itself), became more apparent. From the outset, prime reliance was placed on strategic policy management, which involved establishing horizontal policy networks at the very center of the executive branch (including officials from the Office of Policy Development, cabinet councils, Office of Planning and Evaluation, Office of Management and Budget [OMB], and the Council of Economic Advisers). The success of this strategy, at least during the first Reagan administration, was due largely to the strict ideological and political tests that were rigorously applied to the presidential appointments process, especially for Executive Office of the President personnel. Its collapse during the earlier years of the second administration was due to the departure of able key orchestrators of the strategy.

Overall in the personnel area, vigorous efforts were mounted to reduce the supply of professional managers and of other Federal workers in domestic agencies by a combination of appointment of noncareer managers, slow or no replacements for retirees, downgrading of middle- and senior-level positions, parsimonious pay and retirement policies, skillful manipulation of the Senior Executive Service, barring of professional managers from policy-formulation activities, and agency eliminations. In the end, the size of the Federal civilian work force, however, was larger than it had ever been in peacetime. Its total rose by over 349,000 between 1981 and 1988, thanks largely to the DOD expansions.

Some observers have contended that the "hollow, incompetent government" that resulted from the starving of the non-DOD agencies that drove the Reagan years constituted a "quiet crisis" that threatened the county's capacity to solve economic and social problems. "Hollowness," for Walter Williams, signifies "too few staff overall, too few specialists, inadequate working conditions,... and weak information and analytical systems"; incompetence implies "lack of experienced capable staff."[9] Horror stories like the HUD scandals, the savings and loan debacle, and even the collision of a jetliner and a smaller commuter plane in Los Angeles (1 February 1991) can be traced to "inept, malfeasant" government. Moreover, the gradual loss of premier status by such formerly acclaimed agencies as the Food and Drug Administration (FDA), the Social Security Administration (SSA), and the National Institutes of Health (NIH) was due to a combination of personnel cuts, hikes in service demands, and losses of top staff and specialists because of the growing gap between Federal and private pay for comparable work.[10]

The budget process initially was the focal point of implementing many of the administration's supply-side management objectives. It was used, chiefly in 1981, to achieve some program eliminations (hence some devolutions), some program mergers, rollbacks in the administrative costs of Federal grants and other programs, limits on strict Federal supervision of many third-party implementers of national policies, and a reduction in Federal collection and dissemination of information. Yet as is noted elsewhere, Congress from 1982 to 1988 did not accept many of the president's domestic cutback proposals. During these years, budgeting was a top-down process in the executive branch, but once the product reached Congress, the pluralistic pressures of domestic program politics asserted themselves, though all within the confines of the deficit dilemma.

With procurement, the Reagan administration began early a drive against waste, fraud, and abuse in various domestic (notably social welfare) programs. Yet its own management of the defense buildup produced some of the most extraordinary examples of poor procurement practices (and of the resulting waste and fraud) the nation has ever seen. With its campaign to reduce the Federal regulatory role, a mix of personnel, procedural, and centralizing actions (OMB serving as the authoritative sifter of proposed and amended regulations pursuant to Executive Orders 12291 and 12498) succeeded in reducing the number of issuances. Yet as is detailed elsewhere, the administration's own support for tough, retrenching grant conditions, new probusiness constraints on certain state activities, and intrusive conservative social-agenda-inspired regulations undercut much of this effort.

In short, Reagan management practices in the strategic planning, personnel, budgetary, procurement, and regulatory spheres, although initially successful in many instances, frequently encountered opposition in the form of conflicting administration policy objectives, congressional hostility, and pressure-group politics. At the same time, they did succeed in rendering top professional managers even more defensive, deflated, and demoralized than they had been in the seventies; no "bamboo-fence" metaphor could apply here.

The *Reagan intergovernmental initiatives* achieved more than what was deemed possible in 1980 but far less than what in late 1981 seemed likely after OBRA. With his drive to reduce the Federal role in the federal system, an absolute reduction in grant outlays of over $8 billion (from the proposed FY 1982 Carter figure) and in the number of grants by more than 140 was achieved with OBRA. Proposed additional deeper cuts, more eliminations, and most new consolidations, however, were mostly rejected by an increasingly assertive Congress. Hence, Federal aid totals rose gradually in both constant and current dollars, from $88.2 billion in FY 1982 to $122.0 billion in current dollars by FY 1989, or by nearly 6 billion constant dollars. The number of Federal grants also increased from 393 in FY 1982 to 435 in FY 1987, and ultimately to 492 by FY 1989. New grant programs enacted during the Reagan administration included Biofuels and Municipal Waste Technology; Fossil Energy Research; State Heating Oil; Asbestos School Hazards Abatement; Marine Sanctuary; Minority Business Development: State and Local Government Program; Urban Mass Transit: Capital Improvement Grants; Emergency Shelter; and Housing Development Grants. It is hard to believe the Reagan presidential pen signed all these and other new Federal grants.

The concomitant Reagan goal of devolving Federal program responsibilities scored slightly better. In addition to OBRA's program eliminations and block grants, greater management responsibility was delegated to some of the states in some of the environmental regulatory programs; categorical conditions in non-social-welfare programs were loosened administratively; and the new block grants during their early years were implemented in a highly permissive fashion. Moreover, two more block grants were added between 1986 and 1988. At the same time, no devolutions of total responsibility in any major grant area (multistate regionalism and certain housing programs excepted) occurred, and categoricals, not block grants or General Revenue Sharing (which was scrapped in 1986), continued to dominate the grant scene throughout these years, accounting for more than 87 percent of total aid dollars in FY 1989, while discretionary Federal aid declined significantly, which suggests a continuing centralization with the entitlements and a de facto unilateral devolution with the shrinking aid for grant programs of assistance to state and local governments.

The deregulation drive, as noted previously, scored some successes and some real losses. The administration did not focus on actively eliminating intergovernmental or other regulations as much as on softening the process — by its appointments (for example, James Watt and Anne Gorsuch Burford) as well as by personnel cuts (for example, between FY 1981 and FY 1986, the Federal funds for state administrative costs under the Clean Air Act were reduced by 15 percent, under the Endangered Species Act by 38 percent, under the Flood Disaster Protection by 35 percent, under Historic Preservation by 40 percent, and under Safe Drinking Water by 25 percent). Other approaches included changes in rules and procedures (for example, Age Discrimination in Employment; Davis-Bacon, which stipulated that prevailing wage rates must be paid to workers employed in a Federally aided project or program; Uniform Relocation, which standardized the rates of compensation for those forced to move as a result of Federal or Federally aided program acquisitions of private property; and the National Environmental Policy Act) and a centralized review of proposed or modified regulations.[11]

The last was achieved by the promulgation on 16 September 1981 of E.O. 12291, which expanded the earlier central regulatory clearance requirement and went way beyond the procedures established by Ford and Carter. The order stipulated that all "major"-agency regulatory proposals must survive cost-benefit analyses,[12] and this responsibility was given to the Office of Information and Regulatory Affairs (OIRA) within OMB. This assignment to an agency with eighty-four positions and the absence of outside participation or even clear information on the process generated considerable controversy. Yet despite congressional and Federal court criticisms, the regulatory clearance drive continued, and over its first four years a sharp reduction in the number of prepared rules appearing in the *Federal Register* occurred. With E.O. 12498 (1985) all significant regulatory actions "planned or under way," including background documents that could trigger rule-making procedures, had to be submitted to OIRA in annual "regulatory program" reports from each relevant agency.[13] Although there was some later opening up of the process, OMB's control over it was assured, and this centralized "review of regulations would take its place with budgetary review as one of the principal management tools available to the President."[14] The private sector, however, benefited much more from this relief than the intergovernmental.

In addition and totally contrary to the Reagan regulatory strategy, twenty-one new major "social-regulation" enactments occurred during Reagan's two terms.[15] From Age Discrimination in Employment (1986), Handicapped Children's Protection (1986), Highway Safety Amendments (that is, minimum national drinking age of twenty-one), and the Surface Transportation Assistance Act (which, for example, set uniform truck size and weight limits) to Lead Contamination Control (1988) and the Ocean Dumping Ban (1988), regulatory legislation involving antidiscrimination, health and safety, and environmental protection continued to be as significant a congressional concern in the 1980s as in the 1970s. The president either passively or with relish signed these measures, all of which heavily impacted state and local government.

Moreover, conditions in social-welfare grants got tougher, and congressional preemptions of state regulatory authority picked up: one hundred were legislated between 1980 and 1988. No frontal legislative assault was ever mounted by the administration on behalf of regulatory relief. For Federal managers of social programs, all this meant a much heavier administrative load. For those in the environmental and block grant areas, it involved some lightening of their responsibilities. For state and local officials generally, it meant more headaches.

The push to return to *the old Federal-state partnership* was reflected in all of the thirteen new block grants, wherein the states were the sole recipients; in the number of theretofore Federal-local programs that were merged in the blocks; in the unsuccessful 1982 administration effort to achieve the "Big Swap" in program responsibilities between the national government and the states; in the delegations of environmental administrative responsibilities; and in the decline in the proportion of grant monies that bypassed state governments (table Int-2, pp. 6–7). All of these, save for the ill-fated 1982 proposal, eased the job of affected Federal grants managers. On the opposite side of the ledger, states and their administrators bore the brunt of the increased conditions and fiscal curbs in the social-welfare area. They also were most affected by the new preemptions and crossover sanctions (for example, the tandem-trailer-truck regulation and teenage drinking bans) and they felt more than the other subnational governments did the adverse effects of the administration's and Congress's unilateral intergovernmental initiatives.

Finally, the need to *curb governmental activism* at all levels proved to be a need that no level honored. In overall expenditure terms, Federal expenditures soared from $617 billion in 1980 to over $1,214 billion by 1988; state outlays from own-revenue sources increased from $143.3 billion in 1980 to $280.5 billion by 1988; and the local figures for the same years were $223.6 billion up to $421.7.[16] As a percentage of GNP, total Federal-state-local spending rose from 32.56 percent in 1980 to 33.94 percent by 1988, a share that exceeded that of most of the seventies.

To sum up, Reagan policies in the managerial area fared far better than those in the fiscal or federalism fields, and in the overall scheme of things federalism proved to be the least lustrous of the various stars in the galaxy of Reagan concepts. The total of Federal actions from 1981 to 1988 did impact domestic policy activism in Washington, however, and in a serious fashion. The failure of the president and Congress really to come to grips with the runaway budget deficits even in years of prosperity did more than any of the intergovernmental initiatives to curb, though not control, the expansionist entrepreneurialism of Federal policymakers.

On the federalism front as such, the narrowing of the Federal aid package's programmatic breadth (as gauged by the number of grant programs), of its jurisdictional reach (as indicated by the severe slashing of direct Federal-local grant links), and of its fiscal size (as measured by the meager 5.7 percent increase in constant FY 1987 dollars between FY 1982 and FY 1989) constituted a partial victory for Reagan's original reductionist goal. Yet the Reagan record in no way included the severe rollbacks envisaged by OBRA. In specific program terms, the elimination of 140-odd programs, the curbing of countless others, the withdrawal from the multistate and most other substate regional programs, the stringent slashes in housing aid, and the scuttling of aid for the working poor and for poor local jurisdictions also were in conformity with the Reagan downsizing strategy. Yet outlays for transfer payments soared during this same period, which largely explains the overall hike in domestic outlays. Moreover, after 1981 most of the constrained actions were of the decremental, "de facto" type, not outright line-outs.

The failure of the "Big-Swap" proposals ended the last major Reagan effort to reform the system. Its sorting out strategy was remarkable for its boldness and its lack of balance. AFDC and food stamps were to be devolved and Medicaid nationalized; a $28 billion trust fund was to be established to replace forty-three Federal grants in five broad program areas; the states were to have the initial option of keeping the grants in their categorical form or accepting "no-strings" monies from the trust fund; but a phaseout of the fund and the taxes support- ing it would occur in four years, thus leaving it to the states to pick up or pass on the devolved program responsibilities. The timing of the proposal was not good: in the midst of the recession. Moreover, it lacked programmatic sense. Food stamps were and are 95 percent Federally funded, and to propose a de- volution of the program made no political or fiscal sense. The devolution of AFDC raised other major questions. Additionally, the proposed phaseout led to the states' labeling — which was to apply to more than this endeavor — of "shift and shaft."

The conflicting Reagan regulatory record with its stiff curbs from within and several new presidential signings forced mostly from without left the level of Federal involvement in this area roughly where it was in 1980 or even higher. One authority summed it up: "In regulation as elsewhere, the Reagan adminis- tration has left a complex but often disappointing legacy when measured against its original objectives.... [I]ts long-term commitment to this goal [of reducing the IGR regulatory impact] proved surprisingly superficial and its deregulatory accomplishments did not extend beyond its first two years in office."[17]

As a partial result of the above, the states continued to revitalize their his- toric roles of serving as independent centers of policy initiatives. The renaissance of state governing systems began in the late 1960s and continued unabated through the 1970s.[18] Several states enacted education reform and finance, economic development, health-cost control, welfare reform, and consumer pro- tection legislation. During the Reagan years, these and other state innovations (for example, foreign trade missions, filling gaps caused by Federal grant reduc- tions, and solid waste disposal) continued to be enacted. Moreover, the really revolutionary feature of Reagan's economic and intergovernmental policies was that few state and local officials by 1988 looked to Washington for solutions to many of their most pressing problems, as they had tended to do in the 1970s. At the same time, they did not ignore the national scene either. Too many actions were taken there — fiscal, programmatic, administrative, regulatory, and judi- cial — that could affect them adversely or favorably to permit a closing down of the IGR lobby and the various individual state and local offices in Washington.

In short, Reagan's and Congress's impacts on intergovernmental relations from 1981 to 1988 were mildly surgical from a conservative perspective, though drastically so from the liberal vantage point. They constituted more a reaction than a revolution because neither the politics undergirding the earlier public ex- pansionism nor most of the major programs that symbolized that activism were eliminated. To achieve a kind of "de facto," "decremental" federalism in some areas by the drastic device of triple-digit (in billions) budget deficits suggests an approach that did not make sense fiscally or, in the long run, for federalism. No return to dual or even the simple cooperative federalism of 1960 occurred. When the regulatory, preemptive, political, and judicial developments of the Reagan years are combined, the net result was a greater centralization in the system, with the more balancing trends in the operational area not enough to outweigh the crushing centripetalism in the others. More on this in the succeeding chapters.

### Errors of Omission and Commission

While achieving much more than had been expected in 1980, Reagan pulled off no revolution, in large part, as David Stockman explained in his *Triumph of Politics*, because the president "was a consensus politician, not an ideologue. He had no business trying to make a revolution, because it wasn't in his bones."[19] In more specific terms, Reagan would have achieved a revolution had he been more visceral about his goals and had those goals been clearly hammered out by knowledgeable experts. For example, there should have been one tax cut in 1981, not two (the indexation of the Federal income tax brackets amounted to another major tax cut).[20] There should have been no more than a 5 percent annual hike in real growth terms for defense from 1980 to 1986, as Reagan had promised in the campaign. Yet based on figures that failed to recognize that Congress already had enacted a FY 1981 DOD package that had 9 percent real growth built into it, Stockman and his aides went on to increase Defense's real growth by 10 percent annually through to 1986, double what Reagan had promised.[21] There should have been presidential and cabinet support for Stockman's "Chapter Two," which would have slashed subsidies to upper- and middle-income folk and corrected the image that the Reagan program was simply against the working poor.[22] This would have meant a second round of cuts but involving items like the oil depletion allowance, grazing and timber fees, the "mansion tax," and "squeezing the yacht owners," as well as curbing the big middle-class entitlements — Social Security, Medicare, and Federal retirement pensions.[23] All this was rejected with the president leading the defense for the depletion allowance. Finally, the failure of the "Big-Swap" federalism reform proposal would not have occurred had the president intervened personally in midsummer 1982 to break the impasse between the governors and divided administration spokespersons. Out of these actions and inactions, the genie of greater and greater deficits was unleashed and a rare moment for real federalism reform was lost.

## The Bush Aftermath

Another legacy of Reagan's was the Bush administration, because the 1988 election results were interpreted by most analysts as a vote for continuity. But what was to be continued? Would the new president honor his campaign promises to cut regulatory red tape, to rein in the Federal government, to reduce the deficit, and to keep "Washington off the backs of business"? Would he thus resume Reagan's initial radical thrusts to reduce surgically the Federal role in the federal and private-sector systems? Or would he, like the later Reagan, in fact, accommodate to and compromise with the plethora of congressional and interest group pressures bent on expanding or at least not contracting the Federal role? Would he, in fact, be a standpat conservative, a role with which he was most comfortable? As it turns out, he assumed various of these guises, like his predecessor and like Congress. If this conveys the impression of a less than clear articulation of the president's federalism precepts, it is an accurate impression. Bush had few of the intellectual, if not ideological, insights of his chief of staff, former governor John Sununu. Moreover and less obviously, the congressional role during this period reflected new and committed Democratic leadership and a resurgence of the congressional federalism values of the seventies, though always within the confines of the budgetary constraints.

In *the operational side of Federal-state-local relations* and its fiscal component, the dominant conditioner obviously was the longest recession since the thirties. It produced a "deficit-driven federalism" at all levels of government, not merely at the national, as was the case prior to 1989. From that in turn came the "fend-for-yourself" variety of federalism, though outside help was not always lacking. The Federal debt soared to new highs: from $2.8 trillion in FY 1989 (three times the 1980 figure) to nearly $4 trillion in FY 1993.

Obviously, the deficit was the basic backdrop of the continued constraint in budget outlays, both foreign and domestic. It also was the prime prompter of the famous November 1990 Budget Reconciliation agreement, which hiked revenues by $137 billion over a five-year period, cut $182.4 billion from discretionary spending, and established a new budget process (scrapping Gramm-Rudman-Hollings) that stipulated three categories of spending (defense, international, and domestic), placed caps on each, and required across-the-board cuts within fifteen days after a congressional session if a cap was exceeded. This, in effect, plugged some loopholes in the earlier Gramm-Rudman-Hollings procedure.

In the domestic-program sphere and despite these severe fiscal contrasts, the number of Federal grants rose to an all-time high of 593 by FY 1993, 101 more than its FY 1989 counterpart. In current-dollar terms, $71.6 billion was added to the aid total between FY 1989 and FY 1993. As a percentage of state-local expenditures, this figure produced a slight hike of 4.9 percent from FY 1989 to FY 1993, and as a proportion of total Federal outlays it represented a 3.0 percent increase between FY 1989 and FY 1993. Most of this, it should be stressed, is explained by the $42 billion jump in Medicaid outlays from FY 1990 to FY 1993.

Major new enactments were few but included the Clean Air Act Amendments of 1990 and the Intermodel Surface Transportation Efficiency Act (ISTEA-1991). The first was largely a presidential initiative — one of very few in the domestic-program area — that resulted from a series of compromises between and among various affected parties, including the White House and subnational governments. It stands as probably the best (critics would say the only) example of Bush's cooperative leadership skills in the domestic-policy area.[24] Among its provisions were ones that would help state and local governments to achieve tougher air-quality standards for ozone, carbon monoxide, and particulate pollution. With ISTEA, $115.9 billion went for highway work and $31.5 billion (the largest authorization ever) for mass transit through FY 1996. The measure also cut several earlier programmatic and spending constraints on states and metropolitan-area bodies, thus converting most of the mass transit program into a block grant.[25] In a far less prominent fashion, Congress and the president hammered out similar and dissimilar grant priorities in health, education, welfare, and other areas.

Still within the operational sphere of intergovernmental relations but in regard to the *regulatory and mandating parts of the story,* another totally conflicting ethic — a co-optive one — partially prevailed. Six major new social regulations were enacted between 1989 and 1992, including Americans with Disabilities Act (1990), Clean Air Act Amendments (1990), Education for the Handicapped Act (1990), mandated expansions of Medicaid's coverage, and the Civil Rights Restoration Act. Of these, the ADA, Clean Air Act, and Medicaid mandates were the most controversial and costly.

A look at *the state-local fiscal picture* is necessary to gauge the bad timing of these new Federal regulations. The prolonged recession and the Federal budgetary crisis took their toll at these levels, and added mandates were not appreciated. Most states contended that they faced the "bleakest fiscal conditions" since 1983. Twenty-nine had to cut spending to balance their FY 1991 budgets, and thirty had to increase revenues for FY 1992.[26] The total state revenue shortfalls were increasing, largely because of (1) the slowdown in the national economy, which was decreasing state tax revenue and raising the demand for as well as the cost of "safety-net" programs that states partially finance, and (2) "continuing mandates from the Federal government" — mainly Medicaid program expansions — that were forcing the states to exceed estimated expenditures for those programs.[27] Earlier tax and spending decisions also were a factor to be reckoned with here.

From 1981 to 1989, it is to be remembered, states and localities financed the bulk of their expanding outlays from hikes in their own general revenue (thanks to their healthy economic condition from 1984 to 1989). The states' total general revenues grew by 96 percent and the localities' by 102 percent between 1982 and 1989. A new factor, then, had been added to the intergovernmental picture: "deficit-driven" federalism was found at all three levels of government, not just the Federal. By 1992, state revenues were down, Federal aid was meager in light of state program responsibilities, mandates mounted, and most localities were begging for more help from the states, in light of the Federal slashing of direct aid to local government programs but with little reprieve on local regulations.

The pressures on the states to spend had been tremendous. During the eighties state outlays for primary and secondary education reached $187 billion, double the 1980 figure, and this made the states the senior financiers of this fundamental governmental responsibility (the Federal contribution in 1990 was $13 billion). Corrections — prisons, prison personnel, parole, and related costs — is another basically state-financed function, though with some local contributions in some areas. Changing attitudes toward crime had focused on punishment, incarceration, mandatory sentences, and a broadening of the definition of crime. All this combined to push upward what used to be an average state outlay of 3.5 percent of the budget for corrections, and there was no Federal aid then for this function. With Medicaid and AFDC, there was a Federal role, but it seemed mostly coercive, as noted above in the case of Medicaid.

Of the sixty or more crosscutting conditions that in 1980 applied to all relevant Federal grants, most were still in place during the Reagan-Bush years, for the simple reason that nearly all were rooted in statutory provisions. And the figure for these grew during these years. One new crosscut was Reagan's E.O. 12612 (26 October 1987), which required federalism assessments by implementing Federal grant agencies. In it, nine basic federalism principles and administrative procedures were identified. Among the latter: Federal actions curbing state discretion should be taken only where constitutional authority for such moves is clear and certain, and where the national scope of the problem requires Washington to act; where national policies are state administered, maximum discretion should be granted; Federal executive agencies should encourage states to develop their own policies to implement policy objectives; should states abstain, to the maximum extent possible, Federal agencies should desist from issuing uniform national standards; where such standards are required, the agencies should engage in consultation with affected state and local officers; and any Federal preemption of state law shall be narrowly targeted. President Bush indicated his support for E.O. 12612 in a 1990 memorandum to heads of Federal executive departments and agencies. What little evaluation there was of this "federalism by fiat" executive order suggested a mixed-to-pessimistic assessment of its impact.[28]

In terms of *regulatory costs,* most studies indicate their steady increase during the eighties and into the nineties, despite efforts within the Executive Office of the President to control them. Total regulation spending in 1991, for example, was more than 20 percent higher, after accounting for inflation, than when Carter left Washington for Plains. The *Federal Register* ran 68,000 pages of new regulations in 1991, up a quarter from the 1990 total.[29] The Congressional Budget Office in May 1988 found that new regulations adopted since 1983 imposed a cumulative estimated cost of approximately $9 billion on states and localities and that these costs have risen rapidly since 1986, surpassing the rate of growth of Federal aid itself. CBO also found that certain regulatory enactments have been estimated to produce net savings for state and local governments, but that these have been eclipsed by the costs of new grant conditions and regulatory expansions.[30]

To cope with the mounting number and costs of regulations, the processes for curbing government regulations within the Bush administration were nearly as stringent as those under Reagan. The Council on Competitiveness, chaired by Vice-President Dan Quayle, was empowered by the president in 1989 to scrutinize regulations with a view toward lightening the regulatory burden placed on businesses and sometimes on subnational governments. Staffing at the regulatory agencies in early 1992 was 20 percent higher than it was in 1985. Some of the Bush appointees to these regulatory slots were not the ideologues their Reagan predecessors had been but instead were competent professionals.[31] Quayle and his crew focused on fifty to sixty proposed new regulations, chiefly from the Environmental Protection Agency and the Food and Drug Administration. This produced intraadministration squabbles that Quayle sometimes lost and sometimes won. The alleged gutting of the implementation of the Clean Air Act Amendments of 1990 has been described by some as the council's greatest coup. Just prior to and during the presidential primaries and campaign, the Quayle Council became embroiled in political controversy, in part because of assertions the vice-president made concerning the council's accomplishments.[32] Bush's ninety-day freeze on key regulations only added to the partisan battle over the Federal regulatory role in 1992.

The bulk of the proposed rules and regulations, of course, were still reviewed by OMB's OIRA, and the private sector, not state and local governments, were the prime beneficiaries of the Bush administration's deregulatory activities. Quayle's council was, in a sense, a "court of last resort" for businesspeople who believed they were not receiving fair treatment elsewhere.[33]

Both OIRA and the council were cited in Bush's 1990 regulatory program as the two central units involved in providing regulatory relief. Moreover, while enunciating Reagan's regulatory ideas and program, Bush had to face some of the poor results of his predecessor's permissive regulatory record, including the savings and loan scandal, which some felt was caused by lax governmental regulation.[34] Additionally, some businesses were seeking reregulation in their respective areas of concern. The broadcasters, for example, favored regulation of the cable industry, which in turn affected franchising local governments. Some changes in procedures, few ideological appointments to key regulatory slots, slight cuts in some agencies operating budgets, but greater funding for others like the Food and Drug Administration (FDA) and the Economic Development Administration (EDA) — these were Bush's key changes in the regulatory realm.[35] Not to be overlooked here was how Court cases, like *Dole* v. *United Steelworkers of America*,[36] also served to set limits on some of the more aggressive administration deregulatory procedures, in this case OIRA's.

Despite the efforts to sustain a "kinder and gentler" regulatory reform drive, the figures on the number of regulations that were found to be consistent with the president's regulatory policy plan, the number that were withdrawn by the agencies involved, and the number retained by OIRA for reconsideration suggest little difference between the Reagan and Bush records in this area.[37]

Congress proved to be as much a shaper of intergovernmental relations during the Bush years as the president. All of the major new social regulations (with the partial exception of the Clean Air Act Amendments), the Civil Rights Act of 1991, the 1990 budget agreement, the Child Care Act, new education programs, the measures that were vetoed (twenty-five plus), even the beefed-up drug strategy were largely or exclusively shaped by Congress.[38] With most of the measures that passed, and were signed, presidential imprints can be found here and there. Yet generally the format was congressionally crafted.

To sum up the brief but eventful Bush years, finances tended to dominate domestic policy during this period. The Reagan legacy of supersize payments on the national debt, the downturn in the economy, the accompanying shortfall in revenues, and the parallel need to retrench at all levels forced public finances to the fore. The bold bipartisan budget agreement of 1990 was the chief national governmental response.

Yet alongside this seemingly coherent and connected story, there lay a series of other developments that underscore the continuance of "conflicted federalism." Some programs were cut, again mostly discretionary ones, and others, mostly entitlements, were increased, all to the continuing consternation of state and local officials. Attempts to deregulate were continued and even strengthened within the Executive Branch, even as the president signed six new major social regulations. The fifty state-local operational systems were all living under a "deficit-driven federalism" along with its "fend-for-yourself" corollary. Yet the 1990 Medicaid mandates that hiked required state outlays for the program, as well as the Federal outlays, exacerbated these already constrained conditions.

Both the political and to a somewhat lesser degree the judicial arenas witnessed continuing centralization, as subsequent chapters will demonstrate, and the public persisted in its love affair with certain Federal programs and its animosity toward the national government, its administrators, and its taxes.

## Clinton, Congress, and the Current IGR Condition

The current phase of this intergovernmental chronicle began with the swearing in of Bill Clinton as president on 20 January 1993. At that time, nearly all of the conditioners of the late Bush years were still in place, except for the fact that Clinton faced a Congress of his own party. At present, nearly all of the adverse economic and fiscal and even some of the centralizing judicial and regulatory features of 1993 are gone. This suggests that some significant developments have occurred since 1993, developments of crucial consequence for our federalism. If one looks at the sharp shifts and turns, sometimes U-turns, that occurred in the political and policy areas during this period, the likelihood of a really productive national policy and intergovernmental record would seem quite slim. Despite early presidential efforts to advance many moderate and some clearly liberal policies, notably health care reform, and later congressional Republican attempts to enact a long list of conservative, if not ultraconservative, agenda items in 1995, extremism did not prevail most of the time and centrism as a result of compromise or shared policy commitment frequently carried the day, though by 1995 the center was to the right of where it was in 1992.

### Clinton's First Two Years

As a "New Democrat," a plurality (43 percent) presidential winner, and a chief executive bound by the 1990 budget agreement constraints, Clinton faced many obstacles in his attempt to assert presidential leadership. His middle-class-oriented New Democratic creed called for an honoring of those "basic values of opportunity, responsibility, and community, of work, responsibility, and faith."[39] His federalism precepts reflected a genuine effort both in theory and practice to achieve a real balancing of powers and responsibilities between and among the levels. A pair of Domestic Policy staffers detailed seven principles governing the president's approach to IGR:

- federal leadership should entail establishing national goals but leaving maximum feasible authority to states and localities in choosing the means of achieving them (as Clinton did with reference to educational standards in his Goals 2000);

- by using existing legislative and regulatory authority, the national government should make heavy use of authorized waiver authority to permit state and local governments to devise their own implementation designs for intergovernmental programs (more than forty-one states had welfare reform waivers by 1996 and eleven had them for Medicaid experimentation, thanks largely to Clinton);

- the Federal government should enhance its efforts to improve coordination and collaboration among categorical grants and, where appropriate, propose mergers and block grants (Vice-President Gore's National Program Review [NPR] called for the consolidation of 55 categoricals involving $12.5 billion in the fall of 1993, and the president in his FY 1997 budget proposed the consolidation of 271 grants into 27 block grants, but by this time the Republicans were in firm control of Congress and had a different blueprint for intergovernmental reform);

- the Federal government should assume a greater fiscal role in problem areas that fall within its legal authority (the president's anti-crime and anti-drug drives illustrate applications of this precept);

- while continuing to meet its constitutional responsibility to ensure equal citizenship and opportunity for all, the national government should reduce uncompensated fiscal impacts of Federal mandates on state and local governments (the president was an early supporter of the Unfunded Mandates legislation, which became part of the Gingrich Contract with America, and signed it as soon as it reached him in early March 1995, much to the irritation of some congressional Democrats and a host of environmentalists); and

- the achievements of states and localities as "laboratories of democracy" should be noted and publicized so that other jurisdictions may benefit from the success stories of sister jurisdictions (the vice-president's NPR effort and to a certain degree the Department of Housing and Community Development have attempted to fulfill some of what is envisioned here).[40]

If a label were to be placed on these principles taken as a whole and as applied, the term *New Cooperative Federalist* might be the most appropriate. In theory at least, if not always in practice (his Motor Voter act, which authorized voter registration as part of applying for a state driver's licence, family leave legislation, and Brady bill, which required local law enforcement offices to conduct background checks on prospective gun buyers, all contained mandates), Clinton has been the most devolutionary and the most intergovernmentally collaborative of all the Democratic presidents going back to Woodrow Wilson. His two major, if not historic, legislative achievements in his first year were primarily geared to demonstrating his New Democratic creed in practice and not his IGR instincts, though states and localities were significantly affected, albeit indirectly. When he decided to apply an "anti–tax cut, anti-spending" approach to his budget for FY 1994, he encountered little else but dire warnings of inflation, depression, and soaring unemployment from his political opposition. By biting the budget deficit bullet and calling for $211 billion in tax hikes and $255 billion in spending cuts, he underscored the New Democratic doctrine of fiscal responsibility and belief that low interest rates, solid economic growth, and more jobs hinge on acceptance of these tough budget proposals. Of immediate worry to state and local governmental leaders was the prospective continuance of the decremental grant growth of the Reagan-Bush years. In the long run, it now seems clear to most economists and others that the narrowly won budget victory for the president along with private-sector restructurings were the two key factors explaining the extraordinary economic growth since 1993. This, of course, helps explain those budget surpluses now being enjoyed by most states and some localities. The courage of this act and the political damage it did to the Democrats in 1994 has received meager recognition from the experts and the public alike.

Clinton's other major 1993 congressional victory was, of course, NAFTA (the North American Free Trade Agreement), which already had been hammered out by the Bush administration. While traditionally a "free trade" party, the Democrats were deeply divided over NAFTA.[41] Organized labor, "rust belt" politicians, Ross Perot, and most of the House Democratic leadership opposed it, sometimes vociferously. The administration had to reach across the aisle to get Republican support to assure passage of a measure Clinton believed would produce more, not fewer, jobs and would signify American acceptance of the economic implications of globalization. With 132 Republican "ayes" and 43 "nays" and only 102 Democratic affirmatives and 156 in the negative, the measure passed and the "New Democracy" won another victory over an embittered "Old Democracy." Clinton's personal lobbying for the measure was a real factor in gaining its passage. In American regional terms, states bordering Mexico seem pleased with the ratification, but some leaders in the older industrial states fear it and cite it as a cause for slower economic recovery.

The major liberal initiative of the Clinton administration obviously was the president's ill-fated health care reform package. From late 1993 to late summer of 1994, this issue consumed the attention of the administration, especially of the First Lady. The twin goals of the president and his wife were to cut health costs (outlays in this area had risen from 9 percent of total Federal revenues in 1971 to 21 percent in 1991) and to extend coverage to the 15 percent of the population without health insurance.[42] In retrospect, it is easy to criticize Clinton's policy development process (for its secrecy, exclusivity, arrogance in ignoring friendly key health experts, political ineptitude, bad timing — the budget and NAFTA battles consumed much of 1993, but an election year was not an auspicious time — and the ignoring of state officials and their Medicaid reform experience was foolish). After its unveiling some state skeptics viewed the measure as "one massive unfunded mandate." In the final analysis, the excruciatingly complicated politics and number of players that are involved when one-seventh of the economy is affected, the nearly impossible task of producing a "competitive managed care program" that would achieve universal coverage but avoid the bureaucracy and cost of a universal system, and the stark fact that the vast majority of Americans, as Senator Bob Dole constantly reminded us, had good health care and that the crisis was simply a sectoral one, guaranteed a very rough journey to even a partially successful result. But the willingness to compromise was not there on the part of the administration.[43] Its failure to meet head on the clever but misleading TV ads of the national small business and small insurance national associations in the winter and spring of 1994, its inability to win over a respectable number of Republicans, and its loss of big business support, which was there at the beginning, brought matters to a point where the plan was shelved without even a Senate vote.[44] A return to an incremental approach occurred in health policy making in the 104th and 105th Congresses, and it scored some successes. The most prominent among these was the 1997 State Children's Health Insurance Program (SCHIP), which authorizes states to spend their Title XXI allocations through Medicaid, a SCHIP, or a combination of both. Under a SCHIP, states may vary eligibility and benefits to target special regional health problems or according to any other criterion. Federal funding under this option is more generous than that of Medicaid.

With his anti-crime omnibus bill, the president after considerable wrangling got a version that reflected more of his centrism than his liberalism. In his 1994 State of the Union message, he called for a crime bill that was both "tough and smart." Given the negative image on crime generally of the Democrats, he viewed his bill as a necessary corrective and a reflection of a New Democratic approach to the problem.[45] Its more conservative initial provisions included funding for hiring a hundred thousand additional police officers, procedural reform of death-row appeals, the "three strikes and you're out" sentencing policy, and authorization of the death penalty for an enlarged list of Federal crimes. State and local law enforcement and judicial officials clearly were directly affected by most of these changes as well as by the more liberal proposal for gun controls, including a ban on assault weapons.

No Congress during the previous six years of attempting to move on this front had succeeded, and compromise on sharply contrasting differences between liberals and conservatives was not easy. Given the level of discontent with the final product from groups all over the ideological spectrum, special efforts were needed to conciliate many of the potential opponents. A \$3.3 billion cut was made in the Conference Report's total figure, and an energizing campaign of rallying folks who favored specific provisions in the bill was mounted. These administration and congressional efforts ultimately proved successful. Unlike the other key measures analyzed here this one had a significant and direct impact on subnational governments. And not all reactions from their officials were favorable, since mandates and some actual as well as de facto preemptions were part of the measure.

In addition to these major measures, a cluster of educational bills was enacted (e.g., Goals 2000, Schools-to-Work, and an expanded Head Start program), along with family leave, "empowerment zones," which was of importance to the urban interests, the Brady bill, and the Motor Voter act. Most of these cost very little money, and total outlays for Federal grants rose by only \$31.4 billion between FY 1993 and FY 1995; moreover, most of this increase went for entitlements. The number of grants passed the 600 figure by 1993, and the amount of Federal aid going directly to local governments rose very slightly from 11.22 percent in 1992 to 11.49 percent in FY 1995, reflecting the success of a few of the Clinton urban initiatives, especially in the anti-crime area. Little of his "New Cooperative" Federalism was reflected in his push for at least six intrusive regulations and an unfunded mandate (in the Brady bill) that the Court later overturned in *Printz* v. *United States* (1997).

Many of the president's collaborative efforts occurred in the administrative area and by executive fiat.[46] His early Executive Order 12866, which required relevant Federal agencies to begin planning for regulatory relief; his later promulgation of Executive Order 12875, which set up an intergovernmental consultative process with regard to regulatory issuances; the acceleration in his granting of waivers, noted earlier; and his launching, with the vice-president, of a National Performance Review, which had an intergovernmental dimension were but a few of the executive branch actions that won commendation from most state and local leaders. By late fall of 1994, most of these spokespersons indicated their satisfaction with their treatment from the White House but also their anger with various attitudes and actions of the Democratic Congress.

### Clinton and the Republican 104th Congress

In November 1994, the Republicans captured control of the Congress, the first time since the election of the 83d in the 1952 Eisenhower sweep. It was the first time since Harry Truman that a Democratic president confronted a Republican Congress. The fairly steady obstructionism to the Clinton agenda of the opposition throughout most of the 103d continued with the party decision to make the Clinton presidency the basic issue in the midterm elections. To draw a starkly contrasting picture of the differences between the presidential and the congressional platforms, Newt Gingrich, the emerging GOP House leader, drew up his Contract with America, with ten major subheadings subsuming over thirty specific proposals. Whether the Contract actually figured prominently in the Republican victory is open to conjecture. In any event, the Contract was a remarkably clever way to capture the attention of the media and others. With all but a handful of the GOP House candidates signing on in public in front of the Capitol, a rare high degree of national party programmatic cohesion seemed to manifest itself in a nonpresidential election year. Senator Bob Dole's seven-point program received far less coverage, and it focused far more narrowly on defense and fiscal issues.

The Contract called for a balanced budget amendment, a line-item veto, a capital gains tax cut along with several other tax reductions, tax credits, even stiffer sentencing guidelines than Clinton's anti–trial lawyer legislation, term limits, welfare reform, and mandate relief, to mention a few of its planks. Compared to the Dole package, it was much more inclusive, potentially incendiary, and mostly reflective of both social and economic conservative viewpoints. When combined, the proposals added up to a revolution advocated by a party that received 53 percent of the 38 percent of the electorate that actually turned out on Election Day. At the time, the House leaders interpreted the Contract precisely that way. Newt Gingrich described himself as a "revolutionary" and House Appropriations Committee Chair Bob Livingston declared after the election "we are all revolutionaries."[47] And they were correct in their characterizations, since they contemplated nothing less than "a comprehensive ideological, structural, and policy transformation that goes to the foundations of the American political order."[48] The dismantling of the "Welfare State" was the grand goal.

Initially, it appeared that a real revolution would occur. Speaker Gingrich, armed with stronger powers than any other Speaker since "Uncle Joe" Cannon, succeeded in getting all of the Contract's agenda save one (term limits) enacted by spring. A remarkable legislative feat, no doubt! But from the state and local perspective most of the bills were not of any great help. The Republican win in popular terms was viewed as a clarion call for "smaller government, lower taxes, less power in Washington, and greater emphasis on individual responsibility and personal morality."[49] But a balanced inclusion of items for the subnational governments as well as for the private sector was not achieved. The modest Unfunded Mandates bill was helpful, but certainly no panacea. It did not bar mandates and it was prospective, not retrospective. Yet it did help to reduce unfunded enactments. Pursuant to the legislation, any member may raise a "point of order" if a measure comes up that contains a mandate costing subnational governments more than $50 million. In the welfare, crime, children, and product safety liability areas, states and to a lesser degree localities were clearly affected, but frequently in intrusive and preemptive ways. These measures after all reflected certain strongly held conservative social values for the most part, values that could not be left to state or local determination. So here we begin to understand the conflict between the ideological conservative approach to change which is not comfortable with devolution in all policy areas and that of institutional conservatives who are concerned with systemic balance and trust state and local judgments more and hence have far fewer worries about more devolutions.

By June, the press, media, many political pundits, and much of the public were treating the Speaker as if he were a prime minister and as if Westminster had been transported to Washington, D.C. Senate Majority Leader Dole had become the leader of an impotent House of Lords and Bill Clinton had been transformed into a constitutional monarch with no real authority, or so it seemed at the time to many who knew not our Madisonian political/governmental system. That for a while included even the Speaker himself. But by December only four minor items in the Contract had been enacted. The president discovered what he always had — namely, a spine — and he penned his first veto in August and was prepared to use it again, if the need arose. The Senate, with its eleven moderate Republican committee chairs (out of twenty-one) plus the majority leader who disagreed with many of the Gingrich reform proposals, began to develop substitutes for, or to bury, or to adopt with perfecting amendments the thirty-odd parts of the Contract.

The continued ideological posturing of the House freshmen, hence of their leaders, led to the adoption of a debt limit hike and two omnibus budget bills, all of which contained provisions unacceptable to the president, notably in the Medicare, Medicaid, education, and environmental areas (which ultimately became the Clinton reelection mantra in 1996). Each produced presidential vetoes and failure on the part of the Congress to enact continuing resolutions to permit the government to continue to function. The congressional leaders were convinced that the president would be blamed for the resulting shutdowns. Instead, it was Congress that was singled out for chastisement. By the summer of 1996, some political realism began to set in. The enactment record of the first session of the 104th was after all the worst since World War II, and that along with continued impasses between the branches and the houses over the spring only added to the image of a "do-nothing" Congress. So the legislative machinery was lubricated, then enactments occurred, and presidential signings multiplied. Not all the legislation was conservative, as we shall see.

What does the record of the 104th Congress and its relations with the president tell us about our current politics, our actual stance with regard to devolution, and our federalism? Analysis of the measures passed and those rejected reveal some expected and a number of quite unexpected findings.[50] Among those that were enacted and that had clear devolutionary characteristics were the historic welfare reform omnibus package (more on it later); the Unfunded Mandates measure, discussed above; the Safe Drinking Water amendments, which among other things permit small town water systems to meet alternative treatment and monitoring standards; the Clean Air Act Commuter Programs, which make voluntary those provisions under the 1990 Clean Air Act Amendments that required states with ozone and carbon monoxide nonattainment areas to set up employee trip-reductions for companies in the areas involved; and the new food safety legislation, which scrapped the earlier adopted "zero cancer risk" standard for pesticide residues on raw agricultural and processed food. The loosening up on the two environmental and the food safety regulations was made at the specific urging of state and local lobbyists. In addition, the Native Indian Housing program was converted into a block grant, and the Selected Housing Program

Extensions measure assigned various needed powers to managers of local housing authorities. They included the right to evict drug and alcohol abusers and to designate certain projects solely for the elderly and disabled. Such were the various laws enacted by the 104th Congress that enhanced state and/or local program discretion. Certainly not a roll call of dramatic devolutions in a dozen or more program areas that would constitute a complete revamping of our federal system, as early House proposals promised! Nor does it add up to the "Devolution Revolution" that some Republican leaders and academics were trumpeting in the spring of 1995.[51]

Of the lot, welfare reform clearly stands head and shoulders above the others, which almost constitutes an insult, since the rest — save for Unfunded Mandates and Safe Drinking Water — are really pygmies. This new and still highly controversial measure is in fact a massive nine-title omnibus piece of legislation — the Personal Responsibility and Work Opportunity Reconciliation Act (PRWORA) of 1996 — which contains many compromises, some devolutions, and some Federal dictates and was passed with a major assist from the National Governors' Association (NGA).[52] It also contains the first repeal of a New Deal welfare law, and this is the key title (Title I) in the act. Under it, the Temporary Assistance for Needy Families (TANF) replaces the old Aid to Families with Dependent Children (AFDC). It is a block grant, which means a fixed amount of money is allocated to each of the states and the District of Columbia according to a congressionally dictated formula. It also assigns the states considerable discretion in determining eligibility and benefit levels, in developing workfare programs, and in experimenting with ways of achieving the act's basic objective of reducing dependency by job preparation, actual work, and marriage. These three areas of discretion were carved out by eliminating several conditions that formerly applied to AFDC recipients. Discretion was further enhanced by specifically giving the states the option of making payments or using vouchers for employment placement programs, of using electronic benefits transfer (EBT) programs, of shifting TANF funds to the Child Care and Development grant, and of treating for a year families that moved from another state as being under the cash assistance rules of that state. All this is salutary in terms of meeting some of the definitional requisites of a block grant. But unlike any other such grant enacted since 1966, when the first block grant (the Partnership for Health Act) was enacted, this one begins with a number of constraints and dictates. Moreover, when the other titles of the omnibus measure are examined, the prescriptive side of the ledger gets even heavier. So what we have here is a bastard block, not a genuine or legitimate one.

On the prescriptive side of the ledger, under PRWORA states are required to

- impose a five-year lifetime limit on benefits;

- stipulate that parents and caretakers engage in work after twenty-four months of receiving benefits if they are to continue to receive full funding;

- establish and act on goals to reduce out-of-wedlock pregnancies;

- provide education and training on the problem of statutory rape; and

- set forth objective criteria for determining eligibility and paying benefits.

The several very specific prohibitions include the following: states may not provide TANF aid to single parents under eighteen unless they live under adult supervision; they may not help single parents under eighteen who have not completed high school unless they are enrolled in an equivalent program; and they may not provide TANF monies to children who have been absent from home for 45 days or at the state's discretion for 30 to 180 days. Regarding work participation, single parents must work twenty hours a week within a year of the signing of the act. With welfare rolls, 25 percent of a state's caseload must be off the rolls by 1997 and 50 percent by 2002. If states fail to meet TANF deadlines, they may suffer fiscal penalties. There are loopholes in some of these prohibitions, but not many. The goal with these and other Federal dictates in the legislation was and is to force liberal states to "terminate welfare benefits and put teeth into work and related family and school behavioral requirements," as Richard P. Nathan has explained it.[53] During its first year, TANF achieved a remarkable one million reduction in the number on welfare rolls, which represented a 25 percent overall decline,[54] though the buoyant economy must be given some share of the credit. This reduction more than doubled the next year. At the same time, welfare experts know that not all those off the rolls are working. The generally cited guesstimate is that about half of those not on welfare are not working. The real question then is where are they? Reliable answers must be provided to this query before we may make any firm early judgments about TANF's effectiveness.

Under the other eight titles of PRWORA, a tightening of eligibility was mandated for the Supplemental Security Income (SSI) program in Title II by establishing a new method for determining whether a child is disabled. Title III strengthens the child support program by beefing up the statewide automated tracking system of all new hires, still a source of considerable confusion. In addition, under this title, child support court orders are mandated and states must increase from 75 percent to 90 percent the paternity identification rate. This entire problem of locating and computerizing "dead-beat dads" has been with us since the 1990 child support legislation, and success has not come easy. Witness the cases of California, New Hampshire, and Florida, to cite only a few. Child protection is covered by Title IV, which continues care and adoption, family preservation, child abuse prevention, and other child welfare categoricals; it also raises to 75 percent the Federal match for state child welfare informational and computerized systems.

Title VI created a small new childcare block grant, whose funds will grow as the work requirement deadlines draw near. Title VII reduced the Federal reimbursement for the Summer Food Service program for school children and established a two-tier approach to reimbursing child and adult food allowances. In Title VIII, a reduction in the maximum food stamp benefits and in the levels of eligibility were stipulated along with the requirement that able-bodied adults between the ages of eighteen and fifty must work if they are to be eligible for food stamps. In a similar fashion, Title IV restricts welfare and other social welfare benefits for legal aliens during their first five years in the country. These last restrictions were repealed by the 105th Congress at the behest of the governors and others, including many who questioned their constitutionality. Title IV also requires states to establish systems for verifying immigration status when determining eligibility, another part of the welfare package of doubtful constitutionality in light of *Lopez* (1995), as the next chapter will indicate. Finally, under several of the titles states may deny Medicaid benefits to adults dropped from welfare rolls because they failed to meet work requirements.

Clearly this 502-page multifaceted omnibus measure is neither a heavily devolutionary nor a continuously centralizing package of programs, but combines elements of both. The original House welfare scheme of a major welfare reform title along with a number of smaller allied block grants was scrapped by the Senate and/or the president. As it stands now, it is composed of one large bastard block grant, one small childcare block, and eight categoricals. In addition at least a dozen mandates are included in the measure. Combining these separate titles in a way that makes administrative sense is no easy task, given the mix of devolutionary and dictatorial provisions in the legislation. Not to be overlooked here is the fact that some of the titles that were included were there to provide a basis for some tough budget cuts, notably those dealing with Medicaid, food stamps, and SSI. Most of the $51.1 billion in savings came from reductions in these three programs. TANF alone generated very little by way of significant budget cuts.

Shifting back to the overall record of the 104th Congress, it is appropriate here to note the various proposed devolutionary bills that were defeated. Chief among these was the proposed Medicaid block grant with a $163 billion cut in funding over five years. Both a public housing blocking proposal and the big regulatory reform measure that would have seriously limited the Federal government's power to issue rules affecting health, safety, and the environment were scuttled. Extension of the Clean Water Act, enactment of a consolidation of eighty-odd manpower training programs, and passage of a revised Endangered Species Act, which eliminated the Federal authority to restrict threatening activities, were all successfully resisted. A rollback of affirmative action, a conservative shift in the Superfund's program and rules, and the proposed Product Liability Legal Reform Act of 1996 were also scuttled. Of the nine here, two died because of Senate rejection; three, because of a presidential veto or the threat of one; two others failed because neither chamber dared take either one up; and the last two died because of a deadlocked Conference Committee and lack of time to consider a Conference Report. In these diverse but deadly actions, the "Republican Revolution" was truncated.

Worthy of notice here were the many moves made by the Republican majorities to enhance the power of the Federal government, which in turn highlights the secondary significance of federalism with them when other more crucial social, moral, and "law and order" issues come into play. (Most Democrats behave the same way, of course; it is only the issues that differ; and with "law and order," the parties tend to respond in the same centripetal fashion.) With the 104th, note the Republican same-sex legislation that allows states to ignore the validity of another state's actions when that state has authorized such unions; the ban in the new Immigration Act that obligates state and local officials to meet new Federal anti-fraud specifications for drivers' licenses and for birth certificates; the exemption in the new Securities Regulation Act of mutual funds from state registration requirements; as well as the prohibition in the Food Safety legislation of state enactments of tougher legislation in that field. In addition, the sweeping new telecommunications legislation nullifies state and local laws, regulations, or legal provisions that bar competition in this rapidly growing field, and another provision in the Immigration Act denies benefits to illegal aliens under any means-tested Federal or state program. Here we have six examples in diverse subject areas of conservative congressional action that undercut state authority one way or another.[55]

In a major field of Federal concern — criminal justice — Congress enacted a maze of mandates and preemptions. Among them were expanding Federal criminal penalties to cover interstate stalking of a person, rape committed during a car-jacking, participation in international terrorism activities within the United States, and targeting Federal employees for harm because of their official duties.[56] Moreover, states were "forced" into having their prisoners serve at least 85 percent of their sentences to avoid losing their prison construction monies. Finally, one of the most dramatic examples of congressional centralization was the undercutting of the much-heralded and state-lauded *U.S.* v. *Lopez* (1995) decision (but more on this in the next chapter). To sum up, did devolution or centralization win out in the array of basically conservative-initiated federalism-related actions taken by the 104th Congress? Obviously, sometimes it was the former, sometimes the latter! But taken as a whole a record emerges that in no way supports the claim that massive devolution occurred as a consequence of bills passed by this Congress. At the same time, this Congress was somewhat more sensitive to state concerns than almost any recent Democratic Congress.

Not to be overlooked in this assessment of the 104th and its ideological directions and achievements was the enactment of three centralizing liberal pieces of legislation late in the second session. Thanks to the collaboration of Senator Nancy Kassebaum (R-Kans.) and Senator Ted Kennedy (D-Mass.) and the anxious political atmosphere at the time, a much publicized minimum wage bill, which required setting aside the Unfunded Mandates legislation, was passed along with two health care measures. One guaranteed workers the chance to continue health insurance coverage if they lost their jobs, and the other barred insurers from denying coverage for preexisting conditions for more than one year. Meanwhile, Congress also made some liberal moves in the appropriations area. Education funding for FY 1997 was 14 percent greater than the FY 1996 figure, with school reform receiving the amounts that the president called for. But the Congress also gutted the heart of the president's program in this field. The Goals 2000 legislation was rewritten, and the integrated state plans containing the performance standards and the nongovernmental peer review of the plans were scrapped, thanks to the energy of the House Republican freshmen.[57] Monies for student aid exceeded the FY 1996 level, and the same was true for Head Start, which had a 12 percent increase. AmeriCorps, a presidential pet program, was cut by 26 percent, which was less drastic than its elimination, which the House had initially voted. The Low Income Energy Assistance Program was funded at $1 billion each for FY 1997 and FY 1998, another case of continuing a grant, but at a reduced appropriation level, when initially it had been slated for extermination. FY 1997 funds for the National Institutes of Health were higher than the president's budget request and 7 percent higher than the FY 1996 level. These and other "liberal" enactments occurred during the final months of the second session. Their passage signified a real taming of many of the Republican freshmen, not to mention the Speaker in January, both of whom in no way would have contemplated letting such measures pass in 1995.

Looking at the Omnibus Appropriations bill for FY 1997 in various ways further underscores how the congressional Republicans and the president were forced to come together late in the second session and to cut deals. The need to avoid supersensational issues and ideological polarization was accepted by nearly all players so that there would be no repeat of the earlier shutdowns. The measure was crucial in that only seven of the regular thirteen appropriations measures had been passed. Given the time crunch for campaigning, Congress gave the president the additional $6.5 billion he wanted for a cluster of programs that he felt had been shortchanged. When the totals for this omnibus bill and the seven already enacted are combined, $502 billion was provided for discretionary Federal spending, or only $3 billion less than what the president had originally called for, but $5 billion more than the House-passed bills would have provided. In intergovernmental terms, aid to state and local governments increased slightly by $6.4 billion. Of the $234.2 billion aid total, Medicaid received 40 percent, and it along with the other eleven safety-net entitlement grants accounted for about 68 percent of the total. Outlays for the remaining 648-odd discretionary grants, which included all aid for state and local governments, came to 32 percent, compared to 33 percent in FY 1966 and 33.5 percent in FY 1995. No big changes here despite the conversion of AFDC into a nonentitlement block grant.

What does this probe of Clinton and the 104th Congress reveal? First and foremost it shows that the congressional record and especially its welfare reform is but one more chapter in the ongoing chronicle of our contemporary "Conflicted Federalism." Devolution after all was but one item on the House leadership's agenda and not always a paramount one. Moreover, the Senate and the president had different perspectives with regard to devolution and centralization. The overall rhetoric of 1995 certainly was heavily devolutionary, but concrete courses of action in this area are most difficult to pursue; after all, such actions amount to relinquishing some presidential, national bureaucratic, and/or congressional power and principles. No easy thing! And to assume that the House of Representatives had become the center of Federal power in 1995 was the height of political and policy folly. But it was understandable, given the remarkable House enactment record up to June 1995. The overall legislative record of the 104th Congress and the presidential role in it are not as bad as many would have us believe. For liberals, the welfare package and the president's need to appear to have fulfilled his 1992 campaign promise of "ending welfare as we have known it" stood out as the blackest mark in this legislative record. Yet some liberal measures were passed, and several conservative initiatives were defeated. For the fiscally prudent, the failure to follow through with the promised severe 1995 Republican cuts in Medicare and Medicaid with less stringent but meaningful entitlement reductions in 1996 was bothersome. But entitlement growth and more managed care did occur. For conservatives, the fundamental dilemma of seeking to achieve radical change in a system that loads the dice against such actions proved to be their biggest headache. Their frustration was intense; their anger with fellow party members who were more moderate was great; and their self-righteousness was viewed by some as pharisaic, but given their ethical goal of cleansing the system it was understandable. The great paradox here, of course, is that it was a conservative governmental system that thwarted the hard-right conservative Republican revolution. Yet the internal rules changes were mostly meritorious and should not be forgotten.

## Our Federalism's Current Condition

The reelection of Bill Clinton and of a Republican Congress, albeit with smaller majorities, begins this final and current phase in this tracing of the evolution of American federalism. But given the rebukes that both parties received from the voters in the 1994 and 1996 elections, caution and relative calm have characterized the relations between the national government's political branches since the election in 1996. The president's eloquent 1997 State of the Union message, echoing his campaign rhetoric, touched on some of the nation's and federalism's key issues (e.g., educational excellence, racial reconciliation, a balanced budget, restructuring Medicare and Social Security, expansions of health care coverage, charter schools, curbing juvenile crime, campaign finance reform, and protecting Medicaid, Medicare, education).[58] The hard choices involved with restructuring Social Security and Medicare, with achieving racial reconciliation, with reforming campaign finance and education, and protecting his four "sacred cows" were not spelled out and probably should not be in an address of this kind. Nevertheless, some suggestions of the sacrifices that will be needed to effectuate most of his domestic program goals would have been helpful. Some compared the speech to a "State of the State" message of a governor, because most of the themes were the ones he dealt with in Little Rock — crime, welfare, taxes, health care, the environment, and especially education. These are perennial gubernatorial and state concerns and they were at the heart of the Clinton national message as he began his second term. But the fact that they are state and local concerns suggests that most of them require state and local action as much as, if not more than, national action.

In retrospect, the 1993 to 1996 years were busy ones with major initiatives from the left, center, and right dominating the legislative agenda. The 105th Congress lacked the excitement and some of the time the rabid partisanship of the previous two Congresses. The president from early on was criticized for his "Incredible Shrinking Agenda"[59] and Congress for its "do-nothing" record. The basic reason for both of these caustic criticisms was that big new programs were out of the question, given budgetary and political constraints. Incremental approaches then were about the only feasible ones for both branches, given the absence of a clear programmatic mandate for either. In the president's case, the memory of the health care fiasco only reinforced his cautious tendency.

The chief accomplishment of the first session of the 105th Congress and the president was, of course, the balanced budget agreement. The leaders of both branches came together by early August to agree on how the Federal budget would be balanced by the year 2002 (actually it technically was balanced by the fall of 1997). Traditional strategies for achieving such a goal involved tax hikes and spending cuts, but this one produced tax cuts and credits, the largest since Reagan's 1981 bonanza, and spending increases in a range of mostly social programs as well as some program cuts. An extraordinary mix of diverse associations and people were pleased with the omnibus measure, from noted economists to the Children's Defense Fund and Families USA, to the rich and middle classes. Those constituencies facing negative consequences of congressional actions — Medicare recipients, providers of Medicaid, frequent fliers, and smokers — were and are not so happy. On the social welfare and educational fronts, significant enactments occurred, most of them at the behest of the president. They included a hike in Medicare outlays that was earmarked for tests to help prevent seniors from coming down with an illness; establishment of a $1.5 billion block grant to the states to assist poor Medicaid enrollees in paying their Part B premiums; a $23.4 billion appropriation to expand health coverage for uninsured children, allowing parents with incomes as high as $110,000 to claim a $400 tax credit for each child beginning in 1998 and up to $500 in subsequent years; authorizing low- and middle-income families a tax credit for college tuition costs and other education expenses — the largest increase in Federal education spending since the GI bill; and restoration of disability payments to legal immigrants who had been in residence when the welfare reform bill became law, at a cost of $11 billion over five years.[60] The Medicaid provisions here were of major assistance to the states. The child health provisions assist low-income families, while the child tax credit hike and the education tax credit assist both middle- and low-income folks. Liberal advocacy groups, while not displeased, felt more could have been done for children, while conservative think tank analysts described most of this group of measures as the "most decisive liberal victory in twenty years."[61]

On the tax cut front, an amazing variety of "goodies" was given to diverse but mostly well-to-do citizens. They included a reduction to 20 percent from the previous 28 percent in the top individual tax rate on profits made on sales of stock and other assets held for more than eighteen months, expansions of tax-deferred individual retirement accounts, and an increase to $1 million from the previous $600,000 in the exemption from Federal estate taxes. The measure also includes dozens of smaller breaks for specific interest groups. With regard to spending, it will drop below projected levels by roughly $263 billion, with most of the savings coming from curbing the growth in Medicare, as was suggested above. The tax cut portion of the agreement was largely crafted by congressional Republicans, though the White House helped to moderate some of the earlier, more generous reduction proposals.

How did this agreement come about? It resulted from the amazing condition of the Federal fisc, whose robust health required steady upward revisions of tax revenues, hence the ability to avoid most of the pain usually associated with efforts to balance the budget. The focus of attention became increased outlays for liberal programs, and $95 billion in tax cuts over five years and $274 billion over ten. By the end of the fiscal year in October 1997, Treasury announced a surplus of some $16 billion.

The rest of the record of the 105th Congress was relatively nondescript, with deadlock or defeat for tobacco legislation, campaign finance reform, education revitalization, school construction aid, "fast track" trade negotiating authority for the president, and the expansion of child care programs — to cite a few of the more obvious. Most of the last half of the second session was spent debating spending priorities and patients' rights, handling the budget surplus, and posturing for policy positions that would help in the November elections, as occurred with the House vote to abolish the Federal tax code by 2002. Nevertheless, the Transportation Efficiency Act-21 (TEA-21) and one major and two minor manpower training block grants were passed. Scandal, of course, was the dominant concern of the second session of this Congress.

So what is the condition of American federalism as we approach the millennium? In fiscal terms, as the above discussion suggests and as chapter 8 amply demonstrates, it is in better shape than it has been at any other point in living memory. In terms of Federal-state-local relations, some of the earlier intense distrust between and among the levels has subsided thanks to some actions of the president and some by Congress as well as the more assertive representational efforts of the states and localities. Regarding the two areas — the judicial and the political — in which the subnational governments have fared badly over the past quarter of a century or more, these jurisdictions have won a greater percentage of Federal court cases in this decade than during the previous two. This is not to say that the Supreme Court has become a totally even-handed umpire of Federal-state legal disputes. As the next chapter shows, in certain but not all crucial areas of constitutional adjudication the Court still adheres to a centripetal course. In the realm of politics, subnational leaders have in no way recaptured the clout they possessed even a generation ago. The aggressive representational efforts of the Republican governors in 1995 were an amazing feat, but in the final analysis they did not get anywhere near what they wanted in all nine titles of PRWORA or in other program areas. As chapter 10 explains in depth, the key actors in our political system today are mostly national ones whether we like it or not. The paramount position of state and local political figures from 1828 to roughly 1968 has eroded to the point that they cannot even control their own nominating processes, never mind those for national officers. Yet in the realm of government operations, states and localities are more important than ever before.

Regarding the centralization-devolution conundrum, the simultaneous tendency to centralize and to devolve clearly continues. The welfare reform case study provides ample proof that neither centripetalism nor centrifugalism dominates national policymaking today; instead both condition the process. Gingrich's New Federalism III, like its Nixonian and Reaganite predecessors, never even approached a major reassignment of power to the states and localities. To devolve in a federal system like that of the United States is always difficult. Unitary and parliamentary systems can do it more easily, for power is more concentrated in both. Moreover, devolution presupposes heavy centralization, and this has not been the case in America, political rhetoric notwithstanding. When looking at the present sad political, administrative, and institutional condition of the national government, some of us wonder whether a sufficient strengthening of its authority and capacity can be achieved if and when the challenges abroad and the monolithic business mergers and other sharp signs of unbridled private power at home necessitate it.

So the present state of our intergovernmental relations indicates there has been something of a real "rebirth of federalism" in the nineties. Yet the system is still a "conflicted" one, but not to the extent that it was in 1980 or even in 1992. The remaining chapters further highlight the dimensions of our current "Conflicted Federalism."

*Part 3*

# Some Dynamics
# of Today's System

## Chapter 7

# The Federal Judiciary:
# Centralizer or Umpire?

Each of the three earlier periods in the evolution of U.S. federalism revealed a significant, if not dominant, role for the Federal judiciary, and the current post-1960 period obviously is no exception. Any notions that the federal principle and intergovernmental relations are discrete and somehow disconnected, that the judges deal with the former but exert little impact on the latter, are swept aside by the Supreme Court's record of the past four decades. Moreover, the nearly complete demise of dual federalism and the concomitant activist tendency from the late sixties until now, with the early Reagan years and the first session of the Republican 104th Congress excepted, to shove nearly every type of public policy question — large or small, paramount or puny — into the intergovernmental arena were heavily conditioned, if not actually shaped, by decisions of the Court.

Although the activism of the Warren Court obviously predated 1960, it was the addition of four new members (Byron R. White, Arthur J. Goldberg, Abe Fortas, and Thurgood Marshall) by Presidents Kennedy and Johnson that strengthened the Court's libertarian and equalitarian tendencies. To a far greater degree than in the fifties, the Court of the sixties not only sanctioned controversial congressional enactments but assumed "a novel role as a leader in the process of social change quite at odds with its traditional position as a defender of legalistic tradition and social continuity."[1]

For the most part, the decisions "expanded Federal power fundamentally by placing much stricter limits on the states,"[2] and this centralizing tendency did not cease with the appointments of Warren E. Burger in 1969 or even of William H. Rehnquist in 1986 to the chief justice position. Yet some of the Warren Court and Burger Court cases, notably in the reapportionment, racial equity, and educational finance areas, had the effect of strengthening the states. One of the Court's most pronounced libertarians, Justice Hugo L. Black, in 1971 could still speak fondly of "Our Federalism" and of the necessity of understanding that "the entire country is made up of a Union of separate state governments."[3] He went on to caution in dual federalist terms that "the National Government will fare best if the States and their institutions are left free to perform their separate functions in their separate ways."[4]

The Court during some of the Warren and especially the early Burger years revealed some sensitivity to the concept of state autonomy in certain areas. At the same time, it also relied on such phrases as "cooperative federalism" and "state cooperation in a joint federal-state program" to underpin some of its decisions in the grants-in-aid area.[5] During the late Burger and Rehnquist years, much greater emphasis was placed on governmental and societal rights and less on those of individuals. In terms of the principal constitutional bases used to extend national authority, Congress's commerce, conditional spending (that is, the ability to enact grants for any purpose and with any conditions), and taxing powers were and are pivotal. In addition, the supremacy, necessary and proper, and the Fourteenth Amendment's due process and equal protection clauses must not be overlooked here. The guarantee clause of Article IV and the Tenth and Eleventh Amendments are used chiefly to protect states' rights. Federalism cases involve reconciling the conflicting values reflected in these two constitutional clusters with each other, as well as with other values embodied in other parts of the Constitution.

Finally, the Court on many occasions, especially during the sixties, appeared to be totally oblivious to the systemic effects of its decisions. The issue has reared its head again in the Court's present battles relating to efforts to overturn earlier liberal decisions. The following will attempt to ascertain how these varying judicial views on federalism fared with the "new" Warren Court (1960–69), with its successor under the uncertain leadership of Chief Justice Burger (1969–86), and the current tribunal headed by Chief Justice Rehnquist (1986–), initially overwhelmingly conservative but with the two Clinton appointees (Ruth Bader Ginsburg and Stephen G. Breyer) now moderately conservative.

## The Warren Court in the Sixties

### The Goals

Four basic commitments, as Archibald Cox pointed out, dominated the Warren Court and especially its decisions during the sixties: achieving greater racial justice, securing civil liberties, reforming criminal procedures, and strengthening political processes.[6] Far oftener than not, it was the states and their localities that were affected most directly by the Court's actions in these four areas.

What emerges from the Warren Court's record of the sixties is a Federal judiciary determined to end racial discrimination and segregation; to carry the protection of civil liberties to the outermost bounds of the individualistic ethic; to reform criminal-justice procedures totally; to afford new and controversial protections to the accused and to the convicted; and to establish an egalitarian standard for representation in all of the nation's deliberative bodies, save for the U.S. Senate. National judicial power was asserted in ways and by means never before contemplated or practiced. Frequently, the Court was ordering respondents, especially subnational governmental respondents, to do something, rather than simply negating what was held to be unconstitutional. Throughout, the Fourteenth Amendment became a vehicle for revising the Constitution and for transforming the federal system.[7] Not only the First Amendment but most of the procedural guarantees of the Bill of Rights were "absorbed" within it, and even new constitutional rights were found that could be brought within its orbit. The Warren Court generally "seemed to come down squarely on the side of progress for individual rights, even if these decisions were harmful to the principles of federalism."[8]

The basic dilemma that this reformist record raised was how far a tribunal whose authority ultimately rests on a historic national consensus regarding the nation's purposes, philosophy, and frame of government can move into essentially controversial political areas. Judicial lawmaking is as old as the system itself, but continuous lawmaking on several, not a few, controversial fronts suggests a faith in the results and in the stability of the system that many have questioned. If the Court serves as the steady instrument of social change, what, then, are the roles of a responsible citizenry operating through the representational processes and of the political branches of the national government, not to mention those of subnational units? To this, Warren Court defenders would query: How can an electorate that is not fully enfranchised make its individual and collective views known in the halls of power if the representational processes that constitute the means of expression of the views are flawed, given their favoring of only certain portions of the citizenry?

## Questions Raised

The Warren Court, more than any of its predecessors, furthered the cause of individuals' rights and racial justice but in the process left a legacy of institutional problems that its critics have highlighted and its defenders have argued were necessary and, in any event, only temporary. One result of the institutional dilemma was the cluster of problems the Court faced as a result of its particular style of activism. Its abandonment of the traditional "step-by-step process that long characterized the common-law and constitutional forms of adjudications" and its alternative preference for carrying nearly "every proposition ... to its logical extreme" and "to write codes of conduct rather than resolve particular controversies" were manifestations of this bold activism.[9]

Another manifestation was the Court's failure to acknowledge the weaknesses in its own structure: its difficulty in gathering the data required for the broad rule making, its difficulty in administering the broad rules it promulgated, and its difficulty in commanding the support of the political branches of the national government when its rules affected those who had not resorted to the judiciary for their protection — to cite only some of the more obvious.[10] Above all, perhaps, was the tendency of the Warren Court (like others, before and since) to ignore the counsel from Hamilton to Brandeis that a judge may advise and persuade, but should not coerce or comment.[11]

As this Court came to a close, its critics raised some fundamental questions concerning its record:

- Can individual liberty and social equity be merged in either judicial decisions or philosophic debate when the long history of both suggests that the concepts are antithetical, not complementary, and certainly not identical?

- Can the political branches of any level of government behave more responsibly if basic policy questions confronting them are judicially preempted?

- How successful can new judge-made laws be in changing citizen and official behavior when multiple counterefforts on diverse fronts are mounted at the same time?

- Can a federal system survive if the ultimate umpire of the system assumes that practically all of the subnational governments are undemocratic and if the principle of interlevel comity becomes the principle of preemption?

The Warren Court's defenders, on the other hand, point to several positive aspects of its evolution and of its decisions:

- While unanimously ruling against school segregation in perhaps its most famous decision, *Brown v. Board of Education,* the Court developed an implementation formula that was anything but radical or precipitous, thanks in part to the fact that four of its members were southerners.

- The doctrine of "a political question" is a "cop-out" when the political realm affords no means of resolving a basic institutional issue, as was the case with reapportionment.

- The nationalization of the Bill of Rights did achieve a revolution in Federal-state relations in that it extended the protections of the Fourth, Fifth, and Sixth Amendments to state and local criminal-justice systems, but the genesis of this effort began with Justices Douglas and Black, and subjecting the systems that administer the overwhelming majority of criminal-justice functions to a common standard of fairness arguably is an enhancement of the constitutional rights of the citizenry.

- The "substantive justice" that was achieved with the various decisions relating to criminal procedure, reapportionment, racial discrimination, and so forth justified the aggressive assertion of judicial power in some of these cases, and in most instances there was no other recourse, given the political and interest group system of the day.

- On the federalism issue, the Court did as much as any force in the land to rehabilitate the states and their localities; the old charges of their being racist (not all, of course), rurally dominated, and reactionary were no longer possible once the relevant decisions (sometimes with congressional help, as with voting rights) took root.

The Warren legacy has not been repealed by an ever more conservative Court in the nearly three decades that have elapsed since Earl Warren retired. Moreover, from the perspective of 1998, not 1969, one wonders how the advancement of these rights could or would have occurred in any other arena but the judicial, given the restricted and unresponsive character of many of the nation's political systems through to the midsixties.

# The Burger Court

In June 1968 Chief Justice Warren announced his resignation, to take effect once his successor had been confirmed by the Senate. President Johnson's appointment of Justice Fortas to the chief justiceship, however, was defeated by a Senate filibuster, and in December Warren indicated he would retire the following June. Judge Warren Earl Burger of the U.S. Court of Appeals for the Eighth Circuit was selected by President Nixon to succeed Warren. The forced resignation of Fortas in May[12] and the retirements of Justices Black and Harlan in September 1971 ultimately brought about three other Nixon appointments: Judge Harry Blackmun, Judge Lewis Powell, and Deputy Attorney General William H. Rehnquist. Some observers believed the five, along with Justice Potter Stewart, an Eisenhower appointee, would constitute a new conservative majority. The appointments of John Paul Stevens in 1975 by President Ford, following Justice Douglas's reluctant retirement, and of Judge Sandra Day O'Connor in 1981 by President Reagan only buttressed this impression for some.

## Continued, If Not Greater, Activism

Analysis of a cluster of key cases in the civil rights and civil liberties areas suggests an activism and sensitivity to the libertarian and racial justice norms nearly as great as, if not in a few instances greater than, its predecessor, at least during the seventies.[13] The decisions reflected no major retreat from the Warren Court's egalitarianism, especially when issues of racial justice were involved. Pretty much the same generalization applies to a range of civil liberty questions.[14] Most of its cases in the civil liberties and rights areas during the seventies indicate no major counterrevolution on the part of the Burger Court. If anything, they suggest strong lines of continuity and, in some instances, some logical (and liberal) extensions (as with the death penalty, antipatronage, abortion, and equal employment opportunity decisions). No special consideration was given to the states and their police powers here. Yet the Burger Court obviously was no carbon copy of its predecessor. Its own special positions and policy preferences, then, must be found largely in its decisions relating to other constitutional issues, particularly those relating to the scope of the provisions of the Fourteenth Amendment, and in its approach to its own procedures.

## Some Contrasts, a Different Assertiveness, and Some Sensitivity to the Federal Principle during the Seventies

One clearly identifiable area where the Burger Court instituted significant changes involved the procedural guarantees of the Bill of Rights. In a series of cases beginning in 1971, the Court began to narrow the Fourth Amendment's protections by limiting its exclusionary rule. As a result, it expanded the discretion of state and local law-enforcement officers.[15] Although *Miranda* was never overturned, its strict rules against forced disclosure of evidence by a criminal suspect were weakened, but not to the extent declared by the most vociferous critics of the Burger Court.[16] The right to counsel in pretrial interrogations, another *Miranda* standard, was also limited.[17] Yet the Warren Court's extension of the jury-trial right to all state criminal cases was further expanded during the transition to the Burger Court to cover petty misdemeanors punishable by six or more months' imprisonment.[18] Later decisions voided the twelve-person and unanimous-verdict requirements.[19] Both of these actions marked a rediscovered recognition by the Court's new majority that the diversity of state criminal justice procedures and practices need not lead to injustices.

With the new injunctive procedures initiated by the Warren Court, its successor in 1971 began to curb the availability of Federal injunctions against alleged state violations of civil rights.[20] In most of these cases, however, some form of state action already had commenced, unlike the situation in the earlier *Dombrowski* case (1965), wherein the Warren Court sanctioned Federal injunctive relief in a situation where no state prosecution was pending.[21] In a somewhat similar vein, the Burger Court severely curtailed Federal habeas corpus relief for prisoners who asserted Fourth Amendment violations.[22] Federal habeas corpus review of seizure-and-search assertions of convicted and incarcerated criminals had been pioneered by the Warren Court as a means of ensuring the "integrity of proceedings at and before trial where constitutional rights are at stake."[23] In *Schneckleth v. Bustamente* (1973), the Burger Court held that this "collateral relief" practice tended to ignore societal values that are significant for individual justice, including "(i) the most effective use of limited judicial resources, (ii) the necessity of finality in criminal trials, (iii) the minimization of friction between Federal and state systems of justice, and (iv) the maintenance of the constitutional balance upon which the doctrine of federalism is founded."[24]

In its decisions relating to pornography, the Burger Court stepped back from the "constitutional quagmire" its predecessor had created and been caught in. The concepts of a national community standard for obscenity was rejected, and trial courts were urged to gauge obscenity by local community values, which clearly vary from locale to locale.[25]

With school desegregation, the Court sounded no retreat but trumpeted a blast for busing. Yet when it confronted the question of approving a multidistrict affirmative action plan as a remedy for de jure segregation in a single district (Detroit), the strategy was rejected.[26]

In an entirely different area — state taxation as it affects commerce — the Court in 1976 upheld state levies on all imports, as long as they "were imposed equally on all goods foreign and domestic" and were not applied to goods still in transit.[27] Decisions to the contrary going back for more than a century were overruled here, and the states clearly were strengthened as a result.

The Burger Court's handling of Federal preemption marks another area of contrast with its predecessor. In a number of cases, the Court permitted state law "to govern questions thought preempted by the national lawmaking power."[28] All of these decisions had the practical effect of expanding the authority of the states' police power. Yet this trend was by no means consistent or across the board.[29]

In its reapportionment cases, the Burger Court was less literally equalitarian that its predecessor. Slightly larger disparities in the size of electoral districts were upheld than would have been permitted in the sixties.[30] Moreover, the "one-man, one-vote" rule was not extended to invalidate various extraordinary majority requirements.[31]

Of critical import from the vantage point of those concerned with the federal principle during the seventies was a small cluster of cases wherein the Court refused to extend Federal authority. In the pivotal case *San Antonio Independent School District* v. *Rodriguez* (1973), the Burger Court by a 5–4 vote refused to hold that the local-property-tax method of financing public education necessarily operated to the disadvantage of some "suspect class." Whatever discrimination that might arise as a consequence of unequal property values in various school districts is relative, not absolute; hence, the equal protection clause does not require "absolute equality or precisely equal advantages."[32] The Court, however, noted that all state constitutions had an equal protection or comparable provision, and this was the appropriate basis for settling the educational financial equity issue. Subsequently, several state suits were initiated.

The Burger Court also was cautious in automatically holding that sex is a suspect classification in state statutes.[33] Moreover, in a cluster of local zoning cases, the Court reflected a significant "degree of deference to referendums and other forms of state and local government decision-making designed to distill and reflect the particular will of local majorities."[34] It left to the states and localities the task of deciding the proper balance between majority wishes and minority rights in the zoning area, just as it did in the educational finance realm.

Of greater significance was the Court's dismissal in 1978 of the appeal generated by a ruling of the Pennsylvania Supreme Court that state laws forbidding the state treasurer from disbursing Federal aid funds unless they have been specifically appropriated by the legislature do not violate either the state or U.S. Constitution.[35] During the seventies, the question of legislative appropriation of Federal grant monies had become a major issue between the executive and legislative branches of certain states (and some localities) as the proportion of state (and local) revenues coming from Washington grew. In addition to this separation of powers issue, Federal-state questions also were raised because some grants (in the instant case, the 1968 Omnibus Crime Control and Safe Streets block grant) focused on executive branch recipients and overtly or tacitly ignored the state legislature. The Court dismissed the appeal "for want of a Federal question." In effect, the traditional theory of a grant-in-aid was used here to reject the appellant's claims that the supremacy clause and the intent of an act of Congress had been subverted by the state statute.

Finally, in the most controversial federalism decision in the seventies (*National League of Cities* v. *Usery*, 1976), the Supreme Court voided the 1974 amendments to the Fair Labor Standards Act that extended the wages and hours provisions of that act to nearly all state and local employees.[36] Justice Rehnquist in writing the majority opinion held that such an extension displaced the states' discretion to structure "traditional governmental functions" and thus interfered with functions essential to the states' "separate and independent existence."

Some of the Court's liberal critics dubbed *National League of Cities* an aberration that would be corrected by later decisions or the addition of another liberal justice to the Court; others viewed it as a welcome signal that the Court finally had begun recognizing the need for federalism-based constraints on what theretofore had been a largely unchecked congressional power to regulate state conduct and to impinge on state autonomy.[37] It was the later correcting case option that proved accurate. By 1981 the question of whether *National League of Cities* was a "glass half full, or half empty" prompted the retort that it was a "smashed glass."

### The Later Burger Court, 1978–86

Beginning in the late seventies and early eighties, some surprising decisions were handed down, thanks in part to the growing moderation of certain Nixon and Ford appointees — especially Justices Blackmun, Powell, and Stevens — and the coalition-building skills of Justice Brennan, the most senior and one of the most liberal members remaining on the Court.

By the late seventies, for example, a shift took place from the Court's earlier efforts led by Chief Justice Burger to curb the judicial activism generated by heavy use of Section 1983 as a basis of plaintiffs' appeals. The legal foundation of these actions is found in Section 1 of the Civil Rights Act of 1870 ("The Ku Klux Klan Act"), now codified as U.S.C. Section 1983. In modern times, the section has been extended beyond cases of racial discrimination to include almost any kind of alleged deprivation of a constitutional right.[38] By the mid-seventies, Section 1983 actions had produced a "flood of litigation" against state officers in the Federal courts. In 1976 roughly a third of all "private actions" (that is, not by or against the United States or its officials) were civil rights suits asking for constitutional protection against state and local officials. The complaints ranged from dress codes in schools to conditions in mental hospitals and prisons. This was the background against which the Burger Court initially began to rein in the reach of Section 1983 (for example, by excluding states and municipalities as "persons" under the section; by deferring to state courts before accepting jurisdiction; and by defining the underlying substantive Federal right because Section 1983 is merely a process for enforcing such rights; if no such right is involved there is nothing to enforce).[39]

By the midseventies civil libertarians were complaining of the Court's Section 1983 decisions, and a corrective omnibus measure was introduced in Congress in 1977. But a year later the Court overturned the holding in a major earlier decision (*Monroe v. Pape*)[40] that a municipality could not be sued under Section 1983.[41] In *Owen v. City of Independence*,[42] it ruled that municipalities being sued under Section 1983 may not plead as defense that the governmental official involved in an alleged wrong had acted in "good faith" (a defense that the official could make if sued personally). And in *Maine* v. *Thiboutot* (1980), the Court dramatically decided that the plaintiffs (a family denied welfare benefits) could use Section 1983 to seek redress of claims based generally on Federal statutes.[43] All these decisions triggered strong conservative dissents that cited the resulting perils to local and state governments. To indicate its awareness that threats to state and local finances could result from such cases, the Court in 1981 held that a judgment against a municipality need not include punitive damages.[44]

In an entirely different area, *municipal antitrust liability,* the Burger Court during this period decided a cluster of cases that, in effect, placed localities under certain circumstances within the purview of the Sherman Anti-Trust Act.[45] Until the seventies, the act was deemed to be directed against private, not public sector, parties. But in *City of Lafayette* v. *Louisiana Power and Light Co.* (1978), the Court decided that the city could be exempt only if the alleged anticompetitive practices fell within the state authorization.[46] Two years later, a California statutory plan for pricing wine was held to be a violation of the Sherman Act. And in the famous *Boulder* case (1982), the chartered Colorado city had acted to stop expansion of a local CATV in order to ascertain the possibility of greater cable company competition. The Court ruled the city's moratorium was not exempt from antitrust scrutiny, and the state's delegation of home rule powers did not constitute the "clearly articulated and affirmatively expressed" grant of state authority required by the *Lafayette* decision.[47] More than two hundred localities faced antitrust suits in the wake of *Boulder.*

Another area in which the seemingly unlimited power of the national government has been manifested is *the conditional spending power.* The Warren Court did invalidate certain conditions relating to receipt of welfare benefits,[48] but throughout the Burger years Federal courts adhered to their deference to Congress in this sphere of ever increasing Federal-state-local interaction. In a time when the conditions appended to grants became more intrusive, no Federal court action was taken to reduce or constrain this basic threat to conventional cooperative federalism. While praising the virtues of a balanced federalism in other areas, the courts upheld Federal grant conditions that — among other things — mandated public sector collective bargaining in a state where it was barred by state statute,[49] required state government reorganization and/or the creation of new state agencies,[50] directed the bypassing of states in distributing Federal grant funds to local school districts despite a state prohibition of such,[51] required welfare recipients to submit to warrantless home inspections,[52] and stipulated living arrangements of food stamp recipients.[53] The Court in 1984 also sanctioned conditions that required recipients of Federal educational aid to register for the draft, even though late registration involves self-incrimination and the possibility of criminal prosecution.[54] Despite the violations of civil and states' rights in various of these aid requirements, the Court throughout the Burger era refused to curb Congress's increasing propensity to utilize grant conditions for intergovernmental regulatory purposes. Under any other guise, at least some of these provisions would have been found unconstitutional.

This review of Section 1983 cases, municipal antitrust liability cases, other commerce power regulatory cases, and conditional spending power cases decided during the later Burger years (1978–86) underscores a continuing centralizing propensity of the Federal judiciary in many areas of crucial concern to advocates of a more balanced system. All of this occurred during a period that was ostensibly conservative and with a Court sensitive to state prerogatives.

Obviously, *this centripetal propensity did not extend to Court decisions in all areas.* In the antitrust area, some authorities have seen a return to a "deferential federalism" in the Court's efforts during the later Burger years to develop and apply tests that sort out private activity, which is subject to Federal antitrust laws, from state public activity, which is exempt under the "state action doctrine."[55] In three cases decided near the end of the eighties, the Court held that when a sovereign state acts directly, a state action exemption exists as an automatic result. But in the remaining instances wherein a state delegates regulatory authority to a municipality, a state agency, or an individual, the Court modified its earlier tough review test in favor of a lenient process review before a state action exemption was accorded.[56]

In certain Section 1983 cases, the broad scope of *Thiboutot* was narrowed somewhat. The leading decision here was *Pennhurst v. Halderman* (1981), in which the Court held that the Developmentally Disabled Assistance and Bill of Rights Act of 1975 did not create a substantive right in favor of the mentally retarded to "appropriate treatment" in the "least restrictive" setting because the act did not specifically grant it.[57] As a result, the Court was not obliged to answer the question of whether, assuming such a substantive right, there would be a private right of action under Section 1983 to enforce it. Two months later, in the *Middlesex* case, the Court utilized the "exclusive-remedy" approach to limiting Section 1983 suits.[58] The two statutes involved — the Federal Water Pollution Control Act and the Marine Protection, Research, and Sanctuaries Act — expressly authorized private persons to bring citizen suits to enjoin statutory violations, and these, the Court held, supplanted the remedy otherwise available under Section 1983.[59]

In light of the accelerated pace of *Federal preemptions* in the past two decades (one hundred in the 1980s alone), the Federal courts inevitably became involved. Preemption, or the displacement of state law by Federal law based generally on the supremacy clause and specifically on the commerce power or the necessary and proper clause, takes place when Congress overrides a state statute.[60] Preemptive intent is not clearly ascertained unless Congress includes an "express" declaration in the pertinent act. Yet this is not always the case, and the Court has found that preemption may be "implied" when the pervasiveness of the Federal regulation leaves no room for state supplementary action. Or it may be rooted in "conflict" when Congress has not totally displaced state regulatory authority, but to the extent that conflict arises between the two, the Federal regulation prevails.[61] Over the long history of Federal preemption, the Court has shifted from the general position of finding broad preemptive intent on the part of Congress (that is, prior to the New Deal) to one wherein preemptive intent had to be "clearly indicated" in the statute (the thirties), to a return favoring implied congressional preemption (the forties), to the current period, in which the Court has once again sought to narrow the standards under which Federal takeover may be presupposed.

Increasingly, the Court has adhered to the so-called dual compliance doctrine, according to which less emphasis is placed on whether a state law frustrates some broad Federal purpose and far more emphasis is given to ascertaining whether conformity with both Federal and state law is literally impossible.[62] Thus, in the now-famous *Silkwood* v. *Kerr-McGee* case (1984), the Court had to balance the states' traditional authority to afford tort remedies to their citizens against the Federal government's express goal of maintaining exclusive regulatory authority over the safety features of nuclear power.[63] The Court decided that Congress's silence regarding remedies for radiation injuries and its failure to establish Federal recourse for persons injured by corporate nuclear misconduct were sufficient basis for permitting state-authorized redress. In the *Pacific Gas and Electric Co.* case, the Court upheld a California statute establishing a moratorium on certification of new nuclear plants pending development of ways of disposing of high-level radioactive waste.[64] Again a unanimous Court deferred to a traditional state power, recognizing that although national preemption of the nuclear field was total, the state's economic reasons for the plant stoppage lay outside the Federally occupied field. By not inferring preemption in the face of congressional ambiguity in these implied preemption cases, the Court raises the question "Is this compatible or in conflict with *Garcia?*" Legal scholars come down on both sides. But the fact that state authority is being upheld, however tenuously, is unarguable.

Yet another field where the states have been aided is the Court interpretation of the *dormant commerce clause,* which assumes no particular congressional role but instead relies on the commerce clause itself as a prohibition of discrimination against interstate commerce, regardless of its form or method.[65] In cases involving this clause, the Court, in effect, makes legislative determinations as to whether this or that form of commerce requires exclusive regulation. Beginning around 1976, the Court started to fashion a "market-participant" exception to the clause. In *Hughes* v. *Alexandria Scrap,* it ruled that where a state acts not as a regulator but as a "purchaser," it frees itself from dormant commerce scrutiny because without a congressional enactment, nothing in the clause prohibits a state from participating in the market and utilizing the right of favoring its own citizens.[66] In two later cases, *Reeves* (1980) and *White* (1983), the Court clarified its position in *Alexandria Scrap* by holding that a state seeking immunity from the clause must play a role analogous to a private trader (not a public regulator) and that a state has the right to act as "guardian and trustee" for its citizenry.[67] Some qualms about its collective position in these cases was reflected in the *South Central Timber* case (1984), wherein a plurality of the members refused to grant exemption to Alaska's stipulation that timber produced within the state must also be processed there, citing the foreign commerce dimension of the issue.[68] From one perspective, the Court's dormant commerce clause jurisdiction has produced a historic and theoretical quagmire;

from another, it constitutes a means of protecting certain state interests, albeit within bounds.

The record of state and local governments as direct parties before the Supreme Court is another area where these governments fared well with the Burger Court, both in the seventies and the eighties. Witness the fact that there was a tripling of their appearances as appellants before the Court from the early sixties to the eighties. A quantitative analysis of some 6,800 areas stretching from 1953 to 1989, involving state and local governments voluntarily as respondents appearing before the Court, underscores their increasing success rates as the Burger years unfolded and especially in cases where they appeared as appellants.[69] Only minorities, unions, and the national government exceeded their record of case victories in appellant cases. The state and local government success rate in decisions where they were respondents was surpassed only by that of the national government.[70] In terms of the character of these cases, steady improvement was made during the seventies and eighties in the criminal procedure and civil rights areas; their improvement over the sixties in the First Amendment and economic issues cases slipped during the eighties; and a ragged record on federalism decisions prevailed throughout.[71] All this suggests that with the changes in the Court's membership, in the very character of state governments themselves — thanks in part to some Court-instituted reforms and to the growing willingness of states and localities to litigate — subnational governments overall have fared much better during the Burger (and Rehnquist) years than the federalism focus of this and other analyses would suggest. Yet the outcomes of the federalism decisions in the final analysis determine the constitutional status of state and local governments under the system, and that remained bad until the early nineties.

Finally, the emergence of a "new judicial federalism" during this period can be interpreted only as another good omen to those worried about greater balance in the system. Partly as a result of certain Supreme Court cases that were interpreted by some as "retreats" on the civil rights and liberties fronts and partly as a result of other Federal court cases that encouraged state assertiveness, states, beginning in the seventies, rediscovered their own Bills of Rights and placed increasing reliance on them. Acting on "independent and adequate" state constitutional grounds, a state supreme court can grant greater protection of rights under its own declaration of rights than the U.S. Supreme Court deems permissible under comparable provisions of the U.S. Bill of Rights.[72] Since 1975, according to John Kincaid, there have been more than five hundred such state supreme court decisions, thus prompting the "new judicial federalism" designation. Under it, the U.S. Supreme Court cases involving the national Bill of Rights establish a national standard of protection, and the states may not fall below this level, but they may raise rights to a higher plane and set standards in areas not touched by Supreme Court or congressional protective actions.[73] Beginning in the seventies, then, and continuing to the present, Madison's "double security of the rights of the people" has — for the first time — found actual expression in the judicial area.

The most notable action in the federalism field taken by the Burger Court in the eighties dealt with the commerce power. In regulatory actions under this power, the Court began to clarify the meaning of *National League of Cities* and, in effect, began its evisceration.[74] In the *Hodel v. Surface Mining and Reclamation Association* case (1981), the Court attempted to explain its position in the earlier decision by constructing an elaborate "Tenth Amendment Test":

First, there must be a showing that the challenged statute regulates "states as states." Second, the Federal regulation must address matters that are indisputably "attributes of state sovereignty." And third, it must be apparent that the states' compliance with the Federal law would directly impair their ability "to structure integral operations in areas of traditional functions."[75]

A year later, the Court found that the operation of interstate passenger and freight railroads and mass transit systems was traditionally a private, not a public, function,[76] and in one major lower court decision it was held that a local transit authority receiving Federal grant funds was subject to the wages and hours provisions of the Fair Labor Standards Act.[77] Yet in other cases, there were words of warning about a "static historic view" of what was a "traditional" state or local function. Nonetheless, the historical factor continued to condition Federal judicial determinations throughout the early eighties.

Perhaps the clearest clue as to the ultimate fate of *National League of Cities* came with *Equal Employment Opportunity Commission v. Wyoming* (1983), in which the Supreme Court in a 5–4 decision ruled that the extension of the Age Discrimination in Employment Act (ADEA) to cover state and local governments was a "valid exercise of Congress' powers under the commerce clause."[78] Such action was not precluded by the external constraints imposed by the Tenth Amendment, even though the operation of a state park (the plaintiff was a game warden who was facing mandatory retirement under Wyoming law) was conceded to be a "traditional state function." But the Court's majority contended that the state had failed to show that the ADEA would directly impair its capacity to structure its "integral operations." The issue then was not the stark fact of Federal intrusiveness but rather the degree of its intrusiveness.[79] *National League of Cities's* dicta clearly were not determinative here.

Finally, in 1985 the Supreme Court specifically overruled *National League of Cities* in *Garcia v. San Antonio Metropolitan Transit Authority*.[80] By so doing, the Court virtually abandoned any specific constitutional defenses against national regulation of state (and local) functions. "If there are to be limits on the Federal Government's power to interfere with state functions — as undoubtedly there are — one must look elsewhere to find them," wrote Justice Harry Blackmun for the five-person majority. That "elsewhere" was to be found in the national political processes:

[T]he Framers choose to rely on a Federal system in which special restraints on Federal power inhered principally in the workings of the

National Government itself, rather than in discrete limitations on the objects of Federal authority. State sovereign interests, then, are more properly protected by procedural safeguards inherent in the structure of the Federal system than by judicially-created limitations on Federal power.[81]

Liberals and others viewed this decision as a necessary elimination of the exceptional *National League of Cities* decision and as a mere codification of the conventional Court treatment of Congress's use of the commerce power since the New Deal Court. Pragmatists were worried about its cost to state and local governments, which some asserted could amount to $2–$4 billion annually. Conservatives and others castigated the case on several grounds, including (1) its violation of the basic constitutional precept that no branch of government should be the final judge of its own powers; (2) its denial of the Court's fundamental systemic role as umpire in disputes between the national and subnational governments; (3) its embodiment of the worst fears of the original critics of the Constitution that the states ultimately would be relegated to a "trivial role"; and (4) its apparent unawareness of the fundamental fact that in the areas of political and representational federalism, the states and localities have not enjoyed a potent position for well over a generation now.[82] More will be said about this in a later chapter.

## An Assessment

As the foregoing suggests, the Burger Court, especially during the seventies, was neither completely unmindful of its role as inheritor and interpreter of its predecessor's racial justice and libertarian legacy nor oblivious to some of the institutional difficulties that this legacy generated. Hence, there was no real retreat from the Warren Court's defense of the First Amendment and of the equal protection clause, especially in matters involving racial justice. The Burger Court, however, was less prone to place all of the procedural guarantees of the Bill of Rights on the same plane as the First Amendment or to apply them with the same degree of vigor as its predecessor in order to constrain the police power of the states and their localities. Moreover, the Burger Court was more sensitive to the concept of state autonomy than its predecessor ever was, in part because some of the reformist decisions of the latter now permitted such a stance and in part because more of its members trusted the states.

In any event, some sense of the older judicial concepts of intergovernmental comity and forbearance clearly are reflected in the Court's efforts to bar Federal court interference in state judicial proceedings in order to protect individual constitutional rights and to narrow the scope of constitutional protection in decisions wherein a state or local government might be found in violation of a right protected by the Fourteenth Amendment. Court attempts to gauge the possible effects of its decisions on state and local governments in its approach to remedies for still other alleged constitutional violations (as it did in *Milliken v. Bradley*)[83] further illustrate this concern with judicial comity.

Other pro-state Burger Court actions, taken mostly during the eighties, included efforts to narrow the scope of Federal preemptions, the number and reach of Section 1983 cases, and the breadth of the dormant commerce power. Throughout the Burger years, state and local governments appeared more frequently before the Court, especially in the role of appellant, which involves Court acceptance for review of a state's appeal, an action that usually signifies a willingness to reexamine, if not overturn, an earlier decision.

Yet continuing and new centralizing actions were taken by the Court: *Garcia's* dramatic overturning of *National League of Cities;* the rapid growth in Section 1983 cases, especially during the late seventies (even as the chief justice was attempting to curb actions that circumvented state judiciaries); the extension of Federal antitrust coverage to local governments; the Court's upholding of intrusive national regulations (as in *EEOC* v. *Wyoming* and *FERC* v. *Mississippi*, which upheld a Federal statute requiring state utility officials to consider and implement certain Federal regulatory standards);[84] and its failure to begin setting some curbs on the increasing congressional tendency to use its conditional spending power for regulatory purposes. When the pro-state and pro-local are placed opposite the pro-national decisions on the scale of federal systemic balance, the tilt clearly was still very much toward Washington when the chief justice stepped down. As with its predecessor Court, the overall record of the Burger Court raises some basic questions, but of a different kind:

- How can judicial conservatives reconcile their desire to achieve certain ideological goals requiring the overruling of earlier "liberal" decisions with their conservative institutional concerns that such actions, especially when numerous and frequent, can undermine the image, integrity, and institutional continuity of the Court?

- How realistic or relevant is it to discuss judicial philosophies and tests of Court fitness in "activist" as opposed to "strict constructionist" or "deferential" terms? Is not the plight of the federal system today in part due to the Supreme Court's long-term, essentially passive interpretation of the commerce and conditional spending powers of Congress (under liberal and conservative Courts alike) and to its activist stance (albeit more moderate of late) regarding the scope of the Fourteenth Amendment? Has not the combined result of these differing interpretative approaches been the further enhancement of national authority and a steady erosion of that of the states?

- How can the Court continue to perform its historic role of umpire of the federal system if it defers to a political system and the policy outcomes of that system that are heavily conditioned by centripetal forces that reflect no awareness of or concern for the indispensable roles of state and local governments in our contemporary system of governance?

# The Rehnquist (or Post-Powell) Court

A deeply conservative Court was seemingly established with the elevation of Justice Rehnquist to the chief justiceship in 1986 and the appointments of Antonin Scalia to replace him, of Anthony Kennedy to take Justice Lewis Powell's seat, and of David Souter and Clarence Thomas to fill the positions of the Court's oldest and most authentic liberals, Justices William Brennan and Thurgood Marshall. In point of fact, with the swearing in of Justice Kennedy, a Reagan Court was finally in place, but just as the president was ready to leave the White House. Not all of the many Reagan policy proposals involving the Court were implemented, and many opposition positions were sustained by it.[85] Nonetheless, major changes were expected by most students of this Court. As one authority put it, "With regard to the legal philosophy of federalism, the audience, though in some cases surprised at the *direction* of changes was not to be disappointed in the *extent* of change."[86]

## Unconditional Grant Conditions?

Shortly after the elevation of Justice Rehnquist, a major reiteration of the Court's nearly seventy-year-old interpretation of Congress's spending power occurred. Despite great changes in the regulatory, fiscal, and programmatic features of Federal grants-in-aid, the Federal courts have steadily adhered to the doctrine first enunciated in the 1923 cases: the decision to enter into a financial contract, being voluntary on the part of both parties, gives the grantor considerable discretion to attach the conditions it sees fit, provided the grantee "knowingly accepts the terms of the 'contract.' "[87] Hence, state and local parties to Federal grant programs have been denied relief from allegedly unconstitutional conditions on grounds that they voluntarily submitted to the Federal assistance statute; their participation was really at their option, and acceptance of the grant was not compulsory.[88] The conditional spending power, then, is deemed by many to confer a broader, more sweeping grant of power to Congress than any other provisions of Article I, Section 8. The implication is an insidious one for the constitutional goal of an ordered, balanced federalism, since it has been used to violate rights and to assert congressional authority in cases that otherwise would be found unconstitutional.

In *South Dakota* v. *Dole* (1987),[89] the Court upheld the congressional use of a "crossover sanction" as a means of encouraging states to raise their minimum drinking age to twenty-one.[90] The 1984 amendments to the Surface Transportation Act, known as the National Minimum Drinking Age Act, stipulated that 5 percent of a state's Federal highway monies would be withheld (note this program has a 90–10 cost-sharing arrangement) if the state failed to enact the necessary prohibiting legislation within one year after the bill's enactment and 10 percent if compliance was not achieved in the second year. In its challenge, South Dakota contended that Congress cannot bring about indirectly through conditioned spending what it cannot bring about directly through other enumerated powers. The Court rejected this argument out of hand, as it had in the past, contending that Congress may use its spending authority to achieve local objectives as long as its activities are (1) in pursuit of the general welfare, (2) unambiguous in that states are aware of the implication of participation, and (3) separate from constitutional provisions that may provide an independent barrier to the conditional grant of Federal monies.[91] To South Dakota's argument that the 1984 act was unconstitutional in that it violated the Twenty-first Amendment's provision that the regulation of liquor falls "squarely within the ambit of those powers reserved to the states," the chief justice, speaking for the Court, held that the "independent constitutional ban" (that is, the Twenty-first Amendment) was not a prohibition on the achievement indirectly of objectives that Congress could not effectuate directly. Rather, he contended, the language of "our earlier opinions stand[s] for the unexceptional proposition that the power may not be used to induce the states to engage in activities that would themselves be unconstitutional."[92]

At what point does the lure of Federal financial largesse turn into compulsion? In the *Dole* and *Nevada* v. *Skinner* cases,[93] the cutoff of Federal highway funds came, in practical terms, very close to a gun at the head of the legislatures. Yet the Federal courts ignored the actual degree of coercion. In *Clarke* v. *U.S.*[94] a Federal court for the first time did establish a limit in this area. At issue was Congress's appending to the District of Columbia's annual payment a requirement that specific legislation had to be enacted by the D.C. Council. Noting that previous conditional spending challenges had never reached a "level such as to render inevitable the state's submission to Congress' will," a U.S. district court held in *Clarke* that such conditions violated the free speech rights of D.C. Council members. A U.S. court of appeals upheld the district court's action.

The 1991–92 term of the Court produced another case dealing with a grant condition that infringed on the First Amendment. In *Rust* v. *Sullivan* (1991),[95] the Court upheld a highly controversial condition attached to an almost equally controversial Federal grant program. A sharply divided bench sanctioned executive-branch-imposed restrictions placed on the abortion-related speech of medical professionals working in Federally funded family planning clinics. The constitutionality of the "gag rule" was questioned on many grounds, including First Amendment rights, but the chief justice, speaking for the majority, held that a ban on specific medical advice did not violate the amendment, arguing that the government had "merely chosen to fund one activity to the exclusion of the other."[96] The sweep of the constitutional spending power is indeed broad and susceptible to constraints only in the most egregious circumstances. Again the now-ancient dictum of the *Mellon* case was restated:

> [G]rant recipients can choose between accepting Title X funds — subject to the Government's conditions that they provide matching funds and forgo abortion counseling and referral in the Title X project — or declining the subsidy and financing their own unsubsidized program. We have

never held that the Government violates the First Amendment simply by offering that choice.[97]

Thus was the broad scope of the conditional spending power demonstrated by a chief justice ostensibly concerned with a better balancing of state and national rights in the judicial sphere.

## Threatening and Assisting Tax Cases

Just before Justice Powell stepped down, another landmark case involving inter-governmental tax immunity was decided. In *South Carolina v. Baker,*[98] the Court held that the Federal income tax could be constitutionally applied to interest on state or local bonds. Any assumption that *Garcia* would be overturned or at least restricted to commerce power–related cases was swept aside by this re-markable decision. More specifically, South Carolina, supported by the National Governors' Association, charged that the section of the Tax Equity and Fiscal Responsibility Act of 1982 (TEFRA) that authorized withholding of the Federal income tax exemption on long-term bonds issued by state and local governments, unless such bonds were in registered form, was unconstitutional. Abrogation of the Tenth Amendment and violation of the doctrine of intergovernmental tax immunity were cited as the basic reasons for the charge. The Court by a 7–1 vote rejected both contentions. In response to South Carolina's assertion that in light of *Garcia's* political-process reasoning the sections of TEFRA in question were "imposed by the vote of an uninformed Congress relying upon incomplete information," the Court declared that "nothing in *Garcia,* or the Tenth Amend-ment authorizes courts to second-guess the substantive basis for Congressional legislation."[99] Regarding the intergovernmental tax immunity issue, the Court interpreted the doctrine to mean only that the national government is prevented from imposing directly certain taxes on the states and may not reach state bond income.[100] The decision clearly further weakened the constitutional defenses of the states and was enunciated in a way that reflected no serious assessment of the Federal issues involved. Only in Justice O'Connor's lone dissent was any consideration given to these issues.

A tax and civil rights case proved to be nearly as significant as *Baker.* In *Missouri v. Jenkins,*[101] the Court took the extraordinary action of upholding a U.S. district court order to a local school district to pay for the implementation of a magnet-school desegregation plan. Although some scholars found the case restricted wholly to the desegregated school sphere, others believed it potentially served as a major new weapon for the courts to enforce their decrees. This was the first time the Court upheld a direct mandate to a legislative body to raise funds for a specific valid purpose.

In two state tax cases, the Court adopted a permissive position. Michigan is the only state that has enacted a value-added tax (VAT), and an Ohio firm al-leged that the formula used to tax the portion of the company's receipts due to its business in Michigan as well as the VAT were significant interferences with interstate commerce.[102] The Court upheld the formula as being fair and the tax as not being an undue burden on interstate commerce. In *Leathers v. Medlock* (1991),[103] an Arkansas tax on cable television was also upheld. The Court found that although Arkansas taxed no other form of media, the tax was not a violation of the First Amendment rights of the cable television companies, in that the tax was one of general applicability and not based on program content. More recently, the Court in an 8–1 decision upheld Ohio's denial of state tax exemption for natural gas companies to nonlocal distribution companies.[104] Yet at nearly the same time, it voided a Maine tax provision that limited tax exemption for charitable organizations whose services primarily benefited out-of-state residents.[105] The basic argument made by the majority was that in isolation the provision in question posed no threat to the health of the national economy, but to sanction such "discrimination," Justice Breyer wrote, "would invite significant inroads on our national solidarity."

## Preemption

In the area of preemption, the Rehnquist Court pretty much adhered to its earlier stances. In two cases involving the Employee Retirement Income Security Act of 1974 (ERISA), the act's broad and express preemption provisions were recognized in Justice O'Connor's opinions and were upheld.[106] But in *Wisconsin Public Intervenor v. Mortier*,[107] the Court found that the Federal Insecticide, Fungicide, and Rodenticide Act (FIFRA) did not preempt local governmental regulation of pesticide use because the Court found no clear statement of Congress's intent to preempt and no clear and manifest intent indicating any implied Federal supplanting of local pesticide control. Moreover, Justice White, writing for the majority, found no actual conflict between the Federal and local regulators in the pesticide area. Thus, the earlier "dual compliance" test was met.

In its later cases, the Court continued on the course begun with *Silkwood.* In *Goodyear Atomic Corp. v. Miller*,[108] the Court upheld an Ohio constitutional provision requiring payment of additional damage awards if any injury resulted from an employer's violation of a state safety requirement as it applied to a worker in a Federally owned nuclear power plant. The relevant Federal statute authorized such action, the Court reasoned; hence, there was no preemption in this specific area, therefore no conflict. And in *English v. General Electric Co.*,[109] it was found that the state law claim of a nuclear plant employee for intentional infliction of emotional stress stemming from the alleged retaliation of his employer for his reporting of nuclear safety violations was not preempted by the Energy Reorganization Act of 1974 and did not conflict with that act's remedies. The Court in both these cases underscored the need for Congress, when preempting, to state its intent clearly and the specific area(s) of regulation it intends to take over. In one of its most recent preemption cases, the Court in *California Division of Labor Standards v. Dillingham* (1997) ruled against an employer's claim that the Employee Retirement Income Security Act of 1974 (ERISA) preempted California's wage law as it applied to apprenticeship programs.[110] Justice Thomas, writing for the Court's majority, declared: "Where federal law is said to bar state action in fields of traditional state regulation, we have worked on the assumption that the historic police powers of the States were not to be superseded unless that was a clear and manifest purpose of Congress." Not finding such a congressional intent, the Court proceeded to rule in favor of California and against extending ERISA's coverage to nonfederal apprentice programs.

## Section 1983

The Rehnquist Court's handling of appeals under Section 1983 revived some of the earlier Burger precedents and also carved out new ground. In *Wilson v. Seiter* (1991), the Court considered a prison case.[111] For two decades the Federal courts have intervened in cases brought under Section 1983 as they related to alleged unconstitutional deprivations in hospitals, mental health facilities, and prisons.[112] Resulting injunctive decrees placed the courts, most notably Federal district courts, in a position where they were intervening in state-run systems and were grappling with questions of program operations and funding. Thus, both federalism and separation of powers issues were involved, not to mention heavy-duty judicial activism.

In the instant case, the question was whether a prisoner must show more than "cruel and unusual" conditions for Eighth Amendment rights protection and also must demonstrate a "culpable state of mind" on the part of the prison officials involved in order to be entitled to relief.[113] The Court decided that proof of unconstitutional conditions was not enough and that at least the "deliberate indifference" of prison officials to such conditions also had to be shown. Ignoring the question of whether funding was adequate, the Court here set forth a standard — the need to inquire into the prison official's frame of mind — that will constitute a high hurdle to surmount in future challenges to alleged unconstitutional conditions in state facilities.

A very different Section 1983 issue was settled in *Dennis v. Higgins* (1991).[114] The section traditionally applied only to interests secured by the Constitution in general and the Fourteenth Amendment in particular. Beginning in 1980 with *Thiboutot*, however, the Court began to expand the scope of civil rights law to interests created by Federal statutes. This continued throughout the decade, and in the instant case the Court found that violations of the commerce clause may be brought under Section 1983 and that a lower court had erred in interpreting it too narrowly, in that a "broad construction of Section 1983" is "compelled by statutory language which speaks of deprivation 'of any rights, privileges, or immunities recurred by the Constitution or laws.'"[115] Regarding the commerce clause claim, Justice White writing for a 7–2 majority held that although it clearly is a substantive restriction on permissible state regulations, individuals injured by state action that violates this feature of the clause may sue and obtain injunctive and declaratory relief. The commerce clause, he asserted, was designed not merely to allocate power between the Federal and state governments but also to benefit those engaged in interstate commerce.

In *Suter* v. *Artist M*,[116] the Court returned to the issue of whether Congress created rights in one of its enactments that are enforceable against state agencies and officials under Section 1983 actions. The chief justice found that the Adoption Act of 1980 did not create enforceable Section 1983 rights in that its language at most directed that the states have a plan for "reasonable efforts" to assign case workers in a timely manner, which applied to all political subdivisions. But the act did not specify how such efforts were to be measured or how the state was to effectuate them. Hence, the Court found that Congress did not intend to create an implied cause of Section 1983 action in the act itself. The Court thereby continued its earlier course in regard to this issue.

In another Section 1983 case, the basic question was whether the estate of a municipal employee killed in an on-the-job accident may sue the city under the section.[117] The petitioner, the widow of the dead worker, alleged that the city's failure to train its employees properly was the cause of her husband's death and part of a policy of deliberate indifference to his constitutional rights. In a unanimous opinion, written by Justice Stevens, the Court found that because the plaintiff had failed to allege a constitutional violation, the case was not acceptable under Section 1983 and, further, the due process clause did not impose a duty upon municipalities to provide certain minimum levels of workplace security and safety. The plaintiff could not assert that the city deprived her husband of his liberty when he voluntarily accepted an employment offer.

*Hafer* v. *Melo* (1991)[118] posed the question as to whether personal liberty of state officials arose under Section 1983 when a newly elected auditor general of Pennsylvania fired several employees in her department. The Court in a unanimous opinion by Justice O'Connor held that state officials can be held personally liable for damages under Section 1983 based on actions taken in their official capacities, a decision here that tends to run counter to the restraining position taken on most of the other cases in this field.

### Civil Rights

During the first two years of the post-Powell Court, three highly controversial *civil rights* cases were decided. In *Wards Cove Packing Co.* v. *Antonio*,[119] in which plaintiffs alleged discrimination in hiring and promotional practices, the Court found that the burden of proof was on the plaintiffs to show a disparate racial effect but also that the effect was the direct result of the defendant's employment practices. This overturned *Griggs* v. *Duke Power Co.*,[120] which had placed the burden of showing the business necessity of such practices on the employer. In *Martin* v. *Wilks*,[121] the Court held that whites who were not parties to a consent decree in an employment discrimination case are permitted to make later challenges of enforcement actions pursuant to the decree. In *Richmond* v. *Croson*,[122] it limited set-asides of public works funds for minority contractors. State and local governments' reactions to the two decisions were very mixed because *Croson*, after all, involved overturning portions of a municipal ordinance. On the other hand, civil rights forces took alarm and mounted a congressional campaign to overturn these and related decisions. In 1991 after a previous presidential veto, the slightly modified Civil Rights Act of 1991 was signed into law, and these and other civil rights decisions were thus nullified. Yet in June 1995 the Court in its *Adarand* decision held by a 5–4 vote that the Federal government cannot rely on race alone as the criterion for awarding contracts.[123] This, in effect, reinstated *Croson* and the principle that to be constitutional any set-aside program must serve a compelling governmental interest and must be clearly designed to address past discrimination.

Still in the civil rights area but involving the Federal habeas corpus procedure were two cases — the opinions written by Justice O'Connor — that favored the finality of state proceedings. When a state defendant seeks to attack a state conviction through the Federal habeas corpus procedure by alleging violation of Federal constitutional rights, the Federal court must confront the potentially differing claims of two sovereigns: the Federal and state governments involved. In *Coleman v. Thompson*,[124] the petitioner raised several Federal claims in state habeas filings, and a number of claims were denied at the trial level. On appeal, the intermediate appellate court barred the claims on grounds that they were filed three days after the thirty-day filing requirement had expired. The Virginia Supreme Court dismissed the appeal but failed to indicate whether the dismissal was based on a review of the Federal claims or whether the state procedural filing requirement was not met. This is not a matter of splitting legal hairs; the Supreme Court will not review an appeal from a state where the state high court's decision was based on an "adequate and independent state ground" (here, the thirty-day filing requirement), even when a national constitutional issue is involved. Justice O'Connor held that because it was not clear that the state supreme court had rested its decision on Federal claims, it could be implied that the decision rested on a state procedural claim — an independent and adequate state ground — and thus the decision should not be overturned.

With *McClesky v. Zant*,[125] there was a further erosion of the "Great Writ of Liberty." The petitioner here had filed a postconviction relief action which among other items stressed the right-to-counsel issue. When relief was denied, he filed for Federal habeas corpus relief but did not include that claim in his appeal. The Supreme Court decided it would be an "abuse of the writ" now to allow review of the claim at the highest level. "Finality has special importance in the context of a Federal attack on a state conviction," the Court maintained. Reexamination of a state conviction on Federal habeas corpus "frustrates . . . both the state's sovereign power to punish offenders and [the state's] good-faith efforts to honor constitutional rights." Here was a resounding victory for a position former Chief Justice Burger had frequently enunciated, but it did not always prevail.

These habeas corpus decisions are significant because of their relationship to substantive United States constitutional law in the field of criminal defendants' rights. On the face, they appear to be dealing with mere technicalities, but in fact substantive constitutional claims to access to Federal courts are involved, and these have been diminished. In effect the Republican 104th Congress in enacting habeas corpus reform as part of its Anti-Crime legislation followed the

Court's lead in this matter. One of the most controversial provisions in the so-called reform bill required Federal judges to defer to state court rulings regarding what the United States Constitution means in this area, unless those state decisions are unreasonable.[126] Critics of this legislation have pointed out that it could easily result in undercutting the power of the Federal courts in maintaining uniform nationwide constitutional protections. This legislation nevertheless was passed and constitutional challenges arose almost immediately, since it raised the basic issue of the ability of prisoners to file for second and successive habeas corpus applications and changed the rules of procedure Federal courts utilize when considering such applications. A unanimous Court held in *Felker* v. *Turpin* (1996) that the act was constitutional and found no infringement on its own powers under Article III.[127] "The added restrictions which the Act places on second habeas petitions," the Court declared, "are well within the compass of this evolutionary (regarding access) process and we hold that they do not amount to suspension of the writ contrary to Article I, Section 9." So spoke a unanimous, if not unctuous, Court on a matter of crucial importance to its jurisdictional integrity.

Quite different was the Court's thrust in *City of Boerne, Texas* v. *Flores* (1997), which involved an extension by Congress of Federal power in the realm of religion.[128] At issue was the free exercise clause of the First Amendment and its ostensible support from the contentious Religious Freedom Restoration Act (RFRA) of 1993. This law was designed to bar the national government and the states from implementing laws in such a way as to undermine religious freedom unless a "compelling need" can be demonstrated for doing so. The case arose out of the efforts of a family parish to expand their church to accommodate their rapidly expanding membership. The proposed architectural changes encountered opposition from the city's landmark commission on grounds that the plans violated the preservation of the historic setting in which the enlarged church was to be erected. Parishioners claimed this constituted a denial of their religious freedom under the First Amendment, as reinforced by the RFRA. This conflict between states' (and local) rights and religious rights produced a 6–3 decision against RFRA. The Court majority found that the Act not only infringed on states' rights, thus undermining federalism, but also violated the separation of powers at the national level in that Congress went beyond its appropriate role to legislate "remedial and preventive" legislation of "confined scope" in order to correct past violations of constitutional rights inflicted by state actions. More importantly, the Court found that the act threatened the fundamental authority of the Court itself to determine the ultimate constitutionality of Federal and state laws. With this decision, both the states' police powers and the integrity of its own power of judicial review were upheld. Quite a contrast to the stance assumed in *Felker*.

The Court both favored and curbed state and local authority in a pair of speech cases involving politics. In *Austin* v. *Michigan Chamber of Commerce*,[129] a state campaign finance law that prohibited the use of corporate funds for expenditures for or against candidates running for state office was upheld. But in *Republican Party* v. *Rutan*,[130] the Court considered whether various political patronage practices — "promotion, transfer, recall, and hiring decisions" — as they relate to low-level public employees, may be based on political affiliation and support. It decided that the practices run counter to the First Amendment. Columnists as diverse as George Will and David Broder condemned the decision on grounds that it further weakened already feeble state and local party organizations.

In the early nineties, a cluster of civil rights and civil liberties cases were decided, not always in a conservative fashion. A New York State statute that barred criminals from profiting from their crimes by selling their stories to the media was found to be a violation of the First Amendment.[131] The act set up an escrow fund from the sales of such stories, which in turn was used to help satisfy civil judgments favoring crime victims. The eight concurring justices agreed that the law singled out speech on a particular subject — works by criminals about their crimes — and subjected it to a financial burden placed on no other speech. This was an unusual case with an unusual level of agreement on an issue that usually produced divisions.

In a major speech case, the Court held the St. Paul, Minnesota, ordinance outlawing "hate crimes" violated the First Amendment. The ordinance prohibited placing on public or private property a symbol that one has reasonable grounds to know arouses anger, alarm, or resentment in others on the basis of race, color, creed, or gender. The justices unanimously agreed that the ordinance violated the First Amendment, but that was all.[132] Writing for a five-member majority, Justice Scalia found that although the Court was bound by the state court's finding that the ordinance was limited to the unprotected category of "fighting words," the city could not single out particular kinds of "fighting words" because of hostility to their content. In other words, some "fighting words" were covered by the ordinance but not others, and the ordinance went beyond mere content to actual discrimination against certain viewpoints.

The Court in *Burson* v. *Freeman* (1992)[133] ruled as constitutional a Tennessee statute that prohibited campaigning activities on election day near the entrance to polling places. The Court held that although the act represented a "content-based restriction" on political speech and as such had to be subjected to exacting scrutiny, a long-standing consensus existed among the states that some restricted zone around polling places was necessary to protect the right to vote freely.

As a follow-up to the Voting Rights Act of 1965 as amended, the Justice Department in the late eighties and early nineties sought to persuade states when redistricting and pursuant to the act that they should assure that certain minorities are adequately represented. The focus of the Justice Department's strategy was to achieve the creation of "majority-minority districts," that is, districts whose boundaries are drawn in a way to encompass a population of which a majority are of minority group background. In the case of the Bush administration this strategy enhanced the prospect of increasing the number of Republican Congresspersons from the South. Beginning with *Shaw* v. *Reno* (1995), the Supreme Court paid close attention to the weirdly drawn electoral districts resulting from the Justice Department's ostensible civil rights concerns.[134] In *Shaw,* the Court held that North Carolina would violate the Fourteenth Amendment's equal protection clause if any of the redrawn districts in its plan primarily reflected race as the pivotal determinant of their respective boundaries. Such traditional electoral districting considerations as compactness and territorial contiguity were not to be excluded. Later in a Georgia case, the Court voided the state's plan because its Eleventh District clearly indicated near exclusive reliance on race in the shaping of its boundaries.[135] In 1996, a revised North Carolina plan was struck down for the same basic reason, and the same fate was experienced by a Texas redistricting proposal.[136] During its 1996–97 term, the Court upheld a revised Georgia plan that contained only one ostensibly "majority-minority" district, noting that all three black members of Georgia's congressional delegation were reelected in the 1996 elections despite the conversion of two of the districts into majority white ones. This, Justice Kennedy maintained, proved the weaknesses of the Justice Department's methodologies for calculating the likelihood of a black winning based on strictly racial percentages.[137]

## Roe *Revisited*

More obvious signs of the Court's new conservative cast were reflected in three cases that upheld state regulation of certain abortion practices and raised questions about the durability of *Roe* v. *Wade.*[138] In the most famous, *Webster* v. *Reproductive Health Services,*[139] Missouri's requirements for ascertaining the viability of the fetus before an abortion when the doctor has reason to believe the fetus is more than thirty weeks old were upheld. This amounted to a partial modification of *Roe* v. *Wade* because it permitted intrusion into the middle trimester of a pregnancy, during which state regulation is supposed to be restricted to protecting the health of the mother. Two state requirements for parental notification with a judicial bypass then were upheld.[140] All this generated great ferment among state legislatures as well as pro-choice and anti-abortion groups.

In the fall of 1992, the long-awaited case involving Pennsylvania's comparatively tough curbs on abortions was decided. *Planned Parenthood of Southeastern Pennsylvania* v. *Casey*[141] tells us a great deal about judicial coalition-building, conservative judicial philosophies in conflict, and the centrality of the Court when its interpretation of the Constitution calls upon the contending sides of a national controversy to end their national division by accepting a common mandate rooted in the Constitution.[142] It tells us less about federalism, although the reach of state authority in abortions was the basic issue at stake here. Five provisions of the Pennsylvania Abortion Control Act of 1982 were said by the plaintiffs to be unconstitutional. A U.S. district court agreed with them, and a U.S. court of appeals struck down the husband-notification provision but upheld the others. Justice O'Connor, joined by Justices Kennedy and Souter, delivered the opinion of the Court; Justices Blackmun and Stevens supported key portions of the decision but not others.

The crucial character of the case was noted at the outset: "Liberty finds no refuge in a jurisprudence of doubt. Yet 19 years after our holding that the Constitution protects a woman's right to terminate her pregnancy in its early stages . . . , that definition of liberty is still questioned."[143] The opinion then moves directly to *Roe*, and after considering the fundamental constitutional questions resolved by it, the "principles of institutional integrity, and the rule of stare decisis," arrives at the conclusion that "the essential holding of *Roe* v. *Wade* should be retained and once again reaffirmed."[144] The decision of a woman to terminate her pregnancy is protected by the due process clause of the Fourteenth Amendment, and this is a substantive, not a procedural, right.

Yet the state's important and legitimate interest in protecting the potentiality of life and "the health of this woman" was also recognized in *Roe* and in this case. But these state interests must not produce regulations that can constitute an "undue burden." Among those sanctioned were requirements that truthful information regarding the risks of abortion and childbirth be made available to the woman; that a doctor inform a woman seeking an abortion of the availability of materials relating to the consequences to the fetus; that there be a twenty-four-hour waiting period; that there be informed consent in writing; that in the case of a minor there be the consent of at least one parent, but with a judicial bypass where this proves necessary; and that clinics maintain records and provide reports on their activities. The notification-and-consent-of-spouse requirements were rejected. The landmark decision came about because Justices O'Connor, Kennedy, and Souter exhibited "an act of personal courage and constitutional principle," as Justice Blackmun noted in his concurring opinion.[145]

## Undercutting Garcia?

The most significant victory for federalism thus far in the record of the Rehnquist Court was *Gregory* v. *Ashcroft* (1991).[146] It was triggered by a challenge by two septuagenarian state judges to a Missouri constitutional mandate that state judges retire at age seventy. The actual decision, written by Justice O'Connor and in which seven justices concurred, held simply that the two Missouri judges fell within an exemption to the Age Discrimination in Employment Act (ADEA), thus permitting Missouri to prescribe retirement ages, unless such prescriptions violated the equal protection clause. Such was the core of the case. But the eloquent elaboration of federalist arguments to buttress the final conclusion was of an order rarely found in any Federal court decision during the three decades under review here. The Framers' dual sovereignty principle, its reiteration in *Texas* v. *White* (1869), and Madison's exposition on the limited nature of national powers were cited to highlight our federalist tradition. A listing of the perennial special advantages of such a system was made to indicate their contemporary relevance. "It assumes a decentralized government that will be more sensitive to the diverse needs of a heterogeneous society; it increases opportunity for citizen involvements in democratic processes; it allows for more innovation and experimentation in government; and it makes government more responsive by putting the states in competition for a mobile citizenry."[147]

Then came warnings that "one can dispute whether our federalist system has been quite as successful in checking government abuse as Hamilton promised" and that the supremacy clause "is an extraordinary power that we must assume Congress does not exercise lightly" — tongue in cheek here, no doubt, in light of Congress's accelerating rate of preemptions. Citing certain recent cases, Justice O'Connor concluded that "the States retain substantial sovereign powers under our constitutional scheme with which Congress does not readily interfere."[148] Here the central thrust of *Garcia* is blunted. The "authority of the people of the States" to establish the qualifications of their most important government officials is a "power reserved to the states under the Tenth Amendment and guaranteed them by that provision of the Constitution under which the United States 'guarantee(s)' to every state in this Union a Republican form of Government."[149] This second foundation for O'Connor's federalist defense of the states has become a gradually recurring theme in her opinions and may well serve as a new source of state constitutional safety. She clearly serves as the Court's most ardent defender of a more balanced federalism.

Three other cases of the nineties also relied on the Tenth Amendment and resulted in state victories. In *New York v. United States* (1992), by a 6–3 vote the Court found that the national government could not force a state that had not provided for the disposal of low-level radioactive waste produced within its borders to "take title" to such waste.[150] Justice O'Connor, again writing for the majority, declared that with the pertinent provision of the Federal Low-Level Radioactive Waste Amendments Act of 1985, Congress "has crossed the line distinguishing encouragement from coercion"; hence, it violated the Tenth Amendment. In his dissent, Justice White contended that the law "was very much the product of cooperative federalism" in that it "reflected hard-fought agreements among the states refereed by Congress." As its final case decided in its 1996–97 term, the High Court handed down *Printz v. United States* (1997), which voided that provision of the Brady bill that mandated background checks by state and local officials of prospective gun buyers.[151] Justice Scalia writing for the majority asserted:

> It is incontestable that the Constitution established a system of "dual sovereignty." Although the states surrendered many of their powers to the new Federal Government, they retained a "residuary and inviolable sovereignty." ... [S]uch commands [as the required background checks] ... are fundamentally incompatible with our constitutional system of dual sovereignty.

Justice Stevens in his dissent warned: "Unelected judges are better off leaving the protection of federalism to the political process in all but the most extraordinary circumstances," thus echoing the basic thrust of *Garcia*.[152] The executive branch subsequently began to establish its own national computerized background check clearinghouse.

In a very different Tenth Amendment case, the Court in *U.S. Term Limits v. Thornton* (1995) found that if the Founding Fathers had wanted term limits, they had ample opportunity to transfer the existing limiting provision of the Articles of Confederation and to insert it into the new Constitution, as they had done in various other instances.[153] The failure to do so, the majority held, must mean that they did not find term limits a new qualification that was appropriate or necessary. Moreover, the majority also interpreted the Tenth Amendment as covering only "the original power of sovereignty," thus going back to Justice Story's antebellum view that the Amendment reserves to the states only those powers that existed prior to the adoption of the Constitution.[154] Hence, an additional qualification for members of Congress cannot be deemed a "reserved power" since the national government did not exist prior to the Constitution. Because there was no "original power" in establishing Federal legislators' qualifications, the states cannot impute one. Here we have a nationalist, even a Hamiltonian decision producing a curb on the reach of the Tenth Amendment as well as a loss for those some deem to be "populist federalists."

The Supreme Court in *Seminole Tribe* v. *Florida* (1996) struck down a provision of the Federal Indian Gaming Regulatory Act of 1988, which allowed tribes to sue states in Federal courts to force negotiations over Indian gaming on reservations.[155] The Eleventh Amendment was cited as the basis for voiding the provision, in that it protects states from being sued in Federal courts by citizens. The Court conceded that Congress had plenary authority to legislate in the field of Indian affairs and the states had none. But the Court access provision of the 1988 law was found to be in conflict with the Eleventh Amendment protection. In so doing, the Court struck another blow against national authority in a currently heated area of public policy, which was repeated the following year.

Finally, perhaps the most striking blow against *Garcia* was the Court's decision in *United States* v. *Lopez* (1995).[156] Equally remarkable were the reactions of the political branches of the national government to the decision. This was only the second time since 1935 that Congress invalidated an act of Congress on the basis of the commerce power, and the first — *Usery* — was later overruled. The act in question, the Gun-Free Zones Act of 1990, was found to be in violation of this power in that both education and criminalizing fire arms possession have long fallen within the purview of the states' authority. Congress, the majority held, had not made clear findings as to the linkages between the two functions and interstate commerce. The chief justice in his majority opinion pointed out that prior case law was uncertain as to whether intrastate activities such as those involved in this case must "affect" or "affect substantially" interstate commerce in order to be regulated under the commerce power authority. Yet he concluded that the weight of precedent favored the latter, more restrictive interpretation.

The chief justice then set forth a four-part test for whether an intrastate activity "substantially affects" interstate commerce. These include (1) Does it fall primarily within the commercial or noncommercial sphere of activity? (2) Does it have an explicit connection with interstate commerce? (3) Did Congress make a formal finding as to the substantial burden that the intrastate undertaking imposes on interstate commerce? And (4) does the regulated activity result in a

Federal plenary police power by encroaching on a sphere of regulation heretofore left to the states?

*Lopez* was challenged almost immediately after it was handed down. The president and certain members of Congress, notably Senator Herb Kohl (D-Wis.) began to prepare corrective legislation that would meet the tests cited by the chief justice.[157] Legislation was introduced on 10 May 1995. Its declared basic purposes were to show the direct connection with commerce of the two intrastate activities affected by the bill and to make it clear that the proposed legislation in no way facilitated Federal regulation of education. The bill became law when the president signed the massive fall 1996 omnibus authorization measure. The remedial bill had been languishing after earlier hearings staged by a subcommittee of the Senate Judiciary Committee. But it was inserted into the massive spending measure with some members being in a state of ignorance regarding this legislative stratagem. It then became law when the president signed the omnibus legislation on 30 September 1996. Here we have a conservative Court decision set aside by a very conservative Congress and a centrist president. The questions now are whether follow-up cases will arise and whether the justices will stick to the four-part test. If they do, the new legislation probably will be negated, since it fails two of the four component test parts.

## The Rehnquist Court in Retrospect

The record to date of the Rehnquist tribunal is not quite as conflicting and inconsistent as its immediate predecessor's. The Court's interpretation of certain constitutional provisions that have been used steadily to chip away at the powers of the states are on a par with or in some cases more assertive than those of either the Burger or Warren Courts. For example:

- The conditional spending power has been upheld in cases that involved abrogations of state or individual rights that otherwise would have been declared unconstitutional under any other provisions of Article I, Section 8; the Warren Court exhibited more concern for the protection of rights and a restraining of Congress's intent to violate them in its conditional spending power cases, though the recent *Clarke* case suggests that outrageous congressional dictates could be curbed by the Federal courts.

- The reach of the commerce power vis-à-vis the states is not as expansive as it was when *Garcia* was decided, but Justice Rehnquist's dissenting promise of a fast overruling once the Court acquired a new justice has proved to be a hollow threat.

- The traditional doctrine of intergovernmental tax immunity has been scrapped by the Rehnquist Court, and some contend this is of more serious consequence to state and local governments than *Garcia*.

- The Court's negating of state-enacted term limits and Congress's attempt to expand the scope of religious freedom with RFRA indicated its capacity to resist varying dimensions of "populist federalism."

- The Court's discovery of a new body of rights, notably for business, under the commerce clause that are susceptible to relief under Section 1983 is another remarkable court action, as is the 1994 case in which a Clarkstown, New York, "flow control" garbage ordinance was invalidated for being in conflict with the "dormant" commerce clause.

- Finally, the Court's outlawing of patronage in low-level governmental jobs surely put the final nail in the coffin of the "political-question doctrine" in constitutional if not political terms.

On the more state-sensitive side of the ledger, many more signs of an emerging more protective federalism can now be detected than was the case even five years ago. This is despite the arrival of the Clinton appointees, the liberalization of Justice Souter, and the continuing liberal stance of Justice Stevens. Witness the following:

- The Rehnquist Court has continued and clarified the efforts of its two predecessors in the preemption areas by seeking a clear congressional statement of preemptive intent; by emphasizing the need for a clear delineation of the functional activities to be preempted; and by determining whether there is in fact a conflict between Federal- and state-authorized activities in the preempted program area under the "dual compliance doctrine"; all this is of aid to the states in the exercise of their police powers.

- In Section 1983 individual prisoner and state institutional cases, the Rehnquist Court has erected some high barriers for those seeking injunctive or declaratory relief from alleged violations of constitutional rights, all to the benefit of state judiciaries and the integrity of their procedures.

- Regarding Federal habeas corpus proceedings, the Court, with Congress later following its lead, also has adhered as rigorously as possible to the doctrines of interlevel judicial comity in such proceedings by stressing the legitimacy of state court actions based on "objective and independent state grounds."

- In a cluster of abortion-related and civil rights cases, there has been a curbing or even a rolling back of earlier decisions in these two areas, presumably to the benefit of state legislative discretion, though there are those who would deny this vigorously.

- The murky and still controversial dormant commerce power, although involving unilateral judicial determinations of constitutionality because no congressional legislation is involved, has in some cases expanded state discretion as a participant in commerce and in others denied it; yet it still must be labeled a pro-state development and in conflict with *Garcia.*

- Turning to *Garcia* directly, the Court's actions in voiding various Federal orders and mandates to states and localities as in *Ashcroft, New York v. United States, Lopez, Printz,* and *Flores* — all decided in the nineties, and four of them involving the Tenth Amendment — underscore the Court's gradual emergence as an umpire of the federalism system, not merely a perennial player on the national government's team.

- The Supreme Court's extraordinary upholding in *Missouri v. Jenkins* (1990)[158] of a Federal district court's decree that a school district must raise the revenues needed to implement a magnet school desegregation order was, in effect, set aside in a revisiting of the issues raised in the case in 1995.[159] The later case also left several other desegregation plans in limbo.

- The Rehnquist Court has continued the tradition of the Burger Court by being sympathetic to hearing state appeals and sanctioning the state position in several areas of concern to subnational governments, but the record of growing empathy has not been extended to some of the most crucial, namely, where there is a direct confrontation between the national and subnational governments. These include conflicts in the regulatory and mandating areas. Moreover, the states and localities inevitably lose in all cases involving the conditional spending power and in those containing clearly stated preemptions. Moreover, the recent 5–4 decisions setting some parameters around the commerce power have not involved crucial assertions of Federal authority, so there have to be some caveats raised about the recent judicial push to protect state rights.

- The federalist eloquence and principle expressed by Justice O'Connor in her *Gregory* opinion, exempting state judges from ADEA, and her revitalizing of the substantive significance of the Tenth Amendment and the guarantee clause of Article IV were perhaps the strongest indicators of some shift in Court opinion on the basic federalism questions (though only four other justices agreed with the federalist positions in her opinions).

To conclude this assessment of the Rehnquist Court, it seems clear at this point that while ambivalence and inconsistencies still exist in some judicial areas, a trend toward a somewhat greater sensitivity toward the states (and their localities) has clearly emerged during the nineties. This is not to say a parity of legal status implied in Justice Scalia's "system of dual sovereignty" has arrived. Far from it, most of the balancing cases have involved reining in the national government when it has acted in an arbitrary fashion through unilaterally imposed mandates and regulations. This in turn has helped to restore some of the trust between and among the levels that has been in such short supply during the past three decades. It also suggests that the Court itself has acquired a somewhat greater trust in the subnational governments, as well it might given its own major contributions to the reform of the states beginning with *Baker v. Carr* (1962).

# The Supreme Court in Retrospect

The Supreme Court, despite extraordinary changes in its membership, has chalked up a record over the past three decades indicating a degree of judicial leadership in so many areas of public policy that it is safe to state that none of its predecessors matched its degree of assertiveness. In effect, four very different interpretations exist as to the essential nature and direction of this record. The differences between and among the interpretations relate to the contrasting ideological stance of their formulators and their concomitant capacity to be highly selective in their reading of the cases.

With Nathan Glazer, a *neoconservative critique* of the Court emerged in the midseventies and continues to the present. For him (and others), there was little difference between the Warren Court and the Burger Court. Instead, the entire period was characterized by the emergence of a seemingly permanently activist, nonconservative Federal judiciary.[160] This continuing activism was a result of the decline, especially in the seventies, in "angry reaction from the people and legislatures," the favorable image of the Court projected by the mass media, the expansion of government itself (especially its regulatory role), and the proliferation of legal advocacy groups of all kinds. The continuing nonconservative course was rooted more in the need for the later Court to work out "the logic of positions...taken" by its predecessors and in the difficulty of withdrawing from the implications of earlier decisions. Both situations clearly confronted the Burger and Rehnquist Courts in their consideration of certain classes of cases. The record, then, suggests that this neoconservative view was partially correct, especially as it pertained to decisions of the Burger Court relating to racial justice and certain facets of the First Amendment but less to the Rehnquist Court, which, as it acquired more conservative members, showed a greater propensity to restrict Section 1983, Federal habeas corpus, and certain earlier Fourteenth Amendment civil rights precedents.

For *orthodox conservatives*, the failure of the Supreme Court, especially a conservative Court, to severely narrow Federal power, to strike a better balance in its weighing of national against state and local interests, and to provide the Tenth Amendment with a hard core of residual substantive content produced anger at and frustration with various key decisions in the eighties. Most notable among these, of course, were *Garcia, Baker, Croson,* and *Jenkins.* After *Garcia,* various efforts were mounted to place federalism on a firmer constitutional foundation. The commerce, conditional spending, and supremacy clauses were their chief constitutional focus of attention. In one such effort, four basic approaches to amending the Constitution were advanced as ways of resolving the "federalism contradictions" the Court had created.[161] These included (1) amending the Tenth Amendment to include a section requiring the Federal judiciary to decide questions of jurisdictional conflict between the levels; (2) adding to the Tenth Amendment a section that would detail specific criteria for determining the limits of congressional power vis-à-vis the states; (3) again adding new sections to the Tenth Amendment that explicitly prohibit Congress and the Supreme Court from requiring states "to take any action that is not otherwise required expressly and explicitly by this Constitution," from restricting the power of states under the commerce clause unless such law is expressly for the purpose of regulating the free flow of commerce, from interpreting the necessary and proper clause to mean convenient rather than absolutely necessary, from preempting when the takeover is not explicitly stated and without it the Federal law could not be implemented, and from enacting or upholding certain grant conditions; and (4) amending Article I of the Constitution to authorize collective state nullification of alleged unconstitutional national legislation and to limit Federal revenue-raising capacity.[162] The range of these proposed constitutional curbs on congressional and Supreme Court authority underscores just how frustrated constitutional federalists of the old school are with most developments on both fronts during the Reagan-Bush years. Parts of the Republican governors' "Williamsburg Resolves" (1994), the heavy constitutional thrusts of the recommendations advanced at the governors' "Federalism Summit" in 1995, and certainly the recent attempts on the part of congressional conservatives to enact legislation that would facilitate enforcement of the Tenth Amendment reflect some of the continuing frustrations of orthodox conservatives. Yet this frustration generates a purist perspective that tends to overlook the gradual but certain "conservative" achievements of the Burger and Rehnquist Courts: for example, the fact that 47 percent of all lower Federal court judges were Reagan appointees by 1988, the gradual narrowing of the number and scope of Fourteenth Amendment civil rights cases, the curbing of unfettered Federal preemption, the revitalizing of the dormant commerce clause, the gradual revitalization of the Tenth Amendment by the Court, and various other centrifugal developments of the nineties.

A simpler reform proposal still falling within this school of interpretation is that the Constitution should be amended to require a three-fourths vote of the Court before a state law can be negated.[163] And this writer in a moment of philosophic desperation not so long ago called for a constitutional amendment to sanitize the alternative state approach to amending the Constitution set forth in Article V so that all the current confusion about the procedures, the scope of a constitutional convention's agenda, and the role of Congress are clearly spelled out. Such an amendment would provide a traditional Madisonian correction to what now is a process dominated by Congress in its initiating phase.[164]

The Burger and Rehnquist Courts' *liberal* opponents have not been wholly in error. Their charge of a "retreat from the vigorous defense of liberty and equality" has not been entirely without foundation, though their assertion that "the primary victims of this shift in judicial attitude have been our society's oppressed" is subject to considerable doubt and debate.[165] The Burger Court's stance on habeas corpus and injunctive relief procedures and its less rigid stand on the need to incorporate all of the procedural protections of the Bill of Rights within the confines of the Fourteenth Amendment are what usually is cited to buttress this contention. The continuation of these practices along with its general treatment of Section 1983 cases, certain Fourteenth Amendment civil rights cases, the close judicial scrutiny given "majority-minority" electoral districts and their outlandish configurations, and even freedom of speech under the conditional spending power suggest an even greater retreat by the Rehnquist Court.

But what of the Burger Court's equalitarian decisions on busing, equal opportunity, compensatory educational programs, and the vote? What of its libertarian stands on abortion, speech, age discrimination, and the spoils system? The Court's explicit support for the "New Judicial Federalism" should also be noted here.[166] These cannot be dismissed in any overall assessment of the complex behavior of this divided Court. Fewer "individual rights" victories have obviously occurred during the Rehnquist years, though the *Rutan* (antipatronage), *Hafer, St. Paul, U.S. v. Virginia* (1966),[167] and *Casey* decisions must be classified as clear wins in this area, and the Court's "discovery" of commerce clause rights that may be protected by Section 1983 action also should not be ignored in this connection. In addition, institutional liberals clearly were delighted with the failure to overturn *Garcia,* the striking down of term limits, the curbing of the Religious Freedom Recovery Act, and the voiding of Colorado's 1992 Constitutional Amendment 2, which barred state legislative, executive, or judicial action to protect the status of persons based on sexual "orientation, conduct, or private relationships, and the continued elimination"[168] of intergovernmental tax immunity. Only by focusing on some decisions and by ignoring other equally significant ones can the liberal charge of judicial "counterrevolution" begin to be fully sustained. Neither the neoconservative, orthodox conservative, nor the liberal assessments tell the whole story, then.

A fourth perspective is provided by *those who assess the Court in terms of its capacity to balance institutional needs and individual rights* — to return to the basic dilemma raised by Cox in his analysis of the Warren Court nearly thirty years ago.[169] For some, like McFeeley, the Burger Court concerned itself more "with the protection of the traditional institutional relationships such as federalism."[170] In support of this view, the Court's decisions in the obscenity, fair labor standards, Federal preemption, privacy as it relates to personal reputation, and school finance cases were highlighted.[171] Also, the Court's efforts to restrict the jurisdiction of Federal courts by limiting class actions, Federal injunctive relief, and "standing" are cited as procedural ways by which the Burger Court, in contrast to the Warren Court, served to reduce the Federal judicial role in the interpretation and protection of individual rights. Yet though the evidence cited demonstrates a greater sensitivity to the Federal principle and to the notion of state autonomy than the Warren Court exhibited, it is at least arguable that civil rights and liberties did not fare that much worse and federalism that much better under the Burger regime of the seventies. For the eighties, one could argue that both civil rights (given the continuation of the restrictive rights trend cited above) and federalism (in light of *EEOC v. Wyoming* [1983], *Garcia* [1985], *Baker* [1988], and *FERC* [1988]) fared poorly.

In truth, however, the overall general record of the Burger tribunal during the period 1969–81 suggests rough continuing attempts at balancing institutional needs against individual rights, at reconciling societal concerns with minority protections, at toning down the Court's role of progressive and persistent law-making and elevating somewhat its traditional one of serving as a stabilizing agent for the entire system. The attempts inevitably infuriated both the liberal and conservative critics of this Court, given their respective mind-sets and fairly rigid values.

The balancing act, of course, was reflected in and was the by-product of the fairly diverse ideological makeup of the Court during Burger's first twelve years. The presence of two old-style liberals, two new-style conservatives, one unpredictable but tending conservative, one traditional moderate, two evolving moderates, and one "lawyers' lawyer" (that is, one who focuses on the facts of a case, assesses them in light of relevant precedents, and seeks to harmonize the two — Justice Lewis Powell) helps explain this. On different issues, there were different "swing persons," and on federalism questions the chief justice was as frequently in the minority as the majority.

With the changing composition of the Court during the eighties and the resulting shift to the right, the Court tended to place more emphasis on governmental authority and processes, social and governmental stability, and judicial intergovernmental comity. The statistical findings of the study cited earlier corroborate this trend; state and local governments achieved their greatest successes in the criminal procedure and civil rights areas during the eighties.[172] At the same time, their fewer successes in the First Amendment, economic, and federalism areas compared with the seventies suggest continuing conflicts relative to individual vis-à-vis institutional rights. The low federalism rating directly highlights the ongoing, if not increasing, success of the national government in cases in which it directly confronts state and local governments.

In the nineties, there appear to be at least two major judicial balancing acts being performed. The first involves the one that dominated the Warren Court and that has arisen again because the Court, especially since 1981, has come down so steadily on the side of governmental authority, processes, and immunity that one could conclude there has been an overreaction to the alleged libertarian and egalitarian excesses of the Warren era and even the early Burger Court. Hence, the reappearance of a conflict of individual rights against protective institutional actions.

The second balancing act, which obviously is being played out now in a more equitable fashion, is the continuing challenge to the Supreme Court to weigh national as against state and local interests in a way that does not reflect a persistent favoring of national power. The Court's support for "dual compliance" and clear congressional expressions of intent with preemptions; for lenient review of state actions protective of local governments in municipal antitrust proceedings; for the "exclusive relief" doctrine in Section 1983 cases and other devices for reducing the number of such cases; for developing a dormant commerce clause basis; for sanctioning a state participant role in certain aspects of commerce; for recently resurrecting the Tenth and Eleventh Amendments and citing the guarantee clause of Article IV as bases for providing substantive constraints on assertions of expanded national power; for exhibiting a deference to state judicial proceedings in various ways; for a greater receptivity to accepting and hearing state appeals; and, above all perhaps, the use of the mostly antebellum phrase "a system of dual sovereignty" in at least two decisions handed down in this decade — all reflect a new and growing Court awareness of state and local concerns and their indispensable operational role in the overall system of governance.

At the same time, the Court still adheres to powerful national positions in its interpretations of the commerce and conditional spending powers, the chief constitutional bases for the most dynamic and disruptive of all forms of current intergovernmental relations: the Federal regulation of state and local governments. Intergovernmental tax immunity was scrapped by a Court chaired by Chief Justice Rehnquist, and that case gave hardly a glance at the transcendent federalism issues raised therein. This Court's extension of Section 1983 relief to the economic areas even as it curbs the relief in the civil rights sphere also should be underscored here.[173] Of the twenty-two most important cases involving key federalism issues from 1980 to 1991, the Court favored the national government in fourteen. Most remarkably, of the fifteen decided since *Garcia* (1985), eleven were decided against subnational governments or bodies.[174]

Where stands this Court, then, on federalism? In 1993 one astute observer, after surveying the twists and turns of the Court since 1980, declared: "[T]he Supreme Court of the 1980's and early 1990's may be characterized in terms of its collective equivocation on questions of federalism."[175] Another view came in 1992 from Charles Wise and Rosemary O'Leary: "Is federalism alive in the Supreme Court? The answer to that seems to be, Yes. As with Mark Twain, the federalism principle can declare 'the reports of my death are premature.' Whether it is well, however, will depend on where the Supreme Court goes from here."[176]

From the vantage point of the late nineties, the judicial federal principle is stronger than it has been at any time since the retirement of Justice Felix Frankfurter in 1962. What is more, the Court, in effect, has curbed the basic remedial course enunciated in *Garcia.* Justice Blackmun in the majority opinion held that the states had ample opportunity to protect their Tenth Amendment rights by relying on their representational (lobbying) skills in Washington, D.C. The justice, of course, failed to concede that despite the presence of major generalist public interest groups (PIGs) in the nation's capital, neither singly nor in combination were they able to thwart most of the highly intrusive Federal regulatory mandates enacted in the seventies and early eighties. Moreover, the basic argument in the dissenting opinion of Justice Powell now seems to be accepted at least by key judicial and political policy actors. His warning in *Garcia* was an elemental Madisonian one: no branch of government alone should be able to determine the scope of its own powers. Hence, the Court should not abdicate its ultimate role of judging the constitutionality of acts of the Congress, the executive branch, and the states. The willingness of the present Court to void coercive acts and commandeering provisions of congressional legislation and to abandon its earlier deference to the national government's political branches in crucial areas of public intergovernmental policy signifies a new activism — one that contributes to the better health of our federal system. The only major exception is the Court's continued adherence to the de facto fictitious contractual interpretation of the conditional spending power. Here deference to Congress still persists. It is time for a greater realism in interpreting this now most centralizing provision of the United States Constitution.

# Chapter 8

# Fiscal Federalism:
# The Fateful Dynamic

One of the most important conditioners of the federal system today is the status of its public finances, which until quite recently were very uncertain.

## Galloping Public Sector Growth

Total governmental outlays soared from 1960 onward, but not at quite the same rate as during the years 1930–60. As a percentage of the gross domestic product (GDP),[1] the figure rose by 3.5 points during the sixties; by 2.2 points to 29.2 percent between 1970 and 1980; but rose to 31.9 percent in 1992. Then came a gradual decline from the 1992 watermark to 29.5 percent by 1997.[2] The overall 5.9 percent increase for the 1960–97 period, however, does not match the 1930–60 expansion.

On a per capita dollar basis, public outlays more than quadrupled between 1962 and 1980, and from 1962 to 1994 grew more than tenfold, slightly above the 9.4 rate from 1934 to 1960.[3] The total expenditure growth rate in constant dollar terms is even more striking. The 1960 figure had multiplied more than six and a half times by 1980 and fourteen times by 1991. It had reached a level by the midseventies that some economists found alarming and that some politicians brought into campaign debate. Reagan's domestic retrenchment efforts obviously were a failure, given the figures for the eighties. The 1.3 per capita dollar rate during the Bush and early Clinton years compares quite favorably with Reagan's 1.7 rate.

### The Intergovernmental Split

The manner in which the national public outlays were divided among the governmental levels, in terms of expenditures from their own funds (grants excluded), reflects some previous trends as well as some different developments. For example, although the Federal government had assumed the dominant overall fiscal position by the late thirties, it went on during the late sixties to ascendancy in domestic outlays as well: the Federal proportion had risen to 58.2 percent of these outlays by 1977; the combined state-local share was 41.8 percent (see table 8-1). After 1987, however, there was a steady though gradual

## Table 8-1
### Federal, State, and Local Shares from Own Funds of Total and Domestic Governmental Expenditures, Selected Years, 1962–94

| Calendar Year | Federal | | State | | Local | |
|---|---|---|---|---|---|---|
| | Total (%) | Domestic (%) | Total (%) | Domestic (%) | Total (%) | Domestic (%) |
| 1962 | 68.4 | 49.5 | 14.4 | 23.0 | 17.2 | 27.5 |
| 1967 | 68.1 | 51.1 | 15.9 | 24.4 | 16.0 | 24.5 |
| 1972 | 63.7 | 51.4 | 18.6 | 24.9 | 17.7 | 23.7 |
| 1977 | 67.2 | 58.2 | 17.9 | 22.9 | 14.9 | 18.9 |
| 1982 | 69.4 | 58.3 | 17.5 | 23.8 | 13.1 | 17.8 |
| 1987 | 69.1 | 57.7 | 17.2 | 23.5 | 13.7 | 18.8 |
| 1990 | 66.7 | 55.3 | 18.3 | 24.5 | 15.0 | 20.1 |
| 1991 | 61.6 | 45.8 | 20.9 | 29.5 | 17.5 | 24.6 |
| 1994 | 59.3 | 49.5 | 23.2 | 28.8 | 17.4 | 21.7 |

Sources: Adapted from Advisory Commission on Intergovernmental Relations, *Significant Features of Fiscal Federalism*, vol. 2, *Revenues and Expenditures*, 1993, M-185-II (Washington, D.C., September 1993), 58–59, 70, 72; and American Council on Intergovernmental Relations, *Significant Features of Fiscal Federalism*, vol. 2, *Revenues and Expenditures* (Washington, D.C., October 1997), 8, 9.

Note: Federal domestic outlays exclude outlays for defense, foreign affairs, and interest on the debt.

decline in the Federal share of total domestic expenditures, to the point that in 1994 it was less than the state-local proportion.

The earlier expansion in state expenditures continued fairly steadily. The states' 23 percent of the domestic total in 1962 had risen slowly to 23.5 percent by 1987, and to 28.8 percent by 1994. Local outlays show a less regular pattern: 27.5 percent in 1962; 23.7 percent in 1972; 17.8 percent in 1982; 24.6 percent in 1991; and down to 21.7 percent in 1994. In other words, the earlier gradual decline in the local share of the total governmental expenditures as a proportion of the total was halted only temporarily in the current period. State and local shares together were more than 50 percent of the total in 1994, matching for the first time their initial 1962 share, a most welcome development in terms of fiscal balance.

### Shifts in Federal, State, and Local Shares

The changes in the Federal, state, and local shares of total outlays and of domestic expenditures provide yet another way of highlighting certain broad intergovernmental fiscal trends of the current period. Unlike the previous three decades, the figures here reveal a slightly shifting but comparatively stable Federal share of total outlays, with only a 10 percentage point spread between the low mark in 1994 and the high one in 1982. In the domestic sphere, there was

Table 8-2
### Selected Federal Revenue Sources as a Proportion
### of Total General Revenue, Selected Years, 1960–95

| Year | Personal Income (%) | Corporate Income (%) | Social Security and Medicare (%) | Others (%) |
|------|------|------|------|------|
| 1960 | 46.8 | 24.9 | 12.2 | 16.1 |
| 1965 | 43.2 | 22.5 | 14.8 | 19.5 |
| 1970 | 48.1 | 17.5 | 20.5 | 13.9 |
| 1975 | 45.2 | 15.0 | 27.9 | 14.9 |
| 1980 | 49.1 | 12.9 | 28.0 | 10.0 |
| 1986 | 47.2 | 8.5 | 34.8 | 9.5 |
| 1989 | 46.2 | 10.7 | 35.2 | 7.9 |
| 1990 | 46.5 | 9.3 | 36.0 | 8.2 |
| 1991 | 45.4 | 9.5 | 36.7 | 8.4 |
| 1995 | 40.5 | 12.5 | 39.8 | 7.2 |

*Sources:* Adapted from Advisory Commission on Intergovernmental Relations, *Significant Features of Fiscal Federalism,* vol. 2, *Revenues and Expenditures, 1993,* M-185-II (Washington, D.C., September 1993), 58; and American Council on Intergovernmental Relations, *Significant Features of Fiscal Federalism,* vol. 2, *Revenues and Expenditures* (Washington, D.C., October 1997), 32.

a steady rise from the early sixties to the early eighties, then a gradual decline. The state proportion of domestic outlays, on the other hand, remained fairly stable during the first two decades, then experienced a gradual increase. The local share declined by about 9 percent but then began to rise irregularly, so there was only a 5.8 percent overall drop in the local share between 1962 and 1994.

If comparisons are made with the previous period, the stable state pattern appears to be a long continuation of what prevailed from 1929 to 1960. The local share also reflects a projection of the earlier trend line, but instead of a mere 5.8 percent decline, more than 32 percentage points must be subtracted from the 1929 figure. Moreover, the Federal share of domestic outlays not only surpassed the combined state-local proportion by the early sixties but the spread between them was more than 15 percentage points in 1982. By 1994 the gap was a mere .5 percent.[4] In terms of fiscal balance, these trends also look good.

## Revenue Sources: Changes and Continuities

In regard to specific revenue sources, the Federal government relied to an even greater extent on personal and corporate income taxes during the 1960–95 period than it had in the previous thirty years. This reliance was not all that steady, however. Personal income taxes during the 1960–95 period actually declined a bit, while the dependence on corporate income levies was cut by nearly two-thirds, thanks in part to the 1981 Tax Act (see table 8-2).

Contributions for social insurance have been another major source of Federal revenues (see table 8-2) since the early seventies, the second largest ($588 billion in 1995, or nearly 40 percent of general revenues). In the early fifties it had been the smallest of the big four (personal income taxes, corporate income levies, excise taxes, and contributions for social insurance). The change was caused by expansion of the nation's work force, changes in wage rates, enactment of Medicare, coverage of existing and additional social insurance programs, and periodic enactment of higher tax rates to finance liberalization of benefits (most recently, the 1982 Social Security bailout). Social Security, Medicare, and Medicaid are all facing most severe fiscal challenges.

The Federal government has also relied increasingly on another funding source: deficit spending. To a far greater degree than ever before (wartime years excepted), large annual Federal deficits were incurred from the late seventies to the late nineties. The seventies, in large part because of the recession of 1975 and 1976, inflation, and indexation of the entitlements, witnessed an annual growth in the deficit in percentage and absolute dollar terms that would have been unacceptable in the fifties and early sixties. Moreover, annual interest payments on the national debt soared from $8.9 billion in 1965 to $14.0 billion in 1970, up to $61.3 billion by 1980, and then to $202.7 billion by 1994. The last figure is more than twenty-two times its 1965 counterpart. It is now the third-largest expenditure item in the Federal budget, right after Social Security and defense; this is reflected in the ever increasing proportion that interest payments constitute in Federal budget outlays: 10 percent in 1980, 13 percent in 1990, and 21.9 percent in 1995. As a proportion of GDP, the Federal debt declined steadily from 111.8 percent in 1946 to 46.9 percent in 1960, then to 26.5 percent in 1980. But beginning in the eighties and continuing through to 1997, there was a steady and increasingly alarming soaring of deficit figures, from 34.1 percent in 1983 to 51.4 percent in 1995.[5] For many, this development was the preeminent challenge not only to our entire system of public finance but also to our entire system of governance because it mirrored a country politically out of control, though the recent balanced budget accord (1997) was most encouraging. Yet the tax cuts and spending hikes in this agreement along with the looming fiscal impact of the aging "boomers" on Social Security and Medicare as well as the inevitable downturn in the economy raise potentially serious questions about our capacity to sustain a favorable Federal budget balance in the near future.

## State Taxes: More Growth but Continuing Diversity

State taxes experienced major shifts during the most recent four decades, with the state share of the state-local total tax surpassing the local tax for the first time ever in the late sixties. The margin widened steadily from 4.6 percent in 1968 to 20.8 percent in 1977, down to 10.2 percent in 1994.[6] The sustained strength of both general and selected sales taxes and the significant hike in the income tax's share of total state taxes (22.4 percent in 1967, more than 38 percent in 1994) help explain the emergence of this dominance of state revenue over local (see table 8–3).

As the above suggests, the adoption of new state taxes during this period was a key factor producing this dominant fiscal position. Between 1960 and 1998, twelve states adopted personal income taxes[7] (joining the seventeen that did so between 1930 and 1960, and the sixteen between 1911 and 1929). Ten enacted corporate income levies (joining the thirty-seven, including Hawaii, that did so between 1901 and 1961).[8] In addition, eleven moved on the general sales front. These thirty-three major enactments helped produce a fiscal picture in 1998 in which forty-five states had an income tax (forty-two with a broad-based tax), forty-six a corporate income levy, and forty-five a general sales tax. Overall, thirty-eight states possessed all three of these levies in 1998, compared with nineteen in 1960.

The steep rise in state collections, especially in the seventies, prompted fourteen states in that decade to enact tax or expenditure lids (TEL); seven more did so in the eighties, and one in the nineties.[9] Of the twenty-two, ten lack a constitutional basis, which makes it easier to ignore them. All but four were passed in regions outside the Northeast and the Great Lakes. In addition to the tax and expenditure lids, six states in the late seventies (Arizona, Colorado, and California in 1978; Wisconsin, Iowa, and Minnesota in 1979), along with Utah in the eighties, indexed their personal income taxes. By requiring that certain fixed-dollar features of the income tax code be adjusted annually in light of the rate of inflation, these states sought to curb the collections "windfall" that occurs simply by inflation's capacity to push a family's income into a higher tax bracket. These various actions, then, along with the growing pressure for fiscal restraint in various of the states not enacting such measures, were expected in 1980 to produce some lowering of the rate of increase in state collections in the upcoming decade. State tax collections in 1980 were 2.7 times greater than in 1970, and the 1990 figure was only 2.3 times larger than that in the 1980s. The 1994 figure was 1.25 times greater than the 1990 one, suggesting a repeat of the seventies perhaps and certainly the eighties.

## Local Levies: Modest Diversification and More Limits

Among the local levies, the property tax has retained its traditional predominant position (see table 8-3). Yet the erosion in its earlier near-monopoly that began in the forties and fifties continued; its 86.7 percent share in 1957 had slipped to 80.5 percent by 1977, to 74.8 percent by 1994. The somewhat greater diversification of the local revenue base provides one explanation for this. In proportional terms, the sales tax share of total local revenues doubled between 1957 and 1994, but the local income tax share rose by only a little over 3 percent. The two combined accounted for less than 20 percent of total local general revenues in 1991 and 1994, but this was more than double the 1957 percentage. By 1976 twenty-two states had authorized some or all of their general units of local government to levy a sales tax; by 1991 the figure had risen to thirty-one. In 1976,

## Table 8-3
## Distribution of State and Local Revenue Sources, Selected Years, 1957–94

| | State | | | Local | | | |
|---|---|---|---|---|---|---|---|
| Year | General and Selected Sales (%) | Personal and Corporate Income (%) | Other (%) | General and Selected Sales (%) | Income (%) | Personal and Corporate Property (%) | Other (%) |
| 1957 | 58.1 | 17.5 | 24.4 | 7.2 | 1.3 | 86.7 | 4.8 |
| 1967 | 58.2 | 22.4 | 19.4 | 6.7 | 3.2 | 86.6 | 3.5 |
| 1977 | 51.8 | 34.3 | 13.9 | 11.1 | 5.0 | 80.5 | 3.4 |
| 1985 | 48.9 | 37.7 | 13.4 | 15.6 | 5.9 | 74.2 | 4.3 |
| 1990 | 48.9 | 39.2 | 11.9 | 15.3 | 5.7 | 74.5 | 5.5 |
| 1991 | 49.4 | 38.5 | 12.1 | 14.9 | 4.7 | 75.3 | 5.1 |
| 1994 | 49.8 | 38.2 | 12.0 | 14.9 | 4.6 | 74.8 | 5.7 |

*Source:* Advisory Commission on Intergovernmental Relations, *Significant Features of Fiscal Federalism*, vol. 2, *Revenues and Expenditures*, 1992, M-185-II (Washington, D.C., September 1993), 70, 72; American Council on Intergovernmental Relations, *Significant Features of Fiscal Federalism*, vol. 2, *Revenues and Expenditures* (Washington, D.C., October 1997), 72–75.

4,150 cities and 685 counties levied a sales tax; in 1991, 4,234 cities and 1,429 counties did so.[10] Municipalities in Alabama, California, Kansas, Missouri, Oklahoma, and Texas accounted for nearly two-thirds of the total in 1991; nearly two-thirds of the county total was collected in Alabama, Arkansas, Georgia, Kansas, Missouri, North Carolina, Ohio, Tennessee, Texas, and Virginia. Moreover, sixteen states now authorize some or all of their cities or counties to levy a local income tax. Nearly 3,000 cities and towns had an income or payroll tax[11] in 1976. The figure was roughly the same in 1991: cities, boroughs, and towns in Pennsylvania accounted for roughly three-quarters of the total; Ohio ranked second, with all of its 512 municipalities having a payroll tax; and Kentucky ranked third, with 87 cities taxing income. One hundred thirty counties, including all of the counties in Maryland and Indiana, now have access to this tax, more than twice the number in 1976.[12]

Another source of local revenues is selective sales or excise taxes, which more and more states have authorized for local use. By the late eighties, local taxes on transient lodging were permitted in forty-three states, on utility services in thirty-three, on amusement admissions in twenty, on alcoholic beverages in seventeen, on gasoline in fifteen, and on cigarettes in eight.[13] All this suggests a limited broadening of the local tax bases, and largely in about one-third of the states.

Still another factor explaining the lessening role of the property tax beginning in the seventies was enactment of various kinds of limits on its usage; seventeen states took such action in the seventies, most notably California with Proposition 13 (1978). In 1994, only six states had no limits. Fifteen had enacted limits on property tax revenue (in one case for counties only, in another for cities only); ten had local revenue rollback statutes; and three had general expenditure limits, in one case for cities only.[14] These newer, more stringent forms of state mandates and local revenue restraints were in part a reaction to the rapid rise in local property values and assessments during the seventies and eighties and in part to the comparative ineffectiveness of traditional property tax rate limits, which thirty states have legislated. When the old and new are combined, all but four states (all in New England) in 1998 have one or more forms of constraint on local property taxation.

## State-Local Tax Efforts

The rates and specific combination of various state and local taxes differ considerably from state to state, of course, just as they did in the previous period. Indices from the representative tax system model can be used as a measure of tax effort to highlight the differences.[15] Seven states (New Hampshire, Nevada, Florida, Tennessee, Arizona, Alabama, and Delaware) fell in the 66 to 85 range between 1967 and 1988, well below the national average (100); New York, Arkansas, and Wisconsin fell in the extraordinary 115 to 155 bracket, far above the average tax effort category.[16] In both groups the same effort trends can be traced back for at least a decade, with one exception. With the middling forty that fall within the 86 to 114 range, five (Massachusetts, Rhode Island, Hawaii,

New Jersey, and Arizona) experienced a 10-point or more reduction in effort between 1980 and 1988 (in one case by 37 percent and in another, 30 percent). Eight others (Ohio, Iowa, North Dakota, Louisiana, New Mexico, Oklahoma, Texas, and Wyoming) witnessed a 10-point hike, with Texas having a 23 percent increase during the eight-year period and Wyoming having a 20 percent hike.[17] All this suggests a range of state-local tax endeavors — some up and some down; some to correct for past excesses; some to make up for past parsimony. Compared with 1978, the number of states that fell below the 85 level was smaller in 1988 (by five), and the number above the 108 level was the same (eight). The overall typical tax bite of 7.6 percent of state personal income in 1953 had risen to 12.8 percent by 1977 but was down to 11.5 percent in 1990.

In the three earlier decades probed here, the combined results of revenue actions at both the state and local levels were that the total state-local tax burden rose almost 40 percent between 1961 and 1990. Most of the growth occurred in two periods: the late sixties and early seventies, and 1983–86.[18] Meanwhile, the Federal tax burden during the late sixties and early seventies rose by 10 percent (as a percentage of GNP) and then declined in the early eighties — due to OBRA and other developments — before leveling off. Without the resilience of the state-local revenue system during the eighties, the overall condition of public finance would have been infinitely worse.

In terms of the degree of deep dependence on one or another of the major direct taxes, nine states in FY 1990 put high emphasis on the personal income tax: Massachusetts, Delaware, Maryland, New York, Ohio, Minnesota, North Carolina, Virginia, and Oregon.[19] By FY 1994 the list included Kentucky and Wisconsin as well. All were four or more points above the national average. Low utilizers included the nine states with no or only a nominal income tax: New Hampshire, South Dakota, Florida, Tennessee, Texas, Wyoming, Alaska, Nevada, and Washington, as well as Alabama, Louisiana, Mississippi, New Mexico, and North Dakota (all of which are 9 percent or more below the national average rate of usage).[20]

In FY 1994 high general sales tax states included eleven states with rates of 4 or more points above the national average of 13.5 percent: Missouri, Arkansas, Florida, Tennessee, Arizona, New Mexico, Texas, Utah, Hawaii, Nevada, and Washington.[21] Of the forty-five states having a broad-based sales levy, eighteen as of FY 1994 did not exempt food. Nine states made no or only minor use of this tax: Delaware, Vermont, New Hampshire, Maryland, Massachusetts, Montana, Wyoming, Oregon, and Alaska. Few states make any significant use of the corporate income tax for the obvious reason that it can influence business location decisions. Those brave souls who ignore this potential risk are Connecticut, Massachusetts, Delaware, New York, Indiana, and Michigan (all of whom have a 3.5 percent or higher rate, the national norm being 2.6 percent).

Five of the six New England states plus four others — New Jersey, Illinois, Michigan, and Wisconsin — made heavy use (that is, 4 percent above the national average of 17.9 percent) of the property tax in FY 1994.[22] Of the remaining forty-one that have it, seventeen rely on it minimally (that is, 4 percent below the national average), nine of which are southern or border states. Another dimension of recent state revenue diversification has been increased reliance on nontax revenues (that is, user fees, lotteries, special assessments, mineral royalties, and interest earnings), beginning in the late seventies almost simultaneously with the numerous TEL enactments (tax and expenditure lids) and lasting through the 1990s. Such revenues soared by more than 300 percent between 1980 and 1990. Interstate differences, with all their equity, economic development, grant-in-aid, and servicing implications, clearly have not been eliminated by the tendency during this period of more states to adopt more balanced revenue systems.

## How Regressive?

Widespread state efforts were also made to render two of the main and more regressive components of state-local tax systems more equitable. By the mid-seventies, all states had enacted some sort of property tax relief measure, most of them by 1970. Forty-four are of the homestead-exemption type, thirty-four are of the "circuit-breaker" variety, and thirty-two states in 1994 had both versions. With homestead exemptions, reductions generally are by a certain amount (sometimes all) of the assessed valuation of a homestead to which the property tax is applied. The exemption may or may not be restricted to certain classes of beneficiaries (such as the disabled, veterans, the elderly), owner-occupants, or those with incomes below specified limits. Perhaps more to the point, almost half of the homestead exemption programs provide no reimbursement to the affected local governments, and in ten others state reimbursement is only partial.[23]

Like its counterpart in an electrical system, the "circuit-breaker" approach kicks in when there is an "overload," that is, when the property tax reaches a certain percentage of family income that the state deems to be onerous. More-over, the state finances the program either by a state income tax credit or by a rebate to the beneficiary so that affected local governments do not suffer revenue losses. Of the thirty-four state-financed programs in 1991, five began in the sixties, twenty-seven in the seventies, two in the eighties, and one in the nineties.[24] Nearly all of these enactments, it should be noted, occurred during the seventies, when property tax values and rates were rising rapidly. In addition to these efforts, of the forty-five states with a general sales tax in 1990, thirty-seven exempted food and drugs; seventeen of these exempted clothing as well. These overall figures represent a distinct improvement over their counter-parts of the late seventies.[25] In connection with the personal income tax, twelve states after the 1986 Federal tax reform removed the poor (those whose income placed them in the bottom fifth of all family categories) from their rolls, joining Louisiana, Mississippi, and New Mexico in this move toward greater tax equity.[26]

Despite these reforms, most states did not possess progressive state-local tax systems by the nineties. By determining the percentage gap in the proportion of family income allotted for state-local taxes between the 20 percent of the families in the lowest income bracket and the 1 percent in the highest, one

## Table 8-4
## Changes in Effective Federal Taxes, 1977–96
### (in Percentage Points)

| Income Group | Personal Income Tax (%) | Payroll Tax (%) | Corporate Income Tax (%) | Excise Tax (%) | Total (%) |
|---|---|---|---|---|---|
| **Bottom Four-Fifths** | −2.2 | 2.4 | −0.9 | −0.1 | −0.8 |
| First | −6.3 | 2.6 | −0.6 | 0.1 | −4.2 |
| Second | −1.7 | 2.1 | −0.9 | 0.0 | −0.5 |
| Third | −0.8 | 2.1 | −1.0 | −0.1 | 0.2 |
| Fourth | −0.8 | 2.7 | −1.0 | −0.2 | 0.7 |
| **Top Fifth** | 0.3 | 2.4 | −1.7 | −0.2 | 0.8 |
| 81–90% | −0.6 | 3.1 | −1.0 | −0.2 | 1.3 |
| 91–95% | −0.6 | 3.4 | −1.2 | −0.2 | 1.4 |
| 96–99% | −0.3 | 3.2 | −1.8 | −0.3 | 0.8 |
| Top 1% | −0.8 | 1.8 | −3.8 | 0.0 | −2.8 |
| **All** | 0.1 | 2.4 | −1.2 | −0.2 | 1.1 |

CBO projections of 1996 income levels under 1996 tax law are used here.

*Source:* Lawrence Mishel, Jared Bernstein, and John Schmitt, *The State of Working America — 1996–97*, Economic Policy Institute (Armonk, N.Y.: M.E. Sharpe, 1997), 121.

can measure progressivity. In no instance in 1991 did the highest-income family in any state pay a larger proportion of its income in combined state-local taxes, for the elemental reason that the majority of those taxes (the personal income excepted) are not based on income as such (see table 8-4). The question here is, to what extent do state-local revenue systems rely on progressive levies in a meaningful though modest fashion? The seven most progressive state-local systems in 1991, as indicated by their having only a zero to 2.5 percentage point gap between the lowest and highest family-income groupings, were, in rank order, Vermont, Hawaii, Maryland, Montana, Delaware, Minnesota, and Oregon. With Vermont there was no gap; with the others the highest figure was for the lowest-income family group.[27] A moderately progressive group, with a 2.5 to 5 percent gap, again with the lowest tax share going to the highest-income family, included, in rank order, Alaska, North Carolina, and Maine. The least progressive, that is, the states in which there was a gap of more than 10 percent, included Texas, Washington, South Dakota, Tennessee, Illinois, Pennsylvania, Florida, and Connecticut.

Some of these differences reflect traditional contrasts between and among the fifty state-local systems in terms of revenue and expenditure preferences. Others reflect responses to the fiscal challenges these jurisdictions had to face in light of the 1990–93 recession as well as cuts in the midnineties. The variations here among the fifty states seem to outweigh the commonalities suggested by the emergence of more balanced state-local revenue systems and efforts to render sales and property taxes less regressive.

The foregoing generalization applies with comparable force to the taxes imposed by local government. The pressure during the seventies and eighties of nonschool taxes on a per capita basis, for example, was heaviest in the central cities of the East, heavy in the West, somewhat lighter in the Midwest, and lightest in the South. The most recent study of central city as against outside central city per capita total taxes indicates, however, a continuation of the long-term trend of some gradual decline in the tax disparities between cities and their suburbs,[28] thanks to increased and better-targeted educational aid, the emergence of inner-ring suburbs with "leveling-down" problems, greater revenue diversification, and central city revitalization in some cases.

## The Toll on the Taxpayer

Perhaps the most vivid evidence of the overall impact of the many changes that have taken place in intergovernmental finances during the current period is their effect on the citizenry. First, in terms of international comparisons, the United States' total tax revenues as a percentage of gross domestic product came to 29.7 percent in 1997, compared with 25.8 percent in 1965 and 28.8 percent in 1979. The comparable figures for nineteen other Organization for Economic Cooperation and Development (OECD) nations exceeded the 1993 U.S. figure. Only three of the twenty-four nations' totals fell below the U.S. percentage: Japan, Australia, and Turkey.[29] Federal taxes have become much less progressive since 1977 because of the mix of a less progressive personal income tax, higher Social Security payments, and a lower incidence of corporate taxes. The 1981 tax legislation began the erosion in the Federal revenue system, and although the 1986 tax reform restored some progressivity to the system, it was not enough to make up for the prior tax cuts, as reflected in Federal rates between 1977 and 1996 (see table 8-4, p. 221). Such rates for the bottom 80 percent declined by 0.8 percent. But the rate also fell for the top 1 percent by 2.8 percent. OBRA '93 hiked income taxes for the wealthy, but it left Middle America largely untouched. This injected slightly greater progressivity into the system.

A comparison of Federal and state-local tax burdens from 1959 to 1994 highlights the growing role of the latter in the overall family tax burden (see table 8-5). For reasons noted earlier, the trend only adds to the overall regressivity because these jurisdictions depend to a far greater degree on regressive levies than does the national government, though the latter's tendency of late is to pursue a similar revenue course (see table 8-6).

Even with OBRA '93, all this means that the burden of government now, to a greater degree than in the seventies, is primarily on middle-income and lower-middle-income Americans. It means that the overall revenue system is still regressive, despite state-local diversification efforts. It means that the overall tax burden is modest especially for the wealthiest compared to most

### Table 8-5
### Federal versus State and Local Tax Revenue as a Percentage of Gross Domestic Product, Selected Years, 1959–94

| Year | Federal (%) | State & Local (%) | Total (%) |
|------|-------------|-------------------|-----------|
| 1959 | 17.9 | 7.5 | 25.4 |
| 1967 | 18.3 | 8.9 | 27.2 |
| 1973 | 19.1 | 10.5 | 29.6 |
| 1979 | 20.0 | 9.8 | 29.8 |
| 1989 | 19.8 | 10.3 | 30.2 |
| 1994 | 19.9 | 10.8 | 30.7 |

Source: Lawrence Mishel, Jared Bernstein, and John Schmitt, The State of Working America — 1996–97, Economic Policy Institute (Armonk, N.Y.: M.E. Sharpe, 1997), 102.

### Table 8-6
### Tax and Nontax Revenues as a Percentage of Gross National Product, Selected Years, 1959–94

| Type of Tax | 1959 (%) | 1967 (%) | 1973 (%) | 1979 (%) | 1989 (%) | 1994 (%) |
|-------------|----------|----------|----------|----------|----------|----------|
| **Progressive**[a] | 13.0 | 12.7 | 13.2 | 13.9 | 13.0 | 12.7 |
| Federal | 12.3 | 11.7 | 11.4 | 11.9 | 10.6 | 10.4 |
| State & Local | 0.7 | 1.0 | 1.8 | 2.0 | 2.3 | 2.3 |
| **Regressive**[b] | 12.3 | 14.2 | 16.1 | 15.5 | 16.7 | 17.3 |
| Federal | 5.5 | 6.5 | 7.6 | 7.9 | 9.0 | 9.1 |
| State & Local | 6.8 | 7.7 | 8.5 | 7.6 | 7.8 | 8.2 |
| **Nontaxes**[c] | 0.2 | 0.3 | 0.3 | 0.3 | 0.5 | 0.6 |
| Federal | 0.1 | 0.2 | 0.1 | 0.2 | 0.2 | 0.3 |
| State & Local | 0.1 | 0.1 | 0.1 | 0.2 | 0.3 | 0.3 |

a. Personal and corporate income taxes; estate and gift taxes.

b. Customs, excise, sales, and other taxes; property taxes; contributions for social insurance. Other taxes include vehicle licenses, severance taxes, etc.

c. Fines, certain fees, rents, royalties, tuition, hospital fees, etc.

Source: Lawrence Mishel, Jared Bernstein, and John Schmitt, The State of Working America — 1996–97, Economic Policy Institute (Armonk, N.Y.: M.E. Sharpe, 1997), 130.

advanced countries. The political implications of each of these by-products of our revenue-raising systems cannot be ignored; they have been almost with impunity so far.

## Some Summary Observations

What do the various trends and shifts in intergovernmental finance mean? Among other things, they show that

- the Federal government began this period with a much stronger revenue system than that of the states and localities, but during the past three decades, the state-local systems (especially the state component) achieved a greater degree of strength and resiliency than they had possessed in 1960;

- the heft of Federal finance in the sixties was based on its reliance on the broad-based income tax, the responsiveness of this levy to conditions of economic growth and inflation, the growing acceptance of deficit spending, the separate system for financing social insurance, and the ability to shift funds from defense to the domestic sector; by the late seventies the earlier illusion of a Federal cornucopia was beginning to disappear because of the troubled condition of the Social Security system, the growing demands of the Department of Defense, and mounting concerns about inflation, Social Security taxes, Federal spending generally, and Federal deficits specifically;

- during the eighties and early nineties, the widening Federal expenditure-revenue gap, the continuing rise in entitlement costs and in revenue shortfalls because of the 1981 OBRA and despite four fairly major tax hikes, the resulting escalation in costs of servicing the national debt and cleaning up the savings-and-loan scandals, and an anemic economy from 1989 through the early nineties made the feeble state of Federal finances the number-one issue for most observers of the Washington scene; these factors prompted initially the Bush-congressional 1990 budget agreement and subsequently the Clinton 1993 budget victory, these two acts of courage that along with Federal Reserve decisions and business restructuring had a lot to do with the rolling economy we have enjoyed since 1994;

- the growing state-local fiscal strength was a by-product of the emergence of more balanced and somewhat less regressive tax systems in thirty-eight states, the emergence of the states as the senior[30] partner (that is, the state accounts for 55 percent or more of combined state-local revenue) in all but seven instances (as of 1994, with two still acting the junior role [New Hampshire and New York] and five others only barely over the line), the rise of the income tax as a major state revenue resource, and the moderate rise in local fiscal efforts;

- despite this picture of growing state fiscal power, many states have experienced and continue to confront strong pressures because of their heavy tax, Medicaid, corrections, and education burdens; their constitutionally stipulated balanced budget requirements in all but one case; and the earlier slow or nonexistent growth in their economies, which has now evaporated;

- state revenue systems have become more responsive to economic growth and less in need of rate hikes in "good" or inflationary periods, thanks to the growing reliance on income taxes (17 percent of the FY 1994 total general state revenues);

- local revenue systems have become somewhat more diversified, have relied somewhat less on intergovernmental fiscal transfers — given the gradual rise in own-source revenues during the eighties — and have provided a declining local proportion of overall domestic outlays, until the late eighties when the trend was reversed;

- tax effort and tax burdens still vary widely among states and among localities within states, even though state per capita income differentials have narrowed greatly;

- most major cities in the Northeast and Midwest are in worse fiscal condition than most of their counterparts in other regions,[31] though New York, Boston, Cleveland, Indianapolis, and Columbus have all recently experienced something of a renaissance;

- the view of the late fifties and early sixties that the public sector was starved has returned; even with servicing cuts and far better program management than before, wide gaps between revenues and expenditure needs continued in some states and at many local levels, with the national government continuing a decremental pattern of domestic aid program funding and most state governments, until quite recently, having to rely on servicing cuts, tax hikes, or both;

- finally, the public's clear preference for a range of governmental services and benefits and its equally strong preference for low taxes are a basic conditioner of this fiscal crisis. They have contributed to the greater reliance on regressive (not-so-visible) tax levies and the severe difficulty in cutting certain services. The intergovernmental fiscal system and the politics that sustain it have a desperate need to end this schizoidal citizen syndrome and to confront head-on the paralysis that projected Social Security and Medicare deficits can produce at all levels, especially the national. Enactment of the 1993 Clinton budget package and the 1997 balanced budget agreement were really only a first down payment.

# Intergovernmental Fiscal Transfers: Dramatic Expansions, Then Some Constraints

As the foregoing analysis suggests, the explosive growth in intergovernmental fiscal transfers from 1964 to 1978 signified shifts in Federal outlays, radically reshaped both the revenue and expenditure actions of state government, and provided the fastest-growing revenue source for most local governments during the sixties and seventies. During the Reagan-Bush years, the rate of grant expenditure growth was much lower than in the seventies, but there was not the absolute permanent rollback that had been envisaged by OBRA in 1981. The great growth in grant outlays during the Reagan-Bush years, of course, was in the Medicaid and food stamps programs, with Medicaid alone soaring from 17 percent of total Federal aid in 1980 to 42 percent by 1992 but down to 40 percent by 1995. This kind of program development with its increasing matching demands on state budgets and the accompanying cuts in Federal discretionary grants (i.e., aid for state and local programs, not entitlements) illustrates the basic point that Federal grants may be as much of a burden as they are a source of help. The administrative, programmatic, regulatory, and political implications of these extraordinary Federal aid developments — as much as their fiscal implications — have conditioned and characterized much of this period's intergovernmental relations.

## State Aid

Although attention all too frequently focuses on Federal assistance programs, the state aid story cannot be ignored. It tells much about the role and increasing fiscal and operational strength of the states in this period, and it highlights intergovernmental trends that both differ from and parallel Federal aid actions.

The rate of increase in state aid was more impressive for these years than earlier ones (a more than nineteenfold increase from 1964 to 1996 as compared to a tenfold hike from 1930 to 1960). In constant dollars, the growth rates were nearly the same (427 percent from 1940 to 1960, 422 percent from 1960 to 1990, and 72 percent from 1990 to 1996). Despite the impressive growth, however, Federal aid by 1971 surpassed it as the dominant component of intergovernmental fiscal transfers, which has continued until 1982, when state assistance again became dominant, and this has continued to the present. Still, the reported figures overstate the amount of own-source state aid. In any recent year, 29 to 34 percent of the total (see table 8-7) represents Federal aid channeled to the states and then "passed through" to localities, four-fifths or more of it typically going into the traditional state assistance programs. In 1990, for example, pass-through funds made up an estimated 29.3 percent (or $51.3 billion) of state aid. The proportions were higher in the sixties and early seventies, when the bypassing percentages were comparatively small (see table 8-7). The pass-through phenomenon also suggests that the figures on Federal aid to the states exaggerate (by two-fifths or more) the extent of exclusive state reliance on this funding source.

## Table 8-7
## Pass-Through Federal Aid as Proportion of Federal to State Aid
## and State to Local Aid, Selected Years, 1957–90

| Year | Federal to State Aid (%) | State to Local Aid (%) |
|------|--------------------------|------------------------|
| 1957 | 57.7 | 27.7 |
| 1962 | 58.1 | 37.8 |
| 1967 | 55.0 | 39.3 |
| 1972 | 47.1 | 34.2 |
| 1977 | 43.3 | 31.9 |
| 1987 | 42.9 | 30.3 |
| 1990 est. | 40.0 | 29.3 |

Source: Communication from G. Ross Stephens, University of Missouri–Kansas City, 20 January 1993. Later data not available.

State aid developments in the eighties reflect the new stance of the states in the system. In the first place, the role of state aid as the prime mechanism for achieving fiscal transfers came about because of the steadily growing role of the states in education and corrections throughout this era and the deficit-induced decline of Federal discretionary grants-in-aid. This state aid to public education even held true in lean recession years (1981–82 and 1989–92). Some of this in some states represented efforts in the early eighties to compensate for Federal aid cuts, but most of it reflected continuing strenuous state efforts to upgrade educational systems to keep up with the Medicaid matching and to cope with the heavy expansion for corrections. Among the basic evolving state aid trends over the past three decades are the following.

First, the functional areas assisted remained pretty much the traditional ones (education, highways, public welfare, and general support), but the proportionate shifts among them reveal some important developments (see table 8-8, p. 228). The steadily increasing proportions for education aid stand out; by 1974 for the first time states had become the major provider of funds for primary and secondary education. The proportionate decline for welfare through the mideighties was partly a by-product of the upward surge in educational outlays and growing state assumption of the full non-Federal welfare responsibility for Medicaid (forty states), AFDC (thirty-nine states), and general assistance (twenty-three states). The hike in the "other" category is partly suggestive of the growth of aid to urban jurisdictions in some states, but it chiefly reflects environmental grant outlays. In the time span from 1985 to 1991, some significant trends appeared: state aid for corrections and health soared by 78.9 percent and 68 percent, respectively, but general support, highways, and "other" were down a bit.[32] The aggregate figures in table 8-9 (p. 229) suggest that these contrasting trends continued through until at least 1996.

Table 8-8
**State Aid to Local Governments, Selected Years, 1964–96**

| Year | Total (Millions) | Education (%) | Public Welfare (%) | Highways (%) | General Support (%) | Other (%) |
|------|------------------|---------------|--------------------|--------------|--------------------|-----------|
| 1964 | $ 12,968 | 59.1 | 16.3 | 11.8 | 8.1 | 4.8 |
| 1969 | 24,779 | 60.0 | 17.7 | 8.5 | 8.6 | 5.2 |
| 1974 | 45,600 | 59.4 | 16.2 | 7.0 | 10.5 | 6.8 |
| 1978 | 65,815 | 61.0 | 13.0 | 5.8 | 10.4 | 9.8 |
| 1981 | 91,307 | 62.7 | 12.1 | 5.2 | 10.5 | 9.5 |
| 1985 | 119,608 | 62.7 | 10.6 | 5.8 | 10.3 | 11.4 |
| 1988 | 149,009 | 64.0 | 11.9 | 4.7 | 10.0 | 9.5 |
| 1990 | 175,028 | 62.5 | 12.4 | 4.4 | 9.5 | 11.2 |
| 1991 | 186,469 | 62.3 | 13.1 | 4.4 | 9.1 | 11.1 |
| 1992 | 201,313 | 62.1 | 12.9 | 4.2 | 8.1 | 12.7 |
| 1993 | 214,095 | 61.3 | 14.6 | 4.3 | 8.3 | 11.5 |
| 1994 | 222,635 | 61.0 | 13.8 | 4.3 | 8.1 | 12.8 |
| 1995 | 240,978 | 61.5 | 12.8 | 4.3 | 8.2 | 13.2 |
| 1996 | 252,102 | 62.3 | 12.4 | 4.2 | 7.9 | 13.2 |

*Source:* Adapted from Advisory Commission on Intergovernmental Relations, *Significant Features of Fiscal Federalism*, vol. 2, *Revenues and Expenditures, 1993*, M-185-II (Washington, D.C., September 1993), 41. American Council on Intergovernmental Relations, *Significant Features of Fiscal Federalism*, vol. 2, *Revenues and Expenditures* (Washington, D.C., October 1997), 44. Council of State Governments, *The Book of the States, 1998–99*, vol. 32 (Lexington, Ky.), 433.

Second, as in the earlier period, school districts and counties tended generally (though not in New England) to be the *prime local governmental recipients* of state aid, given their special functional foci and servicing arrangements in most states (see table 8-9). State aid as a proportion of city, county, and school district general revenue from own sources presents a slightly different picture (see table 8-10), with cities over time but irregularly receiving more than normally would be expected and school district dependence on state aid expanding to the point that it exceeds own-revenue-raising efforts.

Third, the figures for *general-support payments* clearly indicate that although this "no-strings" assistance grew slightly in percentage terms during the seventies (compared to the sixties), the bulk of state aid continued to be of the conditional type (92.1 percent in 1996). Moreover, the overwhelming proportion of these categorical funds was distributed according to a formula, not on a competitive project-grant basis.

Fourth, *equity considerations* (that is, efforts to compensate for variations in local fiscal capacity, effort, or service need) received somewhat greater attention in some state aid formulas during the seventies, eighties, and nineties than during the sixties or during the earlier period. It is difficult to evaluate effectively the various ways states may promote equity in their aid programs because the

## Table 8-9
## State Aid to Local Governments, by Jurisdictional Category, Selected Years, 1960–96

| Year | Total (Millions) | Cities (%) | Counties (%) | School Districts (%) | Other (%) |
|------|------------------|------------|--------------|----------------------|-----------|
| 1960 | $  9,443 | 19.6 | 23.6 | 50.9 | 5.9 |
| 1965 | 14,174 | 19.6 | 23.7 | 49.0 | 7.7 |
| 1970 | 28,892 | 22.9 | 26.0 | 47.9 | 3.2 |
| 1975 | 51,976 | 25.5 | 23.2 | 47.4 | 3.9 |
| 1980 | 84,504 | 21.5 | 24.4 | 51.2 | 2.9 |
| 1984 | 108,373 | 19.4 | 23.3 | 53.4 | 3.9 |
| 1989 | 175,028 | 19.8 | 24.0 | 52.2 | 4.8 |
| 1991 | 186,469 | 18.7 | 26.7 | 51.1 | 3.5 |
| 1995 | 237,362 | $21.7^e$ | $24.6^e$ | 52.0 | 4.9 |
| 1996 | 248,206 | $20.7^e$ | $24.2^e$ | 52.7 | 4.9 |

Source: Adapted from Advisory Commission on Intergovernmental Relations, *Significant Features of Fiscal Federalism*, vol. 2, *Revenues and Expenditures, 1992*, M-180-II (Washington, D.C., September 1992), 59. Council of State Governments, *The Book of the States, 1998–99*, vol. 32 (Lexington, Ky.), 438–39.

e. estimated.

## Table 8-10
## State Aid as Proportion of Local Own-Source General Revenue, Selected Fiscal Years, 1960–91

| Fiscal Year | Cities (%) | Counties (%) | School Districts (%) |
|-------------|------------|--------------|----------------------|
| 1960 | 20.1 | 52.2 | 69.3 |
| 1965 | 22.2 | 53.7 | 64.8 |
| 1970 | 33.0 | 67.4 | 75.1 |
| 1975 | 43.2 | 65.3 | 90.3 |
| 1980 | 33.4 | 63.6 | 121.9 |
| 1984 | 28.6 | 52.1 | 111.9 |
| 1989 | 29.3 | 49.8 | 107.0 |
| 1991 | 29.3 | 60.2 | 106.4 |

Source: Adapted from Advisory Commission on Intergovernmental Relations, *Significant Features of Fiscal Federalism*, vol. 2, *Revenues and Expenditures, 1992*, M-180-II (Washington, D.C., September 1992), 59. Bureau of the Census, *Government Finances*, GF 90-5 (February 1992), 2, table 2. Later data not available.

factors involved can and do vary from program to program, and the servicing-assignment patterns still vary considerably from state to state (as chapter 9 indicates). In the forty states that have assumed the full non-Federal costs of Medicaid, in the thirty-nine that have done the same with AFDC, and in the twenty-three that have assumed all the costs of the state's own general assistance programs, equity is promoted by state administration (counties now still actually implement most of the programs) and funding of the program, and the heavy incidence of the poor in certain local jurisdictions is to some degree neutralized by these "takeovers." Similarly, in the eleven states whose own direct expenditures for public services amounted in FY 1994 to more than 55 percent of the combined state-local total — in short where a centralized state-local servicing/funding pattern is operative — equitable formulas are no longer such a big problem.

Yet all states (except Hawaii, where education is a state function, and California, New Mexico, Washington, and recently Michigan, where education funding is centralized) have aid to public education programs, and all, to a greater or lesser degree, have attempted to make them fairer, beginning really with the California educational-finance case *Serrano v. Priest* (1971).[33] As cited earlier, state outlays for education rose significantly in the seventies and eighties, accompanied by moves to modify traditional allocational formulas, usually in the direction of meeting special needs or advancing equity directly (e.g., by confronting the fiscal disparities reflected in the low property-tax support of a youngster in one school district compared with that of another in a more affluent district). In the first *Serrano* decision (there were two more), the California Supreme Court found the state public school finance system unconstitutional. Since then well over thirty other states have been involved in school finance litigation. By 1996, the school finance systems of thirteen states had been ruled unconstitutional, while in sixteen instances challenged school finance arrangements were upheld by their state's highest court.[34] The complexities of educational aid programs, their goals, and their levels of state funding render analysis of the state-local legal and financial reform undertakings in public education hazardous. The only sure findings are (1) more money is being spent on public education than a generation ago, (2) state involvement is deep in all but a handful of instances (only three states in FY 1994 still provided less than 35 percent of the total school bill compared to eight in FY 1991), (3) school systems with a disproportionate number of poor youngsters and/or meager property tax support have been aided in many instances, (4) disparities are fluctuating phenomena because their causes can shift and even move, and (5) Michigan has turned to a state-funded school arrangement (largely its sales tax), while Vermont is experimenting with a state property tax plan with the goal of reducing the disparities between the poorer and more affluent (ski) districts.

In the state *programs of general support* (General Revenue Sharing) a clearer case of less than adequate targeting has been identified. A 1990 General Accounting Office report found that "most states reduced disparities less than did Federal general revenue sharing" in 1985.[35] Although the national average for such state general support programs amounted to only about 10 percent (8.2 percent in FY 1994) of the total of state aid, four states in FY 1994 had programs that exceeded 20 percent of the total, compared to ten in FY 1990. At the other end of the scale is the astounding fact that thirteen states in FY 1994 had general support programs involving 0 to 1 percent of their respective grant assistance.[36] The problem is that most states have yet to merge a number of the programs and to develop an allocational formula that includes a fiscal capacity factor; only seventeen had programs with such a distributional conditioner.

Another study, this one of *central-city/outside-central-city disparities* over time, offers some basis for greater optimism. It looked at state aid to jurisdictions within sixty-eight of the largest metropolitan areas. In 1970 the central-city and suburbs figures were nearly the same, suggesting no efforts in state targeting. In 1977, 1981, and 1987 the central-city figures were greater, indicating a better state effort toward alleviating central-city "overburden" problems (see table 8-18, p. 254).[37] State aid in 1970 was most central-city-focused in the East, less so in the Midwest, and had a more suburban focus by slight margins in the West and South. In 1981 the same general pattern persisted, though the South had moved out of the suburb-oriented sector by a small margin.[38] The figures for total educational aid, largely composed of state funds, reflect the same pattern, but with a few exceptions. First, the margin of difference between central-city and suburban per capita aid is much smaller than that for state aid generally, and second, both the South and West in 1980 still reflected a prosuburban bias in the educational area. Regarding total noneducational aid, all regions reflected a strong central-city focus, but this form of aid included a much larger Federal component, which suggests a greater targeting capacity then of Federal compared to state aid; the functional orientation of state aid, however, must be remembered when comparisons of the two are made. Nonetheless, overall during the seventies, the targeting capacity of most states within which the sixty-eight largest Metropolitan Statistical Areas (MSAs) were located clearly improved. Moreover, the aid figure for 1987 (see table 8-18, p. 254), which was largely state aid because Federal-local aid had been severely cut, demonstrates that this tendency has slackened somewhat but not significantly. No data exist for the nineties, unfortunately.

To summarize this brief analysis of state aid over the past thirty years:

- It has become the chief source of major grant assistance to localities.

- It grew significantly both in absolute and constant dollar terms; though it lost its first-rank position to the Federal aid system in the early seventies, it regained that position in the early eighties, and a rough parity now exists between the aid systems.

- Its functional focus shifted somewhat, with education, corrections, and the environmental categories gaining and highways and welfare slackening off in the seventies only to rebound in the late eighties and nineties.

- Its prime beneficiaries nationwide continued to be school districts and counties, though the cities' share increased slightly and irregularly during the seventies, eighties, and nineties.

- Its preferred device for transferring funds continued to be the conditional grant (chiefly the cost-sharing type of categorical).

- Its capacity to focus on unequal local fiscal capacity, effort, and need (especially in the education field) has improved somewhat since the seventies.

- Compared with Federal aid, it is far less diversified in functional scope, has experienced far fewer program shifts over time, and is far more dominated by a single function, by conditional cost-sharing grants, and by the alternative ability of smaller states to provide a function directly.

- Despite the commonalties suggested above, each state still has an aid system that is unique, reflecting its own politics, policy preferences, and fiscal attitudes.

## Federal Aid: Explosive Expansion Initially, Then a Return to Incrementalism

As the introduction to this book emphasizes, the extraordinary expansion in Federal assistance and a series of directly related developments, including regulatory efforts, more than any other single factor or force "explains" and symbolizes the near-total transformation of the intergovernmental system since 1960. Federal assistance to state and local governments grew phenomenally from 1964 to 1978 in dollar amounts, number of programs, types of aided functions, and eligible recipients. Equally significant, it experienced major changes in program emphasis, in forms of fiscal transfer, in kinds of conditions and regulations attached thereto, and in allocational disbursements. From 1979 to 1994, a slow tapering off took place, marked by a sharp rollback in FY 1982. Then came a resumption of gradual growth in grant outlays with a slightly accelerated rate during the Bush and Clinton years. Combined, these crucial changes in Federal assistance, along with many intended and unintended effects, highlight the remarkable expansion, slight contraction, and continued rise of the Federal government's role in the federal system over the past three decades. These trends in Federal aid help identify another source of ambivalence in the current intergovernmental system.

### Dimensions of Growth

For state and local recipients, *the annual growth rate of Federal aid* was greater than that of their own revenues for fourteen of the years between 1960 and 1978 (see table 8-11). The tapering off that began in the late seventies led to eleven straight years (from 1979 through 1989) in which the growth rate of

## Table 8-11
## Growth Rate of Federal Grants and
## State-Local Own-Source Revenue, 1960–94

| Year | Increase in Federal Grants (%) | Increase in State-Local Own-Source Revenues (%) | Year | Increase in Federal Grants (%) | Increase in State-Local Own-Source Revenues (%) |
|---|---|---|---|---|---|
| 1960 | 7.7 | 11.8 | 1977 | 15.7 | 11.3 |
| 1961 | 1.4 | 7.8 | 1978 | 13.9 | 10.3 |
| 1962 | 11.3 | 9.7 | 1979 | 7.1 | 8.9 |
| 1963 | 8.9 | 6.6 | 1980 | 9.6 | 11.6 |
| 1964 | 18.6 | 9.0 | 1981 | 3.7 | 11.3 |
| 1965 | 6.9 | 7.7 | 1982 | 6.7 | 11.1 |
| 1966 | 18.3 | 10.9 | 1983 | 5.0 | 7.1 |
| 1967 | 17.8 | 8.6 | 1984 | 5.5 | 12.4 |
| 1968 | 23.4 | 10.8 | 1985 | 8.5 | 10.2 |
| 1969 | 8.6 | 13.4 | 1986 | 6.0 | 7.0 |
| 1970 | 19.3 | 14.2 | 1987 | 3.7 | 8.3 |
| 1971 | 16.6 | 9.2 | 1988 | 6.4 | 7.6 |
| 1972 | 22.4 | 10.9 | 1989 | 5.8 | 7.6 |
| 1973 | 21.5 | 10.9 | 1990 | 11.0 | 7.5 |
| 1974 | 3.8 | 9.0 | 1991 | 14.1 | 4.9 |
| 1975 | 14.8 | 9.2 | 1992 | 15.3 | 6.1 |
| 1976 | 18.7 | 10.7 | 1993 | 8.7 | 5.8 |
| | | | 1994 | 8.8 | 5.4 |

*Source:* Adapted from Advisory Commission on Intergovernmental Relations, *Significant Features of Fiscal Federalism,* vol. 2, *Revenues and Expenditures, 1993,* M-185-II (Washington, D.C., September 1992), 13, 70, 72. American Council on Intergovernmental Relations, *Significant Features of Fiscal Federalism,* vol. 2, *Revenues and Expenditures* (Washington, D.C., October 1997), 38, 66–67.

own-source state-local revenue — not surprisingly, perhaps — exceeded that of Federal grants. But FY 1990 saw a return to the earlier pattern.

Somewhat similarly, Federal aid *as a percentage of state-local outlays* experienced a fairly steady increase between FY 1960 and FY 1978 (see table Int-1, pp. 4–5). Yet the proportional decline that began in FY 1979 again signaled that the salad days of Federal aid were largely over. A sharp single drop in FY 1982 was followed by glacial growth until 1989, when under Bush a moderate boost began. The rapid rise and then precipitous plunge of direct Federal aid as a proportion of total local resources tells a slightly different story: 9 percent in FY 1978 fell to 3 percent in 1989, but rose to 4.1 percent by FY 1994, thanks in part to some of the Clinton urban initiatives. Obviously, however, this constituted no return to the pre-1981 era.

The expansion in Federal aid also was reflected in *the variety of assisted activities* (see table 8-12). Creative Federalism, as noted earlier, moved beyond the Federal efforts in traditionally aided program areas (largely certain state functions) into new state efforts, a range of novel and familiar services, as well as activities previously provided by the private sector.[39] Many of the grant programs were attempts to move state and local governments into new fields in light of what was deemed a national need. National purpose, of course, had always been a rationale for launching grants, but with Johnson's Creative Federalism it extended to so many new areas — economic and regional development, transportation (especially urban mass transit), community development and housing (notably water and sewer facilities and model cities), dozens of education and job-training programs, health (particularly mental health, health services delivery, and medical assistance), and income security (with Medicaid, child nutrition, and special milk and food stamps predominating) — that the concept bore little relationship to the one that had been applied previously.

The proliferation in aided program thrusts did not end with Johnson's departure, as has been indicated. Despite attempts by both Nixon and Ford to curb the categoricals, their number increased, their level of subfunctional and even subsubfunctional specializations became deeper, and older aided efforts of secondary concern became major ones — such as environmental, social services, job training, and income-security programs. With the congressionally initiated and presidentially embraced countercyclical programs (under Carter), in the mid-seventies states and especially localities assumed a major role in implementing national economic policies in a time of serious recession.

In short, by 1980 hardly any governmental activity at the subnational levels was ineligible for some form of Federal assistance, albeit in many instances meager, and many of the mostly national services were caught up in the grant-in-aid system, as were the plainly intergovernmental services (such as energy, education, the environment, and transportation) along with an array of presumably local, if not private, concerns. The last included programs from urban gardening and aquaculture to rural fire protection and pothole repair. National purpose as defined through the new pressure-group-conditioned national political process of the seventies clearly had come to encompass just about everything, though only the programs with broad support got good funding. The pygmy projects were pacifiers for small (and sometimes larger) pressure groups, and they were not always renewed.

In FY 1981, 142 categorical grants — mostly small in dollar terms — were eliminated: 65 by outright repeal, and 77 by merger into the 10 new block grants. But from FY 1982 to FY 1993, 182 new categorical grants were enacted — mostly small, some medium, a few large in fiscal terms.[40] Among the new FY 1991 pygmy project categoricals were Urban Parks and Recreation ($19.4 million), Pollution Prevention Incentives for States ($7.0 million), Animal Damage Control ($24.6 million), Technology Education Demonstration ($1 million), Rehabilitation Short-term Training ($0.4 million), Nurse Anesthetist Education ($0.5 million), and the Congregate Housing Services Program ($14.5 million).

## Table 8-12
## Federal Grants as Proportion of Total Aid, by Function,
## Selected Fiscal Years, 1960–95

| Fiscal Year | Health | Income Security | Education, Training, Employment | Transportation | Community and Regional Development | General Government | Other[a] |
|---|---|---|---|---|---|---|---|
| 1960 | 3.0 | 37.5 | 7.5 | 42.7 | 1.6 | 2.4 | 5.3 |
| 1965 | 5.7 | 32.2 | 9.6 | 37.6 | 5.9 | 2.1 | 6.9 |
| 1970 | 16.0 | 24.1 | 26.7 | 19.1 | 7.4 | 2.0 | 4.7 |
| 1975 | 17.7 | 18.8 | 24.4 | 11.8 | 5.7 | 14.2 | 7.4 |
| 1980 | 17.2 | 20.2 | 23.9 | 14.2 | 7.1 | 9.4 | 7.9 |
| 1985 | 23.1 | 25.6 | 16.8 | 16.1 | 4.9 | 6.5 | 7.0 |
| 1990 | 32.4 | 26.0 | 17.3 | 14.2 | 3.7 | 1.7 | 4.7 |
| 1991 | 36.1 | 23.2 | 17.2 | 12.8 | 2.8 | 1.4 | 3.9 |
| 1992 | 40.1 | 24.4 | 16.1 | 11.8 | 2.5 | 1.3 | 3.9 |
| 1993 | 41.1 | 24.3 | 15.6 | 11.5 | 2.9 | 1.6 | 3.5 |
| 1994 | 41.0 | 24.5 | 15.5 | 11.2 | 3.7 | 1.0 | 3.1 |
| 1995 | 41.6 | 24.5 | 15.2 | 11.5 | 3.2 | 1.0 | 3.0 |

Source: Advisory Commission on Intergovernmental Relations, Significant Features of Fiscal Federalism, vol. 2, Revenues and Expenditures, 1992, M-180-II (Washington, D.C., September 1992), 61. American Council on Intergovernmental Relations, Significant Features of Fiscal Federalism, vol. 2, Revenues and Expenditures (Washington, D.C., October 1997), 39.

a. Includes natural resources and the environment, agriculture, energy, veterans' benefits and services, administration of justice, and national defense.

Of the 82 new categoricals funded for FY 1991, 67 were allocated $20 million or less, and only 3 received more than $100 million.[41] It should be noted that 17 grants funded in FY 1989 were not funded in FY 1991, which highlights another feature of the proliferating categorical sector: in any one year several small programs may be scrapped, but others are added, reflecting the less-than-serious nature of many of them. Typically the number of programs added exceeds the number deleted. During Reagan's first three years, for example, 142, 124, and 71 tiny grants were scrapped, even as 48, 31, and 58, respectively, were added. In later years, the numbers have been reversed. In short, the old myth that Federal grants never die is precisely that. The servicing utility of nearly all of these clearly is questionable, but the symbolic and political positives reflected in these enactments cannot be discounted, especially in a time of rugged retrenchment. For 37 programs in FY 1994, this was not the case because they accounted for over 90 percent of the total of grant outlays, and in FY 1997, 22 grants consumed 83.7 percent of the total of Federal aid.

From 1964 to 1980, as the foregoing suggests, an explosive expansion in eligible recipients of Federal grants also occurred, but it was followed by an equally dramatic contraction. From the overwhelming state focus of 1960, when only 8 percent of Federal aid went directly to localities (chiefly a comparatively small number of cities and some special districts), there came into being by 1980 a "pinwheel" pattern of direct Federal aid disbursements to all 18,856 cities, 3,042 counties, and 16,822 towns; to practically all of the 16,500 public school systems and four-fifths of the private ones; to at least one-third of the 26,140 special districts; to an undetermined but sizable number of nonprofit organizations; and to the fifty states.

All told, about 60,000 (or 73 percent) of the approximately 81,000 units of state and local government were directly receiving Federal aid funds by 1980. Between 25 and 29 percent of all such aid (depending on the year) bypassed state governments in the late seventies, compared to 8 percent in 1960 and 12 percent in 1968, thanks to the fact that localities were directly eligible for over 60 percent of the five hundred authorized and funded grants.[42] Moreover, larger local jurisdictions typically "participated" in far more than one aid program. In the midseventies an ACIR-ICMA (International City Management Association) survey of 490 cities (with populations of 50,000 or more) and 100 counties (with populations of 100,000 or more) revealed that the average number of Federal grants received by cities rose from 4.1 in 1969 to 8.8 in 1974; by counties from 7.7 to 18.4, respectively.[43] These figures, if anything, understate the expanded rate of participation because jurisdictions that did not receive any Federal grants funds in 1969 were excluded from the comparison.

Various factors combined to produce the broadening pattern of bypassing the states. Creative Federalism's focus on cities and urban programs was significant initially, though this gave rise to only 12 percent of the Federal aid total's going directly to local governments in 1968, as noted above. General revenue sharing, the Comprehensive Employment and Training Act (CETA), and Community Development block grants (CDBG) were just as significant during the

Nixon years because they were the first assistance programs, other than Title I of the Elementary and Secondary Education Act, to incorporate substate allocation formulas; such formulas by their nature tend inevitably to disburse funds more widely, no matter how restrictive their eligibility provisions. Finally, the three countercyclical programs of the midseventies only continued this trend, with the bulk of the funds in each of them going directly to local jurisdictions.

All of this changed with the arrival of the Reagan administration. The large Federal-to-local grants were slashed severely and the bypassing percentages eroded steadily during the eighties (see table Int-2, pp. 6–7). In programmatic terms, it was not so much a major reduction in the number of grants for which local governments were eligible, as table 8-13 (p. 238) highlights, but that nearly all of the 365 grants (the largest number ever) for which local governments (and in 343 cases, other bodies as well) were eligible in FY 1993 were puny project grants. Only the entitlement CDBG, the mass transit, and some drug control programs involved significant amounts of money. According to a special U.S. Census Bureau count, about 17,000 local governments in 1992 received direct or indirect Federal assistance (grants, loans, and insurance).[44] If only ongoing grants, not one-shot awards, had been considered, the number of local recipients would have been a tiny fraction of the estimated 60,000 figure in 1980. The unheralded return to the historic Federal-state connection under Reagan and a not-so-reluctant Congress led to the turnabout. And the fact that it has continued with only a few recent modifications underscores the durability of this facet of the Reagan revolution.

### Critical Changes

In addition to growing in various ways, the *forms of Federal aid changed* during the current period, as the foregoing suggests. The traditional grant type was the categorical with its four variations (discussed in chapter 4). During the sixties, project categoricals expanded rapidly; about four-fifths of the 210-odd new enactments under Johnson fell within this group. By FY 1975 project grants without geographic constrictions and project grants subject to formula distribution accounted for three-quarters of the total of 442 categoricals; three years later they constituted the same proportion of the 492 categoricals then authorized and funded. During the eighties and nineties, this proportion prevailed despite fluctuating totals.[45] The two exceptions were in FY 1984, when the categorical proportion dipped to 72 percent, and in FY 1997, when it fell to 71 percent.

Block grants and general revenue sharing were added to the categoricals, beginning with enactment of the Partnership for Health block grant in 1966. Passage of the Safe Streets Act in 1968, the Title XX Social Services program in 1972, CETA in 1973, and CDBG in 1974 brought the number of block grants to five by the midseventies, and the signing of the General Revenue Sharing measure by Nixon in 1972 brought the first Federal general support program into being. A tripartite aid system thus materialized between the midsixties and

Table 8-13
Categorical Grant Programs by Eligible Recipients,
Selected Fiscal Years, 1975–93

| Recipient | 1975 N | 1975 (%) | 1978 N | 1978 (%) | 1981 N | 1981 (%) | 1984 N | 1984 (%) | 1987 N | 1987 (%) | 1989 N | 1989 (%) | 1991 N | 1991 (%) | 1993 N | 1993 (%) |
|---|---|---|---|---|---|---|---|---|---|---|---|---|---|---|---|---|
| States only | 162 | 36.7 | 191 | 38.8 | 194 | 36.3 | 153 | 39.0 | 164 | 38.9 | 180 | 37.7 | 206 | 37.8 | 213 | 36.9 |
| State and local | 62 | 14.0 | 67 | 13.6 | 69 | 12.9 | 42 | 10.7 | 44 | 10.4 | 45 | 9.4 | 50 | 9.0 | 51 | 8.8 |
| Local only | 20 | 4.5 | 26 | 5.3 | 23 | 4.3 | 14 | 3.6 | 15 | 3.5 | 17 | 3.6 | 21 | 4.1 | 22 | 3.8 |
| State and local, and public and private nonprofits | 198 | 44.8 | 208 | 42.3 | 248 | 46.4 | 183 | 46.7 | 199 | 47.2 | 236 | 49.3 | 266 | 49.1 | 292 | 50.5 |
| Total | 442 | 100.0 | 492 | 100.0 | 534 | 99.9 | 392 | 100.0 | 422 | 100.0 | 478 | 100.0 | 543 | 100.0 | 578 | 100.0 |

Source: Adapted from Advisory Commission on Intergovernmental Relations tabulations based on Catalog of Federal Domestic Assistance, United States Code and Federal Agency contacts, in Advisory Commission on Intergovernmental Relations, Characteristics of Federal Grants-in-Aid Programs to State and Local Governments: Grants Funded FY 1993, M-188 (Washington, D.C., January 1994), 14.

the midseventies — though the paramount position of the categoricals was never really threatened (down to 75 percent of grant funds in 1975, but up to 80 percent by 1980).

In the early eighties, Safe Streets and CETA were given last rites. The Partnership for Health and Title XX blocks were folded into two of OBRA's ten new block grants (nine actually became operational). And CDBG was split by OBRA: a new miniblock grant to the states and the entitlement portion, which remained as the only block grant at that time directly involving local governments. The Job Training and Partnership Act (JTPA, 1982) established a new job-training block grant; Mental Health Services for the Homeless and Community Youth Service were both enacted in 1988; Payments to the States for Day Care Assistance was enacted in 1990; and a new metropolitan transportation block grant was created by ISTEA in 1991 which became TEA-21 in 1997.[46] All told, nine of the OBRA blocks and five later enactments, plus the old entitlement CDBG, produced a total of fifteen by 1992, but the funding for all of these block grants in FY 1991 amounted to only 14.5 percent of total grant outlays, underscoring again the clout of the categoricals. At the same time, the new blocks reflect a far greater congressional willingness to enact these more permissive forms of intergovernmental fiscal transfer than was the case in the seventies. With the enactment of TANF, a child care block grant, and five other block grant enactments, the total number rose to twenty-two by FY 1997 and their funding total reached 17.5 percent of all Federal aid, which began to approach the salad season of the midseventies, when outlays for GRS and the five block grants were at their peak (25 percent in 1975). Yet their greater number has not served to reduce the number of categoricals, and the modest outlays for all but two of the twenty-two block grants in the 1980s tended to underline Congress's continuing unwillingness to use the device for programs of prime concern to most of the members. At the same time, among the twenty-four such grants that were enacted by 1998, only three were big-ticket items.

As with four of the five "old block grants" (the pre-1980 cluster), most of the Reagan period grants gained conditions over time that constrained recipient programmatic discretion in the broad functional area being aided. A General Accounting Office report on eleven of these intergovernmental fiscal transfers in FY 1990 found they accounted for $14 billion (10.4 percent) of the approximately $135 billion total aid, with six surpassing the $1 billion mark and one (Social Services) exceeding $2 billion. GAO researchers discovered that set-asides (which required spending of a specified minimum percentage of the grant on a particular program, target group, or type of organization) and cost ceilings (no more than a specified maximum is to be spent on a particular purpose or group) were the chief constraints imposed on these blocks as years passed.[47] The basic GAO findings were these:

1. When Congress amended the legislation authorizing nine of the eleven block grants examined in the study, new set-asides and cost-ceiling stipulations or changes in existing ones occurred fifty-eight times between FY 1983 and FY 1991.

2. Of these changes, thirteen involved set-aside and cost-ceiling requirements, one set-aside was scrapped, and one cost ceiling was replaced,
   which brought the total of such requirements from thirty-two in 1982 to
   forty-four by 1991 (twenty-seven set-asides and seventeen cost ceilings).

3. Over the nine years studied, the proportion of set-aside funds was increased in three of the block grants, remained the same (at 90–100 percent
   levels) in two, was reduced by 10–18 percent in two, and retained a
   no-set-aside status in five instances.

Five of the nine block grants permitted the waiver of set-aside or cost-ceiling
provisions; of the thirty-four separate such requirements in the five, waivers
could be obtained for seven; waivers could not be procured for a set-aside of
all the requirements in any of the block grants; and although data are incomplete, what evidence there is suggested that few waivers were sought by recipient
governments, but of those submitted, most were approved.[48]

By the late nineties, the number of block grants had crept up to twenty-four,
but nowhere near what the count would have been had the numerous House
mergers been enacted by the 104th Congress and signed by the president. The
funding for twenty-two in FY 1997 amounted to $41.04 billion (17.5 percent of
the total; see table Int-3, p. 10). Moreover, two of the blocks were big-ticket items
(TANF and ISTEA) and three of them were Federal-local in their jurisdictional
character (ISTEA, the HOME Investment Partnership Program, and, of course,
the perennial entitlement CDBG). The first two are both noteworthy developments. In addition, in the summer of 1998, ISTEA became TEA-21 (Transportation Efficiency Act–21st Century) and three new manpower block grants were
enacted with the Job Training and Partnership Act (JTPA) being merged with
them. These actions place the total for block grants at twenty-four in 1998.

Finally, General Revenue Sharing, the other new form of more discretionary
Federal aid, was renewed over some opposition (especially from old-line congressional hierarchs) in 1976 and renewed again in 1980, but the states' one-third
of the funds was struck from the measure (congressional representatives were
angered over state efforts from 1978 on to advance a call for a constitutional
convention to consider a balanced budget amendment). It was reauthorized yet
again in 1983 with presidential blessing (despite retrenchment concerns) and
killed in 1986 with the sanction of the White House as a means of helping to
reduce the budget deficit. Thus, *the most popular of all Federal aid programs with
state and local officials disappeared, and most of the nearly 38,000 units of subnational
government that received GRS funds lost their only fiscal contact with Washington.*

The tripartite system of Federal aid that emerged in the seventies clearly
underwent crucial changes during the eighties. A major reduction of the categoricals and the formulation of several large new block grants as the first phase
in devolving Federal responsibilities in the program areas affected were two of
Reagan's goals. Obviously, he achieved neither, though he did succeed in advancing the number of blocks, as we have seen. The trend lines from 1975 to
1997 are highlighted in table Int-3 (p. 10), and they underscore the basic finding

that categoricals were stronger in dollar as well as numerical terms at the end of this period than at the beginning.

But what difference do the forms make in operational terms? Four factors are critical to any attempt to make sense out of these terms because they have acquired varied meanings both in principle and practice. The first relates to the extent that recipient jurisdictions are permitted unrestricted, wide, or narrow program discretion — that is, whether funds received must be spent on programs at all, or in specific but broadly defined functional areas, or on very specific projects or services. The second factor is the degree to which the grantor stipulates tight, broad, or nominal program conditions (project or plan approval and review, administrative and reporting requirements, and so on). The third is whether a statutorily based or dictated distributional formula or a basically discretionary allocational approach is adopted. The fourth has to do with recipient eligibility and focuses on whether a broad or a narrow range of potential recipients is statutorily recognized. The four factors are not discrete and disconnected but interactive. The manner in which they combine produces the various forms of intergovernmental fiscal transfer now in operation (see figure 8-1, p. 242). None of the old five blocks and few of the new ones had all of the traits of the ideal block grant at the outset and TANF misses several of them. Moreover, nearly all block grants over time experienced significant mutation, largely in the direction of more conditions and greater centralization because of the extreme political difficulties of maintaining a judicious balance between attaining certain national purposes (by conditions) and assuring significant recipient discretion (by stipulating few conditions).

In operational terms, the *different forms of intergovernmental fiscal transfers produce different administrative, program, and fiscal effects.*[49] With *project categoricals,* recipient discretion is constricted; program scope is narrow; fund distribution is determined by Federal administrators; targeting is possible with proper legislative guidelines and enlightened administrative behavior; politicization is easy (if the above traits are lacking); and a stimulative effect on recipient outlays may — depending in part on matching requirements — be produced. *Formula categoricals* also afford low recipient discretion, narrow program discretion, and stimulative fiscal effects, but funds are allocated on a formula basis usually crafted by Congress, which tends to reduce chances for political manipulation and for significant targeting because the money is widely distributed. Historically, categorical formula grants were always Federal-state grants because accurate formula data for substate governments, the inevitable large number of recipient jurisdictions (no matter how narrow the eligibility provisions), and the resulting potential high cost were insurmountable barriers.

*Block grants* in theory and sometimes in practice are intended to cover a broad program area (for example, criminal justice, social services, community development), to maximize recipient discretion, and to be allocated chiefly on a formula basis. Occasionally, however, a discretionary project grant program may be included in the authorizing legislation to help cover small jurisdictions not eligible for the block grant formula funds, as with the initial Community Development

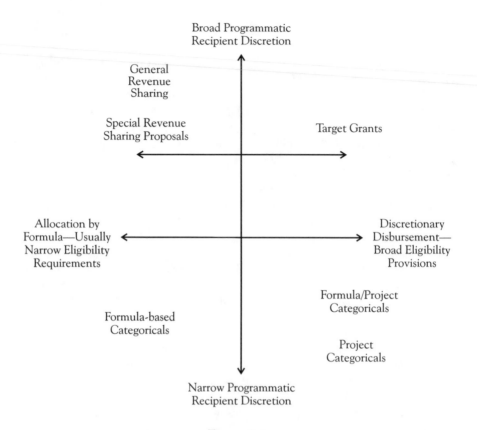

**Figure 8-1**
**Basic Forms of Intergovernmental Transfers**

block grant. Over time, such intergovernmental fiscal transfers tend to acquire conditions, provided Congress or the executive branch is really concerned with the goals of a particular block grant. When they are not, as with the Partnership for Health block grant, then added conditions and money do not materialize. The fiscal effects of these grants usually are additive.

A very recent report of the General Accounting Office (GAO) (see table 8-14) focuses on "Grant Programs" and their differing design features. Its assessment of twenty-one such grants concluded that the national objective involved in a grant may be either performance/service or fiscally oriented, that is, providing funding to expand a program; that the operational nature of the grant may be either to further a distinct national goal by program-specific requirements or to provide funding for what basically is a state or locally oriented program; and that the activities aided may be narrow or quite diverse.[50] This three-factor mode of analysis clearly indicates that there is a wide range of differences among the present family of blocks depending on which option in each of the three pairs is operational in any given program. It also shows that some blocks are closer to

### Table 8-14
### Grant Design Features in Combination

| National objectives | Nature of operations | Diversity of activities | Examples | Characteristics |
|---|---|---|---|---|
| Performance-related | Program | Single major activity | Job Training Partnership Act, titles II-A and II-C<br><br>Special Programs for the Aging – Nutrition Services | Federal role is substantial.<br><br>State or local flexibility is limited.<br><br>Most likely to include national service outcome objectives.<br><br>Most likely to have program performance information at the national level. |
| | Funding stream | Single major activity to diverse activities | Child Care and Development Block Grant<br><br>Preventive Health and Health Services Block Grant | Federal-state balance is established case by case.<br><br>Flexibility varies with diversity of activities.<br><br>Performance objectives and measures may be state or local.<br><br>Less likely to have national performance information. |
| Fiscal | Program (for project) | Diverse activities | Community Development Block Grant – Entitlement<br><br>Byrne Formula Grants | State or local level is dominant.<br><br>Flexibility is broad.<br><br>Likely to have performance and evaluation information at the project level. |
| | Funding stream | Single major activity to diverse activities | Title VI: Innovative Education Program Strategies<br><br>Social Services Block Grant | Federal role is confined to providing funds.<br><br>Flexibility varies with diversity of activities.<br><br>Gives broadest discretion to grantee.<br><br>Least likely to have performance information. |

*Source:* U.S. General Accounting Office, *Grant Programs: Design Features Shape Flexibility, Accountability, and Performance Information* (GAO/GGD – 98-137) (Washington, D.C., June 1998), 17.

some categoricals than to certain others within their family. Moreover, the contemporary concern with both greater accountability and greater flexibility finds no easy answers in the GAO analysis. The former after all now calls for some form of "benchmarking" and the latter still necessitates as few conditions as possible.

Given all the hurdles block grants have faced both in the past and present, why the efforts since the early seventies to enact more? The reasons range from better management, improved implementation, and eliminating categorical duplication to curbing Federal administrators, enhancing recipient discretion both programmatically and administratively, and saving tax payer dollars at both the national and subnational levels. In recent years, the basic reason for the current drive for blocks has been the parallel drive to reduce the national budget deficit. Devolutions — and that is what blocks amount to if properly designed — and deficit reductions have gone together. This happens especially when governors claim that they can put up with a 20 percent cut in appropriations if the costly conditions attached to the merged categoricals are eliminated. Clearly some of the design questions raised in the GAO study run counter to this devolutionary deal. Moreover, the failure of many of the Gingrich-gubernatorial mergers to gain the necessary support for passage in the conservative 104th Congress suggests that the legislative branch's traditional skepticism about this form of intergovernmental fiscal transfer has not disappeared. Not to be forgotten in all this is the instability of blocks as an intergovernmental fiscal and program device. They have proven especially vulnerable to "recentralization, recategorization, and retrenchment," as Paul L. Posner and Margaret T. Wrightson have phrased it.[51]

With General Revenue Sharing (1972–86), recipient discretion was really unchecked, though a few procedural conditions were added in 1976. The funds, in fact, could be spent on anything, even though expenditures for education were disallowed. But given the substitutive fiscal effects of GRS, recipient project discretion was almost boundless, which was why the program was so unpopular with Congress. The funds were allocated by formula (there was, in fact, a choice of one out of two), and despite the participation of 38,200 units of general government, these formulas produced a better allocation to less-well-off jurisdictions than nearly any other conceived in Washington or in state capitals. In short, the forms of Federal assistance do make a difference in operational terms, even though a form may change over time by legislative design or by administrative sleight of hand. In policy-analytical terms, then, special care should be taken when choosing among the intergovernmental means of implementing program goals. Enough experience has been garnered with each of these mechanisms to warrant fairly accurate predictions about implementory outcomes.

Not only did the Federal aid system change in form during the current period, but its *program emphasis also shifted significantly.* According to the broad functional classifications used to report on Federal aid spending over the years, commerce and transportation accounted for more than 42 percent of the outlays in 1960 and income security accounted for 38 percent. By 1980 the former had slipped to 14 percent and the latter to 20 percent, although transportation experienced a rise in the eighties followed by further flat growth (despite ISTEA), and income security paralleled the same course but by larger percentages (see table 8-12, p. 235). The shares of four other functional groupings soared during the earlier two decades: health, from 3 percent in 1960 to 17 percent by 1980; education, training, employment, and social services, from 7.5 percent to 24 percent; general government, from 2.4 percent to 9.4 percent; and community and regional development (chiefly the environment), from 1.6 percent to 7.1 percent. Like income security and transportation, all of these four functional groupings except health lost ground in the eighties and early nineties. Put differently, the cuts in some program areas (for example, community and regional development and job training) and the elimination of GRS explain some of this, but the extraordinary Medicaid outlays alone explain why other program areas — even with increased funding, as with transportation and education — fared feebly in the 1982–95 period. The overall picture that emerges from these shifts and expansions within and among the major aid sectors clearly is one wherein people-related assistance programs (income security, education, training, employment, and health) assumed a far more dominant position (61 percent of the 1980 total and 81 percent of that for 1992, compared with 48 percent in 1960). Not revealed in this broad-brush presentation, of course, is the array of new, narrow, and subfunctional thrusts, noted earlier, that add one more dimension to this pattern of program diversity.[52]

Still another basic change in the Federal aid system occurred within the *conditions attached to grant programs.* Here the perennial congressional tendency to impose "strings" and the more recent habit of adding regulations and mandates, noted earlier, undercut the very foundations of interlevel program collaboration that provided the fundamental framework of the Cooperative Federalism concept and ethic. In the pre-1969 years, grant conditions were almost wholly program specific, hence vertical, in nature, with innocuous institutional ("single state agency") and personnel (Hatch Act and merit-systems) requirements added to some (chiefly in the public welfare and employment security areas). Today, most of these more traditional programmatic conditions still apply — obviously to the categoricals, which still dominate the grant scene, and increasingly to the block grants. Over time, as emphasized earlier, the tendency among block grants was and is to acquire additional conditions. It was mentioned before that with the 1976 renewal of GRS, this presumably least conditional of all Federal aid programs imposed requirements — ranging from citizen participation, audits of all funds expended, restrictions on debt retirement with GRS monies, and compliance with prevailing wages for construction projects to protection against discrimination in recruitment and employment of various population groups — on its 38,000 recipients in the provision of public services, and in the selection of facilities to be financed out of Federal funds.

One of the most significant developments from 1964 to 1980 (a time of "creeping conditionalism") was the piecemeal yet persistent proliferation of conditions that applied generally or selectively to all or most of the Federal assistance programs. By 1980 most of the sixty-two crosscutting national policy requirements clustered under ten broad rubrics: nondiscrimination, thirteen requirements; environmental protection, thirteen; health, welfare, and safety, four; labor and procurement standards, six; public employee standards, two; access to government information and decision procedures, three (but one crosscutting regulation included more than 150 separate citizen-participation requirements in a like number of grants); protection and advancement of the economy, three; general administrative and procedural requirements, four; non-profit recipient-related administrative and fiscal requirements, four; and state and local government-related administrative and fiscal requirements, four. All but six of these sixty-two requirements were enacted or promulgated during 1960–80; thirty-eight, during the seventies.

Thirty-nine of the *crosscutting conditions* took the form of a single congressional enactment, but some were multiple, not always identical, enactments in various grant programs (as with the citizen-participation requirements). Still others included a general requirement along with differing, more stringent enactments in the same topical area for certain aid programs (as with civil rights). Not all of the sixty-two were "intrusive." In fact, some were intended to facilitate the grants-management role of the recipient governments (as with several of the general and more specific administrative and procedural requirements). Yet about three-fourths of the total clearly were of a quasi-regulatory nature and reflected a new thrust in Federal conditions attached to grants — conditions that departed significantly from the older, largely program-specific vertical type.

The shift to new regulatory approaches was manifest in more than the crosscutting category, for crosscutting conditions were only one device to promote this major policy objective of "New Social Regulation." The real focus of these crosscuts was not so much on the informational, procedural, economic, and administrative goals but on regulations in the nondiscrimination, health and safety, and environmental protection areas that gave rise to this "New Social Regulation" designation. As noted in the introduction and chapter 1, other devices were also used to implement this national policy objective of the seventies (and eighties and nineties). These included *partial preemptions* (where administrative authority may be delegated to states if they meet nationally determined standards); *direct orders* (that mandate state or local actions under the threat of criminal or civil penalties); and *crossover sanctions* (which threaten the termination or reduction of aid provided in one or more specified grant programs when the tough requirements of another are not met).[53]

Crosscutting grant conditions not only continued in the eighties but increased. Although a few were scrapped (under Reagan, for example, requirements issued under Circular A-95 and the State and Local Assistance Act of 1972) and others were downplayed (for example, Citizen Participation; Intergovernmental Personnel Act of 1970 as amended by the Civil Service Reform Act of 1978; Architectural Barriers Act of 1968; A-111, covering jointly funded Federal assistance; A-40, covering the management of Federal Reporting Requirements), other crosscuts were enacted or promulgated and handled with vigor (for example, E.O. 12291, centralizing regulatory review; Circular A-129,

## Table 8-15
## New Social Regulatory Enactments by Type and Over Time, 1930–90

|        | Crosscuts | Crossovers | Partial Preemptions | Direct Orders | Mixed |
|--------|-----------|------------|---------------------|---------------|-------|
| 1930s  | 1         | –          | –                   | –             | –     |
| 1940s  | 1         | –          | –                   | –             | –     |
| 1960s  | 4         | 1          | 3                   | –             | –     |
| 1970s  | 9         | 3          | 6                   | 5             | 5     |
| 1980s  | 1         | 6          | 2                   | 9             | 2     |
| 1990   | 2         | 1          | 1                   | 2             | 1     |

*Sources:* Adapted from Advisory Commission on Intergovernmental Relations, *Regulatory Federalism: Policy, Process, Impact and Reform,* A-95 (Washington, D.C., February 1984), 19–21; and Timothy J. Conlan and David R. Beam, "Federal Mandates: The Record of Reform and Future Prospects," *Intergovernmental Perspective* (ACIR) 18 (Fall 1992): 8.

for prescreening of applicants for recovery of delinquent Federal debt).[54] The new-style regulations, which involve more than mandates in the "New Social Regulation" group, number more than seventy. Direct orders, which usually deal with public employment and environmental protection, usually are based on the commerce power or on the equal protection clause of the Fourteenth Amendment. Partial preemptions, which tend to cover environmental protection, natural resources, and health and safety, are authorized under the commerce power and the supremacy clause, though they also are usually components of a Federal grant based on the conditional spending power. Strictly speaking, only the crosscutting, crossover, and the intrusive program-specific conditions are part of the new strategy of using grants-in-aid, their conditions, and the conditional spending power as novel instruments for promoting Federal regulatory objectives. As the analysis in chapter 7 demonstrates, this approach essentially gives Congress unlimited authority to pursue a regulatory course with whatever grant conditions it wishes. This fact is yet to be fully appreciated by both friends and foes of federalism.

Of the major "social regulations" enacted over the past thirty-two years, crosscuts have been the most common, though direct orders experienced a dramatic increase in the eighties (see table 8-15). Partial preemptions and crossovers have nearly the same count, but the former were used more frequently in the seventies and the latter in the eighties. The eight mixed types illustrate the distinctive and more coercive effects of melding these devices: for example, Americans with Disabilities Act (1990), which includes a crosscut and a direct order; Safe Drinking Water Act Amendments (1986), which rely on a partial preemption and a direct order; and the Water Quality Act of 1987, which uses a partial preemption, a crosscut, and a direct order.

All this highlights more of the dimensions of one of the most controversial developments in contemporary intergovernmental relations: Federal mandates to

state and local governments. Such social regulation constituted as large a proportion of regulatory enactments in the conservative eighties as in the prior decade.
Moreover, the figures cited here and most of the discussion have not covered
the costly program-specific conditions that have been more burdensome in fiscal terms than all but a few of the new types of regulation. The 1990 Medicaid
amendments, the workfare requirement in AFDC that came with the 1998 welfare reform, and the hike in local matches for Federal water projects are only
the more obvious of earlier burdensome, vertical, specific-to-a-grant program
conditions.[55]

The costs of these new Federal mandates rose with their numbers. New rules
promulgated pursuant to the regulatory enactments passed between 1983 and
1992 cost state and local governments at least $10.85 billion.[56] Compliance with
Environmental Protection Agency (EPA) regulations alone were estimated to
have cost local governments $19 billion by 1987, and this was projected to reach
$32 billion by the millennium. The march of the mandates was not matched by a
pick-up in the march of grant monies. If anything, the regulations advanced and
the aid funds receded — excluding entitlement monies for individuals. Federal
aid in constant dollar terms was actually cut by one-third in the eighties. Hence
the vigorous move in the early nineties on the part of public interest groups
(PIGs) and other concerned people to mount a regulatory reform campaign.
With it came growing media coverage of the issue.[57]

The Unfunded Mandates Reform Act (UMRA) represented the culmination
of a concerted PIG push to rein in the congressional regulatory romp. It was
the first item in Gingrich's Contract to be passed, and it was immediately signed
by the president. This action was viewed by many as a move toward a more
balanced federalism. But, as stressed in chapter 6, it was in fact a modest measure — one that encouraged a "stop, look, and listen" approach to mandates.[58]
Any such proposed legislation that involved an uncompensated state or local
cost greater than $50 million a year above and beyond savings and direct Fed-
eral funding as determined by the Congressional Budget Office (CBO) can now
be halted by a mere point of order on the Senate or House floor. A simple majority may override the point of order, but the issue of a mandate's cost is raised.
Yet the exemptions must also be noted; these include those regulations that relate to preventing discrimination, grant conditions, preemptions, or provision of
services not having state or local fiscal implications.

How did UMRA fare with the Congress that enacted it? The number of "significant mandates" as determined by CBO proved to be remarkably small, 11 to
be exact — out of an estimated 718 total in 1996. As Paul Posner explained it,
the commitment of the Republican majority to regulatory restraint and the act
itself combined to keep the number of new mandates to a handful, though there
were intrusive grant conditions and dictatorial preemptions that passed during
the second session of the 104th Congress, as indicated in chapter 6. In addition,
in some instances a proposed mandate's cost would be reduced in order to avoid
reaching the $50 million threshold. In other cases, a new mandate prompted
a consensus among all members that a point of order was out of order in that

### Table 8-16
### Federal Grant Matching Ratios by Number of Programs,
### 1960, 1976, 1991

| | 1960 | | 1976 | | 1991 | |
|---|---|---|---|---|---|---|
| *Federal Participation* | N | (%) | N | (%) | N | (%) |
| Less than 50 percent | 8 | 5.9 | 2 | 0.4 | 4 | 0.7 |
| 50 percent | 36 | 26.7 | 59 | 13.3 | 43 | 7.8 |
| 50–100 percent | 17 | 12.6 | 145 | 32.8 | 193 | 35.2 |
| Some cost sharing[a] | 10 | 7.4 | 42 | 9.5 | 40 | 7.4 |
| 100 percent | 58 | 43.0 | 170 | 38.4 | 268 | 48.9 |
| Other[b] | 6 | 4.4 | 25 | 5.6 | 0 | 0.0 |
| Total | 135 | 100.0 | 443 | 100.0 | 548 | 100.0 |

*Source:* Adapted from Advisory Commission on Intergovernmental Relations, *Regulatory Federalism: Policy, Process, Impact and Reform*, A-95 (Washington, D.C., February 1984), 19–21; and Timothy J. Conlan and David R. Beam, "Federal Mandates: The Record of Reform and Future Prospects," *Intergovernmental Perspective* (ACIR) 18 (Fall 1992): 8.

a. Some nominal or negotiable recipient contribution required.
b. Indeterminable.

particular instance, as with Megan's Law. Whether constraint will continue to win out depends on whether protection of state and local interests against Federal regulation becomes more compelling than the particular goals advanced by mandate advocates.[59] No bets on this one!

Still another marked change in the character of Federal aid is in the area of *matching and maintenance-of-effort requirements,* as well as *"nonsupplanting"* requirements (that is, banning the use of Federal aid funds as substitutes for required recipient outlays). In this realm of recipient fiscal responsibilities, a basic trend toward reducing the dollar match and a corresponding trend toward increasing the number of maintenance-of-effort or "nonsupplanting" of recipient funds conditions can be observed.

The proportion of aid programs having low or fifty-fifty Federal matching declined from 32.6 percent of the 1960 total to 13.7 percent of the 1976 total, to 8.5 percent by 1991. Concomitantly, the proportion of grants calling for high Federal fiscal participation rose from 63 percent in 1960 to more than 80 percent of the 443 programs funded and operational in 1976, even though the sector represented by the full-Federal-funding group declined slightly in proportionate though not in absolute terms. By 1991 the proportion had risen to more than 91 percent, with an increase in the 100 percent, full-Federal-funding sector (see table 8-16).

When the large, very costly Federal grant programs are considered, full Federal funding is much more rare. Air pollution control, wastewater treatment works, urban mass transportation, capital improvements, vocational education, developmental disability, Medicaid, veterans hospital and Medicaid care, and national school lunch programs all require state or local matches and TANF has a maintenance-of-effort requirement. Moreover, the non-Federal match has been increased in some programs over the past twelve years. Even so, the number of programs with generous Federal matching shares is still fairly amazing, given the plight of the Federal purse.

A final group of significant changes in the Federal aid system is highlighted in the various *ways in which the flow of assistance dollars shifted* since 1961. At the most aggregative level, this is reflected in the 54/46 split in 1961 of Federal aid funds between nonurban and urban areas (which, of course, did not correspond with the population division of the time) and the roughly 30/70 split in any recent fiscal year (which reflects population patterns more closely).

On the thorny front of fiscal equalization, other not unrelated changes occurred. In 1960 wealthy states received the lowest grant amounts on a per capita basis, poorer states got the largest amounts, and middle states' amounts were just above the national per capita norm.[60] Middle-income states dropped below the national average by 1962 and below the wealthy states' average by 1968 and have remained there since. Moreover, by the midseventies and because of the fallout from Medicaid, the wealthy states overtook the poorer states, reducing the latter to a second-rank position for the remainder of the decade.

This development relates in part to the ascendancy of highways in the 1960 grant package, in which allocation formulas favored low-population-density states (which then frequently had low per capita incomes). The subsequent shifts were in part a product of the greater grant focus on urban areas and the expansion of public assistance programs (AFDC and Medicaid). With the later urban thrusts, comparatively well-off urban states (and their less-well-off local jurisdictions) benefited. Even with public assistance and its equalization factors built into its cost-sharing formulas, liberal eligibility provisions pushed several high-income states into the largest per capita assistance class — along with some in the lowest income category.[61] It was these trends that produced the situation in the seventies in which the wealthy states ranked first and the poorest states second in their respective per capita assistance receipt rates.

In general, the eighties and early nineties reflected a strange combination of trends from the previous two decades. Wealthy states in 1991 divided, some having high per capita Federal aid figures (for example, Connecticut, Massachusetts, New York, Alaska, and Hawaii), and others having middling to even low figures (for example, Nevada, California, and Maryland).[62] Much of this can be explained in terms of efforts in some of the latter group to institute constraints on Medicaid and AFDC (before it was repealed) spending. The high 1991 figure for Alaska, surpassing all others save for Wyoming, was in part a product of the increase in highway outlays. For the sixteen states that fell in the low per capita income bracket, the figures for per capita Federal aid generally were high. Yet again, there were divisions: three states had comparatively low figures and another cluster of nine had an average per capita grant share that was 25 percent greater than the average for the low three.

Careful examination of table 8-17 (p. 252) indicates that in FY 1994 Federal grant outlays reflected an even more bizarre pattern of allocations than its FY 1991 predecessor. Only five of the eleven high per capita income states were high or upper-middle aid recipients, while another five fell in the lower middle and low aid categories (one very low, Nevada). At the other extreme, the fourteen lower-middle and low per capita income states subdivided into five that were classed as high (three) or upper middle (three) regarding their grant allocations on a per capita basis, while three were low or lower-middle aid recipients. A third of this group were among the middle range of per capita grants; there was not much equalization here.

With the large middling per capita income category composed of exactly half the states, there were only two high aid receivers and five in the upper-middle subgroup. The lower-middle and low per capita grant receivers numbered twelve. The rest (six) were classed as middlers in per capita income and in per capita aid. It's hard to make much sense out of this.

What are the explanatory factors at play here, if any? A clear one is the simple fact that states have different program preferences and contrasting views about services and funding them. The desire to participate heavily in certain social and health programs is still a factor for some, but not for others. Some of the findings of the "Civic Culture" researchers and from Daniel Elazar's political cultural typology come into play here also.[63] With smaller states the program needs frequently appear less severe than those of larger and more urban states, and this can affect rates of grant participation. In his assessment of per capita grant allotments to the states and localities, G. Ross Stephens found that "two thirds of the variation in per capita federal grants is explained by two variables, the reciprocal of state population size and per capita own source receipts of state and local governments."[64] Put more plainly, small and tax-rich states receive higher per capita aid. Much of this is explained by the operation of the senatorial principle of representation: the parity of the states.

Not to be overlooked in this ambiguous description of the interstate equalization effects of Federal aid is the fact that income redistribution was not and is not the prime goal of the overwhelming majority of the aid programs. None of the old five block grants contained a fiscal capacity factor in their allocational formulas, and only GRS and about twenty-five categoricals relied in some measure on the ability of a recipient jurisdiction to finance public services as a factor in allocating aid funds in the seventies. In FY 1991, none of the 14 block grants contained a fiscal capacity factor in its formula, and of the 146 categorical formula grants, only 28 (10 percent) had an income factor in their allocational formula and only a few of these were big-money items (for example, Medicaid and formerly AFDC).[65] There has not been much change here since the seventies.

The shifts in the program composition of the Federal grant package explain

## Table 8-17
### Federal Per Capita Grant Allocations by States (FY 1994)
### Ranked by Per Capita Income

| *High*<br>*Per Capita Income States*<br>*($23,000–$30,000)* | | *Upper Middle (11)*<br>*and Middle (14)*<br>*Per Capita Income States*<br>*($19,000–$22,000)* | | *Lower Middle (8), Low (4),*<br>*and Very Low (2)*<br>*Per Capita Income States*<br>*($15,000–$18,999)* | |
|---|---|---|---|---|---|
| Connecticut | UM | Virginia | UM | South Dakota | UM |
| Massachusetts | UM | Minnesota | M | Alabama | M |
| New Jersey | LM | Colorado | L | North Dakota | H |
| Maryland | L | California | UM | Idaho | LM |
| New York | H | Washington | LM | Louisiana | H |
| Delaware | LM | Michigan | M | South Carolina | M |
| New Hampshire | M | Pennsylvania | LM | Kentucky | M |
| Hawaii | UM | Rhode Island | UM | Oklahoma | L |
| Illinois | LM | Ohio | M | | |
| Nevada | VL | Wisconsin | LM | Montana | UM |
| Alaska | H | Florida | L | Utah | LM |
| | | | | Arkansas | M |
| | | Kansas | LM | New Mexico | M |
| | | Georgia | LM | | |
| | | Texas | LM | West Virginia | H |
| | | Nebraska | LM | Mississippi | UM |
| | | Indiana | M | | |
| | | Oregon | UM | | |
| | | Vermont | H | | |
| | | Iowa | LM | | |
| | | Tennessee | M | | |
| | | Missouri | LM | | |
| | | Arizona | LM | | |
| | | Wyoming | H | | |
| | | North Carolina | M | | |
| | | Maine | UM | | |

*Sources:* Adapted from American Council on Intergovernmental Relations, *Significant Features of Fiscal Federalism,* vol. 2, *Revenues and Expenditures, 1995* (Washington, D.C., October 1997), 27, 110, 111.

**Legend for Per Capita State Grant Allocations:**

| | | |
|---|---|---|
| H | High: | $1,000 or more |
| UM | Upper Middle: | $900–$999 |
| M | Middle: | $700–$899 (U.S. average: $735) |
| LM | Lower Middle: | $600–$699 |
| L | Low: | $500–$599 |
| VL | Very Low: | below $500 |

some of the distributional changes, along with its focus on four allocational principles, not one: political fairness (with its emphasis on population and jurisdictional equality); program need (with its reliance on sometimes doubtful proxies in the formulas); recipient program effort (which involves some variation of the cost-sharing approach); and fiscal capacity or equalization (which even when emphasized usually conflicts with one or more of the above factors). The growing emphasis on more environmental and more social welfare grants, then, along with the shifting interaction among the four allocational factors, produced the seemingly random shifts in interstate distribution of Federal assistance from 1960 to the present.

A final facet of the changed allocational patterns of Federal assistance is the degree to which local jurisdictions have been cut out of the picture. As recently as 1978, some of the more hard-pressed central cities, notably in the Northeast and Midwest, came to depend heavily on Federal financial aid. In municipalities such as St. Louis, Newark, Buffalo, Cleveland, Baltimore, Philadelphia, Detroit, and Chicago, direct Federal aid as a percentage of own-source general revenue ranged from 42 percent (for Chicago) to 75.9 percent (for Buffalo) and 76.8 percent (for Detroit).[66] There is still some disagreement about the extent to which Federal aid was or could be targeted to local jurisdictions encountering a range of economic, social, and fiscal challenges, but the figures in the seventies indicated a growing reliance on direct Federal aid (from a range of grant sources) by several central cities, with some of the most "pressured" having the highest "reliance" rates. The one major caveat to be noted here is that the higher percentages for FY 1978 were explained partially in terms of funds flowing from the three countercyclical programs and that only one of these (CETA) was reauthorized and was still operational in 1980. In general, then, the 1979–80 figures were lower, reflecting the more stabilized condition of Federal aid during that period. Yet larger central cities still fared better than medium-sized and small municipalities, and all categories indicated far higher receipt rates than had prevailed early in the seventies.[67] The same generalization could be made aggregatively for counties, cities, and towns.

All this now seems to be in the very distant past. General Revenue Sharing is gone, and other programs providing big help to many local governments have been systematically slashed or eliminated. In FY 1978 direct Federal aid constituted 9 percent of local general revenue; by FY 1987, 4.2 percent; by FY 1990, 3.6 percent; and by FY 1994, 4.1 percent. The state share of local general revenue first shrunk somewhat, due to states' added responsibilities because of Reagan New Federalism and their own fiscal difficulties, but later it soared. From 1980 to 1985, it declined from more than 31 percent to less than 29 percent; during the rest of the decade, it hovered around 29 percent but rose to 33.6 percent by FY 1990.[68] But by FY 1994, the percentage had reached a high of 55 percent, thanks to the rolling economy and educational demands.

Most evidence indicates that the disparities between central cities and their suburbs persist.[69] The most recent updating of fiscal disparities between thirty-five central cities and their suburban neighbors indicates a continuation of earlier

Table 8-18
**Average Fiscal Disparities for Common Sample
of Metropolitan Statistical Areas (MSAs)**

|  | 1957 | 1970 | 1977 | 1981 | 1987 |
|---|---|---|---|---|---|
| Per capita expenditures |  |  |  |  |  |
|    Total | 1.32 | 1.39 | 1.47 | 1.40 | 1.51 |
|    Education | 0.77 | 0.86 | 0.95 | 0.90 | 0.91 |
|    Noneducation | 2.07 | 2.13 | 2.04 | 1.87 | 2.17 |
| Per capita taxes | 1.59 | 1.42 | 1.32 | 1.31 | 1.25 |
| Per capita Federal and state aid[a] total | 0.99 | 1.36 | 1.69 | 1.64 | 1.53 |
| Per capita income[a] | – | 0.91 | 0.87 | 0.83 | 0.82 |
| Employment to population ratio[a] | – | – | 2.05 | 1.79 | 1.60 |
| State and Federal aid as a percentage of per capita income[a] | – | 1.58 | 2.06 | 2.12 | 1.98 |
| CC per capita income[b] | – | 3,222 | 5,836 | 7,816 | 11,280 |
| OCC per capita income[b] | – | 3,579 | 6,672 | 8,488 | 13,868 |
| CC employment to population ratio[c] | – | 0.48 | 0.48 | 0.55 | 0.44 |
| OCC employment to population ratio[c] | – | 0.24 | 0.24 | 0.28 | 0.27 |
| CC state and Federal per capita aid relative to income[c] | – | 0.05 | 0.09 | 0.11 | 0.08 |
| OCC state and Federal per capita aid relative to income[c] | – | 0.04 | 0.05 | 0.05 | 0.04 |

*Source:* Roy Bahl, Jorge Martinez-Vasquez, and David L. Sjoquist, "Central City–Suburban Fiscal Disparities," *Public Finance Quarterly* 70 (October 1992): 425. No later data available.

   a. These variables are measured as the ratio of central city to outside central city.
   b. These variables are expressed in current dollars.
   c. These variables correspond either to the central cities (CC) or the area in the MSA other than the central city (OCC).

trends, for example, significant per capita income, employment, and expenditure differences (see table 8-18). At the same time, and as noted earlier, Federal and state aid data suggest an improvement in the capacity of both levels to target the central cities from 1957 through 1977, with a slight slip by 1981 and a larger one by 1987, but this may be partially explained by the emergence of inner-ring, blue-collar suburbs with many of the same difficulties as the central cities. In any event, although the disparities persist, the aid figures for the eighties are better than what one might be led to believe and do suggest a rough attempt to target despite reduced grant funding. Many close observers of the metropolitan scene now believe that central cities can solve many of their problems only within the context of the regions of which they are a part.[70]

The basic grant-related issues confronting Federal policymakers are these: (1) Should prime reliance be placed on a free-market solution to urban problems with some facilitative Federal and state actions, or should there be a return to a revitalized servicing strategy with assistance programs playing a big role? (2) If the latter is the case, should the Federal government work through the states, as it has largely since the early eighties, or return to the direct-access approach of the seventies? And (3) because people in the metropolitan areas, especially central cities, already benefit from various existing people-related Federal grants, should a local-regional governmental as well as a people strategy be part of this ameliorative effort?

To sum up, the many dimensions of the growth of and changes in Federal aid underscore and symbolize the uneven emergence of a still heavily inter-governmentalized system. Yet it is not as marbleized as it was in 1980, though it is far more so than in 1970 or certainly 1960. If the flow of grant dollars is blended with the flow of Federal regulations, then today's level of intergovernmental entanglement probably matches that of 1980. Until 1997 and its budget agreement, over the Federal aid system as well as that of the states and over the revenue systems of all levels was the ever lengthening dark shadow of the ballooning national budget deficits (in the triple digit range since FY 1982). The national debt has more than quintupled since 1981, and the annual interest payment on this debt surpassed the total of all Federal aid to state and local governments in FY 1982. But that is all behind us; the budget actually was balanced at the end of the 1997 Federal fiscal year, and the budget agreement of 1997 promises continued adherence to a budgetary course that will assure that this balance will still be in place by 2002. This represents a remarkable shift in perspective since 1994.

## The Deficit That Disappeared

The earlier dire national-debt dilemma rose out of the application of economic theories in the early eighties that at the very least were questionable. It thrived on the political and even more the interest group policy gridlock in Washington and on the public's appetite for government programs and antipathy to paying for them. It was sustained by the multibillion-dollar savings-and-loan and HUD scandals and the zooming costs of health programs. It took on new life with the lingering 1990–92 recession and the faltering efforts in the late eighties and early nineties to deal with the very serious structural and cyclical defects that afflicted the economy.

In specific terms, how did the country's status as the greatest debtor nation globally impact state and local governments? Deficit-driven federalism at the national level

- kept the rate of growth in grant programs, notably those in the non-entitlement areas, close to a near-static level;

- eliminated any real Federal role in attacking the major new threats to urban or rural America;

- enhanced the propensity of national decision makers to enact unfunded conditions and mandates;

- accelerated the congressional tendency to enact dozens of pint-size project grants that looked impressive symbolically and politically to the naive among us, but did little to help people in subnational governments, given their meager monies, that did nothing at all to enhance trust in government, and that added to the number of interest groups;

- intensified Federal forays into state and local revenue-raising terrain, largely to reduce the number and dollar amounts of items still deductible from the Federal personal income tax; and

- rendered the Federal government reactive, not proactive, and this has underscored the resilience of states and their localities but dramatized the necessity to recognize that there are certain domestic policy areas that only Washington can address.

A reactive Federal government is not one that can confront the cluster of conflicting challenges facing the nation and our governance system. What then is the current state of fiscal federalism? An accurate response, one mindful of the past three decades of pulverizing the public fisc, would have to be a resounding "Pretty good," if not "Excellent, all things considered." But what has made all the difference between 1985 (Gramm-Rudman-Hollings), 1990 (the Bush-congressional accord), 1993 (the Clinton budget victory) and now? All of these were periods when the deficit was in dire straits. The answer to the question, of course, is that the goal of these three deficit reduction endeavors now has been achieved. The earlier enervating anxiety of many that we lack the courage required to correct runaway deficit spending has been reduced significantly. Courage, of course, was shown in 1990 and 1993, but some question arises whether much was required to cut the 1997 budget deal. To balance the budget while increasing educational, health, and workfare outlays and while also cutting taxes and granting tax credits is not quite the kind of pain associated with a big budget summit resolved on ending the deficit spending we have known since FY 1970. So why no sweat, no pain? Enter the economy with its nearly unparalleled expansion, low inflation, remarkably low unemployment, and its capacity to produce unanticipated public revenues of a size that astounds even the most cynical. (CBO's latest forecast for the next ten years is a surplus of $1.6 trillion in FY 2009.) It was these extra revenues that permitted the budget to be described in almost any terms but those of fiscal constraint, which may come back to haunt its authors and all of us as well.[71] The cuts were few after all, amounting to a total of $329.6 billion; the tax cuts and social program hikes were numerous, costing $214.2 billion; and the economic forecasts were fairly rosy. Meanwhile, the basic future budget issues of the long-term viability of Social Security, Medicare, and, in effect, Medicaid were shelved for the time being. Let another commission take on these thankless assignments, as if we have not had our fill of them.

So what of the broader issues relating to all of the facets of our public finances? On the very positive side of the ledger, the balanced Federal budget with all of the questions and criticisms surrounding it must be deemed an unparalleled plus. The hope now is that some of the several negative side effects of the national deficits that hurt state and local governments might begin to be corrected. A second salutary omen is the balance that has emerged between state-local and Federal expenditures from own sources on domestic governance. Who would have believed a generation ago that such a feat could be accomplished? Were it only possible to achieve this same roughly even balance in the realm of American parties and politics? More on this in chapter 10. A third happy development in the field of public finance is the emergence of more balanced state-local revenue systems that are more stable, less volatile, and a bit more progressive than their predecessors of a generation ago. All this is not to say that much more need not be done to eliminate some of the instabilities, inelasticities, and inequities in these systems. It is to say that compared to the sixties, for example, the fifty systems today are a distinct improvement. Other salutary signs are the increases in the number and funding of Federal block grants, in moves to curb Federal mandates, and in the continuing strength of the local sector.

In an overall systemic sense, there is a broad adherence by the various levels to expenditure patterns that reflect a rough division of servicing labor among the three tiers, with the bulk of Federal domestic funds going for redistributive, social, and spillover programs and most state and local outlays allocated broadly to developmental and public safety programs. Many public policy and finance authorities (Alice Rivlin, Paul E. Peterson, Edward M. Gramlich, and Richard M. Bird, among others) find this to be a healthy arrangement for a number of reasons — political, economic, equity-related, and administrative.[72] Peterson has found that most recent intergovernmental fiscal, transfer developments have, in fact, pretty much adhered to this rough division of programmatic labor. The major exception to this functional division, of course, is TANF. Its turning over of much of the public welfare function to the states prompted strong criticism from Paul Peterson and others on grounds that this devolution of an equity function can only lead in the long run to "a race to the bottom." Only time will tell whether Peterson and his many allies or the all-the-way devolutionists are right and whether this action was a good thing for a more balanced federalism or not. Perhaps the most heartening omen for the future and for our federalism was the degree to which the public indicated support for the deficit reduction drive. Some of the efforts and some of the key players in this drama required this support to withstand the many pressures to cave in to the fiscally profligate crowd.

On the more negative side of the public finance ledger, the initial craze to figure out how best to spend the Federal budget surpluses clearly is a source of some alarm. Debt reduction was not mentioned by anybody but Alan Greenspan, and very quietly. The president's wish to save the surpluses for the later needs of Social Security seemed both wise and politically shrewd, but we will have to wait and see. Another negative sign is the degree to which all tax systems, not just the state and local, have recently become more regressive. The House majority leader Dick Armey has been trumpeting the virtues of a flat tax. Examination of the present revenue-raising arrangements would indicate that in practice we are pretty close to one right now. Any suggestion that progressivity in a tax code has social and/or fiscal merit seems to encounter hostility on all sides, or at least from the vocal members of an audience. Thanks to the Earned Income Tax Credit (EITC), the working poor have been relieved of some of their tax burden, though this was an item for repeal in the 104th Congress. The outstanding social fact of our times is the extraordinary and ever growing gap between the rich and poor in this country. More progressive tax codes are a modest way of alleviating some of the potential dissension that steep class cleavages can engender. They are, in fact, a way to enhance social stability. At the moment, however, this clearly is an academic argument, not a feasible plank in a party platform.

Another worry is the failure of most states to take seriously the desperate need to diversify local revenues. The property tax, nuisance levies, and state aid are not the basis of a stable and even roughly fair local revenue system. Some of the failure to take action here stems from the need to avoid politically the local government reorganization question, which almost inevitably arises if the revenue diversification issue is plumbed to its depths. This concern is closely related to the bigger question of how much has the present good shape of Federal and state finances aided local governments? Regulatory relief, state mandate reform, welfare reform, more block grants, and windfalls for state treasuries with the first TANF allocations have not provided many direct benefits for America's localities. The continued decremental spending for discretionary grant programs to the states, the 0.4 percent increase in direct Federal aid to localities (from FY 1992 to FY 1997), and even the arrival of a couple of additional local block grants (HOME, ISTEA, and TEA-21) are not viewed by local officials as having any great significance, though they are welcomed. All in all, the recent increases in state and, to a lesser extent, their own revenues, along with some big hikes in some states in state aid, notably for education, constitute the chief direct benefits accruing to local governments as a consequence of our robust economy and improved public finances. From fiscal years 1994 through 1999, state total year-end balances amounted to $16.9, $20.6, $25.1, $27.1, $24.7, and $20.9 billion, respectively, and this was with several tax cuts.[73] The recent reduction in those state surpluses, especially the one slated for FY 1999, was caused largely by tax cuts, not by any widespread state effort to deal with interlocal fiscal disparities, with the need in at least half the states for a local general support program, with using fiscal incentives to facilitate regional cooperation and joint performance of functions on an areawide basis, or with property tax relief in the sixteen states not having a "circuit breaker." These are some of the ways, along with greater action on the ongoing educational reform front, that local governments really might benefit from the happy condition of our public finances at the Federal and especially the state levels.

So how fares our public fisc? It's mostly fine for now, but it soon must face the future — a future with some storm clouds already visible, including our entitlements, the quiet but very real crisis in our educational systems (which require a lot more than mere money), and uncertainties about the economy, especially in light of the collapse of several East Asian systems and their combined impact on ours.

# Chapter 9

# A Resurgent Role for the States?

The states' strategically crucial role in the administration, financing, and planning of intergovernmental programs and regulations — both Federal and their own — and their perennial key position in practically all areas of local governance have made them the pivotal middlemen in the realm of functional federalism. Yet they enjoy no such primacy in the political, representational, or judicial spheres. It is a paradox that will be probed here, as will be the ambiguity that stems from the states' responsibilities as creators of, competitors with, and protectors of their local governments.

This chapter will deal with several variations on the state theme: (1) recent shifts in the state's relationship to localities, (2) the resurgence of state institutional and operational strength and resulting new roles in the system, especially in the welfare reform area, (3) the current character of state-local financing and servicing systems, and (4) the state as shaper and nonshaper of local and substate regional institutions and processes.

## The Leading Intergovernmental Linkage

The state-local relationship traditionally was the paramount U.S. intergovernmental connection. Significant Federal-state linkages date mainly from the 1930s, and widespread Federal-state-local and direct Federal to local grant and regulatory contacts were pretty much a product of the 1964–80 years. The state-local relationship once was paramount in the system and, with current trends continuing, will again become so.[1] In fact, if the intergovernmental fiscal transfers are the major measure of primacy, then this linkage already has become the paramount one, since state aid surpassed Federal aid in the early nineties.

### Forgetting the Facts

For more than two hundred years, the states have been the chief architects, by conscious and sometimes unconscious action or inaction, of the welter of servicing, financial, institutional, and jurisdictional arrangements that form our fifty state-local systems. Moreover, they have provided the means by which most of domestic U.S. governance is conducted and most domestic policies are implemented. This elemental fact of intergovernmental relations appeared at times

260

to be forgotten or overtly challenged during the 1960s and 1970s. Evidence of this change was apparent in many actions of the national government and its policymakers:

- the increasing bypassing of the states in Federal aid allocations, rising from 8 percent in 1960 to 12 percent in 1968, to double that figure by 1974, and to 29 percent by 1978;

- the parallel development at the national level of a "panoramic partnership principle" during the years 1964–80, wherein practically all categories of subnational governments were accorded eligibility status under an ever expanding number of grant programs;

- the accompanying tendency of Washington policymakers to treat the various major categories of subnational governments as separate, disconnected, and sometimes even equal providers of public goods and services and as contesting supplicants for the Federal aid largesse;

- the parallel inclination in Federal aid programs to assign almost equal status to very different jurisdictions in the same local governmental grouping (for example, towns and townships as well as counties under General Revenue Sharing, metropolitan counties under community development, and counties under CETA);

- the ever greater blurring of private and public issues;

- the mounting habit of the media, the public, and many elected officials at all levels to treat almost any state, substate regional, or local issue as a national issue subject to national alleviation;

- the nearly monolithic focus on intergovernmental fiscal transfers and regulations as the chief means of mounting a response to many challenges confronting local governments.

## Why the Apparent National Unawareness?

The above developments during the 1960s and 1970s directed the eyes of the electorate and of state and local elected officials toward the nation's capital. Decision makers there found it difficult to resist the attention. How could this come to pass? How could the array of legal, fiscal, functional, and political linkages, which in all of the states combine differently to form fifty distinct and diverse polities, be ignored?

In one sense, of course, this fundamental fact of American federalism was not overlooked. The expanding state-local linkages in these years belie the notion that all Washington decision makers were oblivious to this relationship. The Federal aid that was channeled through the states (see table 8-7, p. 227) and on to their localities was always a reminder. But certainly there was a broad trend toward treating these inevitable and sometimes trying relationships in a cavalier or contemptuous fashion. Moreover, the Federal government was looked to by more and more citizens and organizational groups as the prime instrumentality for expressing their respective social, economic, or moralistic goals. Paralleling this development was the continuing proliferation of pressure groups in the nation's capital, including new and expanding public interest groups (PIGs). But, again, the question arises: Why?

The poor national image of most state governments in the 1950s and the mid-1960s is one part of the answer. Racist, rurally dominated, and reactionary were the epithets then thrown at most, but not all, state systems. Even as late as 1968, John Fisher of *Harper's* could describe the voyage to Puerto Rico by the nation's governors for their annual meeting as a "Ship of Fools" (the title of a best-seller by Katherine Anne Porter). It is difficult for most of us to remember the condition of state politics and governmental systems before *Baker v. Carr* (1962), the pivotal reapportionment decision, and the historic Voting Rights Act of 1965. In 1958, only eight of the then forty-eight states had legislatures that roughly approximated the one-person, one-vote democratic representational norm.

Optimistic assumptions in the mid-1960s about the resourcefulness and progressivity of the Federal revenue system also were part of this shift toward Washington. Equally sanguine assumptions about the productivity, management acumen, competitiveness, and rich resource basis of the nation's economy reinforced the belief that the Federal fisc was and would be the fruitful provider of whatever was needed to help fill funding gaps at the state and local levels.

Not unrelated to these centralizing tendencies was the erosion of the traditional political parties as mediating and moderating institutions within the federal system. The steady decline in state and local party influence over nominating and electoral processes at all levels, as well as in the legislative process nationally, cannot be ignored as a factor here. When it was coupled with the simultaneous advent of an increasing array of interest groups located in and focusing sometimes exclusively on Washington, the centralization trend became even more pronounced. This trend is discussed in more detail later in the chapter.

Buttressing all this were overall popular attitudes favoring an expansionist national government role and believing in the capacity of the central government to solve and resolve basic and mundane societal and economic problems. Not to be overlooked was a general unawareness among the citizenry of the structural and functional differences among the fifty state systems. These trends prompted a steady watch on Washington, a hike in public interest group (PIG) representation (for example, National Governors' Association, National Conference of State Legislatures, National Association of County Officials, National League of Cities, U.S. Conference of Mayors), and a parallel downgrading of the state-local relationship.

### The Resurgence of the Crucial Connection

By the late 1970s popular faith in the capacity of the Federal government began to fade, and with good reason. Much of it, after all, had been misplaced to begin with. The optimism regarding Federal revenues and the national economy began to evaporate as early as the winter of 1973–74. Federal aid to states and localities began to taper off by 1979 and 1980; budget deficits continued throughout the decade; and the indexation of various entitlement programs in the early 1970s really began to take a budgetary toll as inflation soared in the last part of the decade. Meanwhile, defense outlays again started to rise, beginning with FY 1979, even as some regulatory curbs were being imposed and new block grants proposed. The latter, of course, indicated a growing awareness of the need for correcting some of the earlier excesses of national interventionism.

All of these later Carter trends continued and were greatly accelerated under President Reagan. The various efforts at devolution during the eighties forced a reexamination and renewal of the state-local relationship. The new block grants, the devolution of administrative authority under some of the regulatory programs, the surgical cuts in direct Federal-local aid, and the elimination of much of the national government's role in the substate regional realm helped generate the shift. In addition, new municipal liability in the antitrust, tort, and other judicial areas also prompted a growing realization of the need for greater state-local collaboration, though occasional confrontation was part of this connection both in state capitals and in Washington, D.C.

Some of the anti-Washington sentiment had nothing to do with actual or alleged Federal failures and ostensible excesses, but rather with significant and salutary Federal successes. Various kinds of folk took exception to certain of these landmark legislative victories. For example, many southerners and others were infuriated by the civil rights legislation of the sixties. As Michael R. Beschloss has noted in his "Taking Charge" (1997), Lyndon B. Johnson predicted that the southern Democratic party would erode as a consequence of these enactments, of which he was the prime architect. This was an accurate forecast from a president who understood the historical significance of these measures, even if later generations did not. With the major surge in the seventies in the environmental protection area and its emphasis on regulations as well as expanded grants, much of the business community and others began an anti-Washington campaign, despite the fact that it was Nixon who supported all but one of these measures enacted during his White House years. Workplace safety and efforts to expand the goal of more equal access went beyond blacks to include women, the disabled, the aged, and others, much to the consternation of conservatives of various stripes and others who resented governmental intrusion. In short, it was the advance of the environmental and the egalitarian principles in this period along with some outright misrepresentations of what Washington had and had not done that set the scene for a venomous antinational shift in public opinion, some of it supported by state and local governments. After all they also were affected directly by nearly all of the reform movements of the seventies and by the racial and reappointment transformations of the sixties.

# The Silent Revolution

Even with the heavy focus on Washington through the seventies, the states
during the years 1964–80 were undergoing a major transformation, the most
dramatic of any two decades in their more than eleven-score-year history. In
practically every state, efforts were made to promote greater efficiency, economy,
and accountability in all branches of government.[2] States were responding to
criticisms directed at antiquated constitutions; malapportioned, amateurish, and
inefficient legislatures; and governors with restricted tenure, inadequate staffing,
and insufficient controls over highly fragmented state administrations. They were
condemned for relying on spoils systems rather than merit systems for personnel
management; for regressive tax systems; for poor methods of judicial selection,
discipline, and removal; and for their shackling of local governments, such that
these jurisdictions were unable to deal with mounting urban problems. Some
states moved ahead of the Federal goal on civil rights; others were woeful lag-
gards. State reform continued after 1980, although not at its earlier fast pace.
Overall, the midsixties through 1990 witnessed many improvements. Here are
some indicators of reform in recent years:

- Eleven state constitutions were totally overhauled, and all but a few
  others were partially modified, in most cases to curb excessive constitutional detail, strengthen individual rights, enhance the capacities of all
  three branches of state government, broaden the suffrage, and extend local
  home rule.[3]

- Legislatures became equitably apportioned and now meet annually;[4] 12
  states do not restrict the length of sessions, down from 20 seventeen years
  ago;[5] 30 (compared with 36 in 1960) do not curb the legislature's power to
  call special sessions and 33 may determine the subject matter of the special
  sessions.

- The number of legislative committees has been reduced; at present, 6
  states have standing committees that number less than 10 in both houses;
  in 23, they number between 11 and 20 in each chamber; in 5 states, each
  had more than 20 but less than 30, while 2 had more than 30 in both
  bodies. In the "mixed" category, 2 states had a senate with less than 10,
  but a house of over 30; 9 had an upper house with less than 10 and a
  lower house with 11 to 20; 2 had between 21 and 29 in the upper body
  and over 30 in the lower, while 1 had a senate of less than 10 but a house
  of more than 40.[6] Clearly, reform has yet to run its full course in this field.
  Thirty-five legislatures have uniform rules of procedure that apply to all
  committees; advance notice of hearings is required in most states; and all
  require open committee meetings.

- All states have legislative reference libraries now; 48 staff professionally all
  of their Senate and House committees;[7] presiding officers in all states have

clerical assistance, and over 80 percent have professional aides as well; a comparable number of legislatures now name the state auditor and have responsibility for the auditing process.

- In 1995, some form of "sunset" review process existed in 27 legislatures (formerly 35); 41 have authority to review proposed administrative rules and regulations, and 21 may veto them; and 37 have established a process for reappropriating some or all Federal grants to state governments.

- Forty-eight governors now have four-year terms, compared with 19 in 1960 (but 40 states limit the governor's term; formerly it was 31); gubernatorial appointment authority has broadened somewhat with the decline in the number of elected administrative officers; 41 governors have the sole authority to prepare an executive budget, and the power is shared in 9 states; 44 governors (1 more than in 1981) have an item veto; reorganization authority has been assigned to 20, with 2 (Virginia and Hawaii) having a limited version, as against 7 in the earlier period;[8] governors' salaries overall, like the legislators', have not kept abreast of inflation, but their staffing, again like the legislators', has improved considerably.

- Ten states have a short executive branch ballot (1 to 3 officers), 15 have a medium length ballot (4 to 5 officers), and the remaining 25 have the old style "laundry list" ballot containing 6 or more slots.[9]

- Twenty-six states underwent major executive-branch reform during the period 1965–91,[10] and the number of multimember boards heading line agencies and departments was reduced; 37 have governmentwide merit systems, and at least three-quarters of all permanent state employees are under such systems.

- All state judiciaries now have a court administrative office; all but 3 require legal training for appellate and trial judges,[11] compared with 33 in the fifties; special disciplinary and removal commissions exist in all but 1 state, compared with 41 in 1980 and only 11 in 1960;[12] and about three-quarters have most of the features of "reformed" integrated state-local systems, compared with 18 in the late 1960s.

- Fiscally, states now have much more diversified revenue systems: 42 have a broad-based personal income tax; 45 have a broad-based sales tax and 46 a corporate income tax. States overall have been the senior partners with respect to combined state-local expenditures for over two decades now.

These and other current indicators certainly buttress the assertions that reform, not standpattism, has dominated much of the recent state institutional and fiscal record; that more managership, greater professionalism, and more unshackling were the dominant goals of this remarkable effort; and that state capacity — whether defined in administrative, fiscal, or programmatic terms — was enhanced as a result.

At the same time, some of the facts relating to contemporary legislatures suggest that the traditional ideal of the "citizen" legislature was by no means replaced totally by the "professional" norm. In fact, there was some slippage on this front during the eighties, reflecting populist fears of legislative conniving. Nothing illustrates this more than the recent decline in the scope of legislative autonomy noted above and the sanctioning, as of 1998, of legislative term limits in eighteen states. This latter populist reform, of course, tends to weaken legislative leadership and experience in an age of multibillion-dollar state budgets and to enhance the clout of lobbyists, who naturally are not subject to any kind of term limits, and of executive branch officials, both elective and administrative. The recent increase in the use of popular initiatives and referenda also underscores the continued strength of populism. With executive reorganization, political, economic, administrative, and sometimes historic factors combined to modify the full application of the orthodox administrative principles. Thus, education departments or boards, attorneys general offices, other constitutional posts, and quasi-regulatory boards and commissions rarely have been touched by executive reorganization plans. Furthermore, a number of reorganizations achieved during this period were of the "traditional type," in that they involved a "reduction of the number of agencies — to some degree within the existing pattern of agencies headed by elected officers, boards, and commissions."[13] Similarly, although judicial reform proceeded more uniformly and at a faster pace than changes in the other branches of state government, all or most of the judicial officers in eighteen states are elected, in eight by partisan ballot and in ten by a nonpartisan one (in one case without opposition). In ten some are selected and others are elected.

All this suggests that the older and populist state values of representativeness (especially in the legislatures), administrative pluralism, achieving accountability through severe institutional and constitutional constraints, and hostility to concentrated gubernatorial or even in some cases judicial power have not disappeared. Instead, these values still compete with the newer managerial and professional values to greater or lesser degrees within each state. A.E. Buck's classical principles of state executive reorganization (that is, concentration of authority and responsibility in the gubernatorial office, functional integration through departmentalization, abolition of multimember boards or restrictions on their roles, coordinated central staff services, an independent audit, and establishment of a governor's cabinet) have been before us for over half a century. Dean Roscoe Pound's counterpart precepts for state (local) judiciaries have been known for a comparable period. Yet the neo-Hamiltonian norms implicit in both have had to contend with neo-Madisonian pluralist and neo-Jeffersonian populist beliefs throughout. And the latter seem more potent than ever since the 1980s: again witness the recent rash of term-limiting legislation and the increase in the use of referenda.

Despite these caveats, however, the statement still can be made that there were more changes on more state structural fronts during the past thirty years than in any other period since the drafting of the first state constitutions.

## The States' Newly Revitalized Systemic Roles

What do the three decades of institutional, procedural, and fiscal changes have to do with the states' position in the federal system? The answer, it seems, is that without them the present role the states play in the system would be inconceivable.[14]

In traditional legalistic terms, the states', not the Congress's, systemic role flowed from the fact that they were the repositories of the reserved powers under the U.S. Constitution. Hence, they served as a source of constraint on efforts to expand national power, as the prime guardians of their citizens' public health, safety, welfare, and order, and as the constitutional source of all local governmental authority.

In policy terms, the states were the paramount arena for devising innovations throughout the nineteenth century and well into the twentieth. They also served as the foremost instruments of popular choice in nearly all policy areas during the first half of the nineteenth century, in most such areas from 1865 to 1932, and in fewer but still significant areas until the early 1960s. These policy areas included public education; regulation of insurance, other businesses, public utilities, professions and intrastate transportation; and most criminal justice functions, to cite only a few.

As administrators of Federal aid programs, the states' role was practically nonexistent in the nineteenth century and involved only 15 relatively minor grant programs by 1930. Some thirty years later, the number of collaborative undertakings had risen to 132. Over 90 percent of the Federal dollars went to the states, but only four departments and agencies of the states were heavily affected.

In political terms, state and local parties traditionally possessed what cohesion and strength there was in the nation's party system. They played a key role in selecting national officeholders, and they exerted a strong noncentralizing influence on national policymaking.

For at least 140 years, the states were far more than middlemen. They were paramount political and policy actors and innovators, the exclusive legal architects of local government, which at the time provided most of the public services available, and they were effective restrainers of national governmental activism.

From Roosevelt through Eisenhower, the scope of the states' police powers lessened somewhat; their performance as policy innovators, because of the Great Depression and badly malapportioned legislatures, severely eroded; and their involvement with national program goals through Federal grants expanded, but in comparatively modest terms. Meanwhile, their superior influence in Washington remained potent; their involvement with and their aid to their localities grew; their paramount position in the nation's electoral processes for the most part went unchallenged; and the fifty state-local fiscal and servicing systems they engineered provided the overwhelming bulk of the funding for domestic governmental services. Thus, as recently as the early 1960s, the states still served as key instruments in certain significant policy areas. They vigorously acted as powerful representatives of fifty sets of geographic interests and had assumed an important administrative and funding role in the comparatively small and inexpensive package of Federal grants then extant.

Since the mid-1960s, the states' role in the federal system has undergone major changes. The states have undertaken new responsibilities on their own initiatives, even as the traditional ones were revitalized. One major authority has contended that in contrast to their earlier basic functions, their current function is to assume two main responsibilities: planning and controlling big and frequently intergovernmental programs and using the state position as the major intermediate level of government and of politics to mobilize political consent for these programs.[15] In this assessment, the forces of modernization — growing interdependence, scientific and technological advances, the concomitant rise of centralizing coalitions and of professional-bureaucratic complexes, and the continuing national effort to respond to public demands for more and better services — transformed the national government into the paramount vehicle for achieving social goals. Yet these forces also led to the assigning of new intergovernmental functions to the states because very few of the many Great Society and post–Great Society programs were administered exclusively by Federal civil servants.

This intriguing intergovernmental interpretation of the states' role is borne out by many of the fiscal, funding, and structural developments since the mid-1960s that have affected the states and their de facto role in the federal system. As the prime recipients of Federal grant funds and as channelers of Federal aid to their localities, states are pivotal intermediaries. They plan, supervise, partially fund, and sometimes directly execute large, costly, and socially significant intergovernmental programs. The shifts, of course, are emphasized in all but two of the twenty-four new block grants enacted since 1981 and in the severing of most of the direct Federal-local grant ties since 1981. Moreover, as the major financiers from their own revenue sources of primary, secondary, and higher public education, primary and secondary public highway systems, and health and hospital functions, the states have carved out still another dimension of this important intergovernmental role almost apart from Federal initiatives. The dominance of fiscal and matching-money issues in state politics over the past twenty-five years or more, along with strong state involvement in nearly all environmental programs, Medicaid, social services, educational standards, special education, and now welfare reform — to cite nearly all the major current examples — clearly demonstrates that the states are forums of political debate over their newly assigned intergovernmental programmatic role.

Alongside the new intergovernmental roles is a cluster of traditional roles. Through their political and independent policymaking processes, the states reflect differing approaches to taxes, servicing preferences, social and environmental legislation, and governmental accountability. They exhibit differing degrees of devotion to the older neo-Madisonian governmental values of fully representative institutions, administrative pluralism, and accountability through tough institutional constraints, as noted above, and to new Jeffersonian populist devices such as initiatives, referenda, recalls, and term limits. They also demonstrate varying commitments to neo-Hamiltonian reform values of executive leadership, bureaucratic rationality, management professionalism, and "unshackling."

The states also revitalized their earlier function as experimental laboratories within the overall system. Witness their pioneering efforts over the past two decades in consumer protection, campaign finance, "sunset" legislation, coastal zone management, hospital cost control, enterprise zones, foreign trade, universal health care, welfare, and educational reform.

With recent Federal efforts to devolve functions and finances by a formal means such as a block grant or a less direct approach such as a decremental budget strategy, states have assumed another new systemic role as compensator for or channeler to local and private sector units of relinquished Federal responsibilities. Both approaches have been utilized by the states in their responses to deficit-driven Federal reductionism. The channeling-downward-to-locals strategy was the dominant one relied on during the Reagan cuts in the 1982–84 period, but the compensating approach was the more prevalent one used in the early nineties.

Out of this broad, differentiated representative role also flow fifty differing functional assignment, taxing, and funding patterns, which are discussed below. Finally, each state addresses idiosyncratically its historically strong responsibilities regarding its local governments.

## The Fifty State-Local Fiscal and Servicing Systems

Despite the continuing major role of Federal aid, Federal regulations and conditions, and their combined conditioning of state-local service-delivery systems, the provision of domestic services has been and still is predominantly a state-local responsibility. Each state has chosen to offer these services in its own way.

For nine broad functional areas, the state and local sectors maintained their prime servicing responsibility in all but energy, commerce, and income security from 1967 to 1987. This, of course, is based on the respective shares of direct expenditures that refer to government spending without reference to which government raises the funds. In short, it includes intergovernmental fiscal transfers as well as own-source revenues.

Within *specific functional arenas,*

- the local role in public education declined somewhat, and the environment and community development and public safety roles increased somewhat;

- the state role grew significantly in income maintenance and, to a lesser degree, debt servicing and public safety; and

- the Federal government clearly increased its direct responsibilities in income maintenance, in the servicing of the national debt, and, to a minuscule degree, in courts and public safety.[16]

A review of the *servicing roles of the various categories of local government,* in direct expenditure terms for thirty program areas in 1987, showed cities led for highways, police, fire protection, sewerage, solid waste management, parks and recreation, housing and community development, air transport, parking facilities, water and power facilities, protective inspection and regulation, and libraries.[17] For all of the remaining categories, save education and natural resources, cities accounted for at least 22 percent of all local general expenditures. Counties led in public welfare, hospitals, health, corrections, judicial and legal, and natural resources. They also accounted for 15 percent or more of local spending for highways, police, solid waste management, parks and recreation, and libraries. School districts were the big local spenders for schools. Nonschool special districts and authorities predominated in 1987 in water transport, transit, and natural resources, and they were responsible for significant shares of housing and community development (38.5 percent), water and power utilities (33.7 percent), hospitals (32.32 percent), air transportation (28.3 percent), sewerage (24.3 percent), libraries (14.0 percent), and parks and recreation (12.0 percent). In the twenty states having township government, the roles of such governments were much greater than their national figures would suggest (the biggest being 10.4 percent of the total local outlays for highways). They were responsible for 21.3 percent of highways, 17.1 percent of solid waste management, 14.2 percent of fire protection, 13.4 percent of libraries, 11.8 percent of police, and 10.7 percent of parks and recreation. In the northeastern towns and township states from Maine to Pennsylvania the figures are even higher.

Over time and overall, the school districts' share of direct expenditures fell 5.8 percent between 1967 and 1987; special districts' share rose by 4.5 percent; counties' share was hiked by 3.0 percent; and municipalities' share rose slightly by 1972, and then dropped for a 1.7 percent loss between 1967 and 1987. The overall picture of the state-local servicing system shows that in 1987 states were the "senior servicing partner" (accounting for 55 percent or more of total state-local direct expenditures for a function) in public welfare (largely Medicaid), highways, hospitals, corrections, judicial and legal, natural resources, and protective inspection and regulation. They shared the lead with municipalities in water transport. Municipalities were the dominant provider for police, sewerage, parks and recreation, fire protection, solid waste management, air transport, and parking facilities. School districts dominated public education, naturally. Neither counties nor special districts accounted for 55 percent or more of total local general expenditures for any function, though both figured prominently in the growing more-than-one-provider category, suggesting the increasing flexibility in service arrangements both at and below the state level. It should be kept in mind that these patterns do not apply uniformly among the states. The distribution of functions between the states and their local governments varies substantially; for example, highways may be primarily a state function in some states and heavily local in others.

*Regional servicing patterns* did not always parallel these national trends. The New England region used state governments as dominant providers, with major roles also assigned to cities and towns but nearly none to counties (Connecticut and Rhode Island have none); the Mid-Atlantic region was the heaviest user of special districts and of the more-than-one-provider program option. Municipalities showed their greatest ascendancy in the West North Central region but also had heavy use in the Midwestern and Western regions. Counties predominated in the Southeast, followed by the Mountain and East South Central regions.

A good way to come to grips with the more-than-one-provider phenomenon is to determine "significant" roles (that is, 15 percent or more of total state and local direct expenditures) rather than only dominant providers. With this refinement, counties in 1987 were significant providers of eight of the eighteen listed services in more than half the states. Special districts also improved their rating over 1987, increasing by more than half the number of services for which they were significant providers, and townships experienced a 16.4 percent increase over the same period.

*Classifying the fifty state-local fiscal and servicing arrangements raises both methodological and interpretative questions,* but dealing with both helps to clarify the subtleties of systems that simultaneously are becoming more alike even while they reflect significant differences from one another. G. Ross Stephens used three factors to develop a typology of state-local fiscal and functional relationships. They involve expenditures as a measure of service delivery; revenues as a gauge of the funding of state and local services; and the distribution of personnel as another factor indicating which level is doing what.[18] From this comes a composite index, showing clearly that over time, and especially during the past twenty-five years, there has been a general trend away from local dominance and toward state seniority in fiscal terms; a gradual emergence of a more balanced state-local sharing of service delivery and responsibilities; and a continuing local ascendancy in work force. There was some reduction in the seemingly inexorable march toward state centralization in 1989 (see table 9-1, p. 272). And well there might be, given the difficult economic decisions that confronted the states (and their localities) that year and the following three. Yet the 1992 figure indicated a resumption of the earlier trend.

From a long-term perspective, what factors seem significant in explaining this generally centripetal course? The amount of Federal aid to a state is considered to be one such conditioner, especially when the grants received encompass a "pass through" of monies to local governments, and higher or lower defense outlays appears to be another. Over the entire period covered by Stephens (1957–92), population size tended to be related to state centralization, with small states tending to be more centralized (see table 9-2, p. 273). Of the eighteen states with less than 2.5 million population in 1992, twelve (one less than in 1989) were consistently above the average in terms of level of centralization (Alaska, Arkansas, Delaware, Hawaii, Maine, Montana, New Mexico, North Dakota, Rhode Island, South Dakota, Vermont, and West Virginia); the only major exception to this generalization was Nebraska, which was regularly below the average (see table 9-3, p. 274). States with a population of 4.4 million or more were consistently less centralized. Seven of the eight largest over time have

## Table 9-1
## Centralized, Balanced, and Decentralized States,
## Selected Years, 1902–92

| State Centralization Index | 1902 | 1913 | 1932 | 1942 | 1947[a] | 1969 | 1977 | 1982 | 1986 | 1989 | 1992 |
|---|---|---|---|---|---|---|---|---|---|---|---|
| Centralized (60.0+) | – | – | – | 1[b] | 4 | 6 | 9 | 16 | 20 | 14 | 16 |
| Leaning toward state (55.0 to 59.9) | – | – | – | 3 | 5 | 9 | 12 | 12 | 14 | 9 | 11 |
| Balanced (45.0 to 54.9) | – | – | 1[c] | 10 | 20 | 24 | 25 | 18 | 15 | 22 | 22 |
| Leaning toward local (40.0 to 44.9) | – | 1[d] | – | 9 | 8 | 6 | 4 | 4 | 1 | 5 | 1 |
| Decentralized (39.9 or less) | 45 | 47 | 47 | 25 | 13 | 5 | – | – | – | – | – |
| Total | 45 | 48 | 48 | 48 | 50 | 50 | 50 | 50 | 50 | 50 | 50 |
| Average state | 17.8 | 19.3 | 25.7 | 40.7 | 47.1 | 51.6 | 54.2 | 56.5 | 58.4 | 56.5 | 57.2 |

*Source:* G. Ross Stephens, "Patterns of State Centralization/Decentralization during the Last Half of the Twentieth Century," paper presented at the annual meeting of the Southwestern Political Science Association, Austin, 18–21 March 1992), 18; and G. Ross Stephens, University of Missouri–Kansas City, private communication, 8 July 1998.

a. Includes Alaska and Hawaii, even though they had not quite achieved statehood.
b. At this time elementary and secondary education were state services in North Carolina.
c. Delaware.
d. Vermont.

been more decentralized than the average (California, Florida, Illinois, Michigan, New York, Ohio, and Texas, with Florida and New York consistently in the much below average category); only Pennsylvania has tended to fall in the middle range.

The updating of state governmental structures and revenue systems, in part because of the impact of heavy flows of Federal aid, also seems to be a factor in this long-term development. Moreover, in a few instances the regional issue rears its head. All midwestern states plus Kansas and Nebraska were steadily below average in terms of the relative state government role. Looking to the future, continuation of this long-term tendency toward state centralization may be in some doubt (see table 9-1). All governments are attempting to downsize, and although states in the past (notably in 1981 and 1982) weathered recessions fairly well, the 1989–92 structurally related recession was an exception to this rule. Since 1979 the number of states with below-average per capita tax capacity has risen from twenty-four to thirty-three, and this highlights another conditioner of the level of future state centralization. Since the slippage in state centralization in the late eighties was probably contingent on whether the country as a whole could cope with the national deficit and underlying economic structural challenges, the rise in 1992 suggests a return to the centralizing norm.

## Table 9-2
## Composite Ranking of the Fifty States
## in Terms of State Centralization, 1957 and 1992[a]

| Category | States | |
|---|---|---|
| (No. of states, 1957/1992) | 1957 Index Rating | 1992 Index Rating |
| Centralized (3/16) | HI 71.6, DE 66.1, NM 60.8 WV 60.4 | HI 83.2, AK 71.0, DE 71.0, RI 70.4, VT 67.1, WV 67.0, ND 65.9, ME 64.6, KY 64.2, MA 63.6, CT 63.2, NM 62.6, MT 62.4, AR 61.7, NJ 60.6, SD 60.5 |
| State services (5/11) | AK 59.9, LA 58.2, NC 57.7, AR 57.1, OK 55.0 | NH 59.9, SC 59.3, LA 58.9, UT 58.1, ID 57.9, MD 57.8, PA 57.7, OH 57.5, OK 57.4, WA 56.7, WY 56.3 |
| Balanced (20/22) | CT 54.4, KY 54.1, ME 53.6, SC 53.1, VT 52.4, MT 51.6, OR 51.5, AL 51.3, MS 51.3, RI 51.3, NH 51.2, NV 51.0, VA 50.9, ND 50.0, WA 49.2, SD 49.1, UT 49.1, ID 48.9, WY 47.0, AZ 45.4 | MI 54.4, AL 54.2, OR 54.0, MS 53.8, WI 53.6, IN 53.5, MO 53.4, VA 53.1, IA 52.5, NC 52.1, IL 51.7, TN 50.9, KS 50.5, AZ 49.5, MN 49.0, GA 48.8, NE 48.8, NV 48.3, NY 47.8, TX 47.5, CA 46.8, FL 45.5 |
| Local services (8/1) | PA 44.9, MO 44.8, GA 44.1, FL 42.5, MI 41.7, TN 41.5, MD 40.6, KS 40.3 | CO 44.8 |
| Decentralized (13/0) | IA 39.8, IN 38.9, MA 38.6, TX 38.0, CO 37.6, OH 37.1, MN 34.1, IL 33.4, NE 33.4, CA 32.4, WI 31.6, NJ 29.9, NY 28.9 | |
| Average State | 47.1 | 57.2 |

Source: G. Ross Stephens, University of Missouri–Kansas City, private communication, 8 July 1998.

a. Alaska and Hawaii are included in the 1957 data even though they had not quite achieved statehood at that time.

The Stephens study suggests both external (that is, Federal aid and defense contracts) and internal (that is, population size and location) reasons for the increasing overall state centralization. At the same time, divergences and differences also are noted, with a centralized system decentralizing, a small state remaining decentralized, and a sustained position not being adhered to over time. It is clear that the Federal-state-local roles are inextricably entangled, but it also is clear that indigenous state-local forces cause differentiated impacts, and variations still persist.

Jeffrey M. Stonecash in his analyses of this same subject has, like Stephens, concluded that states have become more alike in the area of state-local fiscal

## Table 9-3
## Comparison of Individual States with National Trends, 1957–92

| Comparison | States (N) | States |
|---|---|---|
| Consistently much above average | 7 | HI, AK, WV, DE, KY, NM, VT |
| Consistently above average | 8 | RI, SC, ME, ND, LA, SD, AR, MT |
| Mostly above average | 2 | CT, ID |
| Above average to average | 3 | OK, UT, AL |
| Generally average | 4 | PA, NH, VA, WY |
| Above average to below average | 5 | NC, WA, MS, OR, NV |
| Below average to above average | 2 | NJ, MA |
| Below average to average | 1 | MD |
| Consistently below average | 12 | OH, IL, IA, WI, IN, MN, MO, TN, TX, CA, MI, CO |
| Below average to much below average | 2 | GA, AZ |
| Consistently much below average | 4 | NE, NY, KS, FL |

*Source:* G. Ross Stephens, "Patterns of State Centralization/Decentralization during the Last Half of the Twentieth Century," paper presented at the annual meeting of the Southwestern Political Science Association, Austin, 18–21 March 1992, 15.

centralization but that much of this development occurred in earlier times.[19] The growing similarity, he contends, occurs because decentralized states become more like already centralized ones, and the convergence takes place around increasing levels of centralization for the more decentralized but not necessarily for the already centralized. Examination of individual states suggests that a number of them have followed entirely unique patterns of change. The states have pursued different paths to increase their fiscal roles, and this in turn has produced variations in state aid to local governments resulting in variations in services within states.

Two caveats should be added to this assessment of state centralization trends. The first has to do with *operational ways in which state centralization manifests itself.* In essence, two quite different approaches are involved: (1) direct state assumption of program responsibilities formerly performed by local governments, and (2) an expansion of state intergovernmental fiscal transfers to those of its localities that are primary providers of public services.[20] There is here a rough division between the old dual federal and new cooperative federal approaches with their different models of state-local relations.

A *second caveat* is that fiscal, manpower, and grant data do not reflect the extent to which states utilize *regulations and mandates* as means of influencing their local governments and citizens. Like the national government, states in recent years have increased their reliance on regulations to achieve varying policy objectives — usually their own, but sometimes Federal. Moreover, they almost always use "direct orders," unlike their Federal counterparts. Mandates differ from other state policies in that they focus on the distribution of authority, not of resources or levels of expenditure.[21] At the same time, mandates obviously have fiscal implications, and they may be "instrumental" in the carrying out of arbitrary policies that have been enacted.

Catherine Lovell's pioneering study of Federal and state mandating in 1979 found with reference to the latter that such actions had increased greatly since 1960 in the five states surveyed, with 84 percent of the 2,811 total having been instituted since 1960 and 59 percent since 1970.[22] She and her associates found differences in the extent to which the five engaged in mandating, though only minor variations regarding type of mandates adopted. A survey of all the states late in the seventies, however, produced a somewhat different picture of state mandating: compared to states in other regions, southern states generally mandated less, and decentralized states (where local governments contributed more than half of the state-local revenue) showed a greater tendency to mandate more.[23] In addition, of the seventy-seven potential mandating areas surveyed, fourteen were found to be heavy-action areas (in which thirty-five or more states had mandates). These included mandates governing three types of local personnel matters, four public safety areas, solid waste disposal in the environmental protection field, and six educational issues. Minimal mandating (action by fifteen states or fewer) was found in three other local personnel, nine other public safety, and three other environmental protection areas, as well as in nine social service and other fields.

An early-eighties ACIR study found the most common mandates were special education programs (forty-five states), solid waste disposal standards (forty-five states), worker compensation for local personnel (forty-two states), and requirements for employee retirement systems (forty-two states).[24] The most heavily mandating states then were New York (sixty out of a possible seventy-seven mandates), California (fifty-two), Minnesota (fifty-one), and Wisconsin (fifty) — all of which are states that account for a comparatively low share of total state-local outlays but a high proportion of local revenue aid.

Rodney Hero and Jody L. Fitzpatrick have identified other distinguishing traits of states that are most likely to mandate, including greater affluence, less industrialization, greater party competition, and a higher "quality" of state administration. Legislature professionalism, policy innovation, political culture, and state centralization did not prove to be related to mandating "when the impact of other variables" was controlled.[25]

The goals of state mandates may be commendable. As the ACIR has pointed out, "Movements to improve individual rights protection, consumer protection, environmental protection, social welfare, public service provision, governmental efficiency, and public accountability . . . all require governments to behave in new ways. . . . Many of these issues are not subject to local variability."[26] Yet other less noble reasons are also at play here. When funds are short, as they were from 1989 to 1992, there was a "strong temptation to satisfy policy demands by mandating that functions be performed by other governments."[27] In addition, the emergence of the states as powerful policymakers in their own right has attracted far more interest groups to state capitals than was the case a generation ago, and for some of these, state regulation has been a useful technique for circumventing localities. Federal regulations also have been a generator of state mandates (for example, the special education requirements cited above). For these and other reasons, states have been very much a part of the rush to regulate. In the case of Connecticut, in FY 1995, 48.6 percent of local budgets were affected by state mandates, with education accounting for 36.0 percent of the total and property tax exemptions for 9.6 percent. Major mandates in effect at the time numbered eleven, and one more was enacted since then.[28] At the same time, the legislature subsequently repealed two pivotal points of local governmental irritation: "heart and hypertension" as it relates to workmen's compensation and prospectively the elimination of local funding of General Assistance.

Although there are no reliable overall current figures, individual state studies and continuous calls for relief from the national associations of local officials as well as from state leagues during the eighties and early nineties suggest there has been no significant reduction in the number of mandates. In fact, during the early nineties, there were retrenchment reasons for assuming there actually was some increase. Moreover, the hike from twenty-five in 1980 to forty-two by 1990 then to forty-three by 1995 in the number of states that enacted "fiscal note" legislation (requiring estimates of cost be attached to proposed legislation or administrative rules that would impose monetary burdens on affected local governments) is a sign of sustained local concern with this major irritant in contemporary intergovernmental relations.[29] In thirty-six instances, the fiscal notes were required to include a provision identifying the intended source of the extra funding.

This same concern also explains the rise to fourteen by 1988 in the number of states stipulating that there must be reimbursement if the mandate is enacted — seven by constitutional amendment and seven by statutory enactment. Yet there were continuing local outcries in some of these states about loopholes in the reimbursement schemes. A 1991 survey of state municipal leagues by the National League of Cities (NLC) in thirteen of the reimbursing states showed that four state programs were "not equal to the task of stopping unfunded mandates, but generally work to inhibit them" (California, Missouri, Rhode Island, and Tennessee); the Illinois and Michigan enactments "are strong on paper, but not in practice"; Hawaii's and Montana's are good as far as they go but are very limited; and those in Florida, Louisiana, and Maine are unknowns in that implementing legislation had not been passed as of the date of the NLC survey.[30] The later record tended to suggest that in states with constitutional prohibitions of unfunded mandates, localities fared better in the courts and with the legislature. As Deil Wright observed, "Despite ... supposed statutory protections, the anti-mandate assurances provided to local governments do not appear to have been particularly successful."[31] In any event, state mandating remains a significant factor shaping state-local fiscal, programmatic, and jurisdictional relations, though its role clearly is greater in some states than in others. To the degree that it is heavy, there can be no doubt that the administration, delivery, and scope of local services are significantly affected.

To sum up this functional-fiscal analysis, the states in a much more premeditated way than ever before have served as the prime architect of their respective combined state-local servicing and financing systems. During the four decades at issue the systems (1) have become somewhat less professionalized than in the early eighties, given the increase in the number of constraints on legislative sessions and terms; (2) are still very differentiated in their reforms and capabilities; (3) have become increasingly more centralized, but with significant variations in the extent and nature of the centripetalism; (4) have continued to reflect varying and changing preferences regarding local government providers, with counties and special districts experiencing significantly expanding functional assignments and municipalities remaining the most multipurpose of all the local governmental groupings; (5) have exhibited varying forms of centralization in terms of expenditures, servicing, and employment patterns, as well as in the extent to which there is still a centralized and compartmentalized interlevel relationship or a much more heavily interactional pattern for this intergovernmental relationship; (6) have reflected an increase in state mandating that has added an unquantifiable dimension to the challenge of determining the degree and dimensions of centralization and decentralization, in part because there seems to be a linkage between decentralized state systems and a heavier incidence of mandating.

## The States as Implementers
## of New Intergovernmental Programs

Recent state experiences with certain new Federal-state undertakings highlight the challenges involved with assuming their new systemic role of being prime implementers of key intergovernmental programs. Four brief case studies highlight the good, the bad, and the mixed features of their record to date.

We turn first to the cardinal question of the role of information technology (IT) in public policy and public administration. A close reading of the "reinventing government" literature and a cautious analysis of PRWORA indicate that our new informational technology was intended to play a major role in achieving the grand goals of both historic undertakings. One facet of the latter, as noted in chapter 6, is a provision to beef up the child support program. Going back to 1980, Congress mandated the computerization of this program beginning at the state and local levels and ultimately ending up with one massive national data bank. By 1995, only one state had been certified by Washington as having an "up and running" system. Other states, from New Hampshire to Florida to the biggest failure of all, California, were unable to meet minimum standards. California finally gave up a couple of years ago after having spent a half billion dollars on a fruitless effort, though a new try is possible. States in the future may face fiscal penalties if they miss their deadlines.

The problems here are many. One is the difficulty of gathering reliable, accurate, and comparable data from governmental jurisdictions that are not under one's direct control. In the California case, the counties had the initial responsibility of gathering the seemingly simple data regarding "dead-beat dads." A second problem is seeking out private sector computer experts, who may know IT, but know little of government. When the process is privatized, the data-gathering function usually is left to the contracting government. Yet the information-gathering function is a pivotal part of the computerization quandary, and even states have trouble procuring needed information from their localities, despite their constitutional status vis-à-vis these units.

Other more general reasons exist for the difficulties encountered when intergovernmental IT projects are proposed. One is "when it comes to projects that cross Federal, state or local boundaries, there is a greater need for coordination."[32] Coordination is needed to resolve the inevitable conflicts that arise when governmental bodies are far apart, as is "the case with federal-state and state-local projects." Another difficulty with such IT projects is the whole matter of control. Sometimes it is the IT people themselves who seek to dominate; other times it is a level of government. Still another issue, which must be dealt with here, is that "cross governmental projects have failed, because they don't try to rethink how government should deliver services."[33] This stems in part from the failure of the Federal and sometimes the state government to clearly define the mission envisaged for the IT collaboration (which was not a problem with the "dead-beat dads" undertaking). Yet another dilemma is the tendency of IT experts to overestimate their capacity to resolve fundamental interoperable problems so that the project may begin (which was a problem with the child care support program). So much for causes of failure.

All of the above intergovernmental causes of IT troubles are raised in the current effort to implement TANF. Most states have refocused their human service undertakings from determining eligibility and distributing benefits to case management, service delivery, and client support.[34] To effect this elemental change, large amounts of money are being spent now and into the future on the informational technology infrastructure needed to cope with case management and service provision. Yet Federal requirements, deemed "burdensome" by state IT officials, threaten to limit the discretion that welfare reform was supposed to confer. Most states have begun creating standard protocols for data exchange, building data warehouses, linking third party service providers, inserting relevant information into case-workers' desktops, and establishing electronic referral systems and resource directories. Significant interagency and in some cases interlevel collaboration must come into play if these systems are to succeed, which in turn raises for the states all the questions regarding coordination, control, and interlevel distance noted above. Moreover, while states are attempting to define the outcomes they desire, the processes to achieve them, and the information systems required to support service delivery, as well as the evaluation of the outcomes, earlier proposed Federal reporting requirements brought to a halt the development of state human services information systems. Many of the "178 data elements proposed for mandatory reporting are not clearly related to performance outcomes,"[35] which underscores the point made above that the Federal officials must rethink the servicing approach issue when dealing with outcome-oriented intergovernmental programs supported by complete information technology systems. At the same time, states must recognize the Federal need for comparable data, for they still have oversight and reportorial roles in this block grant program. Implementing TANF effectively would appear to convert the "dead-beat dads" undertaking into a matter for child's play.

President Clinton's frequent granting of Medicaid's Section 1115 waivers provides a very different kind of story. Basically such waivers make it possible for recipient states to launch research and demonstration projects within their Medicaid programs without meeting all the strict Federal requirements. The evidence to date shows that the states having the waivers used their discretion to experiment with a variety of health care service delivery, financing, and coverage options. All this has produced greater state leadership in and control over their respective programs. As of April 1997, sixteen states had received Federal approval to begin comprehensive research and demonstration projects within their programs.[36] Ten of these had already completed some part of their projects by the spring of 1997. Despite their great diversity, some commonalties emerge from these state plans. They include a strong interest in various facets of the managed care approach, attempts to reach nontraditional Medicaid beneficiaries, recognition of the fact that experimentation in this area can be politically very controversial, and learning that reforms require new administrative procedures and talented administrators. This brief case study would appear to be a first-rate example of a Federal-state partnership in action, with the states demonstrably serving in a Brandeisian sense as "laboratories of health care experimentation and innovation." And as with all experiments, some have not been successful.

A third case study in state programmatic innovation is provided by early attempts to implement the new Temporary Assistance to Needy Families. Though less than twenty months old at this writing, TANF already has provided us with some state experience that merits attention. An obvious initial generalization is that the plans adopted by the fifty states and the District of Columbia reflect a wide diversity regarding their comparative degree of generosity and of parsimony. A survey of the New England states by Thomas J. Anton and Richard M. Francis found that tiny Rhode Island provided the largest package of benefits when per capita income is considered, while affluent Massachusetts opted for the most frugal.[37] Wealthy Connecticut, another neighboring state, also selected a comparatively paltry package of benefits. The Rhode Island case then at least initially would seem to refute the "race to the bottom" thesis of Paul Peterson.

Earlier findings of welfare policy analysts showed that high per capita income states, surging economic growth states, and legislatures with strong Democratic majorities all tend to favor generous social welfare programs. In the New England case study, economically hard-pressed Rhode Island and Maine supported the most generous plans in light of their fiscal circumstances. Moreover, New Hampshire, the most conservative state in the region — if not the country — with overwhelming Republican majorities in the legislature, supported a fairly generous welfare program. Legislative professionalism also is deemed by many experts to be a key conditioner of more liberal state policies. Yet the least professional of the six legislatures — Rhode Island, Maine, Vermont, and New Hampshire — enacted more liberal welfare plans than the highly professionalized Massachusetts and Connecticut legislatures. On behalf of the latter, it might be noted that traditionally both funded quite generous AFDC benefits and both initiated welfare reforms prior to TANF.

Finally, the various actors who played key roles in hammering out the new welfare programs for their respective states did not conform to the scenario a policy analyst might have postulated. Outside, the business community hardly played any role in any of the six programs, and on the inside the legislature (save partially in the case of Rhode Island) definitely played a secondary role. Governors, along with health and human services secretaries, assumed lead roles in drafting their state plans; advocacy groups in four instances were active collaborative participants and in two instances were confrontational and outside the decision-making process.[38] Overall, this New England case study controverts many analysts' assumptions about policy actors, advocacy groups, economic conditioners of policy preferences, and institutional caliber. Whether New England mirrors the nation is doubtful. But later research no doubt will underscore highly differentiated state policy responses and conceivably other cases of the less affluent helping the less affluent.

A fourth and final case study relates to the handling by some states of their environmental responsibilities. A June 1998 report of the inspector general of the Environmental Protection Agency (EPA) documented widespread failure of state and local as well as Federal officials in six audited states to uphold even the most basic of the nation's clean air and clean water legislation.[39] The chief of this independent accounting unit within EPA found wastewater treatment plants operating without permits or with obsolete ones. Also noted was the fact that authorized inspectors did not conduct visits to potentially polluting factories along with the failure of some states to meet national environmental goals. Senior EPA officials felt that many of the problems identified in the relatively few states that were audited were not isolated but indicative of more widespread violations of the law.

In one border state, three-quarters of its streams did not meet the basic goal of the water clean enough for swimming. The required studies to show why this twenty-five-year objective was unattainable were not performed. Water quality criteria for several pollutants were set by this state at lower than national standards without any justification for taking such action. In two other states in the Pacific Northwest, Federal inspectors had not issued or renewed hundreds of permits required for factories and wastewater treatment plants. In several instances, there had been a lapse of ten years. Only a few permits were issued in order to bolster a strategy of focusing public attention on a few sources of major pollution.[40]

In a southwestern state, roughly half the major air-pollution sources cited in the Clean Air Act were never inspected from 1990 to 1996, and in 1995 and 1996 the state failed to report any significant violations of air-quality regulations to EPA, as required by law. In another state, its environmental officials reported that only 7 of the 178 major sources of air pollution were violating permits. Federal inspectors subsequently found in a sample of 31 locations that 17 were in violation of their permits. These findings suggest a need for beefing up enforcement at both the state and Federal levels. Efforts should be made to determine how much of this is due to the recent craze to downsize agencies, especially the regulatory ones. "Hollow government" and "dead law" do nothing to enhance respect for the law or intergovernmental trust between and among the partners. The role of local pressure groups also should not be discounted here.

## The States as Shapers of Local and Substate Regional Institutions and Processes

The states are the architects, either by commission, permission, or omission, of the structures, institutional character, processes, and powers of their respective local governments, just as they are of their fiscal and functional capabilities — as the foregoing analysis has demonstrated. Nearly a quarter of a century ago in less pressured and more optimistic times, it was written that "if the States are to be 'middlemen with muscle,' not merely 'middlemen with potential,' their sometimes acrimonious and wholly unavoidable relationships with their localities must be reviewed, revitalized, and in many instances reformed."[41]

### An Enervating Evolution

Since 1776, this oldest intergovernmental relationship has been marked by conflict as well as by cooperation. From the ratification of the first state constitutions following the Declaration of Independence until now, local governments have had only the rights and powers conferred by their state constitutions or legislatures.

Applying the principle of state supremacy during the first four decades of the New Republic caused little friction. But then, immigration, industrialization, and urbanization combined to differentiate local jurisdictions. Social, economic, and political groups that were markedly different from those within various localities formed at the state level. State intervention in various forms began to appear in the three decades before the Civil War, and following Appomattox, became more extensive.

Dillon's Rule that local governments have only the powers specifically delegated by the state emerged and gained wide acceptance during that period. In the legislatures, the principle was reflected in expanded state involvement in local affairs through mandating, special local enactments, and the assumption of certain local responsibilities. In addition, the doctrine of expressed powers evolved to enhance the legal supremacy of the states. Under it, localities were viewed as administrative units established by the legislature to carry out specific state policies and programs. What powers they had were delegated, and their use of the powers was to be monitored closely and interpreted strictly. This widespread acceptance of the doctrine generated countless court cases, numerous local efforts to achieve explicit state-empowering authorizations, and occasionally open legislative invitations to groups losing out at the local level to seek redress in the state capital.

The counterthrust to state interventionism, the concept of local home rule (that is, the state grant of discretionary authority in structural, functional, policy, and sometimes other areas to local general governments), had its roots in the Midwest. Iowa was the first to adopt a home-rule statute in 1859, and Missouri was the first to establish home rule by constitutional amendment, sixteen years later. Since then the movement's history has been uneven. By 1915, fifteen states had adopted constitutional amendments providing for municipal home rule, yet by 1930 only one more had done so. After the depression and World War II, interest was rekindled, and in 1948, for the first time, a state supreme court held that a home-rule city acts by authority of conferred constitutional powers, not through powers delegated to it by the state legislature. The decision gave the residual powers approach to home rule some official sanction.

The American Municipal Association drafted a model plan incorporating this principle in 1953; South Dakota was the first to enact the provision five years later. By the midsixties, twenty-eight states had granted home rule to their cities, and fourteen the same for counties. By 1997, forty-eight of the states had enacted some form of municipal home rule, while thirty-seven states had granted similar powers to counties. This contrasts with forty and twenty-six states, respectively, that had taken comparable action as of 1979.

### The Contemporary Ambivalent Condition

Paradoxically, an analysis of the relationship between state reform and local discretion by Vincent Marando and Mavis Mann Reeves produced the general finding that the reform of state government in the ways discussed earlier in this chapter is not related to local discretion.[42] Only when state constitutional reform includes a strong local home-rule article does this kind of move make a difference. The chief reason for this somewhat surprising conclusion is the very understandable fact that state policy activism resulting from institutional and other reforms can simultaneously produce policies that both enhance and curb local discretionary authority.

Overall, as one authority put it, "Although constitutional change (during this period) was limited, many statutory changes were made that gave home rule to local governments. Cities and counties with general law home rule increased by almost 50 percent."[43] In practice, the circumstance has meant that these localities now have more freedom in determining their governmental structures, choosing functions, and deciding how they will be carried out.

All this suggests a salutary resolution of, or at the very least, the beginning of a solution to, a recurring problem in state-local relations. But *certain caveats must be raised before the optimism becomes overwhelming, including the following:*[44]

- Constitutional home-rule authorizations are frequently inoperative if state legislatures fail to enact the necessary implementing statutes.

- Many home-rule authorizations confer discretion over local governmental structure but omit the critical provision that the localities "may exercise all legislative powers not prohibited by law or by charter" (as the Alaska Constitution phrases it).

- The functional features are not always clear, especially under older authorizations; this is especially the case where the primary purpose is to give jurisdictions the right to choose from a range of structural governmental types (for example, optional-forms legislation) as opposed to the residual powers approach.

- Urban home-rule counties tend to provide a significantly greater number of services than do their non-home-rule counterparts.

- Not to be overlooked here are the overriding state regulatory actions in the local personnel, health and safety, and environmental protection areas that were taken in the seventies and eighties.

- Home rule usually is circumscribed by state fiscal constraints with regard to new forms of revenue and to the traditional chief source of local revenue, the property tax, as noted earlier.

- The applicability of home-rule promises frequently hinges on the whims of corporation counsels, lawyers, and judges, and the disputes and informal agreements between and among them.

The caveats suggest *tensions between home-rule advocates and principles and state reformers and policies.* Home rule, after all, was conceived in an age of compartmentalized intergovernmental relations wherein a fairly clear-cut division of state and local functions and funding was deemed to be feasible and desirable. Such clearly is not the case today, given the ever mounting extent of mutual interdependence even in states that are highly centralized and that provide only modest grant assistance to their localities. Moreover, state mandates, controls over local finances, and failure to confront the jurisdictional jungle at many local levels combine to undercut genuine "home rule."

### The Interlocal and Regional Challenge

One of the most problematic topics confronting state and local officials (and, indirectly, Federal officials) is the gap between the natural boundaries of a needed service and the fixed jurisdictional boundaries of most general units of local government.[45] Nowhere is this a bigger problem than in the growing metropolitan areas. These areas and to a lesser degree their nonmetropolitan regional counterparts provide stark evidence of the need to come up with economically efficient, administratively effective, and equitable ways and means of handling the problems, programs, and processes that spill over municipal and county boundaries. They provide the raw materials of which today's substate regional drama in all its manifestations is made. At present this is a prime challenge to the states, although many do not view it as such.

## Current Metro Trends

Metropolitan America is experiencing change on at least ten fronts.

1. There are more metro areas. More metro areas exist in the nineties than ever before (320 in 1990 and 353 in 1995, with over 550 central cities), a nearly 40 percent increase since 1962.

2. There are more people in metro areas. Seventy-eight percent of the total population was located in metro areas in 1990, compared with 63 percent in 1962. More people also live in suburban jurisdictions than previously — some 60 percent of total metro population in 1990, compared with 50 percent in 1960.

3. The big metro areas are getting bigger and more numerous. Although more than half the individual metropolitan areas have populations of 250,000 or less, more than half the metropolitan population lived in the forty-seven metro areas that in 1990 had populations of one million or more.

4. The West is as metropolitan as the Northeast, much to the consternation of the "wide, open spaces" westerners. Not surprisingly, the fastest-growing metro areas are in the South and the West.

5. Metro government fragmentation continues. Growth in metro areas has meant further fractionalization of the local governmental map. More of the nation's local governments in 1992 were located in metro areas: 37.7 percent of the then 86,692 total, compared with 36 percent in 1982 and 20 percent in 1972 (see table 9-4). The average metro area still encompasses about ninety-four governmental units, and there was a slight increase recently in the proportion of larger multicounty metro areas from 55 percent in 1987 to 61 percent in 1992.

6. Metro diversity has increased. Compared with their condition in the 1960s, metro areas now are much more diverse in (a) population and territorial size; (b) the mix of private economic functions and the range of public services offered; (c) the respective position of central cities vis-à-vis outside-central-city jurisdictions; (d) the kinds of jurisdictional complexity; and (e) the varieties of regional bodies and processes.

## Table 9-4
## Local-Level Jurisdictions, Selected Years, 1962–97

| Jurisdiction | 1962 (N) | 1972 (N) | 1977 (N) | 1982 (N) | 1987 (N) | 1992 (N) | % in MSAs (1992) | 1997 (N) |
|---|---|---|---|---|---|---|---|---|
| Counties | 3,043 | 3,044 | 3,042 | 3,041 | 3,042 | 3,043 | 24.2 | 3,052 |
| Municipalities | 18,000 | 18,516 | 18,856 | 19,083 | 19,200 | 19,296 | 39.0 | 19,372 |
| Townships | 17,142 | 16,991 | 16,822 | 16,748 | 16,691 | 16,666 | 30.2 | 16,629 |
| School Districts | 34,678 | 15,780 | 15,260 | 15,032 | 14,721 | 14,556 | 40.6 | 13,726 |
| Special Districts | 18,323 | 23,886 | 26,140 | 28,733 | 29,532 | 33,131 | 43.0 | 34,683 |
| Total | 91,186 | 78,217 | 80,120 | 82,637 | 83,186 | 86,692 | 38.4 | 87,462 |

*Sources:* Bureau of the Census, "Preliminary Report 1992 Census of Governments," GC 92-I P (Washington, D.C., November 1992), table A-3; and Bureau of the Census, Governments Division, *Communications,* 24 July 1998.

7. Federal aid has been reduced. Direct Federal aid to localities — many of them urban — accounted for 29 percent of all Federal grant outlays in FY 1978, an all-time high, but by FY 1997 it was down to 11.6 percent of the total, without much of a concomitant reduction in Federal regulations.

8. The rate of growth in state aid has been reduced. Because noneducational state aid was reduced and other changes were made in state mandates and conditions, metro aid, even when it included Federal "pass-through aid," increased by 226 percent between 1978 and 1988 (compared with a 455 percent jump between 1964 and 1977), and from 1988 to 1996, it grew by only 169 percent.

9. Central-city urban America possesses a smaller proportion of the nation's population now (about 25 percent) than it has in decades. Its combustible mix of poverty, poor schools, minority alienation, drugs, violence, isolation, desperation, and babies with single parents suggests a metropolitan challenge that nearly four decades of social experimentation and market-oriented cures have not overcome — despite some indigenous examples of successful breakthroughs, with or without external help.

10. Academic cacophony prevails. For officials seeking guidance from the academic experts, theoretical harmony is more elusive than ever; more theories are in vogue as to how metro areas should be run — from public choice (market-oriented) and the more governmental providers the better; to a mixed-servicing approach combining public and private provision of services; to diverse efforts to promote regional awareness, collaborative areawide service, communicational undertakings, and sometimes private-public enterprises, all under the auspices of civic-citizen-business alliances; to two- and one-tier regional governmental reorganizations. The many faces of reform have produced little real reform at any time.

These mostly long-term metro area trends point to regionalism in its many forms as a solution because it can (a) handle certain functions (usually of a capital-intensive or regulatory nature) on a multijurisdictional basis; (b) achieve economies of scale in providing various services by broadening the basis of fiscal support and the demand for certain services; (c) handle "spillover" servicing problems caused by rapid urban population growth and sometimes decline; (d) confront the necessity for retrenchment by seeking more effective ways of rendering public services; and (e) help groups that distrust one another learn to "cut a deal." None of these benefits, however, can be had without positive state actions.

In light of recent economic, political, and civic action developments, another cluster of reasons must be cited. Some economists contend that in contemporary America the "real economies are mainly metropolitan-centered regions" and cities and suburbs within each metro area are inextricably linked economically.[46] Hence, if one views a region as an integrated, interdependent economy, it changes the way we look at the economy as a whole and also highlights the near complete disjuncture between the various regional economies and the galaxy of governments that occupy the same space as these unified entities. A variation on this economic theme is the argument that our global competitiveness is endangered when we fail to face the fact that without effective regional governance perspectives, institutions, and processes, the competition for global markets will be undercut.[47]

Some contend that the history of regionalism is really a three-act play: in act one central cities sought to dominate suburbs and potential suburbs; in act two suburbs sought to control central cities in various ways, notably through their clout in legislatures; and in the present act neither side sees a way to dominate the other, and mutual cooperation emerges as the sensible course.[48] Still others see the need for more solid regional governance arrangements to assure a more positive role for local governments and communities in an era of incremental devolution. Thus far, states have benefited most from this erratic but continuing phenomenon. With effective regions, authoritative substate voices would be heard and relied on. For the growing number of growth management advocates, strong regions are a major part of their corrective strategies. Metropolitan Baltimore, St. Louis, Detroit, Cleveland, Chicago, Seattle, and especially Portland, Oregon, are all involved in different ways and through different organizations with this overriding issue. For David Rusk, "growth management" is "regionalism's core issue."[49] These then are some of the totally contemporary reasons for focusing on regions, regionalism, regional processes, and regional institutions. They also indicate we need much clearer conceptions about governance and governments. The latter cannot simply be ignored, as they so frequently are when this topic is discussed.

## Eighteen Approaches to Regionalism

Regionalism encompasses approaches that range from the innocuous, voluntary, and procedural to the dramatic, surgical, and institutional. Eighteen of the approaches to regional service problems can be arrayed on a spectrum from the

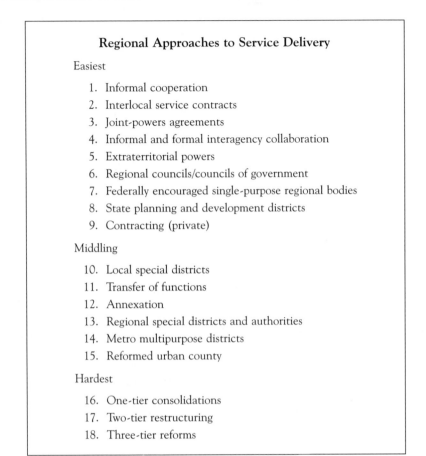

**Regional Approaches to Service Delivery**

Easiest

1. Informal cooperation
2. Interlocal service contracts
3. Joint-powers agreements
4. Informal and formal interagency collaboration
5. Extraterritorial powers
6. Regional councils/councils of government
7. Federally encouraged single-purpose regional bodies
8. State planning and development districts
9. Contracting (private)

Middling

10. Local special districts
11. Transfer of functions
12. Annexation
13. Regional special districts and authorities
14. Metro multipurpose districts
15. Reformed urban county

Hardest

16. One-tier consolidations
17. Two-tier restructuring
18. Three-tier reforms

easiest to the hardest; from the most politically feasible, least controversial, and sometimes least effective to the politically least feasible, most threatening to local officials, and sometimes most effective — at least in the opinion of many in the twenty-seven jurisdictions that have made the "hardest" reforms (see box, above).

### The first nine approaches are not difficult.

1. *Informal Cooperation.* For many hard-pressed localities, this approach is the easiest of them all. It is clearly the least formal and the most pragmatic of the eighteen. It generally involves collaborative and reciprocal actions between two local jurisdictions, does not require state authorization, does not usually require fiscal actions, and only rarely involves matters of regional or even subregional significance. Although reliable information on the extent of its use is generally absent, anecdotal evidence suggests that informal cooperation is the most widely practiced approach to interlocal collaboration.

2. *Interlocal Service Contracts.* Voluntary but formal agreements between two or more local governments are widely used. Some forty-five states now sanction them broadly. Earlier survey data suggest a slight decline (4 percent) between 1972 and 1983 in their use, but well over half the cities and counties polled in 1983 had used such contracts to handle at least one of their servicing responsibilities.[50] Metro central cities, suburbs, and counties generally relied on them to a greater extent than nonmetro municipal and county jurisdictions. A fairly recent Connecticut survey identified over nine hundred instances of interlocal contracting including people-related services as well as the less controversial certain public safety and physical developmental activities.[51] The absence of any counties is a factor to be reckoned with here, but there also is the strong independent, even isolationist tradition of small-town New England to consider. So this is a salutary sign of needed change in an area that big regional thinkers dismiss as "small potatoes."

3. *Joint-Powers Agreements.* These agreements between two or more local governments provide for the joint planning, financing, and delivery of a service for the citizens of all the jurisdictions involved. All states authorize joint-services agreements, but twenty still require that each participating unit be empowered to provide the service in question. Surveys indicate that the number of cities and counties relying on agreements for at least one service rose from 33 percent in 1972 to 55 percent in 1983, making them slightly more popular than interlocal contracting. In 1987 and 1988, the use of "these agreements among American local governments as an alternative service delivery mechanism . . . remained remarkably stable."[52] The chief exceptions were "substantial increases in some health and human services and in various agreements for tax bill processing." The only real decreases were in solid waste disposal and court operations.

4. *Informal and Formal Interagency Collaboration.* This new regional device is one of the by-products of H. George Frederickson's regional research.[53] It entails the emergence in various metro areas of several "metropolitan areawide horizontal linkages which mirror the primary categories and sub-categories of local government." Thus, most metropolitan governance is functional, albeit organized on a separate jurisdictional basis and operated by professionals having a common educational background and sharing a similar set of values.[54] Specific coordinated program areas include public works, law enforcement, some corrections, parks and recreation, emergency services, social services, licensing and business permits, and several other local and potentially regional functions along with their subcomponents. This device is placed where it is in the listing because it involves both informal and formal agreements and is essentially voluntary, but it goes well beyond the unifunctional and single-agreement traits of the approaches cited above.

5. *Extraterritorial Powers.* Sanctioned in thirty-five states, extraterritorial powers permit all, or at least some, cities to exercise some of their regulatory authority outside their boundaries in rapidly developing unincorporated areas. Less than half the authorizing states permit extraterritorial planning, zoning, and subdivision regulation, however, which makes effective control of fringe growth

difficult. Because a number of states do not authorize extraterritorial powers, and because this approach does not apply to cities surrounded by other incorporated jurisdictions, it is used less than other techniques.

6. *Regional Councils/Councils of Governments.* By 1960, in no more than 20 to 25 regions did local jurisdictions come together to create wholly voluntaristic regional councils. That figure had soared to over 660 by 1980, thanks largely to Federal aid and especially to Federal requirements, notably Section 204 of the Model Cities legislation, which required a regional review-and-comment process in all metro areas for certain local grant applications. Title IV of the Intergovernmental Cooperation Act of 1968 built on the Section 204 base to create a "clearinghouse" structure (Circular A-95) at the rural and urban regional as well as state levels. Local participation in regional councils still remained primarily voluntary, however, with jurisdictions resisting any efforts at coercion.

Regional councils, also known as Councils of Government (COGs), which rely so heavily on interlocal cooperation, assumed far more than a clearinghouse role in the late 1960s and 1970s. Federal programs that required a regional plan, used a regional planning organization, or gave preference to regional councils in any pool of eligible recipients numbered nearly forty in 1979. Rural COGs tended to take on certain direct-assistance and servicing roles for their constituents; the more heavily urban COGs usually served a role as regional agenda definer and conflict resolver.

With the advent of Reagan federalism, a drastic reduction in the Federal role in substate regionalism occurred. Reagan's Executive Order 12372 put the prime responsibility for the A-95 clearinghouse role with the states, while providing a backup Federal role; forty-eight states picked up the challenge, but only forty were participating by 1992, and ten of these performed the A-95 Review Process without any regional input.[55] Of the thirty-nine Federal regional programs in 1980, twelve were scrapped, eleven were cut heavily, nine lost their regional component, six were revised, and only one was left fully intact.[56]

In order to survive, COGs had to adapt, and the overwhelming majority did so; only about 60 of the 660 regional councils shut their doors. Some got greater state support both in funding and in power. Those providing significant funding in 1991 included Alabama, Arkansas, Connecticut, Florida, Georgia, Idaho, Iowa, Kentucky, Maine, Maryland, Missouri, New Hampshire, North Carolina, Pennsylvania, South Carolina, Tennessee, Utah, Vermont, Virginia, and Washington.[57] Many other COGs sought more local fiscal contributions and became regional servicing agencies for constituent local units. A majority of regional councils now serve as a chief source of technical services and provide certain direct services under contract to their localities. Some state functions have been transferred to regional councils, and some serve as field administrators of certain state-planned and state-funded services. As of 1991 all still performed some type of clearinghouse function, and some had assumed specialized regional planning and other related functions under roughly six Federal grants and loan programs. Most COGs, then, reflect a greater "nativism," "pragmatism," and service activism than their predecessors of the seventies.

7. *Federally Encouraged Single-Purpose Regional Bodies.* Single-purpose regional bodies came into being when institutional strings were attached to some twenty Federal aid programs (as of 1980). According to the 1977 Census of Local Governments, these Federally encouraged special-purpose regional units numbered between 1,400 and 1,700, depending on definition and classification. A less rigorous, private, and meagerly funded survey identified more than 990 such bodies in 1983. Although the actual number as of 1983 was probably higher, by 1986 the total was probably much less, given the number of regional program revisions, budget cuts, and eliminations during the years 1983–86. Single-purpose regional bodies now exist only in a few Federal aid programs (notably economic development, Appalachia, Area Agencies on Aging, Job Training, and the Intermodal Surface Transportation Efficiency Act [ISTEA, 1991]). Continued Federal fundings make them easy to establish and they play a helpful, nonthreatening planning role; many have been brought under the COG umbrella. ISTEA, with its many block grant features, has proven to be a major tool in region building when implementation is in the hands of clever craftspersons.[58] Metro Seattle provides an excellent example of this. Moreover, ISTEA's successor legislation of 1998 — the Transportation Equity Act for the 21st Century (TEA-21) — authorizes spending of more than $22 billion over five years. It also continues the reforms of ISTEA, including an environmental focus, and provides a boost for better state and regional (MPO) planning processes.[59] While the Federal government still exerts a regional impact with its environmental, welfare reform, and training programs, ISTEA and now TEA-21 clearly are the most influential of these undertakings.

8. *State Planning and Development Districts (SPDDs).* These districts were established by the states during the late 1960s and early 1970s to bring order to the chaotic proliferation of Federal special-purpose regional programs. In 1991 a state's own substate regional goals were a prominent part of the authorizing legislation (thirty-two states, compared with nineteen in 1980) or gubernatorial executive orders (eleven states) that established SPDDs. By 1991, sixteen states had conferred a review-and-comment role on their SPDDs for certain non-Federally aided local and state projects. Eleven conferred such authority for special-purpose district projects, and seventeen authorized SPDDs to assume a direct servicing role if it was sanctioned by member governments or by the regional electorate.

As a matter of practice, nearly all SPDDs adhere to the confederative style of regional councils/COGs. Many regional councils have been folded into the SPDD system, although boundaries have sometimes changed. Approximately the same number of SPDD systems (forty-three) exist today as in the late 1970s, although in the Midwest funding problems have rendered some moribund. All of these states took on the devolved responsibilities under Reagan's E.O. 12372 for the "clearinghouse function," as did five others. In FY 1991, twenty-three of forty-three respondents (seven states did not reply) indicated they funded their SPDDs, but only five in a respectable fashion.[60] At present, the most active states in their support for their SPDD systems include Florida, Georgia, Virginia, North Carolina, and Texas.

Although feasible, SPDDs are somewhat difficult to set up, because special authorizing legislation is required, state purposes and goals are involved, and the establishment of a new statewide districting system can at least initially appear threatening, especially to counties. Yet the number has increased over the past sixteen years, which suggests that these hurdles can be overcome with good state leadership.

9. *Contracting (Private)*. Contracting with the private sector is the only form of public-private collaboration analyzed here and is the most popular of all such forms. Service contracts with private providers are now authorized in twenty-six states — far fewer than their intergovernmental counterparts and usually with far more detailed procedural requirements. Their use has clearly increased from the early 1970s to the present, with scores of different local services sometimes provided under contracts with various private-sector providers. Joint-powers agreements and interlocal service agreements, however, are both more popular than contracting with private firms.

This approach rounds out the cluster of interlocal approaches that may be termed *easiest*. Contracting with private organizations has been placed last because authorizing legislation, especially of the nonrestrictive type, may be difficult to obtain because of the corruption that has arisen with this approach in the past. Moreover, the fears of public sector unions as well as those of certain public employees are aroused when local officials seek to contract services privately. At the same time, for "reinventing government" mayors and county executives, reform usually involves the "contracting out" of services traditionally performed by their own personnel. Witness the case study of Indianapolis–Marion County under Mayor Stephen Goldsmith.[61]

*The middle cluster in the spectrum of regional approaches to services delivery includes four institutional and two tough procedural approaches for new and usually broader territorial service-delivery systems. These approaches present somewhat greater hurdles than those in the easy group, but each is a more stable way to align governmental and service-delivery boundaries.*

10. *Local Special Districts*. These districts, which require state authorization, are a very popular way to provide a single service or sometimes multiple related services on a multijurisdictional basis. Three-quarters of all local special districts serve areas whose boundaries are not coterminous with those of a city or country, a situation that has prevailed for over four decades. At the same time, special taxing districts (for beach condos, lakeside property, and fire protection) sometimes figure in state counts. These are mostly intramunicipal or intratown in jurisdictional terms, and their numbers have been growing. Forty-three percent of all special districts in 1992 were found within metro areas, making special districts the most numerous of the five basic categories of local government in metro America.

11. *Transfer of Functions*. This procedural way to change permanently the provider of a specific service jumped by 40 percent in a decade, according to

a 1983 survey of counties and cities. The larger urban jurisdictions were much more likely to transfer functions than the smaller ones were. More than three-fifths of the central cities reported such transfers, compared with 37 percent of the suburban cities and 35 percent of the nonmetro municipalities. Among counties, 47 percent of the metro type transferred functions, compared with only 29 percent of the nonmetro group. Cities were likely to shift services first to counties, then to COGs and special districts.

Despite its increased popularity, the difficulties involved in transfer of functions should not be overlooked. Only eighteen states in 1995 authorized such shifts (eight more than in 1974), and in half these cases voter approval was mandated. In addition, the language of some of the authorizing statutes did not always clearly distinguish between a transfer and an interlocal servicing contract.

12. *Annexation.* The dominant nineteenth-century device for bringing local jurisdictional servicing boundaries and expanding settlement patterns into proper alignment by including additional territory within municipal boundaries remains popular. The 61,356 annexations in the 1970s involved 8,700 square miles and 3.2 million people. The 65,585 annexations from 1980 to 1989 involved about 7,800 square miles and affected 2.3 million people. Although the vast majority of these annexations involved very few square miles, they are an incremental solution to closing the gap between governmental servicing boundaries and the boundaries of the center city.

A look at the larger-scale annexations of the past five decades reveals at least eleven municipalities that serve almost as de facto regional governments: Phoenix, Houston, Dallas, San Antonio, Memphis, San Jose, El Paso, Huntsville (Ala.), Ft. Worth, Omaha, and Shreveport. Most large-scale annexations have occurred in the Southwest and West because of the large amounts of unincorporated land on municipal peripheries and, until very recently, of pro-city state annexation statutes. Students of public finance point out that central cities that were able to annex substantial land are usually in good fiscal shape; such cities have escaped the hole-in-the-doughnut problems of central cities in the older metro areas of the East and Midwest.

Annexation is limited by the nature of state authorizing laws (most do not favor the annexing locality); its irrelevance in most northeastern states, given the absence of unincorporated turf in their urban areas; and a reluctance to use the process as a long-range solution to eliminating local jurisdictional, fiscal, and servicing fragmentation. Annexation, then, has limited geographic application and is usually used incrementally, but when it is assigned a key role in a city's development, it can transform a municipality from a local to a regional institution.

13. *Regional Special Districts and Authorities.* These big areawide institutions constituted the greatest number of regional governments in the 353 metro areas in 1995. Unlike their local urban counterparts, they are established to cope on a fully areawide basis with a major urban servicing challenge such as mass transit, sewage disposal, water supply, hospitals, airports, or pollution control. Census data showed there were approximately 132 regional and 983 major subregional

special districts and authorities in metro areas in 1982, compared with 230 and 2,232, respectively, in nonmetro areas. In 1992, regional and subregional special districts in rural and metropolitan America totaled 3,767, slightly more than the 1982 figure, according to the U.S. Census Bureau.

Relatively few large regional units have been established because they (a) require specific state enactment and may involve functional transfers from local units; (b) are independent, expensive, professional, and fully governmental; and (c) frequently are as accountable to bond buyers as to the localities and the citizen consumers. Yet where they exist, they are strong regional actors.

14. *Metro Multipurpose Districts.* These districts differ from the regional model in that they involve establishing a regional authority to perform diverse, not just related, regional functions. At least four states have enacted legislation authorizing such districts, but only a comparatively narrow range of services has been authorized. This option clearly ranks among the most difficult to implement, with Metro Seattle the only basic case study until 1998, when it merged with King County. Although multipurpose districts have a number of theoretical advantages (greater popular control, better planning and coordination of a limited number of areawide functions, and a more accountable regional government), political and statutory difficulties have barred their widespread use, despite the growth in single-function regional special authorities.

15. *The Reformed Urban County.* Because county modernization transforms a unit of local government, a move frequently opposed by the elected officials of the jurisdiction in question, new urban counties are difficult to form. As a result, although 37 states have enacted some form of county home rule statutes and 23 have constitutional authorization, only 130 charter counties (generally urban) have been created, but this is 54 more than in 1980.[62]

In metro areas, however, 30 percent of the 689 metro counties have either an elected chief executive or an appointed chief administrative officer. The servicing role of these jurisdictions has expanded rapidly over the past three decades or so. Since 1967, outlays for what used to be traditional county functions (corrections, welfare, roads, and health and hospitals) have declined, while expenditures for various municipal-type, regional, and new Federally encouraged services have risen commensurately. Overall, the range of state-mandated and county-initiated services has grown rapidly in metro counties, which has necessitated a better approach to fiscal and program management.

In the 105 single-county metro areas (as of 1990), this reform county option is excellent. However, because county mergers and modification of county boundaries are almost impossible, in the more numerous multicounty metro areas the option is less valuable. It can provide only a subregional solution to certain service-delivery problems, not a fully regional approach.

*The hardest approaches to metro regionalism are the three general governmental options: one-tier or unitary, two-tier or federative, and three-tier or superfederative. All three involve the creation of a new areawide level of government, a reallocation of local government powers and functions, and as a result a disruption of the political and institutional status quo. All three involve very rare and remarkable forms of interlocal cooperation.*

16. *One-Tier Consolidation.* This method of expanding municipal boundaries has had a lean but long history. From 1804 to 1907, four city-county mergers occurred, all by state mandate. Then municipalities proliferated but city-county mergers virtually stopped for forty years. From Baton Rouge's partial merger in 1947 to 1998 there were some twenty-three city-county consolidations (four since 1980), most endorsed by popular referendum. Among the hurdles to surmount in achieving such reorganizations are state authorization, the frequent opposition of local elected officials, racial anxieties (where large minorities exist), an equitable representational system, concerns about the size of government, and technical issues relating to such matters as debt assumption. Only one in five consolidation efforts has succeeded in the past forty years. Most consolidations have been partial, not total, with small suburban municipalities, school districts, and special districts sometimes left out; however, the new county government generally exercises some authority over some of their activities.

In addition, the metro settlement pattern in some cases has long since exceeded county limits, so the reorganized government may be the prime service provider and a key player but not the only one. This, of course, is another result of rigid county boundaries. To sum up, one-tier consolidation has generally been most suitable in smaller nonmetro urban areas and in smaller and medium-size, ideally unicounty, metro areas (for example, Augusta and Columbus, Georgia; Lexington, Kentucky; Nashville; Jacksonville; and Indianapolis). Yet even when the county is only part of a multicounty metro area, a city-county merger can help simplify things, as is the case with the consolidation involving Kansas City and Wyandotte County, Kansas, in 1998.

17. *Two-Tier Restructuring.* This approach seeks a division between local and regional functions, with two levels of government to render such services. These and other features, notably a reorganized county government, are spelled out in a new county charter that is adopted in a countywide referendum. The Committee of Economic Development advanced one of the most persuasive arguments for this approach in the 1970s. Metro Toronto, which created a strongly empowered regional federative government to handle areawide functions that ultimately led to some local reorganization by the merger of some municipalities, was a model for this approach. But in 1998 Ontario's legislature mandated the creation of a unitary, single-tier metro government for the Toronto region, against the wishes of three-fourths of the affected citizenry. No American state could or would enact such a mandate.

The prime American example of this federative approach is Metro Dade County (the Miami area). Unlike the outcomes of an incremental-reform approach of the modernized or urban county, in this case a drastically redesigned county structure and role emerged from a head-on confrontation over the restructuring issue. Narrowly approved in a countywide referendum in 1957, the new metro government's cluster of strong charter powers and its authority to perform a range of areawide functions were steadily opposed until the mid-1960s. Since then, its powers have grown, and it is widely considered a success. Witness the extraordinary responsibilities Metro Dade assumed during the various waves of immigration since the early 1960s. The level of metro-municipal collaboration is better now than it was a generation ago, but tensions and confrontations are still part of the relationship — as they are in most federative systems. Metro Dade's survival, however, appears to be assured, though some dissident communities recently have raised the banner of secession because of disagreements with the county. Doubtless little will come of this effort.

18. *Three-Tier Reform.* This is a rarely used approach, with just two U.S. examples. The Seattle metro region could well be the third, given recent areawide developments there. This three-tier approach deals with the very special problems of multicounty metro areas.

The first example is the Twin Cities Metropolitan Council in Minneapolis–St. Paul. Launched as a metro initiative and enacted by the state legislature in 1967, the council is the authoritative regional coordinator, planner, and controller of large-scale development for its region, which includes seven counties and several localities. It is empowered by the state to review, approve, or suspend projects and plans of the area's various multijurisdictional special districts and authorities (known now as commissions); it is the regional designee under all Federally sponsored substate regional programs for which the area is eligible; and it has the right to review and delay projects having an adverse areawide impact. Direct operational responsibilities do not fall within its purview, but it directly molds the region's future development because council members sit on and approve plans and budgets of the operational regional commissions (formerly regional special districts). Like any body that possesses significant power over other public agencies and indirectly over private regional actors, the council has become somewhat politicized in recent years, but its rightful place in the governance of the Twin Cities is not questioned. Some of its powers, in fact, have been strengthened recently. In 1994, the Minnesota legislature bound the Met Council very closely to the role of serving as the urban service provider in the metro area. This means the council no longer is just a regional planning and coordinating body, albeit a powerful one, but also is the owner and provider of a range of areawide services. Yet it confronts an elemental challenge now that it did not in 1967: the human settlement pattern of today's Twin Cities region encompasses thirteen counties, not seven. Since effective areawide planning has been one of the Met Council's great strengths, its future role in this field may be somewhat truncated, even as its direct provider role expands.

The other three-tier experiment is the Greater Portland Metropolitan Service District (MSD), or Portland Metro, as it is now designated in Oregon, a regional planning and coordinating agency that serves the urbanized portions of three counties. Approved by popular referendum in 1978, the Metro supplanted the previous COG and assumed the waste disposal and Portland Zoo responsibilities of the previous regional authority. Its basic functions also include consolidated planning, controlling flooding, running Tri-Met, and monitoring air and water quality. The authorizing law empowered the Metro to take on human services, jails, parks, libraries, and cultural facilities. It also is statutorily authorized to enforce the containment boundary set up by the Portland Region and to direct growth into urban areas within its boundaries. Growth management, as noted before, plays a pivotal role in its current operations. Unlike the Twin Cities Council, the Metro has an elected mayor, an appointed manager, and an elected twelve-member council, which provides a popular accountability that the Twin Cities Council has yet to achieve. Both three-tier examples suggest how other multicounty metro areas might approach areawide service delivery and other metro challenges, but they are arduous undertakings and not easy to sustain. Additionally, the state is a crucial player in such efforts.

## Summary Analysis

1. Most of the various approaches to substate regionalism have been on the increase. Since the early 1970s, use of the nine easiest has seen a net increase despite a reduction in the number of regional councils and of Federally supported substate districts. Meanwhile, five of the six middling approaches grew markedly (the exception was the metro multipurpose district). Even the three toughest approaches have been the subject of more discussion and a few enactments.

2. Very few metro areas rely on only one or two forms of substate regionalism. Quite the contrary, the players on the regional stage are so numerous that it is difficult to sort them out; some of this is due to the rise during the Reagan years of the civic-citizen-business alliances and related groups joining the special district, COG, Federally aided regional planning, and in some cases state-supported areawide endeavors.

3. The easier procedural and unifunctional institutional types of service shifts tend to be found more in larger metro areas; the harder restructurings usually take place successfully within the medium-sized and especially the small metro areas.

4. The expanded use of at least ten of the fifteen easiest and middling approaches is largely a product of local needs and initiatives, as well as of a growing awareness of their increasingly interdependent condition, but state authorizing legislation is required in practically all of these approaches.

5. Jurisdictional fragmentation has not been reduced significantly as a result of restructuring successes, but even incomplete forms of cooperation are useful. Such approaches are used extensively; in a majority of metro areas, they are the only feasible forms of regional and subregional collaboration.

6. Like much else in the U.S. system of metro governance, the overwhelming majority of interlocal and regional actions taken to resolve servicing and other problems reflect an ad hoc, generally issue-by-issue, incremental pattern of evolution. Nevertheless, most of the major reorganizations were triggered, at least in part, by a visible crisis of some sort, either functional, as with Nashville and the Twin Cities, or scandalous, as with Jacksonville.

7. The intergovernmental bases of substate regional activities remain as sig-

nificant as ever. The states, which always have played a significant part in the evolution of their metro areas, have moved gradually and reluctantly into a new primary role in this arena, thanks partly to the major Federal retreat from sub-state regionalism. Yet the Feds have returned to the field, notably with TEA-21. The states overall, though with some notable exceptions, have produced a pretty ragged regional record since the time they were expected to pick up the baton of leadership in 1982.

8. Movement, real movement, on this front will come when citizens, civic leaders, community spokespersons, economic elites, and policymakers recognize that various program challenges — whether solid waste disposal, a magnet school, growth management, or improved crime prevention — require a regional solution. Once the functional solution is settled, a steady probe of the resulting procedural and institutional implementation options ought to produce a response that strengthens general units of local government, not the functional variety, of which we have a surplus. But in all this, the many players involved must come together and recognize that processes alone will not suffice, that free market practices alone will not do the job, that collaboration to be effective over time requires authoritative institutions, and that romantic regionalism will never prevail as long as it lacks a good dose of regional reality. Many of the "New Regionalists" possess a faith that borders on the mystical, not exactly the best asset when tough interjurisdictional bargains are required.

## Lingering Questions

What does a state-local partnership in the jurisdictional and institutional areas entail?

- It means identifying common concerns, and the two greatest of these are the rising tide of nonelected functional governments and the incongruence of totally interdependent economic metro regions and the overlay of jurisdictional fragmentation in most of these same regions.

- It means recognizing that elected officials and generalists at the city, county, and state levels have more similarities than differences.

- It means knowing that structural factors are part of the fiscal and functional quandary engulfing most states and their localities.

- It means understanding that further application of the proliferation-is-local-power thesis will necessitate increasing higher-level intervention and will accelerate even more the conversion of multipurpose local governments into limited-purpose units.

- Finally, it means that the large number of substate governments, especially the thousands of tiny local units, and the absence of an authoritative arbiter in most of our metro and rural regions invite a divide-and-conquer strategy from above.

A partnership, to paraphrase Webster, means a relationship between and among government units contractually associated as joint principals in the public's business. The public's business is pressing. The contractual association, however, is only dimly perceived by many of the actual partners, and the concept of joint principals has been pushed to the point where it is difficult to sort out the principals from the bit players, given the number of governmental actors.

## Afterthoughts

This chapter on the states and their localities could not have been written in 1980, nor in 1968, nor obviously in 1960. The institutional and operational state reforms that were highlighted at the outset could be and were recognized in 1980, but their systemic significance was not clearly understood until the Reagan-Bush period, when their new roles were demonstrated. The tendency of states to curb local fiscal and personnel discretion and to play a passive role in the institutional arrangements in substate regional areas also was pointed out. In addition, the scrapping by the Federal government of its role as chief architect of substate regional programs, institutions, and processes from 1962 to 1980 was considered, as was the fact that the states now either by commission or by omission are the authoritative mapmakers for substate regions in rural and metropolitan America — a role some would like to ignore.

Most states, but by no means all, must grapple with a few of the interlocal, regional, and state governmental implications of the following jurisdictional facts:[63] (1) at least 51 percent (42,565) of all local governments are nonviable, given the population size of their jurisdictions; (2) economies of scale and the provision of merely a majority of the local services their citizenries require are not feasible for the 14,669 townships with populations below 5,000, for the 16,868 municipalities with populations below 10,000, and for the 2,257 counties with populations below 50,000; and (3) the same can be said of the 51 percent of all school districts that have fewer than 1,000 pupils. In Sweden in the 1950s, in West Germany from 1968 to 1978, and in the United Kingdom in the early seventies, such figures for local governments produced major two-tier structural reorganizations. But the United States does not have the kind of party system that could achieve this. At the same time, the many kinds of assistance these small jurisdictions need require a much greater focus on forms of interlocal and regional collaboration that will strengthen their status in the system.

A few final words on the states are in order. Most of this chapter trumpeted the achievements and the virtues of the states, and deservedly so. Their transformation since the midsixties has been nothing short of a revolution, albeit a quiet one. But there are also caveats. First, the scope of modernization has not been total. State capacity varies greatly — in resources, financial strength and effort, management, political culture, and degree of politicization. Second, just as the Federal government is not suited to handle all kinds of programs and functions, so it also is with states. They excel in activities that enhance their competitive position vis-à-vis other states and even countries. This means that developmental functions of the usual type, as well as programs like education at all its levels, are normally handled by most states. Health care, environmental issues, and corrections, on the other hand, present greater problems. Moreover, public management matters are also sources of difficulty. A recent Maxwell School (Syracuse University)–*Governing* magazine study of state government performance identified twenty-four states that fell below the overall state norm in public personnel policies and procedures, twenty-eight that ranked below the national average in managing for results with its emphasis on measuring inputs and outputs and on benchmarking, as well as a comparable number that were below the overall score for handling effectively information technology matters.[64] The list of good to exceptional performers included some states not usually deemed to be pacesetters in public management. The four top scorers were Missouri, Utah, Virginia, and Washington. Third, the states' civic cultures, political traditions, and degree of sensitivity to interest groups all make for very diverse political atmospheres, and these condition state policy and administration, and not always in the public interest. Finally, the states are more important to the successful operation of our federal system than ever before. And the Supreme Court in this decade seems slowly to be getting to the point where many of its members understand this. But in the national political and pressure-group realm, centralization persists, and the states are still treated as not much more than one more category of pressure group (as the next chapter demonstrates) — notwithstanding the cordial reception the Republican governors initially received from the leadership of the 104th Congress.

# Chapter 10

# A New Political System?

## The Devilish Dynamics

The current period in U.S. intergovernmental relations has witnessed the culmination of all the debilitating developments of the thirties, forties, and fifties that
had begun to undermine the state-local foundations of the "old party system."
The earlier system, which lasted from 1828 to roughly 1968, was confederative in structure and in interlevel power relationships, generally noncentralizing
(with the exception of the Republicans from 1861 to 1870 and the Democrats
from 1933 to 1938), and coalitional in character, given its multifactional nature. As we have seen, the strength of state and local party organizations varied
over time and from region to region, but these variations never compromised
in a permanent way the capacity of state and local politicians and parties to
make their views authoritatively known in Washington when the need arose nor
their ability to control the nominating processes for their own and for national
offices. The image of strong, boss-led local party organizations, we are discovering, has frequently been overdrawn.[1] But the real point here is that national
party instrumentalities were at no point between 1824 and the early 1960s really
authoritative.

### Dimensions of Decline

In the current period, as one authority put it, "Where once state and local
governments had composed the Federal government, by the 1960's they were
reduced to copying their functional rivals' practice of organizing associations . . .
and hiring Washington lobbyists in order to communicate with federal representatives."[2] The political changes that prompted this fundamental shift were
just as crucial to intergovernmental relations as were the structural changes
in the scope, methods, financing, and degree of sharing of public services. In
fact, without an understanding of the dynamics of recent political federalism
and especially its regulatory component, the evolution of operational federalism
traced in earlier chapters cannot be fully comprehended. Yet in fact, political
centralization came after the heavy centralization of policy initiatives under LBJ,
not before. Moreover, the states' move to set up Washington offices did not
occur until they were aware of both developments, in the late sixties and early
seventies.

The original causes of the collapse of potent state and local politics, parties, and politicians were largely indigenous, although Washington figured in a few (for example, the collapse of the white primary in Dixie, as mentioned earlier, the emergence of Federally funded social services, and consequently the erosion of old-style bossism in the North), and generational changes figured in them as well. The extension of direct primaries; the professionalization of municipal and state bureaucracies; the concomitant decline in political patronage; the election of governors, mayors, and county executives who focused more on their growing official responsibilities and less on politics as such; the rise of powerful functional constituencies (for example, interest groups), with their monied political action arms; and increasing state regulation of state and local party organizations (see table 10-1, p. 302) and processes are all part of this sad saga.[3] So, too, were the increasing suburbanization of politics, the accompanying collapse of strong party identification, and the increase in split-ticket voting. Not to be ignored, however, is the fact that some of these factors, while eroding the clout of state and local political organizations and their leaders, also strengthened the professionalism of state and local administrators and undercut the racism and exclusivity that were so much a part of the old non-centralized party system.

## Signs of Political Centralization

As a few of these state-centered and locally centered factors suggest, nationalizing forces of various kinds began to assert themselves even in the fifties, but more so in the decades composing the current period. And these accelerated the pace of subnational party decline. Even as popular attitudes toward the parties were becoming ever more critical,[4] national party instrumentalities were losing their 140-year-old "politics without power." While the Democrats began promulgating a few binding national rules (on convention delegates) in the fifties and adopted a rule in 1964 that banned the seating of delegations selected on a discriminatory basis, their traumatic 1968 national convention in Chicago prompted the most extraordinary changes in national party rules that ever had been undertaken.

With adoption of the McGovern-Fraser Commission's recommendations and subsequent early compliance by forty-one states, the national delegate-selection process was "opened up"; the role of party professionals was severely curbed; and slates of delegates would approximate the demographic composition of each state insofar as women, blacks, and young people were concerned. State parties were directed to make available written rules of the delegate-selection process, to give adequate notice of all pertinent meetings, to choose at least three-quarters of the delegates at a level no higher than congressional districts, to select no more than 10 percent of the delegates by the state committee, to refrain from awarding delegates slots on the basis of the unit-rule or "winner-take-all" system, and to establish demographic quotas for delegates.[5]

The result was to increase greatly the number of women, black, and young delegates, to reduce the earlier large proportion of elected officeholders, and paradoxically to produce a convention membership that only faintly resem-

## Table 10-1
## Index of State Regulation of Political Parties[a]

| | | *Light Regulators* | | |
|---|---|---|---|---|
| 0 | 1 | 2 | 3 | 4 |
| Alaska | Alabama | | Connecticut | Maine |
| Delaware | Georgia | | | New Hampshire |
| Hawaii | Minnesota | | | |
| Kentucky | New Mexico | | | |
| North Carolina | Oklahoma | | | |
| | Virginia | | | |

| | | *Moderate Regulators* | | |
|---|---|---|---|---|
| 5 | 6 | 7 | 8 | 9 |
| Arkansas | Rhode Island | Pennsylvania | Colorado | Mississippi |
| Florida | | | Idaho | Montana |
| Nebraska | | | Iowa | Nevada |
| | | | South Carolina | Vermont |
| | | | South Dakota | Washington |
| | | | Utah | Wisconsin |

| | | *Heavy Regulators* | | |
|---|---|---|---|---|
| 10 | 11 | 12 | 13 | 14 |
| Indiana | Arizona | Kansas | Illinois | Louisiana |
| Michigan | California | New Jersey | Ohio | |
| North Dakota | Maryland | Texas | | |
| Oregon | Massachusetts | Wyoming | | |
| | Missouri | | | |
| | New York | | | |
| | Tennessee | | | |
| | West Virginia | | | |

a. Index is based on state laws that regulate the parties' internal organizational structure, composition, and procedures.

*Source:* ACIR staff compilation. Advisory Commission on Intergovernmental Relations, *The Transformation of American Politics: Implications for Federalism* A-106 (Washington, D.C., August 1986), 143.

bled the rank and file of the Democratic party. Other by-products of the new rules were the further proliferation of primaries, growing from seventeen for the Democrats and sixteen for the Republicans in 1968 to thirty-nine for the Democrats and thirty-eight for the GOP in 1992, and the enhancing of the powers of activists over loyalists, who ultimately determine whether a party wins. Commission members favored more open caucuses, but in some states these were used in a way that further undercut the representativeness of the nominating process.

Efforts to resist these national party changes by party regulars tended to enhance further national party authority. Witness a unanimous Supreme Court decision that upheld the refusal of the 1972 Democratic National Committee's

Credentials Committee to seat the Daley-led Cook County, Illinois, delegation because of its alleged failure to comply with the new rules.[6]

Other than rule making relating to the delegate selection process, the Democratic National Committee (DNC) promulgated explicit bylaws governing and overseeing state and local parties between conventions. Most of them fell under the goal of fostering "full voter participation" and had diverse affirmative action guidelines covering gender, religious and ethnic minorities, and so on. Critics argued that the one group that was not singled out for extra attention and better representation was registered, authentic Democrats. Critics of this process also sometimes felt the Census Bureau rather than the processes stipulated by the DNC could have more easily implemented its ostensibly more representative goals because the basic assumption of the national rule makers was that the party's membership was essentially coterminous with that of the electorate as a whole — an insult to Republicans and independents, and an error that began the steady Democratic losses of the presidency.

With the Republicans, it was far less a matter of rules than of acquiring more ample resources, though state Republican parties were affected by the Democratic-sponsored state legislation relating to primaries. The Republican National Committee's budget grew by over 300 percent (in constant dollars) between 1965 and 1978. This in turn provided the wherewithal for a much broadened, computerized fund-raising operation, for providing a rich array of services to candidates and state and local parties, for establishing the campaign Management College, for launching an aggressive program of campaign recruitment for pivotal House and Senate races, and for engaging in national television advertising that could serve as a focal point and an umbrella for GOP candidates at all levels.[7]

Ultimately and belatedly, the Democrats began to follow suit with a much more modernized approach to fund-raising; provision of resources, training, and services to congressional candidates; and experimentation with a small program of national party advertisements. All these endeavors enhanced the role of both national committees, obviously by very different approaches, and subjected state and local party organizations to varying degrees of dependency or at most interdependency. Close to the Capitol in Washington, D.C., are the national headquarters buildings of the Democratic and Republican parties. A generation ago there were no permanent headquarters. These offices, their respective chairs, and their professional staffs are at the peak of American political party organization.[8] Both bodies are stronger than they have ever been; their respective resources and staff have multiplied. With the Republicans, it really began with Chairman Ray Bliss of Ohio in the late fifties, and it only took the Bliss example for the Democrats to begin recharging their own national party machinery. While the current Federal-state-local party organizational relationship is essentially a federal one, it is a centralized one, no doubt. With the proliferation of PACs and "soft money" (i.e., unrestricted contributions that may be used for enhancing party activities, but not specific candidates), the national committees now serve as massive money conduits to their state committee counterparts. Pursuant to the 1979 "Soft Money" amendment to the Federal Election Campaign Act, the Republicans' "soft money" outlays rose from $15.1 million in 1980 to $18.9 million by 1992, while the Democratic expenditures in this area soared from $4.0 million to $23.6 million over the same time span. These various fiscal developments enhanced the role of national committees in intraparty affairs.

In addition to the centralizing of party rules and funding, there has been a significant shift to Washington, D.C., of many of the foci of policy development and enactments along with the emergence of critical challenges to the national parties. In the first place, the historical national party practice of suppressing issues from national consideration that would divide the party was pretty much scrapped by the end of the Johnson administration with the expansion of the national policy agenda to include all manner of subjects, from those that clearly were national and intergovernmental to several that belonged in the state and local government or the private sectors. Party efforts to cope with this massive expansion of ostensibly national policy concerns proved to be difficult to impossible. To the extent that they did achieve some success in addressing this extended agenda, the job of reconciling and compromising on these different and usually divisive issues became all the more arduous. Admittedly some of the lesser policy concerns were abolished during the early Reagan years, but by 1988 the number was back nearly to where it was in 1980. Reaction to the enactment permissiveness of the seventies prompted the broad Reagan anti-government thrusts, as we have seen, and these in turn generated moderate to liberal counteractions. The Gingrich-Clinton duel repeated this scenario, but with more drama and extremist jousting. More ideological deadlock, more intraparty friction, and fewer significant policy enactments were the major by-products of this growing party and institutional polarization.

## Other National Actors

While the national party organizations were gaining power vis-à-vis their state and local counterparts, the two major parties as a whole were experiencing an overall decline in voter allegiance, support, and trust. A prime sign of this decline is the fundamental political fact that the nation has experienced divided national government for all but six of the past thirty years. This is the longest such period in our political history, far outmatching the 1877–96 era, when there were only four years of one-party control.

Party affiliation and commitment have experienced fairly drastic shifts since the sixties. The proportion of strong Democrats in the voting electorate shifted from 27 percent in 1964 to 17 percent twenty years later and up to 19 percent in 1996.[9] Weak Democrats dropped from 25 percent in 1984 to 20 percent in 1996. Strong Republicans began at 11 percent, rose a percentage point by 1984 and yet another point twelve years later.[10] The proportion of weak Republicans rose from 14 percent to 15 percent by 1984 and gained another percentage point by 1996. With the two tending groups and the strict independents, the combined figures indicate a hike from 23 percent of the total in 1964, to 34 percent twenty years later, and gaining a percentage point by 1996. This last set of figures, of course, underscores the progressive decline of strong and even moderate party commitment on the part of voters. Accompanying this dealignment in the party system (that is, the weakening of popular attachment to the major political parties) has been the precipitous drop in voter turnout from 62.8 percent of the eligible electorate in 1960 to 48.8 percent in 1996. Midterm election turnouts have been even lower. The "Gingrich Revolution," for example, was based on 53 percent of the total turnout that represented 38.6 percent of the eligible voters. The reasons for this decline are multiple and conjectural. The weakening of strong party loyalty, the confusing personalized and factionalized character of primaries, caucuses, and general elections, along with continued voter disenchantment with politics and politicians are among the key reasons generally cited.[11] In addition, among many there is a feeling that one's vote is useless and without weight.

With the erosion of party loyalty and voter participation, there arose new and, in some cases, revitalized old political actors on the national scene and later at the state and local levels. Functions that parties had previously performed were gradually or suddenly assumed by other political players, even as the national parties assumed new responsibilities, especially in telecommunications, finance, and technical assistance to state and local parties and candidates, most of whom were and are nationally oriented and based. The heightened role of mass media and the ever mounting costs relating to their use are two new factors that translate into key actors first at the national level and then at the state and local levels. Communications now may be seen as the lifeblood of politics, and some have contended each is a side of the same coin.

Nearly every era has had its particular new form for reaching party communicants and others. Today it patently is telecommunications. Not only does a thirty-minute nightly newscast reach 50 to 60 million viewers, but the new round-the-clock cable news reaches an even wider audience, though generally fewer people at any one time than the traditional newscasts. With both, the form and content of the news are different from those of the traditional news media.[12] Despite very conflicting assessments of these phenomena, there is general agreement among most experts that televised news is now more national, much more political, and much more superficial and sensational than the news in most of the other media. This has important intergovernmental, political, and public opinion consequences. In terms of the political party, televised politics has tended to focus on the candidates, not their parties; to replace the party as the main link between the candidate and the voter; to become the prism through which voters perceive the issues; to highlight conflict and downplay consensus; and to provide the opportunity for candidates to bypass party organization completely and establish a personal, media-oriented campaign organization and staff.[13] Above all, perhaps, the indispensability of television as a campaign necessity has exponentially escalated its costs. Martin P. Wattenberg in his research also has found that heavy reliance on the media has contributed to the declining salience of political parties.[14]

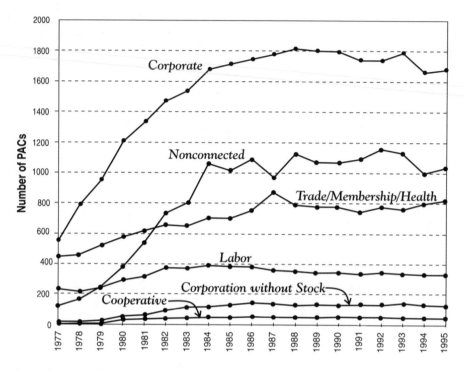

*Source:* http://www.fec.gov/press/pacnum.jpg.

**Figure 10-1**
**Political Action Committee (PAC) Count, 1977 to 1995**

Enter the PACs. Political action committees have been with us since the 1940s, but it is only in the past three decades that they have cast a dark cloud over politics, policies, and politicians. Their rapid recent growth (see figure 10-1) was indirectly but significantly fueled by the campaign finance reforms of the seventies. The Federal Election Campaign Act (FECA) of 1971, its 1974 amendments, a 1975 Federal Election Commission ruling (which held that a corporation could solicit employees and stockholders to contribute to its PAC so long as no coercion was involved), and a 1976 Supreme Court decision that struck down curbs on noncandidate political contributions by groups and individuals combined to unleash the near quadrupling of the number of PACs between 1976 and 1987,[15] while the 1988 to 1995 figures indicate a slight tapering off with both the corporate and trade/membership/health PACs. All told, the total figure in 1995 surpassed the 3,200 mark.

PACs and "soft money" came into their own in 1996. The PACs discovered that they could circumvent the amounts of money going to specific candidates by contributing "soft money" to national and state committees for party-strengthening purposes, including "get out the vote" campaigns and highly visible "issue ad" promotions. The results of the combined lavish campaign fund-

### Table 10-2
### Summary Financial Activity, All Congressional Campaigns, 1996

|  | 1981–82 | 1983–84 | 1985–86 | 1987–88 | 1989–90 | 1991–92 | 1993–94 | 1995–96 |
|---|---|---|---|---|---|---|---|---|
| Raised (in millions) | $354.7 | $397.2 | $472.0 | $477.6 | $471.7 | $659.3 | $740.5 | $790.5 |
| Spent (in millions) | $342.4 | $374.1 | $450.9 | $459.0 | $446.3 | $680.2 | $725.2 | $765.3 |
| No. of Candidates | 2,240 | 2,036 | 1,873 | 1,792 | 1,759 | 2,950 | 2,376 | 2,605 |

Source: http://www.fec.gov/press/canye96.htm (14 April 1997), 1.

ing amounted to more than $2.2 billion for the 1996 presidential canvass, $4.7 million for the typical U.S. Senate race, and $673,000 for the average House contest. The beginning base figure for a presidential run in 2000 now is set at $22 million. Figures for total campaign funding for the 1981–82 cycle to the 1995–96 cycle indicate a steady increase for all but the 1989–90 period. All told the outlays more than doubled during this sixteen-year span (see table 10-2). Outlays for the 1998 midterm elections were the first to pass the $1 billion mark. Large "soft money" contributions to the national and state parties not only undercut Federal donor and spending limits, but they also undermine the efficacy of state and local campaign finance laws. Special interest contributors in most states, while restricted in their donations to individual candidates, may escape these curbs by allocating large contributions to state political parties, which then transfer them to their candidates. Superficially, it would seem that the state organizations are strengthened by these and the national committees' "soft money" donations. But, in fact, the reverse would seem more to be the case, since major ethical issues are raised in both instances. For old "pols," these figures are staggering, if not shameful.

In the wake of the 1996 election, the pressing need to plug the large "soft money" loophole was apparent to many in both parties and among civic and citizens' groups. The earlier corrective measure sponsored by Senators John McCain (R-Ariz.) and Russell F. Feingold (D-Wis.) was defeated in July 1996, falling short of the six votes needed to shut off a filibuster. In the House, a companion bill cosponsored by Representatives Christopher Shays (R-Conn.) and Martin Meehan (D-Mass.) was passed by a comfortable margin. But eight Republican senators had to be converted if it was to pass muster in the upper chamber. This did not happen. Regardless of the outcome, the "soft money" issue will not wither away because it is a major facet of our increasingly more questionable campaign financing practices. Meanwhile, national "soft money" contributions increased by nearly 250 percent between January 1993 and June 1998 (see figure 10-2, p. 308).

In addition to the advent of the national political money suppliers, other new actors include campaign consultants, pollsters, and even state and local party supporters, as long as their efforts dovetailed with those of the individual candidate's stratagems. Another major conditioner here was the parallel proliferation of interest groups on the Washington scene over this period. For the most part

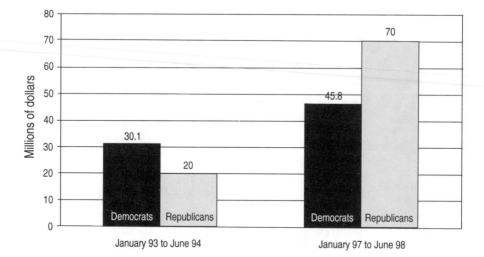

Source: *Newsweek,* 17 August 1998, 13.

**Figure 10-2**
**Soft-Money Contributions (in Millions of Dollars)**

the growth in the number of PACs, grant-in-aid programs, and Federal regulations, as well as public skepticism about politics and policymaking of the major
parties generally, have to be linked to the expansion in numbers, types, purposes,
and strategies of interest groups at the national level. According to one count,
in 1960 there were 523 organizations in Washington, D.C., engaged in representational efforts; by 1980, 2,721 had Washington offices, and a total of 5,769 were
engaged in lobbying.[16] By the mideighties the latter category had soared to more
than 10,000, and by 1991, to more than 14,000.[17] In the first six months of 1997,
there were 9,198 different registered lobbyists in Washington, D.C.[18] This figure
amounts to a decrease of nearly 5,000 since 1991, which may be attributable to
the policy passivity of the 105th Congress.

In terms of composition, only 19 percent of the 11,750 individual lobbyists
in 1990 were active for "special-cause groups" (that is, organizations that are
membership-based); 32 percent had ties to trade and professional associations;
15 percent were from individual corporations; 17 percent were lawyers registered as foreign lobbyists or for big agencies; 17 percent were consultants and
professional managers from client associations and interest groups; and less than
1 percent were from policy think tanks.[19] Despite this heavy tilt toward business, "public interest, welfare, single-issue, intergovernmental lobby, and specific
program groups all expanded significantly during the seventies and eighties."[20]
Analysis of the list of lobbying organizations spending $1 million or more from
1 January to 30 June 1997 reveals that only 7 of the total of 106 were not
in corporate or corporate-related companies or associations. These included
three social welfare groups (AARP, the National Committee to Preserve So-

cial Security, and the Seniors Coalition), one religious association (the Christian Coalition), a quasi-Federal lending agency (Fannie Mae), a conservative single-issue coalition (the National Right to Work Committee), and one big labor body (the AFL-CIO). All the 99 remaining were an extraordinary mix of corporations, trade and professional associations, and business umbrella groups; they were by no means united on most issues.[21]

Why this growth in interest group politics in Washington? Economic growth, soaring specialization in both the economic and societal areas, and higher educational levels have all been cited as explanatory factors. In the political socialization realm, learning from the success of others (for example, handicapped and women's groups learning from the success of African Americans, citizen participation groups learning from labor's success), the advantages of concentrating on a single issue, recognition that a "win in Washington" beats almost any success at the state or local level, and discovering that the national political and policy-making processes had never been more permeable than in the seventies also must be factored in here. The Federal government itself, in its many policy moves from 1964 to 1980, served as a magnet, attracting all manner of groups. The hyperreponsiveness of Congress, especially following the liberal reforms of the midseventies, was yet another facet of this governmental attraction to added pressure-group activities.[22] The further pulverization of Congress's already heavily decentralized power structure in the seventies, the curbing of the powers of standing committee chairs just as northern and western Democrats were assuming these positions, and the steady erosion of presidential agenda-setting authority should not be overlooked when assessing this rise in interest groups' assertiveness.

The textbook theory of how a bill becomes a law was shoved aside in many policy areas. Madison's maze of procedural, institutional, and motivational obstacles continued to prevail when new legislative proposals were advanced. But when the second, third, and fourth round of reauthorizations of Great Society programs came up, the politics of renewal made it easy to expand the scope, goals, recipients, and even the implementation techniques of the original program. With an omnibus bill as the preferred device for reauthorization and with mounting majorities on both sides of the aisle voting for renewal, national activism took on new life — a life that did not appear to have much clear programmatic purpose, as Samuel Beer and John Gardner noted at the time. The system by 1980 was suffering from a severe case of political and programmatic overload, caused by the seemingly unlimited forays of interest groups into national policymaking and the hyperporosity of the national political and policy development system in the seventies.

Provocative but largely persuasive earlier research on the role of pressure groups in the eighties suggests that success for some of them had become more elusive. Paul Peterson developed the argument that pressure-group power of "the Good Old Days" was over. An interest is "special," for Peterson, if it "consists of or is represented by a fairly small number of intensive supporters who cannot expect that their cause will receive strong support from the general public except under unusual circumstances."[23] The test of their strength is the percentage of the gross national product (GNP) the national government has spent on activities not of paramount interest to one or both of the two major parties. Thus, special-interest programs include everything that remains in the Federal budget after interest on the debt, defense, foreign relations, programs for the elderly, the safety net, and agricultural programs have been excluded. Programs not in this listing (that is, pressure-group programs) grew from 3.6 percent to 5.69 percent of GNP from 1962 to 1980,[24] which, for Peterson, meant that special-interest programs accounted for three-fourths of the entire increase in the total size of the Federal budget during the eighteen years. "It was a great time to be a special interest," he concluded.[25]

The special conditions, for him, that supported this "world of special interest politics" (that is, the politically accessible economic resources that arose as a consequence of inflation and the resulting bracket creep, the peace dividend in the form of halving defense outlays, and the decentralization of policymaking both in the congressional and executive branches) did not prevail in the eighties. Instead, real difficulties arose in translating economic resources into public funds because of the 1981 tax cuts, the indexation of income tax brackets, the recession, the resulting sharp fall in Federal revenues, and the arrival of huge deficits.[26] The peace dividend obviously disappeared with the sharp rises in defense outlays, and there was a high level of White House centralization and a major curbing of congressional decentralization because of the riveted attention of nearly all on budget deficits. Relative few players (for example, chiefly the members of the six money committees) dominated that process in both houses. The consequence was a decline in special-interest program spending from 5.6 percent of GNP in 1980 to 3.7 percent in 1989. Most of the consensus expenditures categories, on the other hand, remained the same or expanded, while "special-interest programs" were cut 70 percent on the average, sliding back to 1962 levels.

While the nineties were not covered in Peterson's analysis, it is clear that the constraints imposed by mounting deficits in the 1989–92 period simply continued the earlier course, but with more austerity. The Bush and Clinton budget agreements in 1990 and 1993 respectively produced a mix of tax hikes and service cuts that surpassed anything done in the Reagan years. The outlays then for "special-interest programs" probably would match or surpass the low ones for the eighties. On the other hand, the 1997 budget agreement, as noted earlier, began a new strategy of tax cuts and certain servicing hikes along with some other program reductions, providing more room than had been present for some time for "special-interest" solicitations. In addition, the initial House version of the 1998 highway bill was so loaded with pork that it was nearly impossible to find any real beef in it, prompting moral outrage from some of the Republican sophomores. In the final measure, the special projects for individual members accounted for about 5 percent of the total funds, which admittedly were large. With defense appropriations for the same fiscal year, $10 billion dollars was added to the total for items that DOD did not want, but members of Congress, including the Speaker, did. With the prospect of budget surpluses now and in the future, presumably this special-interest favoritism will accelerate, unless the surpluses are earmarked for Social Security or reduction of the national debt, or both.

Peterson's classification scheme can produce arguments, though it would be difficult to modify greatly his list of consensus programs, given their strong political support. The failure of certain grants to attain this status may be deplorable, but the failure is a political failure of being unable to convert the parochial into a paramount purpose. Some will point to tax expenditures, regulations, trade restrictions, and grant conditions as items that should be considered in any assessment of how lobbyists are faring. The reining in of regulations by administrative means during the Reagan and Bush years and the plugging of many loopholes by the 1986 Tax Reform Act do suggest a kind of replay in these two areas of the pressure-group constraints encountered in the expenditures field. But in all these cases, only some pressure groups are punished, not others. Peterson argues that the stronger national parties and more centralized decision making are not likely to erode in the near future and the interest group liberalism of the seventies will not reappear.[27] Recent events, noted above, suggest this might not be so.

None of the above undercuts the earlier findings that most policies have been nationalized, that pressure groups are more numerous than ever, that they inject excessive amounts of conflict into the decision-making process, that PACs as well as individual giving are more important than ever, and that the wherewithal of reelection to national office is still found in Washington, D.C. Moreover, the checking of some pressure groups in the eighties and nineties was due to the deficit, congressional budget procedures, and institutional centralizations — not to any assertion of greater authority by the national parties as such. Here there is disagreement with a part of the Peterson proposition.

## State and Local Parties Adapting

State and local parties and politicians have lost most of their earlier, much earlier, punch in various national political arenas and still lack any significant influence over national and, in some cases, over state and local nominations and election processes. Yet they have experienced and are experiencing an adaptive kind of renaissance of sorts. Their organizations, services, resources, and strategies have all been transformed to greater or lesser degrees in most states.[28] There are higher staffing and budget levels in state party organizations, though the variations here between and among states are still quite wide. Nonetheless, the overall pattern for the eighties stands in marked contrast to that of the sixties. Fund-raising activities have picked up and been modernized, and the package of services for candidates for state office has been enlarged — more so in the Republican than the Democratic case.[29] There are signs that some elected state officials — notably governors of both parties and Republican legislators — are paying more attention to party matters now than they were twenty years ago. Moreover, state party organizations are playing an increasing role in presidential primaries, particularly during the earlier ones. Governor John Sununu's organization was a critical factor in George Bush's New Hampshire win in 1988.

Many of these state efforts at revitalization have been aided by their respective national committees, a development that would have been unthinkable thirty years ago. Fund-raising help, direct financial aid (especially after 1995), polling and data processing, voter registration drives, candidate recruitment and training, and organizational management help are among the kinds of assistance provided by the two national committees to their state counterparts — the Republicans in all instances to a greater degree than the Democrats. The wide gap here that existed in the early eighties appears to have been narrowed since then, especially during Paul Kirk's and Ron Brown's tenures at the Democratic National Committee.[30]

On the regulatory question, an earlier ACIR survey found that more Republican state chairs than Democratic believed Federal laws interfered with state party activities.[31] The same response pattern was produced by the question "Are state laws regulating political parties and elections in your state generally supportive or unsupportive?"

Accompanying the revival of state parties and paralleling the "advocacy explosion" in Washington, interest groups in the seventies and especially the eighties took on state capitals as an essential "second front."[32] The proportions representing major types of interests at the state level are roughly similar to those at the national.[33]

The number and diversity of the interest groups now found in state capitals — compared with thirty years ago — are much, much greater.[34] This trend reflects the spread of urbanization and suburbanization in heretofore largely rural states, the impact of Federal programs on pressure-group politics at the state level, and, to some degree, one more result of reapportionment. There is some evidence that where state parties have weakened, certain pressure groups have assumed a greater role.[35] There is also evidence that some of this expansion was a direct result of nationally based organizations working to acquire a fifty-state substructure, especially during the Reagan years.

In an exhaustive analysis of interest group power in the fifty states, a five-category classification was devised.[36] The "dominant" label applied to nine states where pressure groups as a whole exerted overwhelming influence on policymaking. The "complementary" label applied to seventeen states where groups are forced to work in conjunction with or are constrained by other forces of the political system. The "subordinate" label would have applied to states where groups are subordinated to other features of the policymaking process, but no states fell under this heading, indicating that pressure groups played some role in all states. The "dominant-complementary" label applied to nineteen states whose interest groups alternated between the dominant and complementary alternatives or were in the process of moving from one to another. The "complementary-subordinate" label referred to a different alternating pattern, one that assigns a greater role to five states' strengthened party systems. Clearly, regional as well as strong-party–strong-governmental factors are conditioners of many of the designations. Increasing professionalism of government and richer social pluralism also seem to be influential in the drift to the "complementary" category. Like many of the other basic findings in this study, nationalizing influences are a major force at work in creating this fifty-state pressure-group picture. But another finding is the state-local variations that mutate the nationalizing forces.[37]

At the local level, valid political generalizations are much more difficult to make. The following are at best tentative:

- Most local officials tend to spend less time on partisan affairs than do most state officials.

- Trust in local government and officials is somewhat greater than in those at the state level.

- Local parties and their organizations and procedures, generally, are even more regulated by legislatures than are their state counterparts.[38] Here and there are signs of municipal political organizations that possess a certain degree of cohesion based on the strong issues orientation of their membership.

- Patronage and pressure-group politics in the contracting, personnel, and zoning areas are certainly known in most larger multicultural municipalities, but none of this adds up to a revitalization of the old, highly disciplined, urban machine. Supreme Court cases banning political patronage in non-policy-making positions, as in *Rutan,* have had minimum impact on local personnel practices.[39]

- The politics of most of the relatively few reorganized metropolitan governments tends to be a cut above that of the unreconstructed ones.

States and their localities are represented nationally both separately and collectively. The latter case, as noted earlier, takes the form of the so-called intergovernmental lobby, or the PIGs, that is, public interest groups. Relations between and among the "Big Six" in Washington are not always fraternal, and the Reagan years made the development of joint positions exceedingly excruciating. The cities and counties, after all, were being forced to relinquish some of the strength they had possessed in the seventies, while the state associations assumed lead roles, especially the National Governors' Association. The slashing of aid to the localities exacerbated friction, and the puny increase of 0.5 percent in direct aid between 1992 and 1997 did not change the earlier course to any appreciable degree.

## What Kind of Party System?

Others may worry whether ours is a dealigning, realigning, decomposing, or declining political system,[40] but the concerns here are whether the parties and/or the entire political system are really nationalized, and whether the operational strength that is now possessed by states and localities can ever be converted into regained power in the political realm. The evolution of both parties from noncentralized, loosely constructed, confederative organizations into what some observers believe are federative structures "under which the different levels of organization share both resources...and functional responsibilities" is not all that obvious.[41] This view does not mean that the parties resemble each other structurally, as Gary Wekkin points out. For him, "Interparty relations within the Democratic party, especially those concerning delegate selection, greatly resemble Deil Wright's *overlapping authority* model" of IGR, "where (1) substantial areas of governing operations involve national, state, and local units simultaneously, (2) the areas of separate, autonomous jurisdiction have shrunken very small, and (3) authority in most policy areas therefore tends to be shared and subject to much bargaining and negotiation."[42] On the Republican side, national-state relations have reached a point where they have gone "beyond 'cooperative federalism' to something approaching Wright's *inclusive-authority model*" of IGR, "where (1) states and localities are dependent upon decisions that are nationwide in scope and are made by the national government, (2) subnational institutions have atrophied, and (3) the functions formerly performed by these subnational organs have been fused into a centralized, hierarchical system."[43]

Wekkin's interpretation seems roughly reasonable insofar as it deals with the parties, except that it seems to somewhat overstate the degree of Republican centralization, which the current period of not having a Republican in the White House ought to demonstrate, and it may well understate the extent of Democratic centralization. Only time will tell how accurate the interpretation is. Of greater concern than these systemic descriptions of the political parties are the roles of the other actors in the political system. The other players in combination and even singly, after all, are just as potent, or nearly so, as the parties in determining policy and political outcomes at the various levels.

One of the most acute observers of political parties has written that a "world without parties" would be one wherein special-interest groups and PACs gain; wealthy and celebrity candidates gain; incumbents gain; the news media, especially television news media, gain; and political consultants gain.[44] To many observers, this is a wholly accurate description of what now prevails in U.S. politics. When one probes the very successful negative media politics of the small insurance and small business associations against the Clinton health care reform proposal, or the remarkable clout of individual large interests like Big Tobacco, Big Insurance, and Big Money during the 105th Congress, one cannot doubt the strength of "pressure-group politics" over "responsible party politics" much of the time.[45] Put differently, ours generally is a system without effective parties, though paradoxically it is one with a strong constitutional basis but an incredibly weak political party component. Such organizations at a very minimum under the old (pre-1968) regime of the traditional parties performed the latter-day Madisonian function of forcing interest groups through rules, procedures, and program review both in the governmental and political arenas to moderate their parochial demands and strident rhetoric. They also provided a territorial counterweight to the vertical functional groupings rapidly gathering in Washington. But there are only a few signs that today's major national parties are attempting to resume this mediating, ameliorating, and filtering function, unlike the situation in some states, where the parties are a check on interest groups. In part, this is because many interests already have infiltrated the parties, thanks to the ease with which they can stage coups in caucuses, primaries, and committee rooms. In addition, a new political animal has appeared recently on the national scene, one that combines some traits of a party with those of a pressure group: the pressure-group party, of which more will be said in the next chapter. The rank and file in both parties have suffered greatly as a result of the ostensible opening up of the nominating processes since 1972 and the congressional processes since 1973.

The emergence recently of greater party voter cohesion in Congress is viewed by some as the basis of a new era of party government and as a potential restraint on the power of the pressure groups. That there has been much more of a tendency among most, if not nearly all, Republicans to vote their party position (when there is one) and a similar voting pattern among the Democrats has been clearly the case beginning in the midseventies. The basic cause for this has been the continuous shift of conservative southern Democrats over into Republican ranks along with a less perceptible, but nonetheless real, increase of Democratic strength in the Northeast. The result, of course, has been to buttress the already strong position of the conservative wing of the GOP and to expand the number of moderates within Democratic ranks.[46] In ideational terms, both parties have on most issues been pushed further to the right, with the GOP becoming much more "hard right" and the Democrats more centrist.

The reasons for this are multiple and include the renaissance of a vibrant, largely religiously based social conservatism in the South, the continuation of deep popular resentment to Federal social programs and Federal regulations, and a general resentment of Federal policy activism and Washington's perceived greater power. In institutional terms, the increase in the number of safe congressional districts, including "majority-minority" ones, and the sometimes arbitrary actions of the House leadership, as perceived by the minority in the seventies through to the early nineties, should be noted. The higher levels of party cohesion began with the 103d Congress with its infusion of a large number of GOP freshmen conservatives and the overall Republican reaction to the Clinton policy proposals, especially his budgetary and health care reform recommendations. The Republican 104th Congress, of course, reflected a voting pattern that looked more Westminsterian in its strictness than Washingtonian. Much of this is explained by the remarkable character of the GOP victory, especially Newt Gingrich's "Contract with America" and the arrival of seventy-three mostly ultraconservative freshmen. As John A. Aldrich and David W. Rohde have noted, it was the bending of strategic party and standing committee appointments and powers to the Speaker's will, as well as his scrapping of the traditional seniority rule and close shepherding of the GOP freshmen and sophomores, that provided the leadership and cohesive support for the enactment by May of all but one of the more than thirty items that were subsumed under the Contract's ten general headings. For Aldrich and Rohde, it was the Speaker's successful adaptation of congressional party instrumentalities and House rules and customs to enhance the chances of passing the basic policy goals of the revitalized congressional Republicans that established this case study of "conditional Congressional government."[47]

Subsequent events obviously have proved this to be a short-lived experiment. In the first place, it was a case study of the House and the House alone. Congressional government, as it was described in the 1880s, presupposed close collaboration between the two legislative branches, their dominance in dictating national policies — to the extent that there were any — and a Presidency that served pretty much as the Clerk of the Senate. The 1995–96 situation in the House in no way paralleled the description given in the 1880s study. Second, the Gingrich strategy, personality, and sense of power produced the farcical situation of assuming that the traditional checks and balances between and among the three national political branches had evaporated and that the House had become the paramount body with the Senate and the presidency reduced to subordinate positions. No Congress in the twentieth century, not even the 80th, assumed this strident stance. The more conciliatory shift in Gingrich's strategy with the 105th Congress and the return under Speaker A. Dennis Hastert of the 105th to according greater authority to the standing committee chairs, greater discretion to the committees themselves, and greater respect for the seniority principle all suggest how temporary the distinctive 104th House record was. What is more, the kind of party cohesion that was the basis of the Gingrich grand enterprise has come asunder, and this applies to both chambers of Congress, not just the House. In short, the special mix of circumstances that permitted the 104th's experiment with "conditional Congressional government" was just that: special and not a permanent political or institutional addition to Congress or the national government.

To sum up, parties, politics, and pressure groups have become nationalized over the past quarter of a century. State and local parties have been adapting to their new role as adjuncts to national parties and, in this more centralized system, are frequently financed by the national parties. But no matter how much revitalized, they probably cannot regain their former dominance and control of the national nominating and electoral processes. With less regulation, perhaps they can capture control of their very own nominating and electoral processes. The stark fact that states and localities have had to resort to setting up their own representational units in the nation's capital underscores how low the formerly mighty have fallen, though the partnership role assumed by some able Republican governors in congressional bill drafting and even negotiating during the 104th Congress indicated a climb to the heights, at least temporarily.[48]

The great irony here, of course, is that this should be necessary in an age when the states are more reformed, responsible, respected, and resourceful than ever before. When, more than three decades ago, at least four-fifths of them could not lay claim to many of these qualities, the states needed no lobbying operations in Washington; their congressional delegations were enough. All this has changed, of course. So, a fundamental question of fairness arises here: Should the states and localities be relegated to subordinate pressure-group status in the political world when most of them are near-indispensable governments performing the nation's most critical domestic functions in the world of governmental operations?

In the political sphere, state and, to a lesser degree, local political parties are beginning to revive and reappear, but the process is slow and dependent on help and in some cases regulatory relief from above. Other political competitors increasingly seem to have greater access to the voters than the parties do. The strengthened national parties have been helpful in many ways, but in the case of both parties, it is a highly centralized form of political federalism that applies because the state and local units have neither the power nor an authoritative impartial party umpire to aid their cause. Their cause, of course, is to strengthen the historic territorial basis of the two parties and to serve as a counterweight to the fragmentation caused nationally by the flourishing functionalists, demographic groups, and special-interest moneymen.

The time has come to put the many centripetal forces in the system in their proper place, one that is commensurate with what the domestic role of the national government has now become. This should produce a more genuine federative structure for the parties, a structure that better matches the real world of contemporary intergovernmental operations. But none of this is likely unless state and local officials who possess the operational clout use it to leverage greater political power within their respective parties, within the political branches of the national government, within the body politic, and before the Supreme Court, where they are beginning to score well. The first step in this direction is achieving a far greater unity among these subnational governments both in the field and in Washington, D.C. Additionally, their leaders must develop the ways and means of engaging in some strategic planning on an ongoing basis. Short-term concerns almost always succeed in shunting aside the bigger questions of what the state and local roles in the federal system will and should be come the millennium.

*Part 4*

# Toward a Rebirth
# of Federalism

# Chapter 11

# What of the Future?

To gauge the condition of our federalism at any particular time is rarely a simple task. And currently it is difficult, though not as difficult as it was as recently as 1994. Why? Because power and influences in the system have been manifesting themselves in more areas of intergovernmental activity and in more inconsistent ways than ever before. Today there are somewhat fewer areas of ambiguity; hence the lead title of this work: "The Rebirth of Federalism," which is far more appropriate now than when it was first used in early 1995. At the same time, the issue of inconsistency, the matter of simultaneously divergent developments, and the still steady "Slouching toward Washington" have not disappeared, as earlier findings have demonstrated. In some instances, they have become more pronounced because centralization in certain areas no longer conquers all. Witness the recent pro-state judicial record. So we still have totally different contemporary interpretations of the character of today's federalism and the intergovernmental relations that flow from it. Single-factor explanations of the evolution of U.S. federalism usually have been found to be faulty, and in federalism's continuing highly conflicted condition, such an approach is at best a way to gain only a partial understanding of what makes the system tick.

To describe the system as still fully centralized or newly decentralized; as cooperative or resurgently competitive; as less regulated or more so; as activistic or retrenching; as overloaded or unburdened highlights the wide range of dynamic and antagonistic impulses that shape it. In the previous chapters, a sustained effort was mounted to discover the extent to which operational federalism (that is, the funding, running, and accounting of public programs, whether intergovernmentally or by separate levels) dovetailed with the dynamics of judicial, representational, and political federalism(s). Each of these facets of federalism was a prime part of the legacy of the Founders, as noted in chapter 2. Moreover, analysis of federal systems abroad confirms the influence of the four factors in shaping the Swiss, Canadian, Australian, and German federal systems. More specifically, these factors are (1) a constitutional division of significant functional and financial responsibilities between the center and constituent governments; (2) the existence of a high court that plays an umpiring role most of the time; (3) direct representation of subnational governmental (that is, territorial) interests in a national upper chamber; and (4) a cohesive, subnationally based party system. And it really makes a difference if trends in each of these four areas are mutually supportive or work at cross-purposes.

## General Findings and Observations

With the above analytical factors in mind, what basic conclusions can be drawn concerning the many dimensions of intergovernmental interaction that compose today's still complex and conflicted system?

1. In terms of power relationships, our system remains mostly a nation-centered one, certainly when compared to that of 1960 or even 1968; yet it is somewhat less centripetal than the system of 1980, thanks to the recent constrained Federal fiscal and programmatic roles (and to some curbs on the regulatory one); to the enactment of some devolutionary measures mostly during the 104th Congress; to certain pro-state Supreme Court decisions; and to the growing state assertiveness, operational responsibilities, and leadership in curbing some of the more arbitrary Federal IGR actions.

2. Regarding intergovernmental operations, the states are far more the middle-level planners, administrators, and partial funders of national domestic programs than they were in 1960, 1970, or even 1980, because the scope of Federal grant programs was smaller in the first two years, and the local role was much larger in the last. This suggests no return to dual federalism but, superficially, a continuance of the pre-1964 cooperative federalism.

3. When some of the core processes that make up the vast operational IGR terrain are explored, the cooperative label is appropriate generally only for the older functions, where program goals have become consensual ones, but not for the newer, costly, and thus more controversial ones. In the financial relationships between and among the levels, the reduced level of Federal funding in non-entitlement, urban, and non-safety-net social programs has left the states and notably the localities in more strained financial shape. In the areas of expanded state discretion, another new kind of unusual program responsibility has arisen — one that requires states to achieve certain quantitative results by a specific date or suffer penalties. But, overall, the direct expenditures of the subnational governments are on a par with Federal domestic expenditures, and despite the pain, this parity is a most welcome omen for those who seek signs of greater balance in any of the areas where federalism functions.

4. In operational federalism's regulatory realm, the weight of unilaterally added mandates by the national government on states and localities has been lightened somewhat compared to the rage to regulate prior to 1995. Before the passage of the Unfunded Mandates Reform Act (UMRA), neither the deficit dilemma nor the State or Local Government Cost Estimates Act (1982) had nurtured a more responsible congressional behavior in this area. If anything, the deficit vise has resulted in more regulations and costly specific program conditions (the expansion of Medicaid coverage, the Safe Drinking Water Act, the Immigration Reform and Control Act of 1986, to note a few of the more blatant examples); all contained provisions that heaped up sizable, unreimbursed fiscal burdens on state and some local governments.[1] Yet this in turn produced instances of states' probing for accounting loopholes in programs such as Medicaid, but more importantly, it led to the united drive for UMRA, which at least ini-

tially dampened the congressional drive to issue "direct orders" to the states and localities. In tandem with the earlier revolution in intergovernmental regulation was the parallel push to preempt, with 280 such actions occurring between 1960 and 1991.[2] In constitutional terms, these actions amount to a steady erosion of the states' police powers and a further enhancement of the reach of Congress's regulatory arm. The effectiveness of the curbs instituted since 1995 depends almost wholly on the attitudinal climate of each Congress, a frail check at best.

5. The proposition that some analysts put forth that with reduced Federal grant funding in most program areas a comparable reduction would occur in the regulatory area has proved to be a myth. If anything, the Federal propensity in the eighties and early nineties to fall back on mandates actually continued at the same high rate as it had in the roaring seventies. To some extent, the same scenario has been played out at the state level, with locals suffering most from the punitive, pass-the-buck policy, a policy that would have been unthinkable in the years of the "old party system."[3] Since UMRA excluded grant conditions, past enactments, and mandates whose estimated cost is under $50 million, there are many loopholes in the measure; equally significant is the tendency to reduce the estimated burden on affected governments to below the threshold figure and to shift to grant mandates rather than direct orders to achieve the regulatory goal.

6. With grants management, the assignments since 1981 have been both easier and tougher. The return to a roughly one-to-fifty Federal-state grant administrative relationship has strengthened the supervisory role of Federal grants managers and the administrative tasks of their state counterparts as well. But the merger of the traditional grant distributive and program oversight roles with the more recent role of administering the new social regulations attached to these programs (with different but equally conflicting roles assigned to the state and local counterparts) violates all rules of proper management. This burden has become the fate of far too many Federal managers, generating tension, if not confrontation, between the administering groups at both levels. Some of the new block grants with their expanded recipient government discretion and their tough Federal reporting and/or performance requirements set the scene for a repeat of this kind of distrustful relationship. Where once the cooperative federalist ethic prevailed in the old grant programs, the seeds of suspicion and of a "fearful new federalism" have been sown with various of the new grant enactments. Witness the battle between state human resource commissioners along with their IT staff and Department of Health and Human Services (DHHS) officials and their desire for over 170 different TANF reportorial items from the states.

7. Regarding the Federal agencies themselves, the full impact of "hollow government" and "government by proxy" at the national level has yet to be fully fathomed by most observers, including propagandists for "reinventing government." Any objective assessment of the domestic agencies — whether direct providers of services or providers of grants and loans to other governments and agencies — would show clearly that the shortcomings of many of these units are largely a result of severe earlier personnel cuts and the extraordinary expansion in Federal reliance on third-party providers to implement policies, prompted

largely by ideological initiatives in the eighties. Agency assignments generally have not been reduced, but staff has; in intergovernmental terms, this Federal personnel condition frequently has produced a situation where state agency people appear more professional, knowledgeable, and numerous than their Federal counterparts. It also has produced fundamental oversight problems regarding the operations of third-party organizations, especially with the proliferating Government Sponsored Enterprises (GSEs) with their billions of outstanding lending authority. A "thin red line" of administrative competence is not the best way to uphold the Federal position in current grant and loan management operations, especially in light of the new regulatory complexities Congress has thrust into the operations. Moreover, it is not inconceivable that a significant impact will result from the increasing number of court cases involving the issue of whether workers employed by private or quasi-private firms performing functions pursuant to government contracts are subject to the same or some of the same protections and liabilities as government employees. If, as some authorities like David H. Rosenbloom believe, this type of work becomes "constitutionalized," some of the major benefits of privatization will be lost.

8. The "new politics" buried two very different theories of Federal bureaucratic behavior. Its centralizing propensities demolished the Grodzins-Elazar thesis that no president, Congress, or administrator would enact or implement grants or conditions that were fundamentally subversive of state and local jurisdictional integrity because the noncentralized political system of the fifties and early sixties placed national policymakers in jeopardy if they took such actions.[4] In addition, Leonard D. White's extension of classical public administration precepts to cover grant administration disappeared somewhere in the middle of Johnson's Great Society years. The White theory held that Federal grant administrators possessed adequate controls to run the programs and to maintain accountability.[5] Given the number, variety, and controversial goals of many of the pressure group–conditioned grants enacted in the late sixties and especially in the seventies, the White precept proved unworkable. And most political developments from Reagan to the present have only served to further weaken the position, professionalism, and power of career Federal administrators.

9. Even more to the point perhaps, the new political system with its coterie of special actors surrounding an individual candidate, the ever present media, and a plethora of pressure groups and PACs — while reflecting the nation's incredibly rich, multicultural, but deeply divided pluralism — nearly took over in the seventies, as Peterson and others have noted. Fiscal constraints placed curbs on some of the smaller groups in the eighties, but the gridlocks of the eighties and nineties were as much a pressure-group-produced phenomenon as they were a mere matter of divided political control of the executive and legislative branches.[6] The phenomenon also was shaped partially by differing ideologies at both ends of Pennsylvania Avenue, with each sustained by its own cohorts of rabid factional partisans and allied assorted pressure groups.

10. Among the pressure groups, the functional and centripetally oriented have tended to dominate, although the professional-technological, regulating,

social-moralistic, and citizens' groups in most cases are not genuinely functional in character but just as centralizing as the other groups. Where does this leave the intergovernmental lobby? It leaves the lobby in a very precarious position: few allies, many actual and potential opponents (including their own program people), and techniques that generally do not differ materially from those of other lobbying groups. On rare occasions, it can score with Congress and the administration. If its members can firmly unite, if they can show they will suffer real fiscal pain as a result of a Federal action, or if they can demonstrate that they actually have a "better way," they generally can be persuasive with national policymakers. But each of these three are tough tests to meet. Moreover, the manner by which they usually must make their cases is demeaning for a group that provides the major means for the national government to carry out most of its domestic policies. The IGR lobby is about all that is left of representational federalism, which once was the bulwark of state-local strength within the very confines of the central government. No one seriously is proposing repeal of the Seventeenth Amendment to restore a direct state role in national policymaking. Yet it would be appropriate and accommodating if the kind of collaborative consultation and mutual deference that characterized the relations between the congressional Republican leadership and certain Republican governors during most of the 104th Congress were to become permanent, pervasive, and bipartisan. But this could occur only if the states' political power matched their functional force.

11. With judicial federalism, an institutional force is encountered that plays a grander and greater adjudicatory function than any high court in any other system, whether federal or unitary. The assessment herein of the Supreme Court's recent record indicates another division, but in this case between institutional and ideological judicial conservatives. There were a few liberal ideologues on the Court earlier, and there are some conservative ideologues now, and neither group placed the Court's role, institutional integrity, and popular acceptance of its decisions at the core of their very different philosophies. Yet the Court is one of the few institutions in our system that can be above politics, politicians, and specific interests — even though its members frequently were nurtured in such an atmosphere. At the moment the former strength of the ideological right has been reduced because of the Clinton appointees (Justices Ginsburg and Breyer), the continuing generally liberal course of Justice Stevens, and the growing independence of Justice Souter. This leaves Justice Kennedy and Justice O'Connor, the Court's most ardent defender of federalist values, as this Court's swing persons, depending on the specific issue. The Court through various recent decisions involving different constitutional provisions has developed a common basic principle: the power of the political branches of the national government cannot be used to issue direct orders to states and their localities. The Supreme Court then has begun to play a salutary role in relieving the nation of some of its worst excesses, including the continuous centralization. That there has been a "rebirth of federalism" in no small part is due to recent decisions of the Court.

12. Finally, if a label is to be put on the current system of federalism, it must

be "a partially permissive federalism," which is an adaptation of Michael Reagan's "permissive federalism." Though coined more than a quarter of a century ago, his description (and John Sanzone's) captured most of the realities of intergovernmental relations until quite recently. There still was a sharing of power and authority between the two constitutionally recognized levels of government, and the states' share rested largely "upon the permission and permissiveness of the national government."[7] For Reagan and others, this version of federalism was both accurately descriptive and normatively prescriptive. The basis for the interpretation was the belief that the national government should be dominant, that the interdependence involved gives rise to mutual leveraging activities, that the states and localities "retain sufficient political strength to ensure that their views will be listened to by the national government," and that considerable discretion will be permitted in the implementation of grant programs.[8] One may quibble with these points, especially those dealing with political strength and program discretion, but the description is all the more accurate because the states and localities do not possess much political clout under the "new political system," and significant program discretion depends on the type of grant — certainly almost all of the big-ticket grants are heavily conditional, and all grants were still enmeshed in crosscutting and other forms of regulation.

Missing in the Reagan and Sanzone analysis was an assessment of the Court's centralizing role, the powerful role of the key nonparty actors in the new political system, and the new regulatory and preemptive roles of the political branches of the national government. Yet all of these trends rendered "permissive federalism" all the more accurate as a description only a few years ago. The only modifiers that needed to be noted were the few instances the intergovernmental lobby overturned or blunted national mandates, the significant but secondary Supreme Court decisions that favored the states and localities, and the informal administrative clout subnational governments possessed as basic implementers of Federal domestic programs, along with the national government's inability to sack anybody working for these governments.

"Permissive federalism," then, was, until roughly 1994, an accurate portrayal of most intergovernmental power, political, judicial, and administrative trends, though it missed the "slouching toward Washington" that arrival of the "new political system" symbolized. But as a normative interpretation, Michael Reagan's view was repugnant to those who were concerned with the long-term vitality of our governance system and who found the centripetal arrangements to be inadequate constitutional, political, and representational protections for state and local governments. National policymaking and implementation must leave subnational governments with a due measure of policy discretion so that they may help cope with the manifold challenges now confronting the country. Neither the Federal policy process, nor Federal finances, nor the centralizing cluster of functional interests in Washington — singly or in combination — could cope with these challenges. Permissiveness was not enough. A freed-up and protected federalism is what was needed, not the conflicts, ambivalences, and overloads that "permissive federalism" had nurtured.

What then prompted the new designation of "partially permissive federalism" for current Federal-state-local relationships? The basic reason, of course, is there has been some tilt toward the states that began earlier in some areas and was strengthened recently by certain judicial decisions and political developments. When these state-favoring trends are combined, a reexamination of the Michael Reagan interpretation must be undertaken. The national government still is authoritative in several intergovernmental fields. But what produced the increase in state power and influence?

First, the High Court has clearly changed its previously steady centralizing course. In 1994 when the first edition of this work was being written, *New York v. United States* (1992) looked like a lone, probably aberrational decision. By 1998, it could be seen as the first in at least five major decisions that together signaled the advent of a new "protective federalism" stance on the Court's part. Second, public opinion has demonstrated a swing to support for the states. Let us recall that Madison relied primarily on shifts in public opinion as the most effective way to correct the imbalance in power that arises when one level of government becomes too strong or distrusted. If polls are any guide, the public feels the Federal government is too strong and untrustworthy, but it has far greater faith in the states. In a January 1997 survey conducted by the Pew Research Center, 17 percent of those surveyed said they had "a good deal of trust in state governments." Fifty-three percent indicated they had "a fair amount" of trust in their states, which is nearly 20 points above the counterpart 1992 figure.[9] The Federal figure is usually about half the state (and local) one. Four decades ago, 73 percent of the public said they felt the Federal government could be trusted to do the right thing most of the time, while a Pew national survey found only 34 percent felt that way in 1998.[10] In-depth analysis of the responses to this poll suggests that when the public is anxious about the economy, public morals, values, and the direction in which the country appears to be headed, then the national government is blamed — this despite the fact most of these issues have very little to do with Federal governmental operations. Moreover, various Federal agencies were exempt from these general anti-Federal attitudes, with some coming up with rave reviews, for example, the Agriculture Department, the FDA, the Post Office, and even the Department of Education and the IRS for some. In any event, the states indirectly have benefited from the generalized anti-Washington worries.

The comparatively modest (in light of initially high expectations) devolutionary enactments of recent Congresses and the attempt on the part of the nation's lawmakers to rein in their previous rush to mandate with UMRA must be interpreted as state-sensitive measures. Moreover, the close Republican gubernatorial-congressional collaboration during much of the 104th Congress cannot be ignored here, despite the fact that it did not extend into the 105th. In addition, there has been the president's personal proclivity to heed state and local complaints and to rely heavily on waivers to encourage state experimentation in welfare and health care reform, as well as his recent acquiescence in meeting the vehement attacks from state and local leaders on Executive Order

13083 on Federalism, which was issued when he was at the May 1998 economic summit in Britain. The complaints included the lack of any prior consultation with their organizational representatives in Washington, D.C. (unusual for this administration), the absence in the order of any language requiring explicit justification of a proposed preemption, and the listing of nine different conditions that would warrant centralization of a governmental function.[11] In truth, six of the nine would be considered by objective observers as reasonable. The three that irritated the state and local officials the most were those relating to calls for centralization when decentralization increases the cost of administration, when states are "reluctant to impose necessary regulations" because they fear adverse economic consequences, and when delegating regulatory authority to state and local governments imposes excessive fiscal and personnel burdens.[12] The White House's withdrawal of the order and willingness to discuss the disputed points indicated that Clinton was willing to go more than half way to accommodate his old friends. By early 1999, it appeared to be dead.

These and other recent developments indicate there is a basis for claiming a resurgence of state influence in Washington and in the system. Yet note that generally the key elements of change here are behavioral shifts by Federal institutional actors. This fundamental fact seems to uphold Michael Reagan's view that the scope of state and local discretion and authority still seems to be determined by national officials. Another interpretation is that the combination of the states' new fiscal, administrative, regulatory, and welfare reform roles now tends to give their spokespersons greater leverage in national policymaking. The key to achieving this clout is the need for state and local leaders continually to stress their indispensability to the effective functioning of our federalism and to continue with their litigation, when required. Regardless of whether the Reagan or independent state action theory is the more accurate, "partially permissive federalism" is still the proper designation, because it captures the curbing of national power in some areas and the increase in state prestige and influence. It also suggests that something of the old spirit of cooperative federalism has reemerged in some areas.

## Five Paradoxes

The above twelve summary findings and observations underscore the continued conflicted condition of federalism, and they clearly reveal antagonisms within and among the four areas of analysis employed here: the operational, political, representational, and judicial. Others, relying on a one- or two-factor approach to assessment, do not find this multidimensional ambivalence in their analyses of the system. To highlight the variety of other contemporary interpretations, five paradoxes found in the recent record of Federal-state-local relations are briefly probed.[13]

One debate that has emerged from very different readings of the record is *whether a state-centered system has been restored (or has always existed) or whether a nation-centered system has been strengthened (or was never really dismantled)*. In the final months of the Reagan presidency, a *Washington Post* headline read "States Assuming New Powers as Federal Policy Role Ebbs," and a lead article at about the same time in a state and local affairs journal carried the title "State Power Needn't Be Resurrected Because It Never Died."[14] John Shannon (see chapter 1) has long and eloquently contended that "De Facto New Federalism [the result of Reagan's economics and federalism] represents a continuous unplanned retreat from federal positions staked out during the Great Society Era" and that for a variety of reasons it has enjoyed considerable success.[15] Most recently, he has suggested that a return to a form of dual federalism has been achieved, with the state-local portion of the layer cake a large one. More recently, the election of the Republican 104th Congress was seen by many as heralding a new age of state ascendancy and a reduction in the Federal domestic role, thanks to "accelerating devolutions."

Others do not dismiss the fiscal difficulties of the Federal government or its reduced domestic fiscal and programmatic roles especially during the era of triple-digit national budget deficits. Yet they emphasize there has been and is no general retreat from the earlier centralizing propensities on the political, regulatory, and even judicial fronts. As the analyses in earlier chapters have documented, the political parties now are pseudofederal in organization and in many operations, but nearly all the other actors in this political system, except the PIGs, are centralizing in their thrusts. Moreover, the congressional record from the early 1970s until 1995 in the regulatory and preemption spheres constituted a continuous aggrandizement of national authority. Moreover, the reining-in reforms of the 104th Congress may well be short lived. The fallout from the various preemptive and regulatory actions taken by that very Congress has yet to be fully gauged. Witness the preemption provision of the telecommunications legislation, which has begun to generate grumbling from states and localities on grounds that it can override state and local land use authority. Vermont currently has taken the lead in raising this complex question. The recent lull in new intrusive Federal enactments may be just that — a short respite in what has been for over three decades an arena of avid Federal activism. What is more, some of the current intrusiveness has been prompted by big business, as in the Vermont case. Finally, anything that depends on congressional forbearance for its survival is relying on a frail faculty of our nation's lawmakers. So the future of constraint regarding Federal mandates and preemptions is at best an uncertain one. Additionally, the Court has nodded favorably in the states' direction, and on matters of more than secondary importance. On the big issues involving the conditional spending and taxing powers, as well as the supremacy clause (as long as the intent to preempt is clear), the Rehnquist Court generally has been centripetal. But a series of cases beginning with *Clarke v. United States* (1989) and ending with decisions from the Court's latest term when viewed in sequence define certain evolving federalism principles that strengthen the states' constitutional status in our system. Now this is a new development, largely a product of the nineties and largely unnoticed by all but federalism fans and constitutional law buffs. Ponder the following: *Clarke* (1988), a Federal district court case, later upheld by a circuit court of appeals, found that a mandate attached to the District of Columbia's annual payment from Congress amounted to a "gun held to the head of the District Council" and as such exceeded the scope of the conditional spending power, the only such case to do so. In *Gregory v. Ashcroft* (1991), as noted earlier, the Court held that the Age Discrimination in Employment Act could not and did not supersede the Constitution of the state of Missouri, which requires state judges to retire at seventy. The right of a state to specify such a provision is one of the sovereign rights of a state, Justice O'Connor wrote, and is protected by the Tenth Amendment. In *New York v. United States* (1992), the provision of the Low-Level Radioactive Policy Act of 1985 requiring states that failed to provide disposal sites by 1996 to take title of and assume liability for all undisposed waste was found unconstitutional. In her majority decision, Justice O'Connor returned to her argument in *Ashcroft* and held that Congress by this requirement infringed on New York's powers under the Tenth Amendment. With *United States v. Lopez* (1995), the Supreme Court declared that there is a four-part "substantial effects on interstate commerce" test and that the Gun-Free School Zones Act met none of the components. The reenactment by Congress of an amended version of the 1990 act sets the scene for a later Court case dealing with the topic, but only two of the four requirements were met by the 1996 legislation. So we shall see. In *Printz v. U.S.* (1997), it was held that the Brady Act's requirement that local law enforcement officials had to conduct background checks on prospective gun buyers violated the commerce power and also was a violation of state sovereignty under the Tenth Amendment. Ours is a system of "dual sovereignty," Justice Scalia declared. In *City of Boerne, Texas v. Flores* (1997), the Court invalidated the Religious Freedom Restoration Act as a violation of its own right to interpret the Constitution and as an intrusion on the sovereignty of the states, notably the right of their localities to enact land use ordinances. With the *Seminole Tribe v. Florida* (1996) and *Idaho et al. v. Coeur d'Alene Tribe of Idaho* (1997), the Eleventh Amendment rights of the states were upheld insofar as in both cases the tribes' suits against the respective states could not proceed in a Federal Court.[16] Finally, with *Maryland v. Watson* (1997) and *Richards v. Wisconsin* (1997), the Court upheld local police actions that would have raised questions of legality in the Warren Court.[17] Clearly the above cluster of cases with its mix of big and comparatively less significant decisions highlights an emerging sensitivity to states' rights under the Tenth and Eleventh Amendments and amounts to an effort to broaden the scope of the states' police power. Finally, this still centralizing attitudinal group should understand that the reduced Federal fiscal role does not mean its elimination; the largest number of grants ever and total outlays for FY 1998 of more than $250 billion are not to be disregarded.

A second federalist debate has erupted over whether ours is or should be *a competitive or cooperative federal system*. One argument for the competitive case holds that the 1981 Federal tax cuts, the repeal of General Revenue Sharing, the rising deficits, earlier and future serious fiscal nightmares plaguing Social Security and Medicare, along with other shackling developments, have produced a situation in which the national government no longer "can move into virtually any domestic area," no longer "possesses a towering fiscal advantage over the state and local governments," and must "now compete head on for the political and fiscal support of federalism's ultimate arbiters — the voters/taxpayers."[18]

A different version of the competitive thesis comes from Thomas Dye, who has enunciated a contemporary theory of competitive federalism that links public choice and the more traditional state-centered federalism theories. Dye finds several signs of the vigor of the competitive ethic in the provision and financing of domestic public services. Yet he also cites the hurdles that hinder achievement of a more ideal free-market model, hurdles that need to be torn down.[19]

Yet another perspective on competitiveness has been advanced by Alice Rivlin. In *Reviving the American Dream*, she called for a wholesale sorting out of governmental functions and assigned to the states a long list of services — education, crime protection, physical infrastructure, job training, and so forth — that would constitute a "productivity agenda" in which differing competitive state approaches to providing these functions would enhance the likelihood of their success.[20]

Contrasting collaborative views of the system come from other thinkers and from experience. Paul Peterson and his associates in an in-depth study of certain Federal grant programs concluded that the vigorous give-and-take among Federal and state and local administrators regarding grant conditions and objectives ultimately produces a rough kind of agreement, even in the case of redistributive aid programs. For Peterson and others, this in practice amounts to a contemporary version of cooperative federalism.[21] To the more historically oriented, the rise, abrupt decline, and gradually renewed growth in the Federal grant system is a fundamental sign that cooperative federalism is alive and well, though not as flourishing as it was in the sixties and seventies. These grants, it should be remembered, were the prime instrumental sign a half century ago that dual federalism was on the wane and a new cooperative version was emerging. Other recent omens that this approach still functions are the emergence of the negotiated method of developing new or modified grant regulations involving affected state and Federal officials and the devolution of greater administrative authority, especially in the eighties, to state environmental administrators pursuant to statutory authorization in cases where individual states meet certain Federal standards.[22] The expanded use of block grants, of waivers, and of negotiated rulemaking in the midnineties is a more contemporary example of the collaborative trusting ethic.

A third controversy generating opposite IGR views is *whether the system has become a co-optive rather than a collaborative, decentralized one.* Proponents of the co-optive interpretation point to the national propensity for a third of a century to preempt and to regulate — and not merely the private sector in the latter regard but subnational governments as well. Those asserting the emergence of a co-optive Federal role in the system usually cite two statistics: (1) there were more preemptions after 1960 than there were between 1789 and 1960, and (2) the number of new social regulations enacted in the 1960s quadrupled in the 1970s and 1980s. The absence of reimbursements also is noted, along with key Court decisions like *Garcia, Baker, Rutan, Rust*, and *Jenkins* — all highly intrusive, radical in the sense of erasing traditional positions (except for *Rust*), and produced by a conservative tribunal. Most analysts who adopt this co-optive assessment believe that such a stance on the part of national decision makers is inevitable, given the weak political and judicial status of the states and localities in Washington, D.C. In the field, most local governmental spokespersons certainly believe that their discretionary power is more shackled than ever before, given state and Federal regulations. State leaders also feel more fettered as a consequence of constraining Federal conditions and regulations. The increase in the eighties of direct orders, the most peremptory of all the newer regulatory devices, is a particularly irritating development and perhaps the most vivid symbol of how vigorous co-optive federalism has become.

Contrary opinion holds that most of the above arguments are exaggerations and do not reflect contemporary operational and judicial reality. This school of thought points to the expanded number of block grants, the Federal exit in the eighties from certain program areas (notably the multistate and substate regional ones), the passive behavior of many Federal regulators, their small number in various of the key agencies, and the practical problem of their insisting on mandate compliance when money is lacking. It also singles out the ten instances during the eighties when Congress overturned or softened judicial mandates and stringent congressional statutes in response to vigorous protests from the IGR lobby. It underscores the internal efforts of the two past administrations to soften — if not to scuttle — regulations, and it singles out the Bush failure to follow up after the signing of the Clean Air Act Amendments with vigorous or even passable enforcement efforts. In the nineties, it cites the Clinton executive orders on mandates and state-local consultation on them. The Supreme Court's actions in narrowing the liability of state and local officials and relief sought under 42 U.S.C. Section 1983, in establishing certain ground rules regarding Federal preemption, and in recognizing concurrent state court jurisdiction in certain cases also are duly noted. The Court's decisions according greater deference to state judiciaries in Federal habeas corpus proceedings, in upholding a new state tax initiative (that is, a VAT), in recognizing the validity of a state constitutional retirement provision in *Gregory v. Ashcroft*,[23] and in voiding the unfunded mandate in the Brady law requiring local police background checks on prospective gun buyers in the *Printz* case are cited as further evidence of shifts from its centralizing stance. The eloquent enunciation of a doctrine of federalist constraints on national power in the *Ashcroft* case by Justice O'Connor is usually singled out for special attention. These factors along with the states' assertion of their own right to experiment and innovate in various governmental program areas, so this argument runs, are ample proof that state and local governments are less constrained now than they were in the seventies.

The question of *governmental activism or governmental constraint* has also been a source of dispute. Activism advocates point to the continuous growth in total governmental outlays as a percentage of GDP from 1960 through 1983 and a little over 1 percent decline from 1983 to 1990, but a rise to 31.9 percent by FY 1992. A further gradual decline then occurred, with the FY 1997 figure hovering around 29.5 percent. The post-1993 period then has been irregular with no big surges or big reductions, suggesting an ambivalent activism in an era of retrenchment. They note that no proposed presidential budget since FY 1983 has been less than its immediate predecessor, and that the same is true of congressional budgetary actions. They emphasize the 42 percent hike in grant-in-aid outlays during the Bush years, thus signaling the end of the Reagan era's slowdown in grant growth. They also stress the 29.7 percent increase in aid outlays between FY 1993 and FY 1998, despite the 1993 budget agreement and two Republican Congresses. The activism group stresses the steady rise in the proportion of total aid for grants involving payments to individuals — rising from 35.7 percent of the 1960 total to 63 percent by FY 1993 and 62.5 percent by FY 1998. Medicaid outlays alone soared by more than 100 percent from FY 1989 to FY 1993, reaching over $80 billion, and then rose to over $103 billion by FY 1997, a 28.8 percent increase from the FY 1993 figure. But there was a 36 percent decline in what formerly went to AFDC and now is allocated to TANF. Finally, this group emphasizes the steady rise during the past decade and a half in combined state and local expenditures as a percentage of GDP compared with the glacially declining Federal domestic percentages. With the earlier downturn in the economy, the state-local trend was temporarily halted. Although conceding the severe constraints generated by the gargantuan Federal deficits in the eighties and early nineties, the advocates of this viewpoint find that the various dimensions of growth cited above are all the more remarkable in light of the deficit-driven politics that have prevailed since 1982 until quite recently. Nothing reveals the strength of this activism, they assert, as much as the sorry restraining record of congressional budgetary reforms from 1974 to roughly 1991.

Those adhering to the governmental-constraint interpretation include supporters and opponents of downsizing public expenditures. Both usually agree that the rate of Federal program domestic growth from 1978 to the present was far below what it would have been if the annual growth rate of the midseventies had continued. Rather, they stress that there was a 16 percent aid reduction in constant dollars between 1978 and 1988 and a 20 percent decline in aid as a proportion of state and local outlays. The mix of aid hikes under President Bush and curbs on aid growth beginning in FY 1991 and especially in FY 1993 combined to produce a meager 4.3 percent increase in Federal aid as a percentage of state and local outlays from FY 1988 to FY 1997 (see table Int-1, pp. 4–5). In constant dollars, the increase amounted to a 16 percent hike.

Liberals in the governmental-constraint group have stressed the ill effects socially of various budget acts, especially in the programs for the working poor, the young, and the environment. They also criticize the growing gap between the wealthy and the poor, both during the Reagan years because of the tax cuts and the slash in benefits for the working poor and in the nineties because of additional tax cuts for the well-to-do. Those who applauded what happened with the 1990 and 1993 budget agreements contend that the tax hikes and personnel and program downsizing in these measures were the only reliable ways to strengthen capital formation and greater productivity, and for building the firm bases for a healthy U.S. economy. And to some extent, they were right, because a surging economy partially aided by these governmental actions did produce a small budgetary surplus as early as October 1997. For this conservative group, the worry now is whether the national politicians of both parties can resist using the projected surpluses for tax cuts or program increases or a combination of both. President Clinton, of course, wants to earmark most of the surpluses for Social Security and Medicare.

A final point of major debate is *whether the federal system is overloaded or not.* By the end of the seventies, systemic overload was diagnosed as the chief malady afflicting the federal system.[24] The evidence cited then was the extraordinary expansion in national programs (that is, grants, loans, subsidies, regulations) — both major and many very minor — in the wide range of recipients, in grant conditions and regulations, in convoluted intergovernmental programmatic linkages, and in grant outlays. At the same time, there were too few Federal supervisory personnel, too few adequate controls, too few dollars, and too little accountability, given the advent of fungibility (that is, the inability to track the final program effects of Federal grant dollars because of their substitutive effect in jurisdictions receiving several grants and especially grants that are non-categorical). These fiscal and administrative signs of overload gave rise to the impression that major policymaking had been centralized, even as implementation had for the most part been devolved.

The reasons for this were largely assigned to the political and judicial actors in the expansionist Federal drama. The Court had been giving a green light to Federal activism on the regulatory and program fronts since late 1937. With the demise of the Conservative Coalition in the midsixties and with the advent of spectacular real economic growth, national policymakers finally found a way to enact and fund expanding national programs. The inflated revenue receipts and the more liberal Democratically controlled Congresses in the seventies partly explain this continued growth. And the increasing tendency of interest groups of all kinds to enter into the very porous national policy-making process of the seventies gave rise to Samuel M. Beer's question of whether the U.S. polity any longer could "impose upon public expenditures any rationale, any coherent view of governmental action, any scale of priorities reflecting an overall view of national needs, if its decision making starts from the extreme pluralism of such a model of public sector politics."[25] There are various primary reasons for these dangerous developments: the Court; an earlier collapse of the old parties, the old congressional procedures, and the power structure; the emergence of public opinion, pundits, and politicians that could not distinguish among a local, state, and federal question; and countenanced governmental scrutiny, aid, and regulation of even the most elemental and most tangential of primary social interrelationships.

From the perspective of the nineties many would contend that the system is still overloaded, not quite as much as it was in 1980 but still overloaded. The gap between service demands and revenue receipts at the national level; the continuing influence of a centripetal interest group–dominated political system in Washington; the concomitant continuance of "slouching toward Washington"; the absence of effective party intermediaries and procedures to force large and powerful pressure groups to heed what is in the public interest; the failure to confront the fearfully large projected expenses of entitlements in the future — all are current signs of an overloaded federal system. In addition, there was a failure on the part of the 104th Congress to stick to its basic goal of reducing the Federal role in the system. When it finally adjourned, the 2 November 1996 cover story of the *National Journal* bore this title: "GOP Confounds Expectations, Expands Federal Authority." It then proceeded to itemize the many centralizing actions of the so-called devolving Congress: from the strict penalties in TANF; to the federalization of such crimes as stalking, rape committed during a carjacking, and participation in terrorist activities; to incentives to states to have criminals serve 85 percent of their sentence; to designating the Federal government as the sole regulator of mutual funds, agricultural chemicals, and most telecommunications.[26]

The Federal propensity to slough off responsibilities to states and localities, to mandate without money (at least until 1995), and to continue to rely on these governments to implement most of its domestic programs remains. No change here! And these continuities are part of the overload problem as well. Perhaps the major cause of this ongoing challenge is the popular habit, acquired largely in the seventies and eighties, of desiring a panoply of public programs but also of adhering to the now-venerable quotation of former Senator Russell Long (D-La.): "Don't tax you, don't tax me, tax the man behind the tree." And politicians did little but respond affirmatively to this populist demagoguery until 1990. Yet another facet of this continuous overload is the fact that the system overall is, if anything, more complex than ever before. From the vantage point of the typical voter, not to mention political analysts, the system cannot be easily, or even with real effort, comprehended. Here arises a popular and an intellectual dimension of this overload indictment.

The opposite view stresses the changes that have occurred since 1981 and especially since 1993 and 1995. Reagan, after all, may not have succeeded in his New Federalism, but he barred a return to the seventies. The soaring deficits injected a kind of discipline into the system — not through a strengthening of parties but of congressional procedures that were intended to discipline. Gramm-Rudman-Hollings and the November 1990 budget procedures, although far from perfect, did allow economy-minded legislators to exercise their franchise, and the Peterson probe showed that marginal (or true) pressure groups did suffer as a result. In addition, many of the administrative nightmares of the "old regime" were largely remedied by the striking reduction in bypassing. The old one-to-fifty formula returned in the eighties, and little was done in the nineties to increase direct Federal aid to localities, as has been emphasized earlier. The signs of greater judicial sensitivity to state and local concerns and the declining, then slightly rising Federal aid figure as a proportion of state and local revenue also suggests a definite shift from the centralization scenario. Not to be overlooked here were "within-house" efforts of the Reagan, Bush, and Clinton administrations to curb the effects of the regulatory rash. Overload in an administrative, regulatory, and practical operational sense is far less burdensome now than in 1980, according to this interpretation. The waivers, new block grants, UMRA and the fewer regulations and preemptions, the Clean Water bill (which gave small local jurisdictions greater leeway in meeting purity standards), the abolition of Federal speed limits, and allocating greater authority to the states in distributing rural development funds are some of the many recent indications that since 1993 a moderate but genuine Federal effort was successfully mounted to devolve and to unload.

## Why These Conflicting Views?

A conflicting condition, according to Webster, is one in which an emotional state exists characterized by indecision, restlessness, uncertainty, and tension. Well might one so describe the range of antagonistic assessments of U.S. intergovernmental relations today. Why this confusion? One answer is that there has been little agreement over the proper role and requisite needs of subnational governments, especially the states, in our federal system for over half a century, and there has been only glancing recognition that the states have been transformed over the past thirty years or so. The memories of rurally dominant, in some cases racist, and generally nonprogressive state governments die slowly. Related to this is the fact that no consensus has arisen since the New Deal over the proper Federal role in the federal system, other than economic action in hard times. The Reagan years, which some thought would settle the matter of proper roles, left us in an even greater quandary about this issue than in 1980.

Some of the difficulty here stems from the varying schools of federalist interpretation described in chapter 1. Particularistic philosophic propensities can scuttle consensus and even provide support for real-world trends that conflict. This is not to say that the ambivalences in U.S. federalism today are a product only of conflicting intellectual interpretations and their impact. Far from it. The system to date, in fact, does reflect a simultaneous series of centralizing and devolutionary tendencies, of a co-optive national government and of less shackled states, of competitive and collaborative administrative and political intergovernmental behaviors, of a centralizing Court and a balancing one, of significant activism and of restraint, and of some systemic overload and greater balance.

But how can this be? Part of the American political tradition has been the propensity to honor values that are basically incompatible, such as liberty and equality, individualism and group cooperation, and more recently, programmatic liberalism (support for individual governmental programs) and philosophic conservatism (hostility to big government). Present-day intellectual, institutional, and operational arenas of our system mirror a rich cluster of contradictions, and this really is nothing new. Yet their number and potentially destructive results are novel and merit attention.

What immediate causes have contributed to this agenda of ambivalence? *The parlous condition of our economy and our public finances* until quite recently was one major explanatory factor. On the one hand, the severe fiscal straits of the national government from 1982 until 1997 generated program cuts, eliminations, and a slow grant growth rate and an undergirding of a whole movement toward devolution. Deficits and devolution have evolved in tandem; ideology alone does not explain the drive for devolving. On the other hand, this same fiscal factor enhanced the earlier centripetal tilt in the system by promoting more regulations, more preemptions, more unfunded grant mandates, and more direct orders (that is, co-optive federalism's prime devices). Through these various means, nationalizing policy initiatives could continue, even if the money were missing. With the advent of quite good economic and public finance times, interlevel conflict moderated somewhat. Yet the continued reduced growth in discretionary Federal aid, the emerging uncertainty regarding the world economy, the accompanying concern about optimistic forecasts of future Federal surpluses, and the new issue generated by the current Federal surpluses of whether to cut taxes or hike program outlays inevitably generate new causes for interlevel fiscal tension.

*The economy, as such, produced a comparable result.* During the 1981–82 and 1990–92 recessions, state efforts to institute self-help programs, attract foreign investment, curb and streamline government programs, and experiment with cost controls in health and hospital programs reflected noncentralizing undertakings and provided further evidence of state revitalization. When it came to matters of further Federal program cuts, prospective new mandates, and the need to curb the dumping by foreign firms and other unfair trade practices harmful to industries in particular states, an inevitable reliance on heavy-duty representational efforts in Washington by members of the intergovernmental lobby occurred and still occurs, and these were and are centralizing actions. The states and their local regional economies must rely on Washington in all those spheres of international trade that require leveraging, loosening up, and retaliating against hostile trade actions by foreign governments. State and private entrepreneurial efforts can achieve a great deal. Yet when rigid protective rules or seemingly innocuous but endless procedural requirements are encountered abroad, the United States, not the Disunited States, must be brought into play. In addition, the collapse of the Southeast Asian economies reminds us that free markets must live by certain "rules" or suffer severe consequences, and these rules must be enforced by a central government. This is a lesson that some of our free marketers here at home frequently forget.

Another conditioner of our systemic inconsistencies is our *recently acquired new political system.* It is risky to generalize about the collective tendencies of the many, many actors in this system: the parties, especially the revamped national parties; the ever expanding nationally based pressure-group complexes; the PACs; the ideological think tanks; the media; the narrowly focused "iron triangles" of specific program concern; the unfocused, broadly constituted "issues networks" of wide policy involvement; and all the hired hands that constitute a candidate's personal campaign organization. But the focus of the overwhelming majority of these active political participants is national, and only incidentally state and local. The dynamics for centralization, national activism, co-optive actions, and systemic overload are all sustained by this unstructured political force, which is not cohesive, monolithic, or without some territorial adherents. Still, the focus of its varied members is Washington, or they would not be there. All want some form of action or inaction on the part of some branch, agency, or individual within the national government. The net effect of this force then has been a centripetal one. Certainly, the small intergovernmental relations generalist lobby, constituting as it does such a small fraction of this gigantic mosaic of American superpluralism, has few allies among the army of functional, citizen, sociomoralistic, and single-issue organizations, as well as free-lancers, and as William Gormley pointed out more than two decades ago, the media has done little to highlight state issues, including threatening Federal actions.

*The reformed states are another new force,* a force that provides one of the few firm foundations for noncentralization and devolution. With the financial, institutional, and representational reforms prompted by forces from both within and without, the states have become operationally indispensable to the overall workings of the system. In the seventies, they became again "the laboratories of democracy" after a forty-year hiatus; heavy revenue raisers despite earlier assertions that this could not or would not happen without a Federal tax credit; prime implementers of most Federal domestic programs; solicitous parents of their local governmental offspring (more so now than in the seventies); and policy innovators (though timid with institutional reforms) in such diverse areas as education and finance, foreign trade and investment, hospital and health care, and consumer protection. Had the states in the eighties and nineties been the states of the early sixties, actual and proposed shifts of Federal responsibilities to them would have been unthinkable. The fiscal supplementation efforts many of them mounted during the mideighties, when certain Federal aid programs were kept on tight or reduced budgets, would have been impossible. And their capacity on occasion to present a better case before the Supreme Court and before congressional committees beginning in that decade was another by-product of their improved image. And this ability only expanded in the nineties.

All this aside, the states by the very nature of our system have had to resort regularly to utilizing all the weaponry they can muster in Washington to ward off new conditions, resist more encroachments into their revenue reserves, avoid costly and undermining Court decisions, and fight off ruthlessly drafted new regulations. At the beginning of the 105th Congress, *State Government News* published a lead article entitled "States Keep Watch on the Hill," which stressed the need to cover upcoming legislative renewals and new program proposals. Little of the state rapport with the earlier 104th Congress was reflected in this analysis. In its final paragraph came a warning: "Although progress has been made in the federal-state relationship, the twin threats of preemption and unfunded mandates remain. States need to be vigilant in the ongoing dialogue with federal policymakers on the impact of new public policy initiatives in 1998."[27] In describing the nature of Federal-state conflicts over policy and power late in the winter of 1998, a more conservative states-righter declared: "States are like rabbits fighting a tiger in their confrontations with federal powers."[28] Quite a different tone from that of Governor Tommy Thompson (R-Wis.) in January 1995! In any event, most of the state actions required to preserve their powers contribute in their own way to centralization because they generally occur in Washington, D.C. Yet overall, the states' recent roles have served to enhance decentralization, cooperation, constraint, and a more balanced system.

The states' recent assumption of major new intergovernmental program roles highlights a new argument for nurturing Cooperative Federalism in an area that presumably would be a state-local matter. A fundamental challenge, as we have seen, is information technology, which is a fundamental factor in implementing child support, PRWORA, and especially the states' key program, TANF. The worry of some experts is that there is a danger of overloading the states.[29] One expert in the IT field feels that "the federal government and the states must work together — and really mean it — for welfare reform to work."[30] Despite the presumed greater discretion allotted the states, the remaining Federal role requires a reliable information system and the right to stipulate the data needed. This seemingly procedural issue, in fact, goes to the heart of the IT systems of the fifty states and in some cases those of the thousands of local governments. Collaboration among the levels is needed to identify appropriate reporting requirements. Without it, the implementation of TANF and the child support program actually will be endangered. Free and full collaboration thus becomes a necessity for both the states and the Federal government.

*The Supreme Court has served as a force* that until the nineties, and like the new political actors, was mostly centralizing. Since the early sixties its prime approach to interpreting the commerce and conditional spending powers and its assertive stance regarding the scope of the Fourteenth Amendment protections produced a cumulative effect that was highly centripetal. Some reining in of the scope of the Fourteenth Amendment did occur during the Burger era, and Federal habeas corpus and Section 1983 appeals were curbed as the Court became more conservative in the eighties. These and other Court actions of the nineties already discussed extensively have balanced significantly the status of the states' police powers, criminal justice processes, taxing authority, and standing before the Court. All this weighs in on the side of decentralization, interlevel comity, and judicial balance. *Lopez* and *Printz* weigh in much more heavily on the side of state sovereignty and the Tenth Amendment. These and other factors add up to a new Court role as defender of a "protective federalism."

Finally, *at the most elemental level of our social and political values,* yet another source of divergence arises. Libertarian concerns can generate a push to Washington when a First Amendment issue crops up, but the localities and states loom large when diversity and differences are the libertarian goals. Equity and egalitarian norms, which frequently conflict with libertarian norms, usually produce a thrust toward the center, but not when it is dominated by conservatives, as it was in the eighties. Promising economic growth can lead to an international focus along with a state and regional one. Fearful economic protectionism, however, can lead only to Washington and the help it can provide. Social issues of a moral, behavioral, or even religious nature may initially be fought out in state legislatures and courts, but if the issue is deeply controversial with vehement protagonists and rabid opponents, Congress and the Supreme Court ultimately will become involved. These battles over different values in our multicultural, superpluralistic society, along with public finance, programmatic, administrative, and broadly systemic disputes, help explain some of the basic reasons for this mix of divergent tendencies within contemporary federalism. And in terms of the conflicting values issue, the emphasis sometimes is on the centralizing, co-optive, activist, overloaded side of the agenda and sometimes on the other, with decentralization, competition, and systemic balance being strengthened. In the main, the latter have not gained in a big way in this current intergovernmental period. But the condition of the system still is better than it was a short decade ago.

## Is Federalism Still a Core Value?

The general findings and observations, along with the intellectual and operational ambivalences in the system, suggest both health and neglect regarding federalism. Tensions can be creative and conflict may be constructive, but hot ideological debates, unilateral power grabs, and resulting efforts to manipulate accounts to discover loopholes in the rules and to ignore whole areas of law are destructive. Moreover, they underscore the ways in which thoughtless neglect of the prerequisites of a resourceful federalism are expressed. A more balanced and better buttressed federalism can be a basis for resolving many of our most serious public issues; a conflicted one is not.

This brings up the question of whether federalism is still a core value in the American creed. It certainly was for all but the past thirty-five years of this republic's history, but what of it now? Intellectually, most of us do not see recent centripetal developments as part of an inevitable evolution to a unitary system. And all but the dreamers see no emergence of a state-centered one. At the same time, compared with all of the older authentic federal systems, ours alone provides continuing examples of a central government moving unilaterally against its own constituent governments. Is this premeditated centralization or a mindless neglect of the fundamental ground rules of a healthy federalism?

In what ways, then, is ours still a federal system? And why are they crucial to comprehend?

1. Societally, the American electorate, although increasingly subject to the pressures of homogenization, is still differentiated territorially. Popular attitudes on a range of topics — taxes, tax effort, social issues, levels of regulation, public services support, civic-mindedness — still vary on a regional and state-by-state basis, although not as much as a generation ago.

2. Attitudinally, the public's belief system even now embodies a hostility to big government, to enhancing governmental power, and to more governmental intrusion, despite its adherence to views regarding programs and regulations that in practice add up to the opposite of all these attitudes. Moreover, recent public opinion polls indicate a far greater trust in the states compared to the weaker faith in the national government.

3. In terms of economic modernization, the extraordinary expansion of small, frequently technically based entrepreneurial firms; of territorially targeted communication systems; and of differentiated state and local responses to educational, economic, public finance, environmental, and consumer concerns suggests that a monolithic centralizing trend is not the inevitable result of increasing specialization, growing interdependence, and greater technological/informational advances. Moreover, states have proven to be more resourceful than the central government in economic development ventures.

4. Among the many interest groups now influencing policy in Washington, there are some that do understand the role of our territorial governments, their indispensability, and their renaissance, and there are some that reflect a deep anxiety about the national and international financial and economic conditions, the need for continued retrenchment, and the dangers of the currently huge gaps between big and small business and between the superrich and the poor.

5. Fiscally, the revenue systems of the three levels are still, to a large degree, separated, and in good times the state-local sector constitutes a major force for fiscal resiliency.

6. Administratively, the national government since the 1960s, and to a greater degree than during the New Deal, has relied on states and, to a lesser degree, the localities to implement most of its domestic service and regulatory programs. If evolution toward a unitary system were really sought and deemed politically feasible, this heavily devolved pattern of implementation would not occupy the paramount position in today's system that it does, and most of state government would be mere adjuncts of fully professional, well-staffed, effectively supervising Federal agencies, which is not the case. Almost thirty years of nearly continuous denigration of the Federal civil service does nothing to enhance either the Federal government or federalism.

7. Judicially, the Supreme Court has begun to enunciate a much clearer conception of the need for states that are not totally shackled, and this could become its dominant stand.

8. Local governments, to a greater degree than has been the case since the early sixties, are more cognizant now of their organic interdependence with and dependence on their states, though they still have

difficulty recognizing that jurisdictional fragmentation does not enhance local power.

These eight noncentralizing features of contemporary American federalism — although significant — still leave the constituent governments and their localities partially at the mercy both of unilateral interventionist actions of national government officials and of the hostile pressure tactics of interest groups in Washington that do not defer to the federalist principle. After more than twenty-one decades of development, federalism ought to mean more than a cultural attachment and sentiment. Its operational, fiscal, educational, testing, and social diversity advantages also should be appreciated. It will be needed as much in the twenty-first century as it was in the eighteenth, probably more so. Our evolving international role, notably as "the keeper of the peace," means that far greater national attention must be allocated to a new range of international concerns, almost whether we want to or not. Neither Europe nor any other combination of powers nor any other single nation is capable of assuming this thankless task.

One basic point in raising questions about the condition of federalism is to determine whether it can serve as a force to free up the Federal government from distracting disputes, policy decisions, and drains on the Treasury caused by the political need to deal with groups whose problems ought to be handled elsewhere. It ought to mean more than the states and localities being victims of a political system that is hardly three decades old. Congress has a tremendously difficult time playing the role of a national parliament. Many of its members dislike confronting the international, national, and big intergovernmental agenda items with which such a body should be dealing. Even a literal reading of Article I, Section 8, in contemporary prose with the additions of health and income maintenance leaves us with a lengthy, expensive, complicated list of national policy concerns. Presidents, also, are not immune from acting less than nationally, for they too are mesmerized at times by the "all-politics-is-local" myth. The unending involvement by national policymakers with secondary state and local issues arises in part out of their delight in having to assume hardly any responsibility for the policy outcomes. This, of course, assumes sufficient funding is appropriated to permit the implementation of even a modest range of the project grants. Yet that is not the case in the hundreds of petty projects where the concern is symbolic and devoid of any serious program involvement. None of these approaches is feasible when confronting the national and major intergovernmental agendas cited above. Washington's responsibility in these tough terrains cannot be avoided easily.

## An Agenda for Reform

A more revitalized federalism, then, is needed to further strengthen the states and their localities as well as to liberate the Federal government from its fixation with minutiae, with concerns and political complexes that are not national, and with all the other distractions that enfeeble it. Can a somewhat more balanced federalism facilitate a strengthening of the federal system and of the national government? Of course it can. But first the new political system needs to be overhauled; it should be clear by now what ought to be done. The states, as has been demonstrated throughout this analysis, have done well in the realm of operational federalism, and their record in this practical world of programs, personnel, and funding would be even better if they were less constrained by the cumulative effects of Federal regulations, preemptions, grant mandates, and judicial dictates. To strengthen the states where they are still weak, to reduce Federal authority where it is still overreaching, but to enhance it where it is enfeebled — these are the three basic goals of any genuine program for federalism reform. All that is sought for the states is to put them on a par with their counterparts in Australia, Germany (insofar as it involves the strong Lander [states] influence on most national legislation), and Switzerland. (Canada's provinces have been given too much power over the past three decades.) A freeing up of the states and of the national government is the thrust of what is needed now, along with the accompanying hope that the localities would also benefit from these systemic liberations.

To circumvent some of the current ambivalences in the system and to end some of the distrustful, destructive, and self-defeating intergovernmental behavioral patterns that are found in so many areas of interlevel activities, a revamped unshackling strategy is required. Changes beyond those already achieved then are needed on four fronts.

First, *focus on the weaknesses of constitutional federalism.* During the nineties the Supreme Court began to take seriously its mandate from Hamilton in *Federalist* No. 78, from Madison and Oliver Ellsworth in the First Congress, and from Marshall as chief justice that the umpiring responsibility in a federal system is one of its most fundamental assignments. It should come to grips with the fact that judicial passivity in the conditional spending area leaves it to the political branches of the national government to determine the reach of their own powers therein. While progress has been made in other areas, this one remains an especially troublesome one.[31]

The country needs Court decisions of a landmark character in these areas to reflect a long overdue balancing of national and federalist values. In addition, Article V's state-initiated amendatory option needs to be sanitized so that it actually may be used. Madison did not deem it appropriate to leave the first phase of amending our basic charter solely to the Congress of the United States. It is time to revive what is dead constitutional law. Such a safeguard is a minimum and traditional one. It is needed now to begin to curb the cavalier and careless approach to asserting national power that has prevailed over the past three decades. It should begin by two-thirds of the state legislatures adopting common and carefully phrased resolutions petitioning Congress to issue a call for a constitutional convention to consider this one fundamental issue.

Second, *mount a variety of efforts to overcome the feeble condition of most state and local parties.* Compared to those of the sixties, state parties today are far more likely to provide services to their candidates, to perform electoral mobilization undertakings, to conduct public opinion polls, to publish newspapers or bulletins, and to raise and funnel money. But vital as these functions are, they are not enough to counteract the arrival in state capitals of a large number of new interest groups that began during the Reagan years nor to help recapture control over formerly party functions. This should mean drives to curb or even eliminate the detailed codes of regulation that govern practically every aspect of party activity at both the state and local levels in those states having such codes of constraint.

In this connection, party reform advocates should probe the broader implications of *Tashjian, Secretary of the State of Connecticut v. Republican Party of Connecticut,*[32] wherein the Supreme Court held that a state law restricting voting in a primary to those registered in the party (that is, a closed primary) was unconstitutional. Although the specifics of this decision run counter to the broad theme of reform developed here, the argument presented by Justice Thurgood Marshall for the majority stressed the private associational character of a political party and the constitutional protection of these attributes. This raises the prospect of a possible legal scuttling of various other state requirements shackling state and local party officials, organizations, and processes.

Specific state items on any reform agenda would include state enactments permitting political parties to determine whether a convention or primary system is the best method of making party nominations and allowing parties in cases where the primary is selected to use preprimary endorsement conventions. Voters should be allowed to vote a straight party ticket, and candidates losing the party nomination should be barred from running under another label in the general election.[33] Laws regarding state registration of lobbyists should be reexamined, with a view toward ensuring, at a minimum, that all actual lobbyists register and that a comprehensive annual report is prepared by the appropriate legislative staff arm and given wide distribution. Section 312 (a) (7) of the Communications Act of 1934 should be modified to require that television stations allow genuine national, state, and local political party units the chance to purchase reasonable amounts of broadcast time to present their positions and platforms to the public and at rates that compare favorably to those for an individual candidate.[34] With the national party organizations, structural and procedural changes should be instituted to convert these bodies into fully federalist organizations, for that is what they are supposed to be. At a minimum, this should mean establishment of joint national-state umpiring units with members equally divided and with authority to arbitrate any outstanding interlevel dispute.

Many of these proposals seem unreal in light of the current condition of state and local parties, and even the condition of their national organizations. Yet the need for stronger and fully representative parties at all levels is clear to those who ponder the negative effects of popular media, pressure groups, and PAC politics in an era of near-partyless politics. As Edward L. Marcus, the chair of Connecticut's Democratic party, succinctly put it: "We have acquiesced in the erosion of party loyalties, solidarity, prerogatives, strength and accountability. And interest groups have stepped in with big bucks and their own axes to grind."[35] Regarding the current and corrupting role of "soft money" campaign financing, which affects state and local races as much as national, the Shays-Meehan bill that passed the House in the summer of 1998 constituted a good beginning, though it was defeated in the Senate. Much more needs to be done to begin removing the mighty influence of campaign monies as they are presently collected and contributed on American politics and policymaking. Perhaps the proper place to begin is with *Buckley* v. *Valeo* (1976)[36] and its dictum that limitations on independent expenditures made by an individual on behalf of a candidate violate the spender's First Amendment right to communicate his or her views. For some, this adds up to "money is speech and speech is free." Without a drastic revision of this plutocratic principle, no effective campaign finance reform will be feasible. The weakened influence of state and local political spokespersons in national political organizational processes, despite their ostensibly quasi-federal organizational character, has much to do with the interest group infiltration of these bodies and processes. Two points, then, should be uppermost in the minds of serious party reformers: (1) the new system, which needs to be replaced, is just that — new, very new — and though aggregatively powerful, it is not monolithic or invulnerable, and (2) states and localities perform roles in the governance system that none of the other political actors do, namely, the implementation of most domestic programs. This should provide the basis for some confidence in the worth of their endeavors. A freeing up and a concurrent strengthening of state and local political organizations accordingly ought to be a by-product of these governments' paramount role in the operational area. Not to be overlooked here is the fact that some of "the Glue" (that is, patronage) which helped solidify earlier state and local organizations is alive and well, Court cases notwithstanding. In some areas, its use has been salutary, and in others, sickening. At a deeper level, some have come to the point where they believe the entire system for nominating presidential candidates — including its processes and length, not just its funding — needs overhauling.

Third, *states and localities need to reassert themselves in the representational sphere.* Although obviously closely connected with the political sphere, the approaches, arenas (much more governmental), and players in the representational sphere are not wholly the same as those in the political. When looking to our own past and to the experience of other federal systems, one sees that the representational strength of subnational politics and governments at the center was crucial for us and still is for our sister systems. Direct representation in the central government or a strong subnational influence over the nominating processes for national officeholders, or a combination of both, were the ways of asserting this power. The irony in this all-important intergovernmental area is that when the states and many local units were malapportioned, closed, and sometimes malignant systems, their voices in Washington were authoritative, and they needed no professional lobbying organization to make protestations or mere representations on their behalf. Why? Because each congressional delegation was usually in perfect harmony with the positions and attitudes of influential state and local elected or nonelected leaders back home. As the states became more representative, responsible, and respected, but without the nominating control, they were forced to set up their associational national headquarters or main offices as well as individual state offices in Washington, as the cities and counties had done earlier.

The initial functions of these public interest groups (PIGs) were to advance and protect their differing jurisdictional interests in an era of expanding Federal grants and regulations. In more recent times, other areas of Federal action commanded their attention: the revenue actions of Treasury and Congress, the rise in regulatory actions of Federal administrative agencies and of Congress, and the mandating and subordinating decisions of Federal courts. In response to these concerns, the State-Local Legal Center, the Council of State Governments' Federalism Index, and other specialized "protective" agencies and procedures were set up. A very recent study of the amicus briefs filed by the center on behalf of some or all of the public interest groups found that out of thirty-one filings the Court favored the center's position some twenty-one times.[37] Fifteen years ago, the success rate would have been more like one out of five, rather than two out of three. All these efforts have helped — though they in no way are an adequate substitute for the power the subnational jurisdictions formerly possessed when dealing with their state delegations; for some prior to 1964, simply relying on the Conservative Coalition was all that was needed to sustain their position.

Nonetheless, the record of recent public interest group efforts show that (1) some threatening rules and regulations can be nipped in the bud if there has been adequate forewarning; (2) some hostile Court and congressional decisions can be modified or even scrapped if such decisions clearly are costly and if the public interest groups are firmly united; and (3) the skilled efforts of the State-Local Legal Center have paid off in some instances, with arguments in its briefs serving as the justification for some Supreme Court decisions. Not to be forgotten here is the one-time, memorable Republican gubernatorial-congressional collaboration in 1995, which ideally would become a permanent and bipartisan practice. Clearly, all these efforts should continue, yet more is needed to combat the centripetal propensities of most of the hundreds of pressure groups in the nation's capital.

On a more aggressive front, state and local organizations should attempt to

- ensure that the Federal regulation of lobbying act (1993) with its exemption of public interest groups and tightened rules for private-sector lobbyists is effectively implemented.

- monitor the procedural and substantive impacts of UMRA, especially the emerging practice of softening a proposed mandate to put it below the $50 million threshold.

- develop specific judicial arguments for State-Local Legal Center briefs that would fix boundaries around the conditional spending. In developing these parameters, certain precepts need to be noted: provisions of the Constitution should not be circumvented, as they were in the eighties, and conditions attached to grants should be clearly related to grant program purposes. Moreover, the fiction that an ongoing formula or cost-sharing grant is a contract voluntarily entered into should be recognized.

- correct, where necessary, deficiencies in their public management so that anti–state-management criticisms can be blunted and their operational roles can be further strengthened.

- demonstrate clearly, when severely provoked, the state's paramount operational role and the impotence of the Federal agencies to carry out the will of Congress by having the remaining states that participate in voluntary partial preemption programs, such as Occupational Safety and Health Administration (OSHA), withdraw in a dramatic fashion from the program. After a decent interval all states would, when cause was shown, file suits in Federal district courts throughout the land citing the Federal agency's failure to implement the legislation. A way is needed to assert the states' operational power in the political and judicial spheres, and this might be one, bold and bloody though it would be.

The last suggestion may sound fairly drastic, but the national government and the politics in which it has been enmeshed must be freed from the follies of petty power plays; of dozens of puny project grants that functionally add up to nothing but pork and politics, for example the 1998 highway bill with its many pet projects; of unreimbursed (though not so costly now) regulations on states and localities; of Federal regulating agencies that lack the personnel and sometimes the professionalism to carry out a direct regulatory role;[38] of a Supreme Court that hands down a decision (*Rutan* [1991]) on patronage that is almost totally ignored, save for the local jurisdiction that figured in the case. There is a strange mix here of real and empty threats, of pretentious and pharisaic behavior, all of which are completely possible, even in an era of fiscal stringencies and small surpluses, because the Federal role in the federal system still seems endless though its resources are finite. Hence the gap between promise and performance in Washington and a basic source of many of the ambivalences analyzed earlier.

A stronger intergovernmental representation, then, is needed at the national level to inject some programmatic reality into the frequently fuzzy understanding there of governmental operations, to voice the territorial perspective amid the cacophony of the functional clusterings, and in this process to help unburden at least somewhat both the Federal and subnational governments from the special pleaders. Perhaps the greatest obstacles to achieving this kind of systemic representational undertaking are the deep divisions between and among members of the state and local generalist groupings, who tend to forget that unity — rare though it is — usually has produced positive results. The natural propensity on the part of state and local leaders is to focus on the immediate and to put off pondering the long-term effects of current conflicting developments, and this has been preeminently the case in recent years.

In this context, establishment of a strategic systemic study center by the states and localities is needed to probe intergovernmental developments in all of the areas covered herein, to spot situations that need high-level attention and action, and to plot alternative future IGR scenarios with a view toward recommending actions geared to a balanced federal result. Farfetched? Perhaps, but it is time for the momentous to drive out the minutiae. The reverse has too long been the case. Equally significant, the public interest groups, Federal officials dealing with domestic programs, policymakers at all levels, and students of federalism desperately need a reliable and current source of statistical data covering intergovernmental finance, institutions, programs, and other relationships. With the dismantling of the ACIR, the elimination of the intergovernmental unit in GAO, and the reduced capacity of Census to do a thorough probe of the many aspects of intergovernmental finance and of state and local governments, along with the failure of academics and university research centers to conduct surveys on at least some of the more troublesome IGR topics of the day, our collective knowledge of the many facts that contribute to understanding Federal-state-local relations has eroded significantly. At present, we have less current IGR information than at any time since 1980. How can the PIGs make an effective case if they lack specific and timely data? How can local governments defend their position when they have no current figures on direct and indirect Federal aid to them, no up-to-date statistics on the extent of Federal aid both channeled through states and going directly to the five categories of local government, no really recent figures on the breakout of state aid by functional and jurisdictional categories, and no refined data to permit the gauging of the various disparities between and among metropolitan jurisdictions? All this information was available up to about 1987, but not now. The public interest groups desperately need and should establish a competent, comprehensive center for collecting program, financial, institutional, and even procedural data that involve Federal-state-local relations. If knowledge is power, then this undertaking would truly enhance the position of the states and localities in the system.

The fundamental dilemma confronting the system is that there is almost a complete absence of parallelism in the political, representational, judicial, and operational spheres of IGR action. In earlier eras, the four tended toward a mutually reinforced pattern of development that enhanced the vitality of federalism. The range of conflicting trends today is simply too wide and too disconnected from fiscal, administrative, and programmatic reality for the health of our system and our people. Hence there is an absolute necessity for a major reinforcement of the intergovernmental representational voice in Washington so that (1) the preferential jurisdictional status of the states conferred by the Constitution is again recognized; (2) the paramount implementing role of the states and localities is also understood and earns for them a special status when national domestic policies are being hammered out; and (3) the unifying effects of strong and generalist-oriented territorial representation at the highest level may serve as a vital counterweight to the welter of single-issue, special, self-serving, or even informative pressure groups that still have far too much say in a faction-laden system Madison would disown. Obviously, all this precludes a return to the supplicant role assumed by many of the public interest groups in the seventies.

Were these strengthening representational reforms to come about, the national government no longer would need to resort to brazenness, bluff, and bluster to convey the image of being the senior partner in the federalism drama, in that the intergovernmental groups would not have to tolerate such unbecoming behavior. The states and localities also would be better protected against unreimbursed mandates, arbitrary grant conditions that are exempt from UMRA, and the divisive politics of petty project grants that denigrate the special jurisdictional and operational status that is theirs. Ideally, a relationship rooted in the rough parity that nearly prevails now in the domestic expenditures programmatic areas should emerge.

*Of prime concern is the operational sphere of intergovernmental relations,* and it is in this fiscal, functional, and administrative realm of shared governmental operations that many of the ultimate results of the dynamics in the judicial, political, and representational spheres are seen. It is also in this sphere that many ambivalent tendencies manifest themselves: centralization and devolution, cooperation and competition, co-option and collaboration, activism and inaction. Yet it also is here that a better balance between the center and the periphery can be clearly discerned.

The healthy signs include the following: the enhanced fiscal, policy, and implementation roles of the states; the Federal-state collaboration in such legislative enactments as ISTEA, TEA-21, the Clean Air Act, and the Safe Drinking Water Act Amendments; the devolution to the states of greater administrative authority under certain environmental programs and collaborative rule making in others; and the improved intergovernmental administration caused by the reduction in bypassing and the disappearance of the "funny-money" syndrome. Above all, the reduced Federal domestic expenditure role coupled with the increasing state-local share of domestic outlays from their own revenues underlies a new and more balanced trend in intergovernmental operations.

The negative aspects of this recent record include the following: a rush to regulate and mandate at both the national and state levels, which engendered anger and distrust at all the subnational levels (although this has subsided considerably since UMRA); a reemergence of deep interlevel entanglements because of this development and the decline in discretionary grants; a rapid increase in preemptions (which has tapered off somewhat beginning in the midnineties); the failure of some states to upgrade the public personnel, benchmarking, and information technology facets of their overall public management systems; a hollowing out of Federal domestic agencies by personnel cuts, regulations, and politicization; the understandable tendency on the part of many states to probe for loopholes in order to avoid compliance or to save money; and the increasing fragmentation of local government, which provides a continuing source of functional weakness for general units of local government.

The Federal aid package has acquired some features that are new and menacing and others that are old and disreputable. Among the former is the ever growing proportion of payments to individuals, soaring from 36 percent in FY 1960 to 62 percent in FY 1993 to 62.5 percent in FY 1998, and a corresponding decline in the share of grant monies going for physical capital projects, which experienced a sharp drop from 47 percent to 17.6 percent between 1960 and 1998. This course dramatizes the extraordinary drop in grants to governments for governmental functions and a remarkable rise in the states' role as administrators and partial funders of transfer payments to individuals, as with PRWORA, and especially with its paramount program, TANF, and with Medicaid. Another vital aspect of the Federal grant package is that although the number of programs continues to grow chiefly for congressional and interest groups' entrepreneurial reasons, in 1993, 37 programs out of 593 accounted for over 90 percent of the FY 1993 dollar total, and just 4 — Medicaid, food stamps, family support welfare, and the highway obligation ceiling — represented over two-thirds of the total. By FY 1997, 33 large programs accounted for 87 percent of total grant outlays.[39] Put differently, there is an extraordinary number of small formula and especially paltry project grants that explains the explosion in the number of grants. Yet their impact, save for those involving highly specialized and objectively targeted research and demonstration projects, is mostly political in the narrowest sense of the word. Moreover, the degree to which many grants (such as higher education project grants and certain highway programs) now are subject to congressional earmarking further undercuts a claim to legitimate national concern with these aspects of the grant enactment process.

Reforms of one sort or another are clearly suggested by the above and other IGR operational findings presented elsewhere. At the very minimum, state and local officials should be granted more discretion in implementing Federal grant programs, and the earlier recommendations dealing with better consultation, mandate review, and preemption should be instituted. Additionally, the earlier IGR machinery within the executive branch should be reestablished. President Clinton has begun doing this, but the existing units nowhere match their predecessors of the seventies.

At a higher level of political risk are recommendations that call for the elimination of all categorical grants that provide less than 5 percent of total state-local program outlays, the merger of dozens of small grants so that they at least reach this threshold level, and the creation of block grants in various areas now dominated by categoricals (for example, education of the handicapped, special education, vocational education, higher education scholarships, library programs).

Shifting to the equally significant state-local relations arena, all states should enact legislation to establish state-level advisory commissions on intergovernmental relations (ACIRs) to provide — as about half the states have — neutral turf on which state and local officials may meet to identify and debate outstanding interlevel sources of tension and, it is hoped, come up with proposals for resolving such issues. Finally, states and their respective city and county associations should join with their ACIRs to probe the fundamental jurisdictional dilemma that excessive numbers of small nonviable local units create and come up with ways and means of overcoming their dysfunctionality, including stronger counties, incentives for interlocal contracting and transfer of functions, and more strongly empowered and more service-oriented regional councils.

If we turn now to the most ambitious and least standpat of the reform propositions, it is clear that many believe the time has come to apply some basic surgery to the intergovernmental system so that federalism becomes part of the solution to, not one cause of, the nation's basic economic, fiscal, administrative, and program problems. In light of the recent Federal deficits, the emerging uncertain economy, the health care industry's sopping up annually of 14 percent of GNP, and the staggering challenge of reconciling the goals of various of our social policies with contrary goals implicit in some of the above, it is time to revisit the "sorting out" proposals.

Unlike its predecessors, the argument here is not made solely on the basis of improved program administration through devolution, as it was in Eisenhower's time; nor solely on the basis of decongesting a heavily overloaded system for the sake of greater functional effectiveness and greater equity, as the Advisory Commission on Intergovernmental Relations proposed in 1981; nor solely on the basis of Reagan's "Big Swap" 1982 State of the Union proposal, which was largely rooted in an ideological thrust to get several grant programs, including most of welfare, back to the states (although Medicaid would have been nationalized);[40] nor solely on the basis of resolving the nation's earlier economic and fiscal nightmares, as Alice Rivlin has persuasively advocated,[41] though this (along with Paul Peterson's closely related functional theory, according to which the two basic domestic functions of government — developmental and redistributive — are assigned to different levels) clearly enters into any current argument for "dividing the job." Among the other reasons for advocating a sensible "Big Swap" now are these:

- The national government's role in national affairs is infinitely more unpredictable, less understandable, and obviously a consumer of unusual amounts of presidential and congressional time, given the wide-ranging uncertainty of a post–Cold War world and such assignments as global "policing" and, with others, the stabilization of a bundle of bungled economies — hence the need to unburden the national government of what now seem to be extraneous or secondary domestic issues that the states and localities are perfectly capable of handling.

- The states still need to be unburdened — of arbitrary grant conditions, of unnecessary preemptions, and of being treated as pressure groups rather than full partners. A realigning of present entangled servicing roles would further underscore the need for this unshackling.

- The functioning local governments — not the feeble, the tiny, or the very limited though ostensibly general-purpose units — need some unburdening too. A sensible realigning of servicing and regulatory responsibilities to the states could reduce Federal intrusions into local America and reestablish a rare singular and constitutionally proper local reliance on the states for various needed aids, freedoms, and proper regulations.

- Above all perhaps, the entire system needs a severe slashing of the extent of interest group focusing on and lobbying in the nation's capital. The much publicized national gridlock, in truth, was just as much a matter of irreconcilable interests and of rigid ideologies as it was of political differences or systemic weaknesses. With the elimination and devolution of at least some of the programs that really do not belong on the national agenda, the scope of national domestic policymaking would be reduced and something of a policy equilibrium could emerge.

What in broad-brush terms should be considered in a "Big Swap" for the nineties? The first thing to ponder is that over the past thirty-four years, as underscored above, *we have already experienced a major sorting out of basic fiscal and servicing assignments.* Despite the jumble of programs and shifts in their objectives, the Federal government's overall domestic focus has been on people, not on place or territorial governments, nor on the program needs of such governments. TANF, of course, reverses this trend, and time will soon tell whether it was a wise or foolish national policy decision. And this sorting out at the Federal level by the allocation of relatively small amounts of aid funds for nontransfer payment programs and the compensating actions at the state and local levels underscore the capacity of the latter governments to cope quite well with a variety of functions that fall under what Alice Rivlin calls the "productivity agenda": public infrastructure, job training, education reform, housing, rural services, and economic development.[42] For profound altruistic, experiential, and self-interested reasons, state and local officials as they confront the rigors of economic restructuring have no difficulty in melding these servicing areas into a scheme that along with those of sister states produces a competitive and productive response to what otherwise would be potentially crippling challenges. These, after all, are program areas where the national government has not been especially successful.

Research and development, central information gathering, Medicaid with a broader reform format, some transportation functions (that is, air traffic control, some highways), some income-maintenance programs, and above all the job of reshaping the most expensive and least administratively efficient health system in the world and of dealing with social equity would be exclusively left to the Federal government. Shared Federal-state programs would continue in the areas of the environment, natural resources, TANF and the rest of PRWORA, higher education, and student grants and loans.

With this swap, the states would acquire full responsibility (in partnership with their localities in some functional areas) for the devolved Federal programs for primary and secondary education, job training, community and economic development, housing, social services, most highways and other transportation, juvenile justice, and drug control. The Federal government would be left with the challenging assignments of reacquiring the capacity to implement its own traditional exclusive program responsibilities in an effective fashion, of meeting the international challenge of being the only great power, of dealing with health-care reform, of managing the economy, and of maintaining the budget surpluses and earmarking them for Social Security, reduction of the national debt, or both. In addition, the time has come for the national government to enhance the capacity of Federal grants managers and regulators to carry out their responsibilities in a professional, authoritative fashion, hence rethinking the "Reinventing" record. This will entail increasing their number in many instances and rethinking the proper Federal role in the intergovernmental fiscal transfer field and in the realm of intergovernmental regulation. Skeletonized staff, deregulation by default, and de facto dead laws do nothing to enhance federalism or the power position of the states and localities, though some would reject this assertion.

At some point, once the dust has settled a bit from the flurry of program reassignments, a Federal-state equalization fund should be established to even out the fiscal discrepancies among the states that emerge after the sorting outs. All this still adds up to a heavy Hamiltonian agenda for the country's central government, but one that with the new freedom that this sorting out provides has a good chance of being addressed.

The foregoing proposals address a range of old and recent problems that have plagued our system. But they do not confront head on the emergence of a new force, noted briefly in the last chapter, that constitutes a very special threat to all the traditional levels of government. Some see in the accumulation of immense preserves of private wealth, in the mounting number of mergers, in the transnational character of some of the conglomerates, and in their highly effective political clout a new power that merges the role of a party with that of a pressure group. These organizations are primarily business-based. Most are dedicated to preserving the status quo. Most are organized nationally, though they may have state affiliates. All have gone immeasurably beyond financing campaigns in order to prevail. They have become, as Haynes Johnson and David Broder phrased it, "crypto-political parties of their own — unelected and unaccountable — employing skilled operatives who at all times run presidential and senatorial campaigns," in addition to new style lobbying drives.[43] It was two such groups that in large measure stopped the Clinton health care reform package in its tracks, though the reasons for its failure are multiple.

This very special phalanx from the much larger group of pressure groups has been very much in evidence during the past three Congresses and especially when health care, insurance, tobacco, environmental protection, and campaign financing — to mention only the more obvious — were being considered. We have a unique version of "interest group liberalism" in operation here. The lack of much of any real countervailing power is what prompts serious questions to be asked. Labor is much too weak to mount an adversarial attack in most instances; the parties lack sufficient cohesion and independent fiscal clout to put up much of a fight; and negative public opinion is not adequately organized to effectively resist a pressure-group party drive.

Over a hundred years ago, there was a roughly comparable scenario being played out in Washington, D.C., and in state capitals. This was an era of nearly unfettered wealth, of political corruption, of monopolies, and of trusts. Out of this came agrarian revolts initially, and ultimately the Progressive move-ment. Unlike the Grangers, the Greenbackers, and the Populists from the 1870s through to the 1890s, the Progressives were preeminently middle class in socio-economic composition. Given their ethical outrage, they wanted to cleanse the bureaucracy, politics, and the marketplace at all levels; hence the merit system, the primary, and antitrust legislation, respectively, were the chief reform goals. The governmental means of achieving change were states that were popularly empowered to act on the reform agenda or the Federal government in instances where the states lacked the strength or the geographic scope to act.

There are only a few parallels between the Progressive period and today, even though some experts predict the rise of a new Progressive-like era. One ele-ment that is missing is an enraged, moralistic middle class to set the climate for our times. A second is the absence of strong governments at both levels that are prepared to provide answers to questions Madison and the other Founding Fathers did not answer. The Founders brilliantly showed how to divide and con-strain governmental power, but they did not address the challenge of heavily concentrated private power, in part because they could not conceive of national minority factions that could dominate the majority. So indirectly the "rebirth of federalism" is a fortuitous event, insofar as it strengthens the "strong states, strong federal government" model. To the extent that the foregoing reform pro-posals bolster this ideal, they should be adopted. In the final analysis, however, it is up to the people to recognize that the goals of our reformed federalism are still those of the Founders' federalism.

## A Last Word

The "partially permissive federalism" designation was used early in this chapter to describe the actual power relations between the national and the state and local governments. It was deemed a somewhat accurate but also an unpleasant description for any faithful federalist. Should the proposals advanced here receive recognition and be acted on in the near future, the designation "protected feder-alism" would be appropriate, and a complete rebirth of American federalism will have been achieved. Moreover, the incidence of "slouching toward Washington" would be slashed significantly. And this would be in keeping with the intent of the Founders, the thrust of our political tradition, the lessons that foreign federal systems teach us, and better coping with the basic policy problems confronting the nation.

# Notes

## Introduction

1. See General Accounting Office, *Block Grants, Increases in Set-Asides and Cost Ceilings since 1982*, GAO/HRD-92-58 FS (Washington, D.C., July 1992); James L. Martin, "The States and Regulatory Flexibility: Win, Lose, or Draw?" *Intergovernmental Perspective* (ACIR) 18 (Fall 1992): 19.

2. Bruce D. McDowell, "The Regions under Reagan," paper presented at the National Planning Conference of the American Planning Association, Minneapolis–St. Paul, 8 May 1984.

3. See Margaret T. Wrightson, "The Road to South Carolina: Intergovernmental Tax Immunity and the Constitutional Status of Federalism," *Publius* 19 (Summer 1989): 39–56.

4. See Susan MacManus, "Financing Federal, State and Local Governments in the 1990's," in *American Federalism: The Third Century* (special issue of *The Annals*), ed. John Kincaid (Newbury Park, Calif.: Sage, May 1990), 31.

5. 108 S.Ct. 1355 (1988).

6. Mavis Mann Reeves, "The States as Polities: Reformed, Reinvigorated, Resourceful," in *American Federalism: The Third Century* (special issue of *The Annals*), ed. John Kincaid (Newbury Park, Calif.: Sage, May 1990), 83.

7. 426 U.S. 833 (1976).

8. Alfred H. Kelly, Winfred A. Harbison, and Herman Belz, *The American Constitution, Its Origins and Development*, 6th ed. (New York: Norton, 1983), 705.

9. Timothy Conlan, "Politics and Governance: Conflicting Trends in the 1990's?" in *American Federalism: The Third Century* (special issue of *The Annals*), ed. John Kincaid (Newbury Park, Calif.: Sage, May 1990), 130.

10. Frank J. Sorauf and Paul Allen Beck, *Party Politics in America*, 6th ed. (Glenview, Ill.: Scott Foresman, 1988), 98–99.

11. 469 U.S. 552 (1985).

## Chapter 1: Federalism and Its Many Faces

1. See Martha Derthick, "American Federalism: Madison's Middle Ground," *Public Administration Review* 47 (January–February 1987): 66.

2. See K.C. Wheare, *Federal Government*, 4th ed. (New York: Oxford University Press, 1964), 35–52.

3. Michael D. Reagan and John G. Sanzone, *The New Federalism*, 2d ed. (New York: Oxford University Press, 1981), 3.

4. Deil Wright, *Understanding Intergovernmental Relations*, 3d ed. (Pacific Grove, Calif.: Brooks/Cole, 1988), 14.

5. Richard H. Leach, *American Federalism* (New York: Norton, 1970), 9.

6. See William H. Stewart, "Metaphors, Models and the Development of Federal Theory," *Publius* 12 (Spring 1982): 5–24.

7. For an alternative interpretation of these theories, see David C. Nice, *Federalism: The Politics of Intergovernmental Relations* (New York: St. Martin's, 1987), 4–5.

8. Reagan and Sanzone, *The New Federalism*, 175.

9. Morton Grodzins, *The American System*, ed. Daniel J. Elazar (Chicago: Rand McNally, 1966), 17–41.

10. See Donald V. Smiley, "Federal States and Federal Societies, with Special Reference to Canada," *International Political Science Review* 5, no. 4 (1984): 48.

11. Terry Sanford, *Storm over the States* (New York: McGraw-Hill, 1967), 80.

12. Advisory Commission on Intergovernmental Relations (cited hereafter as ACIR), *The Intergovernmental Grant System as Seen by Local, State, and Federal Officials*, A-5 (Washington, D.C., 1977), chap. 5, 177–236.

13. See, for example, A.E. Dick Howard, "Judicial Federalism: The States and the Supreme Court," in *American Federalism: A New Partnership for the Republic*, ed. Robert B. Hawkins Jr. (San Francisco: Institute for Contemporary Studies, 1982), 215–37.

14. Eugene W. Hickok Jr., "Federalism's Future before the U.S. Supreme Court," *American Federalism: The Third Century* (special issue of *The Annals*), ed. John Kincaid (Newbury Park, Calif.: Sage, May 1990), 74–83.

15. See Richard B. Cappalli, *Rights and Remedies under Federal Grants* (Washington, D.C.: Bureau of National Affairs, Inc., 1979); ACIR, *Awakening the Slumbering Giant: Intergovernmental Relations and Federal Grant Law*, M-122 (Washington, D.C., December 1980).

16. 426 U.S. 833 (1976).

17. See David B. Walker, *Toward a Functioning Federalism* (Cambridge, Mass.: Winthrop, 1981), 107–13.

18. See, respectively, Ann O'M. Bowman and Richard Kearney, *The Resurgence of the States* (Englewood Cliffs, N.J.: Prentice-Hall, 1986); Ira Sharkansky, *The Maligned States*, 2d ed. (New York: McGraw-Hill, 1978); Martha M. Hamilton, "States Assuming New Powers as Federal Policy Role Ebbs," *Washington Post*, 30 August 1988; Mavis Mann Reeves, "The States as Polities: Reformed, Reinvigorated, Resourceful," in *American Federalism: The Third Century* (special issue of *The Annals*), ed. John Kincaid (Newbury Park, Calif.: Sage, May 1990), 83; Morton Keller, "The Cycles of Federalism," *Governing*, October 1988, 52–57.

19. Samuel H. Beer, "The Modernization of American Federalism," in *Toward '76— The Federal Polity*, special issue of *Publius* 3 (Fall 1973): 80–87.

20. John D. Donahue, *Disunited States* (New York: Basic Books, 1997).

21. ACIR, *Regulatory Federalism: Policy, Process, Impact and Reform*, A-95 (Washington, D.C., February 1984), 1–24.

22. Ibid., 5.

23. See Academy for State and Local Government, *Preemption: Drawing the Line* (Washington, D.C., October 1986); Joseph E. Zimmerman, *Federal Preemption: The Silent Revolution* (Ames: Iowa State University Press, 1991); ACIR, *Federal Statutory Preemption of State and Local Authority: History, Inventory, and Issues*, A-121 (Washington, D.C., September 1992), 7–9.

24. See Barry Bosworth, "The Evolution of Economic Policy," in *The Great Society and Its Legacy*, ed. Marshall Kaplan and Peggy Cuciti (Durham, N.C.: Duke University Press, 1986).

25. Timothy Conlan, *New Federalism: Intergovernmental Reform from Nixon to Reagan* (Washington, D.C.: Brookings Institution, 1988), 133.

26. Ibid.

27. John Shannon, "The Return of Fend-for-Yourself Federalism: The Reagan Marks," *Intergovernmental Perspective* ACIR 13 (Summer–Fall 1987): 34–37.

28. See Richard P. Nathan and John R. Lago, "Intergovernmental Fiscal Roles and Relations," in *American Federalism: The Third Century* (special issue of *The Annals*), ed. John Kincaid (Newbury Park, Calif.: Sage, May 1990), 44–45.

29. See David B. Walker, "American Federalism from Johnson to Bush," *Publius* 21 (Winter 1991): 105.

30. See Everett Carll Ladd Jr., *American Political Parties* (New York: Norton, 1970), 28–34.

31. See Richard P. McCormick, "Political Development and the Second Party System," in *The American Party Systems: Stages of Political Development*, ed. William N. Chambers and Walter Dean Burnham (New York: Oxford University Press, 1975), 112–13; Samuel P. Hays, "Political Parties and the Community Society," in *The American Party Systems: Stages of Political Development*, ed. William N. Chambers and Walter Dean Burnham (New York: Oxford University Press, 1975), 161–63.

32. ACIR, *The Transformation in American Politics: Implications for Federalism*, A-106 (Washington, D.C., August 1986), 17–46.

33. See Gary D. Wekkin, "The New Federal Party Organizations: Intergovernmental Consequences of Party Renewal," paper presented at the annual meeting of the American Political Science Association, New Orleans, September 1985.

34. See M. Margaret Conway, "Republican Political Party Nationalization," *Publius* 13 (Winter 1983): 1–18.

35. ACIR, *The Transformation in American Politics: Implications for Federalism*, B-9R (Washington, D.C., October 1987), 31–34.

36. Ibid., 30.

37. ACIR, *The Transformation in American Politics*, A-106, 227.

38. Ibid.

39. Ibid., 242.

40. Parris N. Glendening and Mavis Mann Reeves, *Pragmatic Federalism*, 2d ed. (Pacific Palisades, Calif.: Palisades Publishers, 1984), 27–28.

41. Ibid., 28.

42. Beer, "The Modernization of American Federalism," 53–95.

43. Ibid., 56–80.

44. Richard P. Nathan and Fred C. Doolittle, *Reagan and the States* (Princeton: Princeton University Press, 1987), 362.

45. Ibid.

46. James Edwin Kee and John Shannon, *Transforming American Federalism: The Role of Crisis, Consensus, and Competition* (Washington, D.C.: Urban Institute, 1992), 1.

47. Ibid., 3.

48. Ibid., 26.

49. Ibid., 33.

## Chapter 2: American Federalism and Its Intergovernmental Relations, 1607–1789

1. Jack P. Greene, "The Background of the Articles of Confederation," *Publius* 12 (Fall 1982): 18–19.

2. Ibid., 20–25.

3. See ibid., 24.

4. Richard H. Leach, *American Federalism* (New York: Norton, 1970), 30.

5. These included contact with the committee on appeals of the Privy Council in cases of judicial appeal; with the Board of Trade on legislative review and disallowance matters; with the treasury and customs commissioners regarding the colonial customs service; with the High Court of Admiralty on marine and violations-of-trade-act cases; and with the secretary of state for the Southern Department on military, foreign policy, and royal gubernatorial matters.

6. Quoted in Alpheus T. Mason, *Free Government in the Making: Readings in American Political Thought* (New York: Oxford University Press, 1949), 130–31.

7. Alfred H. Kelly, Winfred A. Harbison, and Herman Belz, *The American Constitution: Its Origins and Development,* 6th ed. (New York: Norton, 1983), 56.

8. Greene, "The Background of the Articles of Confederation," 29–32.

9. Ibid., 30.

10. Ibid., 33.

11. Ibid., 35.

12. Jack Rakove, "The Legacy of the Articles of Confederation," *Publius* 12 (Fall 1982): 48.

13. Ibid., 50.

14. See Andrew C. McLaughlin, *A Constitutional History of the United States* (New York: Appleton, 1935), 125.

15. Rakove, "The Legacy of the Articles of Confederation," 52.

16. Ibid.

17. See Articles 4 and 6 of the Articles of Confederation.

18. Greene, "The Background of the Articles of Confederation," 43.

19. Rakove, "The Legacy of the Articles of Confederation," 46–47.

20. See Daniel J. Elazar, "Confederation and Federal Liberty," *Publius* 12 (Fall 1982): 1–14.

21. The Founding Fathers generally used the term *federal* as today's students of government use the term *confederal,* that is, a system wherein nearly all basic governmental powers rest with constituent units, thus constituting a league whose basis is a treaty or compact among equals and whose purposes are largely restricted to military and foreign policy concerns. Hence, Madison's description of the proposed new system in *Federalist* No. 39 as being neither wholly national nor wholly federal. In laying claim to the "federalist" designation, the supporters of the new frame, as Deil Wright points out, used a term that the politically knowledgeable of that day understood to be the least centralized of the alternative ways of organizing central government–constituent unit relationships.

22. See McLaughlin, *A Constitutional History,* 184–85.

23. Kelly, Harbison, and Belz, *The American Constitution,* 103–4.

24. McLaughlin, *A Constitutional History,* 185.

25. See Clinton Rossiter, *The American Presidency* (New York: Harcourt, Brace & World, 1959), 76ff.

26. Ibid., 77.

27. Benjamin F. Wright, *Consensus and Continuity* (Boston: Boston University Press, 1958), 34–35.

28. See McLaughlin, *A Constitutional History,* 180–81.

29. See Wright, *Consensus and Continuity,* 32.

30. See McLaughlin, *A Constitutional History,* 185–86.

31. Ibid., 190.

32. Samuel H. Beer, "Federalism, Nationalism and Democracy in America," *American Political Science Review* 72 (March 1978): 14.

33. William H. Riker, *Federalism: Origin, Operation, Significance* (Boston: Little, Brown, 1964), 19–25.

34. Beer, "Federalism, Nationalism and Democracy in America," 10.

35. Martin Diamond, "What the Framers Meant by Federalism," in *A Nation of States,* ed. Robert A. Goldwin (Chicago: Rand McNally, 1964), 35.

36. See ibid., 37.

37. See ibid.

38. See Beer, "Federalism, Nationalism and Democracy in America," 14, 15; Diamond, "What the Framers Meant by Federalism."

39. *Federalist* No. 10, 62. All references are to the Modern Library edition, ed. E.M. Earle (New York: Modern Library, 1977).

40. See Beer, "Federalism, Nationalism and Democracy in America," 12–13.

41. Ibid.

42. Quoted, ibid., 13.

43. See Samuel H. Beer, "Federalism and the National Idea: The Uses of Diversity" (speech delivered at the Harvard Graduate School of Arts and Sciences), *Harvard Graduate Society Newsletter,* Fall 1991, 9, 20, 21.

44. James Harrington, *Oceana (Ideal Commonwealths)* (Port Washington, N.Y.: Kennikat Press, 1968), 185–86, 192–93, 195–97, 205, 384–90, 415–16.

45. David Hume, "Idea of a Perfect Commonwealth," in Hume's *Moral and Political Philosophy,* ed. Henry D. Aiken (New York: Hofner, 1972), 384.

46. Riker, *Federalism,* 20–25.

47. *Federalist* No. 51, 339.

48. *Federalist* No. 46, 304–6.

49. K.C. Wheare, *Federal Government* (New York: Oxford University Press, 1964), 2.

50. *Federalist* No. 45, 303.

51. *Federalist* No. 23, 142; *Federalist* No. 45, 303.

52. Paul Peterson, "Federalism at the American Founding: In Defense of the Diamond Theses," *Publius* 15 (Winter 1985): 23.

53. Martin Diamond, "The Federalist's View of Federalism," *Essays on Federalism,* ed. George C.S. Benson et al. (Claremont, Calif.: Institute for Studies in Federalism, 1961), 22, 24.

54. Peterson, "Federalism at the American Founding," 24.

55. "Essays by a Farmer" (*Maryland Gazette*), in *The Complete Anti-Federalist,* ed. Herbert J. Storing, vol. 5 (Chicago: University of Chicago Press, 1981), 29.

56. Jean Yarborough, "Rethinking the Federalist's View of Federalism," *Publius* 15 (Winter 1985): 31.

57. Ibid.

58. Jean Yarborough, "Federalism in the Foundation and Presentation of the American Republic," *Publius* 6 (Summer 1976): 49. Also see *Federalist* No. 27, 166–68; *Federalist* No. 46, 306.

59. Vincent Ostrom, "The Meaning of Federalism in *The Federalist,*" *Publius* 15 (Winter 1985): 16.

60. Ibid., 18.

61. *Federalist* No. 17, 101–4.

62. *Federalist* No. 32, 193.

63. *Federalist* No. 46, 306.

64. *Federalist* No. 46, 307. For Hamilton's views, see *Federalist* No. 35, 215–16; *Federalist* No. 36, 218–19.

65. For the people, see *Federalist* No. 16, 100; *Federalist* No. 35, 215; *Federalist* No. 45, 301–3. For the courts, see *Federalist* No. 78, 502–11; *Federalist* Nos. 80, 81, and 82, 515–38.

66. Martin Grodzins, *The American System*, ed. Daniel J. Elazar (Chicago: Rand McNally, 1966), 24.

67. Harry N. Scheiber, "American Federalism and the Diffusion of Power: Historical and Contemporary Perspectives," 9 *University of Toledo Law Review* 627.

68. *Federalist* No. 46, 304–5.

69. *Federalist* No. 14, 82.

70. McLaughlin, *A Constitutional History*, 180.

## Chapter 3: Variations on Dual Federalism, 1789–1930

1. Edwin S. Corwin, "A Constitution of Powers and Modern Federalism," in *Essays in Constitutional Law*, ed. Robert G. McCloskey (New York: Knopf, 1962), 188–89.

2. 2 Dallas 409 (1793).

3. 4 Wheaton 316 (1819).

4. See Harry N. Scheiber, "American Federalism and the Diffusion of Power: Historical and Contemporary Perspectives," 9 *University of Toledo Law Review* 619, at 629–30. Also *Gibbons v. Ogden*, 9 Wheaton (1824); *Willson v. Black Bird Creek Marsh Co.*, 2 Peters 245 (1829); *Barron v. Baltimore*, 7 Peters 243 (1829); *Ogden v. Saunders*, 12 Wheaton 213 (1827); *Providence Bank v. Billings*, 4 Peters 51 (1830), respectively.

5. *Cohens v. Virginia*, 6 Wheaton 26 (1821).

6. Alfred H. Kelly, Winfred A. Harbison, and Herman Belz, *The American Constitution: Its Origins and Development*, 6th ed. (New York: Norton, 1983), 204–5; Scheiber, "American Federalism and the Diffusion of Power," 630.

7. *Briscoe v. Bank of the Commonwealth of Kentucky*, 11 Peters 257 (1837).

8. *Charles River Bridge v. Warren Bridge*, 11 Peters 620 (1837).

9. Corwin, "A Constitution of Powers and Modern Federalism," 200–201.

10. Quoted in Scheiber, "American Federalism and the Diffusion of Power," 630.

11. See Kelly, Harbison, and Belz, *The American Constitution*, 240–41.

12. *Gibbons v. Ogden*, 9 Wheaton 1 (1824); *Abelman v. Booth*, 21 Howard 506 (1859).

13. Kelly, Harbison, and Belz, *The American Constitution*, 242.

14. See Morton Grodzins, *The American System*, ed. Daniel J. Elazar (Chicago: Rand McNally, 1969), 24.

15. Ibid., 33–34.

16. *Congressional Globe*, 33d Cong., 1st sess., 3 May 1854, 1062.

17. Scheiber, "American Federalism and the Diffusion of Power," 632; William Anderson, *Intergovernmental Relations in Review* (Minneapolis: University of Minnesota Press, 1960), 142.

18. Laura Jensen, "The Early American Origins of Entitlements," in *Studies in American Political Development* 10 (Fall 1996): 360–404.

19. Paul Goodman, "The First American Party Systems," in *The American Party Systems: Stages of Political Development*, ed. William N. Chambers and Walter Dean Burnham, 2d ed. (New York: Oxford University Press, 1975), 63.

20. Ibid., 71.

21. Frederick C. Mosher, *Democracy and the Public Service,* 2d ed. (New York: Oxford University Press, 1982), 58–60.

22. Richard P. McCormick, "Political Development and the Second Party System," in *The American Party Systems: Stages of Political Development,* ed. William N. Chambers and Walter Dean Burnham (New York: Oxford University Press, 1975), 106–7.

23. Mosher, *Democracy and the Public Service,* 64–66.

24. See William Nisbet Chambers, "Party Development and the American Mainstream," in *The American Party Systems: Stages of Political Development,* ed. William N. Chambers and Walter Dean Burnham (New York: Oxford University Press, 1975), 11.

25. McCormick, "Political Development and the Second Party System," 106–7.

26. Chambers, "Party Development and the American Mainstream."

27. Mosher, *Democracy and the Public Service.*

28. McCormick, "Political Development and the Second Party System," 115–16.

29. See Samuel H. Beer, "The Modernization of American Federalism," in *Toward '76–The Federal Polity,* special issue of *Publius* 3 (Fall 1973): 68–69.

30. See Kelly, Harbison, and Belz, *The American Constitution,* 326.

31. 7 Wallace 700 (1869).

32. See Scheiber, "American Federalism and the Diffusion of Power," 638. Also *U.S. v. Cruikshank,* 92 U.S. 542 (1876); *Ex parte Virginia,* 100 U.S. 339 (1880); *Cummings v. Richmond County Board of Education,* 175 U.S. 528 (1899); and especially *Plessy v. Ferguson,* 163 U.S. 537 (1896) and *U.S. v. Reese,* 92 U.S. 21 (1876).

33. See Scheiber, "American Federalism and the Diffusion of Power," 643–44, 653–54.

34. Kelly, Harbison, and Belz, *The American Constitution,* 416.

35. Scheiber, "American Federalism and the Diffusion of Power," 689.

36. 163 U.S. 537 (1896).

37. The states, after all, realistically could not grapple with great corporate power, even when the legal right was theirs. And, as has been demonstrated, the states' police power was expanded greatly into wholly novel areas during this period, and many of the extensions were upheld.

38. Kelly, Harbison, and Belz, *The American Constitution,* 458.

39. Ibid., 455.

40. Ibid.

41. William H. Riker, *Federalism: Origin, Operation, Significance* (Boston: Little, Brown, 1964), 51.

42. See Kelly, Harbison, and Belz, *The American Constitution,* 412–13.

43. *Pollack v. Farmers' Loan and Trust Co.,* 158 U.S. 601 (1895).

44. ACIR, *Significant Features of Fiscal Federalism,* 1976–77, vol. 2, M-110 (Washington, D.C., 1977), 99–101.

45. See James A. Maxwell and J. Richard Aaron, *Financing State and Local Governments* (Washington, D.C.: Brookings Institution, 1977), 85.

46. See Arthur W. MacMahon, *Administering Federalism in a Democracy* (New York: Oxford University Press, 1972), 72.

47. See Earl Baker, Bernadette A. Stevens, Stephen L. Schechter, and Harlan A. Wright, *Federal Grants, National Interest and State Response: A Review of Theory and Research* (Philadelphia: Center for the Study of Federalism, Temple University, 1974), 25–28.

48. Ibid., 27.

49. Ibid., 28–29.

50. *Massachusetts v. Mellon*, 262 U.S. 447 (1923). See Scheiber, "American Federalism and the Diffusion of Power," 642, 643.

51. *Frothingham v. Mellon*, 262 U.S. 447 (1923).

52. See Harry N. Scheiber, *The Condition of American Federalism: An Historian's View,* study prepared for the Subcommittee on Intergovernmental Relations of the Senate Committee on Government Operations, 89th Cong., 2d sess., 15 October 1966, Committee Print, 6.

53. Federal civilian employees numbered 579,559 in 1927; state-local personnel, 2,532,000.

54. Chambers, "Party Development and the American Mainstream," 14.

55. Ibid.

56. ACIR, *The Transformation in American Politics: Implications for Federalism,* A-106 (Washington, D.C., 1986), 26–27.

57. Samuel P. Hays, "Political Parties and the Community-Society Continuum," in *The American Party Systems: Stages of Political Development,* ed. William N. Chambers and Walter Dean Burnham (New York: Oxford University Press, 1975), 161–63.

58. Ibid., 166–67.

59. Ibid., 168.

60. Ibid.

61. Beer, "The Modernization of American Federalism," 65.

62. Ibid., 67.

63. Ibid., 69.

64. ACIR, *The Transformation in American Politics,* 29.

65. William Riker, "The Senate and American Federalism," *American Political Science Review* 49 (June 1955): 457.

66. ACIR, *The Transformation in American Politics,* 30.

67. See E.E. Schattschneider, *Party Government* (New York: Holt, Rinehart & Winston, 1942), 137.

68. ACIR, *The Transformation in American Politics,* 34.

69. James L. Sundquist, *Dynamics of the Party System* (Washington, D.C.: Brookings Institution, 1973), 158.

70. See Mosher, *Democracy and the Public Service,* 66–73.

71. Ibid., 73–80.

72. ACIR, *The Transformation in American Politics,* 37.

73. Richard J. Stillman II, *Preface to Public Administration: A Search for Themes and Direction* (New York: St. Martin's, 1991), 32–72.

## Chapter 4: The Rise and Maturation of Cooperative Federalism, 1930–60

1. See Morton Grodzins, *The American System,* ed. Daniel J. Elazar (Chicago: Rand McNally, 1969), 17–57.

2. Morton Grodzins, "The American Federal System," in *A Nation of States,* ed. Robert A. Goldwin (Chicago: Rand McNally, 1963), 21–22.

3. Daniel J. Elazar, *The American Partnership: Intergovernmental Co-operation in the Nineteenth Century* (Chicago: University of Chicago Press, 1962), 297.

4. See Joseph E. McLean, "Politics Is What You Make It," Public Affairs Pamphlet No. 181 (Washington, D.C.: Public Affairs Press, April 1952), 5.

5. Alfred H. Kelly, Winfred A. Harbison, and Herman Belz, *The American Constitution: Its Origins and Development*, 6th ed. (New York: Norton, 1983), 481–87.

6. Ibid., 480; Carl Brent Swisher, *American Constitutional Development* (Boston: Houghton Mifflin, 1943), 922–38.

7. See Kelly, Harbison, and Belz, *The American Constitution*, 493–94.

8. Ibid., 496–97.

9. See *NLRB v. Jones and Laughlin Steel Co.*, 301 U.S. 1 (1937); *NLRB v. Friedman-Harry Marks Clothing Co.*, 301 U.S. 58 (1937).

10. *Stewart Machine Co. v. Davis*, 301 U.S. 548 (1937).

11. *Helvering v. Davis*, 301 U.S. 619 (1937).

12. See *Consolidated Edison Co. v. NLRB*, 305 U.S. 197 (1938); *NLRB v. Fainblatt*, 306 U.S. 601 (1939).

13. See Harry N. Scheiber, "American Federalism and the Diffusion of Power: Historical and Contemporary Perspectives," 9 *University of Toledo Law Review* 619, at 643–44, 653–54.

14. Kelly, Harbison, and Belz, *The American Constitution*, 517.

15. *Palko v. Connecticut*, 302 U.S. 319 (1937); see also Kelly, Harbison, and Belz, *The American Constitution*, 536–37.

16. Scheiber, "American Federalism and the Diffusion of Power," 653.

17. Ibid.

18. See *Adamson v. California*, 322 U.S. 46 (1948).

19. See *Morgan v. Virginia*, 328 U.S. 373 (1946); *Shelley v. Kraemer*, 339 U.S. 1 (1948).

20. See *Sipuel v. Board of Regents*, 332 U.S. 631 (1948); *Sweatt v. Painter*, 339 U.S. 629 (1950); *McLaurin v. Oklahoma State Regents*, 339 U.S. 637 (1950).

21. *Brown v. Board of Education of Topeka*, 347 U.S. 483 (1954); *Brown v. Board of Education of Topeka*, 349 U.S. 29 (1955).

22. See Scheiber, "American Federalism and the Diffusion of Power," 654–55; Kelly, Harbison, and Belz, *The American Constitution*, 610–12.

23. James A. Maxwell and J. Richard Aaron, *Financing State and Local Governments* (Washington, D.C.: Brookings Institution, 1977), 18.

24. See ACIR, *Significant Features of Fiscal Federalism, 1976–77*, vol. 2, M-110 (Washington, D.C., 1977), 99–101.

25. See Maxwell and Aaron, *Financing State and Local Governments*, 167.

26. The 1932 figure would have been $2.3 billion; the 1958, $8.1 billion.

27. See Maxwell and Aaron, *Financing State and Local Governments*, 83–91.

28. As of 1957, counties received 27.6 percent of all state aid; school districts, 48.2 percent; cities, 20.2 percent; towns, 3.7 percent; and special districts, .3 percent.

29. Maxwell and Aaron, *Financing State and Local Governments*, 85.

30. The usual overall "guesstimate" for the fifties was 20 to 25 percent.

31. See Scheiber, *The Condition of American Federalism: An Historian's View*, study prepared for the Subcommittee on Intergovernmental Relations of the Senate Committee on Government Operations, 89th Cong., 2d sess., 15 October 1966, Committee Print, 8–9.

32. Ibid., 9.

33. ACIR, *Periodic Congressional Review of Federal Grants-in-Aid to State and Local Governments*, A-8 (Washington, D.C., June 1961), table 4.

34. Ibid., 10–11, table 1.

35. Ibid.

36. Adapted from ACIR, *Fiscal Balance in the American Federal System*, vol. 1, A-31 (Washington, D.C., 1967), 140–42.

37. See ACIR, *Periodic Congressional Review of Federal Grants-in-Aid to State and Local Governments*, 14, table 3.

38. See ACIR, *Fiscal Balance in the American Federal System*, 151.

39. Earl Baker, Bernadette A. Stevens, Stephen L. Schechter, and Harlan A. Wright, *Federal Grants, National Interest and State Response: A Review of Theory and Research* (Philadelphia: Center for the Study of Federalism, Temple University, 1974), 34.

40. Commission on Intergovernmental Relations, *A Report to the President for Transmittal to the Congress* (Washington, D.C.: Government Printing Office, June 1955), 120.

41. See Kelly, Harbison, and Belz, *The American Constitution*, 516–17.

42. Theodore J. Lowi, *The End of Liberalism*, 2d ed. (New York: Norton, 1979), 273.

43. See Louis M. Kohlmeier Jr., *The Regulators* (New York: Harper & Row, 1969), 69–82 especially.

44. See Commission on Intergovernmental Relations, *A Report to the President for Transmittal to the Congress*, 31, 32.

45. See ibid., 32.

46. See William Anderson, Clara Penniman, and Edward W. Weidner, *Government in the Fifty States* (New York: Holt, Rinehart & Winston, 1960), 402–3.

47. Ibid., 404.

48. See Roberta Balstad Millner, "The Federal Role in Cities: The New Deal Years," *Commentary*, July 1979, 11–13.

49. See ACIR, *Fiscal Balance in the American Federal System*, 166.

50. See Samuel H. Beer, "The Modernization of American Federalism," in *Toward '76—The Federal Polity*, special issue of *Publius* 3 (Fall 1973): 71–73; Everett Carl Ladd Jr., *American Political Parties* (New York: Norton, 1970), 180–83.

51. Richard Hofstadter, *The American Political Tradition* (New York: Vintage Books, 1954), 334.

52. See Ladd, *American Political Parties*, 188.

53. Samuel I. Rosenman, ed., *The Public Papers and Addresses of Franklin D. Roosevelt*, vol. 2 (New York: Random House, 1938), 165.

54. See Lowi, *The End of Liberalism*.

55. See Lloyd D. Muslof, *Government and the Economy* (Glenview, Ill.: Scott, Foresman, 1967), 10–33.

56. See Congress, Joint Economic Committee, *Subsidy and Subsidy-like Programs of the U.S. Government*, 86th Cong., 2d sess., 1960, Joint Committee Print.

57. Ibid., 18.

58. See James Q. Wilson, "The Politics of Regulation," in *Social Responsibility and the Business Predicament*, ed. James W. McKie (Washington, D.C.: Brookings Institution, 1976), 139–47.

59. William Nisbet Chambers, "Party Development and the American Mainstream," in *The American Party Systems: Stages of Political Development*, ed. William N. Chambers and Walter Dean Burnham (New York: Oxford University Press, 1975), 22.

60. Samuel Lubell, *The Future of American Politics* (Garden City, N.Y.: Doubleday, 1967), 35–60.

61. Ibid., 29–35.

62. ACIR, *The Transformation in American Politics: Implications for Federalism*, A-106 (Washington, D.C., 1986), 39.

63. James T. Patterson, *The New Deal and the States* (Princeton: Princeton University Press, 1969), 74–81.

64. See V.O. Key, *Politics, Parties, and Pressure Groups*, 5th ed. (New York: Crowell, 1964), 358.

65. Ibid., 443–44.

66. Donald E. Stokes, "Parties and Nationalization of Electoral Forces," in *The American Party Systems: Stages of Political Development*, ed. William N. Chambers and Walter Dean Burnham (New York: Oxford University Press, 1975), 193–96.

67. Louis Harris, *Is There a Republican Majority?* (New York: Harper Brothers, 1954), 15.

68. Ibid., 14.

69. Lubell, *The Future of American Politics*, 22–23.

70. Theodore J. Lowi, "Party, Policy, and Constitution in America," in *The American Party Systems: Stages of Political Development*, ed. William N. Chambers and Walter Dean Burnham (New York: Oxford University Press, 1975), 259.

71. V.O. Key, *American State Parties: An Introduction* (New York: Knopf, 1956), 100–118, 194–96.

72. James L. Sundquist, *Dynamics of the Party System* (Washington, D.C.: Brookings Institution, 1973), 239–44.

73. Ibid, 239.

74. *Grovey v. Townsend*, 295 U.S. 45 (1935).

75. *United States v. Classic*, 313 U.S. 299 (1941).

76. *Smith v. Allwright*, 321 U.S. 649 (1944).

77. Key, *Politics, Parties, and Pressure Groups*, 610–11.

78. James MacGregor Burns, *The Deadlock of Democracy* (Englewood Cliffs, N.J.: Prentice-Hall, 1963), 236–37.

79. See President's Committee on Administrative Management, *Report of the Committee, with Special Studies* (Washington, D.C.: Government Printing Office, 1937).

80. Ibid., 7–8.

81. Mosher, *Democracy and the Public Service*, 89.

82. Ibid.

83. Ibid., 91.

## Chapter 5: Cooperative Federalism's Conceptual Offspring, 1960–80

1. See Richard H. Leach, *American Federalism* (New York: Norton, 1976), 14–17.

2. See Max Ways, "Creative Federalism and the Great Society," *Fortune*, January 1966; Edmund S. Muskie, "The Challenge of Creative Federalism," *Congressional Record*, 89th Cong., 2d sess., 25 March 1966 (bound ed.), 6833–45.

3. Richard Warner, "The Concept of Creative Federalism," doctoral dissertation, American University, 1970.

4. See *Publius* 2 (Spring 1972): 98–146.

5. The term *balanced national partnership*, of course, had been used in some of his campaign speeches.

6. Timothy Conlan, *New Federalism: Intergovernmental Reform from Nixon to Reagan* (Washington, D.C.: Brookings Institution, 1988), 12–13.

7. A block grant is an intergovernmental fiscal transfer that covers a wide functional terrain and seeks to achieve broad national purposes, while maximizing the discretion of recipient jurisdictions.

8. Lyndon B. Johnson, speech to the New York Liberal party, 15 October 1964, *Public Reports,* 1350–51.

9. See Harry N. Scheiber, *The Condition of American Federalism: An Historian's View,* study prepared for the Subcommittee on Intergovernmental Relations of the Senate Committee on Government Operations, 89th Cong., 2d sess., 15 October 1966, Committee Print, 14–16.

10. See David M. Welborn and Jesse Burkhead, *Intergovernmental Relations in the American Administrative State* (Austin: University of Texas Press, 1989), 199–234.

11. Given the difficulty of gauging whether such delegations actually take place, this estimate must be viewed with some caution. See ACIR, *Improving Federal Grants Management,* A-53 (Washington, D.C., February 1977), 187–91.

12. See Office of Management and Budget, *Special Analysis, Budget of the United States Government, Fiscal Year 1977* (Washington, D.C.: Government Printing Office), 256–57.

13. See ACIR, *Categorical Grants: Their Role and Design,* A-52 (Washington, D.C., 1978), 31–43; ACIR, *A Catalogue of Federal Grant-in-Aid Programs to State and Local Governments: Grants Funded FY 1978,* A-72 (Washington, D.C., February 1979), 1.

14. See Samuel H. Beer, "The Adoption of General Revenue Sharing," *Public Policy* 2 (Spring 1976): 127–95.

15. ACIR, *Regulatory Federalism: Policy, Process, Impact and Reform,* A-95 (Washington, D.C., February 1984), 34–44.

16. Ibid., 34–39.

17. See Jimmy Carter, "Address on Urban Policy to the United States Conference of Mayors," 29 June 1976 (copy in author's possession).

18. See Rochelle L. Stanfield, "Is the Man from Georgia Ready to Help the States and Cities?" *National Journal,* 22 January 1977, 137–41.

19. See Jack Knott and Aaron Wildavsky, "Jimmy Carter's Theory of Governing," *Wilson Quarterly* 2 (Winter 1977): 49–67.

20. See David R. Beam, "Public Administration Is Alive and Well and Living in the White House," *Public Administration Review* 38 (January–February 1978): 72–77.

21. See Reorganization Plan No. 1 of 1977 (copy in author's possession); Rochelle L. Stanfield, "The Best Laid Reorganization Plans Sometimes Go Astray," *National Journal,* 1 January 1979, 84–91.

22. See Donald F. Haider, "Zero Base: Federal Style," *Public Administration Review* 37 (July–August 1977): 400–407.

23. See Joel Havermann, "Can Carter Chop through the Civil Service System?" *National Journal,* 23 April 1977, 616.

24. "The President's Memorandum for the Heads of Executive Departments and Agencies: Involvement of State and Local Officials in the Administration's Politics and Programs," 25 February 1977, *Weekly Compilation of Presidential Documents,* 283.

25. "Memorandum for the Heads of Executive Departments and Agencies: Administration of Federal Aid Systems," 9 September 1977, *Weekly Compilation of Presidential Documents,* 12 September 1977, 1318–19.

26. See *Federal Aid Simplification,* White House Status Report, September 1978.

27. David R. Beam and David B. Walker, "Can Carter Cut the Marble Cake?" paper presented at the annual meeting of the American Society for Public Administration, Phoenix, 9–12 April 1978.

28. See *Intergovernmental Perspective* (ACIR) 4 (Winter 1978): 8–9.

29. See Lawrence O. Houstoun Jr., "The Carter Urban Policy a Year Later," memorandum, 8 February 1979, U.S. Department of Commerce.

30. See "The National Policy: One Year Later," *Information Bulletin* (ACIR) no. 79-4, May 1979.

31. See Harold Seidman, *Politics, Position, and Power: The Dynamics of Federal Organization* (New York: Oxford University Press, 1979), 136.

32. See ACIR, *Tenth Annual Report* (Washington, D.C., 1968), 8.

33. Senate Committee on Government Operations, Subcommittee on Intergovernmental Relations, *The Federal System as Seen by Federal Aid Officials*, 89th Cong., 1st sess., 15 December 1965, Committee Print, 98–101.

34. The latter involved a survey of 125 program administrators responsible for disbursing a little more than $12 billion in grants in 1964, 109 of whose responses were used in the subcommittee report. The ACIR surveyed 440 administrators, 276 of whose responses were deemed "usable" for analytical purposes.

35. Senate Committee on Government Operations, Subcommittee on Intergovernmental Relations, *The Federal System as Seen by Federal Aid Officials*, 93–102.

36. Terry Sanford, *Storm over the States* (New York: McGraw-Hill, 1967), 80.

37. David B. Walker, "Federal Aid Administrators and the Federal System," in *Intergovernmental Perspective* (ACIR) 3 (Fall 1977): 10–17.

38. See ACIR, *The Intergovernmental Grant System as Seen by Local, State, and Federal Officials*, A-54 (Washington, D.C., 1977), chap. 5.

39. John E. Schwarz, *America's Hidden Success*, rev. ed. (New York: Norton, 1987).

## Chapter 6: The Reactions to Cooperative (and Co-Optive) Federalism, 1981–

1. John E. Schwarz, *America's Hidden Success*, rev. ed. (New York: Norton, 1987), 17–70.

2. James A. Carroll, A. Lee Fritschler, and B.L.R. Smith, "Supply Side Management in the Reagan Administration," *Public Administration Review* 45 (1985): 805–14.

3. See Timothy Conlan, "Federalism and Competing Values in the Reagan Administration," *Publius* 16 (Winter 1986): 37–42; Hugh Heclo, "Reaganism and the Search for a Public Philosophy," in *Perspectives on the Reagan Years*, ed. John L. Palmer (Washington, D.C.: Urban Institute Press, 1986), 39–47.

4. See Paul E. Peterson and Mark Rom, "Lower Taxes, More Spending, and Budget Deficits," in *The Reagan Legacy: Promise and Performance*, ed. Charles O. Jones (Chatham, N.J.: Chatham House, 1988), 213–38; James Tobin, "Reaganomics in Retrospect," in *The Reagan Revolution?* ed. B.B. Kymlicka and Jean V. Matthews (Chicago: Dorsey Press, 1988), 85–103.

5. Carroll, Fritschler, and Smith, "Supply Side Management in the Reagan Administration."

6. Ibid.

7. See David B. Walker, "Modernized Grants Management: Little Noticed, but Greatly Needed," *Assistance Management Journal* (National Grants Management Association) 7 (Fall 1992): 4–5.

8. Ibid., 13.

9. Walter Williams, "America's Quiet Crisis: Hollow Incompetent Government," DC-13 (Seattle: Graduate School of Public Affairs, University of Washington, 20 February 1991): 1.

10. Ibid., 2.

11. See Catherine H. Lovell, "Reregulation of Intergovernmental Programs: Early Results of Reagan Policies," *Public Affairs Report* (Institute of Governmental Studies, University of California at Berkeley) 25 (1984): 2.

12. Peter M. Benda and Charles H. Levine, "Reagan and the Bureaucracy," in *The Reagan Legacy: Promise and Performance*, ed. Charles O. Jones (Chatham, N.J.: Chatham House, 1988), 114–20.

13. Ibid., 119.

14. Harold Seidman and Robert Gilmour, *Politics, Position, and Power: From the Positive to the Regulatory State*, 4th ed. (New York: Oxford University Press, 1986), 130.

15. Timothy J. Conlan and David R. Beam, "Federal Mandates: The Record Reform and Future Prospects," *Intergovernmental Perspective* (ACIR) 18 (Fall 1992): 7.

16. ACIR, *Significant Features of Fiscal Federalism*, vol. 2, *Budget Processes and Tax System*, M-180-II (Washington, D.C., September 1992), 146–48.

17. Timothy Conlan, *New Federalism: Intergovernmental Reform from Nixon to Reagan* (Washington, D.C.: Brookings Institution, 1988), 201–2.

18. See Daniel J. Elazar, "Opening the Third Century of American Federalism: Issues and Prospects," in *American Federalism: The Third Century* (special issue of *The Annals*), ed. John Kincaid (Newbury Park, Calif.: Sage, May 1990), 14–15.

19. David A. Stockman, *The Triumph of Politics: Why the Reagan Revolution Failed* (New York: Harper & Row, 1986), 9.

20. Ibid., 10–11.

21. Ibid., 109.

22. Ibid., 127.

23. Ibid., 125–27.

24. See Paul J. Quirk, "Domestic Policy: Divided Government and Cooperative Presidential Leadership," in *The Bush Presidency: First Appraisal*, ed. Colin Campbell and Bert A. Rockman (Chatham, N.J.: Chatham House, 1991), 14–17.

25. See "Highway and Transit Overload Is Cleared for President," *Congressional Quarterly*, 30 November 1991, 3518–22.

26. Marcia A. Howard, *Fiscal Survey of the States, October 1991* (Washington, D.C.: National Governors' Association and National Association of State Budget Officers, October 1991), ix.

27. National Governors' Association, News Release (Washington, D.C., 2 January 1991), 1.

28. See ACIR, *Federal Regulation of State and Local Governments: The Mixed Record of the 1980s*, A-126 (Washington, D.C., 1993), 31–40.

29. Michael Duffy and Dan Goodgame, *Marching in Place* (New York: Simon & Schuster, 1992), 95.

30. See ACIR, *Federal Regulation of State and Local Governments*, chap. 4.

31. "A Quayle Hunts the Watchdogs," *Newsweek*, 6 January 1992, 34.

32. See "Move Over, Doonesbury," *National Journal*, 16 December 1991, 3005.

33. Victor Kirk, "Quayle's Quiet Coup," *National Journal*, 6 July 1991, 1676–80.

34. Marshall R. Goodman, "A Kinder and Gentler Regulatory Reform: The Bush Regulatory Strategy and Its Impact," paper presented at the annual meeting of the Southern Political Science Association, Atlanta, 1990, 10–11.

35. See ibid., 13–20.

36. *Dole v. United Steelworkers of America*, 494 U.S. 26 (1990).

37. Goodman, "A Kinder and Gentler Regulatory Reform," 16.

38. See Duffy and Goodgame, *Marching in Place*, 77–88.

39. Paul J. Quirk and Joseph Hinchliffe, "Domestic Policy: The Trials of a Centrist Democrat," in *The Clinton Presidency: First Appraisals*, ed. Colin Campbell and Bert A. Rockman (Chatham, N.J.: Chatham House, 1996), 264–65.

40. William A. Galston and Geoffrey L. Tibbetts, "Reinventing Federalism: The Clinton-Gore Program for a New Partnership among the Federal, State, Local, and Tribal Governments," *Publius* 2, no. 3 (Summer 1994): 24–25.

41. Charles O. Jones, "Campaigning to Govern: The Clinton Style," in *The Clinton Presidency: First Appraisals*, ed. Colin Campbell and Bert A. Rockman (Chatham, N.J.: Chatham House, 1996), 37–38.

42. Quirk and Hinchliffe, "Domestic Policy," 274.

43. Ibid., 275.

44. See Haynes Johnson and David S. Broder, *The System* (Boston: Little, Brown, 1996), for an in-depth analysis of this policy battle.

45. Quirk and Hinchliffe, "Domestic Policy," 278–79.

46. See Office of Management and Budget, "Delivering a Government That Works Better and Costs Less," *Budget of the United States Government, FY 1995* (Washington, D.C.: Government Printing Office), 169–70.

47. Walter Dean Burnham, "Realignment Lives: The 1994 Earthquake and Its Implications," in *The Clinton Presidency: First Appraisals*, ed. Colin Campbell and Bert A. Rockman (Chatham, N.J.: Chatham House, 1996), 383.

48. Ibid.

49. "Republicans Initial Promise: 100 Days Debate on Contract," *Congressional Quarterly*, 13 November 1994, 3216–19.

50. See *Congressional Quarterly's* House Action Reports Fact Sheet No. 104–37, 4, 5, 21, 30, and 32.

51. See "The Devolution Revolution," *Rockefeller Institute Bulletin — 1996* (Albany N.Y.: Nelson A. Rockefeller Institute of Government, 1996), 5–13.

52. For the following analysis of Public Law 104-193, see Carl Tubbesing and Sheri Steisel, "Answers to Your Welfare Worries," *State Legislature*, January 1997, 12–19; and "The Personal Responsibility and Work Opportunity Reconciliation Act of 1996," analysis prepared by the American Public Welfare Association (APWA), the National Governors' Association (NGA), and the National Conference of State Legislatures (NCSL) (Washington, D.C.: APWA, 22 August 1996), 1–23.

53. Richard P. Nathan, "The Newest New Federalism for Welfare," *Rockefeller Institute Bulletin — 1998* (Albany, N.Y.: Nelson A. Rockefeller Institute of Government, 1998), 4–7.

54. Barbara Vobejda and Jon Jeter, "And Now Comes the Hard Part," *Washington Post National Weekly Edition*, 1 September 1997, 29.

55. "Assessing Congress," *Congressional Quarterly*, 2 November 1996, 3120–22.

56. David Hussansky, "GOP Confounds Expectations, Expands Federal Authority," *Congressional Quarterly*, 2 November 1996, 3117–19.

57. David S. Broder, "Muddling Education," *Washington Post National Weekly Edition*, 6 October 1997, 4.

58. Dan Balz, "In Search of an Agenda," *Washington Post National Weekly Edition*, 10 February 1997.

59. David S. Broder, "Thinking Small," *Washington Post National Weekly Edition*, 4.

60. David S. Broder, "Building a Legacy, Step by Tiny Step," *Washington Post National Weekly Edition*, 16 June 1997.

61. Barbara Vobejda and Judith Havemann, "Finally a Budget Deal," *Washington Post National Weekly Edition*, 4 August 1997, 9.

## Chapter 7: The Federal Judiciary: Centralizer or Umpire?

1. Alfred H. Kelly and Winfred Harbison, *The American Constitution: Its Origins and Development* (New York: Norton, 1976), 856.

2. Harry N. Scheiber, "American Federalism and the Diffusion of Power: Historical and Contemporary Perspectives," 9 *University of Toledo Law Review* 619, at 654.

3. *Younger v. Harris*, 401 U.S. 37 (1971).

4. Ibid.

5. See *King v. Smith*, 329 U.S. 316 (1968); *Shapiro v. Thompson*, 394 U.S. 618 (1969).

6. See Archibald Cox, *The Warren Court: Constitutional Decision as an Instrument of Reform* (Cambridge, Mass.: Harvard University Press, 1968), 12–13.

7. See Raoul Berger, *Government by Judiciary* (Cambridge, Mass.: Harvard University Press, 1977).

8. Neil McFeeley, "The Supreme Court and the Federal System," *Publius* 8 (Fall 1978): 12.

9. See Philip B. Kurland, *Politics, the Constitution, and the Warren Court* (Chicago: University of Chicago Press, 1969), xx.

10. Ibid., xxi.

11. Ibid.

12. A minor scandal prompted this.

13. See *Swann v. Charlotte-Mecklenburg Board of Education*, 402 U.S. 1 (1971); *Keyes v. School District No. 1, Denver*, 412 U.S. 189 (1973); *Milliken v. Bradley*, 418 U.S. 717 (1974) (as noted later, this case also rejected a central city–suburban school district merger as a means of further desegregation); *Lau v. Nichols*, 414 U.S. 563 (1974). See also Donald L. Horowitz, *The Courts and Social Policy* (Washington, D.C.: Brookings Institution, 1976), 15–17; *Griggs v. Duke Power Company*, 401 U.S. 42 (1971); *Oregon v. Mitchell*, 400 U.S. 112 (1970); *U.S. Department of Agriculture v. Moreno*, 413 U.S. 528 (1973).

14. See *Cohen v. California*, 403 U.S. 15 (1971); *Elrod v. Burns*, 965 U.S. 2673 (1976); *Hynes v. Borough of Oradell*, 425 U.S. 610 (1976); *Roe v. Wade*, 410 U.S. 113 (1973); *Doe v. Bolton*, 410 U.S. 179 (1973); *Furman v. Georgia*, 408 U.S. 238 (1972); *Gregg v. Georgia*, 428 U.S. 153 (1976); *Coker v. Georgia*, 433 U.S. 583 (1977).

15. *United States v. Harris*, 403 U.S. 92 (1971); *Cady v. Dombrowski*, 410 U.S. 952 (1973); *United States v. Robinson*, 412 U.S. 936 (1973); *United States v. Calandra*, 414 U.S. 338 (1973).

16. *Harris v. New York*, 401 U.S. 222 (1971); *Oregon v. Haas*, 420 U.S. 71 (1975); *Ybarra v. Illinois*, 444 U.S. 85 (1979).

17. *Kirby v. Illinois*, 406 U.S. 682 (1972).

18. *Baldwin v. New York*, 399 U.S. 66 (1970).

19. *Williams v. Florida*, 399 U.S. 78 (1970); *Johnson v. Louisiana*, 406 U.S. 356 (1972); *Apodaca v. Oregon*, 406 U.S. 40 (1972).

20. *Younger v. Harris*, 401 U.S. 37 (1971).

21. *Dombrowski v. Pfister,* 380 U.S. 479 (1965).

22. See McFeeley, "The Supreme Court and the Federal System," 23–34.

23. *Kaufman v. United States,* 394 U.S. 217 (1969).

24. *Schneckleth v. Bustamente,* 412 U.S. 218 (1973).

25. See *Miller v. California,* 413 U.S. 15 (1973); *Paris Adult Theater I v. Slayton,* 413 U.S. 49 (1973).

26. *Milliken v. Bradley,* 418 U.S. 717 (1974).

27. See C. Herman Pritchett, *The American Constitution* (New York: McGraw-Hill, 1977), 213; *Michelin Tire Corp. v. Wages,* 424 U.S. 935 (1976).

28. Louis Weinberg, "The New Judicial Federalism," 29 *Stanford Law Review* 1193 (1977). See *DeCanas v. Bica,* 424 U.S. 35 (1976); *Kewanee Oil Co. v. Bicron Corp.,* 416 U.S. 470 (1974); *Askew v. American Waterways Operations, Inc.,* 411 U.S. 325 (1973); *Goldstein v. California,* 412 U.S. 546 (1972).

29. See, for example, *Ray v. Atlantic Richfield Co.,* 435 U.S. 151 (1978); *City of Philadelphia v. New Jersey,* 437 U.S. 617 (1978).

30. *Mahan v. Howell,* 410 U.S. 315 (1973).

31. See *Gordon v. Lance,* 403 U.S. 1 (1971) at 7; *Bogert v. Kinzer,* 403 U.S. 91 (1971).

32. *San Antonio Independent School District v. Rodriguez,* 411 U.S. 1 (1973).

33. See *Reed v. Reed,* 404 U.S. 71 (1971); *Stanton v. Stanton,* 421 U.S. 7 (1975); *Frontiero v. Richardson,* 411 U.S. 677 (1973); *Kahn v. Shevin,* 461 U.S. 351 (1974).

34. "Developments in the Law: Section 1983," 90 *Harvard Law Review* 1180 (1977).

35. *Thornburgh v. Casey,* 440 U.S. 823 (1979).

36. *National League of Cities v. Usery,* 426 U.S. 833 (1976).

37. See Laurence Tribe, "Unraveling National League of Cities: The New Federalism and Affirmative Rights to Essential Governmental Services," 90 *Harvard Law Review* 1065 (1977), at 1067–68; McFeeley, "The Supreme Court and the Federal System," 22. It should be noted that the lesser Federal judiciary in a series of cases in the midsixties voided the provisions of the Environmental Protection Agency's regulations for the Clean Air Act that mandated state implementation of Federal standards and state regulation of private action on grounds that they were an unconstitutional encroachment on states' rights, and hence beyond the reach of the commerce power. See Jeffrey Kessler, "Clean Air Act," 79 *Columbia Law Review* 990 (1976), 1007–10.

38. A.E. Dick Howard, "The States and the Supreme Court," *Symposium: State and Local Government Issues before the Supreme Court* (Washington, D.C.: State and Local Legal Center of the Academy for State and Local Government, 1982), 379.

39. Ibid., 381.

40. *Monroe v. Pape,* 365 U.S. 167 (1961).

41. *Monell v. New York City Department of Social Services,* 436 U.S. 658 (1978).

42. 445 U.S. 622 (1980).

43. 448 U.S. 1 (1980).

44. *City of Newport v. Fact Concerts, Inc.,* 453 U.S. 247 (1981).

45. Jerry Fensterman, "Antitrust and Local Governments," *Intergovernmental Perspective* (ACIR) 9 (Fall 1983): 7–16.

46. 435 U.S. 389 (1978).

47. *Community Communications Co. v. City of Boulder,* 455 U.S. 40 (1982).

48. See Laura S. Jensen, "Subsidies, Strings, and the Courts: Judicial Action and Conditional Federal Spending," *Review of Politics* 55 (Summer 1993): 491–509.

49. *City of Macon v. Marshall,* 439 F. Supp. 1209 (M.D. Ga. 1977).

50. *Montgomery County v. Califano,* 449 F. Supp. 1230 (D. Md. 1978), aff'd without op., 599 F.2d 1048 (4th Cir. 1979); North Carolina, ex. rel. *Morrow v. Califano,* 445 F. Supp. 532 (E.D. N.C. 1977), aff'd mem., 435 U.S. 926 (1978); *Florida Department of Health v. Califano,* 441 U.S. 931 (1979).

51. *Lawrence County v. Lead-Deadwood School District,* 469 U.S. 256 (1985).

52. *Wyman v. Jones,* 400 U.S. 309 (1971).

53. *Lyng v. Castillo,* 477 U.S. 635 (1986).

54. *Selective Service System v. Minnesota Public Interest Group,* 468 U.S. 841 (1984).

55. See Thomas M. Jorde, "A Return to Deferential Federalism: Antitrust and the New 'State Action' Doctrine," in *Perspective on Federalism: Papers from the First Berkeley Seminar on Federalism,* ed. Harry N. Scheiber (Berkeley: Institute of Governmental Studies, University of California, 1987), 73–74.

56. See *Hoover v. Ronwin,* 466 U.S. 558 (1984); *Town of Hallie v. City of Eau Claire,* 471 U.S. 3 (1985); *Southern Motor Carriers Rate Conference Inc. v. United States,* 471 U.S. 48 (1985).

57. 451 U.S. 1 (1981).

58. *Middlesex County Sewage Authority v. National Sea Clammers Association,* 453 U.S. 1 (1981).

59. Ibid., at 26–27.

60. Cynthia Cates Colella, "Do As I Say, Not As I Do — The Supreme Court, Preemption, and the Dormant Commerce Clause: Mixed Signals in the Age of *Garcia,*" paper presented at the annual meeting of the American Political Science Association, Washington, D.C., 1 September 1991, 6–7.

61. Ibid., 7.

62. Ibid., 9.

63. 464 U.S. 238 (1984), at 248.

64. *Pacific Gas and Electric Co. v. State Energy Resources Conservation and Development Commission,* 461 U.S. 190 (1983).

65. Colella, "Do As I Say, Not As I Do," 14.

66. 426 U.S. 79 (1976).

67. *Reeves, Inc. v. Stake,* 447 U.S. 429 (1980); *White v. Massachusetts Council of Construction Employers,* 460 U.S. 20 (1983).

68. *South Central Timber Development v. Wunnicke,* 467 U.S. 82 (1984).

69. Richard C. Kearney and Reginald S. Sheehan, "Supreme Court Decision-Making: The Impact of Court Composition on State and Local Government Litigation," *Journal of Politics* 5 (November 1992): 1011–12.

70. Ibid.

71. Ibid., 1015.

72. John Kincaid, "The State and Federal Bills of Rights: Partners and Rivals in Liberty," *Intergovernmental Perspective* (ACIR) 17 (Fall 1991): 33; Thomas Anton, *American Federalism and Public Policy* (Philadelphia: Temple University Press, 1989), 202–3.

73. Ibid.

74. See Cynthia Cates Colella, "Mass Transit and the Tenth Amendment," *Intergovernmental Perspective* (ACIR) 9 (Fall 1983): 17–24.

75. *Hode v. Surface Mining and Reclamation Association,* 452 U.S. 76 (1981).

76. *United Transportation Union v. Long Island Railroad,* 455 U.S. 678 (1982).

77. *Kramer v. New Castle Area Transit Authority,* 677 F.2d 308 (3d Cir. 1982), cert. denied, 459 U.S. 1146 (1983).

78. 460 U.S. 226 (1983).

79. Colella, "Mass Transit and the Tenth Amendment," 26.

80. 469 U.S. 528 (1985).

81. Ibid.

82. See ACIR, *Reflections on Garcia and Its Implications for Federalism*, M-147 (Washington, D.C., February 1986), 3–10.

83. See Lewis B. Kaden, "Politics, Money, and State Sovereignty," 79 *Columbia Law Review* 847 (1979), at 847–85.

84. *FERC v. Mississippi*, 456 U.S. 742 (1982).

85. See Elder Witt, *A Different Justice* (Washington, D.C.: CQ Press, 1986), 3–10.

86. Cynthia Cates Colella, "The Judiciary and Regulation in the Eighties," in ACIR, *Federal Regulation of State and Local Governments: The Mixed Record of the 1980s*, A-126 (Washington, D.C., 1993), 71–118.

87. Ibid., 77–78.

88. Ibid., 78.

89. 483 U.S. 203 (1987).

90. See ACIR, *Regulatory Federalism: Policy, Process, Impact and Reform*, A-95 (Washington, D.C., February 1984), 8.

91. Colella, "The Judiciary and Regulation in the Eighties."

92. 483 U.S. 203 (1987), at 210.

93. 884 F.2d 445 (1989).

94. 886 F.2d 404, at 410 (D.C. Cir. 1989).

95. 111 S.Ct. 1759 (1991).

96. Ibid., at 1772.

97. Ibid.

98. 485 U.S. 505 (1988).

99. Ibid., at 515.

100. Ibid., at 533.

101. *Missouri v. Jenkins*, 109 S.Ct. 1150 (1990).

102. *Trinova Corp. v. Michigan Department of Treasury*, 498 U.S. 358 (1991).

103. 111 S.Ct. 1438 (1991).

104. *General Motors Corp., Petitioner v. Roger W. Tracy, The Tax Commissioner of Ohio*, 117, S.Ct. 814 (1997).

105. *Camps Newfound/Owatonma, Inc. v. Town of Harrison et al.*, 117, S.Ct. 1590 (1997).

106. *FMC v. Holliday*, 498 U.S. 52 (1990); *Ingersoll-Rand v. McClendon Corp.*, 498 U.S. 133 (1990).

107. 111 S.Ct. 2476 (1991).

108. 486 U.S. 17 (1988).

109. 497 U.S. 62 (1990).

110. 117 S.Ct. 832 (1997).

111. 111 S.Ct. 2321 (1991).

112. See Richard Cole, "The States before the Supreme Court in the Post-Powell Era: An Ordering of Judicial Federalism," unpublished paper, University of Connecticut, Spring 1992, 9–10.

113. 111 S.Ct. 2321 (1991).

114. 498 U.S. 439 (1991).

115. Ibid.

116. 112 S.Ct. 1360 (1992).

117. *Collins v. City of Harker Heights, Texas*, 112 S.Ct. 1061 (1992).

118. *Hafer v. Melo*, 112 S.Ct. 358 (1991).

119. 490 U.S. 642 (1989).

120. 401 U.S. 42 (1971).

121. 490 U.S. 755 (1989).

122. 488 U.S. 469 (1989).

123. 63 L.W. 4523 (1995).

124. 111 S.Ct. 2546 (1991).

125. 111 S.Ct. 145 (1990).

126. Katy J. Harriger, "The Federalism Debate Is the Transformation of Federal Habeas Corpus," *Publius* 27, no. 3 (Summer 1997): 19–20.

127. 116 S.Ct. 2333 (1996).

128. 117 S.Ct. 2157 (1997).

129. 484 U.S. 652 (1990).

130. 497 U.S. 62. (1990).

131. *Simon & Schuster, Inc. v. Members of New York State Crime Victim Board*, 112 S.Ct. 501 (1991).

132. *R.A.V. v. St. Paul*, 112 S.Ct. 2538 (1992).

133. 112 S.Ct. 1846 (1992).

134. 113 S.Ct. 1732 (1995).

135. *Miller v. Johnson*, 515 S.Ct. 7475 (1995).

136. *Shaw v. Hunt*, L.Ed., 2d, 207 (1996); *Bush v. Vera*, L.Ed., 2d 258 (1996).

137. *Abrams et al. v. Johnson et al.* 117 S.Ct. 1925 (1997).

138. 410 U.S. 113 (1973).

139. 492 U.S. 490 (1989).

140. *Hodgson v. Minnesota*, 497 U.S. 417 (1990); *Ohio v. Akron Center for Reproductive Health*, 497 U.S. 502 (1990).

141. 112 S.Ct. 2791 (1992).

142. Ibid., at 2815.

143. Ibid., at 2803.

144. Ibid., at 2804.

145. Ibid., at 2844.

146. 111 S.Ct. 2395 (1991).

147. Ibid., at 2399.

148. Ibid.

149. Ibid.

150. 60 L.W. 4603 (1992).

151. 117 S.Ct. 2376 (1997).

152. Ibid., 2401.

153. 115 S.Ct. 1842 (1995). See Cynthia L. Cates, "Splitting the Atom of Sovereignty: *Term Limits Inc.'s* . . . Conflicting Views of Popular Autonomy in Federal Republic," *Publius* 26, no. 3 (Summer 1996): 127–36, 139–40.

154. See Michael A. Pagano and Ann O'M. Bowman, "The State of American Federalism, 1994–1995," *Publius* 25, no. 3 (Summer 1995): 12–14.

155. 1996 U.S. Lexis 2165.

156. 115 S.Ct. 1624 (1995).

157. See David B. Walker and Matthew W. Hart, "Lopez: The President, the Judiciary, and the Congress," paper presented at the annual meeting of the New England Political Science Association, Worcester, Mass., 1 May 1998, 14–30.

158. 110 S.Ct. 1651 (1990).

159. *Missouri et al. v. Jenkins et al.*, 63 L.W. 4486 (1995).

160. Nathan Glazer, "Towards an Imperial Judiciary?" *Public Interest* 41 (Fall 1975): 112–21.

161. ACIR, *Reflections on* Garcia *and Its Implications for Federalism*, 43–50.

162. Ibid., 43–49.

163. John Kincaid, "A Proposal to Strengthen Federalism," *Journal of State Government* 62 (January–February 1989): 36–45.

164. David B. Walker, "American Federalism: From Johnson to Bush," *Publius* 21 (Winter 1991): 119.

165. See Tribe, "Unraveling *National League of Cities*," 1065.

166. Cox, *The Warren Court.*

167. *United States v. Virginia*, 518 U.S. 515 (1996).

168. *Romer v. Evans et al.*, 1996 U.S. Lexis, 64 U.S. L.W. 4353.

169. Cited in McFeeley, "The Supreme Court and the Federal System," 6.

170. Ibid., 19–22.

171. Ibid., 23–34.

172. Kearney and Sheehan, "Supreme Court Decision-Making," 1015.

173. Colella, "The Judiciary and Regulation in the Eighties," 100.

174. Ibid.

175. Charles Wise and Rosemary O'Leary, "Is Federalism Dead or Alive in the Supreme Court? Implications for Public Administration," *Public Administration Review* 52 (November–December 1992): 571.

176. Ibid., 561.

## Chapter 8: Fiscal Federalism: The Fateful Dynamic

1. Historical Tables, *Budget of the United States Government, Fiscal Year 1999*, table 15.2, 269–70.

2. Ibid.

3. ACIR, *Significant Features of Fiscal Federalism*, vol. 2, *Revenues and Expenditures* (Washington, D.C., October 1997), 53.

4. See General Accounting Office, *Intergovernmental Relations: Changing Patterns in State-Local Finances*, GAO/HRD-92-87FS (Washington, D.C., March 1992), 17.

5. Historical Tables, *Budget of the United States Government, Fiscal Year 1999*, 53.

6. ACIR, *Significant Features of Fiscal Federalism*, 1997, 72 and 74.

7. Ibid., 212.

8. ACIR, *Significant Features of Fiscal Federalism*, vol. 1, *Budget Processes and Tax Systems*, M-180-I (cited hereafter as *Budget Processes and Tax Systems*, 1992) (Washington, D.C., February 1992), 32.

9. Ibid., 14–17.

10. Ibid., 96–97.

11. A payroll tax is a levy on wages and does not include other forms of wealth.

12. ACIR, *Budget Processes and Tax Systems, 1992*, 73–75.

13. Susan A. MacManus, "Financing Federal, State and Local Governments in the 1990s," in *American Federalism: The Third Century* (special issue of *The Annals*), ed. John Kincaid (Newbury Park, Calif.: Sage, May 1990), 26.

14. ACIR, *Budget Processes and Tax Systems, 1992*, 18.

15. The representative tax system's indexes of tax effort are measures of the relative extent to which states utilize their available taxation capacity or tax bases. An index of 100 is the national average. The tax effort indexes are obtained by comparing actual state-based tax revenues per capita with the states' estimated tax capacities, which are derived from estimates of the per capita amounts of the tax revenues that could be raised in each state if the same state-local tax system (representative of an average tax system) were used in every state. See ACIR, *Revenues and Expenditures*, 1992, 267.

16. Ibid., 269.

17. Ibid. All the states cited here, except for Ohio, Iowa, and North Dakota, are oil states and benefit from oil taxes, most of which are passed on to customers in other states.

18. GAO, *Intergovernmental Relations*, 46.

19. ACIR, *Significant Features of Fiscal Federalism*, 1992, 132–39.

20. ACIR, *Significant Features of Fiscal Federalism*, 1997, 94–95.

21. Ibid.

22. Ibid.

23. ACIR, *Budget Processes and Tax Systems*, 1992, 133–39.

24. Ibid., 124–32.

25. Ibid., 89–91.

26. Citizens for Tax Justice, *A Far Cry from Fair* (Washington, D.C., 1991), 10.

27. Ibid., 19–69.

28. Roy Bahl, Jorge Martinez-Vasquez, and David L. Sjoquist, "Central City–Suburban Fiscal Disparities," *Public Finance Quarterly* 70 (October 1992): 425.

29. Lawrence Mishel, Jared Bernstein, and John Schmitt, *The State of Working America — 1996–97*, Economic Policy Institute (Armonk, N.Y.: M.E. Sharpe, 1997), 103.

30. ACIR, *Significant Features of Fiscal Federalism*, 1997, 100–101.

31. Michael Pagano, *City Fiscal Conditions in 1992* (Washington, D.C.: National League of Cities, 1992), 28.

32. Steven D. Gold and Sarah Ritchie, *State Policies Affecting Cities and Counties in 1992* (Albany: Center for the Study of the States, State University of New York, January 1993), 7.

33. 5 Cal. 3d 584, 487 P. 2d 1241, 96 Cal. Rptr. 601 (1971).

34. National Conference of State Legislatures, *Educational Partners: Working Papers* (Denver, 1996), 4.

35. General Accounting Office, *Communities in Fiscal Distress — State Targeting Provides Limited Help*, GAO/HRD-90-69 (Washington, D.C., April 1990), 35. Payments in lieu of taxes, which are reimbursements to localities for revenue losses due to tax-exempt properties, frequently are included in these programs.

36. ACIR, *Significant Features of Fiscal Federalism*, 1997, 46–47.

37. ACIR, *Fiscal Disparities: Central Cities and Suburbs, 1981* (Washington, D.C., August 1984), 17; Bahl, Martinez-Vasquez, and Sjoquist, "Central City–Suburban Fiscal Disparities," 425.

38. ACIR, *Fiscal Disparities*, 17.

39. See James L. Sundquist and David W. Davis, *Making Federalism Work: A Study of Program Coordination at the Community Level* (Washington, D.C.: Brookings Institution, 1969), 3–5.

40. ACIR, *Characteristics of Federal Grant-in-Aid Programs to State and Local Governments: Grants Funded FY 1993*, M-188 (Washington, D.C., January 1994), 2–3.

41. ACIR, *Characteristics of Federal Grant-in-Aid Programs to State and Local Governments: Grants Funded FY 1991*, M-182 (Washington, D.C., March 1992), 2–3.

42. ACIR, *A Catalog of Federal Grant-in-Aid Programs to State and Local Governments: Grants Funded FY 1978*, A-72 (Washington, D.C., 1979), 3.

43. ACIR, *The Intergovernmental System as Seen by Local, State and Federal Officials*, A-5 (Washington, D.C., 1977), 11–12.

44. Fax communication from Henry Wulf, Governments Division, U.S. Census Bureau (Suitland, Md., 24 February 1993).

45. ACIR, *Characteristics of Federal Grant-in-Aid Programs to State and Local Governments*, 1994, 8.

46. See ibid., 6.

47. General Accounting Office, *Block Grants, Increases in Set-Asides and Cost Ceilings since 1982*, GAO/HRD-92-58FS (Washington, D.C., July 1992), 2–3.

48. Ibid., 10–18.

49. See ACIR, "Summary and Concluding Observations," *The Intergovernmental Grant System: An Assessment and Proposed Policies*, A-62 (Washington, D.C., June 1978), 8–12.

50. General Accounting Office, *Grant Programs: Design Features Shape Flexibility, Accountability, and Performance Information*, GAO-GGD-98-137 (Washington, D.C., June 1998), 14–22.

51. Paul L. Posner and Margaret T. Wrightson, "Block Grants: A Perennial, but Unstable Tool of Government," *Publius* 26, no. 3 (Summer 1996): 92.

52. See Carl W. Stenberg, "Recent Trends in State Spending: Patterns, Problems, and Prospects," *Publius* 24, no. 3 (Summer 1994): 136.

53. ACIR, *Regulatory Federalism: Policy, Process, Impact and Reform*, A-95 (Washington, D.C., February 1984), 7–11.

54. See David B. Walker, "Modernized Grants Management: Little Noticed, but Greatly Needed," *Assistance Management Journal* 7 (Fall 1992): 13.

55. Timothy J. Conlan, James D. Riggle, and Donna E. Schwartz, "Deregulating Federalism? The Politics of Mandate Reform in the 104th Congress," *Publius* 25, no. 3 (Summer 1995): 25–26.

56. Ibid., 27.

57. Paul L. Posner, "Unfunded Mandates Reform Act of 1996 and Beyond," *Publius* 27, no. 2 (Summer 1997): 53.

58. Ibid., 71.

59. Ibid.

60. Sophie Dale, "Federal Grants to State and Local Governments, FY 1975: A Quarter Century Review," *Social Security Bulletin,* September 1976, 30–31.

61. Ibid., 30.

62. Adapted from ACIR, *Revenues and Expenditures*, 1992, 64–65.

63. See Tom W. Rice and Alexander F. Sumberg, "Civic Culture and Government Performance in the American States," *Publius* 27, no. 1 (Winter 1997): 99–114, and Daniel J. Elazar, *The American Mosaic* (Boulder, Colo.: Westview, 1994).

64. G. Ross Stephens, University of Missouri–Kansas City, private communication, 30 January 1995.

65. ACIR, *Characteristics of Federal Grant-in-Aid Programs to State and Local Governments*, 1994, 24–41.

66. See David B. Walker, *Toward a Functioning Federalism* (Cambridge, Mass.: Winthrop, 1981), 12.

67. See Congress, Joint Economic Committee, Subcommittee on Fiscal and Intergovernmental Policy, *Trends in the Fiscal Conditions of Cities: 1978–1980* (Washington, D.C.: Government Printing Office, 20 April 1980), 19–20.

68. See National League of Cities, *City Distress, Metropolitan Disparities and Economic Growth,* combined rev. ed. (Washington, D.C., September 1992), 6–7; ACIR, *Revenues and Expenditures,* 1992, 176.

69. See National League of Cities, *City Distress, Metropolitan Disparities and Economic Growth,* 1–7, and appendix tables.

70. Ibid., 13–19.

71. See Robert D. Reischauer, "Light at the End of the Tunnel or Another Illusion? The 1997 Budget Deal," *National Tax Journal* 51, no. 1 (March 1998): 143–66.

72. See Paul E. Peterson, *The Price of Federalism* (Washington, D.C.: Brookings Institution, 1995); Edward M. Gramlich, "A Policymaker's Guide to Fiscal Decentralization," *National Tax Journal* 46, no. 2 (1993): 229–35; Richard M. Bird, "Threading the Fiscal Labyrinth: Some Issues in Fiscal Decentralization," *National Tax Journal* 46, no. 2 (1993): 207–27.

73. National Association of State Budget Officers and the National Governors' Association, *The Fiscal Survey of the States* (Washington, D.C., May 1998), 8.

## Chapter 9: A Resurgent Role for the States?

1. The following analysis of the state-local linkage is an adapted and updated version of David B. Walker, "The State-Local Connection: Perennial, Paramount, Resurgent," *National Civic Review* 73, no. 2 (February 1984): 53–62.

2. See ACIR, *A Question of State Government Capability,* A-98 (Washington, D.C., January 1985).

3. *The Book of the States, 1992–1993* (Lexington, Ky.: Council of State Governments, 1992), 20.

4. Rick Jones, "The State Legislatures," in ibid., 129.

5. *Book of the States,* 64–65.

6. Ibid., 114.

7. Ibid., 112.

8. Ibid., 49–50, table 2.4, "The Governors: Powers."

9. Ibid.

10. James K. Conant, "Executive Branch Reorganization in the States, 1965–1991," in ibid., 64.

11. Ibid., table 4.3, "Qualifications of States Appellate Courts and General Trial Courts."

12. Ibid., 236–43, table 4.5, "Methods for Removal of Judges and Filling of Vacancies."

13. See George A. Bell, "State Administrative Organization Activities, 1972–73," in *The Book of the States, 1972–1973* (Lexington, Ky.: Council of State Governments, 1972), 139; James L. Garnett, *Reorganizing State Government: The Executive Branch* (Boulder, Colo.: Westview, 1980), 12.

14. See Mavis M. Reeves, "State Activism as a Balance in Preserving Federalism," *Journal of State Government* 62 (January–February 1989): 20–24.

15. Samuel H. Beer, "The Modernization of American Federalism," *Publius* 3 (Fall 1973): 81.

16. Advisory Commission of Intergovernmental Relations, *The Changing Public Sector: Shifts in Governmental Spending and Employment* M-178 (Washington, D.C., December 1991), 26.

17. All figures in this and the four succeeding paragraphs are from ACIR, *The Changing Public Sector: Shifts in Governmental Spending and Employment*, M-178 (Washington, D.C., December 1991), 28–73.

18. All figures in this and the two succeeding paragraphs are from G. Ross Stephens, "Patterns of State Centralization/Decentralization during the Last Half of the Twentieth Century," paper presented at the annual meeting of the Southwestern Social Sciences Association, Austin, 18–21 March 1992, 11–19.

19. Jeffrey M. Stonecash, "Fiscal Centralization in the American States: Increasing Similarity and Persisting Diversity," *Publius* 13 (Fall 1983): 127–37.

20. See Jeffrey M. Stonecash, "Centralization in State-Local Fiscal Relationships," *Western Political Quarterly* 34 (June 1981): 301–9.

21. Rodney E. Hero and Jody L. Fitzpatrick, "State Mandating of Local Government Activities: An Exploration," paper presented at the annual meeting of the American Political Science Association, Washington, D.C., 28 August–1 September 1986, 2.

22. Catherine Lovell et al., "Federal and State Mandating to Local Government: Impact and Issues," draft, University of California at Riverside, 1979, 68–76.

23. ACIR, *State Mandating of Local Expenditures*, A-67 (Washington, D.C., 1978), 40–43.

24. ACIR, *State and Local Roles in the Federal System*, A-88 (Washington, D.C., April 1982), 162–66.

25. Hero and Fitzpatrick, "State Mandating of Local Government Activities," 12.

26. ACIR, *Mandates: Cases in State-Local Relations*, M-173 (Washington, D.C., September 1990), 3.

27. Ibid., 2.

28. Connecticut ACIR, *Cost Estimates for Selected State Mandates on Municipalities in Connecticut* (Hartford, Conn.: February 1995), 1.

29. Ibid., 3; Deil S. Wright, *Understanding Intergovernmental Relations*, 3d ed. (Pacific Grove, Calif.: Brooks/Cole, 1988), 315; *The Book of the States*, 1992–93, 103.

30. Janet Kelly, *State Mandates: Fiscal Notes, Reimbursement and Anti-Mandate Strategies* (Washington, D.C.: National League of Cities, February 1992), 59.

31. Wright, *Understanding Intergovernmental Relations*, 316.

32. David R. Berman, "State-Local Relations: Authority, Finance, and Regional Cooperation," *The Municipal Year Book, 1998*, vol. 65 (Washington, D.C.,: International City/County Management Association, 1998), 64.

33. Tod Newcombe, "Solutions for State and Local Governments in the Information Age — Can Governments Get Along?" *Government Technology* 10, no. 1 (January 1997): 50.

34. Ibid.

35. National Association of State Information Resource Executives, *Welfare and State Human Service Information Systems* (Lexington, Ky., 13 July 1998), 1.

36. Saundra K. Schneider, "Medicaid Section 1115 Waivers: Shifting Health Care Reform to the States," *Publius* 27, no. 2 (Spring 1997): 99.

37. Thomas J. Anton and Richard M. Francis, "Welfare Reform: Lessons from New England," paper presented at the annual meeting of the New England Political Science Association, Worcester, Mass., 1 May 1998, 4, 5.

38. Ibid., 14, 15.

39. "EPA Finds States Ignore Clean-Air, Water Rules," *Chicago Tribune*, 7 June 1998, 14.

40. Ibid.

41. Jeanne Walker and David Walker, "Rationalizing Local Government Powers, Functions and Structure," *States' Responsibilities to Local Governments: An Action Agenda* (Washington, D.C.: National Governors' Conference, October 1975), 39.

42. Vincent L. Marando and Mavis Mann Reeves, "State Reform and Local Discretion: A Preliminary Examination," in *Public Policy across States and Communities,* ed. Dennis R. Judd (Greenwich, Conn.: JAI Press, 1985), 33–48. See also Marando and Reeves, "State Responsiveness and Local Government Organization," *Social Science Quarterly* 69 (December 1988): 996–1004.

43. See Michael Libonati, "State Law Foundations of Local Self-Government: Constitutional, Statutory, and Judicial Issues," ACIR unpublished paper (Washington, D.C., 1991), 172.

44. See Walker and Walker, "Rationalizing Local Government Powers, Functions and Structure," 40.

45. For much of the following, see, with updates, David B. Walker, "Snow White and the 17 Dwarfs: From Metropolitan Cooperation to Governance," *National Civic Review* 76 (January–February 1987): 14–28.

46. William R. Barnes and Larry C. Ledebuhr, "Local Economies: The US Common Market of Local Economic Regions," *The Regionalist* 1, no. 2 (Spring 1995): 8–10.

47. John J. Kirlin, "The Potential to Reframe Regional Policies and Institutions in Ways That Improve Governance and Address Disadvantage," *The Regionalist* 1, no. 1 (Winter 1995): 55–57; Allan D. Wallis, "Regions in Action: Crafting Regional Governance under the Challenge of Global Competitiveness," *National Civic Review* 85, no. 2 (Spring-Summer 1996): 15–16.

48. See Larry N. Gerston and Peter J. Haas, "Political Support for Regional Government in the 1990's: Growing in the Suburbs," *The Regionalist* 1, no. 1 (Winter 1995): 65–73; Allan D. Wallis, "The Third Wave: Current Trends in Regional Governance," *National Civic Review* 83, no. 3 (Summer–Fall 1994): 290–91.

49. David Rusk, "Growth Management: Regionalism's Core Issue," *The Regionalist* 2, no. 4, special issue: Initiatives for America's Regions (Winter 1997): 18–20.

50. Lori Henderson, "Intergovernmental Service Agreements and the Transfer of Functions," *Municipal Year Book, 1985* (Washington, D.C.: International City Management Association, 1986), 194–202.

51. Connecticut ACIR, *Local Government Cooperative Ventures in Connecticut* (Hartford, February 1995).

52. See *Baseline Data Report* (International City Management Association) 21 (November–December 1989).

53. H. George Frederickson, "Beyond the City: Finding Metropolitan Governance in America," paper presented at the spring meeting of the National Academy of Public Administration, Duke University, June 1997, 4.

54. Ibid.

55. J. Eugene Grigsby III, "Regional Governance and Regional Councils," *National Civic Review* 85, no. 2 (Spring–Summer 1996): 55.

56. Bruce D. McDowell, "Regions under Reagan," paper presented at the National Planning Conference, American Planning Association, Minneapolis–St. Paul, 8 May 1984.

57. Patricia E. Salkin, "Consolidation of Services," *The Regionalist* 1, no. 2 (Spring 1995): 35.

58. See Robert W. Gage and Bruce D. McDowell, "ISTEA and the Role of MPO's in the New Transportation Environment: A Midterm Assessment," *Publius* 25, no. 3 (Summer 1995): 133–54.

59. "TEA-21 More Than a Free Refill," *Progress — Surface Transportation Policy Project* 8, no. 4 (June 1998): 1–9.

60. See ACIR, *Report on Regional Councils* (Washington, D.C., forthcoming), table A-2.

61. Mayor Stephen Goldsmith, *The Twenty-first Century City — Resurrecting Urban America* (Washington, D.C.: Regnery Publishing, 1997), 1–74.

62. See Blake R. Jeffery, Tanis J. Salant, and Alan I. Boroshok, *County Government Structure, a State by State Report* (Washington, D.C.: National Association of Counties, 1 July 1989), 8–14.

63. Bureau of the Census, *Government Organization*, vol. 1, GC87 (1)-I (Washington, D.C.: Government Printing Office, September 1988), vi–xii, xiv, and figures xxi–xxiv.

64. Katherine Barrett and Richard Greene, "Grading the States," *Governing*, February 1999, 17–90.

## Chapter 10: A New Political System?

1. Paul Allen Beck, *Party Politics in America*, 8th ed. (New York: Longman, 1997), 73–75.

2. Gary D. Wekkin, "The New Federal Party Organizations: Intergovernmental Consequences of Party Renewal," paper presented at the annual meeting of the American Political Science Association, Washington, D.C., 29 August–1 September 1985, 26–27.

3. See ACIR, *The Transformation in American Politics: Implications for Federalism*, A-106 (Washington, D.C., 1986), 73–81; Wekkin, "The New Federal Party Organizations," 26.

4. See Stephen Earl Bennett, "Changes in the Public's Perceptions of Governmental Responsiveness, 1964–1980," paper presented at the annual meeting of the Midwestern Political Science Association, Milwaukee, 1982, 32.

5. William Crotty, *Party Reform* (New York: Longman, 1983), 50–51.

6. *Cousins v. Wigoda*, 95 S.Ct. 541 (1975).

7. ACIR, *The Transformation in American Politics*, B-9R (Washington, D.C., October 1987), 46–47.

8. Beck, *Party Politics in America*, 85.

9. Harold W. Stanley and Richard G. Niemi, *Vital Statistics on American Politics, 1997–1998* (Washington, D.C., CQ Press, 1998), 108.

10. Ibid.

11. Stephen J. Wayne, *The Road to the White House — 1996* (New York: St. Martin's, 1997), 70–75.

12. Stanley and Niemi, *Vital Statistics on American Politics, 1997–1998*, 179.

13. See ibid., 183–87.

14. Martin P. Wattenberg, *The Decline of American Political Parties* (Cambridge, Mass.: Harvard University Press, 1997) 91.

15. ACIR, *The Transformation in American Politics*, B-9R, 40.

16. ACIR, *The Transformation in American Politics*, A-106, 228.

17. Mark P. Petracca, "The Rediscovery of Interest Group Politics," in *The Politics of Interests*, ed. Mark Petracca (Boulder, Colo.: Westview, 1992), 15.

18. Allan Shuldiner and Tony Raymond, "Who's in the Lobby?" Center for Responsive Politics, http://www.crp.org/pubs/lobby/lobbyindex.htm.

19. Petracca, "The Rediscovery of Interest Group Politics," 14.

20. See ACIR, *The Transformation in American Politics*, A-106, 227.

21. Shuldiner and Raymond, "Who's in the Lobby?"

22. See Howard C. Reiter, *Parties and Elections in Corporate America* (New York: St. Martin's, 1987), 203.

23. This and the two succeeding paragraphs are based on Paul E. Peterson, "The Rise and Fall of Special Interest Politics," in *The Politics of Interests*, ed. Mark Petracca (Boulder, Colo.: Westview, 1992), 327.

24. Ibid., 331.

25. Ibid., 337–38.

26. Ibid., 336.

27. Ibid., 340–41.

28. See James Gibson, Cornelius Palter, John Bibby, and Robert Huckshorn, "Assessing Party Organizational Strength," *American Journal of Political Science* 27 (May 1983): 194–205.

29. ACIR, *The Transformation in American Politics*, A-106, 115.

30. See Larry Sabato, *The Party's Just Begun: Shaping Political Parties for America's Future* (Glenview, Ill.: Scott, Foresman, 1988), 93.

31. ACIR, *The Transformation in American Politics*, A-106, 123.

32. Petracca, "The Rediscovery of Interest Group Politics," 17.

33. Kenneth G. Hunter, Laura Ann Wilcox, and Gregory G. Brunk, "Societal Complexity and Interest Group Lobbying in the American States," *Journal of Politics* 53 (May 1991): 500.

34. Clive S. Thomas and Ronald J. Hrebenar, "Changing Patterns of Interest Group Activity: A Regional Perspective," in *The Politics of Interests*, ed. Mark Petracca (Boulder, Colo.: Westview, 1992), 155, 163.

35. Ibid., 151–52.

36. Ibid., 170–72.

37. Ibid., 172. The states included in each category, discussed below, are these: "dominant": Alaska, Alabama, Florida, Louisiana, Mississippi, New Mexico, South Carolina, Tennessee, and West Virginia; "complementary": Colorado, Illinois, Indiana, Iowa, Kansas, Maine, Maryland, Massachusetts, Michigan, Missouri, New Hampshire, New Jersey, New York, North Dakota, Pennsylvania, South Dakota, Wisconsin; "subordinate": none; "dominant-complementary": Arizona, Arkansas, California, Georgia, Hawaii, Idaho, Kentucky, Montana, Nebraska, Nevada, North Carolina, Ohio, Oklahoma, Oregon, Texas, Utah, Virginia, Washington, Wyoming; "complementary-subordinate": Connecticut, Delaware, Minnesota, Rhode Island, Vermont.

38. See ACIR, *The Transformation in American Politics*, A-106, 129–40.

39. Elizabeth T. Smith, "The Supreme Court and the Spoils System: Political Patronage in the Aftermath of the *Rutan* Case," doctoral dissertation, Department of Political Science, University of Connecticut, Storrs, August 1998.

40. See Reiter, *Parties and Elections in Corporate America*, 283–86.

41. Wekkin, "The New Federal Party Organizations," 24.

42. Ibid.; Deil S. Wright, *Understanding Intergovernmental Relations*, 3d ed. (Pacific Grove, Calif.: Brooks/Cole, 1988), 39–40.

43. Wekkin, "The New Federal Party Organizations"; Wright, *Understanding Intergovernmental Relations*, 43–48.

44. Sabato, *The Party's Just Begun*, 20–21.

45. See Haynes Johnson and David S. Broder, *The System: The American Way of Politics at the Breaking Point* (Boston: Little, Brown, 1996).

46. Philip John Davies, "Political Parties Celebrating the Millennium," in *Political Issues in America Today*, ed. Philip John Davies and Fredrick A. Waldstein (Manchester, U.K.: Manchester University Press, 1996), 96–109.

47. John H. Aldrich and David W. Rohde, "The Transition in Republican Rule in the House: Implications for Theories of Congressional Parties," *Political Science Quarterly* 4 (1997–98): 541–67.

48. John Dinan, "State Government Influence in the National Policy Process: Lessons from the 104th Congress," *Publius* 27, no. 2 (Spring 1997): 138–41.

## Chapter 11: What of the Future?

1. See ACIR, *Federal Regulation of State and Local Governments: The Mixed Record of the 1980s*, A-126 (Washington, D.C., 1993), 41–57.

2. ACIR, *Federal Statutory Preemption of State and Local Authority: History, Inventory, and Issues*, A-121 (Washington, D.C., September 1992), 7–9; Joseph Zimmerman, *Federal Preemption: The Silent Revolution* (Ames: Iowa State University Press, 1991).

3. See Steve D. Gold, "Passing the Buck," *State Legislatures* (January 1993): 36–38.

4. See Morton Grodzins, *The American System*, ed. Daniel J. Elazar (Chicago: Rand McNally, 1966), 254–89.

5. Leonard D. White, *Introduction to the Study of Public Administration*, 4th ed. (New York: Macmillan, 1954), 151–52.

6. See Jonathan Rauch, "Demosclerosis," *National Journal*, 5 September 1992, 1998–2003.

7. Michael D. Reagan and John G. Sanzone, *The New Federalism*, 2d ed. (New York: Oxford University Press, 1981), 175.

8. Ibid., 157.

9. Richard Morin, "In State Government We Trust," *Washington Post National Weekly Edition*, 3 February 1997, 35.

10. Richard Morin, "Less Than Meets the Eye," *Washington Post National Weekly Edition*, 16 March 1998, 35.

11. David S. Broder, "White House to Rewrite Federalism Order, Now with State-Local Input," *Washington Post*, 29 May 1998; "President Clinton's Executive Order on Federalism," *The Federalism Report* (Center for the Study of Federalism, Temple University) 22, no. 3 (Spring 1998): 5–7.

12. "President Clinton's Executive Order on Federalism," 8.

13. See David B. Walker, "Federalism in the 1990's," in *Political Issues in America — The 1990's*, ed. Philip John Davies and Fredrick H. Waldstein (Manchester, U.K.: Manchester University Press, 1991), 127–31.

14. Martha M. Hamilton, "States Assuming New Powers as Federal Policy Role Ebbs," *Washington Post*, 30 August 1988; Morton Keller, "State Power Needn't Be Revived Because It Never Died," *Governing* 2 (October 1988): 53–57.

15. John Shannon, "Fend-for-Yourself (New) Federalism," in *Perspectives on Federalism*, ed. Harry N. Scheiber (Berkeley: Institute of Government Studies, University of California, 1987), 32–33.

16. *Idaho et al. v. Coeur d'Alene Tribe of Idaho*, 117 S.C. 2058 (1997).

17. 117 S.Ct. 882 (1997), and 117 S.Ct. 1416 (1997).

18. John Shannon, "Competitive Federalism — Three Driving Forces," *Intergovernmental Perspective* (ACIR) 15 (Fall 1989): 18.

19. Thomas R. Dye, *American Federalism* (Lexington, Mass.: Lexington Books, 1990), 193–97.

20. Alice Rivlin, *Reviving the American Dream* (Washington, D.C.: Brookings Institution, 1992), 118–22.

21. Paul A. Peterson, Barry E. Rabe, and Kenneth E. Wong, *When Federalism Works* (Washington, D.C.: Brookings Institution, 1986), 15–21.

22. See George Eads and Michael Fox, *Reagan's Regulatory Dilemma: Relief or Reform?* (Washington, D.C.: Urban Institute Press, 1984), 207–34.

23. 111 S.Ct. 2395 (1991).

24. See David B. Walker, *Toward a Functioning Federalism* (Cambridge, Mass.: Winthrop, 1981), 251–55.

25. Samuel H. Beer, "Political Overload and Federalism," paper presented at the annual meeting of the Northeastern Political Science Association, 12 November 1976.

26. David Hoshansky, "GOP Expands Federal Authority," *Congressional Quarterly,* 2 November 1996, 3117–19.

27. Bert Waisanen, "States Keep Watch on the Hill," *State Government News,* January–February 1998, 22–23.

28. Lavarr Webb, "The Tiger vs. the Rabbit," *State Government News,* March 1998, 26, 35.

29. See Tod Newcombe, "Big Project Woes Halt Child Support System," *Government Technology,* February 1998, 34, 35, 61.

30. Larry Singer, "States Need Federal Partner," *Government Technology,* http://govt-tech.govtech.net:80/gtmag/1998/april/welfare/welfare.shtm.

31. See Laura S. Jensen, "Federalism, Individual Rights, and the Continued Threat of Conditional Federal Spending," paper presented at the annual meeting of the New England Political Science Association, Worcester, Mass., 1–2 May 1998.

32. 479 U.S. 208 (1986).

33. ACIR, *The Transformation in American Politics: Implications for Federalism,* B-9R (Washington, D.C., October 1987), 61–62.

34. Ibid., 62–63.

35. Edward L. Marcus, "Parties Protect against Special Interests," *Hartford Courant,* 25 April 1993, C-1.

36. *Buckley v. Valeo,* 424 U.S. 1 (1976).

37. Kenneth T. Palmer and Edward B. Laverty, "The States in the Supreme Court: The Politics of Amicus Curiae Briefs," paper presented at the annual meeting of the American Political Science Association, Boston, 3 September 1998.

38. Cindi Skrzycki, "Deregulation by Default," *Washington Post National Weekly Edition,* 4–10 March 1996, 6–7.

39. Office of Management and Budget, Analytical Systems Division, *The Number of Federal Grant Programs to State and Local Governments* (Washington, D.C., October 1997), 3.

40. Timothy Conlan, *New Federalism: Intergovernmental Reform from Nixon to Reagan* (Washington, D.C.: Brookings Institution, 1988), 179–88.

41. Rivlin, *Reviving the American Dream,* 116–22.

42. Ibid.

43. Haynes Johnson and David S. Broder, *The System* (Boston: Little, Brown, 1996), 630.

# Index

abortion, 191–92, 199–200
Adams, John, 41, 42, 46, 57
Adams, John Quincy, 69
Adams, Sam, 41
administrative federalism, 25
administrators, 136–40
Advisory Commission on Intergovernmental
  Relations (ACIR), 103, 137–39, 351
A-80 process. *See* Circular A-80
A-85 process. *See* Circular A-85
affirmative action, 165, 180
Age Discrimination in Employment Act
  (ADEA), 187, 200, 330
Agency for the Aged, 11
Agricultural Adjustment Act, 108
aid. *See* grants and grants-in-aid
Aid to Families with Dependent Children
  (AFDC): effects on states with different
  income levels, 250; level of, in 1960,
  99; mandates and, 248; the Personal
  Responsibility and Work Opportunity
  Reconciliation Act and, 163; Reagan and,
  150; the states' role regarding, xiv
Aldrich, John A., 315–16
aliens, legal, 165
Amendment 2 (Colorado's 1992 constitutional
  amendment), 208
Americans with Disabilities Act, 153, 247
AmeriCorps, 167
A-95 process. *See* Circular A-95
annexation, 292
anti-Federalists, 22
antinationalists, 47–48, 49, 55
Anti-Recession Fiscal Assistance Program, 129
antitrust proceedings, 81, 184
Anton, Thomas J., 279
Appleby, Paul H., 118
apportionment, 47
Architectural Barriers Act of 1968, 125
Armey, Dick, 258
Articles of Confederation, 39–40, 43–45, 46
Atomic Energy Commission, 104
*Austin* v. *Michigan Chamber of Commerce*, 197

*Baker* v. *Carr*, 205, 206, 262, 332
balanced budgets, 135, 169
bamboo-fence federalism, 25, 136–40
Bank of the United States, 69
Beer, Samuel H., 27, 33, 84, 309, 334
Beschloss, Michael R., 263
Big Swap, the, 8, 149, 150, 151, 351

Bill of Rights: the Burger Court on, 179,
  184, 186, 188, 207; Hugo Black on, 93; as
  restricting national authority, 66; the Warren
  Court on, 176–77, 178
Bird, Richard M., 257
Black, Hugo, xiii, 93, 175, 178, 179
Blackmun, Harry, 179, 182, 187, 199, 200, 210
Bliss, Ray, 303
block grants: Clinton and, 157; conditions on,
  9–10, 245; congressional federalism and,
  130; defined, 366n.7; proportion of, vis-à-vis
  other types of grants, 237–40, 241; Reagan
  and, 9, 144, 147, 148–49; types of, 241–44.
  *See also* grants and grants-in-aid
bonds, 11
bossism, 14, 301
Boston Tea Party, 40
*Boulder* case, 183
Brady bill, 158, 160, 201, 330, 332
Brandeis, Louis D., 123
Brennan, William, 182
Breyer, Stephen G., 176, 193, 325
*Briscoe* v. *Bank of the Commonwealth of Kentucky*,
  67
Broder, David, 198, 353
Brown, Ron, 312
Brownlow committee, 118
*Brown* v. *Board of Education*, 93, 117, 178
Bryan, William Jennings, 76, 83
Buck, A.E., 266
*Buckley* v. *Valeo*, 345
Budget and Impoundment Act, 129
bureaucracy: attacks on, 137–40; Carter's
  reforms of, 133–34; congressional federalism
  and, 129; early federal, 67–68; federal,
  between 1930 and 1960, 109; the new
  politics and, 324. *See also* bureaucratic
  federalism; civil service
bureaucratic federalism, 25
Burford, Gorsuch, 147
Burger Court: activism and, 179; as balancing
  institutional needs and individual rights,
  208–9; centralization and, 14; emphasis on
  governmental and societal rights, 176; liberal
  assessment of, 207–8; national authority and,
  26; neoconservative critique of, 206; from
  1978 to 1986, 182–88; from 1971 to 1978,
  179–82; orthodox conservative assessment
  of, 207; overall assessment of, 188–89; state
  autonomy and, 175–76
Burke, Edmund, 45

Burns, James MacGregor, 118
*Burson v. Freeman*, 198
Bush, George: assessment of the record of,
    151–56; the condition of federalism under,
    121; and federal aid to states, 3; grants and,
    8, 226; intergovernmental relations and, 10;
    Reagan and, 123; role in the evolution of the
    present system, 1, 2; state parties and, 312;
    and states' challenging of changes in federal
    aid, 8
busing, 180

cable news, 305
*California Division of Labor Standards v.
    Dillingham*, 193
campaign financing, 31, 170, 306–7, 345, 353
Carroll, James D., 142
Carter, Jimmy: congressional federalism and,
    129; the New Partnership of, 122, 133–36;
    Reagan and, 141; role in the evolution of the
    present system, 2; the states and, 263
categorical grants: Clinton and, 157; conditions
    on, 245; under Nixon and Ford, 130; patterns
    in federal, since 1960, 234–37; proportion
    of, vis-à-vis other types of grants, 237–39,
    240–41; Reagan and, 144, 147; reasons for
    popularity of, 9
centralization: Congress and, 27; current state
    of, 171; LBJ and, 300; overview of, since
    the 1960s, 1–2; political parties and, 14–15;
    Reagan and, 151; Roosevelt and, 111–12;
    of states, 271–74; the Supreme Court and,
    13–14, 325; theories about modernization
    and, 33
Chambers, William N., 111
*Charles River Bridge* case, 67
Chase, Salmon P., 74
checks and balances, 56
Chicago Democratic Convention (1968), 115,
    301
Child Care Act, 155
*Chisholm v. Georgia*, 66
circuit-breaker approach to property taxes, 220
Circular A-74, 126
Circular A-80, 128
Circular A-85, 125–26, 128
Circular A-87, 126
Circular A-95, 139, 289
Circular A-102, 127
cities: Carter and aid to, 135–36; current
    trends of, 284–86; direct federal aid to,
    253; disparities between their suburbs and,
    253–55; grants and, 236–37, 255; home rule
    and, 282; regionalism and, 288–97; servicing
    roles of, 270; state aid to, 229, 231, 232
*City of Boerne, Texas v. Flores*, 197, 205, 330
*City of Lafayette v. Louisiana Power and Light Co.*,
    183
Civil Aeronautics Authority, 104

civil rights: the Democratic party and, 114–15;
    political effects of legislation on, 263; the
    Supreme Court and, 75, 93, 180, 195–99
Civil Rights Acts, 113, 117, 125, 155, 196
Civil Rights Commission, 114
Civil Rights Restoration Act, 153
civil service: attacks on administrators of,
    137–40; Carter's reforms of, 134; Eisenhower
    and, 119; number of employees in, in 1927,
    362n.53; Reagan and, 145–46
Civil War, the, 74–75
Civil Works Administration, 106
Clark, Joe, 116
*Clarke v. the United States*, 191, 203 329, 330
Clay, Henry, 26, 72
Clean Air Act, 371n.37
Clean Air Act Amendments, 8, 152–53, 155,
    162, 332, 349
Clean Water bill, 336
Cleveland, Grover, 26, 83
Clinton, Bill: attention to state and local
    influence, xv, 327–28; the condition of
    federalism under, 121, 168–71; and federal
    aid to states, 3; federal grants and, 9; first two
    years of the presidency of, 156–60; health
    care reform and, 314, 315; polarization and,
    304; Reagan and, 8, 123; record since 1994,
    160–68; role in the evolution of the present
    system, 1, 2; on Social Security, 258
Clinton, Hillary Rodham, 158–59
coercion, 48–50
*Coleman v. Thompson*, 196
colonies, the: nationalism's rise in, 41–42;
    strength of local government in, 40
commerce clause, 185
commerce power, 14, 26; the Brady bill and,
    330; the Burger Court and, 187, 188,
    189; Creative Federalism and, 125; direct
    orders and, 247; Hoover and, 91; the Labor
    Relations Act and, 92; regulatory actions
    and, 131, 184; the Rehnquist Court and,
    202, 203, 204, 205
Commission on Intergovernmental Relations
    (Kestnbaum Commission), 102
Committee on Administrative Management,
    118
Committee on Detail, 50, 52, 54
*Common Sense* (Paine), 42
Commonwealth of Nations, 41
Communications Act of 1934, 344
Community Development Block Grant Act
    (CDBG), 3, 127, 130, 236, 237, 239
Community Youth Service, 239
compartmentalized federalism, 23
competitive federalism, 330–31
Comprehensive Employment and Training Act
    (CETA), 3, 127, 129, 130, 236, 237, 253
computers, 277–78
concert-of-interests approach, 108, 109

"concurrent powers," 67
conditionalism, 9–10
confederation, 43–45
conflicted federalism, 156
Congress: the Articles of Confederation on the powers of, 43–45; Clinton and, 160–68; the Constitutional Convention on, 46, 47–48, 49; and the current condition of federalism, 168–71; and the current condition of intergovernmental relations, 156–60; governors' lack of effect on the 104th, 15; and the history of federalism, 26–27; increased party cohesion in, 315–16; Reagan and, 150–51; recent centralization and, 27; relations with presidents from 1930 to 1960, 113–15; the Supreme Court's centralizing positions and, 14. *See also* congressional federalism
congressional federalism, 26; overview of, 128–33; as a subspecies of cooperative federalism, 122
Conkling, Roscoe, 85
Connecticut Compromise, the, 47–48
conservation, 105. *See also* environmental issues and regulations
Conservative Coalition in Congress, 109, 113–14, 115, 120, 346
consolidation, 294
Constitution, the: the Civil War and, 74; the Constitutional Convention on the courts and, 49; linkages between the Articles of Confederation and, 45; nineteenth-century interpretations of, 22; the Marshall Court and, 66; orthodox conservative suggestions regarding, 207. *See also* Constitutional Convention, the; Framers, the
Constitutional Convention, the: contested decisions of, 47–51, 53–54; key issues faced by, 45–47; principal features of the system envisioned by, 54–64; uncontested decisions of, 52–53
*Constitutions Construed and Constitutions Vindicated* (Taylor), 22
contract clause, the, 66
contracting, 291
Contract with America, 15, 157, 160–61, 162, 248, 315–16
conventions, political, 72, 301–2
cooperative federalism: beginnings of, 69–70; collaborative theories of federalism and, 23–24; current interpretations emphasizing, 331; from 1960 to 1980, 121–22; postulates of, 89–90
co-optive federalism, 331–32
corporations, 76, 306
Corwin, Edwin S., 65, 67
Council of State Governments' Federalism Index, 346
Council on Competitiveness, 154

Councils of Government, 289, 290
counties: increase in direct federal grants to, 236–37; mergers with cities, 294; reformed urban, 293; servicing roles of, 270, 271; state aid to, 229, 232
Cox, Archibald, 176, 208
Creative Federalism: elements of, 23–24; grants and, 3; New Federalism and, 128; overview of, 123–26; program areas it encompassed, 234; as a subspecies of cooperative federalism, 122
crime, 154, 159–60
criminal justice, 166
Croly, Herbert, 123
crosscutting conditions, 246–47

Daley, Richard J., 303
Davie, William Richardson, 53
dead-beat dads, 164
debt, the federal, 152, 215
decentralization: the Conservative Coalition and, 120; New Federalism and, 126–27; and tensions in the present system, 1–2
Declaration of Independence, 42–43
deficit, the: Bush and, 152; Carter and, 135; disappearance of, 256–59; effects on state and local governments, 255–56; the evolution of the present governmental system and, 1–2; intergovernmental relations and, 30; Reagan and, 143; statistics on, 215
deficit-driven federalism, 30, 153
Deficit Reduction Act (DEFRA-1984), 12
deficit spending, 215
Democratic National Committee, 72, 303–4
Democratic party: centralization of, since the 1960s, 301–2; current state of, 314–15; decline in allegiance to, 304–5; early years of, 71–73, 83, 86; between 1930 and 1960, 111–15, 117; political federalism and, 31; at the state and local levels, 311–13
*Dennis v. Higgins*, 194
Department of Agriculture, 105, 106
Department of Defense, 143, 151
Department of Health and Human Services, 323
Department of Housing and Community Development, 157
Department of Housing and Urban Development, 126
Department of Transportation, 126
deregulation, 147–48, 150
desegregation, 180, 192
Developmentally Disabled Assistance and Bill of Rights Act (1975), 184
developmental theories of federalism, 32–34
devolution: Clinton and, 167; current state of, 171; New Federalism and, 127; the 104th Congress and, 161, 162–63, 166
Dewey, Thomas E., 115

Diamond, Martin, 55, 59, 60, 61
Dickinson, John, 40, 43, 47, 57, 61
Dillon's Rule, 281
Dilworth, Richardson, 116
direct orders, 131, 246, 247, 275, 323, 332, 337
*Disunited States* (Donahue), 27
Dix, Dorothea, 68
Dixiecrats, 114–15
Dole, Bob, 159, 161, 162
*Dole v. United Steelworkers of America,* 155
*Dombrowski* case, 180
dominion theory of empire, 41, 42, 43, 46
Donahue, John D., 27–28
Doolittle, Fred C., 33
dormant commerce clause, 185–86, 189, 204
Douglas, William O., 178, 179
dual-centered federalism, 34
dual federalism: from 1861 to 1930, 73–87;
    the Framers and, 44; history of theories
    of, 22–23; from 1789 to 1860, 65–73; the
    Supreme Court's crushing of the old, 90–94
due process, 75–76
Dye, Thomas, 331

Earned Income Tax Credit, 258
*E.C. Knight* case, 91
Economic Recovery Tax Act (ERTA), 29, 143
education: federal aid for, in the 1950s, 106;
    grants to, early in the twentieth century, 79;
    proportion of federal grants devoted to, 245;
    state aid for, 227–28, 230, 231
Education for the Handicapped Act, 153
Eighth Amendment, 194
Eisenhower, Dwight, 99, 109, 114, 115, 116,
    119
Elazar, Daniel J., 62, 63, 89–90, 120, 251,
    324
elections, 47–50, 85
electoral college, the, 50–51
Elementary and Secondary Education Act and
    Amendments, 130, 237
Eleventh Amendment, 66, 202, 205, 209, 330
Ellsworth, Oliver, 48, 343
Employee Retirement Income Security Act
    (ERISA), 193, 194
Endangered Species Act, 165
*English v. General Electric Co.,* 193
entitlements, 69
environmental issues and regulations, 162,
    263, 280–81. *See also* conservation;
    Environmental Protection Agency
Environmental Protection Agency, 155, 248,
    280, 371n.37
*Equal Employment Opportunity Commission* v.
    *Wyoming,* 187, 189
equity considerations, 228–30
executive federalism, 24–25
Executive Order 12174, 141
Executive Order 12291, 148

Executive Order 12372, 289
Executive Order 12498, 148
Executive Order 12612, 154
Executive Order 13083, 327–28
extraterritorial powers, 288–89

factions, 31, 32, 63–64
Family Assistance Program (FAP), 127, 128
Farm Mortgage Act of 1935, 92
"federal": Founding Fathers' use of the term,
    358n.21
Federal Assistance Review (FAR), 127
Federal Communications Commission, 104
Federal Election Campaign Act (FECA), 304,
    306
Federal Emergency Relief Administration
    (FERA), 112
federalism: an agenda for reform of, 342–54;
    current condition of, xiii–xvi, 170–71,
    322–28, 336–40; the current Supreme Court
    and, 210; defined, 19–20; factors shaping,
    abroad, 321; *The Federalist*'s use of the
    term, 59–62; the Founding Fathers and the
    term, 358n.21; overview of paradoxes in the
    current interpretation of, 328–36; overview
    of relation between intergovernmental
    relations and, 20–21; Reagan and, 149,
    151; status as a core national value, 340–
    42; the various models and metaphors for
    interpreting, 21–34. *See also specific types of
    federalism*
Federalism Summit in 1995, 207
*Federalist, The:* different views of federalism
    in, 58–61; on factions, 31; on the "small-
    republic argument," 55; the Supreme Court
    and, 343
Federalists, the, 22, 70–71
federal judiciary. *See* judicial dual federalism;
    judicial federalism; Supreme Court; *and
    specific courts under the names of the chief
    justices*
Federal Personnel Management Project, 134
Federal Power Commission, 104
Federal Regional Councils, 126, 127
Federal Reserve system, 103, 143
Federal Road Aid Act of 1916, 80
Federal Trade Commission, 104
Feingold, Russell F., 307
*Felker v. Turpin,* 197
fend-for-yourself federalism, 30, 152
*FERC v. Mississippi,* 189
Fess-Kenyon Act, 79
Fifteenth Amendment, 24, 117
Fifth Amendment, 76, 178
First Amendment: the Burger Court and, 186,
    188, 206; the libertarian doctrine and, 93,
    339; the Rehnquist Court and, 191, 192,
    193, 197, 198; the Warren Court and, 176

First American Republic, the, 39–40, 41, 44
fiscal federalism: the deficit and, 255–59; federal aid and, 232–55; overview of, 29–30; public sector growth and, 212–25; state aid and, 226–27
fiscal transfers. *See* intergovernmental fiscal transfers
Fisher, John, 262
Fitzpatrick, Jody L., 275
flat tax, 258
Food and Drug Administration, 146, 155
food safety regulations, 162
food stamps, 150, 165, 226
Ford, Gerald, 129, 130
Fortas, Abe, 175, 179
Fourteenth Amendment, 14, 24, 76; the Burger Court and, 179, 188, 189, 206, 207; direct orders and, 247; overview of the Supreme Court's interpretation of, since the 1960s, 339; Reagan and, 207; regulation and, 125; the Rehnquist Court and, 194, 199, 200; the separate but equal doctrine and, 93; the states and, 339; the Warren Court and, 176
Fourth Amendment, 178, 179, 180
Framers, the, 21, 44
Francis, Richard M., 279
Franklin, Benjamin, 42, 43, 48
Frederickson, H. George, 288
Fritschler, A. Lee, 142
*Frothingham* v. *Mellon,* 80, 191
fruit cake federalism, 107
Full Employment Act of 1946, 109, 114
functional federalism: areas of growth of, between 1930 and 1960, 103–11; governmental finances and, 94–97; intergovernmental fiscal transfers and, 97–103
functionalism, 138
fund-raising, 303

*Garcia* v. *San Antonio Metropolitan Transit Authority* (1985), 15, 208, 210, 332; the Burger Court and, 185, 187, 189; and orthodox conservative critique of the Court, 206; the Rehnquist Court and, 192, 200–203, 204, 205
Gardner, John, 309
General Revenue Sharing (GRS): conditions on, 9, 245; congressional federalism and, 130; devolution and, 127; elimination of, 240; and the expansion in the number of federal grant recipients, 3; problems with states' targeting of, 230–31; proportion of, vis-à-vis other types of aid, 237, 238; range of uses of, 244
general-support payments, 228
George III, King, 42
GI bill, 116
*Gibbons* v. *Ogden,* 67

Gingrich, Newt: Contract with America and, 15, 157, 160–61, 162, 315–16; as failing to shift power to subnational units, 171; ideological approach to government of, 123; polarization and, 304; Unfunded Mandates Reform Act and, 248
Ginsburg, Ruth Bader, 176, 325
Glazer, Nathan, 206
Glendening, Parris N., 32
Goals 2000, 157, 160, 166
Goldberg, Arthur J., 175
Goldsmith, Stephen, 291
*Goodyear Atomic Corp.* v. *Miller,* 193
Gormley, William, 338
Government Sponsored Enterprises, 324
Gramlich, Edward M., 257
Gramm-Rudman-Hollings, 143, 152, 335
Grangers, the, 83
grants and grants-in-aid: Bush and, 152, 154, 226; Carter and, 134; changes in emphasis on various types of, 237–55; Clinton and, 157, 160; congressional federalism and, 129, 130–32; current state of, 350; Ford and, 130; growth of, in the early twentieth century, 78–80; "iron triangles" and, 25; LBJ and, 124; New Federalism and, 127; between 1930 and 1960, 97–103, 105–7, 116; Nixon and, 130; overview of federal, since 1960, 2–15, 234–37; Reagan and, 144–45, 147, 148–49, 226; the Rehnquist Court and, 190–92; states' management of, 323; statistics on growth of federal, 233; the White theory regarding, 324
Great Compromise, the, 47–48, 64, 71
Great Depression, the, 34, 89, 90, 103, 111, 143, 267
Greater Portland Metropolitan Service District, 295–96
Great Society, 20, 23, 123
Greenbackers, the, 83
Greenspan, Alan, 258
*Gregory* v. *Ashcroft,* 200–201, 205, 330, 332
*Griggs* v. *Duke Power Co.,* 195
Grodzins, Martin, 62, 63, 89–90, 111, 120, 324
Gun-Free Zones Act, 202

habeas corpus, 180, 196, 197, 204, 206, 207, 332, 339
*Hafer* v. *Melo,* 195, 208
Hamilton, Alexander, 54; the Constitutional Convention and, 52; different interpretations of his understanding of federalism, 59–62; dominion theory of empire and, 41, 42; Madison compared with, 58; the Supreme Court and, 343
Harlan, John Marshall, 179
Harrington, James, 56, 61
Hastert, A. Dennis, 316

Hatch Act, 79, 102
Hays, Samuel, 84
Head Start, 8, 160, 167
health care: Clinton and, 158–59, 314,
    353; congressional federalism and, 130;
    federal aid to states for, in the 1950s, 105;
    proportion of federal grants for, 245; states'
    experimentation regarding, 279
Hero, Rodney, 275
Highway Beautification Act of 1965, 125
Hill, Lister, 113
*Hodel v. Surface Mining and Reclamation
    Association*, 187
Hofstadter, Richard, 108
hollow government, 146, 323
home rule, 282–83, 293
homestead exemptions, 220
Hoover, Herbert, 91
Hoover Commission, 119
Hopkins, Harry, 112
Hopkins, Stephen, 40, 57, 61
House Rules Committee, 114
Housing Act of 1949, 109, 113, 114
HUD scandals, 146
*Hughes v. Alexandria Scrap*, 185
Hume, David, 56–57, 61

*Idaho et al.* v. *Coeur d'Alene Tribe of Idaho*, 330
*Idea of the Perfect Commonwealth* (Hume), 56–57
income tax: beginnings of, 76–77; between
    1930 and 1960, 95–97; Reagan and, 151;
    shifts in, between 1960 and 1995, 214–15;
    state, 77, 215–16, 219; state and local taxes
    vis-à-vis federal, 12
incrementalism, 128–29
independent collaborative concept of federalism,
    23–24
independent competitive concept of federalism,
    23–24
Indian affairs, 202
inflation, 135
informal and formal interagency collaboration,
    288
information technology, 277–78, 323, 339
Integrated Grant Administration project, 127
interest (pressure) groups: beginnings of, 83–84;
    and the decline of the power of state parties,
    344–45; as the major threat to federalism,
    32; nationalization of, 316–17; in the 1950s,
    116; overview of rise and power of, 307–11;
    parties and, 314–15; at the state level,
    312–13; the states' influence vis-à-vis that of,
    324–25. *See also* pressure-group parties
Intergovernmental Anti-Recession Act, 129
Intergovernmental Cooperation Act, 128, 289
intergovernmental fiscal transfers: the deficit
    and, 255–59; federal aid and, 232–55; state
    aid and, 226–27

intergovernmental relations: beginnings of
    the study of, 103; Carter and, 133–36;
    Clinton, Congress, and the current condition
    of, 156–60; the Constitution on, 62–63;
    Creative Federalism and, 124; defined, 20;
    fiscal federalism and, 29–30; general findings
    and observations regarding current, 322–28;
    overview of, since the 1960s, 1–15, 136–37;
    overview of relation of federalism and, 20–
    21; Reagan and, 147–48, 150–51; regulatory
    federalism and, 28–29
interlocal service contracts, 288
Intermodel Surface Transportation Efficiency
    Act (ISTEA), 8, 11, 152, 153, 240, 290, 349
Interstate Highway legislation, 114
Intolerable Acts, 41
iron triangles, 25, 137

Jackson, Andrew, 26, 72
Jefferson, Thomas, 42, 46
Jeffersonian Republicans, 22, 70
Job Training and Partnership Act, 239, 240
Johnson, Haynes, 353
Johnson, Lyndon B., 113; centralization
    and, 300; Creative Federalism of, 122,
    123–26; and federal aid to states, 3;
    intergovernmental relations and, 10; Nixon
    and, 128; on political effects of Civil Rights
    legislation, 263; Reagan and, 141; role in the
    evolution of the present system, 2
Joint Economic Committee, 109–10
Joint Funding Act, 127
joint-powers agreements, 288
judicial dual federalism, 66–67
judicial federalism, 25–26, 28, 325
judiciary. *See* judicial dual federalism; judicial
    federalism; Supreme Court; *and specific courts
    under the names of the chief justices*
Judiciary Act of 1789, 50, 66, 68

Kassebaum, Nancy, 166
Kee, James E., 33–34
Kennedy, Anthony, 190, 199, 200, 325
Kennedy, John F., 3, 10
Kennedy, Ted, 166
Kestnbaum, Meyer, 25
Key, V.O., 116–17
Keynesian economics, 103
Kincaid, John, 186
King, Rufus, 47
Kirk, Paul, 312
Kohl, Herb, 203

labor-management relations, 104
Lawrence, David, 116
layer cake federalism, 23
Leach, Richard H., 40
*Leathers v. Medlock*, 193
Lee, Robert Henry, 42
libertarianism, 339

Lincoln, Abraham, 26, 79
Livingston, Bob, 161
lobbying/lobbyists, 266, 308–11, 344, 353
local governments: the Burger Court and, 186; Bush and, 153–54; categorical grants and, 238; Clinton and, 157; current dilemma of, 316–17; the current economy and, 258; data on expenditures of, 212–14; decline of powers of, in the 1960s and 1970s, 300–301; direct federal grants to, 236–37, 253; effect of the deficit on, 255–56; fend-for-yourself federalism and, 30; lingering questions regarding their relations to states, 297–98; number of federal grants to, 236; overview of, since the 1960s, 11; overview of finances of, 225; paradoxes in current interpretations of the influence of, 328–36; patterns of their relation to states, 269–77; political parties and, 311–13, 316; regionalism and, 287–98; regressive taxes of, 222; state aid to, 226–32; the states as shapers of institutions and processes in, 281–86; statistics on taxation by, 216–22; suggestions for future actions of, 345–54; the Supreme Court's awareness of concerns of, 209–10
Local Public Works program, 129
local special districts, 291
Long, Norton E., 119
Long, Russell, 335
Lovell, Catherine, 275
Lowi, Theodore, 103, 116
Low-Level Radioactive Policy Act, 330

machines, political: beginnings of, 84–85; the New Deal and, 112–13; in the 1950s, 116; reform movements and, 86
Madison, James, 50; on a "compound republic," 57–58, 65; and the congressional role in shaping federalism, 26; the Constitutional Convention and, 45, 49; current state of federalism relative to the vision of, xiii; different interpretations of his understanding of federalism, 59–62; on factions, 31, 32, 63; Hamilton compared with, 58; and the Judiciary Act of 1789, 66; on the means of electing the president, 50; on the method for electing the Senate, 47; on "mutual forbearance," 63; on the "small-republic argument," 55, 56; on the small states, 48, 53; on "so fatal an omission," 44; the Supreme Court and, 343; the Virginia Plan and, 46
*Maine v. Thiboutot*, 183, 184, 194
majority-minority districts, 198–99, 208
managerialism, 133–34
mandates: Bush and, 156; current state of, 247–49, 323; fiscal federalism and, 29; in the 1980s and early 1990s, 153; the 104th Congress and, 161; from states, 275–77; uncertain future of, 329

Marando, Vincent, 282
marble cake federalism, 23, 90, 103
*Marbury v. Madison*, 66
Marcus, Edward L., 344
Marshall, John, 66
Marshall, Thurgood, 175, 344
Marshall Court, 66
Martin, Luther, 48, 49
*Martin v. Wilks*, 195
*Maryland v. Watson*, 330
Mason, George, 53
*Massachusetts v. Mellon*, 80
matching grants, 249–50
McCain, John, 307
McCarran Acts, 114
*McClesky v. Zant*, 196
*McCulloch v. Maryland*, 66
McFeeley, Neil, 208
McGovern-Fraser Commission, 301
McKinley, William, 26, 83
McLean, Joseph, 90
media, the: and the decline of local-level party organizations, 15; influence in politics, 305; voter contact and, 31
Medicaid, 8; Bush and, 152, 153, 154, 156, 226; challenges to, 215; the deficit and, 257; effects on states with different income levels, 250; LBJ and, 124; mandates and, 248; 105th Congress and, 169; Personal Responsibility and Work Opportunity Reconciliation Act and, 165; Reagan and, 226; states' experiments regarding, 279; states' role in administering, 350
Medicare, 215, 257, 334
Meehan, Martin, 307
Megan's Law, 249
Mental Health Services for the Homeless, 239
mergers, 353
merit system, the, 102, 118, 119
metro multipurpose districts, 293
Metropolitan Planning Organization (MPO), 11
Metropolitan Statistical Areas, 231, 254
*Middlesex* case, 184
*Milliken v. Bradley*, 188, 370n.13
minimum wage, 166
*Miranda*, 179–80
*Missouri v. Jenkins*, 192, 205, 206, 332
Model Cities legislation, 124, 289
modernization, 84
*Monroe v. Pape*, 182
Montesquieu, 39, 56
Morrill Act, 79
Morris, Gouverneur, 46, 49, 50, 53
Mortgage Subsidy Bond Tax Act, 12
Mosher, Frederick C., 71
Motor Voter Act, 158, 160
municipal bonds, 11

Nathan, Richard P., 33, 164
National Defense Education legislation, 106, 114
National Governors' Association (NGA), 163, 313
National Historic Preservation Act of 1966, 125
National Institutes of Health, 146, 167
nationalism: at the Constitutional Convention, 47–48, 49, 55–56; *The Federalist* and, 60–61; pre-Revolutionary, 41–42
National Labor Relations Act (1935), 92
*National League of Cities* v. *Usery*, 14, 26, 181–82, 187, 188, 189, 202
National Minimum Drinking Age Act, 190
National Performance Review, 160
National Program Review, 157
National Republicans, 71
National Urban Policy, 122
Native Indian Housing program, 162
*Nevada* v. *Skinner*, 191
new cooperative federalism, 158, 160
New Deal, the: centralization and decentralization during, 112–13; as fostering the interpenetration of intergovernmental relations, 20; grants and, 99; the Supreme Court and, 91–92; various interpretations of, 108–9
New Democratic creed, 157–58
New Federalism: as activating state governments, 33; Creative Federalism and, 128; dual federalism and, 23; Nixon and, 24; overview of, 126–28; under Reagan, 142–51; as a subspecies of cooperative federalism, 122; success of, 329
New Jersey Plan, 48, 49, 50
new judicial federalism, 186
New Partnership, the, 122, 133–36
*New Partnership to Conserve America's Communities,* 135
new political system, the: as a conditioner of systemic inconsistencies, 337–38; federal bureaucracy and, 324; genesis of, xvi; political federalism and, 31; as prompting major changes in intergovernmental relations, 14–15; states' influence and, 326
New Social Regulation, 246–47
*New York* v. *United States,* 201, 205, 327, 330
Nixon, Richard M.: congressional federalism and, 129; and counteracting bureaucratic "iron triangles," 25; environmental protection and, 263; grants and, 130; LBJ and, 128; New Federalism of, 24, 122, 126–28
North, Lord, 40
North American Free Trade Agreement (NAFTA), 158–59

Occupational Safety and Health Administration (OSHA), 347
*Oceana* (Harrington), 56

O'Connor, Sandra Day, 179, 192, 193, 195, 196, 199, 200, 201, 205, 325, 330, 332
Office of Information and Regulatory Affairs, 148, 155
Office of Management and Budget, 148
O'Leary, Rosemary, 210
Omnibus Budget Reconciliation Act (OBRA), 11, 29, 143, 147, 149, 222, 239
one-tier consolidation, 294
operational dual federalism, 67–69
operational federalism, 2–13, 23, 322–23
Ostrom, Vincent, 60
overload: Congress and, 27; current state of, xiv, 334–36, 338, 339, 340; debate over whether the federal system suffers from, 334; in 1980, 309; overview of recent, 2–15; permissive federalism and, 326
*Owen* v. *City of Independence,* 182–83

*Pacific Gas and Electric Co.* case, 185
Paine, Tom, 42
panoramic partnership, 3
Paperwork Reduction Act, 141
partially permissive federalism, 326, 327, 328, 354
parties, political: beginnings of, 70–73; centralization of, 14–15, 301–4; current state of, 313–17; decline in allegiance to, 304–5; from the 1860s to the 1930s, 82–87; from the 1930s to the 1960s, 111–20; political federalism and, 30–31; state and local, 300–301, 311–13, 343–44; television and, 305
Partnership for Health programs, 130, 237, 239, 242
patronage: between 1866 and 1895, 85; Jackson and, 72; the New Deal and, 112; in the 1950s and 1960s, 119; positive and negative aspects of, 345; the Supreme Court on, 347
Patterson Plan, 48, 49, 50
Payments to the States for Day Care Assistance, 239
Pendleton Act, 86
*Pennhurst* v. *Halderman,* 184
Pepper, Claude, 113
permissive federalism, 22, 326, 327, 354
Perot, Ross, 51, 158
Personal Responsibility and Work Opportunity Reconciliation Act (PRWORA), xiv, 163–65, 350, 352
Peterson, Paul E., 257, 279, 309, 311, 324, 331, 335, 351
Pew Research Center, 327
picket-fence federalism, 25, 136–40
Pierce, Franklin, 68–69
Pinckney, C.C., 48, 54

pinwheel pattern of grant administration, 132
*Planned Parenthood of Southeastern Pennsylvania v. Casey,* 199–200, 208
*Plessy,* 75
political action committees (PACs), 303; political parties and, 31, 314–15; soft money and, 306–7
political federalism, 30–32, 64, 71, 300, 317, 321
Polk, James, 26
*Pollack* case, 76
populism, 266
Populists, the, 83, 85–86
pornography, 180
Posner, Paul L., 244, 248
Pound, Dean Roscoe, 266
Powell, Lewis, 179, 182, 209, 210
power-centered conceptions of federalism, 22–23
Pragmatic Federalism, 32
preemption: the Burger Court and, 180–81, 184–85; current interpretations emphasizing, 331–32; New Social Regulation and, 246–47; the Rehnquist Court and, 193–94, 204; uncertain future of, 329
preferred-freedoms principle, 93
pressure-group parties, 315, 353–54
pressure groups. *See* interest (pressure) groups
primaries: blacks and, 117; closed, 344; and the eclipse of state and local party organizations, 14; increase in, between 1890 and 1928, 86; between 1946 and 1960, 116–18; reason for the proliferation of, 302
*Printz v. the United States,* 160, 201, 205, 330, 332, 339
privatization, 324
procurement practices, 146
professionalism, 138, 139
Progressive movement, 20, 83, 85–86, 87, 354
progressivity of taxes, 222, 223, 258
property tax: the Burger Court on, 181; between 1890 and 1927, 77, 78; experiments with, 230; lessening role of, 216, 218; between 1930 and 1960, 96–97; various states' level of reliance on, 219–20
proportionate representation, 47, 48
Proposition 13, 135, 218
protected federalism, 354
protective federalism, 327
public interest groups: changed role of, 346; and inattention to the role of the states, 262; need for a strategic study center, 348; recent successes of, 346; regulatory reform campaign of, 248
Public Works Administration, 106
Public Works Employment Act, 129

Quayle, Dan, 154

race, 114–15, 176. *See also* racial justice; segregation
racial justice, 14, 176, 177, 179, 188
Railway Labor Act of 1934, 92
Randolph, Edmund, 46
Randolph Plan, 46, 47, 48, 57
Reagan, Michael D., 22, 326, 327, 328
Reagan, Ronald, 335; assessment of the record of, 142–51; campaign themes of, 142; the condition of federalism under, 121; declines in federal aid and, 3, 11; exceptionalism of the federalism of, 122; fiscal federalism and, 29–30; grants and, 8, 9, 226, 237; intergovernmental relations and, 10, 150–51; as narrowing the range of Republican issues, 304; New Federalism of, 23; relation to his predecessors, 141–42; role in the evolution of the present system, 1, 2; the states and, 2, 3, 8, 263
reapportionment, 181
redistricting, 198–99
Reeves, Mavis Mann, 12, 32, 282
*Reeves* case, 185
referenda, 266
reform movement, 85–86
regional councils, 289
regionalism, 286–97
regional special districts and authorities, 292–93
regressivity of taxes, 220–22, 223, 258
regulation: Bush and, 154–55; congressional federalism and, 130–31; current interpretations emphasizing, 331–32; grants and, 9–10; increased, following the Great Depression, 103–4; LBJ and, 125; mandates and, 247–49; modernization and the beginnings of, 84; New Social Regulation and, 246–47; overview of recent, 322–23; Reagan and, 147–48, 150; the states and, 28–29, 274–75. *See also* mandates
regulatory federalism, 28
Rehnquist, William H., 14, 179, 181–82
Rehnquist Court: civil rights and, 195–99; emphasis on governmental and societal rights, 176; *Garcia* and, 200–203; as generally upholding national authority, 26; grants and, 190–92; liberal assessment of, 207–8; neoconservative assessment of, 206; orthodox conservative assessment of, 207; preemption and, 193–94; retrospective view of, 203–6; Section 1983 and, 194–95; as strengthening states' constitutional status, 329–30; tax cases and, 192–93
reinventing government, 323
Religious Freedom Restoration Act (RFRA), 197, 330
representation, 47–48, 53–54
representational federalism, 188, 321, 325

republicanism, 55–64
Republican National Committee, 303–4
Republican party: centralization of, 303–4;
    Clinton and, 160–68; current state of,
    314–15; decline in allegiance to, 304–5;
    between 1860 and 1932, 82, 83, 86; during
    the 1950s, 115–16, 117; political federalism
    and, 31; at the state and local levels, 311–13
*Republican Party v. Rutan,* 198, 208, 313, 332,
    347
Revenue and Expenditure Control Act, 11
revenue sharing, 127, 128
Richardson, Elliot, 130
*Richards v. Wisconsin,* 330
*Richmond v. Croson,* 195, 196, 206
Riker, William, 76
Rivlin, Alice, 257, 331, 351, 352
Rockefeller, Nelson, 123
*Roe v. Wade,* 199–200
Rohde, David W., 315–16
Roosevelt, Franklin D., 23; administrative
    authority and, 118; centralization and,
    111–12; Creative Federalism and, 123; and
    the Democratic senatorial primaries of 1938,
    113; LBJ and, 124; pragmatism of, 109;
    states' rights and, 91; the Supreme Court
    and, 91–92
Roosevelt, Theodore, 83, 123
Rosenbloom, David H., 324
Rusk, David, 286
*Rust v. Sullivan,* 191

Safe Drinking Water Act amendments, 162,
    163, 247, 349
Safe Streets Act, 130, 237, 239
*St. Paul* case, 208
sales tax, 216–17, 219, 220
*San Antonio Independent School District* v.
    *Rodriguez,* 181
Sanford, Terry, 25, 138
Sanzone, John G., 22, 326
savings and loan debacle, 146
Scalia, Antonin, 190, 198, 201, 205, 330
Schattschneider, E.E., 120
Scheiber, Harry N., 62
*Schneckleth v. Bustamente,* 180
school districts, 229, 232, 270. *See also* education
Schools-to-Work program, 160
Schultz, Charles, 126
secession, 74
Second American Republic, 39
Second Continental Congress, 42–43
Section 1983, 182–83, 184, 189, 194–95, 204,
    210
Securities and Exchange Commission, 104
segregation, 93, 176, 178
Selected Housing Program Extensions measure,
    162–63
*Seminole Tribe v. Florida,* 202, 330

Senators, election of, 85
separate but equal doctrine, 93
*Serrano v. Priest,* 230
Seventeenth Amendment, 14, 325
Shannon, John, 30, 33–34, 329
*Shaw v. Reno,* 198–99
Shays, Christopher, 307
Shays-Meehan bill, 345
Shay's Rebellion, 45
Sheppard-Tanner Act of 1921, 80
Sherman, Roger, 47, 49, 55, 56
Sherman Anti-Trust Act, 183
*Silkwood v. Kerr-McGee,* 185
Simon, Herbert A., 119
single-purpose regional bodies, 290
Sixteenth Amendment, 77, 87
Sixth Amendment, 178
slavery, 53–54
slave trade, the, 54
small-republic theory, 56–57
Smith, Bruce L.R., 142
Smith-Hughes Act, 79
Smith-Lever Act, 79
*Smith v. Allwright,* 117
social regulation. *See* regulation
Social Security: budget surpluses and, 334;
    challenges to, 215; Clinton on, 258; the
    deficit and, 257
Social Security Act, 92, 108, 112
Social Security Administration, 146
soft money, 303–4, 306–7, 345
Souter, David, 190, 199, 200, 204, 325
*South Carolina v. Baker,* 12, 192
*South Central Timber* case, 185
*South Dakota v. Dole,* 190, 191
special-interest groups. *See* interest (pressure)
    groups
special-revenue-sharing proposals, 127, 128, 129
spillover coalitions, 84, 87
Stamp Act, 40
standpattism, 138, 139
state-centered federalism, 27
State Children's Health Insurance Program
    (SCHIP), 159
state-dominated federalism, 27
State-Local Legal Center, 346
State or Local Government Cost Estimates Act,
    322
state planning and development districts
    (SPDD), 290–91
states: aid from, to local governments, 226–
    32; and the ambivalence in the current
    system, xiii–xvi, 338–39; the Articles of
    Confederation on, 44–45; the Burger Court
    and, 186; Bush and, 153–54; bypassing of,
    regarding grants, 236–37; categorical grants
    and, 238; challenges to role of, in the 1960s
    and 1970s, 260–62, 300–301; Clinton and,
    157; the Constitutional Convention on, 53,

62–63; current dilemma of, 316–17; current mandates and, 323; data on expenditures of, 212–14; effect of the deficit on, 255–56; *The Federalist* and, 60; fend-for-yourself federalism and, 30; fiscal problems in the 1980s and early 1990s, 153; grants from, between 1930 and 1960, 97–98; as implementers of new intergovernmental programs, 277–81; increased role of, 264–66, 267–69, 322; interest groups and, 324–25; international trade and, 337; lingering questions regarding their relations to localities, 297–98; models for interpreting their relation to the federal government, 21–34; number of federal grants to, 236; overview of federal aid to, from 1961 to 1998, 2–15; overview of finances of, 224–25; overview of their role in the contemporary system, 27–28; paradoxes in current interpretations of the influence of, 328–36; patterns of their relation to localities, 269–77; political parties and, 311–13, 316; primaries in the 1950s and, 116–17; proportions of federal aid received by low-, middle-, and high-income, 250–51; Reagan and, 148–50; recent causes of increased influence of, 327–28; regulatory federalism and, 28–29; Roosevelt and the rights of, 91; as shapers of local and substate regional institutions and processes, 281–86; suggestions for future role of, 343, 345–54; summary of current role of, 298–99; the Supreme Court and, xiii, 209–10; taxation and, 95–96, 215–22, 376n.15; welfare and, 163–65

Stephens, G. Ross, 251, 271, 273, 325
Stevens, John Paul, 179, 182, 195, 199, 201, 204
Stevenson, Adlai, 116
Stewart, Potter, 179
Stillman, Richard J., II, 88
Stockman, David, 151
Stonecash, Jeffrey M., 273–74
Story, Justice, 202
Subcommittee on Intergovernmental Relations, 138–39
subsidies, 110
suburbs, 222, 231, 253–54, 286, 288
Sugar Act, 40
Sundquist, James, 117
Sununu, John, 152, 312
Superfund, 165
Supplemental Security Income (SSI), 8, 164, 165
supply-side approach to public management, 144–45
supremacy clause, 181; and orthodox conservative critique of the Supreme Court, 206; preemption and, 184, 247; the Supreme

Court and, 13, 14, 26, 67, 201, 329; use of, in the 1970s, 131
Supreme Court: and ambivalences in the system, 339; assessments of work of, since the 1960s, 175–76, 206–11; centralizing influence of, 13–14; the Civil War and, 74–75; the Constitutional Convention and, 50; dual federalism's demise and, 90–94; the Framers on, 64; as generally upholding national authority, 26; old-style federalism and, 20; patronage and, 347; the power of the states and, xiii, 75, 327, 329–30; suggestions for future role of, 343. *See also* Burger Court; Marshall Court; Rehnquist Court; Taney Court; Warren Court
supreme Law of the Land provision, 50
*Suter v. Artist M*, 195

Taft-Hartley Act, 104, 114, 115
Taney, Roger B., 22
Taney Court, 66–67
*Tashjian, Secretary of the State of Connecticut v. Republican Party of Connecticut*, 344
Tax Equity and Fiscal Responsibility Act (TEFRA), 12, 192
taxes: the Articles of Confederation on Congress and, 43; the colonies and, 40; the Constitutional Convention on export, 54; in the early twentieth century, 76–78; effects on citizenry of, 222–24; erosion of federal-state comity regarding, 11–12; indexes of, 376n.15; local, 216–22; between 1930 and 1960, 95–97; the 105th Congress and cuts in, 169–70; Reagan and cuts in, 151; the Rehnquist Court and, 192–93; state, 215–22; summary observations regarding, 224–25. *See also* income tax; progressivity of taxes; property tax; regressivity of taxes; sales tax
Tax Reform Act (TRA), 12, 143
Taylor, John, 22
technocratic federalism, 33
technology, 20
television, 305. *See also* media, the
Temporary Assistance for Needy Families (TANF), 257; focus of, 352; information technology and, 278–79, 339; the Personal Responsibility and Work Opportunity Reconciliation Act and, 163, 165; pressure for reports regarding, 323; the states and, xiv, 164, 279–80, 350
Tennessee Valley Authority, 104
Tenth Amendment, 14, 26, 207, 209; the Burger Court and, 187; lobbying and, 210; orthodox conservatives and, 206–7; recent rulings related to, 330; the Rehnquist Court and, 192, 201, 202; the states and, 15, 176, 339; the Supreme Court's nationalistic interpretation of, 22; the Taney Court and, 67

term limits, 266
territorial principle, 19, 52–53
*Texas* v. *White,* 74, 200
third parties, 82, 83
Thomas, Clarence, 190, 193–94
Thompson, Tommy, 339
three-tier reform, 295
Thurmond, Strom, 115
Title XX Social Services program, 130, 237, 239
Townsend Acts, 40
trade deficit, the, 143
Transportation Efficiency Act–21st Century (TEA–21), 11, 239, 240, 290, 297, 349
Truman, David B., 120
Truman, Harry S., 99, 108, 114, 115, 118
Tucker, Raymond, 116
Twain, Mark, 210
Twenty-first Amendment, 191
Twin Cities Metropolitan Council, 295, 296
two-tier restructuring, 294–95

unanimous-approval requirement for amendments, 44–45
Unfunded Mandates Reform Act (UMRA): Clinton and, 157; effect of, 10, 161, 349, 322–23; significance of, 162, 163, 248, 336; as state-sensitive, 327
union government, 59
*United States* v. *Lopez,* 165, 166, 202, 203, 205, 330, 339
*United States* v. *Virginia,* 208
urban aid, 135
Urban and Regional Policy Group (URPG), 135
U.S. Maritime Commission, 104
U.S. Office of Education, 106
*U.S. Term Limits* v. *Thornton,* 201

value-added tax, 192–93
vertical functional autocracies, 25
Virginia Plan, 46, 47, 48, 57
Vocational Rehabilitation Amendments, 130
voter turnout, 305
Voting Rights Act, 198, 262

Wagner Act, 104, 108
Wallace, Henry, 115
*Wards Cove Packing Co.* v. *Antonio,* 195
Warren Court: basic commitments of, 176–77; centralization and, 14; as generally upholding national authority, 26; neoconservative critique of, 206; questions raised by, 177–78; the Rehnquist Court and, 203; state autonomy and, 175–76
Washington, George, 50
Water Quality Act, 125, 247
Watson, Jack, 134
Watt, James, 147
Wattenberg, Martin P., 305
*Webster* v. *Reproductive Health Services,* 199
Weeks Act, the, 79
Wekkin, Gary, 314
welfare: Clinton and, 162, 163–64; federal aid to states for, in the 1950s, 105; Reagan and, 148; state aid for, 227; states' experimentation with, 279–80
Whig party, 71–73
White, Byron R., 175, 193, 194, 201
White, Leonard D., 324
*White* case, 185
white primaries, 14, 117, 120, 301
Wholesome Meat Act, 125
Wholesome Poultry Act, 125
Will, George, 198
Williams, Walter, 146
Wilson, James, 41, 42, 47, 49, 50, 53
Wilson, Woodrow, 83, 123
Wilson-Gorman tariff, 76
*Wilson* v. *Seiter,* 194
*Wisconsin Public Intervenor* v. *Mortier,* 193
Wise, Charles, 210
Women, Infants and Children nutritional program (WIC), 8
Works Progress Administration, 106, 112
Wright, Deil, 21, 276, 314, 358n.21
Wrightson, Margaret T., 244

Yarborough, Jean, 59–60
Yeats, William Butler, xv

zero-based budgeting, 134–35